Advance Praise for *Tam*

"Finally, one of the most interesting boat races in America gets a complete history. The author just happens to be a scion of a racing family who knows first-hand the twists and turns of the Sammamish Slough and the adrenalin rush of competing in the race. I particularly enjoyed the chapter about a driver's perspective of the race and the HUNDREDS of wonderful photographs."
Craig Smith–Retired Seattle Times Sports Writer

"My lifelong love affair with powerboat racing started in the early 1960s when my brother and I picked up a couple of sack lunches and walked two miles from our home to the Bothell Bridge to watch the Sammamish Slough Race. Once a year, the placid little river that ran through our home town, would come alive with speeding hydroplanes as they dashed up the narrow Slough connecting Lake Washington with Lake Sammamish. Jim Benson was one of the racers we used to watch, and now has written a wonderful book that captures all the history, drama and excitement of this amazing race. But this book does more than tell the colorful story of "the Crookedest Race in the World," it gives a fascinating look into the birth of the Seattle Outboard Association; one of the largest and most successful outboard racing clubs in America. I can't recommend this book enough. It is a great read."
David D. Williams–Author & Executive Director of the Hydroplane and Raceboat Museum

"The Sammamish Slough outboard marathon was the most challenging event on Seattle Outboard Association's racing calendar. For much of the twentieth century, it drew crowds witnessing drivers with nerves of steel as they battled each other and the elements. Merely finishing was a major accomplishment. Jim Benson grew up in a family that participated in the race for a number of years. He recounts the history of the event from its inception to the current revival as a spring exhibition. Benson tells the complete story which includes changes to the Slough itself–communities grew up along its shores, farmland became city streets, wooden bridges were rebuilt with concrete pilings. We owe Benson a tremendous debt of gratitude for preserving the memory of an exciting part of boat racing's legacy in the Pacific Northwest."
Craig Fjarlie–Freelance writer, APBA race official, former SOA commodore & raceboat driver

"Jim Benson has captured the curves, climate, color and characters that made the Sammamish Slough Race the most unique boat race to dominate the sport psyche of the "Boating Capital of the World," sharing that with conventional outboard racing on Northwest lakes and rivers, limited inboard racing, unlimited hydroplane racing and University of Washington crew racing. It sadly, but appropriately, ended as the four towns lining the Slough began to grow into populous cities as the Seahawks, Mariners and Supersonics joined to become the dominant focus of local sports fans. On a more personal note; the history and photography of my father, Bob Carver, world renowned for his action boat racing photos, plays an important role in the telling of this story, as it did in publicizing local boat racing in the 50s, 60s and 70s."
Bill Carver–Freelance photographer, son of famous photographer, Bob Carver & retired engineer

Taming of the Slough

*The Intriguing Story of the Sammamish Slough Race
"The Crookedest Race in the World"*

*Plus…The History of the Seattle Outboard Association
and the Seattle to Lake Sammamish Race Course*

By **Jim Benson**

Printed in USA
First Edition
Frist Printing 2018

All rights reserved. No portion of this book may be reproduced in any form without permission from the publisher. For permissions send inquiries to:
Taming.of.the.Slough@gmail.com

Editors:
  Carolyn Benson
  Craig Fjarlie
  Craig Smith

Front, back cover and page layout by Jim Benson

Affiliations:
  American Power Boat Association
  Seattle Hydroplane & Raceboat Museum
  Seattle Outboard Association

Panoramic front, spine & rear cover photo: By Bob Carver of 1962 Sammamish Slough Race incident at the Down River Marina. Race officials reported that the raceboat driver was Don Hansen in the D-Stock Hydro class.

IBSN-13: 9781985666702

Dedication

This book is dedicated to my late mother, Dorothy (Dot) Grace Benson, who for years saved, archived and made scrapbooks about our family's boat racing adventures. And to my late father, Ethan (Al) Allen Benson, for making it possible for us to race boats, befriending the news media, photographers and for collecting hundreds of raceboat and driver photos from West Coast events.

1939: Al & Dot Benson

Credits

Special acknowledgements go to my three tireless editors. First, my wife Carolyn, former boat racer and Seattle Outboard Association Commodore, Craig Fjarlie, and another Craig, retired *Seattle Times* sportswriter Craig Smith. To past APBA President, Rick Sandstrom, of the APBA Historical Society; the son of the late renowned photographer Bob Carver, Bill Carver; my writing teacher, Eileen Crimmin, who wrote the book *Bryant's*; long time Slough racer and fellow historian, John Laird; former Slough Race driver, Phil Williams (owner of Phil's Performax Marine and curator of his private outboard museum); former unlimited crew chief and Slough Race winner Dave Culley; Dave's daughter-in-law, Amberly (Gaul) Culley, who prompted me to write this book; my daughters Saurra and Sonja, Robert Stevens and my brother, Don Benson, for all their contributions.

I also want to thank the following historical societies, museums and other organizations, race drivers and the families of deceased Sammamish Slough Race drivers who provided articles, photos, and other memorabilia for this book:

Businesses-Organizations

American Power Boat Association Historical Society
American Power Boat Association
Bothell Historical Museum
Hydroplane & Raceboat Museum
Kenmore Air Harbor
Kenmore Historical Society
Moses Lake Museum
Museum of History and Industry
Phil's Performax Marine
Redmond Historical Society
Seattle Outboard Association
Seattle Post-Intelligencer
Seattle Public Library
Seattle Times
Woodinville Historical Society

News Reporters

Royal Brougham, Bill Knight, Emmett Watson-*Seattle Post-Intelligencer*
Del Danielson, Tommy Humes, Bud Livesley, Craig Smith-*Seattle Times*
E.A. Jamison-*Seattle Star*

Photographers

Bill Carver, Bob Carver, Bob Miller, Russ Swanson, Lloyd Swanson

Individuals

John Adams	Rick Adams	Al Anderson
Penny Anderson	Mike Alm	Ginny Lea (Lyford) Asp
Tom Ballou	Leslie (Munro) Banks	Kim (Lyford) Bishop
Dave Brown	Jerry Bryant	Amberly (Gaul) Culley
Priscilla Drodge	Annette Eaton	Paul Edgar
Janis (Lee) Ely	Fred Farley	Burt Fraley
Suzi Freeman	Freya Hart	Steve Greaves
Chip Hanauer	Ron Henley	Peter Hunn
Don Ibsen	Effie Ivey	Bev (Schadt) Jacobsen
Ed Jacobsen	Sue Kienast	Erin (O'Neil) Kimbel
Jim Kraft	Bob LaBouy	Dennis Lee
Eric Linderoth	Chuck Lyford	Terry Malinowski
Carolyn Mar	Jay (Pepe) Maxwell	Craig Munro
Kathy Myers	John Paramore	Pat Pierce
Russell Rotzler	Karen & Bob Scheitlin	Billy Schumacher
Clayton Shaw	Jan & Howard Shaw	Darlene Shilling
Nancy (Nims) Spar	Lee Sutter	Joe Townsend
Charley Walters	Bob Wartinger	Charley Williams
Dave Williams	Barry Woods	

Dorothy Benson and first son, Donnie

Table of Contents

Author's Note	1
Prologue	5
Chapter 1: Slough or River?	9
Chapter 2: Pop-Poppers to Wave-Hoppers:	21
Chapter 3: New Club is Born: 1929-1931	31
Chapter 4: Clubhouse of Their Own: 1932 to 1933	61
Chapter 5: The Crookedest Race in the World: 1934	85
Chapter 6: Ladies of the Lakes: 1935 to 1938	107
Chapter 7: Under the Radar: 1939 to 1945	131
Chapter 8: Firewater: 1946 to 1949	183
Chapter 9: Snake Dance: 1950 to 1954	215
Chapter 10: Slaughter in the Slough: 1955 to 1959	253
Chapter 11: A Driver's View: 1960	315
Chapter 12: Disturbing the Peace: 1960 to 1963	335
Chapter 13: The Taming: 1964 to 1965	373
Chapter 14: High Speed Chase: 1966 to 1970	391

Chapter 15: End of an Era: 1971 to 1976 431

Chapter 16: The Bob Carver Story: 485

Epilogue — Return to the Slough: 2014 to present ... 507
   - Slough Race Hall of Fame 523

Appendix: Race Winners, Statistics, Oddities,
          Timeline, SOA Commodores,
          Sportsmanship Awards, Photo Credits 533
Index: 541
About the author (rear cover)

Al and youngest son, future author Jimmy Benson, posing for April 1953 Boat Sport magazine article "Racing Family Style" by Bob Carver & Russ Swanson.

1955 Champion Spark Plug Company add appearing in *Boating Industry*, *Boats*, *Motor Boating*, *Sea & Pacific Motor Boat*, and *Yachting* magazines.

Author's Note
How it all…the book…began

"A Trophy carries dust. Memories last forever"
-Mary Lou Retton-

The genesis of this book began shortly after my parents, Ethan Allen (Al) Benson and Dorothy Grace (Dot) Benson, were married in 1937. My father was fortunate to have a stepfather who owned two homes in Seattle. One was on Queen Anne Hill where he lived during and after high school and the other in Madison Park. He was able to purchase the Madison Park honeymoon home for only $2,000. The two-story home, with a separate living area in the daylight basement, became the place where my older brother Don and I were introduced into boat racing.

The 1930s home was one block west of the Seattle-to-Kirkland ferry dock at the foot of Madison Street. "Pop" as I called my father, had a small storage space behind Fisher's Madison Park boathouse, the early starting location of the soon-to-be-famous Sammamish Slough Race. This is where he kept his race boats and motors, all cramped into a very small storage space, but within 50 feet of the Lake. Pop was racing outboards for more than five years by the time I was born in the early 1940s. He was already a veteran Slough Race driver but never placed or even finished. He was only mentioned in the newspapers as an entry in pre-race articles. Not much notoriety in those days, but Wow, how that changed in the years to come as he became one of the legends of boat racing in the Pacific Northwest.

My father was extremely personable and outgoing, traits he inherited from his mother, Orlena Belle Benson. His enthusiasm for boat racing was infectious which attracted the media, photographers and movie makers alike, resulting in a lot of press photos, clippings and film clips. The local reporters loved to write about him and his sometimes wild and crazy racing adventures.

My mother was the one who saved and archived all the racing memorabilia into scrapbooks and boxes for safe keeping. I inherited all the stuff along with old racing programs, magazines, racing rule books and splendid vintage racing trophies, some of which were handmade by fellow racers.

During our boat racing years, we somehow lived near every Slough Race starting point on Lake Washington, either by accident or some type of divine intervention. As I grew older and continued my racing career, I carried on the family tradition of collecting and acquiring racing memorabilia, which led me to document our family boat racing history. Word got out and I began to receive boxes of other racing mementos that friends and fellow competitors passed on to me for safe keeping.

As it turned out, I was destined to write this book but didn't realize it until fall of 2013 when, Amberly (Gaul) Culley, organizer of the Slough Race revival event in Kenmore told me: "You're the 'missing link'" and encouraged me to write this book, *Taming of the Slough*, about the history of the race.

Plenty is offered to the readers of this book, which was over four years in the making. I hope you all enjoy the book as much as I enjoyed reliving the race's nostalgic history and reconnecting with past and present racing friends.

*The map on the following page shows the various starting locations of the Slough Race. Use this and the map on pages 95 and 250 as a reference throughout the book…

Authors Note | 3

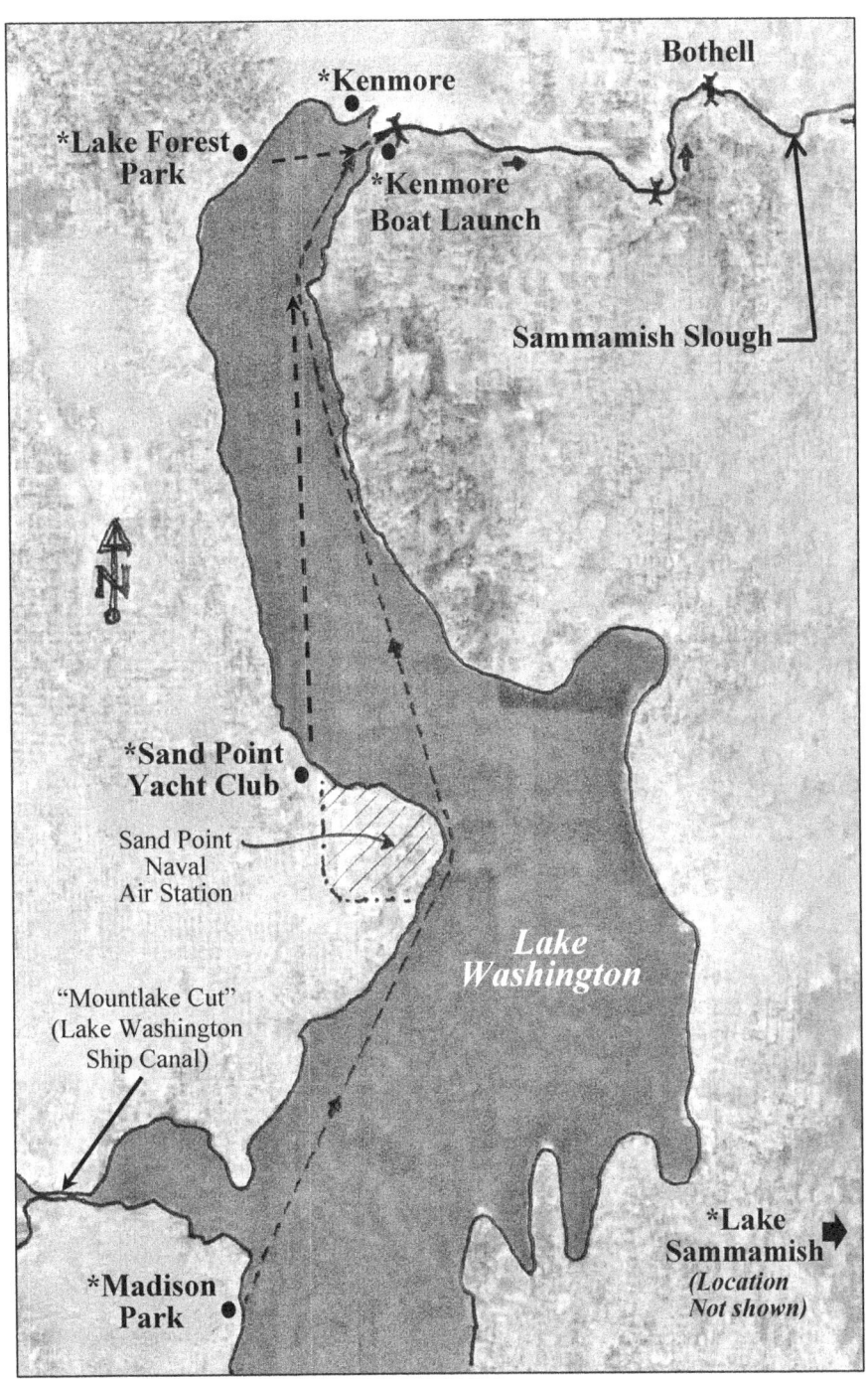

Slough Race Starting Locations (*)

4 | Taming of the Slough

April 1949 Lake Washington: Paramount Pictures cameraman Charley Parryman filming Al Benson (bow of race boat barely visible shooting through middle of fire) and Otis Clinton (boat closest to dock) skirting flames in foreground, from Benson's home on Riviera Place below Lake City, for Sammamish Slough Race pre-race promotion (see story in Chapter 8).

Prologue

As W. C. Fields said, "You can't trust water, even a straight stick turns crooked in it."

It was dubbed the "Crookedest Race in the World," one of the most unusual and challenging boat races in the country. The bizarre Sammamish Slough Race started in Seattle, ran across the windswept waters of Lake Washington and upstream 14 miles through the twisting waterway called the "Sammamish Slough." It traveled through four small towns, under low bridges, around hairpin turns and briefly stopped at a resort on the north end of Lake Sammamish. Then it restarted and reversed course back downstream to the original starting point at various locations.

The race spanned some 40 years which started in the early 1930s and abruptly ended in the late 1970s. It entertained hundreds of thousands of spectators during a time when outboard racing was one of the most popular sporting events in the country. It was the favorite for most of the drivers, some of whom became the greatest legends in boat racing. As intriguing as the race was, it is unimaginable to think that all the land at the Lake Washington starting locations was underwater two decades before the races began–before the lake was lowered in 1916 for the Lake Washington Ship Canal.

A good percentage of its men and women drivers, some who were as young as 9 years old, were forced out of the race because of mechanical breakdowns and unexpected hazards all along the way. Even some of the most famous drivers were never able to master it, no matter how hard they tried. Most drivers considered it a success just to finish, let alone win. The marathon-like regatta was conceived and run by one of the premier boat racing clubs in the country, the Seattle Outboard Association. More than a thousand race drivers participated during its lifetime.

It was a spectacle where unexpected things could happen and usually did. The national and regional press had a field day covering each race with all its wild and crazy antics; crashes, flips, boats running onto riverbanks and sometimes into cow pastures. Hollywood film studios added to the madness by making a number of creative newsreel and short subject movies that were shown to a national audience in movie theaters across the country. The legendary race was witnessed dangerously close by thousands of spectators who lined the riverbanks, sometimes only a few feet away from the high-speed race boats that sped by.

Although the outboard races were the main attraction, the history of the race waters and surrounding land was compelling in its own right. Monumental changes permanently altered the relationship between man, water and land along the race course before the marathon event began. The man-made alterations continued during the race throughout its running.

Each Slough race episode is based on insider insight as reported by local and national news media. Stories of the Sammamish Water-Ski Races, the nostalgic Slough Cruises and the history of the Sammamish River from the late 1880s are included. Intertwined are old business ads, interesting quotations and parallels of history that occurred along the 25-mile long race course between Seattle and Lake Sammamish.

Many revelations are in store for the readers as they make their way through each chapter. Along with each race story, the reader will find results for every race, including all the statistics, driver profiles and a boat-load of humorous stories told by the drivers themselves and the sportswriters who covered the event. The chronological history of the Seattle Outboard and American Power Boat Associations, leading up to the inaugural race, are intertwined with hundreds of photographs, some very rare, from the early 1900s to the present day where the race revival is being remembered as the "Bygone Rite of Spring."

Chapter 1

1909: Steamer *City of Bothell* **with smokestack lowered for bridge clearance.**

A Slough or a River?

Early history of the *Squak Slough*

"Commuters Appeal to United States Attorney for Relief from Continued Nuisance in Lake Sammamish Waterway"

-The Seattle Daily Times, April 4, 1912-

Long before the parents of Slough Race winners Al Benson, Bob Waite and Dave Culley had a twinkle in their eye, the meandering waterway that drains Lake Sammamish was a far cry from what it is now. At one time it was a broad body of water that flowed through the marshy and tree-filled valley where Kenmore, Bothell, Woodinville and Redmond are today. This slow moving, crooked and shallow body of water was originally called the "Squak[1] Slough" by the local Sammamish Valley Native Americans. They were known by early European-American settlers as the *Squak* who inhabited this area in the early 1800s.

It was a great place to live where fish, ducks and other wildlife were abundant in the cat tailed marches and estuaries, even when it routinely flooded. Centuries-old cedar, spruce and fir trees towered nearby, providing makings for village life. In the 1860s settlers began to move in after most of the local Native Americans relocated. Traveling up and down the Squak Slough, known today as the Sammamish Slough (pronounced *Slew*) or Sammamish River, was the main method of transportation through the area.

The Seattle newspapers printed a number of articles recounting stories about how families and individuals traveled from Seattle to the Sammamish valley area under extreme hardship. One story was about L. B. Andrews, a future Washington State

---

[1] Loosely translated, means "marsh" in the local Native American language.

senator, who sailed from California to the Seattle area with his family and settled here in 1861. Their journey continued to the north end of Lake Sammamish when Mr. Andrews acquired government coal lands located in what is now Issaquah. The family's extraordinary adventure began when they left Seattle traveling eastward carrying their goods and belongings with them. They traversed dense woods populated with Native Americans and wild animals to what is now the Leschi area on Lake Washington. Somewhere along the way Mr. Andrews acquired some type of canoe for the rest of their journey traveling across the waters. They began the most difficult part of the trip by paddling north along the shoreline of Lake Washington, then up through the Squak Slough to Lake Sammamish and across the length of the lake to its southern end. Finally, on foot, they completed the last four-miles of their fifty-mile trek to their property what is now, part of Issaquah.

Canoes, rowboats, small scows and larger flat bottom craft traveled on the Slough in the late 1800s. The slow-moving craft bore no resemblance to the high-speed race boats to come. Shallow-draft type boats with flat bottoms were the only vessels that could travel up the 30-mile long winding Slough, which included coal barges to and from Issaquah.

1906: Passenger Steamer *City of Bothell* with smokestack raised.

The steamboats *Bee*, *Everett*, *Duck Hunter* and the little sternwheeler *Minnie May* were making frequent trips on it (the *Minnie May* transported Squak Valley farm goods to the Seattle market place as early as March of 1887). Then craft such as the passenger steamer, *City of Bothell*, *Acme* and the work scow[2] *Squak*, started regularly scheduled runs in 1906. They carried passengers and freight to and from Seattle, Bothell, and settlements on Lake Washington such as Kirkland. The steamers' smokestacks were hinged so they could be lowered to pass under bridges along the way up and downstream. The Minnie May and the Squak occasionally cleared stumps and other debris in the Slough to help keep it navigable.

A number of large boats were built in Bothell. One of them was a 65-foot replica of a Viking ship for the Alaska-Yukon-Pacific Exposition. It was financed by a number of prominent Bothell citizens and launched just below the Bothell Bridge in August of 1909. It included a crew of 22 Sons of Norway oarsmen, Viking warriors and their king, all participating on Union Bay during Norway Day at the Exposition.

---

[2] Flat-bottomed boats built with blunt bows for traveling in shallow water and easily beached to load and unload cargo.

Commercial boat travel in the valley became a secondary mode of transportation with the coming of the railroad. In 1887 the Seattle-Lake Shore & Eastern Railway was extended through the Sammamish Valley, along the Eastern side of Lake Sammamish and on to Issaquah. It served today's local towns and the forgotten communities of Derby, Earlmont, Hollywood and York. Construction materials had to be transported from Seattle, across Lake Washington and up the Squak Slough. One of the vessels used was the steamboat *Bee*, pushing a scow full of construction materials that were loaded at the foot of Madison Street on Lake Washington[3]. The supplies were ordered by the British Columbia firm, Thomas Earle & Co., who were constructing 30 miles of railroad road right-of-way through the Squak Slough valley. Ground breaking began in March and with favorable weather the first 43-miles of the railway were mostly completed by mid-June.

The Squak Slough was also known for its large population of spawning salmon that swam upstream from Lake Washington. The early settlers called the upper valley area Salmonberg. The salmon were so abundant there they, at times, clogged the waterway. Later it was renamed Melrose and finally Redmond when it was platted in 1881. Soon the salmon population would be threatened by a scheme to drain the upper valley of the Squak Slough.

In 1888 W. H. Cowie, George W. Tibbetts and R. M. Crawford explored a scheme to drain the upper area of the Squak Slough. The plan had been under discussion for about four years. The objective was to reduce the constant flooding in the area and reclaim the rich farmland that was submerged most of the time. It was found to be feasible but legal issues, required land subsidies and lack of support from local property owners stalled the effort. Then the passage of a recent drainage law made it more feasible to be carried out and prompted a new effort spearheaded by a local resident named Lauron Ingels. The concept was to straighten and deepen a 17-mile stretch of switchback curves between Woodinville and Redmond. The proposed ditch would drain a 4,500-acre strip of land approximately a mile wide, shorten the water course by seven miles and cost $25,000. Signatures of eight property owners were received, with support from seven others, and the required $100 bond for a survey was secured. Apparently, the effort was stalled at some point because the project never started until years later when more influential citizens got involved.

---

[3] Future starting location of Sammamish Slough Races

Logging in the late 1800s and early 1900s was the major industry in the area. Cut logs were pulled by horses or oxen and then rolled into the Slough, retained by raft-like log booms and eventually transported downstream. Moving the heavy floating logs was extremely difficult. Before the advent of tugboats, they were floated to Lake Washington and then pulled to a mill by using a labor-intensive anchor, cable and winch system called kedging. The towing boat was rowed a distance out into the water where an anchor was lowered to the lake bottom. Then a worker on the log boom pulled the boom back toward the anchored boat using the winch and cable. This arduous process was repeated over and over until the logs were moved to their final destination.

Early loggers showing size of cut old-growth timber.

The loggers created a major hindrance to travel on the Slough. When they dumped their logs into the Slough, they completely clogged up the waterway rendering it impassable. In March of 1899 Congress placed the nation's navigable water courses under the jurisdiction of the Secretary of War. This act made it a severe penalty to divert or block any navigable water course. The penalty was a fine of $500 to $2,500 or one year in prison for violators. Apparently, the loggers were either oblivious to the law or just ignored it because they continued blocking the Slough.

Loggers often blocked boaters by dumping logs in Slough.

Local commuters, home owners, businesses and boaters complained vehemently to the United States attorney's office in Seattle over the years. Wealthy gas industrialist and banker, James Clise, owner of the Willowmoor country estate (now Marymoor Park and eventual Slough Race stopover point) wrote to the Army Corps of Engineers

(C.O.E.) about the loggers' adverse effects on the waterway. He hoped his influence would persuade them to help resolve the situation. Even though the C.O.E. likely was never involved, he eventually was instrumental in forming a drainage district to address the routine flooding in the upper part of the Slough.

Despite the perpetual injunction handed down in 1911 by the U.S. district court and the potential arrest of the perpetrating offenders, the loggers refused to break up their log booms to assist the boaters. Complaints continued for months until county leaders passed a law forbidding this practice, which again the loggers just ignored. Eventually the log boomers had to comply because of threats of contempt proceedings from the U.S. attorney's office that were about to be enforced. Finally, after almost 20 years of frustration, the launches that took parties to the summer homes along the Slough and Lake Sammamish had free passage. An article in the *Seattle Times* on April 18, 1912 printed: "Reports were made to the government that every effort was now being taken by the loggers to keep the Slough clear."

Later in 1912, because of the recent loggers' actions, travelers like the Seattle Knights of Pythias were able to navigate up the Slough unrestricted. A large delegation of the lodge men chartered the Steamship *City of Bothell* for an all-night excursion to Bothell for the purpose of establishing a new lodge. Old-timers of the lodge that served Bothell and Woodinville recalled the joy of the trip; starting from Madison Park, traveling across Lake Washington and winding up the Slough so narrow that one could jump ashore on either side. Scenic voyages like this would unfortunately be gone forever in the years to come.

The *City of Bothell* docked at Bothell Landing-downstream from the Bothell Bridge located on far right.

The continuing saga of draining and straightening the upper area of the Squak was soon underway again. On January 28, 1911, voters in the newly formed King County Drainage District #3 approved the "Sammamish Drainage Project." The project, with King County-appropriated funds of $30,000, was intended to help combat the fluctuating water levels of Lake Sammamish and the flooding in the upper Squak Slough farm areas, just like the scheme proposed in 1888.

The effort was spearheaded by timber magnate F. S. Stimson, J.W. Clise and other wealthy land owners who owned property on the Squak and operated large dairy and farming operations. In turn, Stimson, Clise and real estate dealer Herbert S. Upper, were elected as drainage commissioners by the voters of the new district. The wealthy property owners, other residents and the City of Redmond were fortunate that the project was approved and funded. Unfortunately, it was never started, most likely because of the pending, massive Lake Washington Ship Canal project that would eventually drain the area and mitigate the flooding problem.

Later in 1912, the saga continued. Fed up with all the bureaucratic delays, the upper Redmond valley farmers decided to take responsibility for the whole project and pay for it themselves. They collectively paid $60,000 to straighten and dredge this notorious stretch of the Slough between Redmond and Woodinville. It is the same section of the Slough fraught with continuous switchback curves that restricted the flow of water and caused the surrounding farm areas to flood each year from the overflow of Lake Sammamish. The farmers originally appealed to the county to finance the project but after back and forth haggling, the county turned them down. Again, this was most likely because of the future plan to lower Lake

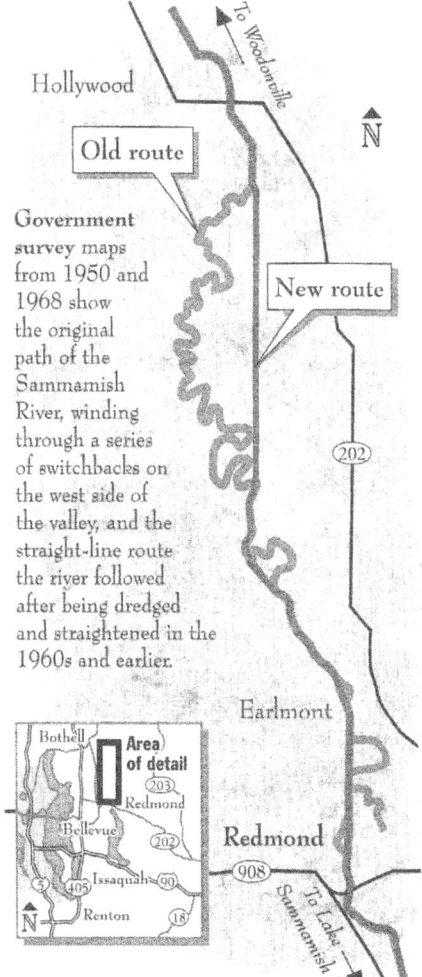

Old, new river routes

Government survey maps from 1950 and 1968 show the original path of the Sammamish River, winding through a series of switchbacks on the west side of the valley, and the straight-line route the river followed after being dredged and straightened in the 1960s and earlier.

Washington. The dredging of this 17-mile section resulted in cutting off seven miles of the 30-mile long Slough and reducing the overall length to about 23-miles. The costly venture brought immediate improvement although some flooding still occurred.

Kenmore area in 1914-The Squak Slough entrance upper right, McMaster shingle mill left center (future Slough Race starting point), Bothell Way in the foreground.

The dairy business was becoming a prominent industry in the valley with world class recognition. The cows and milk of Clise and Stimson won international acclaim. Their dairies along with Herbert S. Upper and steamship tycoon, Charles Peabody's, were helping to keep Seattle in the forefront of the industry. The looming completion of the Lake Washington Ship Canal would make it possible for the Sammamish Valley dairies to ship their product by steamboat down the Slough and directly into downtown Seattle via the new waterway.

During the prohibition period, which began in Washington State in January of 1916, another interesting event occurred in the winter of that year. The heaviest snowfall in memory closed down all the local railways and roads. The snow storm forced some dairies to temporarily transport their milk by boat down the Slough to their Lake Washington and Seattle customers. One might imagine that the bootleggers had to do something similar.

Then in the late summer of 1916, the largest man-made change to ever affect the Slough was completed. Construction of the Lake Washington Ship Canal resulted in the lowering of Lake Washington. The twenty-year project included the building of the Hiram Chittenden Locks, dredging a connecting waterway to Lake Union and excavating another waterway to Lake Washington. The three bodies of water were all at different elevations. The level of Lake Washington was higher than Lake Union and Lake Union's level was higher than Puget Sound (at sea level). The new locks would maintain the existing water level between Puget Sound and Lake Union. The draining of Lake Washington to the level of Lake Union would resolve their elevation difference. The Slough now would be more river-like because the water flow increased due to the change in elevation between Lake Sammamish and Lake Washington. The level drop between Lake Sammamish and Lake Washington increased from approximately 5 to 14 feet.

The federal government was concerned about lawsuits resulting from perceived adverse effects of this far reaching project. Federal officials wouldn't approve the project until the county assured them that they would be protected. The King County commissioners gave that assurance in 1911 by guaranteeing the government protection from any lawsuits resulting from construction of the Lake Washington Ship Canal. In May of 1911 the Bothell Commercial Club gave its endorsement of the county's action in conjunction with other chambers of commerce throughout the county. They resolved to go on record as unanimously approving this action of the county commissioners in passing a resolution guaranteeing to indemnify the U.S. Government against all damages arising from any suit that might be initiated.

In late August of 1916 the final phase of the project was completed when workers breached the earthen dam separating Lake Washington from Lake Union. This was in the Portage bay area location shown in the photograph on the next page. Water from the higher Lake Washington drained into the new canal system and over the flood gates at the new locks for four months until they equalized. Lake Washington was lowered by approximately nine feet. The ship canal opened the following year on July 4, 1917 shortly after the United States declared war on Germany.

The construction eliminated all passenger and commercial traffic on the Sammamish (Squak) Slough from then on. The waterway was transformed into a meandering, narrow and shallow channel less than 50 feet wide. Although the local business and residents knew of the impending change, no one anticipated how dramatic it would be. Once, the broad waterway was deep enough and wide enough to allow coal barges and passenger steamers to travel between Lake Washington and Lake Sammamish. Then, after months of the draining, it was a much smaller snake-like waterway with muddy banks all along its edges. The draining process created a narrow channel, often called a "ditch," only wide enough for smaller boats.

The lowering of Lake Washington also created dramatic and unforeseen changes around the lake. In the months to follow, the receding water exposed an unpleasant muddy and smelly shoreline around the entire lake prompting the once popular boating and recreational areas to be abandoned. The result was similar to the tide going out on Puget Sound, only this was permanent. It's amazing the surrounding cities and communities embraced or at least accepted the plan to lower Lake Washington. A massive project like this with its far-reaching effects seems unthinkable today.

The majority of the recreational activity ceased for the next few years until the shoreline solidified and became usable again. During this time, a lot of boating activity moved into the Puget Sound thanks to the new ship canal. Most of the existing ferry landings and other shoreline facilities were forced to make some type of renovation to resolve any adverse effects of the lake's level change. Ironically, all the future starting locations for the Slough Races were on land that was originally under water. Without this dramatic change, the Slough Races most likely never would have occurred.

August 1916: The dramatic Portage Bay dam breach started the lowering of Lake Washington.

In August of 1920, after the effects of lowering Lake Washington were fully realized by the surrounding Squak Slough communities, the Seattle Port Commission endorsed a proposed plan to dredge the lower portion of the Slough. The plan was to construct a two-mile long public canal between Kenmore and Bothell. It would restore Bothell to its old position as a Lake Washington port as it was before 1916. The canal would be 300 feet wide and 20 feet deep with a staggering cost $1,750,000. The stipulation for approval was that the state legislature would grant the port commission all the land that was originally under water before the Slough was drained and all the future land that would be exposed by the new waterway. In addition, the commission could develop all of the reclaimed land for commercial use. The land which included more than 2,000 acres of rich farming land, would give the port between 200 and 300 acres of industrial sites.

A local improvement district would be established that could levy special assessments to all the surrounding valley property owners to pay for the project. The port commission's plan was a costly attempt by the government to give Bothell something in return for its loss of a navigable transportation route after Lake Washington was lowered. The project never came to a vote because the majority of the residents in the valley were opposed to the adverse commercialization effects it would bring to the area and the cost they would have to bear. The farmers got what they wanted for the upper valley but the City of Bothell lost its port. At about this time, some of the local folks and residents began calling the Squak, the Sammamish Slough or Sammamish River.

The Squak Slough changes described in this chapter and future changes eventually shortened the waterway's length from 30-miles to the approximately 14-miles it is today. Along with the changes in its length, its moniker had also changed over the years. Since the early part of the twentieth century, there's been a controversy among local residents, merchants, and civic leaders about whether we call this important local waterway a "Slough" or a "river."

What you call it depends on your point of view. Many locals prefer "river," because it's more appropriate. Many of them began calling it the Sammamish River after Lake Washington was lowered and the marshy valley was drained. Others prefer to call it a "Slough" because of its storied past and the exciting boat racing events that brought most of the attention to it in the years between 1934 and 1976. The debate will probably continue for the foreseeable future, however for the purposes of this book, it will be called affectionately, "The Sammamish Slough" or "Slough" for short.

Chapter 2

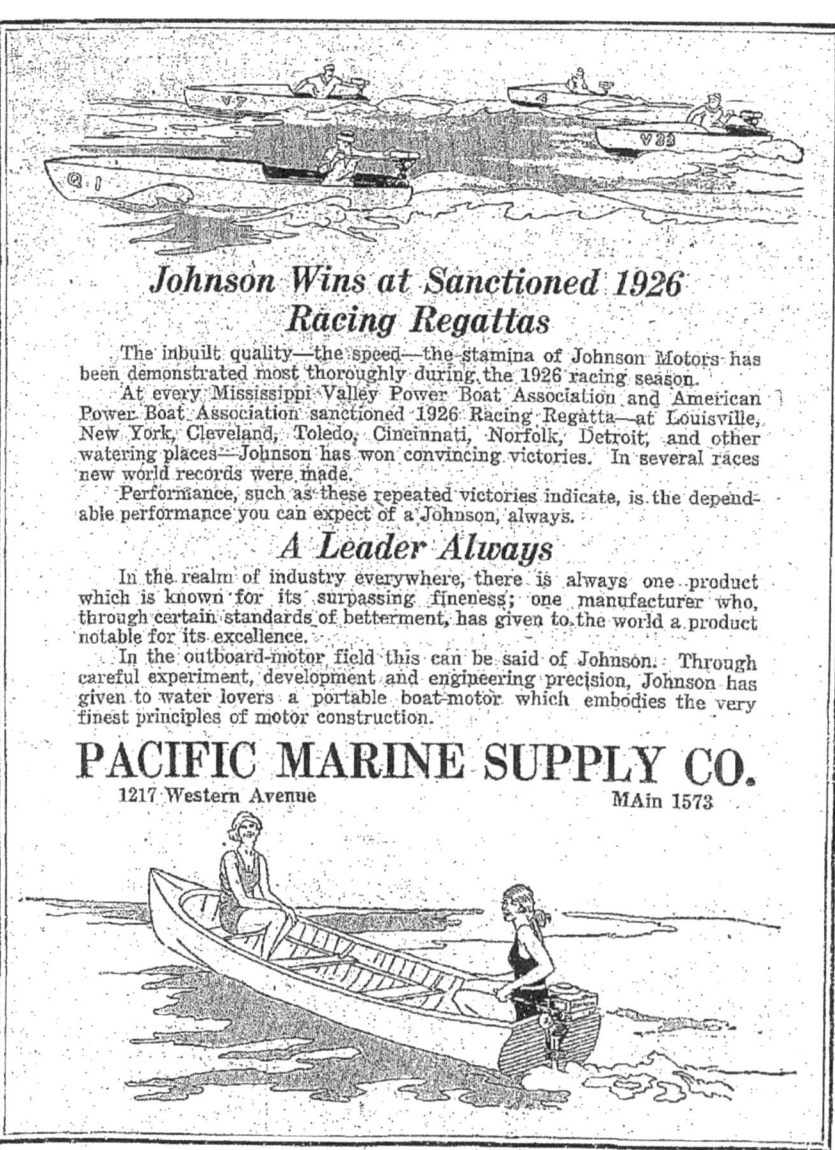

-The Seattle Daily Times, May 22, 1927-

Pop-Poppers to Wave-Hoppers
Outboard Racing History

"SEATTLE DRAWS NATIONAL BOAT BODY'S GLANCE"
-The Seattle Sunday Morning Times, July 15, 1928-

When Cameron Waterman invented his outboard motor[1] and formed the Waterman Marine Motor Company in 1905, the Sammamish Slough Race could never have been imagined. Although he was the inventor of the first outboard motor for sale in the United States, Norwegian-American Ole Evinrude was recognized as the first inventor of a practical outboard motor[2] in 1907. Ole Evinrude sold his original Evinrude Company in 1913 and later formed the ELTO[3] Outboard Motor Company in 1919. In the 1920s Johnson, Evinrude, Caille, Elto and Lockwood-Ash were some of the more common brands sold in the US. During this time outboard motor boats with their loud pop-popping sound, were mainly used by sportsmen for fishing and recreation in the inland waters.

An astute businessman and prominent local sportsman, S.V.B. Miller, was one of the early promoters of high-speed powerboats in Seattle. Miller was an owner of a marine engine supply business that included sales of Elto outboard motors. In 1910 he organized the first-of-its-kind Motor Boat Show in the Northwest where he displayed a number of inboard powerboats that held world records, marine engines and numerous accessories he sold at his business.

---

[1] US Patent No. 851,389 issued April 23, 1907.
[2] Detachable internal-combustion engine mounted on outboard brackets or on the stern of a boat. US Patent No. 1,001,260 issued August 22, 1911.
[3] "ELTO" An acronym derived from the first letters of Evinrude Light Twin Outboard created by Mrs. Bess Evinrude for their Elto Outboard Motor Company in Milwaukee Wisconsin.

By 1911 boats powered with outboard motors were beginning to be used in organized boat races in the Midwest. Seattle's first publicized outboard regatta, as announced in the *Seattle Times*, was held on August 8, 1915. The six-mile free-for-all event started in the afternoon at 2 pm and ran from Leschi Park to Madison Park and back. The race was open to all boats over 14 feet long with a minimum beam of 42 inches and powered by a detachable outboard motor.

Six boats entered the race which was sponsored by the local Chandler-Dunlap Tire Company. J.M. Baird won first place in a 4-passenger clinker boat[4] with a winning time of 40 minutes-eight seconds for the six-mile course. S.A. Carman was second in a 14-foot, 3-passenger clinker boat and S.R. Battenfield was third in a 16-foot, 8-passenger V-bottomed craft. All three of the boats that placed were powered by Evinrude motors.

More is better? Not with 3 unruly outboard motors! Gar Wood: famous 1910s era Gold-Cup racer in first APBA sanctioned Outboard Race held in August of 1924 at Detroit Michigan.

---

[4] Boats built with overlapping planks or boards, also known as "Lapstrake".

During this period Seattle's principle outboard motor dealers were S.V.B. Miller (Elto), Pacific Marine Supply (Johnson), Evinrude Motor Company (Evinrude) and the Walter Bryant Company selling Lockwood-Ash motors. Walter Bryant, whose company was in the ship chandler business[5], was the father of Jerry Bryant, the future patriarch of the Sammamish Slough Race. If you wanted a Caille motor, you had to go to Tacoma and purchase one from Kimball Sporting Goods Company.

The first outboard event run in Seattle with future Seattle Outboard Association members, occurred on August 17, 1924. This was the first-of-its-kind championship outboard regatta to be run on Lake Washington. The event consisted of a series of boat races running between Leschi and Madison Park, including the feature event that would run around Mercer Island. This event was the inaugural 17-Mile Mercer Island Marathon, where drivers started and finished at Madison Park and drove around Mercer Island. Rules required the boats to pass a number of buoys located on the course. The drivers needed to take extra gas to make the entire trip because there was no place for fuel stops along the way.

It was a typical drizzly rain-soaked day on Lake Washington where future Seattle Outboard Club Commodores George Brown, and S.V.B. Miller, along with Victoria, B.C.'s E. G. (Ernie) Adams, competed in the Mercer Island Marathon event. Adams was first with his four-horsepower Evinrude-powered craft, Brown second, also with an Evinrude motor and Miller third with his Elto-powered boat.

In July, 1925, Ernie Adams, by then with Seattle's Pacific Marine Supply, won again but this time he raced a Johnson-powered speedster that he had designed. This race was during Seattle's huge Green Lake "Sportsman Show" where an estimated 350,000 spectators attended the nine-day show. S.V.B. Miller placed second in his Elto-powered craft. The following year, Miller set a world record for 6-1/2 horsepower

---

[5] Retail dealer specializing in supplies or equipment for ships.

outboards on July 31, 1926, in the same Green Lake regatta. His boat was a small flat-bottomed craft weighing 80-pounds powered by an Elto motor (he was the Elto distributor in Seattle). His record average speed was 20.23 mph for a two-mile heat, which bettered the old record by almost 4 mph. It took several days to make it official because a speed adjustment was needed. The course ended up shorter and the speed was lowered based on a subsequent survey by Seattle Yacht Club race officials.

Ernie Adams eventually became a leader at Pacific Marine Supply in the outboard motor sales operation, was vice-commodore of the Northwest Outboard Motor Association and one of the original organizers of the Seattle Outboard Club. S.V.B. Miller was also instrumental in forming the outboard club, where he was commodore for several years and a key promoter of outboard racing.

During this time boats designed specifically for racing were a rarity. Typically, one couldn't just go out and buy a raceboat from a local marine business supplier. They were either designed by a race-driver and then custom-built or built by the driver himself. Most of the boats were rowboats and canoe type craft adapted for outboard motors.

Early outboard racing in the Northwest was mostly an exhibition event combined with sailboat and powerboat (yacht) races sponsored by the Seattle and Queen City yacht clubs. The outboard drivers were mostly individuals who were in the boat and motor business or were well-off financially. By the mid-1920s the races were separate events but still mostly run and sponsored by the yacht clubs.

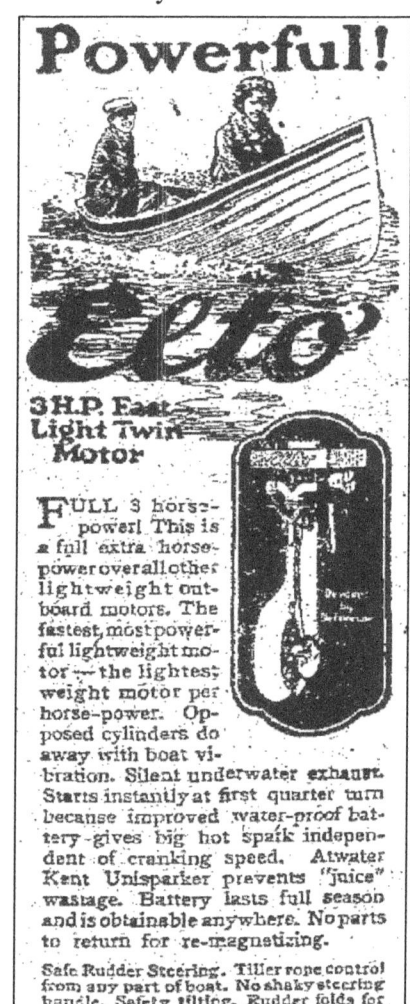

To make the races fair, the racing rules established by the American Power Boat Association (APBA) were adopted. The American Power Boat Association, formed in 1903, was a New York based racing authority for powerboats. It soon became the governing body of national boat racing with the responsibility for establishing and enforcing boat racing rules in the United States.

In the early 1920s there was a need for racing guidelines because the sport of outboard racing was quickly growing and there was considerable public confusion about the motor and boat types for the racing classes. The APBA began the process of establishing outboard motorboat classes based on the engine piston displacement along with guidelines and categorization of larger recreational motorboats for racing. In 1923 they adopted Judge Aaron B. Chon's first-of-its-kind outboard racing rules that he created for his local outboard group, the Mississippi Valley Power Boat Association. The Mississippi racing organization would eventually be recognized as a national governing body like the APBA. Both organizations officially recognized speed records in all their approved classes.

Chon, an Ohio Justus during the weekdays, who was considered by many as "the father of outboard racing," drafted the racing rules to make competitions more equitable and fair. He and his fellow enthusiast's defined classes for small motorboats with detachable motors, starting with the smaller motors designated as "A," "B" and "C." Soon the local outboard groups began adopting Chon's guidelines after they were published in the magazine, *Power Boating*. These guidelines were the basis for APBA's original rules. In 1924 APBA further defined their categorizations of the outboard classes as follows:

"A" under 12 cubic inches
"B" 12 to 17 cubic inches
"C" 17 to 30 cubic inches
"D" over 30 cubic inches

Then a few years later, a further adjustment for engines of the 1928 to 1930 era to:

"A" up to 14 cubic inches
"B" up to 20 cubic inches
"C" up to 30 cubic inches
"D" up to 40 cubic inches
"E" up to 50 cubic inches
"F" up to 60 cubic inches
"G" up to 80 cubic inches

The basic rules were a good start but as boat racing became more popular, there was always someone who'd push the envelope further. This resulted in a lot of disparity between boat contestants with means and those without with respect to their racing equipment. It also caused more public confusion about the types and classes of boats and how a race should be run. In May of 1927, a committee in the boat racing authority came to the rescue. APBA organized the "Contest Board for Outboard Motors" which was chartered with determining rules for how to organize and run outboard motor races along with further clarification of the class descriptions. By 1928 the outboard rules had been expanded by adding classifications for amateur and professional divisions along with classes up to 80 cubic inches of piston displacement.

In 1929 the National Outboard Association (NOA) emerged and joined the likes of the APBA and the Mississippi Valley Power Boat Association. The NOA group, made up of mostly industry leaders, recognized the need to make boat racing equitable for amateurs and professionals to keep the sport prospering. They grouped competitors into three categories:

Division I: Novice amateurs with fewer than 15 races
Division II: Amateurs more experienced with over 15 races
Division III: Professionals who had connections with the industry and were offered cash prizes.

Later in 1929 the NOA merged with the APBA and became a senior partner in the outboard branch where they oversaw the racing activities and provided financial support for the organization. A few years later they simplified the divisions into just amateurs (Division I) and professionals (Division II).

In the late 1920s outboard motor dealers were popping up all over the Northwest. One of them was young Jerry Bryant's first shop. Born Gerome Cordes Bryant, best known as Jerry, he worked for his father's firm and for other business during the summers while attending Queen Anne High School. Then he began learning the outboard motor business working part-time as an outboard motor repairman while attending the University of Washington. In 1928, the year after he graduated, he opened his own outboard motor sales and repair business. The shop was in a corner space of the Seattle Marine Equipment Company at 70 Marion Street where he previously

Jerry Bryant
70 Marion St.
JOHNSON
Outboard Motor Sales, Service and Repairs

Demonstrations Any Time

Tel. MAin 3576

worked part-time as a college student, just down the street from S.V.B. Miller's business. As competitors in the business, the irony of it was that Jerry Bryant would eventually buyout Miller's business in 1947.

Jerry began racing outboards in 1928 to promote his business. His racing accomplishments became known to the public when his name started appearing in the newspapers. In May of 1929, the *Seattle Times* reported that he swept the first regatta of the year, which was held on Lake Washington at Seward Park. In a short time, he became successful in winning his share of races and gained a reputation as a strong competitor. He also competed in the Midwest where he was instrumental in introducing the Midwesterners to the emerging racing regattas in the Northwest and the ideal race sites such as Lake Washington and Green Lake in Seattle.

During this time Bryant was a dealer for Johnson outboard motors but shortly this would change because of an unexpected encounter. Jerry was visited by Ralph Evinrude, the son of renowned outboard motor inventor, Ole Evinrude. Soon they would become close business associates and best of friends.

Jerry Bryant's race boat named *Hinky Dink*-before boat racing rules required safety helmets.

The relationship started when young Evinrude came to Bryant's business all the way from Milwaukee, Wisconsin. He came specifically for the purpose of convincing Mr. Bryant to become an Evinrude dealer. The relationship blossomed and because Jerry had tremendous admiration for the Evinrude family, he was inclined to make the change. It wasn't an easy decision because of his responsibility to his Johnson-buying customers, but Jerry was becoming less enamored with the Johnson Company.

By now Jerry had considerable experience in outboard motor repair and in high-performance tuning of his racing engines. He felt there was a need for improvements to the chronic problems plaguing the Johnson motor. One day he wrote to the factory with suggestions for improvement. The firm's polite but sharp reply included; "until we ask for advice we'll build them and you sell them." Jerry eventually made the decision to change to an Evinrude dealership because of the Johnson rebuff and for his high respect for the Evinrude Company. Bryant's new Evinrude dealership grew successfully over the years into the largest distributorship in the country. Ironically again, S.V.B. Miller at this time was an Evinrude dealer in the Northwest.

In March of 1928, a group of outboard racing enthusiasts gathered in Olympia to form a regional outboard association called the Northwest Outboard Association. Their objective was to represent all the local clubs and be directly affiliated with one of the national associations. They planned to organize regional races open to all outboard clubs and individuals in the Northwest. The group included members of the Tacoma, Everett, Bellingham and Olympia clubs along with individuals from Seattle. J. L. (Joe) Patton was elected commodore; Ernest (Ernie) Adams of Seattle, vice-commodore; Walter Draham of Olympia, secretary, and Henry Long of Olympia as treasurer.

Seattle Outboard Contingent Wooed By APBA

The time was right for the Seattle outboard contingent to have its own organization. They had the largest base of drivers, racing enthusiasts and outboard motor dealers in an area that encompassed ideal inland waters for regattas. During this time, they were loosely affiliated with the Seattle and Queen City yacht clubs, unlike the Tacoma, Everett, Bellingham and Olympia groups that were actual members of their respective boat clubs. The consensus was to form their own club because the national outboard associations required individual boat racers be members of a local organization. Seattle was also emerging as one the nation's hot-spots because of the boat races on Lake Washington and on one of the nation's finest race courses, Green Lake. They were also drawing serious attention from the three national outboard associations–the APBA, the NOA and the Mississippi Valley Power Boat Association.

The American Power Boat Association was the first to court the Northwest. They were known as the oldest and most important official boat racing organization in the world. Because the Northwest was now one of the top three regions in the U.S. for outboard racing, the governing body decided it was time to make an official visit to Seattle. APBA Commodore A.L. Bobrick and *Motor Boating* magazine editor Charles F. Chapman set up a meeting with Joe Patton, commodore of the recent loosely formed Northwest Outboard Association.

The meeting was held at the Queen City Yacht Club in July, 1928, with the Seattle contingent and members of the regional clubs all in attendance. Commodore Bobrick and Chapman expressed the importance of this region as an outboard racing center and asked the association to become a member of the APBA. One of the advantages as a member is certification of speed records and world-wide publicity. Commodore Bobrick also recommended that Seattle racers should immediately form a club of their own. A poll of the attendees indicated that most would approve joining the APBA. Bobrick stated that to become a member, each club within the Northwest Outboard Association would need approval of its membership which eventually occurred. At this time Seattle didn't have an official outboard club but soon it would be in the making.

By the end of the 1920s outboard motors advanced along with the national and local boat racing associations. Many of the old motorboats, powered with slow pop-popping outboard motors, were transformed into faster speedboats. They became wave-hoppers in organized regattas viewed by hundreds of spectators throughout the region. Eventually this sporting event would become one of the most popular in the Northwest and the largest of its kind in the country.

Chapter 3

Winter 1929: Jerry Bryant (rear), his girlfriend Miss Ann Engstrom (front right) and famous boating author, Jack West–early running of the Sammamish Slough.

New Club is Born
SOC Beginning 1929 to 1931

*"Racing Enthusiasts Here to Meet Tuesday Night
at Farwest Boathouse to Plan for New Club"*

-The Seattle Daily Times, January 14, 1929-

Outboard motor dealers, recreational outboard owners and racing enthusiasts scheduled a meeting to organize a new outboard racing club in Seattle on the night of January 15, 1929. The meeting was held at the Farwest Boathouse, located at 2400 Westlake Ave. N., at 8:00 pm under the direction of Pacific Marine Supply's owner, Ernie G. Adams. Mr. Adams ran the meeting until the new club officers were elected. At the time, Adams was a successful outboard race driver and boat builder originally from Victoria, B.C.

Representative boat and motor owners from Seattle, Tacoma, Everett and adjacent cities were invited to attend the meeting to help establish the new organization. The club would be one of many in the region planning to be affiliated with one of the governing national powerboat associations.

Sixty-two individuals had made reservations to attend the inaugural event with the intent of signing-up as charter members. There were as many as ten organizations in the state planning to start clubs during the winter and spring. Their strategy was to foster and direct the outboard motor racing sport throughout Washington State. A plan to hold a Northwest regional race event for all the drivers of the state-wide clubs was in the making. The champions of the regatta would qualify to run in the National Outboard Regatta which would be held in a location to be determined in October.

On January 16, 1929 the *Seattle Daily Times* sports page headlines, highlighted with bold print, were: **"George Brown Named Head of Yacht Body; Race Plans Are Made."** Mr. George Brown, owner of "Brown's Boat House" on Lake Washington in Madison Park, was elected to lead the new boat club as its first commodore. The new organization was called the Seattle Outboard Club (SOC). The other officers elected for the year were Herman Seastrim, vice-commodore; T.C. Andrews, secretary[1] and Harold F. Bolton, treasurer.

Thirty-five outboard enthusiasts from Seattle, Bremerton, Everett, Tacoma, Bellingham and Lake Sammamish signed up to be charter members. The club would schedule and conduct outboard racing events in and around Seattle. The officers and members voted to affiliate themselves with the Northwest Outboard Association (NWOA) which at that time was the regional representative for the National Outboard Association. Race officials were then selected by the membership which would manage the various events organized by the club.

Commodore George Brown

The elected trustees of the club were Ed Mundorf, chairman, Ernie Adams and Ernest Osgood. The membership committee appointees were Gale Roose, chairman with L. J. Vaupell and Charles F. West. Other members included E.M.A. Larrson, Jerry Bryant, Joe Patton, S.V.B. Miller, Jimmy Tregoning, Henry Long, Harold Kuett, "Doc" Morris, Jimmy Harland, "Whiff" Emperor, George Thompson, Johnny Sheriff, Mike Shain and "Curly" Colman.

The next meeting was held again at the Farwest boathouse on Westlake Avenue. During the gathering, a constitution and bylaws were considered, voted upon and adopted by the members. The most interesting item on the agenda was the important business of planning and scheduling the racing events to be run that year. The race schedule, listed on the following page, listed their outboard racing events for the year which was approved by the NWOA and the SOC, which includes races determined later in the year.

```
JOHNSON OUTBOARD MOTORS
          FOR RENT
   DAY—WEEK—MONTH
  Canoes, Rowboats, Sea Sleds, Sail Boats
   Brown's Boat House
   EAst 3782           Madison Park
```

---

[1] Mr. Andrews, without explanation, was not identified as secretary after the meeting. E.M.A. Larrson was stated as the secretary in all future publications.

New Club is Born | 33

1929 Race Schedule & Sponsor

Jan 6	Inaugural Sammamish Slough Cruise
May 5	Seward Park Practice Heats, Seattle by NWOA
June 9	Seattle to Olympia Marathon by NWOA
June 30	100 Mile Mercer Island Marathon by SOC
July 4	Bremerton by SOC
July 20-21	Green Lake NW Championships by SOC
July 28	*Times* Regatta. West Seattle-Lincoln Park by SOC
Aug. 18	Lake Sammamish Regional Championships/Mile Trials by SOC
Sept. 2	American Lake State Championships, Tacoma by SOC
Sept. 22	Lake Washington Movie Promotion by SOC
Oct 12-13	Outboard Nationals in Peoria, Illinois

At this time the Seattle Outboard Club was strictly an amateur organization with all its racing events held under its direction or jurisdiction being conducted on an amateur basis. Officials of the new club extended invitations to anyone interested in outboards to attend the meetings and join. The club planned to coordinate a number of cruising events during the season. These activities were planned for those who were not interested in racing but enjoyed non-competitive outboard events with family and friends.

First Sammamish Slough Cruise

The first documented trip up and down the Sammamish Slough in a motorboat powered by an outboard motor occurred in January, 1929. The photograph at the beginning of this chapter is a historical record of that early journey up the waterway. Jerry Bryant is driving in the rear cockpit. His pretty girlfriend and future wife Ann, along with esteemed boating author Jack West, are in the front cockpit. The purpose of the excursion, other than a remarkable outing in the winter, was to determine the feasibility of cruising up and down the Slough and then have an exhilarating annual cruise that could be sponsored by the Seattle Outboard Club.

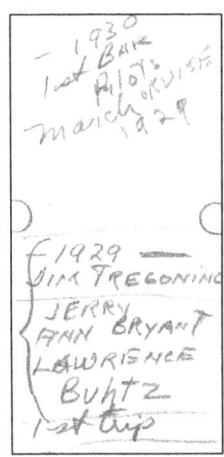

Al Benson notes

My father's old notes indicate that this was the first Sammamish Slough Cruise, to be known as the annual "Old-Timers Cruise," organized by the Seattle Outboard Club. Three boats participated and my father's notes say the three boat parties were: the "Jerry Ann Bryant" boat, the "Jim Tregoning" boat and the "Lawrence Buhtz" boat in the first trip. Jerry, Ann, Jack, Jim, Ellsworth

Simpson along with Lawrence and Eduma Buhtz, "were the public-spirited citizens who personally with ax, saw, brush hook and hatchet, cleared the slough the first Sunday after New Year's Day" in 1929. The inaugural cruise was one of the club's new activities in the planning, an event for all those interested in non-racing outings. An afterthought from this trip most likely led to the planning of the Sammamish Slough Race and nearly 100 annual cruises to Lake Sammamish from 1929 to 1963. This event was also documented in Eileen Crimmin's book *BRYANTS*, except she stated it started in 1930. I believe 1929 was the correct year because my father knew the first slough cruise members well and his notes were written in the 1940s not that long after the event started.

Later in May the club adopted its racing insignia in the form of a flag. The design included a white background with red letters "S.O.C." The plan was for all racing craft to carry the insignia in regattas that summer. It was unimaginable then, but the Seattle Outboard Organization would eventually become the largest outboard club in the Nation.

Seward Park Practice

The first outboard race of the season was held Sunday May 5, 1929 at Seward Park on Lake Washington under the auspices of Northwest Outboard Association. The event was just a practice event, not an official race. Jerry Bryant, called by the local presses "the Barney Oldfield of the Outboards," won most of the races in his *Hinky Dinky II* craft. He swept the opening day race on the two-and-a-half-mile course. Several mishaps were witnessed by the large crowd. Dexter Hunt of Tacoma capsized in his *Homicide* named boat and Seattle's Gale Roose, test driver for Pacific Marine Supply, was unable to finish due to a broken propeller in his custom designed *Cootie*. The race boat categories included Class B, C and a free-for-all.

Seattle-Olympia Marathon

The *Seattle Times* headline on June 6, 1929 was: "WOMEN PILOTS TO FEATURE IN OUTBOARD RACE." The event was the 61-mile marathon run on Puget Sound between Seattle and Olympia that started Sunday morning at 8:00 o'clock on June 9. The race, sponsored by the Northwest Outboard Association, was open to all outboard motor-powered craft with "high powered motors down to fishing skiffs with their one-lung (cylinder) engines. To prove that racing isn't confined to men, driver's entries from several women had been received. Some will race with their husbands while one will pilot a craft by herself. Mrs. A.S. Burr of Seattle filed her entry alone, while Mrs. E.G. Adams and Mrs. Alexander Gow would take part with their husbands." This was the first race in the Northwest in which a woman driver participated and drove her own boat.

The event was reported to have the largest list of prizes of any race to date. Cash and merchandise prizes were supplied by S.V.B. Miller's Elto Company, Pacific Marine Supply, and the Tregoning Boat Company among others. The rule for the boat type was: displacement type boats[2] only–no racing craft. Jimmy Tregoning and Bill Smith in the *Red Streak* won the event in one of the Tregoning boats and received the Governor's Cup as the overall winner. Frank Calvert and Jack West in the *Hoku Boy* were second and Arthur Latimer and Junior Lampson in the *Skippy* were third.

Green Lake Championships

"CALIFORNIANS ENTERED FOR BIG REGATTA" was the headline in the *Times* sports section on July 7, 1929. The third annual running of the Northwest Championships was announced which was run again on Green Lake in Seattle. Entries from Washington, California, Idaho and Oregon were expected. The California sportsmen, Rodney Pantages and George Tait, will try to defend their titles won in last year's event. This year the regatta was sponsored by the new Seattle Outboard Club with assistance from Queen City Yacht club members. Ernest L. Wolfe was appointed race chairman with George Brown and Joe Patton as assistants. The other race officials were: Patton, as referee; Wolfe, starter; Brown, Karl Seastrom and F.L. Meredith, judges; E.M.A. Larsson, measurer, and E.D. Shaw, Carroll Woods and Al Gow, as timers.

The racing categories include Division I: amateurs, Classes "A" & "B," Division II: Classes "A" & "B" and a free-for-all class. The inclusion of the amateur classes was announced as a "special effort to encourage boys" to participate. This was again a combined event with two classes of inboards running on a mile-and-a-half course. National records were anticipated to be broken because Green Lake was becoming Known as one of the finest boat racing courses in the country. A shallow body of water in a natural marine stadium setting with gradually sloping shores that give spectators perfect viewing areas around the entire lake. The *Times* stated: "thousands

---

[2] Boat hull that doesn't plane. It pushes water when moving rather than riding over the top (planing).

and thousands of fans who witnessed the two days of racing last year will be treated to the real thrills of boating." Green Lake's Commercial Club president George Hill got permission from the city Park Board to erect bleachers on the northeast side of the lake for a thousand spectators.

A crowd estimated at 20,000 lined the shores for the two-day racing spectacle. Entries from Washington, Oregon and Idaho made quite a show even though the boys from California never made the trip; maybe they thought the competition would be too stiff. Gale Roose was the big winner in the free-for-all event where he won five of his six heats and was presented a boat for accomplishments. His custom-built speedster was powered by a big Johnson Seahorse four-cylinder motor. Allen Cunningham, Roose's boat builder, was so ecstatic about the performance that he gave the boat to him as a gift for winning the free-for-all championship. Another SOA veteran racer, Jerry Bryant, won the Division II, Class "B" race in his *Hinky Dinky II* craft also powered with a Johnson motor. The Green Lake regatta was one of the major races in 1929 but the main outboard event which would have national implications was about to come.

Lake Sammamish Regionals & Mile Trials

The most important race of the year was the first Northwest Regional Championships held August 17-18 on Lake Sammamish. This race was questionable up to a month before the day of the race because the national body (NOA combined with APBA) was still in the planning stages of establishing outboard racing regions in the country. The NOA group wanted to create a Northwest region that would include Washington, Oregon and Idaho with the possibly of adding Montana and Wyoming. Currently the Northwest Outboard Association and the other independent clubs in the region were not properly organized into one regional entity.

To join the APBA as a regional organization, at least five clubs with a total of 500 members needed to be organized. The current northwest regional association only represented Seattle, Tacoma and Port Angeles. The other twelve clubs in the region decided to stay independent after the Northwest Outboard Association tried to recruit them earlier in the year. In late July the national body suggested that a regional championship "be staged under the auspices of the Seattle Outboard Club, a member of the APBA this year, with other clubs in the three states assisting with financing for the event." They asked E.M. Larrson, secretary of the Seattle club, to be their representative for the region at that time.

Mr. Larrson and Edgar Mundorf, chairman of the Lake Sammamish race committee, inspected the race course site on August 4. It was located in the area were Vasa Park is today. A surveyed 2-1/2 mile race course was laid out in front of three adjacent properties: Lewis Beach, Stafford Park and Vasa Park. The course was approved for APBA world records pending certification after the race. This event was the first regional race run in the Northwest and the first outboard race that was conducted on Lake Sammamish. The key race officials included: chairman, Edgar Mundorf, Issaquah, referee; E.M. Larrson; measurer; Jack West, starter; E.L. Wolfe, and a host of judges, pit men and timers. It is assumed that there was a timer for each boat. Accurate stop watches, called chronographs, were most likely used by a timer who was assigned to a specific boat in each heat.

Chronograph

The two-day race program included three heats consisting of two laps each for both days (5 miles total per heat). The total points accumulated for each event for both days determined the winner and order of finish. Only Classes B, C and DE in Division II were eligible for Nationals qualification. The program was run as follows:

Event 1:	Class A, Division I
Event 2:	Class B, Division I
Event 3:	Class B, Division II
Event 4:	Displacement
Event 5:	Class C, Division I
Event 6:	Class C, Division II
Event 7:	Class DE, Division I
Event 8:	Class DE, Division II

The same program was run on Sunday with the addition of a special event for the inboard speedboats.

The *Times* sports headline on August 19 was "Jerry Bryant of Seattle, Ted Farmin of Sand Point and Jennings of Portland Earn Trips to Peoria." The young speedsters earned the right to represent the Northwest at the National Championships that were to be run in October at Peoria, Illinois. Passage's in the article under the headline read: "Veteran racing drivers in the Northwest fell before the onslaught of youth in the competition. Jerry Bryant, 22-year-old from Seattle, finished first in five straight heats on Saturday and Sunday to earn top honors in the Class B event driving Pat Troyer's

Miss Epps. Ted Farmin, curly haired youngster of Sand Point, Idaho, who yesterday celebrated his 21st birthday, won in the Class C in his *Robbin II* and Talbot Jennings, kid driver from Portland in his first year of racing, piloted his boat named *C-Cow* to first in Class DE. Favored local driver Gale Roose, recent Class DE winner at the Green Lake Championships, was the hard-luck driver of the weekend. He finished a disappointing fifth in three heats on Saturday, finished first in the opening heat on Sunday after the leader, Jennings, tipped over in the *C-Cow* and then while leading in the second heat, he hit a wake and flipped over just before the finish line in the second heat. He was unable to run the final heat because of terminal engine damage sustained in the previous heat. Roose lost the championship due to Jennings' higher accumulated point total even though Jennings failed to finish any heat on Sunday."

Lake Sammamish Regionals – Class-B Event with Jerry Bryant of Seattle leading, followed by Forrest Pollock of Portland, Roy Craig of Tacoma & R.E. Golden of Seattle.

"While Bryant, Jennings and Farmin were earning their right to go east, world records were tumbling before the onslaught of the drivers." Allen Pettrich, a Tacoma youngster, set a new record in Class A with an average speed of 26 miles-per-hour (mph) in one of his 5-mile heats. Then Bryant in Class B set a new mark bettering the existing record of 36.280 on both days. His best record run was on Saturday with the new mark set at 38.864 mph. The third record was set in the displacement Class where Gale Roose and Jerry Bryant, piloting the *A. & P. Flyer*, captured the honors with an average speed at nearly 38 mph. The race was a huge success despite a blinding rain storm, rough water and numerous mishaps during Sunday's mile trials."

Three regional champs were crowned and three world records were established in the first ever official regional championships.

"Seattle Outboard Aces Off to Nationals Meet" was the headline in the *Sunday Times* on September 29. Jerry Bryant and Gale Roose representing the Seattle Outboard Club left the evening of the 28th for Peoria, Illinois, to compete in the

National Outboard Championships being held on October 12 and 13. One could assume that they didn't fare too well because no articles were published giving recounts of their accomplishments after the event or before the event was ran the following year. This was the first National Championship Regatta ever run by the American Power Boat Association.

A number of other outboard races were run by Northwest clubs during the year, including the highly publicized "*Seattle Times* Regatta." Unfortunately, its location on Puget Sound at West Seattle, combined with rough water and drift debris, made it difficult for the entrants, which included all kinds of water craft. It was estimated that about 40,000 spectators lined the shores of Fauntleroy Cove; mostly who arrived in 12,000 cars that jammed the driveways of Lincoln Park.

Seattle outboards competed in a first time "Movie Race" held Sunday, September 22, at Seward Park. The "Movie" regatta was sponsored by the Seattle club as part of the University of Washington crew race scene being produced by the Universal Film Company. Two sectional race winners, Jerry Bryant and Ted Farmin of Everett, along with other types of powerboats, fans and spectators, took part in a mock racing event. Trophy cups were awarded to the outboard and inboard victors in this first of its kind event for Seattle.

In November, new rules for next season were set forth by the national association, placing most of the prominent Northwest outboard champions into the professional Division III category. These were the contestants who were connected with the industry in some way, awarded cash prizes or were paid for racing. This included the recognized outboard pilots; Ernie Adams, Jerry Bryant, Gale Roose, Ted Farmin, and Jimmy Tregoning. Under the new rules they wouldn't be eligible to compete in the nationals, only those in the Division II category were eligible. The local press noted that "fans shouldn't forget that it was the dealers who made the game what it is today. They have always come to the front to assist with advice, with entrants, officials, suggestions and prizes to aid the sport and, with the new changes their aid will be needed more than ever." They still were able to compete in the more or less unlimited division where entrants were allowed to use souped-up motors or specially constructed engines.

Earlier in the year a major event occurred that completely changed the outboard motor industry in the United States. Ole Evinrude and company formed the Outboard Motors Corporation (OMC) in Milwaukee Wisconsin on February 23, 1929. The new company was a merger of the Elto, Evinrude and Lockwood motor companies. The latter two companies were financially in trouble at the time. Ole Evinrude, who orchestrated the partnership, became president; Steven Briggs of Briggs and Stratton, CEO, and Arthur Lockwood, former president of Lockwood motors, treasurer. Ole's son, Ralph, became manager of the export business.

Later in the year, the newly formed OMC was hit hard by the unforeseen stock market crash on Friday, October 28. In the early years of the depression that followed the crash, OMC's sales dropped dramatically. This caused the management team to drop the Lockwood line of motor products. To meet payroll, the company held factory sales of overstock and motors assembled from leftover parts on the weekends. The Depression would continue to affect OMC and the industry in the years to come with the exception of the Northwest, which was becoming the largest and fastest growing outboard motor region in the country.

1929 was a huge success for the inaugural year of the Seattle Outboard Club and for boat racing in general throughout the Northwest. The press was enamored with the new club and gave extensive coverage to all the events and happenings. How the new racing rules, the stock market crash and the following Depression will affect Northwest racing, will only be known next summer after the new season begins.

1930

The Seattle Outboard Club's sophomore year brought in a new cast of officers whose terms began on Friday night, January 3, at the Queen City Yacht Club. They were voted into office during a meeting held the preceding month. L.S. Davis was elected commodore; Jerry Bryant, vice-commodore; Gene Shaw, secretary, and H.L. Baker, treasure. The new officers theme was "a bigger and better racing season and program for the club during the next year."

The Seattle Outboard Club, the newest of the local boating organizations, had grown to nearly 80 members after only a year of existence. In late January, Commodore Davis announced that the club had three events already scheduled. "Despite the fact that ice skaters were now enjoying themselves on Green Lake," the annual speed boat event there during July is one of the big topics for the pilot-house gossip during the winter." New members included future Slough race drivers Orval Skaggs, Lee Stark, Jim Perine, Bill Harrison and future winners Jack Colcock, Bus Sill and Dave Hall. Other new members included Allen Petrich, Art Ridley, Roger

Holman, Steve Easterman, Ted Elberts, Roger De Clements, Norman Ledger and Jim Rautenberg. Rautenberg was an uncle to the young Rautenberg brothers, Bob and Dick, who would continue the family racing tradition later in the 1950s, including being the first members of the Rautenberg family who raced in the Sammamish Slough.

Commodore L.S. Davis changed the location of the SOC monthly meetings to the third floor of the *Seattle Times* building. Their first order of business was to draw up the racing schedule for the year. Last year the first meeting was the inaugural "Old Timers Slough Cruise," but this year it wasn't publicized. It most likely never occurred.

During a meeting in March, the club decided to change their name to the Seattle Outboard Association (SOA). There was no reason stated for the name change but it may have been to align themselves better with the national association. At about the same time, the current secretary and treasurer decided to resign. Because of this, the club decided to combined the two offices and choose Mrs. Frances Burr to fill both positions. In 1929, she was the first woman to pilot a boat in a club-sponsored event. Later in the year the offices were separated and Gene Shaw was appointed treasurer.

The Northwest Outboard Association (NWOA) was finally recognized as one of the national regions within the APBA, when they were officially affiliated in January of 1930. E.M.A. Larrson, the current secretary and past SOC secretary, made the announcement in a January issue of the *Seattle Times*. He also acknowledged that the northwest association now has affiliations with clubs in Washington, Oregon, Idaho and British Columbia. This meant that the national body would sanction and approve all races, records and measures of the newly expanded regional group. The new relationship would allow the Northwest to hold regional races that qualified the drivers and boats to run in the newly formed Divisionals. The competitors who placed first in the divisional races would be awarded an all-expense paid trip to the nationals, the big event that was held in Middleton, Connecticut. The local outboard members felt this was a major benefit that resulted from their association with the regional body. With the later addition of Alaska, the northwest section became the largest outboard region (in area) in the country.

Meanwhile, the newly named SOA was firming up its racing schedule with Green Lake and Lake Sammamish being the major races for the year. Some of the outboarders were off to an early start with new boats. Jerry Bryant and Gale Roose were testing their new boats on Lake Stevens. Ernie Adams built the lightweight

Bryant-designed Division III craft, *Ann How* and Nick Reinell, of the future Marysville boat building family, built Roose's *Cootie III* speedster. Rumor had it that Reinell was building another race boat for a female Reinell family member, young Bertha Reinell.

Bryant, now relegated to the new Division III professional category, didn't have to worry about the new boat weight restrictions with his new Class B craft, Division III boats were exempt. When APBA created the professional class, they allowed unrestricted engine modifications and boat weights as long as the engine displacement was within the classification requirements. Last winter the national association established new rules for Divisions I and II hulls and motors. Class A hulls were to be 100 pounds minimum; Class B and C 150 pounds and Class D and E 190 pounds. Stock motors only were required for both classes and no free-for-all events would to be allowed. A new Family Runabout event was added to the racing categories. These changes and others were added to further level the racing playing field for amateurs, experienced, professional, and recreational race boat drivers. A number of other changes were made for motors, records and prizes.

1930 Race Schedule & Sponsor

May 10	Lake Watcom, Bellingham by NWOA
June 14-15	Lake Sammamish Mile Trials by Lk. Sammamish Yacht Club
June 27	Olympia to Seattle Marathon by SOA
Aug 2-3	Green Lake NW Championships by SOA
Aug 10	100 Mile Mercer Island Marathon by SOA
Aug. 17	Lake Goodwin, Stanwood by SOA
Aug. 23-24	Lake Sammamish Regional Championships by SOA (Div I & II)
Sept 8-9	Lake Merritt, Oakland CA Divisional Championship (Div I & II)
Oct 11-13	Connecticut River, Middleton CT National Championship (Div I & II)

Another new social activity was scheduled for SOA members and their significant others. Mrs. Francis Burr, club secretary and chairman of the entertainment committee, organized the first publicized dance event sponsored by the club. The news headline "Puddle-Jumpers Hop, billed for Outboard Club," was published on March 30. The new event was held on April 26 at the Pioneer Hall in Madison Park. The proceeds from the dance helped support the club's regatta programs.

The first annual Northwest Motor Boat Show was held in the Seattle Civic Auditorium Arena. The first-of-its-kind exhibition started Tuesday April 15 and ran for five days and ended

Sunday. S.V.B. Miller, the innovator who put on the first one-man show 20 years ago in 1910, was chairman of the event that was staged by Northwest Boating Industries, Inc. The show included 80 exhibits, 240 makes of boats, outboard motors of all types and an array of boating accessories. The exhibits were represented by manufacturers and dealers from all over the Northwest and by regions east of the Rockies. Several of the Seattle Outboard club's racing rigs were on display to promote and encourage new members to join. Of course, they were also promoting their own businesses at the same time. The race boats on display were the latest outboard speedboats of Jerry Bryant and Gale Roose. The boat's hulls were built by the Adams and Reinell boat company in Marysville.

Lake Sammamish Mile Trials

This year the speed trials were held Saturday and Sunday, June 14-15. Last year's surveyed one-mile straight-a-way and 2-1/2 mile competition courses located off the shores of Vasa Park on Lake Sammamish were used again this year. The *Times* headline on July 20th was "TWO DRIVERS IN NORTHWEST GET RECORDS." Bertha Reinell and Lyman Doan set national records that were certified by the APBA. In a letter to the *Times*, A.L. Bobrick, member of the National Outboard Racing Commission, approved the marks.

Bertha Reinell, 15-year-old from Everett, set the Class A-I record in the *Lady Luck*, powered by a Lockwood motor. Her raceboat was built by the Adams & Reinell Company in Marysville, Washington. She's the first woman in the northwest to set a national record in a raceboat. The course type and speed for her Class A racing craft was not given in the article. Lyman T. Doan, of Bellingham, set his record in the Class C-II category on the five-mile competition course bettering the existing mark of 39.793 mph. Doan's new record of 40 mph was set with a racing hull powered with an Evinrude motor and built by a boat builder named Ashbridge.

Apparently, Gale Roose's powerful 1930 Johnson motor wasn't enough to break any records in his newly built *Cootie* IV racing hull. He obtained a new Johnson double rotary valve, dual carburetor, motor from Pacific Marine Supply–the first in the Northwest with the latest design. Johnson was still making marked improvements to their outboard motor line

despite being in financial straits at the time. "Some say, Ralph Evinrude and his business partner Steve Briggs" of the newly formed Outboard Motor Company (OMC), kept the critically-ill Johnson out of the morgue through timely infusions of their own personal funds." Recently, Roose sold his *Cootie III* hull to Jim Bleitz, a new SOA member who will be challenging in Class D-II with hopes of being the next speed king!

Green Lake Championships

"To the 40,000 fans that banked Green Lake's shores there was a thrill in every race" was a quote by the *Times'* Peter Salvus on August 4. The fourth annual regatta was run on the weekend of August 2-3 by the Seattle Outboard Association. S.V.B. Miller was the race chairman with assistance from the Queen City Yacht Club. Many of the regular pilots competed along with a number of new faces in the outboard clan. They included the first of the future drivers of the Sammamish Slough Race.

Charles "Chuck" Hickling, future Seattle limited and unlimited hydro driver, took second place in Class A-1 piloting the *Black Streak*. Bill Harrison, driving *½-Pint*, was third in Class A-II, which was won by the now 16-year-old record holder Bertha Reinell in *Lady Luck* and Jack Colcock, future winner in the Slough Race, took Class C-I honors in *Sea Imp*. Mike Shain, veteran local inboard pilot, was fourth in the Division IV class with his displacement boat named *Miss Pat*, and Steve Yates drove the *Miss* Epps to second place in the B-I Class. Lawrence Buhtz, one of the first Sammamish Slough Cruise navigators, was second in the runabout class driving his *Weco Clipper*. The nearly 30 entrants in eight classes made this regatta the largest outboard event ever run in the Northwest.

Lake Sammamish Regional Championships

"OUTBOARD KINGS CRACK RECORDS AT SAMMAMISH" was the *Times'* headline on August 25 with various quotes. "Four world records were split wide open" and six drivers qualified for the Pacific Coast Championships at Lake Merritt in Oakland, California. Chuck McCue from West Seattle, piloting his *Miss West Seattle* to victory in the Class B-II, set two records. The first was the 5-mile mark at 39.045 mph and the second was the 10-mile mark at 39.336 mph. "Bill Harrison, the midget of Northwest outboard racing, was another who bettered world marks." With a brand-new boat, he cleaned-up in Class A, setting his record at 27.297 bettering Bertha Reinell's record set earlier in the year. The fourth record was set by George Wilson of Vancouver, B.C., in Class C-I where he beat out the California entry with a new speed record of 42.795 mph.

Bill (Billy) Harrison was the only future Slough Race driver who won an event and qualified for the Pacific Coast Championships (Region Divisionals). The other Slough drivers were Jack Colcock, Allen Petrich and Steve Yates. Colcock was fourth in Class C-I and fourth in Class DE-II driving *Sea Imp*, Petrich of Tacoma was third in Class B-II driving *Western Spirit*, and Yates was second driving *Miss Epps* in Class B-I. The winning drivers going to California were: Bill Harrison-Seattle, Class A; Vernon Bistrom-Seattle, Class B-I; Chuck McCue-Seattle, Class B-II; G. K. Wilson-Vancouver, B.C., Class C-I; Roy Craig-Tacoma, Class C-II and F.G. Graham-Vancouver, B.C., in Class DE-I.

Lake Merritt Pacific Coast Championships

Seattle drivers, "Jones, McCue and Harrison Qualify for National Outboard Championships by Placing at Oakland" was the *Times* sports headline on Tuesday September 10. Roy Craig of Tacoma was the fourth driver to make the cut. The Northwest outboard pilots made their fellow club members proud by qualifying for the Middletown, Connecticut. Nationals in the Pacific Coast Championships held on Lake Merritt in Oakland, California. Walter Jones and Bill Harrison of Seattle placed second and third in Class A, Charles McCue of Seattle placed second in Class B and Roy Craig of Tacoma placed third in Class C.

Little information was published locally about the outboard nationals that were held in Connecticut. Roy Craig of Tacoma was the only Northwest representative that made the trip to Middletown. He was unable to place in the finals in his Class C-II runabout which was the same case for all the West Coast drivers.

S. V. B. Miller

The second season for the Seattle Outboard Association was very successful, not a down year as some may have expected because of the stock market crash aftermath. Commodore Davis commented on how the club and its many officers and assistants deserve a pat on the back. He was quoted in the *Times*: "During their tenure in office they have pulled the club out of debt and put money in the bank. The membership of the club is in good shape and the program of picnics, dances and so on prepared for 1931, should attract even more outboard followers."

"S.V.B. Miller to Head Club" was the *Times'* headline on Sunday, December 14. Miller, one of the first to race outboards and first to put on a boat show in Seattle, became the third commodore for the Seattle Outboard Association. His strong business sense and first-hand racing knowledge made him ideal for the job, especially for the upcoming year. Joining him was Nick Reinell, Vice-president; Mrs. Francis Burr, Secretary and Steve Yates as Treasurer. The delegates chosen to represent the club with the Northwest Outboard Association were Jerry Bryant, Jack West and Commodore Miller. One item of interest that the officers will have to deal with is next year's Pacific Coast Championships, which in the past were run solely or jointly by the Club. This year they were tentatively awarded to Vancouver, B.C., under the control of the Northwest Outboard Association with the Vancouver boat club, but rumblings are on the horizon that will be costly!

1931

New SOA Commodore S.V.B. Miller called to order a number of meetings during the early part of the year. The purposes of the first meetings were to plan and organize the season's racing events. Newly-elected Jerry Bryant was appointed manager of the regatta committee. Bryant's job was to lead the club in finding potential race sites, firming up the dates and sponsors, as well as working with the regional and national bodies to lobby for staging the West Coast regionals and, it was hoped, the nationals.

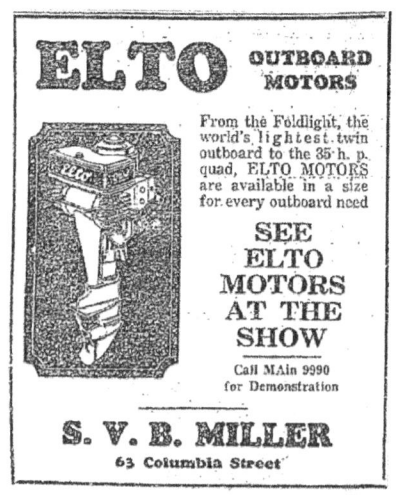

Miller was a good choice for commodore this year. He was also a member of the Queen City Yacht Club and secretary-treasurer of the Associated Boating Industries during that time. His strong business background and pioneering of local outboard racing brought him well-deserved respect from the business and racing communities. Now that the club's newness has worn off and the leadership inadequacies of their associated racing bodies had been exposed, he was ready and willing to make changes or improvements within the club and with their outside affiliations.

One could write a book about S.V.B. Miller. He was born in Indiana in 1882, a mechanical engineering graduate from Purdue University in 1906 and an astute businessman from the Midwest in the motor car business all before his move to Seattle

1914 SVB Miller's Cycle Car add.

in 1908. He then started his own company where he sold and distributed marine engines and related equipment, sold "Cycle Cars" and outboard motors. In 1913 he competed in yachting events when he owned motorboats and competed in the power boat races. He raced boats to promote his business and advertised heavily in the newspapers. He was one of the first to advertise with boat and motor artwork along with text. He was one of the very first outboard racers in the Northwest when he started competing and winning in 1924. At that time, he was married, had a son and two daughters. By now you're probably wondering what Miller's initials (S.V.B.) stood for? The initials have been a secret for thirty years-and still are.

While Jerry Bryant, Miller and other key SOA members were planning and scheduling races, the National Outboard Association was still tinkering with racing rules and their organization. During a January meeting in New York, the delegates decided to only have two race divisions instead of the current four. Officials changed the divisions to Amateur and Professional. The old Divisions I and II were combined into the amateur division, now Division I. And the previous Divisions III and IV were combined into the professional division, now Division II, which makes up those who accepted cash prizes and or those engaged in the profession in some way. Open regattas will be allowed between amateurs and professionals with separate prizes between the divisions, amateurs were not allowed to take any money.

The national group appointed past Commodore A.L. Bobrick of the Los Angeles area to head the rules committee and draw up a set of outboard runabout rules which would be patterned after those used in the Northwest. Selection of the National

Outboard Association Regatta was also left to Bobrick, which would be held on the Pacific Coast during October this year. The race site had been alternating between the East and the West since they began. The site for the Pacific Coast Sectionals would also be named by Bobrick. The new outboard club in Westminster, B.C., was seeking the Sectionals for Lake Barnaby, B.C.

Another event occurred during the first week of the year. During this time period, despite the Depression, the Northwest was experiencing the fastest outboard motor sales growth in the country. W.C. Clausen, sales manager of the Outboard Motors Corporation (OMC), visited the Seattle area to meet with their new Evinrude distributor, Sunde & d'Evers. The meeting was held to discuss the details of OMC's recent expansion of their Northwest distributor territory which now included Washington, Idaho, Western Montana, Oregon and Alaska. Sunde & d'Evers was previously a dealer for the discontinued Lockwood outboard motor.

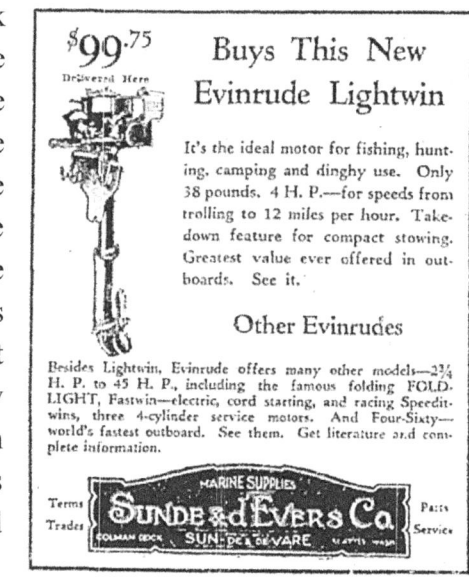

Second Annual Old Timers Slough Cruise

"SAMMAMISH IS OPEN; BOAT TRIP PLEASANT" was headlined in the *Times* on Sunday, March 1. "Lagoons of Florida and bayous and backwaters of Louisiana hold their thrills of motor boating but a trip from Lake Washington to Lake Sammamish in an outboard craft will rival then all" was a passage in the article.

"Twice recently boats have made the journey and those in the party were enthusiastic over the trip. Jimmy Tregoning was the first to attempt it this year and then Mr. and Mrs. Lawrence Buhtz and Mr. and Mrs. Jerry Bryant," married last year on June 20, "made it last Sunday" (February 22). Starting from Western Cooperage Sunday, the four went in a 14-foot *Wecco Clipper*" (outboard runabout) powered by a Class C motor. It took them four hours to dock at Strafford Park, Lake Sammamish, an estimated distance from their start of 45 miles." Strafford Park was next to where Vasa Park is today at the Southwest end of the lake.

On the return trip, they made it in two-and-a-half hours aided by the current. For 25-minutes on the return, traveling was so easy they opened the throttle and sped along at 30 miles an hour. Twelve gallons of gas was consumed on the trip. The boat drew 18-inches of water and the only difficulty encountered was a sand bar at the Lake Washington-end of the Sammamish River.

To make the journey, it was publicized that boating fans should go north and east on Lake Washington. The mouth of the Sammamish River is at the North end of the Inglewood Country Club. Bryant stated "there would be a difficulty at spots because of the overhanging of the trees and some tunneling would be necessary as giant willows form an arch overhead." A log boom across the main channel forced Buhtz and Bryant to take another course at the mouth of the river and shallow water grounded the boat for a few feet. "They waded and put it across the sand bar and at no other time did they touch bottom."

Bryant, chairman of the Seattle Outboard club's regatta committee, announced in early March, "Seattle's outboard racing season will begin in March this year instead of June. With twelve months of boating possible in the Northwest and with surrounding lakes available for racing throughout the year, the outboard club should sponsor regattas both winter and summer." The regatta committee phoned the participants the Sunday morning of each race to confirm if the regatta was to be run. This was to insure the winter regattas, which were conducted between March and May, weren't run in gusty weather.

The first general club meeting of the year was held on Friday evening March 6 at Pioneer Hall in Madison Park. Mrs. Frances Burr, club secretary, announced that the main agenda was to review the race scheduling for the coming season. The tentative schedule was determined by Jerry Bryant's regatta committee during working meetings that winter. They also reviewed the new handicapping system that was attempted for the first time last Sunday in the Runabout Regatta on Lake Washington.

New Outboard Runabout Regatta

Bryant's committee was planning something new for this year, "a year-round affair" which was opened on March 1st with a regatta on Lake Washington. The race was just for outboard runabouts, pleasure boat outfits anyone could purchase. The race course, which was laid out by the committee, started at Madison Park, ran South around a stake buoy at Seward Park and then returned to Madison Park for the finish. Three heats were run, with all classes starting at the same time in the afternoon as an experiment for a new handicapping system. To equalize the competition, the outfits entered were required to meet a minimum weight based on the motor classification as follows:

Class B Motors, outfit minimum 450 pounds, later revised to 500 pounds
Class C Motors, outfit minimum 600 pounds, later revised to 550 pounds
Class D Motors, outfit minimum 700 pounds, later revised to 750 pounds
Class E Motors, outfit minimum 850 pounds, later revised to 950 pounds
Class F Motors, outfit minimum 1,000 pounds, later revised to 1,150 pounds

Entrants whose boats didn't meet the weight limits had to carry extra passengers to make up the difference. All motors had to be equipped with standard mufflers or underwater exhaust to comply with Seattle's nuisance noise law. Only displacement-type runabout hulls were allowed, no hydroplanes[3]. No regulation of deck or length of forward deck was made which opened the class to Family Runabouts[4].

1931: The start of the new Runabout Class at Madison Park on Lake Washington.

Darrell Shain, son of well-known Seattle inboard and outboard driver Mike Shain, won all three heats in his Class E runabout while carrying four passengers. The *Times* wrote, "Darrell Shain is going to be as famous a speedboat driver as his dad." He piloted his runabout aptly named *Dad's Expense*, over the ten-mile course in front of a field of nineteen boats, that all started together. He averaged 25.7 miles-per-hour carrying the four passengers who were needed to make the minimum weight requirement. All the winning boats were weighed immediately after the race. The

---

[3] APBA in the 1920s defined a hydroplane as a boat whose underbody has one or more breaks in the continuity of its longitudinal or transverse immersed surface.
[4] New outboard racing classes open to anyone with displacement type runabout hulls powered by stock detachable motors within the designated classifications as listed above.

total weight of each outfit, including boat, motor, driver and passengers had to meet the motor classification requirement. The other finishers were Carl Blackstock, second, Class C in *Helly-Did*; Ross Marzello, third, Class C in *Risco*; Mrs. Emily Barstad, fourth in *Wildcat*; Paris Robinson, fifth in *Wecco II*; Ellsworth Simpson, sixth, Class B in *Sea Sled*; R.A. Brooks, seventh in *Alahi*; and M.A. Tuthill, eighth, Class B in *Miss Tut*. This was an experimental race to determine if the new rules were adequate, the first of a series of handicapped runabout races that were run throughout the season.

During the SOA's March 6 club meeting the results of the first race were reviewed. A second experimental race was then scheduled and run with some changes to make the competition more equitable, no points[5] were awarded in either race. The second race was modified to include separate heats for Class B because of the disparity in speed with the larger motor classes. The results for the unlimited class were: Shain first again, Emily Barstad in *Wildcat*, second, John Nelson in *Creosote* third; and Ross Marzello in *Risco* fourth. Class B results were Dave Hall in *Nausea* first, Ellsworth Simpson in *Bing II*, second, Orin Rice in *Mister Completely*, third; and Frances Burr and passenger Ann Bryant fourth in *Cockle Burr*. These races turned out to be the model for this type of racing craft that was eventually sanctioned by the APBA.

The following was the final schedule for the year which was revised a number of times throughout the year as priorities and dates changed.

1931 Race Schedule & Sponsor

Feb 22	2nd Sammamish Slough Cruise
March 1	Lake Washington Madison Park-Seward Park Handicap Trial by SOA
April 11	2nd Lake Washington Handicap Trial race by SOA
May 10	Inaugural Monthly Lake Washington Runabout Regatta at Seward Park by SOA
May 17	American Lake by Tacoma Outboard Club & NWOA
June 7	2nd Monthly Lake Washington Runabout Regatta at Seward Park by SOA
June 11-12	Lake Goodwin by Lake Goodwin Outboard Club
June 14-15	Lake Sammamish by Sammamish Yacht Club
July 1-4	Bellingham Regatta
July 7	Elks Club Green Lake Regatta by SOA
July 19	Seattle to Olympia Marathon by SOA
July 26	Lake Stevens by Everett Motor Boat Club

---

[5] National and local club points were given to each registered finisher for all classes which were accumulated and totaled to determine "high point winners" for the season. The winners were awarded plaques or trophies and their accomplishments were permanently recorded in the organization's history archives.

Aug 9	Seattle to Coupeville Marathon by SOA
Aug 15-16	Green Lake Championships by SOA
Aug 22-23	Regional Championships (Div I) by Sammamish Yacht Club & SOA
Sept 14	100 Mile Marathon at Seward Park by SOA
Oct 4	Monthly Lake Washington Runabout Regatta at Seward Park by SOA
Oct 11-12	Lake Merritt, Oakland CA Divisional Championship (Div I)
Oct 14	Lake Merritt, Oakland CA National Championship (Div I)
Nov 8	Monthly Lake Washington Runabout Regatta at Seward Park by SOA
Dec 6	Monthly Lake Washington Runabout Regatta at Seward Park by SOA

"Runabout Race Costly; Bryant Has Details" was the *Times* sports headline several weeks after the second experimental Runabout Regatta. The April regatta proved to be expensive for Jerry Bryant, chairman of the club's regatta committee. His wife Ann just competed in her first outboard race when she rode with Frances Burr, the SOA secretary. The racing experience inspired her desire to have a raceboat of her own. Subsequently, Jerry purchased a complete outfit for Ann, consisting of a new Wecco Clipper and a new Class B Johnson motor, which she raced in the inaugural runabout regatta series which started May 10.

Ann Bryant (left) and Frances Burr before second experimental Runabout Regatta.

Local and National Club Activities

"OUTBOARD GROUP GETS LONG TRIP" was headlined in the *Seattle Sunday Times* on March 8. The first official Seattle Outboard Association cruise to Lake Sammamish consisted of a large party. They pulled out from Madison Park and headed north on Lake Washington to Kenmore, then up the Sammamish River to Lake Sammamish. The route was inspected during a run the week earlier and deemed feasible for the club. It was the first-of-its-kind ever attempted as an official club event. The group consisted of Lawrence Butz, Jack West, Frances Burr, Gale Roose, F.A. (Doc) Harvey, Paris Robinson, Ellsworth Simpson, Ralph Stender, Orin Rice, Jack Thornton and Mr. and Mrs. Jerry Bryant. The group planned to stay the night at Straford Park on Lake Sammamish and return the next afternoon. This was actually the 3rd annual trip which began in 1929.

"N. W. OUTBOARD GROUP OFFENDS SEATTLE BODY" was headlined in the sports section of the *Seattle Times* on Sunday, March 15. "Taxation Without Adequate

Representation Causes Friction; Locals Hold Out for Present." The following *Times* article read: "If time was set back 100 years or so there would be quite a Boston Tea Party in the Northwest. Tea parties in Boston in the eighteenth century weren't cup-and-saucer affairs, but masquerades in which His Majesty King George III was flayed figuratively for his excessive tax burdens upon the colonists. Today the Northwest Outboard Association assumes the 'bogey-man' role of King George III and the Seattle Outboard Association the part of the enraged colonists." The SOA, whose membership is over double that of any other club in the region, currently has three delegates to the NWOA, the same as the other smaller clubs. They also pay over double the dues of any other affiliated club. Club Commodore S.V.B Miller stated that the SOA will not rejoin the Northwest group unless they change their policy.

"CITY'S THREAT TO QUIT GROUP AROUSES FEAR" was another headline in the March 29 *Sunday Times*. Recently the Seattle Outboard Association has been fighting for equal representation in the Northwest Outboard Association. S.V.B. Miller announced yesterday that its membership of 56 was more than the total of the other six clubs associated with the NWOA. The SOA currently was not entitled to equal representation because they didn't have a proportional number of delegates based on the affiliated club's total membership. Therefore, at that time, the SOA refused to continue its affiliation with the NWOA.

The officers of NWOA agreed with Miller's assessment along with the National Outboard Association. A subsequent mail poll of the other NWOA delegates was supportive of the Seattle club's plight and resulted in a reorganization of the Northwest group. One vote was allowed for each ten members of each club giving Seattle six delegates, Vancouver, B.C., two and Lake Sammamish and the others one each. The delegates control the election of officers and all constitution changes within the NWOA. Even though the number of delegates changed in favor of Seattle, the political battle between the NWOA and the Seattle club was not over and serious consequences were about to come in the near future.

While the Seattle club was winning on the home front, the Pacific Coast was taking a beating on the national level. In a recent meeting at the American Power Boat Association, a decision was made to dramatically reduce the funds appropriated for the National Outboard Championships this year. This money was funded by the affiliated National Outboard Association. It was a blow to the West Coast because the nationals would be held somewhere in the West this year. The first nationals held in Peoria, Illinois, were funded for $4,400 and more for the second event in Middleton,

Connecticut. The current reduction of $1,000 was a shock to the West Coast. It will cost more to run this year due to expected higher expenses. The dues were also increased based on the number of members, of which the West Coast had the highest numbers. On the good news side of the ledger, a move to separate the outboard group from the national organization was defeated.

In the past there were two different racing organizations consisting of the APBA and the Mississippi Valley Power Boat Association (MVPBA). They functioned independently with separate racing rules and executive bodies. They have since merged into one central group (APBA) and later were joined by the National Outboard Association which resulted in outboard racing taking great strides over the past three years. An interesting sidelight was that some clubs in the Midwest and West still raced under the original rules of the MVPBA because their boats were designed for right-hand turning courses versus left-hand turning courses per the APBA rules.

The Lake Sammamish Yacht Club also had race events booked for the year. A meeting was held in early March to organize and schedule their racing events for the season. The first regatta scheduled was a two-day event billed for June and another two-day event set for August. Of note was a committee headed by W.J. Lewis who was appointed to pursue the dredging of the Sammamish River. This was another plan in a long line of efforts to clear the waterway for improved navigation.

"Runabout Rules Submitted***Club Offers Suggestions" was a *Times* headline on April 30. At this time Bryant's regatta committee was satisfied with their adjustments to the new runabout class rules and that they had been proven to be equitable in the two experimental races. They submitted the comprehensive set of rules that they had drafted to the National Outboard Association in Chicago where they would be reviewed for incorporation as an official national racing class.

A. L. Bobrick, of the APBA/NOA rules committee, was previously elected chairman of the new runabout rules committee. He allowed the SOA group to draw up the rules because of their local efforts to create and refine the class. Runabout racing had been confined more or less to the West Coast and officials of the APBA realized that the West Coast should establish their own rules. Bobrick's plan was to divide the Pacific Coast into four sections: (1) British Columbia, Washington, Northern Idaho and Montana; (2) Oregon and Southern Idaho; (3) Northern California, including Fresno and Monterey plus Nevada and Utah; and (4) Southern California, all south of but not including Fresno, Monterey and Arizona.

Seattle's new rules were made available to each of these sections for their comments and subsequent approval vote by the majority of the members. The coastal clubs then selected a delegate to represent their club and an eventual commissioner for each of the four sections. Each commissioner was entitled to the same number of votes as there were drivers of runabouts in his section. The Northwest with Seattle's large runabout contingent had the majority of the votes. The commissioners met with Bobrick at the NOA's headquarters in Chicago where the group eventually approved the rules basically as they were submitted by the SOA, as described earlier in this chapter.

New Clock System for Starting Races

The *Times* published an article about the National Outboard Association's new starting system on May 10, 1931. The new system was inaugurated in the Northwest at the American Lake Regatta on May 17, 1931. The system consisted of a large manually operated starting clock and signal flags. The clock most likely had a large second-hand indicator that rotated clockwise from 60 seconds to zero. The hand and clock face would be in contrasting colors, typically a black indicator in front of a white clock face.

A yellow flag was hoisted three minutes before the start of each race which indicated that the boats in that heat could leave the pits and enter the race course. One minute before the scheduled time of the start, the clock would start and a white flag was waved by the starter. Then the white flag was dropped when clock reached zero, which indicated the official start. Any boats crossing the starting line before the appointed time or leaving the pits before the yellow flag was raised were disqualified.

Ann Bryant won for the first time in her racing career during this regatta. She was involved in a duel with Ellsworth Simpson in the Class B event which was reported as "one of the Northwest's best battles ever seen." Ann in her boat named *Wecco Girl* won the first heat, tied for second with Ellsworth Simpson in the next heat and was second to Simpson in the final heat which Simpson won driving his *Bing II* craft. Bryant was determined the winner based on her fastest time in the first heat. Frances Burr, SOA Secretary, was second in the Unlimited Class driving the *Y-Not*.

Elks' Speedboat Regatta

The following was an excerpt from the *Times* on July 8: "Bryant Thrills 9,000 Fans***High Leap Caps Boat Show." "The bespectacled young professional outboard driver, who yesterday returned to racing after a year's absence, provided the thrills and punch for the 9,000 fans who lined the eastern shore of Green Lake for the Elks' Speedboat Regatta. Climaxing a victory in Class C and a second place in the unlimited division, he propelled an outboard craft up a steep 14-foot incline and leaped through a circle" (ring of fire), "the boat landing right side up and Bryant driving straight to the pits." The incline was a boat jump built for staging the side-show.

Bryant had performed his first jump stunt in a previous two-day Green Lake regatta to please some Hollywood film makers who came to shoot the race. They were disappointed that no accidents occurred during the first day of the race and told him they were leaving. So, Bryant, being the showman, he was, and very savvy about how national publicity could help his business, told them to come back the next day and he would give them something worthwhile to film. The next day Bryant made a speeding run over a make shift ramp he and other SOA members quickly constructed. The jump, the first-of-its-kind in the Northwest, was successful and made the day for the film makers.

This regatta was combined outboard and inboard event with entries from all over the state. The outboard classes included Classes; A, CI, CII, and Unlimited. Inboard classes included 151 and 505. Of note are the inboards which usually turned to the right on their courses during the early years of racing. They had to switch to the standard left-hand outboard course in this event. SOA winners included future Sammamish Slough Race participants: Jimmy Harland, Class A, driving *Ruth*; Billy Harrison, Class CI, in *½ Pint*, and Jerry Bryant, Class CII, in *Miss Epps*. Steve Yates placed second in Class CI piloting the *Bing I*, and Bryant was second driving Pat Troyer's new craft *Miss Epps* in the unlimited class. Allen Pettrich of the Tacoma Outboard club, another future Slough racer, was third in Class A driving his runabout named *Keedt*.

Green Lake Championships

The annual Green Lake regatta this year was held August 14-15. The SOA ran the event as usual but this year the Seattle Park Department was a welcome sponsor with deep pockets. This event was a replacement race for the expected Pacific Coast Championships. They were not awarded to Seattle this year because of issues between the club and the regional Northwest Outboard Association. Last year's NWOA commodore and current SOA member, Ernie Adams, was voted out of office. The new elected commodore was from Vancouver, B.C., and subsequently moved their headquarters to Vancouver after the election. The national association's issue was that the vast majority of boat racers were located in Seattle and all the races were run in the

Northwest states, but the governing regional body was in Canada. Consequently, the Northwest Outboard Association's bid for the divisional championships, that it hoped would be run in Burnaby, B.C., was denied because of the two association's separation. The race was subsequently awarded to Oakland, California's Lake Merritt, a convenient location, because the nationals were run the day after the Divisionals on the same lake.

The race was successful because of the substantial prize money awarded by the park department. The purse of $2,500 attracted a strong turnout of entries from all over the West Coast who created "a haze of burning castor oil and gasoline" over the circular mile course. Rookie and veteran Seattle outboard pilots fared well in the wind-swept regatta. New driver and future Sammamish Slough Race competitor, J.C. (Jimmy) Harland, won in the A Hydroplane Class driving the *Ruth Marion* on Saturday. Veteran Jerry Bryant won the 25-mile Marathon event on Sunday in the Unlimited Class piloting the *Miss Epps*. Bryant wasn't as fortunate on Saturday because he flipped, got wet and ruined his motor in his first two heats. That evening he had to burn the midnight oil to make the repairs that were obviously successful. Another SOA newcomer, Frank Le Clair, won the Class B hydroplane event in his *Lady Luck*.

"JERRY LOSES HIS CAP***BUT THAT'S NOT HALF" was an intriguing headline for an article in the *Seattle Times* that read as follows: "A harmless little hat, cap, chapeau or what have you? Caused lots of trouble for the Jerry Bryant family yesterday. Jerry was competing in Class C professional and unlimited hydroplane races in the Seattle speedboat championships on Green Lake. He spilled in his first race but was able to continue in the second-for a time, losing, meanwhile, his yachting cap. The second spill put him definitely out.

"Jerry's wife, Ann, also was driving in Class B for runabouts. She was in third place, rounding past the south buoy, when her propeller became fouled and killed her motor. What fouled the propeller? (This is strictly on the q.t. and don't tell a soul). It was Jerry's lost hat!"

Lake Sammamish Sectionals

The sectional regatta, that qualifies boats and drivers for the divisional and national races, was held again on Lake Sammamish at the same three adjoining property locations: Lewis Beach, Strafford Park and Vasa Park. Two records were set at the two-day event consisting of qualifying races and record mile trial attempts.

Newcomer and hard-to-beat Class-A Hydroplane driver, Jimmy Harland, set a new mile trial mark of 39.647 in his tiny craft *Ruth Marion*. This bettered Los Angeles'

Mrs. Rodney Pantages' Salton Sea record of 37.676 miles-per-hour. The other record was set by F.C. Graham of Vancouver, B.C., driving the *Jennie G* in Class C. He broke the old competition record of 44.776 with an average speed of 46.201 mph on the 2-1/2 mile course. The winners and qualifying drivers were not reported in the papers but Harland and Grahan most likely qualified in their classes.

1929-1931 Summary

The Seattle Outboard Association had another great year despite the second year of the Depression. They continued to grow and were by far the largest club in region, one of the largest in the nation. There were fewer amateur drivers this year, however the Division II professional group was still strong and growing, partly because they were forced into this division because of the new national rules. They had connections to the industry or were financially well off and won prize money opposed to the Division I racers who were not allowed to accept money. The new amateur drivers were mostly either financially able or also connected in some way to the boat and motor industry.

The Seattle club again brought national attention to the Northwest when they created an entirely new category of outboard racing, the family runabout class, which was adopted by the American Power Boat Association. It was a series of regularly scheduled races that ran throughout the year with the winner determined by the highest point accumulation for the year. The club seemed to have gone overboard on the number of races they ran which was a challenge to them and other clubs that led to numerous date changes.

This was the year that Seattle women drivers came of age. Rookie driver Ann Bryant and veteran Frances Burr both had a very successful season in winning their share of races. Frances Burr won the unlimited runabout class and Ann Bryant was runner-up in the B runabout class. The other newcomers, in addition to Ann Bryant were Jimmy Harland, Darrell Shain, Adolph Spreckels, Tommy Humes and Frank Le Clair.

The year also proved to be a transition year for the APBA, SOA and the NWOA. APBA was still making new and revised rules and the individual clubs were becoming independent because of the additional regional membership fees. For the first time, the national body, APBA, was allowing direct affiliations with local clubs, partly for their financial reasons and partly because of conflicts with their regional association. Subsequently, the Divisionals never materialized in Seattle or B.C. because of the national body's concern over the strained relationship and separation between SOA and NWOA. The city boat show was not held this year but boats and motors were displayed at the 5th Ave Theater in place of the annual event.

Interestingly the club was concerned about the noise from outboards with open exhausts. "Outboard Club Warns Against Open Mufflers" was a *times* headlined in April. The Seattle Outboard Association publicly asked its members and recreational boaters to refrain from waking the lakeside dweller with un-muffled outboards. They called to attention Seattle's nuisance noise ordinance which makes un-muffled motors a public nuisance. While modified motors are excusable during racing meets, the club advised that all practice runs should be made on the eastern lakefront and all motors muffled near the city.

1931: Respectful handshake between rookie drivers Darrell Shain (left) and Ann Bryant.

Chapter 4

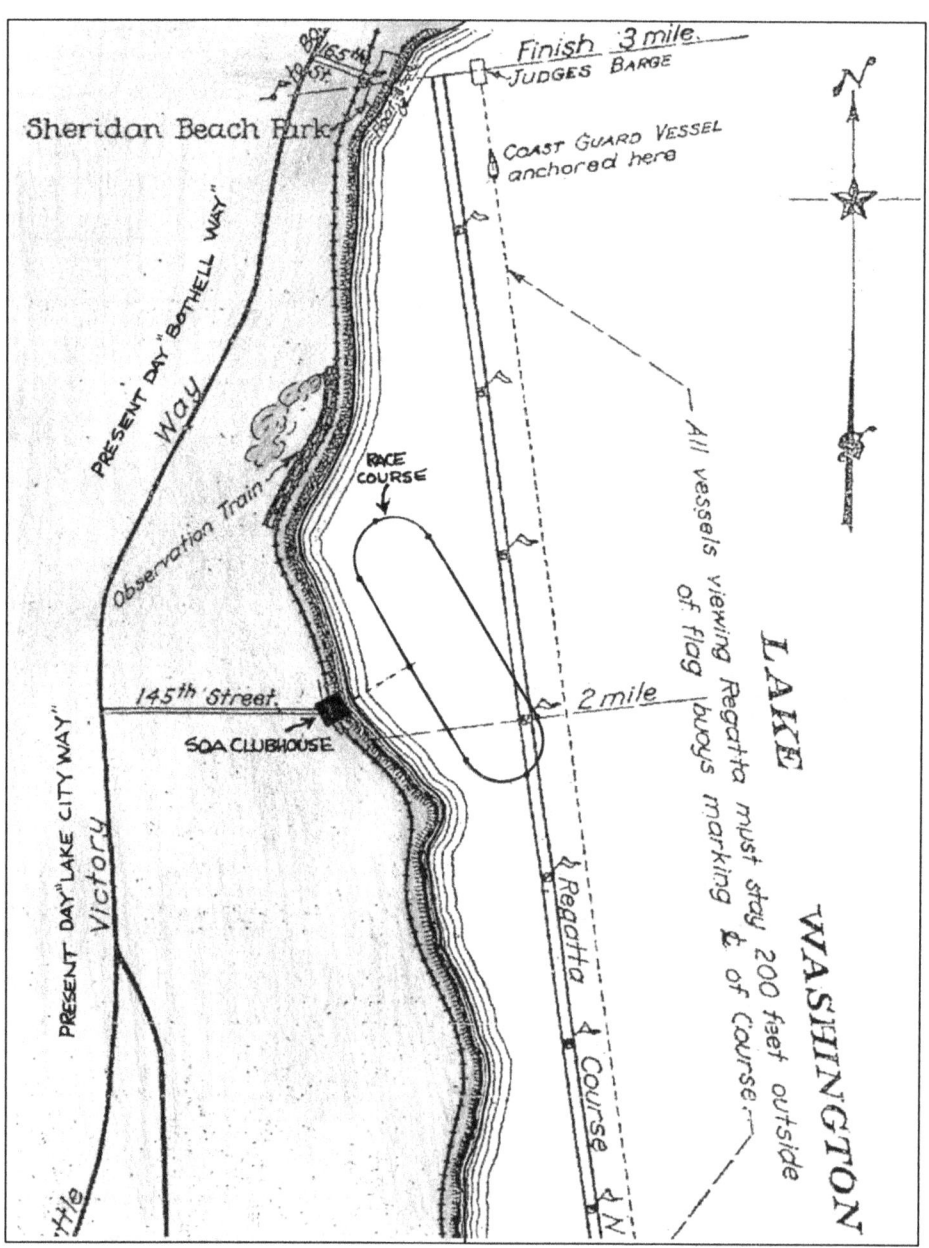

1932: Seattle Outboard Association's Lake Washington clubhouse property adjacent to two-mile mark of University of Washington crew race-course.

Clubhouse of Their Own

SOA 1932 to 1933

*"OUTBOARD CLUB BUYS 60 FEET OF WATERFRONT
Modern Clubhouse Intention of Vigorous Organization,
Which Likes Northern Stretch of Lake as Course"*

-The Seattle Sunday Times, March 6, 1932-

The big news at the beginning of the year was the Seattle Outboard Association's purchase of 60 feet of waterfront property on Lake Washington. The property was located at the foot of NE 145th street (below Lake City of today) just south of Sheridan Beach. This was very near the University of Washington's finish line for their annual Washington crew races. The club's intention was to build a clubhouse and hold outboard races on a permanent race course in front of the clubhouse. Club members felt they needed permanent headquarters and a race course with more protected waters.

The other news was about the new club officers who were elected late last year at the usual meeting place, Pioneer Hall in Madison Park. S.V.B. Miller was elected commodore for a second term, which validated the membership's approval for his strong leadership. The other elected officers were Jerry Bryant, vice-commodore; Jimmy Burton, secretary-treasurer and the trustees, L.S. (Spike) Davis and Tommy

Humes. The officers and the 130 plus members were looking forward to the clubhouse construction, setting up the race course and running regattas.

"S.V.B. MILLER IS HONORED BY OUTBOARDERS" was a major sports headline in the *Seattle Times* on January 29. The sub-heading, "National Association Selects Seattle Man for Three-Year Directorship" along with the rest of the article was supplied by the Associated Press. S.V.B. Miller was chosen along with E. C. Petherick of San Francisco for a three-year term as one of the directors for the National Outboard Association. This was a huge honor for Commodore Miller and the Seattle Outboard Association. He was the first person from the Northwest to become an officer of the national body. The appointment showed the national organization's high respect for Miller, his leadership and the Seattle Outboard Association.

Last year's new club member Tommy Humes, who traded the track of cinders for a track on water, was now a member of the press. Humes, the former University of Washington broad-jumper and driver of the Class B Runabout *Hooper Dooper*, became a sports columnist for the *Seattle Times*. His Sunday column, "Around the Shops" which started in March, was dedicated to the weekly news and gossip of local outboard racing, a valuable resource for the SOA and boat racing enthusiasts. Humes is the grandson of Thomas J. Humes who was mayor of Seattle in 1899. This year in addition to being one of the club trustees, he competed in his new and improved *Hooper Dooper II*.

The club held its first membership drive which began in April. As typical of race drivers, it turned into a competition for bragging rights. Trustee Tom Humes, the outboard columnist, won the prize for recruiting the most members. He may have had an unfair advantage because of his *Seattle Times* connection. The extremely successful drive resulted in adding 68 new members. The SOA was now one of the nation's largest clubs with 200 members at season's end.

Annual Slough Cruise

This year as in the past, a boat party inspected the Sammamish River before the cruise. Jerry and Ann Bryant with the company of Mrs. Burr were the inspectors. After returning they declared the waterway was clear to navigate and "still excellent fun."

The first official club event of the year, held Saturday, January 23, was the third annual Slough Cruise. Club secretary, Frances Burr, announced that the event would be a "weekend affair with an overnight stay at Stafford Park on Lake Sammamish." It included a series of informal races that were run the next day before the boats returned to Seattle. A fleet of ten outboards carrying 20 club members launched and departed from Brown's Madison Park Boathouse in the afternoon. Their trip upstream took about 2-1/2 hours and a little less time on the return. This was the club's first organized overnighter where they used their outboard runabouts for transportation.

Jimmy Harland, in a weak moment, decided to drive his little A-Hydro along with the party. He made it up and back but not without some mishaps. He was thrown out once and turned-over in the river another time. He said after his water-soaked trip that his hydroplane was better suited for racing rather than "navigating meandering rivers."

School Boat Building Program

The creative juices of the Seattle Outboard Association were at work during the final months of the previous year. They started a school boat building contest to promote outboard recreation and racing to the younger generation, a plan to keep the sport popular for years to come by involving youths. The club provided an "ideal" boat-building plan, known to be successful, to local schools. The plans called for boat 15-1/2 feet long that was safe enough for all members of a family, yet capable of sufficient speed with larger powered outboard motors to make it adaptable to the bourgeoning runabout racing class.

The following was the June 26 headline and article in the sports section of the *Seattle Times*. "JAMES MADISON SCHOOL STUDENTS AWARDED PRIZE FOR CONSTRUCTING BEST CRAFT":

"Acclaimed by contestants, their parents, their school instructors, and by its sponsors alike as one of the most successful, interesting and beneficial competitions held here in years, the boat-building contest, conducted in the schools of King County the last school year by the Seattle Outboard Association, has closed. Winners have been announced, and the finest examples of amateur boat building go on display in a special window at the Bon Marche this week together with the three motors which the prizewinners are to receive.

"There were two divisions to the contest, one between pupils who built the boats actually within the school shops, and the other where there was insufficient room in the shops and the boats had to be built at home. The latter division, having the greater number of entries, was awarded two prizes, the first going to Bob West and Charles North, pupils of James Madison School, and the second prize to Herbert Fleischmann and Frank Klinkam, pupils of Franklin High School. Honorable mention was given to the third best boat, built by Tom Page and C. E. Smith, pupils of West Seattle High, whose boat was only slightly behind that of the second prize winner. The prize in the contest of builders in the school shops was won by Lester McIntyre of Roosevelt High School.

"Each winner was awarded a new outboard motor, one being donated by S.V.B. Miller, commodore of the Seattle Outboard Association, and one each by Pacific Marine Supply Company and Sunde & deEvers Company. These three donors were the local distributors for Elto, Johnson and Evinrude motors, respectively. It is interesting to note that the boat which ranked highest was built by 'North' and 'West,' very appropriate for things nautical. This boat is really a work of art, as all could agree, when it was viewed at the Bon Marche. The three judges, all boat builders, Lawrance Buhtz of Western Cooperage Company, Vic Frank of Frank & McCrary and M. G. Shain of Trimmer Ships, Inc., agreed that the boat built by the North-West team rated 100% in true lines, 100% on joiner work and 100% on perfect finish.

"Exactly twenty-five boats were built in the contest, making a very impressive showing for the first of its kind in the world. In more favorable circumstances, it is believed fully 100 boats would have been entered. The most gratifying thing to the sponsors is that the boats are really remarkable in the quality of workmanship put into them. Most amateur boat builders succeed in spoiling lumber and go very little further than that. These school boys, however, turned out beautiful boats.

"Cognizance has been taken of the Seattle contest by the National Outboard Association, and it has been praised as the one most constructive movement for the proper stimulation of small boat building ever devised!"

1932 Cruise and Race Schedule:

March 20	Unofficial Runabout Series at Seward Park-Lake Washington
April 3	First Seward Park Runabout Series (25-mile marathon)-Lake Washington
May 8	First Runabout and Hydroplane Race at New SOA Course-Lake Washington

May 29-30	Holmes Harbor Cruise-Race-Luncheon
June 5	100-mile Runabout and Hydroplane Marathon-Lake Washington
June 19	American Lake SOA Regatta (Tacoma)
June 25-26	Lake Sammamish Regatta
July 2-3	Annual Green Lake Regatta
July 17	Annual Fletchers Bay Cruise
July 30-31	Annual Coupeville Marathon
Aug 7	Club Picnic and Hydroplane Races
Aug 20-21	Pacific Northwest Championships (Sectionals)-Harrison Lake, B.C.
Aug 28	Annual Olympia Marathon
Sept 3-5	Vancouver B. C. Regatta
Sept 8-9	Coast Championships & Runabout Nationals-Lake Merritt Oakland, CA
Sept 11	Lake Washington Runabout and Hydroplane Regatta
Sept 18	Runabout Race at SOA Lake Washington Course
Oct 2	Seward Park Runabout and Hydroplanes-Lake Washington
Oct 10-11	National Championships-Bay City Michigan
Nov 6	Seward Park Runabout and Hydroplanes-Lake Washington
Nov 22	Green Lake 25-mile Marathon
December	Third Annual Sammamish Slough Cruise

First Regatta at New Headquarters on Lake Washington

The Seattle Outboard Association ran the first regatta on their North End Lake Washington course (south of Sheridan Beach) on Sunday, May 8. It was a christening of sorts for the club's new six-buoy race course and the unveiling of several new "fast-stepping boats." The competition started at 2 o'clock and included three heats each of A-I[1], C-I[2], C-II[3] and Unlimited Runabouts and three heats of the A-I Hydro class. A large floating dock was built and towed to the property where it was moored in front of the clubhouse. It provided members a set-up and launching area for boat race testing and competitions.

A thousand or more spectators on shore and in yachts and other boats outside the one-mile course, witnessed the "poppers reel off an average five miles an hour faster" than when they ran at the south end of Lake Washington according to the *Times*. The sheltered water was the major contributor to the faster times. The winner of note was *Times* sports writer, Tommy Humes, who won the A-I and Unlimited Runabout classes. A spill and collision occurred in the first Unlimited heat shortly after a field of 15 boats had just started. Roger Holman and Pat Cummins traded their fins when

---

[1] A-I denotes outboard racing category: Class A Division I (Amateur)
[2] C-I denotes outboard racing category: Class C Division I (Amateur)
[3] C-II denotes outboard racing category: Class C Division II (Professional)

Holman's boat turned over and Cummins boat ran over it. Cummins' metal bottom fin sliced into the bottom of Holman's boat and Holman's fin into Cummins' boat resulting in each fin stuck in the other boat. Neither was injured but both boats were out of commission and in need of major repairs.

Adolph B. Spreckels, Jr., grandson of the Spreckels Sugar magnate, showed up with the first 55-horsepower motor in the Northwest, the most powerful outboard motor available at that time. He ran a demonstration of the powerful Class-E engine on his new runabout aptly named *Miss Hi-Flex*. Another new rig was Gene Hatton's Western Cooperage runabout that was "fashioned" with a 5/8-inch step[4] on the bottom, the first of its kind in the Northwest. Other regatta winners were Wendell Trosper in C-II Runabout and Jimmy Harland in his A-I Hydroplane.

1932: Adolph Spreckels in *Black Cat II* at Green Lake with unknown rider.

---

[4] Forward bottom surface that steps down providing lift-allowing surface behind the step to become free of the water at high speeds reducing drag and friction.

New Clubhouse

Construction of the new clubhouse, which had been in the planning stage for several years, was finally underway in April. Club members "rejoiced" when the foundation timbers were laid and the wall framing began in May. Bill Harrison's father, who was the carpenter in charge, was helped by many of the club members who rolled up their sleeves and provided the majority of the labor.

Tom Humes' May 8 news column stated: "Next week the boys will drop their wrenches, pistons, etc., and turn to the saw and hammer. Construction has started on the new clubhouse and most of the labor will be done by the members of the SOA. Feminine members will have hot coffee as well as iodine and bandages on hand." Former driver, Pete Lippert and his old riding partner Al King completed the wiring.

The modern building faced the lake and incorporated a judges' viewing platform above the roof. Adolph Spreckels, Jr. donated a new public-address system that was used to broadcast continuous coverage of the races. Vacant property on both sides of the building provided parking and viewing areas for the spectators. The railroad tracks located behind the property, owned and operated by the Seattle, Lake Shore and Eastern Railway also provided viewing areas to the north and south.

During the beginning of the clubhouse construction, the bi-annual University of Washington (UW)-California rowing regatta was held which ran along the lakeside in front of the property. The two-mile mark of the three-mile racecourse[5] was near the clubhouse and the finish line was a mile north at Sheridan Beach Park.

It was the first time in rowing history that spectators viewed the event from railroad observation cars. A special train was chartered by the university to accommodate the fans who purchased tickets. Observation and open gondola cars, jammed with spectators, were pulled by a steam locomotive that traveled in tandem with the shells. It's very likely the club was envious of the huge extravaganza and imagined utilizing some of those train cars (only parked) for viewing their races.

Unfortunately for the UW fans, the Husky varsity and jayvee crews met a stunning defeat in the choppy waters of Lake Washington. The only good news was the up and coming Washington freshman pulled to a thrilling victory over a strong California crew.

In June, the National Outboard Association praised the clubhouse undertaking and their extremely successful membership drive. The club was showing outstanding lead-

---

[5] See the crew racecourse and clubhouse map at the beginning of this chapter.

ership and innovation which made them one of the elite, and most likely, the largest outboard club in the nation.

The opening ceremony occurred on July 17, 1932, before a crowd of proud club members and friends. Tom Humes made the formal announcement in his July 17 "Around the Shops" column: "Sore thumbs, slivers, paint-stained clothes and all other ailments connected with amateur carpentry are in vogue with the outboarders this week. The opening ceremony today at the newly completed clubhouse necessitated conscription of labor in order to complete the quarters, and many of their spare moments helping the cause." A "picnic in the afternoon with special races and stunts along with a dance at night" made it a special time for all. But a devastating event would soon temper the joy of the club members.

Jerry Bryant

If the loss of their new loudspeaker system wasn't enough to dampen their spirits, the loss of their new headquarters was! The loudspeaker system was stolen shortly after the clubhouse was constructed but the devastating blow came later. The building was completely destroyed by a fire of undetermined origin. The following was the *Seattle Times* headline in the sports section on September 28: "Outboard Clubhouse Burns Down *** Was Completed Only Recently." Insurance covered the loss of the construction materials valued at $1,500 but not the memorabilia and mementos inside. "Jerry Bryant was called by a neighbor during the night and was told that the building was in flames. He proceeded at once to the scene, accompanied by S.V.B. Miller." Bryant and Miller attempted to determine the cause but nothing was published in the months following the fire. The incident was a serious setback to the club since the building was the culmination of several years' planning and work. It was a sad ending to the huge effort of so many.

Harrison Lake B. C. Pacific Northwest Championships

The Pacific Northwest Championships (sectionals), which had been held on Lake Sammamish the past two years, were run this year in Canada, on Harrison Lake at Harrison Hot Springs, B. C. This regatta, the region's most important outboard race for 1932, was awarded to a British Columbia location for the first time. It was a nod to the Canadian outboard organizations that they were recognized by the American Power Boat Association.

A contingent of 25 Seattle outboard racing teams traveled across the border to the race. They were part of over 50 outboarders who traveled from different parts of the Northwest to participate in the two-day program that started on Saturday August 21. Fifteen Seattle drivers qualified for the national events and three set world competition records. Ellsworth Simpson, driving Jimmy Mandas' *Ahepa*, set a new C-I mark at 39.811 mph, Jerry Bryant raised the C-II record in the *Pacific Phantom* to 40.984 mph and Carl Blackstock, Jr., upped the F-I speed to 42.253. The drivers qualifying for the divisionals and nationals, listed with class first, boat number second and drivers last, were as follows:

Class	Boat #	Boat Name	Driver
A-I	R-131	*Ruth Ann*	Jim (Jimmy) G. Harland
A-I	R-138		Walter Jones
C-II	R-176		William (Billy) H. Harrison
F-I	R-131	*Black Cat II*	Adolph B. Spreckels
C-I Runabout	R-336		Jim (Jimmy) G. Harland
C-I Runabout	R-313	*Ahepa*	Ellsworth E. Simpson
C-I Runabout	R-324		Roger Holman
C-II Runabout	R-328	*Pacific Phantom*	Jerry Bryant
C-II Runabout	R-334		Wendell Trosper
C-II Runabout	R-326		James J. Tregoning
F-I Runabout	R-336	*Miss Hi-Flex*	Adolph B. Spreckels
F-I Runabout	R-305	*Hellydid*	Carl Blackstock, Jr.
F-I Runabout	R-313		Tom R. Humes
F-I Runabout	R-334		Wendell Trosper
F-I Runabout	R-328		Jerry Bryant

(The drivers above received expense money if they traveled to the championships.)

Oakland, California, Divisionals and Runabout Nationals

The Divisionals or Pacific Northwest Championships were held once again in Oakland, California, on the Lake Merritt one-mile course. All the drivers listed above were eligible to compete in the event which was held on September 8-9. Three of the bunch from Seattle won in their respective classes. "SEATTLE GAINS RACING HONORS IN BIG REGATTA," was the *Times* headline in the September 18 edition. "Competing against drivers of the highest caliber from all over the country, Seattle drivers Adolph Spreckels, Jimmy Harland and Jerry Bryant brought home no less than six championships and plenty of honor for the Northwest."

Spreckels took the Pacific Coast Championship in F-I Hydroplane, and Jimmy Harland did even better bringing home two titles. He won the Pacific Coast Championship for Class A-I Hydroplane as well as the C-I national title for service runabouts. Bryant, not to be outdone, proceeded to win the Pacific Coast title in C-II service runabout and the national title for the same class. The only note that marred the event was an auto accident involving Harland and his wife. They were run off the road and hit a tree on the way home. Jimmy was uninjured but his wife injured her hip and both boats were damaged on the trailer.

Bay City, Michigan, Nationals

Jimmy Harland was the only qualified driver who made the long trip to Bay City Michigan, to compete in the National Outboard Regatta. This event, which was the outboard association's biggest race for the year, was held on October 10-11. Harland towed a larger load than expected because it included Adolph Spreckels' F-Hydroplane and his hefty four-cylinder motor. Earlier, Spreckels had asked Harland to take his equipment and compete for him because he was unable to make the trip.

The fourth annual event, most likely held on Saginaw Bay, was marred by days of rain, snow and wind. Officials delayed the regatta for two days in hopes of more favorable conditions but the weather never cooperated. They finally had to run the regatta in the ongoing adverse weather because many of the drivers were about to return home. The postponements and bad weather added to Harland's seemingly bad luck ever since he left the California Divisionals in September when he had the car accident on the way home to Seattle.

Harland's misfortunes continued at the nationals where he competed in two events driving his class A-I Hydroplane and Spreckels' new speedy F-I Hydroplane, now named *Black Cat III*. This was a hot boat, originally named *Irish*, which he purchased at the California Divisionals from the successful female driver, Carmen Pantages. The re-naming of boats has been said to be bad luck which played out in this case during the stormy weather in Lake Huron's Saginaw Bay. Harland struck a concrete pier and

Adolph Spreckels, left and JimmyHarland

"completely wrecked" Spreckels' craft while rounding a buoy during the race. The Associated Press headline, published in the *Seattle Times* on October 12, stated: "HARLAND GIVEN WALLOP; CRAFT HITS BIG PIER." Luckily, he was only treated for some minor injuries and shock before being released from medical care. He returned home with a friend's crashed boat and nothing to show for it except for some bruises. He was unable to finish in the F-Class and wasn't in the money in the A-Class.

Sammamish Slough Cruise

That hardy bunch of Seattle outboard clan tried the Slough once again, albeit very late this year. The excursion, the fourth publicized run up the snake-like water-way, was recapped in Tom Humes' "Around the Shops" column on December 25 and February 5. "The first trip up the Lake Sammamish River was made last week by Gene and Joyce Hatton, Jerry and Ann Bryant, and Ted Engstrom and George Wiggans. The weather was none too good, yet these rabid outboarders insist they had a world of fun, and the trip was worthwhile in spite of weather conditions." The group stayed the night at Strafford's Resort enabling them to refresh and recover from the inclement weather they encountered on the way up.

Carl Blackstock's world record certificate for Class F-I Runabout set June 26, 1932 on Lake Sammamish.

SOA Sportsmanship Award

A race driver was awarded a perpetual trophy for the first time by the Seattle Outboard Association this year. The prestigious award was given, based on a vote of the club's drivers, to the individual who showed the most sportsmanship during the 1932 racing season. First year club member Gene Hatton, Jr., was the first recipient of the plaque that was donated by Carroll Jewelry. He started racing in the *Hellydid* and then campaigned with his new C-Runabout that he named *Mad Hatter*.

Retired SOA Sportsmanship Award trophy given to Al Benson in 1944 and 1945.

1933

The following comments published by club officers summed up S.V.B. Miller's past two-year reign over the club: "Nineteen thirty-two will be remembered by Seattle Outboard Association, Inc., members as the year of greatest accomplishments in the six-years of its history. For the two years under the leadership of retiring Commodore S.V.B. Miller, the club forged ahead, eliminated destructive forces, built up the membership and enjoyed almost an excess of boating activity."

This year the new commodore was L.S. "Spike" Davis, a commodore of the past who came back for another term. Davis was commodore in 1930, the second year of the club's operation. M.A. "Pop" Tuthill was voted as vice-commodore; Ann Bryant, secretary-treasurer; Bob Otis, measurer; and two trustees, S.V.B. Miller and Jerry Bryant. The new officers, who were elected last December, will be taking over an "enthusiastic going concern, with several hundred dollars in the treasury, equity in real estate and all the debts paid in full." Their first order of business was organizing the daring boat trip between Seattle and Lake Sammamish.

Sammamish Slough Cruise

During January, the year after Washington's congress abolished Prohibition, those who loved the adventure of the Slough were at it again. The fourth annual journey began on the 14th when a party of fourteen club members, very cozy in five outboards, left Lake Union for a 60-mile excursion some might call a "cruise of the tortuous Sammamish River."

January is usually cold, wet and windy but the harsh weather never stopped the hardy men and women of the Seattle Outboard club. The group congregated at Lake Union in Seattle where they began their voyage to the southwest end of Lake Sammamish, just like the early pioneers in the 1800s except for their luxury of contemporary equipment. They stocked food, blankets and extra fuel into their launches, all powered by outboard motors. And most importantly, the hot beverage of choice, usually spiked with something extra to keep them warm. The armada proceeded through the Mountlake Cut, across Lake Washington to Kenmore and up the twisting Sammamish Slough to Stafford's resort on Lake Sammamish. The group stayed overnight and then returned to Seattle the next day, concluding the unique and exhilarating adventure (see log and overhanging brush blocking Slough on page 81).

Gordon Stewart, also a member and scribe of the Queen City Yacht Club, was part of the outboard entourage. He originally planned to be the first one to make the trip in an inboard powerboat but found his cruiser full of water while preparing to leave. So, he took his "putt-putt" outboard instead and was reported saying: "First time I ever outboarded in anybody's back yard" while recalling the narrow Slough and its tortuous course.

1933 Cruise and Race Schedule:

Jan 14-15	4th Sammamish Slough Cruise
April 7	University Bridge Opening Celebration -Lake Union
April 9	Green Lake
May 7	Green Lake
June 4	Green Lake
July 4	Lake Kitsap-Bremerton
July 4	Vancouver, Washington
July 4	Lake Stevens
July 16	Annual Seattle to Olympia Marathon
July 22	Green Lake
July 30	Lake Meridian
Aug 5-6	Lake Sammamish Regatta
Aug 13	Annual Coupeville Marathon
Aug 19-20	Harrison Lake, B.C. Pacific Northwest Championships (Sectionals)
Sept 23-24	Pacific Coast Championship & Runabout Nationals-Green Lake
Sept 25	Lake Washington Mile-Trials
Oct 7-8	Chicago Nationals
Oct 22	Green Lake 100-Mile marathon (Cancelled due to bad weather)

University Bridge Celebration

The *Times'* headline: "NEW UNIVERSITY SPAN OPENED BY ROOSEVELT" told the big news for Seattle vehicle drivers on April 8. The University Bridge, seven-years in the making, was opened by President Roosevelt from the White House Oval Office. The new six-lane bridge alleviated years of traffic congestion and frustration for residents traveling between Seattle and the north end. Several thousand residents gathered along with members of the Seattle Outboard Association to celebrate the event.

The outboard club commemorated the opening by running several heats of staged races on Lake Union that included fly-overs by Boeing Field pilots and entertainment from the University of Washington band and glee club. Mayor John F. Dore and other dignitaries were speakers at the gala hosted by the University Commercial Club. The outboard drivers included Bus Tuthill in *Miss Tut*, Dave Hall in *Miss Pat*, Jim Mandas in *Ahepa*, Otto Espesith in *Goofus*, Ellsworth Simpson in *Ahepa II*, Stanley Donogh in *Zimmie Special*, Carl Blackstock, Jr., in *Skunk* and Steve Yates with Ted Engstrom in the *Black cat*.

April 8 was also the Seattle Outboard Association's weigh-in day. Every boat that raced in nationally sanctioned outboard races was required to be weighed before it could be registered. This was a requirement by the National Outboard Association for all boats entered in a local or national event.

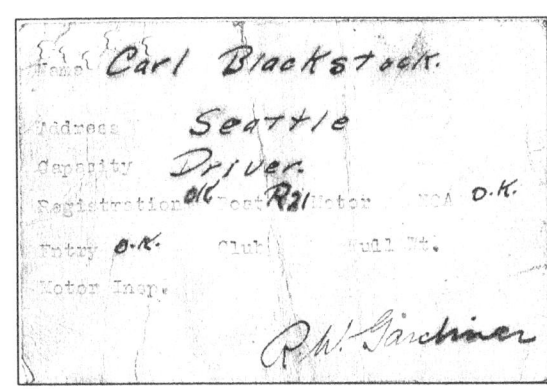

1933 Carl Blackstock NOA Registration card.

Harrison Lake Northwest Championships

The Northwest Championships were run on Harrison Lake at Harrison Hot Springs, B.C., on August 19-20. "TUTHILL MAKES NEW RECORD IN OUTBOARD MEET" was the headline from Harrison Hot Springs, B.C., Monday, August 21. Seattle driver, Bus Tuthill, set a new world record in the C Runabout class and he along with his SOA teammates won 12 out of 18 qualifying classes in the two-day event. Tuthill, who is the son of future SOA Commodore, M.A. "Pop" Tuthill, set a new C-I Runabout competition mark of 37.942 mph, bettering fellow Seattle driver, Gene Hatton's record of 37.815 mph. The following were the Seattle drivers who won the right to compete in the Pacific Coast Championships on Green Lake in August:

Class:	*Driver:*	*Class:*	*Driver:*
A-I	Tom Redfield	C-I Service Runabout	Bill McFadden
A-I	Walter A. Jones	C-I Service Runabout	Bus Sill
A-II	Jimmy Harland	E-I Service Runabout	Carl Blackstock, Jr.
C-II Hydro	Pat Cummins	E-I Service Runabout	Ellsworth Simpson
C-II Hydro	Bill Harrison	E-I Service Runabout	Jim Mandas
F-I Hydro	Jerry Bryant		

New Seattle club member and veteran outboard driver, Stanley Donogh, was severely injured in a mishap while driving his E-II Runabout. He was treated locally for a compound fracture in his leg and was eventually transported to Seattle for further treatment and recovery.

Earlier, in June, he set a new Class E-II Runabout record in the mile trials on Lake Washington piloting his *Zimmie Special*. The Sears executive raised the speed to 42.860 miles per hour with his attractive passenger, Mrs. Ann Bryant. Mrs. Bryant had retired as a successful Class B Runabout driver late last year for medical reasons. But fortunately for the northwest racing community she continued her duties as a respected race official and SOA officer.

Pre-Championship Green Lake Regatta

The most electrifying outboard event of the year transpired during the monthly Green Lake regatta held on June 4. The bold print in the sports section of Monday's *Seattle Daily Times* for June 5 read: "RUNAWAY BOAT THRILLS CROWD." Along with the possibility of several new world records, the thrilling capture of a runaway speedboat was the highlight of the day. The paper printed several photos of the event along with an artist's concept drawing (below) of the hero leaping into a driverless speeding boat much to the amazement of thousands of spectators on shore.

Ellsworth Simpson, driver of Jim Mandas' *Ahepa I*, was the hero of the day. "He succeeded in subduing the *Keedt III*, the berserk craft of Allen Petrich, which had thrown its driver into the lake and was caroming madly about, endangering spectators on the beach. The accident happened when Petrich's craft threw him from the cockpit

Ellsworth Simpson jumping into driverless *Keedt II* from *Ahepa I* driven by Jerry Bryant.

as he attempted to make a sharp turn at the north end of the lake. Roaring over the water at more than 30 miles an hour it headed for the crowded beach as Petrich struggled to swim from the path of the oncoming racers. Suddenly the boat struck a wave in the water and roared out into the lake again as loudspeakers screamed frantic warnings to the spectators near the shore.

Jerry Bryant, a driver who was waiting at the moorings for his race to start, took "Horse" Simpson aboard his craft and headed into the lake for the unmanned craft. Simpson clambered to the bow and Bryant pulled alongside the rampant racing craft, only to have it veer away. Again, he pulled alongside and this time Simpson, riding the bow of Mandas' boat like a cowboy, leaped for the deck of Petrich's racer and in a moment the roar of its motor died when his hand reached and closed the throttle.

Later, Simpson, nicknamed "Horse" by his fellow drivers, completed his second exploit of the day. He was rewarded for his heroic first feat earlier by winning the professional division of the E Service Runabout class and setting a new record at 39.045 mph in the same boat in which he performed his cowboy act. It was a fitting end to a day of excitement for fans and relief to the race officials because no one was injured in the cowboy boat adventure.

A new starting clock, similar to the NOA clock used at American Lake in 1931, was built and tested by the SOA members during the next Green Lake race that occurred July 22. This marked the first step of preparations for the coming championship event. The official clock, which was employed at all the championship regattas, was built in S.V.B. Miller's shop. The construction materials were donated by Blackstock Lumber, Pacific Marine Supply, Jerry Bryant, S.V.B. Miller and Sunde d'Evers Company. The carpentry work was completed by William Harrison, a former race driver and Billy Harrison's father.

Pacific Coast Championships-Runabout Nationals

"THREE SEATTLE DRIVERS WIN IN COAST CONTEST" headlined in the *Times* on September 25. The Pacific Coast Championship Outboard Regatta was finally a reality in Seattle in 1933. It was the first time the Divisionals and the bonus event, the Service Runabout Nationals, were held in the Northwest and run on Green Lake. It's very fitting that the Service Runabout Nationals were part of the contest since they were invented here by the Seattle Outboard Association. The Coast Championships had all been run in the west up to now because these classes were run mainly in this region.

The same regatta, which was held in Oakland the previous year, had been sponsored by the Sears Roebuck & Co. Now, Sears was the sponsor again, primarily because Stanley Donogh, Sears Pacific Coast advertising manager and new member of the Seattle Outboard Association, recently moved to the Seattle area.

Sixty-nine contestants from up and down the coast, including eight world-record holders, converged at the lake in North Seattle to compete in a program of twelve classes under the rules of the National Outboard Association. Green Lake, a natural amphitheater, was considered one of the finest, if not the finest, race course in the country.

Local record holders who entered their world-class boats were Jimmy Harland, holder of three world records; Carl Blackstock, Jr., and Pat Cummins, each the holder of one and Wendell Trosper, who held two marks. Among the California-area record holders entered were Marty Martin, Phill Raber and R. V. Collins from Los Angeles; Set "Slim" Ruhland, Alhambra; Herman Wright, Oakland and Joe Bansi, A. E. Blohm, Bill Downey and James Rudy of San Francisco.

The 69 drivers who entered the regatta were faced with wind, rain and rough water on the first day. They thrilled the enthusiastic crowd estimated at more than 45,000 fans despite the adverse weather conditions. Seattle drivers won five out of the 16 classes in the championship heats run on Saturday through Monday. Saturday's C-Service Runabout heats were postponed to Monday due to the bad weather.

Tom Redfield, Jimmy Harland, Jerry Bryant, Bus Tuthill and Steve Yates were the local "speed maniacs" who proved their superiority by becoming the Pacific Coast champions in their respective classes. Aldoph B. Spreckels III, now from Eugene, Ore. also won a championship in one of the most thrilling Sunday races. Mrs. Set Ruhland, wife of Set "Slim" Ruhland of Alhambe, California and the only woman in the regatta, won and retained her coast title in the B-I Hydro event.

Pacific Coast Championship (Divisional) Results-Sept. 22-23

A-I Hydro 1st	Tom Redfield-Seattle	C-I Service Run	Bus Tuthill, Seattle
A-I Hydro 2nd	Walter Jones-Seattle	C-II Service Run	Steve Yates-Seattle
A-II Hydro 1st	George Letcher-California	C-I Racing Run	Ward Angilly-Marysville, CA
A-II Hydro 2nd	Jim Harland-Seattle	C-II Racing Run 1st	Ernie Millot-Stockton, CA
B-I Hydro	Mrs. Set Ruhland-Alhambra,CA	C-II Racing Run 2nd	Pat Cummins-Seattle
B-II Hydro	Jim Harland-Seattle	F-I Racing Run	John Kovacevitch-Arwin, CA
C-I Hydro	Ward Angilly-Marysville, CA	F-II Racing Run	A. Gilberto-Martines, CA
C-II Hydro	Ernie Millot-Stockton, CA	E-I Service Run	Charley Warner-Modesto, CA
F-I Hydro	Adolph Spreckels-Eugene, OR	E-II Service Run	Jerry Bryant-Seattle
F-II Hydro	R.V. Collins-Los Angeles, CA		

National Outboard Championship Results-Sept. 24

C-I Service Run	Dave Hall-Seattle	F-II Service Run	Slim Ruhland-Alhambra, CA
C-II Service Run	Steve Yates-Seattle	E-I Service Run	Carl Blackstock, Jr.-Seattle
F-I Service Run	A.E. Blohm-El Monte, CA	E-II Service Run	Jerry Bryant-Seattle

Mostly California runabouts are pictured here in the pits at the Pacific Coast Championships and Runabout Nationals held on Green Lake.

The outboard pilots representing the Seattle Outboard Association performed better in the Runabout National Championships run on day three of the event. Monday's program started with the mile-trials on Lake Washington in the morning and continued with the championship races on Green Lake in the afternoon. Four new mile straightaway world records were set in front of the SOA property located at the northwest end of the lake. The two-mile marker and the Sheridan Beach finish line, surveyed years earlier for the UW crew races, were used for the start and finish lines for the record attempts.

Seattle's Pat Cummins set the first record of the day in his CII-Racing Runabout. He established the first world record for the new runabout class at 43.688 mph. A. E. Blohm of El Monte, California, was next with a new mark of 48.517 in the F-I Racing Runabout class. The third record was by California driver H. P. Burpee at 38.793 mph in class C-I Runabout and the final mark of 48.648 mph, the fastest of the day, in the F-II class by 6-foot-7-inch Slim Ruhland of Alhambra, California.

1934 Christmas card photo from Ann and Jerry Bryant (daughter Betty in middle) to Carl Blackstock.

Remember when Jerry Bryant lost his cap in the Green Lake race back in August of 1931? Yes, that's when his wife Ann ran over that "harmless little hat" that fouled her propeller and "killed" her motor. She was in the money while driving her B-Runabout toward third place. But suddenly she was fouled by Jerry's hat, unable to finish and lost her chance for a trophy. Well, she finally got even, so to speak!

Husband Jerry and rider Ellsworth (Horse) Simpson, apparently won Sunday's division II F-Racing Runabout championships by handily defeating all the hot California boys. Jerry was driving Stanley Donogh's fast Class F-Runabout *Zimmie Special* while Donogh was recovering in Providence Hospital from a severe leg injury, a consequence from his accident at the qualifying Divisionals at the Harrison, B.C. divisional regatta. They thought they made a great start, crossed the starting line precisely as the clock closed and the gun fired. But not in the eyes of the chief scorer, you guessed it, Mrs. Ann Bryant! She had to disqualify them because they beat the starter's gun by half a boat length, thus ending the continuing saga of that "harmless little hat" affair.

The men of the SOA represented Seattle well again by winning four of the six runabout classes in Monday's national event. Dave Hall took the honors in C-I Service Runabout, Steve Yates in C-II Service Runabout, Carl Blackstock, Jr., in E-I Service Runabout and the veteran, Jerry Bryant, in the E-II Service Runabout class. These races, witnessed by the largest crowds in Seattle history, were described by the *Times* as being "The most spectacular racing event that this town has ever seen."

Seattle Outboard Association's SOA Sportsmanship Award for 1933, as voted by fellow drivers, was given to Bill "Billy" Harrison for his outstanding contributions toward the betterment of the club and its members. Harrison, small in stature but larger in life, was a mentor to new drivers and along with his father, fabricated the new SOA starting clock.

1929-1933 Summary

The years leading up to the first Sammamish Slough Race since the Seattle Outboard Association was formed couldn't have been more successful. The club which had grown more than 200 members and was full of talented individuals, had become one of the largest and most respected boat racing organizations in the nation. The SOA had been able to separate itself from the regional association to become independent and directly affiliated with the national governing bodies of the APBA and NOA. By the end of 1933, SOA club members held more than half of all the world records in the nation and were highly regarded by the local newspaper reporters.

1933 Woodinville: Ken & Keith Ross. Fallen tree completely blocking Slough.

Northwest outboard racing grew from no organization with a few races in 1915 to numerous races each season conducted by one of the nation's strongest organizations, all in the short time of four years. The Seattle club had the nation's first woman race referee in (Ann Bryant) and an officer in the national body (S.V.B Miller). At this time, Commodore S.V.B. Miller's initials were still one of the club's best kept secrets. Up to now, photographs of the club's accomplishments were a rarity. This year that changed when former race driver and *Outboard Row* salesman, Al King, started taking photos instead of trophies. "Camera Al" as he was called, could be found in his boat, anchored at his favorite "hot" racecourse corner. There he took photos of his fellow outboarders with his trusty Graflex camera.

Seattle was one of the few cities to hold a national regatta and the majority of the regional championships, a remarkable achievement for any time period but especially during the Depression. Worries about the failing economy most likely had some effect on the local drivers who recently won the right to compete in the 1933 Chicago Nationals. The absence of any information about their travels for the nation's biggest outboard race, is likely evidence they never made the trip east unlike in the past when the local newspapers always published articles about the event and their experiences.

The Northwest had quickly become a mecca of boat racing with the best waters in the nation. The success of the Seattle Outboard Association was clear–they had money in the bank, equity in property and their own permanent racecourse. Boat racing life for the Seattle Outboard club members couldn't have been much better! Bill "Billy" Harrison was the second recipient of the SOS Sportsman Award.

1933-Lake Sammamish Regatta at Lewis Beach.

Clubhouse of Their Own | 83

1933 Stanley Donogh & lady mechanic in C-Service Runabout

The Commander McDonald Trophy left, designed by McClelland Barclay, was the most valuable trophy in outboard racing. It was first presented by Commander Eugene F. McDonald, Jr., in 1929 to winning driver Frank Royer of Chicago who drove a raceboat powered by a Johnson "Sea Horse 32."

Chapter 5
"Steeplechase On Water!"

1934-Orval Skaggs (R-81 *Pegasus*) in C-Service Runabout roars around first Slough bend (upstream from Lake Washington) in third place with an unknown 2-man E-Service Runabout behind. Skaggs finished sixth overall after running out of gas and paddling across finishing line at Enos' Gateway Grove on Lake Sammamish.

The Crookedest Race in the World
1934 First Running

"The event will be the Lake Washington–Lake Sammamish Outboard Steeplechase, something new in the way of outboard competition being tried for the first time, according to Jerry Bryant, association commodore."

-The Seattle Sunday Times, February 25, 1934-

The Seattle Outboard Association, now in its fifth year as a boat racing club, elected Jerry Bryant, age 24, as commodore succeeding outgoing commodore, "Spike" Davis. Gene Hatton was elected vice-commodore and E.E. Simpson, secretary-treasurer. The elected committee chairmen were: Orval Skaggs, Entertainment; E.E. Simpson, Publicity, and Otto Espeseth, Membership. Bryant appointed S.V.B. Miller as chairman of the regatta committee with Gene Hatton, Ted Engstrom, Lee Stark, Bob Otis, Fred Durland and Ann Bryant as committee members. Jerry's wife, Ann, said "Jerry could handle anything from a national regatta to the most simple club competitions."

Jerry Bryant was also elected as vice-president of the American Power Boat Association. He was the second representative from the Northwest to be an officer for the national body and the first to be in a high position.

1929-Jerry Bryant

The first official activity for the club was organizing and running a race from the University Bridge, up the Sammamish Slough and ending on Lake Sammamish. The race, which was planned for the latter part of February or early March, was categorized as a marathon event.

The club membership was contemplating whether to run such a unique race during a club meeting in 1932. With Commodore S.V.B. Miller presiding, Ellsworth Simpson, put forth a motion to have the SOA sponsor the novel event. Miller, a very conservative commodore, was opposed to the idea but the majority of the members voted for it after arguments, pro and con, were heard. The vote set the race planning process in motion and laid the groundwork for the "Crookedest Race in the World."

A number of outboard members were preparing for the first running of the Slough Race. Jimmy Harland, Seattle owner of Jimmy Harland Outboard Motors, was observed tuning up a rebuilt C-Racing Runabout *Lion Head* near his shop on the protected waters of Lake Union. Steve Yates gave one of his *Black Cats* a workout and Lee Stark had gained speed in his boat *Apache* during the winter months. Two newcomers, Jack and Jim Perine, had been gaining experience in driving their E-Service Runabout *Painter's Devil*.

Race start location at Madison Park (Brown's Boat House is next to the ferry terminal.)

In a late February news article, Commodore Bryant announced that the Seattle Outboard Association's first official point race of the 1934 season would be staged on Saturday, March 3. The new event was named "The Lake Washington-Lake Sammamish Steeplechase," something new in the way of competition being tried for the first time. The start was to be from Brown's Boat House on Lake Washington at

Madison Park instead of the previously mentioned University Bridge location due to speed restrictions in Portage Bay and the Mountlake Cut. Sixteen or more boat drivers were expected to start at 3 o'clock from the Seattle Boat House on a torturous 25-mile long journey.

On the morning before the first race, Commodore Jerry Bryant and his wife Ann traveled up the Slough to the Lake Sammamish finishing point in preparation for judging the race. It reminded them of the trip they had taken November to verify that the route was still passable. They started from Portage Bay in Seattle, checked out the finishing point at Gateway Grove on the Northwest end of Lake Sammamish and then returned to Seattle. "It is an unusually beautiful trip," Mrs. Bryant said in a *Seattle Times* article. "Those who have only gone part way up the Slough by canoe or rowboat in the early morning or late evening in summer time, with the green banks on either side and the trees swaying over the water, and now and then a silver fish jumping, will agree with her."

The following drivers were expected to enter the March 3rd race:

Driver:	*Class:*	*Number:*	*Boat Name:*
Bill (Billy) Harrison	C-Service Runabout	R-36	Full Paint
Pat Cummins	C-Service Runabout	R-8	Here's How
James (Jimmy) Harland	C-Service Runabout	R-2	Lion Head
M.A. (Bus) Tutthill, Jr.	C-Service Runabout	R-3	Miss Tutt
Lee Stark	C-Service Runabout	R-25	Apache
Orval Skaggs	C-Service Runabout	R-81	Pegasus
Jack Colcock	C-Service Runabout	R-87	Sea Imp III
Jack Lyman	C-Service Runabout	*	*
Allan Petrich	C-Service Runabout	*	*
George Wiggins	C-Service Runabout	*	*
Howard McDonald	C-Service Runabout	*	*
Ellsworth Simpson	C-Service Runabout	*	*
Dave Hall	C-Service Runabout	R-9	Dark Horse
Jim Mandas**	E-Service Runabout	R-7	Ahepa III
Latham Goble**	E-Service Runabout	R-13	Zimmie Special
Jim Perine**	E-Service Runabout	R-79	Painter's Devil
Buster (Bus) Sill**	E-Service Runabout	*	Corsair II

* *Rider-mechanic names, some boat numbers and boat names unavailable*

<u>Patrol Boats:</u>
Jerry Bryant and Steve Yates

** E-Service Runabouts require two persons in the boat, a driver and a rider-mechanic, to make the National Outboard Association's minimum weight requirement.

Inaugural Sammamish Slough Race

The speedsters would start by traveling about 10 miles north on Lake Washington from Madison Park. This stretch of the lake, which varied from about two-miles to one-mile in width, could be extremely rough during that time of the year due to windstorms. The steeplechase[1] element began when the drivers entered the mouth of the Sammamish Slough (Kenmore area), where they ran over a hazardous shallow bar. The "steeplechase" moniker most likely originated with Jerry Bryant, from his participation in college track and field. Then they traveled up another 14 miles through winding switchback curves, under low bridges, alongside flooded pastures, through and over logjams and along two long straightaways. This is all the while they were dodging drift debris, low hanging branches and other obstructions left by the recent high waters. Then the final mile to the finish at Claude Enos' Gateway Grove on the northwest end of Lake Sammamish. Many thrills and spills were expected in the day's action. Automobiles could follow the race on roads by the side of the Slough for a good share of the distance and still arrive at Gateway Grove in time to witness the finish.

Rules of the race established that when a driver approached from the rear and signaled to pass, the lead boat had to move over to allow the pass. Blocking an attempted pass automatically disqualified the driver. The drivers entered in the race were given final instructions during a meeting of the Seattle Outboard Association at the Seattle Yacht Club the evening before Saturday's race.

Race officials determined the race starting time well before the day of the race which included the time for the drivers' meeting. The meeting took place the day of the race at about one-hour before the starting time. The race referee reviewed all the specific racing rules, how the race would start and answered questions.

A typical outboard race was run on a one to two-and-a-half-mile closed course with all the boats running counter-clockwise around a series of buoys and each class running separately. The race drivers entered the race course during a three or five-minute warm-up period and then begin positioning themselves for a running start when the one-minute clock starts or a white flag was waved. Legal starters are boats that do not cross the starting line before the clock reaches zero or when the starting flag is waved– boats crossing the line early are disqualified for that heat.

---

[1] The name is derived from early races in which orientation of the course was by reference to a church steeple, jumping fences and ditches and generally traversing the many intervening obstacles in the countryside or in this case the waterway.

This Sammamish Slough Race was anything but typical, all the classes started together at the same time and the course was a 25-mile-long route from Madison Park to Lake Sammamish. The boats were lined up along a floating dock before the start. A crew member or friend held the boats in place by the back of the motor with the bow pointing toward the race course. Drivers prepared their engines during the count-down by locking their hand-throttle in a closed position (this opens the motor carburetor valve) and primed the engine with fuel to enable a quick start. They accomplished this by chocking fuel into the cylinders with a rag in the throat of the carburetor and pumping the motor's flywheel back and forth with the starting cord (and it was hoped, remembering to remove the rag before starting).

Pat Cummins ready for start. See starting cord knot in flywheel (lower left)-his right hand is holding the handle (not visible).

The starting cords were made of cotton wound rope with a wooden handle on one end and a knot at the other end. The driver repositioned the flywheel with a cylinder just starting compression and then inserted the knotted end of the starting cord into one of the flywheel notches and wrapped it one full turn around the flywheel just before the race start. The cagey drivers always had a spare cord in their life jacket pocket in case it broke, which happened often, especially with the four-cylinder motors. The cotton rope was strong enough to withstand the compression forces but weak enough to break in case of an engine backfire. A strong backfire has been known to break an arm!

As the starting time approached the race starter announced pre-determined time intervals leading up to the start, possibly a 10-minute alert, then the five-minute alert and each succeeding minute up to one minute before the start. The final count-down in seconds begins at one minute to the start...45 seconds...30...15...10-9-8-7-6-5-4-3-2-1-zero, the starting gun fires, "Bang!"

Only then could the drivers start pulling forcibly, sometimes madly, at their pre-wound starting cords. Most used both hands to overcome the strong compression forces of the two and four-cylinder engines. Instantly, one could hear the whip of the starting cord and the firing of the engines, first a low muffled "Oowaaaaa" growl, sometimes sputtering, as the propeller started pushing water away, then a louder higher revving "Waaaaa" as the underwater exhaust opening was exposed when the boat starts moving faster and starts planing[2] up over the water. At the same time the crew and spectators were greeted with a powerful whiff of burnt gasoline and castor oil exhaust from the engines. For an outboard enthusiast it's a wonderful and addicting aroma that you never forget! This all the while they were hoping their engine would start on the first pull. If not, they were already behind because of the precious seconds lost from rewinding the starting cord and re-pulling.

But not to worry, they hoped and expected to make up for the lost time by being faster and driving the shortest path toward the north end of the lake. The first milestone was rounding the tip of Sand Point, about four miles north past Union Bay and Laurelhurst, where the Sand Point Naval Air Station was located, then due north along the east side of Lake Washington, past O.O. Denny Park, St. Edwards Seminary and Arrowhead Point. Then the final mile to the next milestone, the entrance to the Sammamish Slough. The boat that entered the Slough first had the distinct advantage because it was very difficult to pass in the treacherous narrow and winding waterway.

Seattle resident Jack Colcock was the winner of the inaugural Lake Washington-Lake Sammamish weekend steeplechase in his Western Cooperage *WECCO Phantom* boat. He made the remarkable time of 46 minutes flat over the 25-mile distance or an average speed of 32.609 miles per hour driving his Class C entry. Dave Hall was second; Lee Stark, third; Jim Perine with Brother Jack as mechanic, fourth; George Wiggin, fifth and Orval Skaggs sixth. All were members of the Seattle Outboard Association, the sponsor of the race.

Jack Colcock in early 1950s

As advertised, thrills and spills provided excitement for the spectators who watched the start and the hardier who watched from a vantage point somewhere along the Slough. Knowledge about the race was limited since this was the inaugural Slough Race. The starting point, the best viewing areas and the finishing point were not well known, only what was published in the newspapers. The best and easiest places to view the boats in the Slough were on the street bridges[3] that crossed over the Slough

---

[2] See photo in previous chapter of Adolph Spreckels starting to get on a plane from the pits at Green Lake in 1933.
[3] See the map in the middle of this chapter for the racecourse layout for 1934-1946 & 1952.

which included: The Kenmore Bridge (at the Slough entrance), the Juanita Highway Bridge (between Kenmore and Bothell), and the Bothell, Woodinville, and Redmond Bridges. Two accidents occurred in the first-time event. Lathan Goble and girlfriend mechanic Dorothy Dennis, who left the starting line late, were thrown from their Class E-Service Runabout into Lake Washington. They took a chilly bath just off Sand Point after catching up with the leaders. The Harbor Patrol picked up the unhurt but shivering racers who had encountered rough water, the cause of the accident. Dorothy Dennis was the only woman to ever participate in a Slough Race until the 1950s.

1934-Dorothy Dennis, Goble's mechanic.

Latham Goble in "Zimmie Special"-without mechanic.

The second mishap also occurred in the choppy waters of Lake Washington when the craft of Ellsworth Simpson and Adolph Spreckels, in third place at the time, narrowly missed a spill. Then they almost swamped passing over the Slough entrance bar and eventually broke down in Bothell shortly after their restart from the bar. Steve Yates, who was one of the first two employees at Bryant's shop, was the patrol boat pilot who followed the racers up to the finishing point at Lake Sammamish. He was driving one of Bryant's boats and provided assistance to drivers with mishaps along the way–helping them to re-start or towing them to safety.

Only six drivers out of the 16 who entered, finished. They branded it as "the most interesting marathon ever staged by the Seattle Outboard Association." All were eager to stage it again in the near future when water conditions were improved, giving them a better chance to lower Colcock's record. Incidentally, Colcock's C class rig used a 2-cylinder motor, slower than the more powerful E class that had a four-cylinder motor. None of the big Class E rigs finished, showing that the fastest and most powerful didn't always win. Driving consistency, dependability and some good fortune were usually more important to winning a marathon. The following were the race results:

1934 Sammamish Slough Race Results (First Race):

Place	Driver	Class	Boat #	Boat Name	Time
1	Jack Colcock	C-Service Runabout	R-87	Sea Imp III	46.00
2	Dave Hall	C-Service Runabout	R-9	Dark Horse	
3	Lee Stark	C-Service Runabout	R-25	Apache	
4	George Wiggins	C-Service Runabout	*	*	
5	Lee Stark	C-Service Runabout	R-25	Apache	
6	Orval Skaggs	C-Service Runabout	R-81	Pegasus	

*Some boat numbers, boat names and times unavailable

1934

Second Running

"Skippers of the roaring, jumping, skittering outboards come into their own again tomorrow."

The Seattle Times, March, 1934

The club was unsure whether they could run a second race because the water covering the bar at the Slough entrance was two-feet lower than the first race and was becoming dangerously low. But the water level didn't go any lower. It maintained its present depth, which allowed the race to be run as scheduled. This brought renewed expectations for the Class E drivers. They hoped that their equipment would be dependable enough for them to finish the second race and give them bragging rights for beating Jack Colcock's time in the first race of 46 minutes flat. The boys in their boats would start again at Brown's Madison Park Boathouse on Lake Washington and finish at Claude Enos' Gateway Grove at Lake Sammamish.

The following drivers were expected to enter the race:

Driver:	Class:	Number:	Boat Name:
M.A. (Bus) Tutthill, Jr.	C Service Runabout	R-3	Miss Tutt
Dave Hall	C-Service Runabout	R-9	Dark Horse
Rogers Holman	C-Service Runabout	R-15	Nertz III
Lee Stark	C-Service Runabout	R-25	Apache
Orval Skaggs	C-Service Runabout	R-81	Pegasus
Jack Colcock	C-Service Runabout	R-87	Sea Imp III
Jack Lyman	C-Service Runabout	*	*
George Wiggins	C-Service Runabout	*	*
Howard McDonald	C-Service Runabout	*	*
Ellsworth Simpson	C-Service Runabout	*	*
Jim Mandas	E-Service Runabout	R-7	Ahepa III
Latham Goble	E-Service Runabout	R-13	Zimmie Special
Jim Perine	E-Service Runabout	R-79	Painter's Devil
Buster (Bus) Sill	E-Service Runabout		Corsair II
Norman Ledger	E-Service Runabout	R-312	Dad's Expense

Some rider-mechanic names, boat numbers, boat names unavailable

<u>Patrol Boats:</u>
Jerry Bryant and Steve Yates

Buster Sill received his redemption in the second running of the Sammamish Slough Race. "Bus," as he was called by his follow competitors, not only won the marathon, but he set a course record with his big Class E motor. Sill, who was unable to complete the first race, covered the treacherous twisting and turning Slough in 44:43 or 33.544 miles per hour average. This beat the old record of 46:00 minutes set the previous month by Jack Colcock. Second to Sill was Jim Perine, also driving a Class E-Service Runabout, in his R-79 *Painters Devil*. The first C-Service Runabout class to complete the route was driven by Lee Stark, in R-25, *Apache* who reached the finish line in 51:48. Orval Skaggs was the second Class C driver to finish, while Colcock was third in 1 hour, 3 minutes. His luck ran out for a second win as he was stopped several times when his propeller was fouled by weeds.

The Lake and Slough again took a heavy toll with only five of the 15 starters finishing. Carl Blackstock, Jr.'s fast Class F-Runabout, R-71, *Helly Did III*, turned over in the Slough, but no damage to the driver or boat was reported. Bus Tutthill, who never finished the first race, continued his misfortunes in the next day's sprint races. The lengthy six-foot-five State Patrolman, turned over completely but landed right side up. He continued on to a remarkable second place finish.

Second Slough Race: Jim & Jack Perine take 2nd place in R-79 *Painter's Devil*.

1934 Sammamish Slough Race Results (Second Race):

Place	Driver	Class	Boat #	Boat Name	Time
1	Buster Sill	E-Service Runabout	*	Corsair II	44.43
2	Jim Perine	E-Service Runabout	R-79	Painter's Devil	*
3	Lee Stark	C-Service Runabout	R-25	Apache	51:48
4	Orval Skaggs	C-Service Runabout	R-81	Pegasus	*
5	Jack Colcock	C-Service Runabout	R-87	Sea Imp III	63:00

Some boat numbers, boat and rider-mechanic names unavailable

Crew members or friends of the racers would drive to the race's finishing point shortly after the start. There were two routes they could take. The longest was along the north end of Seattle through Kenmore, Bothell, Woodinville and Redmond more or less along the race course to Lake Sammamish. The shortest route was across Lake Washington on the ferry *LESCHI*. The ferry landing was right next to the race starting point at Madison Park. They would drive onto the ferry with their vehicle and empty race boat trailer in tow and ferry across Lake Washington. Then drive off in Kirkland and either head directly east toward Redmond or a much longer route to Kenmore and up the Slough route to the Lake Sammamish finishing point at Gateway Grove. Many times, the crew would take the longer route to look for their boat and driver in case they were conked-out along the way. The boat drivers usually beat their cars to the finish unless there was trouble along the way, and often there was!

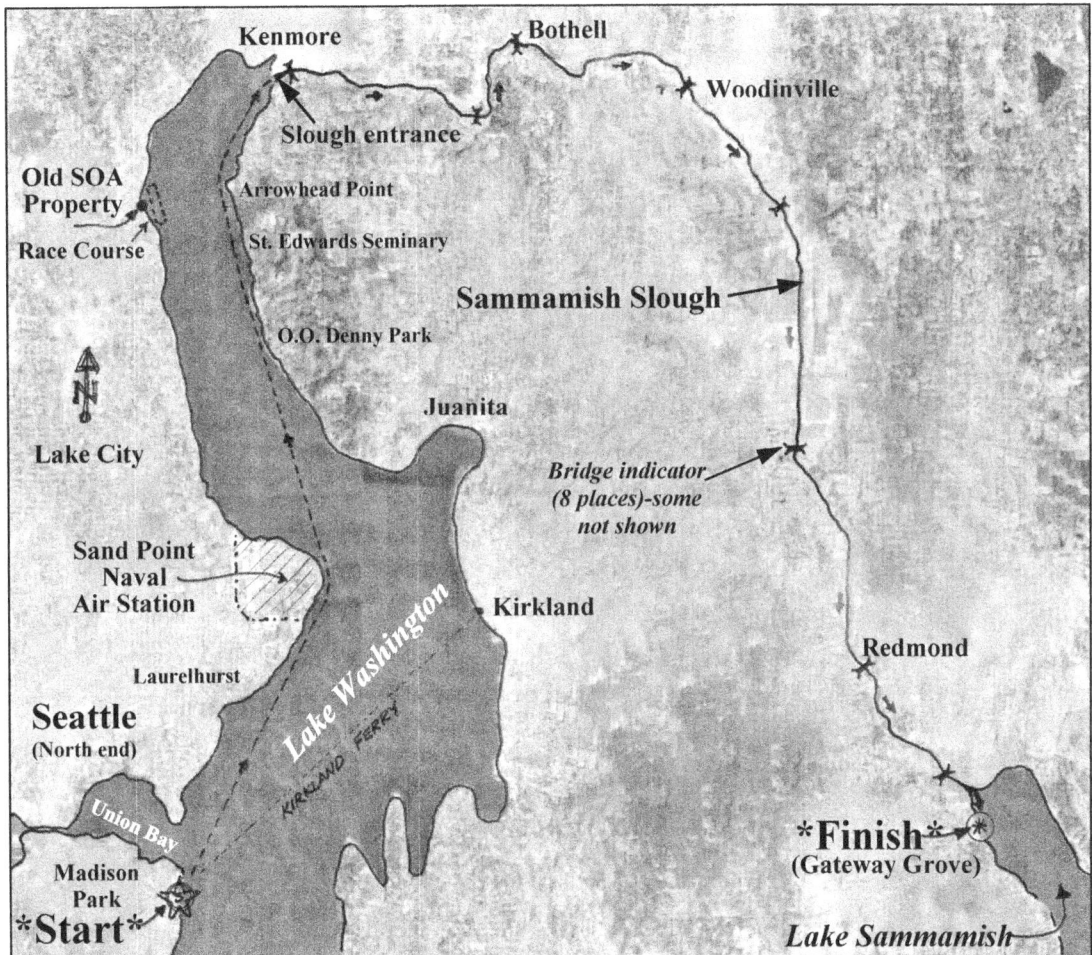

1934-1946 & 1952 Sammamish Slough Race course (Madison Park to Lake Sammamsih).

The ferry service across Lake Washington began in 1891 with the *Elfin*, a 60-foot passenger-only ship. It made round trips between Kirkland on the east side of Lake Washington to the foot of Seattle's Madison Street on the west side for a fare of 10 cents each way. A number of passenger ships made trips across Lake Washington after the *Elfin* was destroyed by a fire in 1900.

That same year the King County Port Commission established a public ferry service on Lake Washington because of the strong insistence from Kirkland residents and business owners. The current steamers were incapable of carrying wagons and horses and made too many stops along the way. A number of larger ferries were used, including the first double ender *King County of Kent* and the larger *Washington of Kirkland*, which made direct routes between Kirkland and Madison Park.

Then ship builder entrepreneur, Captain John Anderson, bought up all the little steamboats and started his own ferry business. Because the county-run ferry ran a regular schedule, he would show up before the public ferry arrived and steal passengers. This didn't sit well with the port commission and City of Kirkland as they were losing fares. The commission forced Anderson away from their docks. By 1920 the ferry system was in financial trouble and the public lost confidence in the county-run system. So, the county appointed Anderson superintendent of ferries where he kept the system in the black from 1922 to 1935.

Ferry service also ran to Juanita and farther north to what is now the O.O. Denny Park area. Orion Denny (son of Arthur Denny) and his wife purchased the park area originally as a 46-acre waterfront country estate (they named "Klahanie") in the late 1800s. Guests were ferried from Seattle aboard their 100-foot Steamer, *S.S. Orion*, which at that time was the largest private motor yacht on the Pacific coast. In the early 1920s, after Orion Denny died, the property was willed to the City of Seattle and became a public park that opened in 1922. Slough Race drivers passed close by the O.O. Denny Park on their way north to the entrance of the Sammamish Slough.

When the new Lake Washington Floating Bridge opened in 1940, the *Lincoln*, which had been the only ferry operating the Kirkland-Madison Park run for 25 years, was retired. It was replaced ironically by the *LESCHI* an older ship originally built by Captain John Anderson. The *LESCHI* was originally constructed as a side-wheeler in 1931 but had been rebuilt into a ferry-boat with power converted from steam to diesel.

The steamer ferry *LESCHI* heading to Kirkland.

After the war the demise of the *LESCHI* was imminent. She was considered too old, too slow, and her passengers dwindled.

By 1949 the bridge was paid for and the tolls were removed. Ferry service would have ended right there, if not for the perseverance of a coalition of residents who refused to let go. But alas, the commissioners decided to retire her. The boat's last run was in August 31, 1950, which ended ferry service on Lake Washington. In 1968 the *LESCHI* was sold to a fishing company in Alaska and was towed north for use as a salmon cannery. After years of hard labor, she was abandoned and capsized. She now lays listing in the muck near Valdez, Alaska.

1934 Cruise & Race Schedule

March 4	Inaugural Sammamish Slough Race
April 14	2nd Sammamish Slough Race
April 15	Lake Sammamish Regatta-1st Miller Cup
April 29	Club Treasurer Hunt on Lake Washington
May 20	American Lake Regatta-2nd Miller Cup
June 10	Green Lake Regatta-3rd Miller Cup
June 17	Lake Sammamish Regatta
July 29	Olympia-Seattle Marathon
Aug 11-12	Harrison Lake Regional Championships- Harrison Hot Springs, B.C.
Aug 25	Green Lake Potlatch Regatta
Aug 30-Sept 1	Pacific Coast Championships- Astoria, Oregon
Sept 14-15	Outboard National Championships-Philadelphia, PA
Sept 23	Silver Lake Regatta
Oct 14	Mercer Island 100-Mile Marathon
December	5th Sammamish Slough Cruise/Clearing

Lake Sammamish Miller Cup Races

Sprint races, featuring the first competition for the S.V.B. Miller class C Runabout Cup, were scheduled to be held on Lake Sammamish the following day after the second Slough Race regardless of whether it was run. The two-day event, Slough Race Saturday and Sprints on Sunday, opened the regular outboard racing season. Rains, similar to those of the previous month, would need to continue in order to allow the Slough competition due to low water conditions. The sprint races were the first official Seattle Outboard Association event of the season where the feature race was the Miller Trophy competition.

Miller, former driver, past SOA commodore and current owner of an outboard motor dealership in Seattle, had put up the cup to settle the Class C Runabout championship of Seattle, an outboard class where there was an on-going heated rivalry. The Miller trophy would be won by scoring the most points in three separate races to be held through the first half of the season. The April 15 race would be the first "leg" of the three competitions. American Lake was the second in May and the final competition at Green Lake on June 10. Furnished cabins at Gateway Grove on Lake

Sammamish could be rented for participants and spectators who wished to witness both days of the season's opening events.

Outboard Club Sponsors Hunt for 'Treasure'

"Hunting for treasure in a speeding motorboat will be the novel stunt staged by the Seattle Outboard Association next Sunday on Lake Washington. For SOA members who possess boats capable of traveling at least 10 miles an hour, the hunt will offer a list of prizes for the winners. There will be no regatta next Sunday."

-The Seattle Sunday Times, April 22, 1934-

Green Lake Regatta-June 10, 1934

"DARK HORSES SWEEP REGATTA" was the bold print headline in the sports section of the *Seattle Daily Times* on June 11. The regatta, which attracted over 6,000 outboard racing fans to the shores of Green Lake, was a huge success. The weather and water conditions were perfect with a sunny day and a slight ripple on the lake providing ideal racing conditions. In addition, there were fewer breakdowns of the motors than in any regatta so far this year, a testament to the drivers and mechanics who were learning how to make their equipment more reliable.

"Horse" Simpson leading the start with Dave Hall in the R-9 *Dark Horse* in foreground and Latham Goble near the shore (notice the white faced starting clock in the upper right which the Seattle Club built in 1933.)

Dave Hall and mechanic-rider Norman Ledger, in Ledger's R-9 boat *Dark Horse*, won the E-Runabout class. Ellsworth 'Horse' Simpson in the R-7 *Ahepa III* with mechanic-owner Jimmy Mandas was second and Latham Goble in his R-13 *Zimmie Special*, with mechanic girlfriend Dorothy Dennis by his side in the cockpit, was third. With the exception of Wenatchee's J. Finlay Webb's win in the F-Hydro class, Seattle pilots rode off with firsts in every event. Up and coming driver, six feet seven-inch-tall Bus Tuthill, won the third S.V.B. Miller Cup race and the overall championship based on having the highest point total during the three separate racing events. Tuthill was awarded the Miller Cup trophy for winning the C-Runabout class, a special event sponsored by Miller and his outboard sales business.

Harrison Lake Regional Championships

"CUMMINS RACES TO NEW RECORD" was the United Press sports headline in the *Seattle Daily Times* on August 13. Cummins of Seattle was also a double winner in the Pacific Northwest Championships held at Harrison Hot Springs, B.C. during the two-day regatta run August 11-12 on the picturesque waters of Harrison Lake. He was the only driver to set a record during the northwest regional race where Seattle drivers won eight out of ten events. He set a new world record of 44.12 mph while driving his boat *Bottom's Up* in the C-Service Runabout class bettering the old mark of 42.482 mph. He won the C-II Service Runabout and C-II Hydroplane classes in *Here's How*, which qualified him for the Pacific Coast Championships to be held at Astoria, Oregon.

The other winning Seattle drivers were Tom Redfield piloting his *Floating Power* in Class A-I Hydroplane; Latham Goble with mechanic Dorothy Dennis; *Zimmie special* in Class E Runabout; Carl Blackstock Jr. *Hellydid III* in F-I Service runabout and *Hellydidn't* in F Hydroplane; Jack Colcock, *Sea Imp III* in C-I Service Runabout and Lee Stark *Apache* in C-I Racing Runabout.

Latham Goble's boat C-4, the *Zimmie Special*, was purchased from Stanley Donogh, which held the 1933 world straightaway records for Class F-II and E-II Runabouts. Donogh, the Sears & Roebuck executive from Seattle, lost a leg last year due to an accident in the Harrison Lake regatta when he was flipped out of his boat and was run over by another competitor. Goble, who previously tried-out Donogh's boat in the Slough Race before the purchase, was competing regularly in the E-II Runabout class with girlfriend rider-mechanic Dorothy Dennis.

Green Lake Potlatch Regatta-August 25, 1934

A sports headline in the *Seattle Post-Intelligencer* on August 26 read "SEATTLE ACES TAKE HONORS IN OUTBOARDS." Seattle outboard drivers were superior against their invading rivals from California and other northwest cities on Green Lake during Seattle's 5th International Potlatch Festival. Carl Blackstock, Jr., in his *Helly-Did III*, triumphed over the previous national champion, Al Blohm in *Big Chief Red Feather* of El Centro, California, in the F-Runabout. He also took the honors in the F-Hydro class driving his *Hellydidn't* craft (shown in the photo below). Rough water and breezy winds made for a number of mishaps and spills throughout the day.

Carl Blackstock, Jr., in his F Hydro R-11 *Hellydidn't*.

Pacific Coast Championships-Astoria, Oregon

The headline on September 1 in the *Seattle Daily Times* stated "Seattle Drivers Win Events of Outboard Meet." Pat Cummins and Carl Blackstock, Jr., of the Seattle Outboard Association, won the honors in the Class C-II and Class F-I Service Runabout classes respectively. The regatta, sponsored by the American Power Boat Association and supervised by E.J. Petheric, racing commissioner of the National Outboard Association, was run in the backwaters of the Columbia River on Young's Bay just southwest of Astoria, Oregon. More than fifty of the fastest outboard pilots on the West Coast competed for the titles in hydroplane and runabout classes during the three-day event run on Friday August 30 to Sunday September 1.

Officials of the A.P.B.A. made a nationwide announcement in the newspapers before the regatta, on August 24. They issued orders to regatta committees throughout the country to disqualify on-site any outboard driver competing in a regatta without a life belt (jacket).

Outboard Nationals-Philadelphia, Pennsylvania

The sports headline in the *Daily Times* on September 1 was "Cummins, Watkins Head for Races***Outboard Titles Are Their Aim." Pacific Coast champions Pat Cummins of Seattle and Bob Watkins of Hoquiam left Seattle for the national championships that were to be held in Philadelphia, Pennsylvania, on September 14-15. Both drivers would run in the C Runabout classes, Cummins as the professional class record holder and Watkins as an amateur class record holder. They were accompanied by Mrs. Pat Cummins and Dave Hall, Cummins' mechanic.

The only west coast driver in the money at the Philadelphia Nationals was California driver and record holder, Al Blohm, in his Class F-II racing runabout *Big Chief Red Feather*. Local pilot Pat Cummins did not place but ended up sixth in the nation with a total of 5,936 racing points for all the classes he competed in, a significant honor for the Seattle driver.

Sammamish Slough Clearing

In October, after an eventful year of outboard racing, members of the Seattle Outboard Association slipped into their reliable outboard outfits and cruised up to Lake Sammamish. This was a necessary trip to inspect the Slough and clear away any obstructing debris that would prevent the next year's annual events. Leading the caravan was newly-elected Commodore, Latham Goble, who headed the association's activities for 1935. As it turned out, this excursion became an annual club event to prepare the Slough for the upcoming seasons.

1934 Summary

Latham Goble, Padilla Bay Oyster Company executive and recent Pacific Northwest Champion in class E-Service Runabout joined the ranks of the Seattle Outboard Association along with Jim Perine and Buster Sill. Gobles' infectious personality won him immediate respect among his fellow club members. He was voted club sportsman of the year and elected club commodore for 1935. He was the third recipient of SOA Sportsman Award. Rounding out the accolades for the year were Pacific Coast Champion Pat Cummins and Jack Colcock. Cummins was the only driver from the Northwest to set a world record this year and the first to rank in the top ten (sixth) in the national point standings. Jack Colcock, northwest regional champion, came out of nowhere to win the inaugural Sammamish Slough Race.

Financially speaking, the Seattle Outboard Association, sponsor of the Green Lake races, failed to succeed in its attempt to raise enough money to cover their prize money debt incurred in last year's Pacific Coast Championships. Although the volunteer service organization, New Order of Cincinnatus, had a large crew of salesmen working the crowd at this year's Green Lake races, only 600 of the 6,000 fans bought the 24-cent tickets which totaled just $144. They would try again next year to raise money from program sales. Members hoped the economy from the lingering Depression years would improve and more fans would purchase programs. The SOA was unable to raise any funds by an admission charge for the races because Green Lake is a public park.

This year, under the direction of Commodore Jerry Bryant, the first and second running of the Sammamish Slough Race was held which eventually was run over a span of forty-years. Had the SOA clubhouse not been destroyed by fire in the fall of 1932, the first Sammamish Slough Race most likely would've started at the clubhouse property location near Sheridan Beach on the northwest end of Lake Washington.

In the years to come the short-subject movie makers will dub this race "The Crookedest Race in the World," a testament to the national and international attention that this wild and crazy race would receive by the press, movie studios and the tens of thousands of local race enthusiasts.

Second Sammamish Slough Race: Driver Norman Ledger and mechanic George Ledger in R-312, E Runabout *Dad's Expense*, encountered engine trouble and were unable to finish.

SEATTLE INTERNATIONAL POTLACH OUTBOARD REGATTA

SUPERVISED BY SEATTLE OUTBOARD ASSOCIATION, INC.

It is the object of the Potlatch Festival to point out advantages of living in our city and state. In no other city in the world can be found such a variety of water for boating. Green Lake is the finest natural race course in the world for outboards with the advantage of being within the city limits for easy access. It is also true that the largest boats in the world can be transported via the canal to fresh water, within the city limits.

COME ON YOU BOATERS!

EXPLANATION OF BOATS AND MOTORS

CLASS A HYDROPLANE—8 h. p. racing motors with 100 pound boats.

CLASS C SERVICE RUNABOUTS—21 h. p. service motors with underwater exhausts and hulls having no step. Total weight of outfit must be at least 550 pounds.

CLASS E RUNABOUTS—31 h. p. service motors with four cylinders. Total weight, including mechanic and driver, not less than 775 pounds.

CLASS C RACING RUNABOUTS—30 h. p. racing motors, two cylinders, no muffler and one person.

CLASS C RACING HYDROPLANE—30 h. p. racing motors which are usually changed from runabout to hydroplane, giving driver chance to enter two events with the same motor. The hydroplane has a step in the bottom and the total weight is 550 pounds.

CLASS F RACING RUNABOUTS—59.2 h. p. racing motor, four cylinders, no muffler and two persons. Fastest stock racing motor made in the United States. Total weight 775 pounds.

CLASS F RACING HYDROPLANE—59.2 h. p. racing motor on step boat weighing 190 pounds. These boats attain speeds of 60 miles per hour and better.

Green Lake .. Saturday .. 2 p. m.

1934 Green Lake Potlatch Race Program-Front Page.

300 Col... Ph...

GENERAL MACHINE WORK **SHAW & MERCILL, INC.** OUTBOARD MACHINE ... ECIALISTS 722 East Pine St. Telephone EAst 1133	"USED BY THE WINNERS" **SPEEDEX — RACING FUEL** JERRY BRYANT, *Distributor*

Boat	Number	Class	Driver
Gilmore	R-22	A Hydroplane	James Harland
Floating Power	R-23	A Hydroplane	Tom Redfield
Conner's Special	R-	A Hydroplane	Sid Sowers
	R-	A Hydroplane	Dorothy Campbell
Miss Tutt	R-3	C Service Runabout	M. A. (Bus) Tutthill, Jr.
Dark Horse	R-9	C Service Runabout	Dave Hall
Nertz III	R-15	C Service Runabout	Rogers Holman
Apache	R-25	C Service Runabout	Lee Stark
Pegasus	R-81	C Service Runabout	Orvel Skaggs
Here's How	R-8	C Service Runabout	Pat Cummins Div. II.
Old Smoothie	R-85	C Service Runabout	Roger DeClemens
Sea Imp III	R-87	C Service Runabout	Jack Colcock
Full Pint	R-36	C Racing Runabout	Bill Harrison
Here's How	R-8	C Racing Runabout	Pat Cummins
Lion Head	R-2	C Racing Runabout	James Harland
Big Beef	R-	C Racing Runabout	Tom Carstens
Miss Mahoney	C-40	C Racing Runabout	Chet Livingston
Half Pint II	R-34	C Racing Hydroplane	Bill Harrison
Bottom's Up	R-6	C Racing Hydroplane	Pat Cummins
Gilmore	R-56	C Racing Hydroplane	Allen Petrich
Ducky	R-17	C Racing Hydroplane	Bob Watkins
Little Snort	R-55	C Racing Hydroplane	Tom Carstens
Jennie "G"	R-	C Racing Hydroplane	Guy Graham
	R-	C Racing Hydroplane	Bob Arlington
Boots	R-14	C Racing Hydroplane	W. B. Earlscourt
Mehitabel	R-58	C Racing Hydroplane	E. E. Richert
Pop-Eye	R-	C Racing Hydroplane	L. Keller
Baby Mahoney	C-88	C Hydroplane	Chet Livingston
My Sin II	R-69	C Hydroplane	Paul True
Stardust	R-61	C Hydroplane	R. F. Driscoll
Skip III	R-39	C Hydroplane	Jack Clark
Ahepa III	R-7	E Service Runabout	James Mandas
Zimmie Special	R-13	E Service Runabout	Latham Goble
Dark Horse	R-9	E Service Runabout	Norman Ledger
Printer's Devil	R-79	E Service Runabout	Jim Perine
Corsair II	R-	E Service Runabout	Bus Sill
Spider Webb	R-	F Hydroplane	Finley Webb
Wenachee Ace	R-	F Hydroplane	Harold Fiel
Miss Wenatchee	R-61	F Hydroplane	Carl Joplin
Flying Cloud	R-	F Hydroplane	Harold McCarty
Hellydidn't	R-31	F Hydroplane	Carl Blackstock
	R-	F Hydroplane	Jim Shannon
Flamin' Mamie	R-	F Hydroplane	L. Richert
Mahoney	C-54	F Hydroplane	E. Millot
Helly Did III	R-71	F Runabout	Carl Blackstock
Miss Stockton	C-44	F Runabout	E. Millot
Big Chief Red Feather	C-71	F Runabout	A. E. Blohm

REPITCHING and STRAIGHTENING **COOLIDGE PROPELLER COMPANY** 1608 FAIRVIEW NORTH	Tutthill (World's Record Holder), De Clemens, Colcock and Harland DRIVING WECCO PHANTOM BOATS "BOATS FOR ALL PURPOSES" **WESTERN COOPERAGE CO.** 1341 Northlake

1934 Green Lake Potlatch Race Program-Back Page.

The Crookedest Race in the World

1934 Harrison Lake Regatta newspaper cartoons by Jack Boothe.

Chapter 6

February 1938 Bar Pilots Induction: Chairman Bryant and Simpson (center of crowd) leading *Bar Pilots Oath* at Southwest side of Bothell Bridge on Sammamish Slough (taken from bridge by unknown).

Ladies of the Lakes
1935-1938

"DOT DENNIS IN OUTBOARD WINS - tiny Seattle miss, won the Class A hydroplane championship"

-The Seattle Daily Times, August 26, 1935-

Under the promising leadership of its seventh Commodore, Latham Goble, the Seattle Outboard Association was looking forward to another great year of boat racing and related events. The club planned to organize and hold a number of cruising events. These activities were planned for those who were not interested in racing but were enthusiastic about outboards. Cruising as opposed to racing up the Sammamish Slough was still an extremely challenging event.

1937: Latham Goble

In December, 1934, the outboard club, now in its sixth year, elected Padilla Bay[1] Oyster Company Sales Manager, Latham Goble, as its new commodore succeeding outgoing commodore, Jerry Bryant. The other elected officers included Edward A. Bassett, vice-commodore; Dorothy Dennis, secretary; Jimmy Burton, treasurer; S.V.B. Miller and Jim Perine, trustees, and L.F. (Spike) Davis as measurer. Goble and the other newly elected officers were installed during the club's first meeting of the year on January 18 at a meeting room in the Seattle Gas Company at 1511 Fourth Avenue.

---

[1] Protected bay on Puget Sound East of Anacortes Washington.

Goble, who eventually became Vice-President of the Bryant Company in 1937, "worked as the sales manager for the sale of the 'lush' oyster lands for the Padilla Bay Oyster Company (east of Anacortes). Latham would give spell-binding lectures on the value of Padilla Bay Oyster land and was responsible for the training of perhaps more than 100 salesmen…to help sell this land. People by the hundreds bought the land to make their millions."[2]

"Sammamish To Be Inspected by Lake Outboards" was the quote from the *Sunday Times* in the December 16, edition. "The first Sunday old Jupe Pluvius[3] lets up and the wind dies down enough, members of the Seattle Outboard Association will climb into their trusty craft and putt out to Lake Sammamish inspecting the Slough and clearing away whatever possible debris and obstructions." This was in anticipation of the upcoming Sammamish Slough Race.

The first official club activity of the year was clearing the channel of the Slough. Inspecting and clearing, if needed, was usually an annual event to prepare for the upcoming race, which was less than two months away. Although there were no reports about a Slough Cruise for 1935, it most likely occurred sometime early in January as that was beginning to be the tradition, a cruise on January 1st, no matter what the weather conditions! The other cruise was the annual "Bar Pilots" cruise that occurred on or near Washington's Birthday, on February 22.

The big event in the river was the Slough Race. But for some reason the race, which was run twice in 1934, lost its luster and was not run in 1935, 1936 or 1937. The most recent publication about the race after 1934 was printed in the *Seattle Times* in 1937. The article stated that the drivers were more interested in racing for points at Blue Lake (near Wenatchee, Washington) than in the Slough as both races were scheduled for the same weekend.

1935 Cruise & Race Schedule

March 24	3rd Sammamish Slough Race-*Cancelled*
Feb 24	Seward Park Tune-up Regatta
April 28	Seward Park Regatta
May 12	Blue Lake-Wenatchee
May 26	American Lake Regatta
June 16	Lake Sammamish Regatta
June 23	Lake Meridian

---

[2] Excerpts from Eileen Crimmins' book *BRYANTS* published 1978 by the Bryant Corporation.
[3] Jupiter Pluvius was the Roman God of Weather.

July 4	Vancouver, Washington
July 7	Lake Chelan
July 14	Lake Meridian-Seattle
July 21	Hayden Lake-Idaho
July 26-28	Devils Lake-Oregon
July 28	Seattle to Olympia Marathon
Aug 4	Seward Park Potlatch Regatta
Aug 11	Service Runabout Regatta-Coupeville, Whidbey Island
Aug 13	Lake Sammamish
Aug 24-25	Harrison Lake Regional Championships- Harrison Hot Springs, B.C.
Sept 1-2	Astoria-Oregon
Sept 7-9	Coast Championships & Runabout Nationals-Lake Merritt Oakland, CA
Sept 21-22	Nationals-Tulsa, Oklahoma

The first part of the Lady of the Lakes chapter is mostly about a very successful woman driver of the Seattle Outboard Association who competed in 1934 and 1935. The first significant woman driver was young Bertha Reinell, followed by Mrs. Francis Burr, Mrs. Ann Bryant and then Dorothy Dennis. We've discussed all of these women earlier with the exception of Miss Dennis who began to shine in outboard racing early in 1935, not just as a rider-mechanic but as a driver in her own boat. These women made a real impact in outboard racing and connected well with the race fans even though none of them drove in the Slough Race. Dorothy Dennis was the only woman competitor in that race until Ginny Lea Lyford drove her small runabout in the 1950s.

Dorothy Dennis-Goble

Dot Dennis as she was called by her fellow racers, began as a rider with boyfriend, Latham Goble. She was the required rider-mechanic for the E-Service Runabout class that Goble was competing in, the *Zimmie Special,* a very fast rig he purchased from Stanley Donogh through his acquaintance with outboard boat and motor expert, Jerry Bryant. National Outboard Association rules required a mechanic or rider in this class to make up the minimum weight requirement of 950 pounds for boat, driver and mechanic.

Dorothy (Dot) Dennis

The dynamic duo of Goble and Dennis began when they attempted to run last year's first Sammamish Slough Race but were thwarted by the rough water on Lake

Washington. Their day ended when they took a very cold bath because of a spill in the lake. Knowing this, one realized that Miss Dennis was not just a pretty face, but a real competitor, one who wasn't satisfied with just participating. This was evident because her spill and resulting bath only inspired her to want her own racing outfit and to compete as an equal, or even better, with the men. So, with the learning experiences she gained while riding in the *Zimmie Special* and with the help of Goble, Bryant and others, she began competing in the A-Hydro Class as an amateur.

1934-Dorothy Dennis in her class A-Hydro at Lake Sammamish

"OUTBOARD RACES RULED OFF LAKE" was a headline in the *Seattle Sunday Times* on April 14, 1935. The following article included: "Green Lake's pestiferous algae have snarled up plans of the Seattle Outboard Association it was announced today. The algae are quiet now, said the Park Board in refusing to allow the association to hold its annual regatta on Green Lake two weeks from today. If the regatta were to go on, the board continued, the algae would be stirred up to such an extent as to make the lake unsuitable for swimming when the season opens.

"So now the association is in a quandary as to where its big annual motor festival will be carried on. Silver Lake is too small, officials say; Sammamish is too far away, and besides this meet is supposed to be a Seattle event."

The regatta was held, however, as the SOA decided to run the program at Seward Park on Lake Washington. Until this year, all the Seattle Outboard club's big regattas were held on Green Lake, "but it looks like the algae are on top this time" and possibly into the future?

Seward Park Regatta-April 28

"Gobles's Outboard Boat Runs Wild***Driver tossed Out at Seward Park" headlined the *Seattle Daily Times* sports section on April 29, 1935. "Racing an outboard on dry land doesn't do it much good. Commodore Latham Goble of the Seattle Outboard Association found to his sorrow at the SOA regatta at Seward Park yesterday. Goble had just opened up the throttle on his F-Runabout when he was tossed out. The craft made several wild circles on the course, and then wound up on the beach. The landing damaged its hull and motor considerably."

Gobles's girlfriend, Dorothy Dennis, faired a lot better as she placed third during her first race in the A-I Hydro class. Another local driver, Jim Rautenberg, uncle to future SOA commodore and Sammamish Slough Race veteran Dick Rautenberg and brother, Bob Rautenberg, placed second in the fast Utility Novice driver's class. The Rautenberg brother's father, Allen, was one of the first outboard racers to run on Green Lake back in the mid-1920s.

Sammamish River Dredging Plans Again in the Works

"County Engineers Survey Sammamish" was an article run in the *Seattle Daily Times* on May 27. A crew of fifteen men was sent to the Sammamish River by County Chief Engineer, Joseph P. Dodd. They were to survey the waterway in preparation for a possible start of flood control for the upper Lake Sammamish area and the Sammamish River Valley. The flood control plan included shortening, widening and dredging the river along with construction of nine new bridges. This effort was part of a broader plan of King County flood control to be financed with federal aid of $3 million for work on the Green River and $500,000 for the Sammamish. The funds were approved by the National Rivers and Harbors Congress committee on flood control who were appointed by President Franklin D. Roosevelt. The Sammamish project includes dredging the river from Lake Washington to Lake Sammamish and shortening the channel to eleven-miles. This was the first of the efforts that eventually drug-on to the middle of the 1960s when the project was actually completed, a very long wait for the residents of Lake Sammamish and the Sammamish River.

Seward Park Potlatch Regatta

Leonard Keller, soon-to-be well-known boat racing instrument maker from Wenatchee, Washington, started racing outboards at the August 4 Seward Park regatta. He placed second in the C-Hydroplane class behind veteran Pat Cummins, who won the Pacific Marine Supply Trophy for first-place in that class. Dave Hall won the A-Hydroplane class and the Sunde & d'Evers trophy, Harold Feil of Wenatchee won the Class F-Hydroplane event and the Schoenfeld Perpetual Trophy, Jerry Bryant was awarded the Callender and Sampson Trophy for taking first in C-Service Runabouts and Bus Tuthill won the Unlimited Runabout event.

Two small Class-C drivers-Billy Harrison and Dorothy Dennis

Harrison Hot Springs Regatta, August 24-25

"DOT DENNIS IN OUTBOARD WINS" was a special headline in the *Daily Times* on August 26. The article under the headline read: "The thousands of fans who lined the shores of Harrison Lake for the final heats of the Pacific Northwest Outboard Racing Championships here yesterday saw another Loretta Turnbull[4] in the makings as Dorothy Dennis, tiny Seattle miss, won the Class A-Hydroplane championship. Miss Dennis started an all-Seattle parade which included drivers from the Queen City taking eight out of the twelve first places and two Seattle drivers setting world records."

The Seattle girl racer, barely weighing 100 pounds and the only woman driver in the regatta, turned in Seattle's first heat victory when she won the opening event leading from start to finish. She won her first championship regatta with an average speed of 36.749 miles per hour for three heats. "She won the first two heats handily and finished the third heat through the gallantry on the part of her male rivals. In this heat her motor refused to respond in the given starting time; here opponents Dave Hall and Jimmy Harland, were privileged to start the race without her, but instead they delayed the race to help her repair her sea horse and all start together. Though Miss Dennis did not win this heat, she scored enough points to lead for the three heats." Not to be outdone Dennis' boyfriend, Latham Goble, won the F-I Runabout class.

Two world records were set. The first was by veteran Pat Cummins who won the C-II Hydroplane championship and bettered the world's competition record with a speed of 44.843 miles per hour. He also won the C-II Racing Runabout class championship. Bus Tuthill set the second record with a new world mark of 38.278 mph in the third heat of the C-I Service Runabout class. The winners representing the Seattle Outboard Association were as follows:

Harrison Race Results

Driver	Class	Speed
Dorothy Dennis	A-I Hydroplane	36.749
Dave Hall	A-I Hydroplane	37.206
Pat Cummins	C-II Hydroplane	44.843
Carl Blackstock, Jr.	F-I Hydroplane	51.784
Latham Goble	F-I Service Runabout	47.284
Jerry Bryant	C-II Service Runabout	38.199
Lee Stark	C-I Racing Runabout	37.100
Pat Cummins	C-II Racing Runabout	44.843

---

[4] Loretta Turnbull was an attractive teenage sensation outboard racer from California in the 1930s era winning national and international outboard racing events.

All the winners qualified for the Pacific Coast Championships that were held on Lake Merritt in Oakland, California, on September 7-9. They also qualified for the Nationals. The other Seattle entries going to the Oakland race were hopeful at seeking qualifying places for the National Outboard Association's National Regatta that was run in Tulsa, Oklahoma September 21-22.

Astoria Oregon Regatta, September 1-2

Dorothy Dennis won just about everything she could during the season, including an unwanted award during the Astoria regatta on Young's Bay off the Columbia River. Thousands of spectators received an added thrill when they watched the rescue of Miss Dennis of Seattle who was thrown into the water from her speeding motor boat. If that wasn't enough, a trophy for her bath added to the insult. The tiny Seattle miss received the "Hell Divers Trophy" for her first spill in her Class A-Hydroplane. Dave Hall was the eventual winner.

Three competition records were set by Seattle drivers. University of Washington student, Bobby Watkins a racing rookie, broke the amateur Class C-Hydroplane mark at 51.255 mph. Then Jerry Bryant established another of his many world records in the professional division of the C-Runabout Class with a speed 38.610 mph. Pat Cummins was not to be out done by Bryant as he set another of his many records in the C-II Racing Runabout class with a speed of 45.965 mph. Dave Hall was awarded the trophy for having accumulated the most points during the regatta.

Pacific Coast Championships-Runabout Nationals

"OUTBOARD ACES GO TO OAKLAND COAST REGATTA" was another headline in the *Times*. The pick of Seattle's outboard motorboat drivers was in route to Oakland to compete in the Pacific Coast Championships and the Outboard Runabout Nationals to be run on Lake Merritt September 7-9. All told, seven of the local speeders were either on their way or set to leave. The contingent from Seattle included Jimmy Harland, Jack Colcock, Dave Hall, Carl Blackstock, Jr., Pat Cummins, Bus Tuthill and Jerry Bryant. Mrs. Ann Bryant was also en route to Oakland, not to race but to be an official for the races.

Nearly all the Seattle drivers are coast or ex-coast champions. Jimmy Harland has held the Class A-Hydro title, Dave Hall is the defending Class C-Service Runabout champ, Carl Blackstock, Jr., has held the Class F-Hydro crown and Pat Cummins is defending his Class C-Racing Runabout title he won last year. And Jerry Bryant, dean of the local group, won the C-Service Runabout Championship in 1933.

Dorothy Dennis, Seattle's girl racing champion who earned fame in the Northwest through her numerous victories for the year, was unable to make the trip even though she was the top contender in the A-Hydroplane class from the Northwest. But not to worry; she was honored and awarded appropriately for her regional accomplishments during the Seattle outboard meeting at the end of the year. The rookie miss was voted "Sportsman of the Year" and was awarded the coveted plaque by a vote of her peers. She was the first woman to win the annual award. The trophy, which was donated by the Carroll Jewelry Store, was presented for the fourth time and kept in the family because Dorothy would soon become Mrs. Latham Goble and Latham won the award for 1934.

One of the *Seattle Times* sports headlines on September 9 was "SEATTLE LANDS 3 COAST TITLES." Two drivers from Seattle won two national championships on Saturday and three Coast titles on Sunday. A large crowd of 50,000 witnessed the event from the shores of Lake Merritt, a small lake in the back waters of the Oakland Inner Harbor.

The outboard nationals were run on Saturday with Seattle drivers winning two of the events and two others placing second. Pat Cummins, driving his Class C-Racing Runabout, set a new speed mark of 45.330 mph in his first heat and broke it again in the next heat at 45.544, making him not only a world record holder but the new national outboard runabout champion as well. The winner of the C-Service Runabout race was again, who else but Jerry Bryant, during the final event of the day. Jack Colcock was second behind Bryant in his craft named *Sea Imp III*. Former SOA member Adolph Spreckles, Jr., now a resident of Oakland, won the F-Runabout event in his *Black Cat IV* and Seattle's Latham Goble won the second-place trophy in the same event driving his trusty *Zimmie Special*.

Three Seattle drivers won Coast Championships in Sunday's program and two others placed second, all earning the right to compete at the Nationals at Tulsa, Oklahoma. Latham Goble won the F-I Hydroplane class with Carl Blackstock, Jr., second, Pat Cummins won his C-II Hydroplane class and Jack Colcock won the C-I Racing Runabout class. Dave Hall was second in the A-II Hydro class. All the winners were awarded travel money, which is typical for the divisional qualifying regattas.

Miscellaneous Notes for the Year

The National Championships were held in Tulsa, Oklahoma, on September 21-22. The 300 entries that were expected for the event most likely raced somewhere on the Arkansas River. A *Seattle Times* article reported that Dave Hall and Jimmy Harland were the only Seattle drivers who would make the trip to the event. It's unclear if they actually went because the news report only listed the winners and no one from the West Coast was in the money.

Leonard Keller was another rookie driver for 1935. Keller would soon be admired and nationally known as a manufacturer of top-of-the-line boat racing instruments and hardware. He also was a boat designer and craftsman builder for an entire class of midget hydroplanes that were campaigned by Northwest drivers in the 1940s.

Another Seattle driver, Bus Tutthill, son of future SOA Commodore M.A. "Pop" Tutthill, was declared a world record holder by the National Outboard Association in mid-September. He raised the Class C-Service Runabout competition speed record to 39.475 during the June 16 regatta at Lake Sammamish. This obviously was better than the previously-noted record he set at Harrison Hot Springs, B.C. in August. Records are set and claimed throughout the year at various courses around the nation. It's typically not known which driver was the fastest for each class until all the submissions are examined and accepted by the national authority at the end of the year. Tutthill's Class C record set at Lake Sammamish was fastest for the year.

1935-Carl Blackstock in his F-Runabout

1936

American Lake Regatta

S.V.B Miller was elected as commodore of the Seattle club for the third time. Miller along with the other officers and membership chairman Jerry Bryant, held their first meeting of the year at Queen Anne Hall. Their first nationally sanctioned outboard race of the year was the annual American Lake Regatta south of Tacoma on May 30. Seattle speedsters won almost all the heats of racing during the contest. Dorothy Dennis placed second and fourth in the Class A-Hydro event, a good showing because she was competing with all of last year's male drivers along with this year's new aspiring pilots.

Green Lake Sportsman Regatta-June 14

Adolph Spreckels and the Seattle Sportsman Show made the front page of the *Seattle Times* on June 15. The headline read, "SPRECKELS HEIR IS UNDAUNTED BY OUTBOARD CRASH." "I can take it and I'm not going to quit this racing game." That was the statement of pain-ridden Adolph B. Spreckels, 26-year-old wealthy sportsman, as he was taken to Swedish Hospital yesterday. He was injured when his speeding outboard race boat leaped a bank and plowed through a throng of spectators who were watching the Sportsman Show at Green Lake.

Spreckels was one of nine people injured as his F-Hydroplane powered by a 60-horsepower motor and driven approximately 45 miles per hour, zoomed out of the water, struck a bank, flew over the heads of thirty spectators and crashed into a sound truck parked 30-feet from shore. Spreckels was thrown into the air and impaled by his arm to a spike on a pole, fifteen feet above the ground. He was taken unconscious to Swedish Hospital but later recovered sufficiently to continue his racing endeavors.

S.V.B. Miller, commodore of the Seattle Outboard Association, under whose direction the outboard race was being held as a feature of the Sportsman's show, said that the accident apparently was caused when the gasoline throttle on Spreckels' motor stuck. Spreckels was the grandson of the late John D. Spreckels who built a fortune as a California sugar king.

This was the first race of the season in Seattle and the first to be held on Green Lake in three years since the Seattle Park Board banned boat racing on the lake. Seattle drivers dominated the races which included Dorothy Dennis. She finished out of the money for one of the few times in her racing career. It's most likely that her mind was on something much more important than racing that day because her beau, Latham Goble, and she were planning to tie the knot. Dorothy and Latham soon married sometime between June and early July. The former Dorothy Dennis traded her racing clothes for a wedding dress and then retired from her short but very successful career in boat racing following the Seward Park P.I. Regatta.

1936 Race Schedule

May 10	Blue Lake Regatta-Wenatchee
May 30	American Lake-Tacoma Regatta
June 14	Green Lake Seattle Sportsman Show Regatta
July 4	Anacortes Fourth-of-July C-Runabout Race
July 4-5	Lake Chelan Regatta
July 12	Seward Park Post Intelligencer Regatta- Lake Washington
August 9	Coupeville Water Festival-Whidbey Island
August 16	Seattle-Olympia Marathon
August 29-30	Harrison Lake Regional Championships- Harrison Hot Springs, B.C.
Sept 7	South Bend Washington Regatta
Sept 12-13	Coast Championships-Lake Merritt Oakland, CA
	Astoria, Oregon Regatta
Sept 19-20	National Championships-Chicago, Ill.

Post-Intelligencer Regatta-July 12

Twenty-thousand spectators lining both sides of the Seward Park race course watched the usual key Seattle drivers win most of the events. They included Pat Cummins, Jimmy Harland, Jerry Bryant and Bus Tuthill. Newly married Mrs. Dorothy Dennis Goble and rookie Chuck Hickling were also among the entrants.

Cummins and Tuthill took baths while leading in one of their heats along with Hickling when they spilled to the entertainment of the crowd. The most interesting event of this race, sponsored by the *Seattle Post-Intelligencer*, was the water polo event. The outboard water polo game was quoted by the *Times* as "something never before seen in these parts." Seattle's veteran drivers, Steve Yates (Red team) and Billy Harrison (Blue team) led their respective teams making it a real spectacle to watch when the driver's tried to hit a floating ball into a goal area while piloting their boats.

Later in the year, members of the Lakewood Community club at Seward Park protested against the outboard events during a Seattle Park Board meeting. Their attorneys said the residents were entitled to "quiet Sundays." Don Dunton, respected

SOA spokesman and SOA "Sportsman of the Year," declared that the outboards would be muffled and races would not be started until after 11:30 in the morning. No further action or decisions on the matter were taken by the board, but the outboard club was worried that their noise would continue to be an issue by residents near race courses. Outboard motor mufflers and how they could be implemented would continue to be a topic of discussion for the club in the future.

Regional-Divisional Championship Results

Information about outboard championships for this year was very sparse. Jim Harland, Jerry Bryant, Bus Tuthill, Tom Redfield and Tom Carstens all won their respective classes at the Harrison Regatta qualifying them for the Pacific Coast Championships in Oakland, California.

Pat Cummins was the only Seattle winner at the Oakland Championships which were run on Lake Merritt. He won the honors in the C-Hydro class and was second in the C-Runabout Nationals. Jimmy Harland had second wrapped up behind Cummins in his C-Hydro but had to stop to cool his britches after flames erupted from his engine and over-warmed his trousers from behind. No information was published about the national races that were held this year. Pat Cummins was the only qualifier at Oakland but most likely did not travel to the Nationals, which were held in Chicago, Illinois.

Other Items of Note

The Slough Race was most likely not run in 1936, like in 1935, because there were no records found showing it was ever run. Chuck Hickling, future Sammamish Slough Race and unlimited hydro driver, was one of the year's rookie drivers. Carl Blackstock, Jr., Lee Stark and Dorothy (Dennis) Goble all retired from racing during this year. Hard-working race official, Don Dutton, was given the SOA Sportsmanship Award for the year.

Jerry Bryant acquired the Seattle Boat Works facility, located on the north shore of Portage Bay, where he began his nationally known marina business with his headquarters still at the downtown Seattle location. This was the property where many of the Sammamish Slough Cruises originated and eventually became Bryant's Marina, the largest boat and motor sales company in the Northwest.

The following chart lists the notable Seattle-area "Ladies of the Lakes" drivers who participated in outboard races from the 1920s through the 1930s.

Driver Name	Racing Period	Classes
Mrs. Francis Burr	1929-1933	B Runabout, Unlimited Runabout
Ms. Bertha Reinell	1930-1932	A Hydro, Unlimited Runabout
Mrs. Ann Bryant	1931-1933	B Runabout
Mrs. Emily Barstad	1931	B Runabout
Ms. Dorothy Dennis	1934-1936	A Hydro
Ms. Dorothy Campbell	1934	A Hydro

1937

The *Seattle Daily Times* sports headline on December 8, 1936 was "Brown to Head Outboarders Next Summer." George Brown, the inaugural SOA commodore of 1929 was elected "high chief of the speed drivers and neck riskers in these parts" for 1937, the associations ninth year in existence. Brown who succeeds S.V.B. Miller "made no glowing promises for the upcoming year but bids fair to be a popular leader."

Jimmy Harland was elected vice commodore; James Burton, Treasurer; Bea Yates, Secretary; Steve Yates, Measurer; Lee Stark, keeper of the pot (membership money for a drawing at meetings end) and Jerry Bryant and M.A. Tuthill (father of multiple record and title holder Bus Tuthill), trustees.

The Seattle outboard group was the guest of Bert Fisher at radio station KOMO February 4. George Brown and others spoke about the organization and upcoming races for the season. This was a first for the outboard group.

Jimmy Harland-vice commodore & 1937 Seattle Outboard sportsman of the year

The club was wrestling with, to some, the unpleasant sound of their outboard motors during the first meetings of the year. The members admitted that the "noise of outboard motors is the blight of our association." Harland and other club members had been publicly addressing the issue and trying to determine a reasonable method of muffling their motors without sacrificing performance. They knew their days of racing on the waters around Seattle were numbered if they didn't. Harland had been kicked-off Lake Union several times by the

Seattle Harbor Patrol during his days of testing–So had other drivers who had been testing on Lake Washington. The outboarders weren't alone in this matter. A number of loud recreational boaters had been cited and even jailed in the past for public noise nuisance during late evening boating parties.

1937 Race Schedule

Feb 21	Sammamish Slough Cruise
May 2	Emigrant Lake-Medford, Oregon Regatta
May 16	Sammamish Slough Race-*Delayed, then Cancelled*
May 16	Blue Lake-Coulee City Regatta
May 30	Upper Klamath Lake Regatta
June 18	Seward Park-Post-Intelligencer Regatta
July 4-5	Soap Lake Regatta
July 18	Bumping Lake-Naches/Yakima
Aug 8	Seward Park Potlatch Regatta
Aug 28-29	Harrison Hot Springs Northwest Championships
Sept 4	Young's Bay-Astoria, Oregon Regatta
Sept 4-6	Clear Lake Coast Championships & Outboard Nationals-Lakeport, CA
September	National Championships-Richmond, Virginia.

Sammamish Slough Race Debated

"SLOUGH RACE IS BEING DEBATED" was headlined in the *Seattle Daily Times* on May 19. Excerpts from the article are in quotes. "Now that the Blue Lake Regatta is in the books and the Northwest outboard season is officially under way, the next thing facing the wave-hoppers is what to do about the Sammamish Slough Race." The event, a so-called annual race that so far was only run in 1934, was originally set for the same day as the Blue Lake affair. Too many drivers, however, decided to take on the Eastern Washington event which led to the Slough Race postponement.

The high-speed boys suggested dropping the race entirely and substituting a regatta to be held on Lake Washington. "The Slough, they maintain, is all right for rowboats, but they'd rather do their racing out in the open where they can turn the heat on." The race was eventually cancelled and never run in 1937. The race that Jerry Bryant and company had dreamed up in 1934 that was so intriguing and eventful, was in jeopardy of never being run again.

Harrison Hot Springs, B.C Regional Championships

"OUTBOARD MEN SMASH RECORDS IN B.C. REGATTA" Headlined the *Times Daily* sports page on August 30. Four Seattle drivers copped titles during the annual two-day regatta which was billed as one of the largest regattas ever held in the Northwest. Jimmy Harland won the professional Service Runabout crown, rookie Wes Loback won in the amateur A-Hydroplane championship, Pat Cummins took the honors in the professional division of the C-Hydroplanes and Latham Goble was the amateur champion in the F-Racing Runabout event.

1937 - Harrison Lake Regatta Pits, Harrison Hot Springs, B.C.

NOA Divisional and National Championships

No race results were found about the Pacific Coast Championships held on Clear Lake at Lakeport, California, except that SOA member Bobby Watkins of Hoquiam set a record and Jimmy Harland had another accident, was hospitalized and released. Watkins had a great year in Division 1 driving his Class-C Hydroplane aptly named *Trouble*. He won the Pacific Coast Championships, set a new world competition record at 51.623 mph and had the Nationals in Richmond, Virginia, sewed up until his tiller line broke. Gar Wood, Jr., son of the famous *Miss America* Gold Cup owner-driver, Gar Wood, eventually won the C-Hydroplane event adding the crown to his A and B national titles he'd won earlier in the regatta.

Future Sammamish Slough Race drivers, Pope Howard, Wes Loback, Otto Dreger, Les Langlie, George Thompson and Ted Alberts were new SOA members this year. Leonard Keller and Wes Loback accompanied Watkins at the Richmond Nationals, the final racing event of the year for the Northwest outboard clan. The well-deserved SOA Sportsmanship Award was given to veteran driver Jimmy Harland.

1938

Last year's commodore, George Brown, was reelected commodore for a second consecutive term. This was his third term as head of the Seattle Outboard Association, the longest reign to date. The club's first meeting of the year was held Friday evening, January 7, at Brown's Boathouse in Madison Park. The other officers were not publicized, except for M.A. "Pop" Tuthill, who was chairman of the utility and cruising committee.

Sammamish Slough Cruises

This year the outboarders didn't wait until the mercury rose before taking to the water. The first cruise up the Sammamish Slough by SOA members was on New Year's Day. This was an unofficial jaunt by Ellsworth Simpson, George Thompson, Jimmy Harland, Tommy Au and Jim Perine, all of whom reported "the going was good" after they completed their zig-zagging through the hairpin turns of the narrow waterway. This year there was renewed interest in cruising and racing up and down the river that had been lacking the last four years.

"OUTBOARD EVENT UP *** Cruise Scheduled Tuesday" was headlined in the *Sunday Times* sports section on February 20. The article went on: "The air, insofar as the outboard clan is concerned, will be filled with music up Lake Sammamish way Tuesday afternoon for if the roar of racing motors isn't music to their ears, what is? The occasion: The inaugural cruise up Lake Sammamish Slough of the Lake Sammamish Bar Pilots' Association.

"Lake Sammamish Slough is no ordinary waterway. It twists and turns like a boa constrictor doing the Big Apple; its banks, for the most part, are close together, and the entire route leaves no great margin for misjudgment or error.

"Yearly, a few pilots have made the jaunt up the Slough. Yearly they have returned with glowing reports of the fun they had traversing it. So, just to start the competitive season out right, the boys and girls decided they'd turn the affair into a major undertaking and invite everybody with any kind of an outboard to make the trip. Judging from the response, everybody is going to take part. There were more than fifty entries on file yesterday."

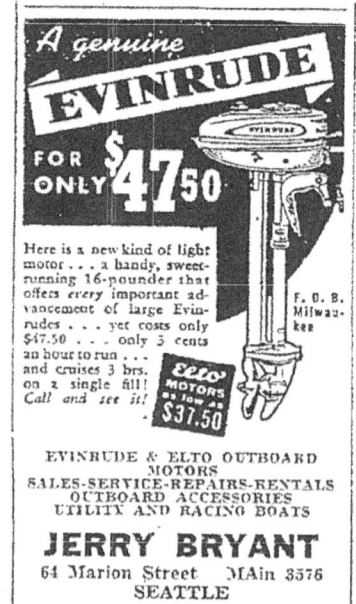

Twenty-five entries made the start at 10 o'clock from the foot of Madison Street at Commodore Brown's boathouse. All the clan were instructed to stop at the entrance of the Slough and wait for instructions from the cruise captain, veteran dare-devil driver, Jimmy Harland, who gave instructions necessary to navigate to the Bothell Bridge, the point on the Slough where the induction ceremonies took place. Jerry Bryant and Ellsworth Simpson were in charge of that department. The new tradition they set forth for the ceremony required all the boaters who completed the course to drink "Slough Juice" from a jug and take an oath given by Bryant with a following confirmation from the inductees stating…"So help me Sammamish Slough!"

The newly-inducted members included Jack April, Glen Jones, Bill Russell, Duane Hinshaw, Tommy Au, Hugh Duncan, Barney Giancoli, Jack Corcoran, Don Ibsen, Ev Thomley, Bus Tuthill, Jack Abenroth, Steve Yates, Ray Zuppe, Jim Perine, R. White, Lee Stark, Jack Colcock, Lin Ivey, Les Lang Val Hallum, Harry Tuttmark, John

Stadlman and Commodore George Brown. All were given an official certificate to commemorate the occasion at the next club meeting.

Cold weather, rain, fog and various motor issues notwithstanding, the outboard group roared its way through the narrow winding course and held an impromptu regatta on Lake Sammamish. Bits of driftwood, ranging from twigs to timbers, led to "sheared pins" providing the greater portion of the woe for virtually all the wave-hoppers.

"The pins being little gadgets easily replaceable, break when the propeller smacks into something" were protecting the prop from damage. George Brown alone had to replace 12 of the little pins all along the way through the Slough.

A *Seattle Times* sports writer with the "The Timer Has the Last Word" column, was one of the participants. He wrote the following in the Friday, March 4 edition: "Ever think of the effect a paddle held broadside in the water over the side of a speeding outboard can produce? The Timer was riding with Jimmy Harland in the Sammamish Slough run Washington's Birthday. All was serene, albeit a bit cold. From down the Slough came the official boat, Jerry Bryant, Ellsworth Simpson and company, banging along at plenty of knots an hour, and with Simpson enthusiastically waving a paddle overhead.

"Maybe," suggested Harland after a quick look astern, 'he thinks he's a drum-major.' Just before passing the Harland craft, Simpson stuck the blade of the paddle broadside in the water. Result: a small but very effective tidal wave, most of which landed on Harland and the Timer."

A second Bar Pilots cruise was run on March 20 for those who were unable to participate in the first event along with some of the same drivers from the first event. "Outboarders Have Fun on Slough Trip" was another sports headline on Monday, March 21. "It just wasn't Billy Harrison's day yesterday, as fourteen outboard drivers piloted their tiny craft through Sammamish Slough from Lake Washington to Lake Sammamish."

Billy, a veteran wave-hopper, landed in the water on the way up the Slough, and in the trees on the way back. The first mishap occurred during the initiation ceremonies into the Lake Sammamish Bar Pilot's Association, which were held at the Bothell Bridge, when Harrison took a header while replacing his shear pin. Then, on the return jaunt, Billy and the boat parted company while negotiating a hairpin curve, the driver landing in some trees on the bank, and the boat continuing down the waterway, driverless.

3rd Sammamish Slough Race

The third Slough Race was delayed this year which was explained per the following article written on April 13 by the *Seattle Times* sports columnist (The Timer Has The Last Word). He wrote: "COOPERATION note: There are, fishermen will tell you, fish in Sammamish Slough. There are too every now and again, outboards on the same waterway, the wave-hoppers liking the jaunt from Lake Washington to Lake Sammamish. For the immediate future, however, the fish will have it all to themselves, the Seattle Outboard Association having decided to stay away for a while.

"Why? The fishing season opens Sunday, April 24. 'If we go tearing up the Slough it will muddy up the water and scare all the fish,' the outboarders explained, and that would be a dirty trick on the fisherman. So, we've decided to stay off the Slough for the time being." The delay may have also been due to the new Kenmore Bridge construction. The bridge opened on May 14 to a crowd numbered in the hundreds after the ceremonial ribbon cutting by the 7-year old daughter of master of ceremonies, King County Commissioner, Tom Smith. The next day on May 15 the Sammamish Slough Race was run.

"CORCORAN WINS SLOUGH RACE" was headlined in the *Seattle Times* on Monday May 16. The article below stated: "Jack Corcoran with mechanic, Duane Henshaw, led a dizzy parade through the Sammamish Slough yesterday, hitting the Lake Washington entrance in front of eleven other boats and crossing the finish line first to take top money in the Seattle Outboard Association's Slough Race. A high-speed jaunt through the Slough is nobody's picnic, yet there were no spills, and, which is amazing, no accidental attempts to climb any trees lining the banks."

Corcoran, a recent inductee into the Lake Sammamish Bar Pilots Association and new Seattle Outboard club member, easily won the event by staying out in front once they entered the Slough piloting his craft named *Flop O*. Other new members, Ray Zuppe was second and Lin Ivey was third. The race boats, likely all utility runabouts, started together just like in the first two events run in 1934. Race chairman Don Dutton, started the race at 10:30 AM from Brown's Madison Park Boathouse while the other half of the Seattle club was racing the same day on the Columbia River in Battleground, Washington. The other drivers Billy Harrison, John Stahlman, Jim

Perine, Val Hallum, Jerome Hallum, Morey Carroll, Morris Gates, Tommy Au and George Thompson finished behind the leaders in the order listed.

1938-Slough Race Winner Jack Corcoran jumping log in C-Service Runabout *R-43* alongside Lin Ivey

1938 Race Schedule

Jan 1	Sammamish Slough Cruise
Feb 22	Inaugural Washington's Birthday Sammamish Slough Bar Pilots Cruise
Mar 20	3rd Sammamish Slough Bar Pilots Cruise
April 10	Madison Park Regatta
(May 14	New Kenmore Bridge completed)
May 15	3rd Sammamish Slough Race
June 12	Bellevue Strawberry Festival Regatta-Lake Washington
June 26	Lake Sammamish Regatta
July 3	Coeur d'Alene, Idaho, Regatta
July 17	Mercer Island 100 Mile Marathon
July 31	Seward Park Potlatch Regatta
Aug 6-7	Anacortes Regatta
Aug 14	White Bluffs Regatta
Aug 21	Northwest Championships-Green Lake
Aug 27-28	Pacific Coast Championships-Harrison Hot Springs, B.C.
Sept 17-18	National Championships-Chattanooga, Tennessee.

Green Lake Northwest Regional Championships

The regatta started at 12:30 pm sharp despite the moans and groans from the drivers who usually warm up their rigs in the morning before a race. Regatta chairman, Carl Blackstock laid out the law to the drivers before the event started, "Listen, we'll have none of you bright lads waking up the Green Lake householders Sunday morning, early or otherwise. Anybody who starts a motor before 12:30 gets disqualified." So were the orders from the race chairman as the Green Lake Regatta was resuming since it had been banned in 1930. The Seattle Park Board approved the races as long as it was quiet until afternoon to appease the local residents who lived around the lake.

The Sectional Championship winners, who all qualified for the Harrison Lake Divisionals were: A-I Hydroplane, Wes Loback; A-II Hydroplane, Pope Howard; C-I Service Runabout, Lin Ivey; C-II Service Runabout, Dave Hall; C-II racing Runabout, Pat Cummins; F-II Runabout, Latham Goble and C-II Hydroplane, Dave Hall. The second and third-place winners also qualified for the Divisionals.

Harrison Hot Springs, B.C., Divisionals and Runabout Nationals

The Western Divisionals and National Runabout Championships held on September 17-18 at Harrison Hot Springs, B.C., was the first time in history that a national outboard event was held outside of the United States. The California drivers that made the long trip north took most of the honors except for two pilots from the Northwest. Pat Cummins and Pope Howard of the Seattle clan kept the men from the south from making a clean sweep. Cummins won the professional C-Hydroplane crown and Howard won the A-Hydro event also in the professional division.

Latham Goble and Pat Cummins both won heats in the runabout nationals but lost their chance of an overall win because of engine trouble in the other heats. They both had the fastest times in their winning heats and were poised to win championships, Goble in F-II Racing Runabout and Cummins in C-II Racing Runabout. Goble was second in the F-II Hydroplane class and Dave Hall second in C-II Service Runabout followed by Jack Corcoran in third place. Wes Loback, SOA "Sportsman of the Year" was third in the A-I Hydroplane event.

Most likely no Northwest drivers traveled to the outboard nationals in Tennessee as no information was published about the results of the regatta. Future Slough Race winners, Lin Ivey and Al Benson were new SOA members this year along with other

Slough Race competitors Ray Zuppe, George Jennings, Fred Carlson, John Stahlman, Val Hallum, Jerome Hallum, Morry Carroll, Morris Gates and Tommy Au.

1934-Carl Blackstock driving his Class-F Runabout *Hellydid III* with mechanic Dave Hall, both Northwest champions and record holders, winning the Green Lake Potlatch Regatta

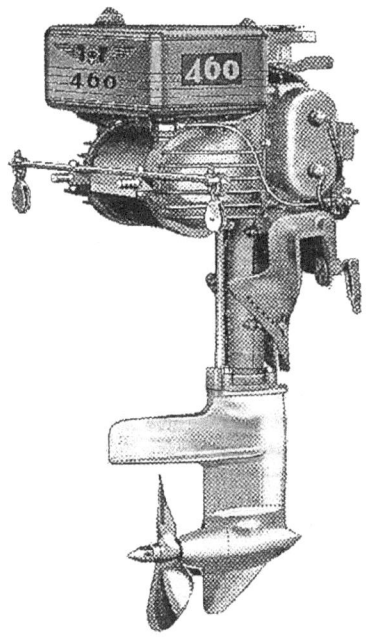

Johnson 460, 4-cylinder, 60 cubic inch factory racing motor used in Class-F

Chapter 7

1941-Sammamish Slough Race newspaper promotion photo taken by *PI* staff photographer from Woodinville Bridge with George Lansing R-36 leading, Bill Rankin R-25, followed by Al Benson R-63 and Lin Ivey R-27.

Under the Radar
War Years 1939-1945

"HOWARD TAKES OUTBOARD RACE - EASY WIN -
Drivers Wind Up Behind Various Eight Balls"

-The Seattle Post-Intelligencer, February 26, 1940-

The Seattle Outboard Association quietly celebrated its 10-year anniversary during the first war year. Their officers kept behind the scenes as none of their names appeared in any publications. Jerry Bryant, who was named the club's race chairman in a news article, was the only club management person who was publicized. Apparently, they were staying "under the radar" because the public thought they were using rationed gas for their racing activities. The club's meetings were now being held at a clubhouse location on Northlake Avenue, which was in the vicinity of Bryant's new marina on the north side of Portage Bay.

Annual Slough Cruise

"SLOUGH DRIVERS TO CRUISE TODAY"- *Seattle Sunday Times*, January 8, 1939. "The outboard motorboaters, who have no regard for wind, waves, wetness or weather, are at it again. The so-called tenth annual cruise was run again where the SOA members and guests traversed that narrow, snaky waterway the full distance from Portage Bay, Seattle, to Lake Sammamish no matter what kind of conditions the weatherman bestowed."

The pilots included Lin Ivey, Jack Corcoran, Jimmy Harland, Jim Perine, George Thompson, Ray Zuppe, Dave Hall, Johnny Michaels, Tommy Au, Forrest Gates, Frank Wiley, Latham Goble, Jerry Bryant, Ellsworth Simpson, Duane Henshaw, George Jennings and Don Dunton,

The outboarders started from Bryant's Marina near the University Bridge at 10 am. The weather was its usual cold, rainy and windy self, which was typical for this time of year. So, as standard operating procedure, the group would bundle-up and most importantly keep warm by consuming their favorite hot beverage spiked with a popular spirit of choice.

The now warmer and lubricated entourage began by motoring slowly through the narrow Montlake Cut, carefully avoiding the watchful eye of the Seattle Harbor Patrol. This was the first dangerous segment of the trip which had a posted 5 MPH maximum speed limit. Strong currents and eddies moved through here that were caused by the runoff entering Lake Washington and its discharge over the Hiram Chittenden Locks into Puget Sound. When together with other boats, they merged into the waves that bounced back and forth off the channel's concrete side walls. This coupled with two-way traffic in a 150-foot wide space, made for extremely difficult navigating. It was especially true when they dodged boats coming and going and battled a mess of water turbulence all at the same time. The boaters were trying to travel the same narrow channel that the University of Washington crews rowed during Seattle's "Opening Day" festivities. Once through the cut they entered Union Bay and then the waters of Lake Washington that were usually very rough due to the typical winter storms.

On Lake Washington they moved north ten miles to the Slough entrance at the town of Kenmore. The windblown, teeth-rattling, body-jarring boat ride on this segment was a challenge all to itself. At the Slough entrance, they had to cross the dangerous shallow sand bar area just like when they competed in the Slough Race, then up 14-miles through the narrow Sammamish Slough. It included navigating countless switchback curves, under a host of low bridges, over flooded cow pastures, through log jams, under overhanging branches all the while dodging drift debris. The outboarders were very lucky they avoided shearing a propeller pin along the way to the finishing point at Lake Sammamish.

The final mile was a straight run to their destination, Gateway Grove, just south of Redmond. By then everyone's bladders were filled up to their eyeballs unless they were relieved somewhere along the way. When this happened, an empty coffee can was a blessing, except for the sorry soul sitting in the rear being doused when it was emptied while under way!

There were usually reports about a boat being customized after losing a part of its windshield or deck that resulted from squeezing under a low bridge. Luckily for most of the boaters, they recognized the hazard and stopped beforehand. They would take on passengers, from other boats behind to lower the craft in the water, allowing it to clear under the bridge.

3rd Annual Bar Pilots Cruise

The Lake Sammamish Bar Pilots Association was open for new members on Washington's Birthday, Wednesday, February 22. Men and women outboard pilots become eligible for membership by successfully navigating the Sammamish Slough and completing the induction ceremony, usually held at Bothell next to the Bothell Bridge. The Slough, now about 14-miles long was described in a *Times* article: "It's no picnic as it's full of twists and turns as a large bowl of spaghetti, Italian style."

The event started from Jerry Bryant's Marina in Portage Bay near the University Bridge at 10 o'clock. The group then congregated in Bothell at 11 o'clock to take part in the initiation proceedings led by the club's "Grand Admiral" Bryant, himself.

4th Sammamish Slough Race

"Outboarders To Race In Slough Today"–*Seattle Sunday Times* March 5, 1939. "Approximately fifteen of Seattle's top-notch outboard drivers have their sights set on Lake Sammamish today." They were to start at 10 o'clock from Brown's Boathouse in Madison Park and end at Claude Enos' Gateway Grove on the north end of Lake Sammamish. They were hoping to better Jack Colcock's record time at 48 minutes he set in the inaugural race of 1934. Jimmy Harland, George Thompson and George Jennings, all driving new 60-horsepowered jobs, were expected to compete for the honors at speeds ranging from 30 to 50 miles an hour. The Slough race this year was problematic due to recurring log jams, a big deterrent that plagued the early settlers of the past.

"OUTBOARD RACE OFF TOMMORROW–*Seattle Daily Times*, Saturday March 11, 1939. The article read "Seattle Outboard Association officials, having noted the damage done to various outfits in last Sunday's frustrated Madison Park-to-Sammamish race, have decided against rerunning the contest tomorrow. They'll wait at least two weeks before trying it again. The various drivers of the shooting shingles started from Madison Park last Sunday, intent on cracking Jack Colcock's record…but found a log boom blocking the mouth of Sammamish Slough. That stopped some of them, but others optimistically dragged their outfits over the obstructing logs only to have another log boom greet them at Woodinville, stopping them for good the rest of the way."

"OUTBOARDS TRY SLOUGH TODAY" was headlined in the Sports Section of the *Seattle Sunday Times*, April 2, 1939, the day of the race. Finally, the race was completed albeit fewer boats were available after the earlier boondoggle. The original roster included such "shingle-shooters" as Billy Harrison, M.A. (Pop) Tuthill, Jim Perine, Leif Buckman, Barney Giancoli, Chuck Richardson, Jack Corcoran, Tommy Au, Jimmy Harland, George Thompson, George Jennings, Johnny Michaels, Ray Zuppe, Wally Hanlon and Dave Hall. A later entry included first-timer Al Benson. The race was divided into three classes-unlimited, utility and outlaw.

The eventual race winner was Dave Hall and George Thompson in a "460 Runabout." It was unclear who was driving and whose boat they were in. This information was published two years later by the *Seattle Times* in their Friday edition on February 21. It stated that Thompson and Hall set a new course record, but the time was never given or any other results. Anything could happen and usually did, good or bad, in an outboard event run between Seattle and Lake Sammamish.

Sammamish Slough Race boats passing by the Windermere community, in background, still bunched together while heading north toward Sand Point, shortly after the start at Madison Park.

1939 Sammamish Slough Race Results

Place	Driver	Class	From	Boat #	Boat Name	Time
1	Dave Hall & George Thompson	Unlimited F-Runabout	Seattle	*	*	New Record

*Some boat numbers, times and boat names unavailable. Classes were Unlimited, Utility & Outlaw

Advance entries included Billy Harrison, M.A. Tuthill, Jim Perine, Leif Buckman, Barney Giancoli, Chuck Richardson, Jack Corcoran, Tommy Au, Jim Harland, George Thompson, George Jennings, Johnny Michaels, Ray Zuppe, Wally Hanlon, Dave Hall, Al Benson

1939 Cruise & Race Schedule

Jan 8	Annual Slough Cruise
Feb 22	3rd Annual Lake Sammamish Bar Pilots Cruise
Mar 5	4th Sammamish Slough Race-*started but not completed due to log jams*
Mar 12	Slough Race rescheduled-*not run due to lack of undamaged boats*
April 2	4th Sammamish Slough Race completed
May 21	Mercer Island 100-Mile Marathon-*postponed due to bad weather*
June 11	Bellevue Strawberry Festival Regatta
July 16	Coos Bay, Oregon Regatta
Aug 6	Pacific Northwest Championships-Anacortes
Sept 2-4	Coast Championships & Runabout Nationals-Lakeport, CA
Sept 24	Mercer Island 100-Mile Marathon-*makeup race*
Sept 21-22	Outboard Nationals-*Location unknown*

1939 Summary & Tidbits

Seattle's Blue Mouse Theater

News about outboard racing in 1939 was very limited, a hint of things to come during the war years even though during this time the United States hadn't yet entered the war. Obviously, this would change in the next two years. Nothing spectacular occurred during the rest of the racing year. No information was available about how the Seattle drivers faired at the Pacific Coast Championships and the Runabout Nationals in California, or whether anyone competed. Also, no information was found about the Outboard Nationals, except that San Francisco, Knoxville, Tennessee, Long Beach and Brownsville, Texas were considered as potential sites by the Chicago-based NOA.

Pope Howard, lanky 6'-7" driver from Everett, Washington, and future Sammamish Slough Race winner, won the SOA Sportsmanship Award honors for the year. Bill Tenney, a nationally-known driver from Bend, Oregon, was an amateur this season and won his share of regattas in the A-Hydroplane class during the year. In the entertainment genre, Seattle's Blue Mouse Theatre showed a new newsreel release in October, *Hydro Maniacs*, a Ted Husing production covering "Outboard Motor Boat Racing."

1940

The Seattle Outboard Association received an infusion of new members in 1940. They elected Linton (Lin) S. Ivey, an amusement entertainment businessman, as their 12th commodore. Ivey's, wife Effie Violet (Vi), was elected secretary; Art Warnell vice-commodore; James Burton treasurer and Don Douglas was appointed publicity chairman. The group held its meetings in their clubroom at 1117 E. Northlake Ave. in Seattle for the second year, the same facility near Jerry Bryant's new marina on the north side of Portage Bay.

SOA Commodore Ivey

Lake Sammamish Bar Pilots Cruise

"OUTBOARD FANS TO TAKE JAUNT," was the headline of the following article in the *Seattle Times* on February 18, 1940. "At 10 o'clock next Thursday morning, a roar and a rattle will arise from the immediate vicinity of Jerry Bryant's wharf near the University Bridge, and if you're an outboard driver or rider, you'll be making part of it.

"That's the day when the Seattle Outboard Association sponsors the annual Lake Sammamish Bar Pilots Association cruise to Shamrock Cottage on Lake Sammamish. At 10:00 o'clock in the morning you'll gun your motor with the rest of the fleet and head through the Mountlake Cut. Once past Webster Point light you'll veer to port and bounce northward in the general direction of Bothell. That part is easy. There are no floating tree limbs or sunken logs to wrap yourself around.

"Then you bang into the entrance of the Slough and unless you have your pockets loaded with highly powerful luck charms, ranging from a nosegay of four-leaf clovers to a stables' supply of horseshoes, your troubles begin. The Slough was never meant for a race course. It twists and turns and writhes and winds like a fifteen-mile long python with a misplaced sense of direction. Thursday's event, of course, will be just a cruise, not a race. The race itself is scheduled for next Sunday." Jerry Bryant, acting as "Grand Marshall" for this event and his wife Ann, originated the idea back in 1929 when they made the initial Slough jaunt in Jerry's fast boat.

5th Annual Sammamish Slough Race

George Pratt of the *Post-Intelligencer* wrote, "Two-cylinders popped in concentric rhythm, the rain fell in desultory drops, a crowd of race boat fanatics raced along the shore of Lake Sammamish in high excitement and Pope Howard hauled his six foot-seven-inch frame out of his cramped position in his outboard and said: 'I've never been so cold in my life! Has anybody got any canned heat?' It was the 1940 Sammamish Slough Race run in near record time by the lanky Everett throttle-gunner, in spite of a terrific rain storm that made the thirty-nine-minute race a severe test of endurance and mental fortitude.

"Eleven other boats followed Howard across the finish line out of a starting field of fourteen which braved the cold and rain for the race. Howard's boat was only kicking on two of its four cylinders when he hit the finish line and was ready to conk-out entirely. But the other drivers were having less good fortune as they finished far back. Wes Loback, figured as a major threat, froze up his motor which delayed his finish and Pat Cummins was in the lead but careened off a log, sheared a pin and ran aground to fall out of contention. Lin Ivey made a poor start with a cold motor and then sheared a pin ending his run. Jimmy Perine stopped for repairs as his motor also froze up and Dave Hall skidded around a turn and hit the bank-the river bank, not the Bothell Bank!

"Despite Howard's troubles, he still finished ahead of Pat Cummins, the second-place boat, by nearly five minutes. Al Benson was first in the C-Utility class (third overall) driving his *Muy Pronto* runabout and Les Langille won in the C-Service class driving the *Flamin Fanny*. The race started at Fishers Madison Park Boathouse, last year's Brown's Boathouse, and ended at Shamrock Grove, last year's Enos' Gateway Grove, on Lake Sammamish."

"The Sammamish Slough Race wasn't yet a household name but it soon would be."

1940 Sammamish Slough Race Results (in order of finish per class)

Place	Driver	Class	Boat #	Boat Name	Time
1	Pope Howard	Unlimited F-Runabout	R-66	Starfire I	39.00
2	Pat Cummins	Unlimited C-Hydro	R-18	Ball Of fire	44:00
3	Dave Hall	Unlimited F-Runabout	*	*	*
1	Les Langille	C-Service Runabout	R-5	Flamin Fanny	*

138 | Taming of the Slough

2	Ray Zuppe	C-Service Runabout	R-1	*	*
3	Lin Ivey	C-Service Runabout	R-25	Poison Ivey	*
1	Al Benson	C-Utility Runabout	R-61	Muy Pronto II	3rd Overall
2	Jim Perine	C-Utility Runabout	*	*	*
3	Lloyd Nicholas	C-Utility Runabout	*	*	*

Some boat numbers, times and boat names unavailable

Al Benson's class winning C-Utility runabout for 1940 Slough Race.

1940 Cruise and Race Schedule

Feb 22	4th Lake Sammamish Bar Pilots Cruise
Feb 25	5th Sammamish Slough Race
May	Juanita Beach Regatta
June 2	Lake Quinault
June 9	Bellevue Strawberry Festival Regatta
June 16	Devils Lake Oregon Regatta
June 30	Tacoma narrows Bridge Opening Water Carnival Regatta
July 2	Lake Washington Floating Bridge Opening Regatta
July 20-21	Anacortes Mariners Pageant Regatta
July 28	Moses Lake Regatta
Aug 4	Pacific Northwest Championships- Coos Bay, Marshfield Oregon
Aug 18	White Bluffs-Columbia River Regatta
Aug 29-30	Astoria Oregon Regatta
Aug 31-Sept1	White Fish Montana Regatta
Sept 1-2	Coast Championships & Runabout Nationals-Long Beach, California
Sept 15-16	National Championships Lake Quinsicamond, Worcester, MA
Sept 22	Mercer Island 100-Mile Marathon
Oct 27	Willamette River 100-Mile-Marathon

Tacoma Narrows Bridge Opening-Water Carnival

July 2, 1940-Tacoma Narrows Bridge Opening

Nov 7, 1940-Tacoma Narrows Bridge Collapse

A Water Carnival and outboard race were run on Sunday, June 30, as part of the Tacoma Narrows Bridge opening ceremonies. The actual bridge opening was held on July 2, 1940 to thousands of people and hundreds of cars that lined up on the new bridge as shown in the photo above.

Al Benson participated in the boat races that were part of the water carnival event several days before the dedication. He placed second in the C-Hydroplane class that

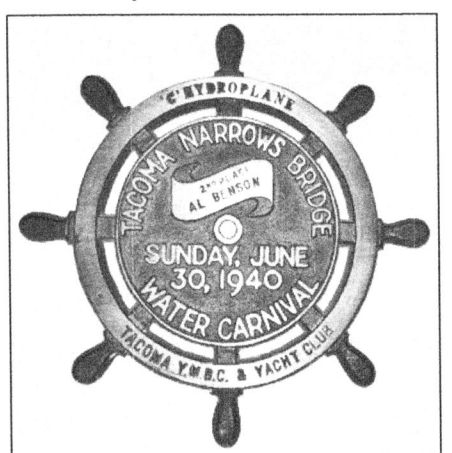

was part of the boat races that were held in the waters below the bridge and sponsored by the Seattle Outboard Association. His trophy, shown here, was cast out of bronze metal and polished to expose the molded-in text and engraving, symbolic of the classic awards given in that era. The bridge opening and later catastrophic collapse was national news along with the Sammamish Slough Races in 1940.

My father, Al Benson, told me about the Tacoma Narrows Bridge collapse in 1983 at my home in Bellevue. He said: "At the time when the Tacoma Narrows Bridge went down, the newsreel companies–there were four of them–were taking pictures of the Slough Race. They said the biggest news that came out of the Northwest was the Narrows Bridge falling down and the Sammamish Slough Race. So that was quite the deal and that was national! Of course, we made a lot of phony shots for the newsreel you know, we'd go up there a week early and make all these phony shots and then they'd dub them in for the race, you know, run through chicken coops and run over boats-about kill ourselves! It was a wonder we didn't get hurt doing that."

"NARROWS BRIDGE CRASHES IN WIND!" Was the headline across the front page in large bold print of the Thursday edition of the *Seattle Times* on November 7. Unfortunately, the excitement of the new bridge opening vanished when the bridge collapsed during a strong windstorm. Forty-plus mile per hour winds were the fateful speeds to upset the balance of the structure that was built inadequately due to the selection of an inferior design concept to save taxpayers' dollars. They would pay dearly for the rebuild.

Lake Washington Floating Bridge Opening-Outboard Regatta

Thousands of spectators, completely filling the new tunnel plaza, witnessed the Lake Washington Floating Bridge opening on July 2. The bridge later was named the *Lacey V. Murrow Memorial Bridge* honoring the director of the Washington Toll Bridge Authority. Some citizens had hopes of being the first to make the crossing of the 6,627-foot-long bridge in their vehicles by paying the 25-cent toll at the Mercer Island toll station following the afternoon bridge opening.

July 2, 1940: Lake Washington Floating Bridge Opening

Governor Clarence D. Martin and Seattle Mayor Arthur B. Langlie spoke to the crowd on a very windy day on Lake Washington. The bridge dedication for the $8,854,000-dollar world's largest floating structure commenced when an urn containing water from every major lake, bay and stream in the state was broken over the west pylon at the Seattle bridge entrance.

The wind caused the accompanying outboard regatta, which began at 11 o'clock and was run on a triangular course near the center span, to have many of its heats of racing canceled. Al Benson, member of the sponsoring Seattle Outboard Association, was one of twelve pilots who signed up for the event. He was one of those who braved the whitecaps and took second-place in the C-Hydro event. This information was written in three pages of my mother's 1940 Race Results that summarized my father's first full year of racing.

1940 Summary & Tidbits

Lin & Vi Ivey, along with other Seattleites, Pat Cummins, Johnny Michaels, Wes Loback and Leonard Keller planned to make the trip to the Long Beach Outboard Championships but no reports were published. Most likely they either never made the trip or were unsuccessful in the regatta. Also, no reports were found about Seattle drivers traveling to the Nationals in Massachusetts. The SOA drivers voted for Fred W. Carlson to be their SOA "Sportsman of the Year." He was the ninth club member to be presented the annual award plaque. Al Benson purchased a trailer-load of race boats, motors and propellers, including the trailer, from "Pop" and Bus Tuthill.

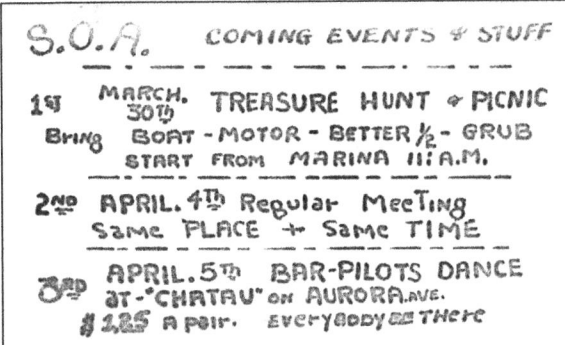

This marked the retirement of Bus Tuthill from outboard racing and his transition to a full-time career as a 6 foot 8-inch-tall Washington State Patrol officer. And the beginning of Benson's car-radio business and his extraordinary boat racing career. Bus Tuthill's father (Pop) would continue his passion as club commodore, engine builder and mentor for aspiring outboard drivers such as the likes of young "Benny" Benson.

1940-Bus and "Pop" Tuthill with their racing equipment they sold to Al Benson late in the year.

1941

During the year when the United States entered World War II, the popular and highly respected M.A. (Pop) Tuthill was elected SOA Commodore for the 1941 season. He received the honor for the next three years, the first person to run the club three consecutive years. "Seattle Elects Officers" was headlined in the *Seattle Post-Intelligencer* at the beginning of the season. Leonard Keller, the newly elected secretary of the Seattle Outboard Association, provided the results of the election to the newspapers. The officers of their Association for the ensuing year among Tuthill and company were: Fred W. Carlson, vice-commodore; Treasurers, Jim Burton and Les Langille, and Leonard Keller, secretary.

M. A."Pop" Tuthill-Seattle Outboard Club Commodore

The sergeant-at-arms was Ralph Sandal; Trustees Lin Ivey and George Brown; regatta chairman Seattle meat cutter Wes Loback; publicity chairman Al Benson, and entertainment officers Billy Harrison, George Lansing and Ralph Sandal. The club meetings were held on the first Friday of each month at the Casa Italiana, 1520-17th Avenue in Seattle. Visiting drivers were invited to attend. Commodore Tuthill promised big doings for the coming year as the club hoped to host the National Outboard Association's Pacific Coast Championships for the year.

Annual Sammamish Slough Cruise

This year the annual Slough Cruise was on Sunday January 5. The following excerpt was from the *Seattle Star* Newspaper on Monday: "If the cows in the pastures adjacent to the Sammamish Slough suffer from stiff necks this morning, it's all from watching a bewildering pilgrimage of outboard drivers yesterday who drove their snarling sea steeds from Portage Bay and Lake Washington up through the Slough and to Lake Sammamish in sufficient numbers to make the bovine inhabitants think they had suddenly been transported to 4th and Pike.

Meaning there was a crowd of people puttering around the Slough yesterday, and not without incident, too. Jimmy (Gimme back my boat!) Perine got tossed out of his sea scooter on one of the hairpin turns near Bothell. George Lansing hit the bank when a steering rope broke and Ted Alberts and Les Lang both burned out (motor) coils in route. The rest of the folks hereafter delineated had a good, cold time and are looking forward to the next spasm at the Slough, scheduled February 22.

<u>The men cruisers included:</u> Steve Yates, Lin Ivey, Bill Harrison, Val Hallum, Ralph White, Les Lang, George Jennings, Bill Ingstrom, Ted Alberts, Ralph Chambers, Sam Stearns, Johnny Sheriff, Ralph Sandall, Bill Finical, Bill Bryant, George Thompson, Ralph Brown, Art Losvar, George Lansing, Jack Zerreuner, Pope Howard, Moritz Libby, Art Lindholt, Pat Cummins and Claude Monroe.

<u>The women cruisers included:</u> Mrs. Dot Benson, Mrs. Dot Lansing, Mrs. Lin Ivey, Mrs. Audrey Seidelmann, Mrs. Edna Brown, Mrs. Ann Loback, Mrs. Ralph White, Mrs. John Bradwill, Miss Mary Navis Pratt and Miss Lillian Berger. Guests included: Mr. and Mrs. Seidelmann, Mr. and Mrs. John Bradwell, Mr. and Mrs. Ralph White and Mr. and Mrs. Ralph Brown.

Sammamish Slough Dredging Continues

"CONTRACT LET TO DREDGE SLOUGH" headlined in the business section of the *Seattle Daily Times* on January 27. In addition to outboard proceedings, the King County powers-to-be awarded a $16,150 contract to the Puget Sound Bridge & Dredging Company for completion of the first phase of a huge flood-control project in the Sammamish Slough. "Commissioner Tom Smith, original sponsor of the project, said the straightening of the Slough, which runs between Lakes Sammamish and Washington, not only would eliminate recurrent floods, but would increase farm revenues by $200,000 annually. Smith said prevention of floods would enable Sammamish Valley farmers to plant crops from sixty to ninety-days earlier, thus making early spring markets available to them."

The first phase, which didn't provide immediate improvement, was essential to the huge project as it involved widening and straightening the Slough's channel downstream of the Kenmore Bridge. The second phase, the main dredging between the lakes, was slated to start within a year depending on weather.

<u>1941 Cruise and Race Schedule</u>

Jan 5	Annual Slough Cruise
Feb 22	5th Lake Sammamish Bar Pilots Cruise
Feb 23	6th Annual Sammamish Slough Race
Mar 30	SOA Cruise & Picnic-Lake Washington, Bellevue
May 25	SOA Sammamish Regatta-Alexander's Beach

June 1	Lake Quinault Derby Regatta
June 15	Strawberry Festival Regatta-Bellevue, Meydenbauer Bay
June 28	Strawberry Festival Marine Pageant-Kirkland, Lake Washington
July 4-6	Coeur d'Alene Lake Motor Boat Race-Idaho
July	Redondo Beach Regatta-Seattle
July 26-27	Anacortes Mariners Pageant Regatta
July 30	Potlatch Mountlake Canal Water Carnival
Aug 2-3	Coos Bay Regatta, Marshfield Oregon
Aug 3	Kennewick-Columbia River Regatta
Aug 9-10	Pacific Northwest Championships-Devils Lake, Oregon
Aug 16-17	Pacific Coast Championships & Outboard Nationals-Seward Park
Sept 13-14	National Championships-Austin Texas
Sept 21	Mercer Island 100-Mile Marathon- Lake Washington

5th Annual Lake Sammamish Bar Pilots Cruise

This year the annual Lake Sammamish Bar Pilots Association cruise was run the day before the Slough Race on the traditional day of Washington's Birthday, February 22. The annual event which was advertised in the local papers, called for all outboarders to join the cruise and anyone successfully navigating the Slough and passing the Bar Pilots ceremony would be eligible for Bar Pilots certificates and pins.

The outing was slated to start from Jerry Bryant's marina at 10:30 am. The entourage traveled out through the Montlake Cut into Lake Washington and north to the mouth of the Slough in Kenmore where they would assemble for further instructions from Steve Yates, the cruise chairman. They usually stopped in Bothell for the ceremony and then motored up to Shamrock Grove at the northwest end of Lake Sammamish to complete the festivities.

6th Annual Sammamish Slough Race

"Eggbeater Racing Costly Sport" was headlined in H.E Jamison's "Along the Waterfront" column in the sports section of the *Seattle Star* newspaper[1] on February 24, 1941. "That roar you folks heard on Lake Washington Sunday that sounded like a squad of bombing planes, was the noise made by the outboarders, holding their annual Lake Washington-Sammamish Slough race.

---

[1] The *Seattle Star* (1899-1947): Of the three Seattle circulation dailies (*Seattle Post-Intelligencer* and *Seattle Times* being the other two) it was the smallest newspaper in circulation, but the largest in the city around 1900. For most of its life the paper was known as the "working man's paper"–staunchly-pro-labor.

"Once a year the lads who ride the aquatic bucking broncos bounce eight-miles across Lake Washington and 13-miles up the winding Slough for the sheer joy of seeing how fast it's possible to make a shingle, propelled by an egg beater, go. Being somewhat addicted to languor and preferring to take my frequent doses of boats and water in the quiet, lazy sailboat fashion, I've neglected the energetic souls who prefer outboarding.

Star's H. E Jamison

"However, when Jerry Bryant told me that there were 10,000 outboard motors in the Seattle area and that they are increasing by about 500 motors a year, it occurred to me that I'd better get busy and tell our readers something about them. Most of us are familiar with the standard outboard that the fisherman use for trolling and the larger units that propel speed and pleasure boats, but few folks know anything about the racing engines that drive the tiny racing boats a mile a minute.

"Take that Sammamish Slough race for example. There were three classes: The Overall class, comprised of boats mounting engines of 40 horse-power and over. These boats have a speed up to 55 miles an hour. The C-Service class boats mount engines averaging 22 horsepower and have a speed up to 45 miles an hour. Then there's the Utility class-boats mounting engines from nine to 22 horsepower and with a speed ranging from 20 to 35 miles an hour. The F-Class (there were none in the Sammamish race) mount 60 horse power engines and their speed is from 56 to 63 miles an hour.

"Now here's an interesting fact regarding these racing engines. All motors, from the 22 horsepower C-Service class and up, burn alcohol instead of gasoline. The reason for this is because castor oil is the best lubricant and it will not mix with gasoline. Alcohol costs $1 a gallon which makes the sport rather expensive. Incidentally, using alcohol instead of gasoline gives each contestant about a mile-and-half an hour more speed. And Jack Corcoran says that an outboard racing enthusiast will work all summer trying to coax and extra half mile out of his motor.

"The boats are divided into two classes–the hydroplane and the flat-bottomed runabout types. The runabout is an exclusive West Coast product. It was developed from the 16-foot fishing boat by the speed demons who began to flatten, shave and polish their craft so that their motors would drive them over the water faster. The net result of years of designing and improving is the present racing machine–13 feet long and 38 inches wide. The hydroplane is approximately the same size, except that the bottom of this craft boasts a 'step' and the step is what gets them up out of the water and gives them their speed.

"While the hydroplane is the fastest design present, the runabouts are not so far behind. With the hydroplane doing 60 miles an hour, the runabout will do about 55 miles an hour. The runabouts are a bit sportier than the hydroplanes. It takes more skill to drive them and they are more thrilling to watch for it's the runabout that bounces so much when under way. This bouncing brings us to the secret of successful design-balance, and one of the things the drivers are always striving for.

"In the F-Class, the mile-a-minute boys, the runabouts rate two men and the hydroplanes rate only one. Because of their slight difference in speed, the hydroplanes and runabouts are never entered in the same race. Usually a driver has one engine and a boat in the prescribed number of heats in the hope of piling up points.

"In order to compete in the local races, you have to be a member of the Seattle Outboard Association. It has approximately 100 members and is affiliated with the National Power Boat Association. Jack Corcoran says that outboard racing is like a disease. A fellow starts out fishing, usually, and then he gets the bug and buys a big engine. A 40-hosepower engine costs $350 and he says that you usually spend another $200 trying to get an additional five miles an hour out of it. The name of his boat is *More Trouble*, which may give you an idea. That the lads have no illusions about this sport is borne out by some of the names. Lin Ivey calls his craft the *Poison Ivey*, Les Lang's is the *Flamin Fanny*, Ted Alberts calls his *Bottoms Up* and an enthusiast in California calls his *Idiot's Delight*.

"In addition to the cost of taking your boat by trailer to the various racing centers, it costs about $10 a race for fuel. But like all sports, when it gets you, it gets you and there are those who will save for the entire year to make the trip to California in the hope of bringing home a trophy."

Sammamish Slough Race Results

"CUMMINS WINS SLOUGH CLASSIC," was a sports section article written in the *Seattle Times* on Monday, February 24. "Pat Cummins of Everett, Pacific Coast C-Hydro champion, proved the champ wild-man of all the outboarders yesterday, when he zoomed at a logjam near Woodinville at fifty miles an hour, shot clear-over and continued the snakelike run of Sammamish Slough successfully to check in at Lake Sammamish in 36 minutes and 3 seconds. His flat-bottomed C-Hydro job was

1941-Pat Cummins

particularly suited for this 'log-hurdling' act and Cummins made the best of his advantage in winning the annual Sammamish Slough race in record time." Lin Ivey, tagging close to Cummins' wake, was second also riding a C-Hydro craft and tried the aerobatics when the log obstruction loomed suddenly ahead, but his carburetor broke off and another "also-ran" was added to the list.

Twenty-two entries roared away from Fisher's Madison Park Boathouse at 11:00 o'clock, all with the hopes of being first into the Slough, a distinct advantage as passing in the narrow waterway was extremely difficult. Cummins was the first in and set the pace by crossing the finish line first at Shamrock Grove on Lake Sammamish. Polson, Montana's, Ray Boettcher, who traveled 600 miles to enter the "classic of crooks and turns," placed second. Boettcher piloted a 16 horsepower Class-B outfit, one of the smallest boats ever to place in the race. Bus Tuthill, returning to the race after a long absence, drove Lin Ivey's boat to first place in the C-Service Runabout class.

Several thousand spectators lined the Slough getting a close-up view within a few feet of the "flying shingles." George Lansing made his exit as a contender trying to hurdle the log jam in Woodinville; Fritz Tietz of Camas, was well ahead in the Utility class until he tried to carve half of a bank out in the Woodinville S-curves and slivered into a pasture; Barney Louthan caught fire at the mouth of the Slough and Wes Loback duplicated last year's performance by "freezing up" off Sand Point. Cowan Pickens did a dipsy-doodle at the Bothell Bridge and took a dunking with a grin to the delight of several hundred race fans as they cheered while the newsreel boys were shooting motion pictures from the bridge.

Pat Cummins' race boat trailer: His winning C-Hydro on opposite side.

1941 Sammamish Slough Race Results (in order of finish per class)

Place	Driver	Class	Boat #	From	Time
1	Pat Cummins	Unlimited C-Hydro	R-2	Everett	36:03**
2	Ray Boettcher	Unlimited B-Hydro	U-43	Polson, MT	*
3	George Thompson	Unlimited F-Runabout	*	Seattle	*
1	Bus Tuthill	C-Service Runabout	R-18	Seattle	*
2	*	C-Service Runabout	*	*	*
3	Johnny Sheriff	C-Service Runabout	R-26	Tacoma	*
1	Ed Hadnett	C-Utility Runabout	*	Seattle	*
2	Les Langille	C-Utility Runabout	R-5	Seattle	*
3	Ralph White	C-Utility Runabout	*	Seattle	*

* *Some driver names, boat numbers and times unavailable*
** *New record time*

Advance entries included Jack Corcoran, Wes Loback, Jimmy Harland, George Lansing, Lester Lang, Ray Zuppe, Lin Ivey, Al Benson, Tommy Au, Ralph Sandell, Pope Howard, Ralph Chambers, Ted Alberts, Dave Hall, Fred Carlson, Bill Rankin and Leonard Keller.

1941 Slough Race: George Lansing driving R-61, *Miss Tutt* in C-Service Runabout Class, heading upstream after passing under the Bothell Bridge (engine trouble prevented him from finishing the race).

The Slough race winners and Sammamish Bar Pilots Association inductees were presented their prizes and certificates during the March meeting at the club's Casa Italiana meeting place. Pat Cummins, winner of the Unlimited Class received the Schorn Paint Trophy; Bus Tuthill C-Service winner, the Preservative Paint Company Trophy and Ed Hodnett, Utility Class winner received the Jerry Bryant Trophy. The new Bar Pilots Association members who received their certificates included:

> Judy Wright, Ann Loback, Mrs. Florence Zerreunier, Bee Yates, Mrs. Ray Zuppe, Bobby White, George Lansing, Austin DeFreece, Frank Francisco, F.A. Fletcher, Fred Carlson, Leonard Clark, Harry O'Conner, Jack Zerreunier and newly appointed SOA publicity chairman, Al Benson.

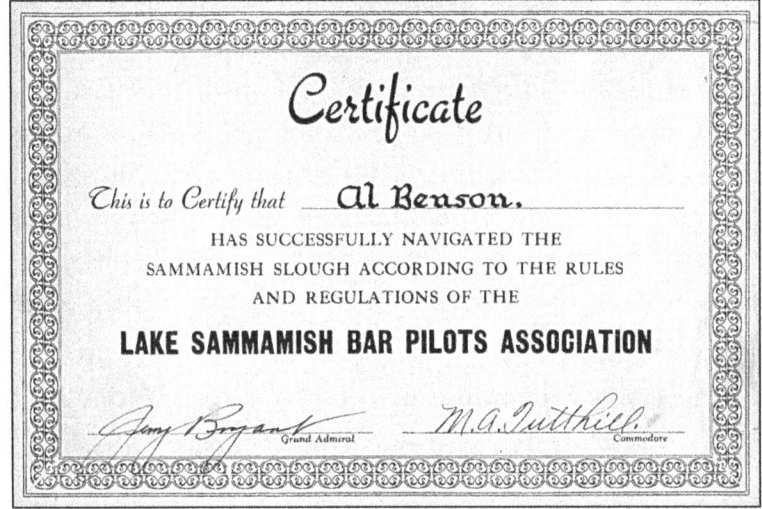

Mystery! - Race Driver Vanishes After Starting Slough Race

This is a first for boat racing. Driver starts race, doesn't finish and is never seen again for several days. My father told me about this mystery when I interviewed him about his boat racing history in 1983. We were talking about the Slough Race and I commented, "You must have lost drivers at times?"

"Oh, yeah, we lost Jimmy Harland for two days once," he said.

He laughed and said, "He was floatin' around somewhere." Dad laughs again." He broke down and got tangled up with some people over in a house across the lake. They got in a big party, and his wife is looking all over for him, we didn't know where he was!"

I said, "That's a big lake to be looking around for people."

He said, "Yeah, and all the way up the Slough!"

This event likely occurred in the 1941 Slough Race when dad was the SOA publicity chairman. You may recall earlier in the book, that Harland had a knack for getting involved in mishaps, especially during his racing and travels. Anyway, Harland and his boat were rescued, either by his wife, or friends, and eventually all was well, except Harland was in the "doghouse" at home front!

Outboard Gals Take Honors in Men's Boats

The women of the Seattle Outboard Association put on the show in the feature part of the club's cruise and picnic instead of the guys during their club festivities in Bellevue on March 30. Margie Wold, driving Fred Hughes' Utility Class boat, was first among six women jockeys in a wild balloon race event when the masculine members turned their wave-hoppers over to the gals as a feature part of the event.

Second place went to Jeannette Asby in Billy Harrison's boat, followed by Mrs. Ray Zuppe (Rosie Qualheim's boat); Madine Scott (Herb Haines's boat); Dot Benson (Austin DeFreeze's boat) and Dot Lansing (Ray Zuppe's boat). In another event, "the wild-eyed balloon race," the women were featured again. But this time they were in the runabout front cockpits trying to puncture five floating balloons with long needle-like pointed sticks while their respective pilots jockeyed close. Ray Zuppe and companion were the winners.

Pacific Coast Championships and Runabout Nationals

"SEATTLE GIVEN U.S. OUTBOARD COAST CLASSIC" was the headline in the *Times* Sports section on May 2. Memories of the Pacific Coast Outboard Championships and the National Runabout title meet, run on Green Lake in 1933, an "all around financial flop" were forgotten and Seattle was again stepping forth to host one of the headlined national outboarding events.

Seattle Outboard Regatta Chairman, Wes Loback, announced that he had received the official sanction for the national event from E.G. Pethrick, National Outboard Racing Commission chairman. Loback, Dr. O.J. Blende and Jack Corcoran of the SOA regatta committee arranged the outboard show for its running at Seward Park with the plan that the regatta was to "pay its freight" through admission fees. Named race officials were: SOA Commodore, M.A. Tuthill, chief starter; James Burton, chief timer; Ann Bryant, head scorer and California's John K. Wagner, referee with Herman Wright as motor inspector. Judges included Leo Weisfield, Elmer Nordstrom, Stanley Donogh, Allen Morgan, Jerry Bryant and Frank Hawkins.

The biggest outboard event on the West Coast this year was run at Seward Park on Lake Washington. The site was the Seattle Outboard Association's second choice because Green Lake was still banned (off-limits) for boat racing by the Seattle Park Board due to the so-called persistent algae growth issues. Pacific Coast competition in all classes, bringing drivers from California, Oregon, Washington and British Columbia were staged on Saturday, August 16. The National races in C-Service, F-Runabout and C-Racing Runabout were held the next day and mile-trials the following day.

Outboard racing articles filled most of the newspaper sports pages during the weeks preceding Seattle's "greatest outboard show." "REGATTA TO AID DEFENSE SPORTS" was another sports headline in the *Times* on July 22. Seattle's Defense Athletics Committee agreed to sponsor this regatta along with other sporting events. The Seattle Park Board granted permission to sell spectators admission tickets to help pay for the regatta's expenses. Proceeds from the championship event went to the Defense Athletic Committee to be used in the recreational program for the service men. Admission tickets were sold at both Ben Paris Recreational stores and at the Spring (street) Cigar Store for 30 cents.

As part of promotion day on August 7, a few C-Service outfits cruised along Lake Washington near the docks at Seward Park in preparation for the upcoming event. Al Benson along with Wes Loback and Pat Cummins were out pretending to be testing and warming up their rigs. Their real objective was to coerce the unsuspecting newspaper reporters, who were covering the event in a cruiser, into being riders and then scaring the daylights out of them. This began when they were told to ride on their boat decks while starting out to keep the outboards from swamping. Benson picked up Dick Williams of the *Times*; Loback, Gail Fowler of the Associated Press, and Cummins, George Pratt of the *Post-Intelligencer*. All of them regretted the experience except for Bob Cahn of the *Star* who was left on the cruiser. The following is the *Times'* Dick Williams' account of the ordeal:

"Outboards Have Their Place, But It's Not With Us" was the editor's headline in the *Times* on August 7. "So, they're outboard motorboats, are they? The heck they are. They're nothing but a disguised, seagoing edition of those pneumatic trip hammers that break up concrete pavement, bark like oversized machine guns and drive people crazy. Don't look now, but we had a ride in one just at sunset on Lake Washington yesterday, at the invitation of the sponsors of the Pacific Coast and

National Outboard races which will be held at Seward Park August 16 and 17. We say don't look now because we are a mass of bruises as a result of said ride.

Seattle Outboard Club drivers: R-37 Wes Loback with AP reporter Gail Fowler, R-39 Pat Cummins with PI reporter George Pratt and R-7 Al Benson with Times reporter Dick Williams giving demonstration rides.

"The outboard people probably thought they were pretty smart, asking a quartet of sports writers to act as supercargoes on a quartet of 'C-Service Runabouts' as they call them during a brief demonstration race. Our share of this reenactment of 'Death in the Afternoon' began when Al Benson, a harmless-looking youth in greasy brown coveralls, grabbed the gunwale of our cruiser and told us, 'Hop aboard.' The only place to hop was a cockpit the size of an apple box, already containing cushions, a wheel, the fore half of a 24-horsepower motor, and Al Benson. We hopped and he said, 'Now shove yourself ahead there on the deck-quick, before we sink!' We shoved ahead, lying prone, grabbed a rope that stretched back from the bow, and had time for half a deep breath before the cannon went off, the torpedo was launched or whatever it was that happened.

"The following ten minutes aren't very clear. One minute

Al Benson's boat *"NO FOOL'N"* with wife Dot as the deck rider

the runabout was wallowing lazily beside the cruiser, and the people who had strapped a lifejacket on us were laughing and waving and wishing us well. Nothing to it, obviously, Why, anybody can ride a boat. Sure, sure. The next minute we were five hundred yards away, going like what Poe, or someone, called a bat out of hell, and enjoying all the delightful sensations of a cookie trying to stay on a tossed plate. The outboard's nose was slamming the surface and bouncing into the air about sixty times a minute. With each slam and each bounce, our chest smacked the deck, our breath went 'oof!' and our teeth rattled. Shoreline was whisking by, boats were grazing us and the motor, turning up some seven thousand revolutions, was trying to sound like the Battle of Smolensk (the first battle during the war in Russia).

"There was a tug at one foot, which was dug into a corner of the cockpit, and Benson beckoned us back with him. It was better there, with legs instead of chest taking the punishment, but our teeth rattled just the same. Then the motor popped weakly and died. 'Going too slow,' said Benson, 'fouled the plugs.' 'Too slow? Just how slow?' we asked him. 'Oh, not more than forty. These things do fifty-two, but we don't usually carry a crew.' Fifty feet away Wes Loback, a former world champion, skittered past with Gail Fowler of the AP bouncing wildly on the deck, opening his mouth to shout something but unable to get it out. We had two more demonstration runs before Benson emptied his tank. They were just like the first, only we had less strength to meet them and came closer to slipping off, into the lake and oblivion. What good's a lifejacket if you break your fool neck hitting the water?

Coast Championship C-Racing Runabout heat won by Seattle's Pat Cummins in R-34, third boat above

"Ashore at last, we smiled weakly when Benson said he was sorry he'd run out of his evil-smelling, $1-a-gallon fuel, about 50 cents worth of which was clinging to our clothes, skin and hair. 'I used to drive in roadster races down in California,' he said. 'Motorcycle races too. I like this best.' That's the kind of motomaniac who had held our life in his hands… We got a look at the name of his boat as they led us away. It was '*NO FOOL'N.*' That's our motto from here on in–no foolin' with outboard racers. We'll go to the big races, but we'll stay ashore, thanks. On second thought, we may not live that long."

The Sports headline in the *Seattle Times* on Monday, August 18, read "U.S. OUTBOARD TITLES GO SOUTH"; the sub-headline read "CUMMINS, TWO SEATTLEITES WIN COAST LAURELS." Chick Garrett of the *Times* wrote under the headlines the following story: "A miss is as good as a mile in outboard racing, too. As California's roaring outboard pilots headed southward today, toting all six national runabout titles, a couple of Seattle pilots were dreaming in the realm of 'if-I-had-only.' Three Pacific Coast titles were the best the locals could do as one of the most successful championship outboard regattas ever held concluded yesterday before a packed shoreline audience off Seward Park Peninsula.

"Pat Cummins of Everett captured Coast C-Racing Runabout honors Saturday and yesterday (Sunday), Art Losvar of Seattle, took first in the professional Midget Class Hydro division and Leonard Keller, also a home towner, emerged professional titlist in A-Hydroplane competition.

"About those just-by-a-whisker misses in the nationals: Ray Zuppe of Seattle bounced to a first and a second in the two heats of amateur C-Service Runabout competition but was nosed out for the national title by Harold Ashkey of Marysville California., who had an elapsed time margin in taking third and first. Herb Hadfield of Los Angeles, defending champion, could do no better than third. The other two Seattle threats for national honors that "fizzled" came in the two heats of professional C-Racing runabout. Both Cummins and Wes Loback of Seattle, regatta racing chairman, making their first driving appearance in the meet, had open-door opportunities to wrap up the title. But Herb Rimlinger of Los Angeles, the defending champion, packed it away.

"Loback, who finished with two second places as compared to Rimlinger's third and first, sheepishly admitted after the second heat that he failed to remember that elapsed time was the deciding factor and took the last lap of the second heat at three-quarters throttle. He lost to Rimlinger by 12.5 seconds. Cummins had his big chance after winning the first heat by 150 yards, showing more speed on the straightaway than either Loback or Rimlinger, but the second heat was a sad story for Pat. He was last over the starting line and dropped out of contention when he missed a buoy and had to go back.

Art Losvar- Midget Champion

Pat Cummins-C Racing Runabout Champion

Leonard Keller: A-Hydro Champion

"The 'into the drink' action was plentiful as the outboard herders dished up the thrills. Hamp Thompson of Napa, California, qualified for 'swimming champ' by sun fishing into the lake both Saturday and Sunday. Al Benson of Seattle did a spine-tingling upsy-daisy in the amateur C-Racing Runabout first heat yesterday while hitting the far-east turn in third place. (Funny how those guys can smack into the water going forty-miles an hour, then come up with a toothy grin for every drip from their coveralls.) 'Guess we did a little bit of all right. Dr. O.J. Blende, general regatta chairman, can take a bow!'"

Pacific Coast Championship (Divisional) Results (local drivers)-Saturday August 17

C-I Service Run 2nd-Glenn Barr, Bellingham, WA
C-I Service Run 3rd-Ray Zuppe, Seattle
C-I Racing Run 3rd-Al Benson-Seattle
C-II Racing Run 1st-Pat Cummins-Seattle

National Hydro & Runabout Championship Results (local drivers)-Sunday August 18

M-II Hydro 1st-Art Losvar-Seattle
A-II Hydro 1st-Leonard Keller-Seattle
A-I Hydro 2nd-Val Hallum-Seattle
C-II Racing Run 3rd-Pat Cummins-Seattle
C-II Hydro 1st-Barney Loutham-Aberdeen, WA
C-II Hydro 2nd-Pat Cummins-Seattle
C-I Service Run 2nd- Ray Zuppe, Seattle
F-I Hydro 3rd –Fred Carlson-Seattle
C-II Racing Run 2nd-Wes Loback-Seattle

First page of 1941 Championship Program

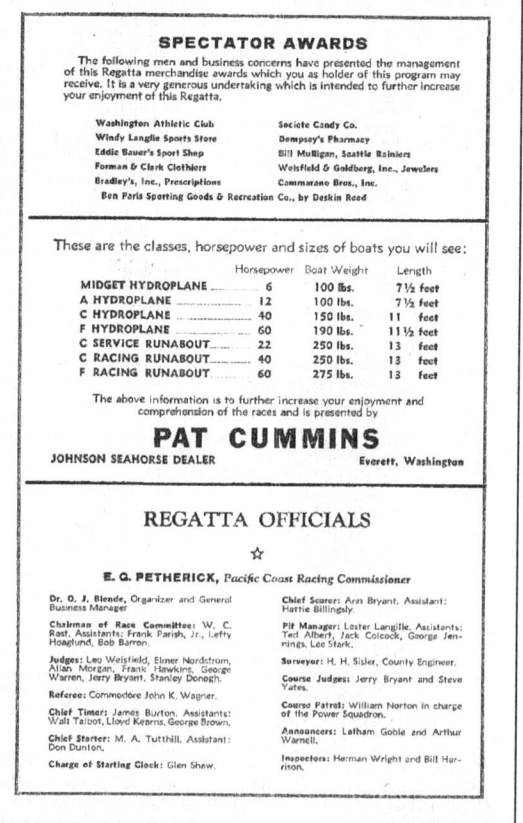

Fifth page of 1941 Championship Program

Rockey Stone-Willamina, OR

Dick Hubbard, Seattle

Val Hallum, Seattle

Leonard Keller, Seattle

1941 Summary & Tidbits

Future Slough Race drivers, Duke Polk, Art Losvar and Dick Hubbard were new SOA club members for the year. Fred Bloom was SOA Sportsman of the Year. The season ended with a worldwide event that adversely affected boat racing and all other sporting events in the United States for the foreseeable future–the U.S. enters WWII.

1942

M.A. "Pop" Tuthill was re-elected as the fourteenth SOA Commodore for a second consecutive term. No articles were published about his officers, trustees or appointed positions. News was sparse this year as the war broke-out and boat racing took a back seat to world affairs.

Gas rationing rumors were a subject of concern for the club members. Soon they would have to get creative to continue their racing activities. This eventually led to the use of car top boat hauling or sharing boat trailers to comply with the minimum tire allocations.

Boat trailers required a minimum of two tires. This combined with four tires for automobiles exceeded the five-tire limit. Fuel rations were also a restriction, so

Commodore M. A. "Pop" Tuthill in his garage re-building outboard motors.

members would eventually share their gasoline supplies by traveling to races together. Use of alcohol blended fuels became more widespread because alcohol was not rationed. This necessitated running the *racing* classes which used alcohol blended motor fuels.

Annual "Old-Timers" Slough Cruise

"Old-Timers Of Outboard Clan Slate Cruise" was headlined in the Saturday edition of the *Seattle Times*. The article read: "Ice and ear-snapping cold regardless, members of the Seattle Outboard Association are looking with enthusiasm to the staging of the annual Old-Timers' Cruise tomorrow."

The outboarders left Jerry Bryant's Marina at 10 o'clock; checked-in at Fisher's Boathouse on Lake Washington at 10:30 and then headed up the Sammamish Slough for Shamrock Grove on Lake Sammamish making stops along the way at Bothell and Woodinville. This was the first year that the annual Slough Cruise, the first SOA event of the year, was named the "Old-Timers Cruise" which became its moniker for the rest of its running.

"BOATMEN IN ICY SPILLS" was the headline in the *Seattle Star* on January 5. "No less than four outboard drivers took plunges into icy water yesterday on the ride up Sammamish Slough. Staged by Seattle Outboard devotees, the boatmen returned with icicles in their whiskers and a new chapter of hard knocks to write into club history. Only one outfit reached Lake Sammamish, that being the boat driven by Jim Harland and Bruce Rogers."

A log jam at Woodinville accounted for a number of casualties, including Billy Harrison, who fell off the logs into the water. George Lansing and Al Benson also hit the drink at Woodinville, right adjacent to a flooded field where a flock of surprised youngsters were skating-not looking for outboard thrills. Art Losvar, who attempted the trip alone in a tiny Midget hydro, fell out and into the water at Bothell to be one of the first "all-out entries." Those who made the trip, or a portion thereof, included:

> Bill Rankin, alone; Jim Harland and Bruce Rogers; George Lansing and Al Benson; Bill Finical and Bill Harrison; Bruce and Betty Bartlett; Art Losvar, alone; Dick Barden and Tillie Wentworth; Billy Bryant and Adelle Smith; Barney and Elma Giancoli; Wes Moore, Mrs. Moor, Dot Benson."

7th Annual Sammamish Slough Race

On Sunday, March 1 the Seattle Outboard Association held its annual Sammamish Slough Race. It was said that any stops made between the start at Madison Park to the finish line at Shamrock Grove on Lake Sammamish were mainly involuntary.

A *Times* article on February 22 stated: "The waterway, over which the drivers matched their abilities to make their mechanized shingles do tricks, has been rated the world's crookedest race course. It had, among other things, not much water, not much width, a profusion of varied objects which can easily wreck a boat if hit, and more twists than an energetic boa constrictor with a full stomach."

Approximately 40 drivers were expected to try their luck in this, for the first time a nationally sanctioned contest sponsored by Ben Paris[2]. "All of them won't finish, what with it needing only a split second of miscalculation in taking a curve to wind up studying bird life in the bushes 20 feet up the bank." Several men in the service are

---

[2] Ben Paris was a well-known Seattleite and avid sportsman whose namesake store was a destination for area sportsmen. By 1932 Paris owned four first-class billiard parlors, a cigar store and a restaurant with locations in Seattle on First Avenue, Pike Street and Westlake Avenue, and in the towns of Bremerton and Mt. Vernon. He sold sporting goods and sponsored many sporting activities including Seattle's first fishing derby, semi-pro baseball teams and the Sammamish Slough races. He published the iconic *Fishing and Hunting Guide to the Northwest*, which ran from 1935 to 1980.

due to compete, including Pvt. Bob Wirostek, former Portlander, now of Camp Lewis, in C-Service class. Ray Boetcher, Montana State champion has entered, as has Spook Griffiths of Idaho.

"LIN IVY OUTBOARD CHAMPION" headlined in the *Seattle Star* on March 2. "Lin Ivey, former SOA Commodore, driving his R-27 Unlimited hydro named *Over Easy*, kept his ears pinned back and his throttle all out, racing a fast field of thirty competitors into defeat in the annual Sammamish Slough Race by the Seattle Outboard Association." He clipped 1-1/2 minutes from Pat Cummin's record set in last year's competition with a time of 34 minutes and 31 seconds. He was the first recipient of the *Ben Paris Perpetual Trophy* which was awarded to the over-all winner of the contest, which out of 31 starters, only 12 were able to cross the finish line. Once again, the hairpin turns, lurking sandbars and floating debris took a heavy toll among the outfits trying to negotiate the tortuous course.

1941 winner-Pat Cummins

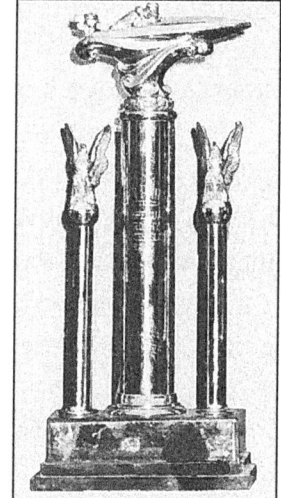
Ben Paris Trophy

Rex Louthan, of Aberdeen, was the winner in the C-Service class, beating out Bob Carpenter of Oregon City and Glen Barr of Bellingham. Bill Bryant of Seattle, half-brother of Jerry, took the honors in Super Utility, with Bert Wilson of Tacoma second and Dick Barden of Seattle third. Art Losvar of Mukilteo beat Bill Snyder of Tacoma and Wayne Crawford of Seattle in the Utility Class. Two former champions, Pat Cummins, who won last year and Pope Howard, who led the field the season before, ran into tough luck before even getting to the Slough entrance. The motors of both drivers froze-up.

SOA Publicity Chairman, Al Benson, who led the pack across the lake and into the Slough, wasn't able to finish either as "after about a mile up, he proceeded to lose his fin and then took a leap at a wholly unoffending dock, knocking the diving board for a loop and polishing off a chunk of shrubbery. Mr. Benson, it can be added, was unhurt. They grow 'em tough out here," the *Star* reported.

1942 Sammamish Slough Race Results (in order of finish per class)

Place	*Driver*	*Class*	*Boat #*	*From*	*Time*
1	Lin Ivey	Unlimited Hydro	R-27	Seattle	34:31**

1	Rex Louthan	C-Service Runabout	R-64	Aberdeen	*
2	Bob Carpenter	C-Service Runabout	*	Oregon City, OR	*
3	Glenn Barr	C-Service Runabout	R-18	Bellingham	*
1	Bill Bryant	Super Utility	*	Seattle	*
2	Bert Wilson	Super Utility	*	Tacoma	*
3	Dick Barden	Super Utility	R-31	Seattle	*
1	Art Losvar	Utility	R-42	Mukilteo, WA	*
2	Bill Snyder	Utility	*	Seattle	*
3	Wayne Crawford	Utility	*	Seattle	*

* *Some driver names, boat numbers and times unavailable*
** *New record time*
   Pat Cummins, Pope Howard and Al Benson did not finish

1942: Lin Ivey's winning Slough Race boat *R-27* on Al Benson's trailer in his car radio shop.

1942: Al Benson C-Hydro *Yehudi* entering Slough in first place.

1942 Race Schedule

Jan 4	Annual "Old-Timers" Slough Cruise
Feb 22	6th Lake Sammamish Bar Pilots Cruise
Mar 1	7th Annual Sammamish Slough Race
Mar 8	1st Sammamish Slough Water-Ski Race
April 5	Oregon Outboard Easter Regatta on Willamette River
May 10	SOA Spring Opening Regatta-Lake Sammamish at Alexander's Beach
May 24	Battle Ground Lake Regatta-Vancouver, Washington
May 31	SOA 2nd Spring Regatta-Lake Sammamish at Alexander's Beach
Jun 28	Lake Goodwin Regatta-Everett
July 4-5	Pacific Coast Championships-Oakland, Calif.
Aug 3	Columbia River Regatta-Kennewick, Washington
Aug 23	Annual Redondo Beach Outboard Regatta on Puget Sound, Seattle
Sept 5-6	Pacific Northwest Championships-Devils' Lake, Oregon
Sept 27	Lake Sammamish Wash. State Championships at Alexander's Beach

The United States Enters WWII and Rationing Begins

Following the bombing of Pearl Harbor by the Japanese on December 7, 1941, the United States declared war against the "Axis" countries, those nations who aligned to oppose the "Allied" forces consisting of the U.S., Britain and other allied countries. The U.S. war effort began to affect the Seattle Outboard Association like all other clubs and associations soon after. All the members either enlisted in a branch of the armed services or began civilian work in support of the military.

In the summer of 1941, the British appealed to Americans to conserve food to provide more for the Britons fighting in World War II. The U.S. office of Price Administration[3] (OPA) warned Americans of potential rubber, gasoline, steel, aluminum and electricity shortages. It believed that with factories converting to military production and consuming many critical supplies, rationing would become necessary if the country entered the war. It established a rationing system after the attack on Pearl Harbor.

Tires were the first item to be rationed by the OPA, which ordered the temporary end of sales on December 11, 1941. There was a shortage of rubber for tires since the Japanese quickly conquered the rubber-producing regions of Southeast Asia. Rationing of gasoline was motivated by a desire to conserve rubber as much as by the desire to conserve gasoline. Civilians first received ration books in May of 1942.

To receive a gasoline ration card, a person had to certify a need for gasoline and ownership of no more than five tires. All tires in excess of five per driver were confiscated by the government. An "A" sticker on a car was the lowest priority of gasoline rationing and entitled the car owner to 3 to 4 U.S. gallons per week. "B" stickers were issued to military workers for up to 8 gallons. "C" stickers were granted to essential persons for the war effort such as doctors, "T" rations were made available to truckers and "X" stickers were given to the highest priority in the system with unlimited supplies such as ministers, police, firemen and civil defense workers. As a result of the gasoline rationing, all forms of automobile racing, including the Indianapolis 500, were banned.

---

[3] Office of Price Administration: A government agency set up by President Franklin D. Roosevelt. It became an independent agency under the Emergency Price Control Act, January 30, 1942. The OPA had the power to place ceilings on all prices except agricultural commodities, and to ration scarce supplies of other items, including tires, automobiles, shoes, nylon, sugar, gasoline, fuel oil, coffee, meats and processed foods.

Gas rationing registration in the Northwest was postponed until November of 1942. Obviously, this affected the outboarders and encouraged them to minimize auto travel and get creative by sharing resources. Local outboard races, which were not banned and required minimal auto travel, continued to be held although they too were scrutinized by the public. The Seattle Outboard club began to race "under the radar," so to speak, to not stir up public resentment. News articles about races and results became few and far between even though the famous Sammamish Slough Races and Slough Cruises continued.

Fired Upon by Base Sentry

The Sand Point Naval Air Station[4] at the north end of Lake Washington in Seattle became a strategic military facility supporting training and air defense for the war. This impacted local boaters on Lake Washington because all public boating activity was restricted on the shore side of the base. Boaters were restricted to keep 50 yards or 150 feet from shore. Seattle outboard cruising and racing continued to pass by the air station and must have kept a safe distance as no reports were made of violations although some boaters did manage to enter the restricted area.

SP NAS insignia

The restriction was not originally posted by signs visible from the water and didn't seem to be an issue for the Slough racers if they stayed a safe distance away. Seattle Outboard member Duke Polk had enlisted and was stationed at Sand Point in 1942 and may have alerted the base about the race and cruises as mishaps could happen and stalled boats could float within the forbidden zone. There was no mention found in any press articles about staying clear of the base or about the wartime restrictions. There were numerous articles about recreational boaters and snoopers who were fired upon by the base sentries. No one was injured but several boats sustained bullet holes in their sides.

---

[4] See the history of the Sand Point Naval Air Station and the Sand Point Yacht Club in the 1946 section of chapter eight.

"Reporter Needed Armor When Two Russian Planes Arrived" was published on September 5 in the *Seattle Times*. The article read: "Two members of the Times staff, Paul O'Neil and Harold Smith were fired on by a Navy sentry late yesterday when they took their speedboat inside the prohibited zone at Sand Point Air Station as they photographed the arrival of Russian aviators. Neither was injured." Here is O'Neil's account of the incident:

"It is hard to realize the importance clothes play in the modern scheme of things until you blunder into a situation incorrectly garbed, and suddenly discover that you are being regarded as socially undesirable.

"For instance, take yesterday's arrival of two Russian airplanes at the Naval Air Station at Sand Point. This turned out to be an affair of some pomp and circumstance, but when Harold (Smitty) Smith, a *Times* photographer, and I set out to watch the planes and photograph them, we were driving a very informal sixteen-foot speedboat and were wearing trench coats and plain business suits.

"The correct costume for photographing Soviet aircraft in the vicinity of a naval establishment should consist of a bullet-proof vest, cut quite long, and a good thick coat of some kind of invisible paint. Speedboats are out. It is best to approach the air station on something which does not throw up so much spray. A middle-aged sea lion would be proper. Perhaps it would be well, however, to coat the lion with invisible paint, also.

Bullets Splash Waves

"We discovered our error after making pictures of the first Soviet plane–a flying boat which bore the red star of the Soviet republic and also a couple of machine guns. We were proceeding in a westerly direction, bound back to the boathouse, where we had rented our craft, when we noticed something splash in a wave, uncomfortably close, and heard a faint bang over the sound of the engine. The wave, plugged squarely through the lip of a .45-caliber slug, sank without a sound. Then something hit closer to the boat. All you have to do to stop a boat of that type is to jerk down the gas lever. You would be surprised how quickly this can be accomplished when you have seaman in a rolling motor-sailor banging away at you with a pistol.

"It all came about like this: The Russian flight–by way of Nome and the Alaskan coast was very hush-hush. At the request of the Russian embassy, the Navy excluded photographers from the air station, though the planes had been photographed at Nome. I got a boat to try to get pictures on the lake. The first airplane landed far ahead of us and by the time we drew up it was within a few feet of the air station's ramp.

"Civilian boats are not supposed to get within a certain distance of the station. The publicity officer said 100 yards, the chief petty officer who captured us said 50 yards, and the State Patrol said the boundary was farther out in the lake. But since nobody on shore seemed to care, we approached and made our pictures.

1931-Sand Point Naval Air Station on Lake Washington, Slough racers pass close to upper shoreline.

Shot Might Have Hit

"As we drew off to leave, a Navy boat rounded a dock astern of us, to take us–and two men from the *Post-Intelligencer*, Arthur French and Robert Berman, who were in another boat, into custody. The chief petty officer in command of the boat had been ordered to stop us. I hadn't seen the Navy boat and didn't know he was shooting until what must have been the third shot hit the water to the right. The fourth shot, which came very close, the chief petty officer said later was fired directly at us. 'It was a line shot and it must have ricocheted off the water right near you,' he said. 'If it had been a little higher it might have hit you.'

"Naval authorities seized the pictures, which showed a hanger that can be viewed by motorists from the road adjacent to the air station. However, they allowed us to set forth again and make pictures of the second Soviet airplane."

1942 Summary & Tidbits

This was the first year the U.S. was directly involved in World War II. It adversely affected the Seattle Outboard Association's membership participation in their boat races. The gas and rubber rationing mentioned earlier played a major role of limiting travel to and from regattas that required significant driving distances.

"ROUGH RIDER Skiers to Go Sloughing" was in bold print in the *Seattle Times* on Saturday, March 7. The Olympic Water Ski Club held their first organized ski-race up the Sammamish Slough when they teamed up with Seattle Outboard pilots. The entourage left Kenmore at 10:00 o'clock Sunday, March 8, in tow with short ski-ropes by their outboard counterparts. They navigated up the tough winding and cold Slough course dodging each other along the way when trying the difficult maneuver of passing. The skier being passed would come dangerously close to the passing boat and the motor's propeller and then have to look out for the skier coming from behind, not for the weak at heart!

Leonard Keller was voted as the eleventh "Sportsman of the Year" by the members of the Seattle Outboard Association and was presented the SOA Sportsman Award plaque by Commodore "Pop" Tuthill.

1943

During the year in which your author was born, M.A. "Pop" Tuthill was re-elected as the fifteenth SOA Commodore for a third consecutive term. He was the longest consecutively-elected commodore of the Seattle Outboard Association to date. Leonard Keller was elected vice-commodore with Al Benson as treasurer and Dorothy "Dot" Benson, secretary. No articles were published about the trustees or appointed positions.

Commodore Tuthill was a mentor for new aspiring drivers and officers such as Al "Benny" Benson. He took Benny under his wing and educated him about engine building, driving, club management and officiating. By this time rationing was in full swing. War bonds were a way for individuals to help finance and support the war. Along the same theme, the SOA decided to donate all their prize money and proceeds to the servicemen's recreational funds–a class act by the outboard club.

8th Annual Sammamish Slough Race

The sports headline in the *Seattle Times* on February 14 read, "OUTBOARDS TO ROAR, Slough Race Due Next Sunday." The article read as follows: "The Seattle Outboard Association's annual Sammamish Slough race will be held next Sunday, with all drivers confronted by the difficult proposition of keeping their fingers crossed and their hands on the throttle at the same time for 25 miles of snaky running.

"They'll start from the Madison Park Boathouse at 11:30 o'clock, and, less than an hour later (they hope) the most fortunate will come shooting out of the Slough onto the comparative calmness of Lake Sammamish and roar past the finish line opposite the Shamrock resort on the west shore.

"This will be the annual 'Washington's Birthday' race, stepped ahead a day. In the past years, the outboard drivers have slithered through the Slough on February 22, but always the night of the race has found boats stranded along the course-here one with a stove-in hull, there another with a burned-out motor-and this year the boys in charge decided that an attempt to do something about such a situation was in order.

"They'll race Sunday and have all day Monday to take care of the casualties. The race is no picnic. It's rated in the outboard fraternity as 'the world's most hazardous course,' and the Northwesterners who boast about it have a talking point. From the time a driver enters the Slough until he emerges, some 14 miles farther on, into Lake Sammamish, it's a case of split-second judgement on the turns and keeping his fingers crossed as he turns on all the power he has for the straight stretches.

"The Slough course itself has all the twists of a jitterbugging boa constrictor with a tummy-ache, and every now and then there'll be a water-soaked log or tree branch resting just enough below the surface…Your hull gets over it nicely but the leading edge of your motor cracks into it, and all of a sudden you're stalled there, hurrying to install a new shear pin…Or you decide that you can take the next turn wide open and you miscalculate your speed…just a trifle…and all of a sudden there you are, with your boat's prow in the willows and your prop beating air, and you're wondering if that hole in the hull can be repaired.

"Despite the hazards involved there'll be quite a number of pilots on hand as the race opens. Included will be Sgt. Wes Bell in a C-Hydroplane job, Lt. J.G. Griffith from Idaho in an F-Class speedster, Billy Bryant of the Coast Guard in an A-Hydro, George Siegal of the Navy in a Super Utility, Jim Emmie in a C-Hydro, and Al Benson in a C-Hydro, which he will have out on its first speed run.

"This, of course, will be strictly a test of speed, and probably there will be a few eyebrows raised here and there because of a 'waste of gas.' The eyebrows should stay in place, for the boys won't be using gas. They'll burn *Dynax*, a fuel especially designed for outboard racing craft, each driver using approximately three gallons of the store they have left since the sale of it stopped about a year ago. When the present supply is exhausted, there'll be no more racing.

"What's more, a chunk of glory will be all that goes to the winner of this race–or any others which are held during the coming season. The outboarders have voted to donate all prize money and proceeds to service men's recreational funds."

"Outboards In Slough Run Tomorrow" was headlined in the small sports section of the *Times* on February 20, 1943. The article stated: "The newspapers during the war were a lot smaller than usual as they too, were being affected by rationing and manpower (some reporters and staff had enlisted). For a brief time, tomorrow morning, there'll be the sound and the fury of numerous outboard motors being warmed up in the immediate vicinity of Madison Park on Lake Washington.

"Then at 11:30 o'clock, there'll be one final, concerted blast and the boys will be on their way to Lake Sammamish in the annual Slough Race. All of them won't get there, for the Slough is rated as 'the world's most hazardous outboard course,' and the winner of those that do will have to have plenty in both speed and luck if he betters the time turned in by Lin Ivey last year." Ivey made the run in 34 minutes and 52 seconds and establish a new record for the one-way Madison Park to Lake Sammamish course.

SOA's Publicity Chairman, Al Benson, reported to the *Times* in a 1944 article that his good friend, George Lansing, won the event this year and was the second recipient of the Ben Paris Trophy driving his C-Service Runabout, R-36, as shown on Benson's trailer (on next page) in a photo taken in 1945. No other results were published.

1943 Sammamish Slough Race Results

Place	Driver	Class	Boat #	From	Time
1	George Lansing	Unlimited C-Hydro	R-36	Seattle	*No times

(No other finishers or entries were published)

Al Benson's trailer during weekend in Long Beach, Calif. with George Lansing's C-Service Runabout R-36.

"Outboarders Are a Trifle Miffed…"

The following article written in the *Seattle Times* on July 15, 1943, by columnist Alex Shults, depicts the views of the Seattle Outboard Association's members concerning their use of gasoline in their outboard regattas during the wartimes. "The outboarders are a trifle miffed. 'When we pull a race meeting,' explained Art Douglas, the spokesman for the Seattle Outboard Association, 'a lot of the townsfolks turn up their noses as though we're blocking the war effort by burning up gasoline.'

"The truth of the matter is a racing outboard is rationed on fuel just like any other motor and if Uncle Sam OK's our racing by granting us 20 gallons of gasoline each, every three-month period we don't feel that we're doing wrong by racing. 'Just the contrary, we entertain a lot of persons with our races which are more than a fisherman does when he burns up his 20-gallon allotment by dragging a salmon plug miles and miles around Puget Sound just to catch a few salmon that he could buy for half his fishing cost.

"'Why the last time we raced at American Lake there was a regular army of soldiers down to watch us go; they estimated the crowd from Camp Murray and Fort Lewis at from 5,000 to 20,000. Some of the Army recreational officers offered to help us obtain gasoline if we'd come back and race for them again.' The youngsters who drive the speeding hydroplanes are having their troubles getting along this year, besides gasoline rationing. There are no new motors to be had and no parts for old ones. When something bursts, it's a case of junk motor unless a used part can be found to repair the damage. When we get through, we'll know more about outboard motors than the manufacturer,' grinned, Dick Hubbard.

SOA's Dick Hubbard

"Twenty gallons every three months doesn't permit much racing. Three of four meetings and a limited amount of running for tuning-up purposes is the best a driver can hope to get out of his craft. Besides the American Lakes show, outstanding events were a race meeting at Shady Beach on Lake Washington (next to Juanita Beach) and the annual run up the Sammamish Slough. Still to come are return engagements at Shady Beach and American Lake, a show at Bremerton and one at the Boeing picnic when it is held.

"'We'd like to put on a Green Lake show for the benefit of the Civilian Defense Council,' said Douglas. The "we" includes Pop Tuthill, commodore of the association; Dorothy Benson, Leonard Keller and Al Benson, the other officers and some 38 drivers including youngsters like Bus Tuthill, Bill Rankin, Dick Barden, Fred Bloom, Fred Carlson, Bruce Bartlett, Val Hallum, Art Losvar and the rest. But since Adolph Spreckels went out of control and climbed a telephone pole, Green Lake has been out. There'll be no meets this summer, though, except where all receipts go to the U.S.O. or Civilian Defense."

1943 Race Schedule

Feb 21	8th Annual Sammamish Slough Race
	(In place of annual Bar Pilots Cruise)
Aug 29	Redondo Beach Water Carnival-Puget Sound, Seattle
Sept 26	Mercer Island 100-Mile Marathon on Lake Washington

(All other racing events were canceled due to rationing, public objections or orders from the local Office of Price Administration.)

1943 Summary & Tidbits

Articles in the *Motor Boating* magazine echoed the trials and tribulations of the Seattle Outboard Association that were published in the *Seattle Times* in the previous writings. Excerpts from the National Outboard Association meeting in 1942 were published in the *Pacific Motor Boat* magazine. Discussions were made about gas rationing issues along with restrictions from government agencies such as the Office of Price Administrations with their orders to stop boat racing (even though boating recreation was encouraged by the Office of Civilian Defense). The national meetings also maintained the current racing rules until the war was over and racing was back to normal. No national championship events were run or national awards presented.

M.A. "Pop" Tuthill was given the well-deserved SOA Sportsman Award for his outstanding work during the early war years as the first three-consecutive-year Commodore. The now aging silver plaque, awarded for the twelfth time, donated by the Carroll Jewelry Store in 1932, was out of room for more recipients' names as Tuthill's was barely scrunched in below Leonard Keller's, who won the previous year.

> *Keller . . .*
> ★ Boat Speed Indicators
> ★ Automatic Throttles
> ★ Steering & Engine Controls
> *Made by Race Drivers for Race Drivers*
> **KELLER MANUFACTURING COMPANY**
> 18340 Ashworth Ave.   Seattle 33, Washington

No other information of note was published as this year there were only a few boat racing articles in the newspapers and boating magazines, mainly because the club still was operating below the radar. They would continue this policy for the foreseeable future until the war was over and local boat racing was back to normal.

1944

Commodore Leonard Keller

Leonard Keller was elected as the sixteenth Commodore of the Seattle Outboard Association along with Al Benson, vice-commodore and "Dot" Benson, secretary. The other officers were not mentioned in any publications. It was about this time that commodore Keller started working at Bryant's Marina[5]

"One of the interesting sidelights of wartime side deals, which benefitted all concerned, involved Leonard Keller, master instrument maker. For part of World War II, Keller operated his business at Bryant's Marina located on Portage Bay.

---

[5] Excerpts from Eileen Crimmin's informative book, Bryant's, the historical story of a 50-year-old business outliving its founder, Jerry Bryant, employing many Seattle Outboard Association members between 1920's through 1970's (published 1978 by Bryant Corporation).

"He continued to maintain his custom instrument building business at his North End home but placed much of his shop machinery and materials in one of the marina cubbyholes for the duration. Keller took on repair and maintenance plus some custom construction of marine instruments for Bryant's while keeping his personal customer list separately at home. Why this arrangement? Bryant was able to get on the basic materials list for war effort raw materials, but a small operator like Keller was unable to get such a priority rating.

"By working in, with and for Bryant's, Leonard could acquire, with the marina's sanction, enough raw material to keep his own business going" where he made speedometers, steering wheels, hand-throttles and other custom hardware for race boats. I remember well how fascinating his shop was in North Seattle where he cast his products and that familiar smell of sand and aluminum that permeated the shop.

The Last Sammamish Slough Cruise

"OUTBOARD SWAN SONG * * * Last Cruise Next Sunday" was printed in the sports section of the *Seattle Times* on February 13, 1944. The article stated: "Outboards motor boat drivers will have their last fling for the duration next Sunday, when they hold their annual Washington's Birthday cruise up Sammamish Slough into Lake Sammamish. Some 30 boats were expected to start from Madison Park at 10 o'clock and finish approximately an hour later at Shamrock Park on Lake Sammamish.

"In former years the event has been held on the holiday, but this year all the pilots will be working: hence the Sunday date. And in former years the event has been a race, but this year it will be just a cruise, so more members of the Seattle Outboard Association may dig out their last cans of hoarded fuel. They get no more for the duration." George Lansing won the event last year. There'll be no winners this time but wait, as it turned out, a race was still being in the works-but way under the radar!

9th Annual Sammamish Slough Race

Despite the gloomy announcement in the *Times*, the Sammamish Slough Cruise turned out to be a race after all! The race was won by Oregon City's Don Critser, in his C-Service Runabout, R-43 named *Floppo*. Results for this race were not published; the winner was only listed on my mother's "Slough Race Winners List" (see opposite page) which covered the races from 1940 to 1959. Critsers' boat, which was originally owned by 1938 winner, Jack Corcoran, was specially designed for the Slough with two keels on the bottom, deep enough to protect the engines propeller when running over logs or in shallow water–a distinct advantage in the Slough.

1940	1. Pope Howard
1941	1. Pat Cummins
1942	1. Lin Ivey 34.31 Unlimited 25 miles
1943	1. George Lansing
1944	1. Don Critser
1945	1. Dick Barden
1946	1. Dick Barden
1947	1. Al Benson
1948	1. Al Benson
1949	1. Johnnie Sherriff
1950	1. Bob Jacobsen
1951	1. Elgin Gates
1952	50,000 People 1. Bob Jacobsen
1953	1. Al Benson
1954	1. Bill Fart
1955	1. Bud Sullivan
1956	1. Bob Waite
1957	1. Dick Brunes?
1958	1. Dick Brunes
1959	1. Howard Anderson

Dorothy Benson's Slough Race Winners List for years 1940-1959.

"PUTT-PUTT? TUT-TUT! Outboard Race Meet Off" was the article headlined in the *Seattle Times* on September 3, 1944. "There'll be no Northwest Championship meet to climax the local outboard motorboat racing season. The SOA announced yesterday that the Northwest races, scheduled for today at Shady Beach[6] on Lake Washington, had been canceled at the request of the Office of Price Administration.

---

[6] Private resort that became part of King Counties *Juanita Beach Park*-now owned by City of Kirkland.

"Although virtually no outboards burn gasoline, their stepped-up motors operating on non-petroleum-based fuel, the O.P.A. reasoned that the outboarders were inviting criticism by their racing while gasoline rationing for automobiles is so stringent. The outboarders have held several lesser regattas here this summer, although none to compare with their prewar extravaganzas."

1944 Race Schedule

Feb 20	9th Annual Sammamish Slough Race
Feb 27	Redondo Beach Water Carnival-Puget Sound, Seattle-*Canceled*
Sept 3	Shady Beach Regatta on Lake Washington-*Canceled*

(All racing events except the Slough Race were cancelled based on orders from the local OPA)

1944 Summary & Tidbits

As you can see by the writings, 1944 was not well publicized as the war effort continued and boat racing regattas and participation declined substantially. The OPA had ordered the Seattle Outboard Association to cease boat racing for the duration, which they did to some extent. But the club was still able to pull off the annual Sammamish Slough Race. By now most of the club's members were either enlisted in the service or working civil service jobs supporting the war. Al Benson was awarded the prized SOA Sportsman Award for his outstanding contributions to the Club.

1945

Al Benson was elected as the Seattle Outboard Association's seventeenth commodore during the last year of the war. The club organized the first of the few races that year, the annual Sammamish Slough Race. Benson, now married for 7 years with 2 young boys, was a civilian worker for the Army at Seattle's Port of Embarkation.

The Slough race was run again during the Washington's Birthday weekend for the third year in a row. The following race report was published in the *Seattle Times* on February 27, 1945.

SOA Commodore Al Benson with Secretary Dorothy "Dot" Benson

10th Annual Sammamish Slough Race

The report headline was: "Going Tough as Outboards Travel Slough." "Once the war is over, and public life settles down to normal channels again, the Seattle Outboard club plans to petition the King County commissioners to clean and dredge Sammamish Slough for its entire length so that outboarders and canoeists may get the fullest use of the long waterway. The outboard drivers reported numerous mishaps during their annual Washington's Birthday speed run through the Slough, held Sunday, with John Trembley's eye injury the most serious. Trembley was switched in the eye by overhanging brush.

"Dick Barden, King County deputy sheriff, driving a Class C-Service Runabout, steered the 25-mile course from Madison Park on Lake Washington to Shamrock Cottage on Lake Sammamish in 39 minutes. Second was Charles Hickling in a tiny A-Class Hydroplane. The boats use non-petroleum-based fuel, developed to comply with gasoline rationing."

1945 Sammamish Slough Race Results (in order of finish per class)

Place	Driver	Class	Boat #	From	Time
1	Dick Barden	C-Service Runabout	R-31	Seattle	39:00
2	Charles Hickling	A-Hydro	R-29	Seattle	2nd Overall
1	Bill Rankin	C-Service Runabout	R-25	Seattle	*
2	Howard Nelson	C-Service Runabout	R-8	Seattle	*
3	Charles Shirley	C-Service Runabout	R-90	Oregon City, OR	*
1	Johnny Sheriff	Unlimited Runabout	R-26	Tacoma	*
2	Stan Young	Unlimited Runabout	*	Seattle	*
3	Dick Hubbard	Unlimited Runabout	*	Seattle	*
4	John Trembley	Unlimited Runabout	*	Seattle	*
5	Rockey Stone	Unlimited Runabout	*	D-Lake, OR	*
1	Mike Shain	Utility	*	Seattle	*
2	Lt. Leach Phillips	Utility	*	Seattle	*
3	Clayton Shaw	Utility	10-R	Tacoma	*

* *Some driver names, boat numbers and times unavailable*

Advance entries included: Lin Ivey, Don Critser, Barney Louthon, Leonard Keller, Val Hallum and Al Benson all of whom did not finish (DNF)

Slough Race winner Dick Barden at the finish line in his C-Service Runabout R-31

Chuck Hickling 2nd overall in his A-Hydro R-29

Al Benson in his C-Service Runabout R-85 (DNF)

Inaugural Regatta at Sand Point Yacht Club

"OUTBOARDS WILL RUN OFF RIVIERA" was the headline in the sports section of the *Seattle Times* on July 29, 1945. Seattle Outboard Commodore, Al Benson, a resident of Riviera Beach below Lake City, provided the announcement above to the newspaper. The regatta, which was not restricted by the OPA, is the first outboard regatta since the Germans surrendered on May 8 1945. The regatta was held on Lake Washington just off shore from the outboard club's new headquarters at the Sand Point Yacht Club, next to Matthew's Beach. The property is just north of the Sand Point Naval Air station where Seattle pioneer, John G. Matthews established a homestead near what is now Matthews Beach, now a part of Seattle's Parks and Recreation.

Commodore Benson, with the support of the membership, leased the club facility from Mr. John G. Matthews, Jr., the son of the original property owner, John G. Matthews, pioneer and homesteader of the property in the 1880s.

In the late 1930s, the area south of the main beach was the site of Pan American World Airways' offices, and the dock for Pan American's "Clipper Ships," the world's first amphibious commercial air transports flying over the ocean. The City of Seattle purchased the first ten acres of Matthews Beach in 1951 and made it a city park.

1955-Matthews Park Beach during Matthew's Creek flood: Large dock on right was starting point for Seattle Outboard's Slough Races during years 1946-1951, the same dock used by Pan American "Clipper Ships."

<u>1945 Race Schedule</u>

Feb 20	10th Annual Sammamish Slough Race
April 29	Shadow Lake Regatta-Renton
July 29	Inaugural Sand Point Yacht Club Riviera Beach Regatta
Sept 16	Veterans of Foreign Wars Regatta-South Bend, Washington
Sept 30	Annual Mercer Island 100-Mile Marathon on Lake Washington
Oct 21	Navy Week Regatta-Madison Park Beach, Lake Washington

"SPEED-CRAZY TEENAGERS"
"Put Them In An Outboard Racer says Pop Tuthill"

The headline above was above a large article published in *Seattle's Weekly Sports Round-Up* on Thursday November 8, 1945: "M.A. (Pop) Tuthill, veteran leader of the Seattle outboard putt-putt enthusiasts, has a simple solution to the problem that has been worrying the law enforcement and school officials concerning the speed-minded teenagers who burn up Seattle streets in ancient jalopies, that is a thousand times more constructive than any plan to haul the youthful violators into jail.

"Pop has been helping mechanical minded and speed crazy youngsters along that line for many years and has started more than one on to fame and a career. Tuthill, the commodore of the Seattle Outboard Association, is more than the figurehead of the speed boaters. He is the backbone of the racers in this area.

"Pop started promoting the utility speedsters back in 1930, by buying a two-cockpit utility craft with a stock motor for his son, Bus Tuthill, to tinker with. Bus was then 15 years old and was some shucks as a tinkerer too, for he mastered the sizzling skippers for a C-Service world record one-mile straight-away burst and held several Pacific Coast titles at various times for various classes. Bus Tuthill is no longer pounding waves in souped-up outboards. He is a Washington State highway patrolman, but Pop is still directing other youths in the thrilling hobby.

"'The way I see it,' Pop says, 'if the kid's spare time is taken up tinkering with a stock motor, making it kick out with a few extra units of horsepower, he won't have time to get into trouble. I always try to impress upon a youngster, interested in racing, to save his speed for the race on the water, which is much more thrilling than a race on the highway where there is a good chance that some innocent motorist will be injured. It's safer for the driver, too, because I can't recall any serious accidents in all my years on Northwest waters.'

1946: Bus Tuthill's C-Service Hydro before Slough Race start.

"Since the end of the war, the local putt-putters have held only one major meet, the 100-mile marathon, won by Al Benson (mentored by Pop Tuthill) in an A class hydro. During the war, the speed-boating was necessarily halted because of the lack of gasoline. With gasoline plentiful again, the outboarders will be skimming over Lake Washington water in an age of increased interest in the sport. And more than one person agrees with the advisability of Pop Tuthill's plan to direct teenage spare time to the building and racing of the speed shells.

"Just how does a youngster go about entering upon an outboard racing event? He scrapes up enough money to buy a stock hull and a motor from a marine supply company. The hull is the regular pleasure craft type with two cockpits enabling him to take his friends for a ride. The motor is a 22-horsepower unit. In order to make the motor more powerful, he may add a racing propeller, ream and revise the carburetor until he believes he has obtained the maximum amount of speed from his craft. He is then ready to race in the utility class.

"From utility he advances to the C-Service class with a shell that can be used for pleasure but has a slightly more powerful motor. He improves the motor also, into which he pours his mixture of castor oil, some chemical with a long technical name, and gasoline for attempts in that class. A hydro is his next boat. This is a small, flat one-cockpit craft with plenty of zip. If his thirst for speed is not quenched by this time, he will acquire an F hydro which has a 75-horsepower motor and a speed of 68 miles per hour–and that is the next thing to flying on water. There is a faster outboard, an X hydro, to be handled by an expert. It is a roaring hellion capable of 90 miles an hour that most of us would like to watch from a safe distance.

"The Seattle Outboard Association racers will be out of competition until February, when they will churn the water of the Sammamish River with other top drivers of the country. The Sammamish Slough event is a nationally known feature, tabbed the crookedest race course in the world. The Sammamish is twisted and not always clear of logs and other debris, and every turn produces a chill for the bystanders. Should any of our Seattle youths who find a racing jalopy has its disadvantages, it might be well worthwhile to contact Pop Tuthill at this event. He will be on shore cheering his youngsters whom he started in outboards in the past years."

Benson Learns War Ending–Hightails to California

A few weeks before the war ended, Al Benson was still employed at Seattle's Port of Embarkation. The following is a story he told me during an interview in 1983 when I asked, "Where were you when the war ended?"

"I worked for the Army as a civilian at the Port of Embarkation, must have been for several years, it's gotta be in '43, '44." (Actually, it was 1943-1945).

"In fact my general told me all the big wigs were all Army–the war was going to be over in a week and so we (good friend and Boeing worker, George Lansing) quickly gathered-up all the gas we could get and the race boats and Lansing, his wife, your mom and I, we jumped in the Buick (his souped up 1939 4-door Buick Special) that pulled the trailer like nobody's business, loaded up and went to Long Beach, California, the Marine Stadium, because there was going to be a boat race down there. We'd heard about it by the grapevine and about the second day we're down the coast, here come planes ripping down the beach and we knew (the war was over)." See photo of trailer and rear of Buick in 1943 section.

World War II Ends

The war in Europe ended with the invasion of Germany by the Western Allies and culminated in the capture of Berlin by the Soviet and Polish troops and the subsequent German unconditional surrender in May 8, 1945.

The United States dropped atomic bombs on the Japanese cities of Hiroshima and Nagasaki on August 6 and 9. With an invasion of the Japanese archipelago[7] imminent, the possibility of additional atomic bombings, the Soviet Union's declaration of war on Japan and the invasion of Manchuria, Japan surrendered on August 15, 1945. This ended the war in Asia and finalized the destruction of the Axis bloc ending World War II. To this day the global conflict was the most widespread war in ever, resulting in an estimated 50 to 85 million fatalities, the deadliest conflict in history.

1945 Summary & Tidbits

Al Benson was voted the recipient of the prized SOA Sportsmanship Award for a second year in a row. He led the club, found a new site for their clubhouse and won the Mercer Island 100-mile marathon all in the same year.

Army veteran Art Losvar

The sportsmanship award, a silver plaque first awarded in 1932, was the first perpetual trophy presented by the Seattle Outboard Association. My father never was able to have his name engraved on the plaque in 1944 or 1945 because there was no room. Because of this, it was retired and given to him for keeps. He was the fourteenth and final recipient of this particular trophy.

Usually a perpetual trophy is only retired after it's won three times by the same recipient. This time was different as there was no more space for names. The trophy was lost between the shuffles of future commodores and meeting places for a few years after Dad became its final owner. He found it later after it was uncovered in storage with other club memorabilia. It presently is proudly displayed in my office, one of a few of his trophies that remain after donations and abuse from storage and moving (see present day photo in the 1932 section).

The club staged a regatta off Madison Beach on Lake Washington as part of the Navy Week celebration. The races included drivers of seven C-Hydros, eight C-Service Runabouts and six A-Hydros. The pilots were Barney Louthan, Pacific Coast Champion; Art Losvar, former champion, on furlough from the Army, and Al Benson,

---

[7] Japanese Archipelago: A string of more than 3,000 islands to the east of Asia extending 1,300 miles between the Sea of Japan and the western Pacific Ocean.

winner of the recent 100-mile Seattle Outboard Association marathon. A water-ski exhibition event was run as part of the regatta headed by Tommy Brown and Don Ibsen. Ibsen, an exhibitionist with his Skiquatic Follies, is credited as the inventor of the water ski.

The trophy below was made by rookie Seattle Outboard Association raceboat driver and hobby machinist Otis Clinton. It was awarded to the overall winner of the 1945 Mercer Island 100-Mile Marathon in the Unlimited Class. The race, won by veteran boat racer Al Benson, started in Madison Park, circled around Mercer Island five times in a counter clockwise direction and ended back at the Madison Park starting point.

Otis Clinton

Most of the boats were equipped with larger gasoline tanks, but not large enough to finish the entire race. The drivers had to refill at least once by returning to the Madison Park starting point for fuel and possible repairs and then continue finishing the remaining laps around the Island. All this took extra time which gave an advantage to the pilots who had the largest fuel tanks and the least amount of problems along the way. Clinton eventually won this race September 21, 1947.

Thus, ends the Seattle Outboard Association's era of "Under the Radar" during the World War II years, including the challenging rationing and racing restrictions administered by the Office of Price Administration. Following the war, the Seattle Outboard Association and outboard racing would soon experience a resurgence of members and races more than ever before.

Mercer Island 100-Mile Marathon trophy: made by Otis Clinton and won by Al Benson on September 30, 1945

Chapter 8

Published in Seattle Post-Intelligencer April 4, 1949

1949: "Firewater" Al Benson, R-25, flying through flames on Lake Washington with Otis Clinton, R-141, for Paramount Pictures promotion of upcoming Sammamish Slough Race.

Firewater
Post War Resurgence 1946-1949

"PUTT-PUTT 'SCREWBALLS' TACKLE SLOUGH AGAIN"

-The Seattle Daily Times, March 31, 1946-

During the 17-year anniversary of the Seattle Outboard Association, Al "Benny" Benson was elected commodore for a second term with charming wife, Dorothy as secretary. The other officers were not published except for Lou Proctor who was listed as chairman of the regatta committee. The day before the annual Sammamish Slough Race, 5,000 veterans were scheduled to return to the East and West Coasts from their tour of war duty in WWII.

Commodore Benson

11th Annual Sammamish Slough Race

"Sammamish Slough To Attract Top Speedboat Drivers Sunday" was the big headlines in Seattle's new little newspaper, the *Weekly Sports Roundup*. They advertised that they were the Northwest's only all-sports newspaper, reaching 75,000 readers weekly. The following are excerpts from an article published on Thursday, February 21, 1946 by Ken Benham:

"The 1946 outboard motorboat season will be officially on next Sunday at 10:30 when 30 or 40 high-powered racing skimmers roar away from Madison Park for the 11th annual Sammamish Slough Race over the "world's crookedest race course." Boats from all motorboat points in the West will compete in this grueling 25-mile roar, 14 miles of which are through the log and sand bar filled Sammamish River which connects Lake Washington with Lake Sammamish. Each year on Washington's Birthday, local motorboaters take a leisurely cruise up the Slough as a prelude to the famous race on the following Sunday.

"This year there will be drivers here from California, Oregon, Montana, Idaho and British Columbia trying to capture the Ben Paris perpetual trophy and the $100 first prize money. Lin Ivey, Seattle, set the record for the event in 1942, tearing up the ditch in 34 minutes and 32 seconds in a C-Hydro. Ivey is going to attempt to break his own record this year with an F-Hydro, the fastest outboard built. An F-Hydro has a four-cylinder, 60 horsepower engine which drives a 12-foot-long, 48 in. wide shell at 60 miles per hour.

1946: Al Benson leading Dick Barden in trial run, passing Walter's Feed Mill at Bothell Bridge.

"The first 10 miles of the course takes the put-putters from the Madison Park Boathouse past Sand Point to the mouth of the Sammamish in Kenmore. This straightaway is no cinch, because often the water is rough, windy and treacherous. Then upstream where the narrow Slough is snarled by overhanging branches, floating logs, hidden sand bars, and a maze of curves and banks. 'Drivers say the cows stand on the bank and view the daring man-things with a great deal of alarm. Let's hope none of the cows decide to go for a swim on the day of the race.' For 25-miles the drivers ride their bucking broncos on the toughest course known to the sport. Of the 30 or 40 that will begin the race Sunday morning, only 10 or 12 will complete the run.

"The finishing drivers come out of the Slough at the north end of Lake Sammamish near Redmond and then sprint one half mile to Shamrock Inn where those that are fortunate enough to finish are treated to a banquet and party. At this time the Ben Paris Trophy and the cash prizes are awarded. In 1934, the first official Sammamish Slough Race was run, but local outboard drivers have been testing their skill on the course for many years. This treacherous ditch has a peculiar fascination for putt-putt enthusiasts and on many an idle Sunday afternoon dairy cows say to one another, 'Oh-Oh, there they go again.'

"It is the ambition of the Seattle Outboard Association, the main force behind the promotion, to build the event until it will focus national attention on the sport and on Seattle. They are perplexed that national magazines and news reel companies show more interest in the novel race than the people of Seattle and its newspapers. "Pop" Tuthill, Al Benson and Dick Barden of the Seattle outboarders would like to see more young men become interested in the thrilling sport of racing and maintaining their own skimmers. After the initial outlay for a boat, the expense is comparatively small."

"The northwest is fortunate to have many bodies of water near the larger cities. It is the aim of the outboarders to pave the way for speed-crazy youngsters into the speedboat sport. Through racing events such as the Sammamish Slough, the racers hope to attain their goal. Barden, King County sheriff, driving a C-Service Runabout, topped the field last year, Don Critser, Oregon City won the year before and George Lansing did the trick in 1943. Ivey set the course record in 1942. These and other former trophy holders including Pat Cummins and Pope Howard will be spinning their props Sunday in an effort to repeat.

"Boat fans and Sunday motorists may view the race from several points; at Madison Park at 10:30 when the event begins or at Bothell, Woodinville or Redmond a few minutes later. The Slough follows the highway for the most part, through dairy pastures and wooded stretches. For the finish, spectators will need to be at Shamrock Inn on Lake Sammamish along about 11 o'clock."

"Barden Ends Rough Trip, Finds Out He's Winner"

The following news story published on February 25 was written by Jack Fraser of the *Seattle Times*: "Dick Barden of the King County sheriff's office was an exceedingly surprised young outboard driver yesterday as he checked in at the finish line of the annual Sammamish Slough Race and was informed he had won the perilous event for the second straight year. 'I win it?' he exclaimed. 'Who you kidding? Why, there were a lotta boats ahead of me.' Having blown a spark plug right at the start and being forced to pause for repairs, Barden's amazement was understandable. But where Barden's blown plug proved his major misfortune in the 25-mile grind from Madison Park on Lake Washington through the snake-like windings of the Slough, other drivers encountered assorted woes of more serious nature.

"With the lake kicking up, several spilled before getting to the Slough entrance and had to be hauled out by the Coast Guard. Others failed to follow the Slough channel and suddenly found themselves high and dry after running out of water on which to run. Barden's time for the journey was 58 minutes and 44 seconds, much slower than the record of 34 minutes, 32 seconds established by Lin Ivey several years ago.

1946: Slough Race winner Dick Barden R-31 *Thru Foolin* approaching Wayne Golf Course heading upstream.

"Barden's shooting shingle, the *Thru Foolin*, was a C-Service job as was that of Charles Shirley of Oregon City, who finished second, 4 minutes and 20 seconds behind the winner. Shirley too, was greatly surprised at doing as well as he did, having been thrown 30 feet when his craft went through instead of over one of the higher waves on Lake Washington. He swam back to the craft, spent the following 15 minutes or so bailing it out and then continued. Thoroughly soaked and being unable to change his position during the rest of the route, Shirley found his legs wouldn't hold him when he crawled out of his boat at the finish and collapsed on the dock. Fast work by a pair of emergency masseurs put him back on his pins shortly, however.

Charles Shirley finished second place overall

Bill Rankin finished third place overall

"Bill Rankin, Seattle, made it three in a row for C-Service speedsters, checking in a bit more than ten minutes after Shirley, and Mike Shain, Seattle, brought in the first utility job three minutes later after that. Art Losvar, Seattle; Art Pierre, Raymond, and Duke Polk, Seattle, finished five, six and seven respectively, but there the list of those managing to make the full trip ended. Seventeen other craft were scattered over the lake and Slough, including Howard Nelson, Portland, who led the way into the narrow Slough only to find himself conked out on the bank. The largest number of persons ever to watch the event lined the course wherever there were vantage points, hoping to see some speed and spills. They saw 'em."

1946 Sammamish Slough Race Results (in order of finish)

Place	Driver	Class	Boat #	Boat Name	Time
1	Dick Barden	C-Service Runabout	R-31	Thru Foolin	58:44
2	Charles Shirley	C-Service Runabout	R-90	*	63:04
3	Bill Rankin	C-Service Runabout	R-20	Soupy	73:04
4	Mike Shain	Utility	*	*	*
5	Art Losvar	Utility	*	*	*
6	Art Pierre	Utility	*	*	*
7	Duke Polk	Utility	*	*	*

*Some boat numbers, times and boat names unavailable

1946: Sammamish Slough Race starting dock at Madison Park Boathouse 30 minutes before the start

1946: Hundreds of spectators at Bothell watch Slough Race while Art Losvar in third place approaches

The field for the race grew during weeks leading up to the race as it was "old home week" for a lot of former star speedsters. The following other drivers entered but failed to finish: Art & Betty Douglas, Hovey Cook, George Lansing, ex-Navy Harry Axtell, Pacific Coast Champion, Pat Cummins, WWII vets Eddie Schott, Stubby Sheppler, Pope Howard, Jimmy Miller, Rex Loutham, John and Ernie Inman, plus Lin Ivey, Dick Barden, Don Critser, Howard Anderson and Al Benson.

1946 Race Schedule

Feb 24	11th Annual Sammamish Slough Race
May 20	Shadow Lake Regatta
June 7	Portland, Oregon Regatta
June 9	Newburg, Oregon Regatta
June 26-27	Gig Harbor Regatta
July 4	Moses Lake Regatta
July 6	Columbia River Regatta-Pasco
July 21	2nd Annual Riviera Beach Pageant
July 28	Anacortes Water Carnival Regatta
August 4	Lake Washington Regatta
August 10-11	Coos Bay, Oregon
August 18	Columbia River Regatta-Vancouver, WA
Sept 2	Devil's Lake, Oregon Regatta
Nov 9-12	National Outboard Championships-Salton Sea & Long Beach, CA

A *Times* news article after the race described a plan by the SOA to rerun the race. It would give the many drivers who were thwarted by the rough water on Lake Washington a second chance to make it into the Slough. The plan was to start at Kenmore to avoid the hazards on the Lake. It probably never occurred because no further news articles were published.

Aside from the rough water conditions, passing close by Sand Point (the shortest path to the Slough), was another dangerous challenge for the drivers because the Naval Air Station's shore restrictions still applied after the war.

Sand Point Naval Air Station History 1920-1970

A peninsula of land, Sand Point, that juts out into Lake Washington eastward from the View Ridge district was in the way of the Sammamish Slough drivers. Sand Point was located three miles north of the Madison Park starting point. The raceboat pilots and local residents needed to be very careful to stay at least 150 feet away from the shores of the Sand Point Naval Air Station; otherwise they would be shot at by the base sentries guarding the facility around its perimeter. As discussed in the previous chapter *Under the Radar*, there were numerous incidents where the public was fired upon and bullet holes in their boats, thankfully, were their only souvenirs of the encounters.

The only fresh water naval base in the United States, the Sand Point Naval Air Station (SPNAS) began with humble beginnings in the early 1920s. After World War I, a movement to build Naval Air Station (NAS) Seattle at Sand Point began when King County started acquiring surrounding property. In 1922 the U.S. Navy commenced construction on the site, which was leased from the county. In 1926 the Navy was deeded the 413-acre field outright that amounted to a public gift of $5 million from the county to the Navy.

1937: Consolidated Navy PBY *Catalina* "flying boats" on Sand Point Naval Air Station runway.

The former grass runways were paved during 1940-41, just prior to the U.S. entering World War II. The primary runway was just under a mile in length at 5050-feet. During its years of operation, Naval Station Puget Sound, as it was called later, was used as a facility to train naval aviators for day and night flying. Several aircraft were forced to ditch into Lake Washington over the years because of aircraft malfunctions or pilot error. Some of the wrecks of these aircraft still remain submerged near Sand Point (now Magnuson Park), where they are often visited by local divers.

The last Slough Race that passed by SPNAS was on April 6, 1952, eighteen years before the station's deactivation. NAS Seattle was deactivated in 1970 and the airfield was shut down. In 1975 a large portion of the Navy's land was given back to the City of Seattle and to the National Oceanic and Atmospheric Administration (NOAA). The city's land was mainly developed as a park and named Magnuson Park in honor of longtime U.S. Senator, Warren Magnuson, a former naval officer from Seattle. The airfields were demolished in the late 1970s and new construction on the north end for NOAA was completed in 1982. The base was formally closed in September 1995.

Aerial view of Sand Point NAS during late 1940s Sammamish Slough races. Raceboats traveled around point (bottom left to right) not far from shore as this was the shortest path north to the Slough entrance.

Aircraft Operated at Sand Point

PBY's, shown on the previous page, were one of the most widely used seaplanes in WWII, serving every branch of the US armed forces. Other aircraft flown at Sand Point included the Grumman *Hellcat* fighter, Beechcraft *Expeditor* trainer, Vought *Corsair* Fighter, Pan American Sikorsky *Clipper Ships* and the experimental Boeing amphibious patrol bomber *Searanger*. In 1927 Charles Lindberg, in his Ryan built *Spirit of St. Louis*, flew in and out of Sand Point in September five months after his non-stop flight from New York to Paris, France. He was flying around the country, promoting aviation, after his historic transatlantic solo flight of May 21, 1927.

Tidbits from 1946

"**Seattle Outboard club has opened swank new quarters at Mathews Beach**" was a bold line item in Alex Shults' "From the SCOREBOOK" column in the *Times* on June 27. He was referring to the club's new digs on the Lake Washington waterfront just south of Mathews Beach, named the Sand Point Yacht Club. The facility was dedicated during the 2nd annual Riviera Beach Water Pageant, Sunday July 21.

1946: Seattle Outboard's new headquarters at Sand Point Yacht Club (taken from end of long dock).

Normally the annual "Old-Timers Cruise" and the annual "Bar Pilots Cruise" preceded the Sammamish Slough Race except that this year the Slough Race was the only event on those waters. The only SOA member going to the nationals, scheduled for November 9-12, was "a one-man invasion of Al Benson."

Benson towed his boats with his trusty '39 Buick Special' some 1300 miles to the National Outboard Championships at Salton Sea Calif. He represented the Seattle club well by placing second in both the C-Service Runabout and C-Hydro events. The race started on the Salton Sea but due to adverse weather conditions, race officials moved and ended the regatta in the calmer waters of Long Beach Stadium at Long Beach, California. The SOA Sportsmanship Award for this year was presented to Bill Rankin.

1947

The year 1947 was a huge one for the outboarders. The excitement was high because they once again had their own dock for starting their annual Slough cruises and Sammamish Slough races. They first purchased waterfront property in 1932 near Sheridan Beach on Lake Washington, then built a clubhouse and held regattas off their dock. But at that time the Slough races had not yet been considered.

Commodore Ivey

The eighteenth Commodore of the Seattle Outboard Association was Lin Ivey, now retired as a successful race driver. Ivey, who was elected as the club's leader for a second time, first ran the club in 1940. Another known officer was last year's Commodore, Al Benson, now vice-commodore and Ivey's wife, Effie, was most likely secretary again. This year, the second year after the war ended, the club grew its membership and increased the number of regattas held the prior year.

Old-Timers and Bar Pilots Cruises

The traditional Old-Timers and Bar Pilots Cruises resumed this year after a hiatus over the past several war years. This year's route was shorter because they started and ended for the first time at the club's new Sand Point headquarters. The first event, labeled as "opening-day cruise", departed at 10 o'clock from their dock at 90th street and Sand Point Way on Sunday, January 5.

This excursion, comprised of about twenty boats, included stops at Bothell, Woodinville and Lake Sammamish. Old Man Winter was cold as usual and a good share of the boaters kept their insides warm by partaking in their favorite beverage, usually spiked with a spirit of choice. This helped them cope with an occasional stoppage due to their motors freezing up. Usually this was rectified by chipping out the chocking ice that formed in the outboard motor's carburetor.

The Lake Sammamish Bar Pilots Association cruise (name shortened to Bar Pilots Cruise) was run on Sunday, February 23, also starting from Sand Point. Another twenty boats took part in the excursion with six new Bar Pilots completing the trip unassisted, a requirement for initiation into the association. The drivers included:

Bob Watson, Jim Miller, B. Blanchard, Carroll C. Cook, Ed Shott and Duane Pulsefir.

12th Sammamish Slough Race Altered

Race officials for the first time dramatically altered the course for the 1947 Slough Race. In all the years past the event started in Madison Park at the same boathouse with various names and different proprietors. This year they moved the starting point to the Kenmore Boathouse at the extreme north end of Lake Washington. Their reasoning, which was unanimously approved by the club members, was obvious when one thinks about all the past year's entries who failed to even reach the Slough.

1947: Kenmore Boathouse during day of Sammamish Slough Race (later Ward's Resort & Uplake Marina).

The officials were confident that the race would be much more exciting and more boats would finish. The starting line was only a few hundred feet from the mouth of the Slough and the thought of all the boats starting at once and entering the narrow waterway together would be a real crowd-pleaser. Of course, they were a little devious, as they knew that some pilots would end up either in the bushes, on the bank or in the drink, because they all couldn't fit together in such a narrow space.

"Putt-Putt In Slough Race" was headlined in the *Seattle Post-Intelligencer* sports section on Tuesday, March 25. "Outboard racers try their luck on the exciting but dangerous annual Sammamish Slough Race Sunday. The race was originated in 1934 with every run over a 25-mile course from Madison Park to Lake Sammamish. From 1934 until 1940 only utility boats were used, as the hairpin turns and hidden logs were at that time thought too dangerous for the faster racing runabouts and hydros, which averaged about 15 miles per hour faster than the utility class.

So that the spectators may have a better opportunity of viewing the boats all in action along the Slough, it has been decided to start the race at the Kenmore Boathouse (later called Ward's Resort), which is located at the mouth of the Slough, at exactly 2 pm, Sunday. The race will be finished at Shamrock Cottage at Lake Sammamish, where the trophies will be presented."

1914: McMaster Shingle Mill on land where Ward's Resort was located during Slough races.

"Al Benson Braves Fire, Water in Taking Sammamish Slough Race"

The above headline was in the *Seattle Daily Times* on March 31. "Burning Gasoline on Surface Hazard to Outboarders." "Al Benson went through fire and water to capture yesterday's spectacular Sammamish Slough outboard race.

"Racing his C-Hydro with which he won second in the nationals at Salton Sea, California, last November, Benson covered the 14-mile twisting, log-strewn course from Kenmore Boat House on Lake Washington to Shamrock Cottage on Lake Sammamish in 22 minutes, 32 seconds. As usual, there were several accidents though no individuals were hurt, and Benson was confronted with the most spectacular of the bunch. Coming up along the Wayne Golf Course, Barney Siegel's gas tank dropped off and spilled gas over the water. In an instant the Slough was ablaze with flames three to four fee t high. Benson was right behind but went through the fire; otherwise he might have lost the race. Siegel saved his boat by submerging it. Other crackups included Bill Bryant's, Chuck Hickling's and Charley Shirley's. Shirley, of Oregon City, Oregon, was leading at the Bothell Bridge, but hit a log shortly thereafter." Bryant turned over and hit the drink and Hickling ran over a log.

The crowd that lined both sides of the course was estimated at 10,000 to 15,000 spectators. Each of the four classes started together from the resort's outer dock, which was a sunken barge about 200 yards off the mouth of the Slough. All the boats that started were racing to get in the front before they entered the narrow channel where passing was extremely difficult. The Slough entrance looked wide from the drivers view but only the narrow channel in the middle was safe to navigate. If the drivers' strayed much from the center they could run aground or hit the submerged objects.

Fourteen-year-old Dave Wolf of Sheridan Beach won the midget class with his M-hydro. Dick Phillips, running in the Utility Runabout class, powered his rig with a Japanese Storm Boat Motor[1] captured during the war. Benson is vice-commodore of the Seattle Outboard Association, sponsor of the annual race. His time will be the target of the boats in future races because the 1947 was shortened. Previously the boats crossed Lake Washington before entering the Slough.

1947 Sammamish Slough Race Results (in order of finish)

Place	Driver	Class	From	Boat #	Boat Name	Time
1	Al Benson	Unlimited C-Hydro	Seattle	R-11	Bennie	22:32
2	Otis Clinton	A-Hydro	Bellevue	R-58	*	25:11
3	Otto Dregger	C-Service Runabout	Seattle	R-37	*	27:02
4	Howard Nelson	C-Service Runabout	Portland	R-8	*	*
5	Dick Barden	C-Service Runabout	Seattle	R-31	Thru Foolin	*
6	John Zonich	C-Service Runabout	Raymond	R-25	*	*
7	Bud Yeapie	C-Utility Runabout	Oregon City	R-61	*	*
8	Jimmy Mills	C-Utility Runabout	Seattle	*	*	*
9	John Sheriff	Utility Runabout	Tacoma	R-28	*	32:44
10	Tommy Gauld	Utility Runabout	Seattle	*	*	*
11	Dan Dority	Utility Runabout	Oregon City	*	*	*
12	Rob Watson	Utility Runabout	Seattle	*	*	*
13	Dave Wolf	M-Hydro	Seattle	*	*	*
14	Dick Phillips	Utility Runabout	Seattle	*	*	45:00

*Barney Siegel, Bill Bryant, Charles Shirley, and Chuck Hickling DNF-Some boat numbers, times and boat names unavailable

---

[1] Small personnel attack boat powered by 50 horsepower 4-cylinder Evinrude outboard motor-designed for beaching or to "storm the shores" during WWII

Al Benson: C Hydro R-11, 1st overall

Otis Clinton: A Hydro R-58, 2nd overall

Al Benson: "Bennie" waiting for start

Otto Dregger: C-Service Runabout R-37, 3rd overall

Pre-race promotion boats entering Slough; Barden in front, Shirley, unknown, Benson, Sheriff and Clinton

Slough Race winners: L to R-Otto Dregger, Al Benson, John Sheriff, Otis Clinton, Dave Wolf; tall center trophy is R.O. Smith class perpetual, next tallest is Ben Paris overall perpetual; smaller trophies were keepers.

1947 Race Schedule

Jan 3	"Old-Timers" Slough Cruise
Feb 23	Sammamish Bar Pilots Cruise
March 30	12th Annual Sammamish Slough Race
May 25	Shadow Lake Championships-Renton
June 28	Lake Washington Association Regatta
July 4	Deep Lake-Olympia
July 5	American Lake-Tacoma
July 6	Gig Harbor
July 26	Anacortes Water Carnival Regatta
Aug 2-3	Kirkland Water Carnival-Lake Wash.
Aug 16	Columbia River-Vancouver, WA
Sept 21	Mercer Island 100-Mile Marathon

Al Benson awarded Trophies by Lou Proctor

Shortwave Radio Experiment

Past SOA commodore Al Benson, a radio sales and service businessman and longtime amateur radio enthusiast, began experimenting with shortwave radio transmissions to assist communications for the Sammamish Slough races. He enlisted a few of his fellow amateur radio club members, some whom worked for him in his Seattle and Bellevue shops, to join the SOA. Together they began broadcasting back and forth from various places along the race course to test the feasibility of wireless communication to track the race progress.

Initially they positioned a radioman at the starting and finishing points to report driver positions and their finishing times for race officials on either end of the course. Some of them purchased racing outfits of their own and began competing.

John Michaels' C-Service Runabout R-39

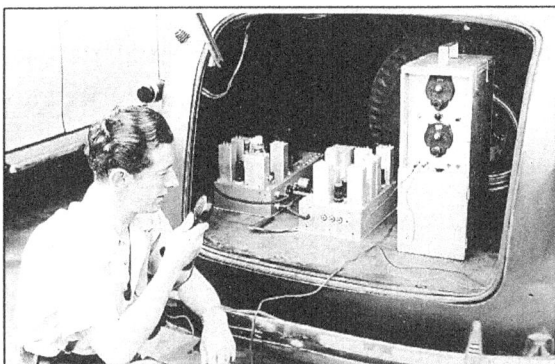

Michaels making shortwave transmission

Tidbits from 1947

Big changes were in order for the "Old Timers" and Bar Pilots Cruises this year. They started for the first time at the Sand Point Yacht Club and reconnected at Pete's Place on Lake Sammamish. Pete's Place was a bit north of Gateway Grove and Shamrock Cottage, the stopping points in earlier years. The "Bar Pilots" ceremonies, directed by Jerry Bryant, were completed at their Sand Point headquarters. Bill Rankin won the SOA Sportsmanship Award for the second year in a row.

The annual Mercer Island 100-Mile Marathon, which started at Madison Park, was won this year by Otis Clinton, second-place overall finisher in the Slough Race. The Olympic Water Ski Club joined forces with the Sand Point Yacht Club which is owned by a "cousin" to the water-skiers, the Seattle Outboard Association. There was talk about them teaming-up to run a water-ski race through the Sammamish Slough, maybe it will happen next year?

1948

This year veteran outboard driver, John Michaels, was elected club commodore along with Donald Olsen as secretary. The names of the other officers were not published. The following article written by Bob Sutton of the *Times* was published April 6: "Sammamish Slough Race Due April 18. Known the country over through the newspapers and newsreels for its dare-devil features, is the annual speedboat race up the twisting, log-strewn 14-mile Sammamish Slough from Lake Washington to Lake Sammamish, and the spectacle will be held again this spring, Sunday, April 18."

The race would start, for the first time from the SOA headquarters at Sand Point, in the afternoon at 1 o'clock. The daring drivers would head out for 5-miles across the open waters of Lake Washington to Kenmore, through the shallow winding Slough, passing by Bothell, Woodinville and Redmond, and finish at Shamrock Inn on Lake Sammamish.

Approximately 30 entries were expected from Washington, Oregon and possibly California, to compete in four classes: unlimited hydro or runabout, C-Service Runabout, A-Hydro and Utility. The utility class was open to any ordinary outboard boat, as used by fishermen, with a stock motor. The event was co-sponsored by the Disabled American Veterans who sold programs to thousands of spectators lining the course. Last year's winner, Al Benson, had to brave driving through 3-foot high flames after spilled gasoline ignited when the gas tank fell off the boat just ahead.

13th Sammamish Slough Race

"Benson Cops Slough Race" was the *Times* headline Monday, April 19. "Al Benson, veteran Seattle Outboard motorboat racer, considers Sammamish Slough's 14-mile narrow, twisting, debris-strewn course 'just a breeze,' and that's the way he took it yesterday to win the annual race spectacle from Lake Washington to Lake Sammamish." It was Benson's second straight victory. Benson took the lead at the outset as the boats left the Sand Point Yacht Club, held it during the five-mile run up the lake to the entrance of the Slough and then never allowed a boat to pass him as he breezed onto Pete's Place on Lake Sammamish with a time of 24:57 for the 19-miles.

"Rockey Stone of Willamina, Oregon, finished second in the unlimited class, only a fourth of a second behind. Benson was driving a Class F hydroplane. Otis Clinton of Seattle won in Class A hydro with a time of 33 minutes, 12½ seconds. Howard

Cole of Auburn, making his first trip up the Slough, came in half a second later to win among the C-Service runabouts. In the utility class, Jack Hall, of Seattle, won in 37 minutes, 40 seconds." No other results were reported. The Ben Paris perpetual trophy was awarded to the overall winner and the winners of each class received the R.O. Smith printing company perpetual trophy.

Al Benson at the start

Benson 1st overall at Lake Sammamish finishing point

Rockey Stone R-80, 2nd overall Unlimited Class

Utility Class boat

Al Benson, driving his step hydro powered by a rebuilt 4-cylinder motor, was the overall winner for the second time, a feat only one other driver could claim. Dick Barden was the other two-time winner and both of their wins were for two consecutive years of the Sammamish Slough Race. Benson's engine, like last year's, was made up of used parts from old surplus engines left over from the pre-war days, a common situation that all boat racers faced after the war.

```
HOME RADIOS                    ELiot 5363
AUTO RADIOS
PHONOGRAPH
COMBINATIONS      CAR RADIO Company
REFRIGERATORS
SOUND SYSTEMS        415 Lenora Street
TELEVISION
ALL MAKES        AL BENSON      SEATTLE 1, WASH.
Serviced and Installed
```

The pre-war supplier, the Outboard Marine Corporation, was ordered to stop sales of their outboard motors in 1941. When the company resumed production after the war, they were undecided about whether to restart production of their racing motors. But because of the outboard racing fraternity's persistent nagging about when they would start building again, the Vice-President (soon to be CEO) blew his top! He was cornered by some outboarders in a New York restaurant during a big boat show, got mad about their badgering, and vowed to "never make another Evinrude or Johnson racing motor again" and furthermore "he guaranteed they'd never make any more spare parts!" This ironically paved the way for a tiny outboard motor company in Fond du Lac, Wisconsin, the Kiekhaefer Corporation, which introduced a complete line of *Mercury* stock outboard motors and racing add-ons within the next few years.

1948 Sammamish Slough Race Results (in order of overall finish)

Place	Driver	Class	Boat #	From	Time
1	Al Benson	Unlimited F-Hydro	R-16	Seattle	24:57
2	Rockey Stone	Unlimited F-Hydro	R-80	Willamina, OR	24:58
3	Otis Clinton	A-Hydro	R-141	Bellevue	33:12
4	Howard Cole	C-Service Runabout	R-65	Auburn	33:13
5	Jack Hall	Utility	*	Seattle	37:40

Pan-American, Seattle Outboard, Use Same Facility

Pan American Sikorsky S-42

The Seattle Outboard Association's headquarters at the Sand Point Yacht Club was on land previously occupied by Pan-American Airways (Pan-Am) who flew Clipper Ships (flying boats) to Alaska between 1938 and 1940. The large dock that extended several hundred feet out into the lake (see photo on next page) once was used for loading seaplane passengers. Now it's being used by the outboard club and hundreds of spectators who watched with anticipation, the start of the Sammamish Slough Race.

Five years earlier, Alaska bound passengers also waited on the dock with anticipation while the shore crew pulled in a Pan-Am "Clipper" with a long rope. The 37-passenger, 4-engine Sikorsky seaplane had been warmed up and taxied close by from its mooring buoy or moved from a hanger on land from Sand Point Naval Air

Station. The airline company only flew from Sand Point for a year or so with a total of eleven flights. In 1940, Pan-Am moved their flight operations and closed the facility.

Pan American "Clipper" pulled to dock for Alaska-bound passenger loading.

The vacant terminal building, which was uphill on the property adjacent to Sand Point Way, eventually was used by the Seattle Outboard Association as a nightclub for their members and guests during the evening hours. Al Benson and his boat racing "arch rival" Lin Ivey, teamed up to rent the old terminal building and transformed it into a "Bottle Club" for the nighttime entertainment of club members and their guests. The club ran their races by day and their meetings and nightclub by night.

Bottle clubs, which sprang up all over Seattle, were a new local phenomenon. This was because private nightclubs were taking advantage of a recent change to a city liquor law in 1947. The law revision omitted requiring licenses for private clubs that served liquor. Club members in the new establishments brought their bottle of liquor into the club and give it to the bar tender who mixed their drinks for a nominal fee.

Ivey, who was in the coin-operated amusement machine business, installed several slot-machines for the entertainment of the members–all the profits were placed into the club's operating fund. The yacht club facility, which was a separate building from the bottle club and near the lakeshore, was built a few years after Pan-Am ceased operations. It is not clear who built it or owned it.

1948 Race Schedule

Jan 4	Annual "Old Timers" Cruise
Feb 22	Annual Sammamish Slough Bar Pilots Cruise
Jan 25	Green Lake Water-Ski Carnival
April 18	13th Sammamish Slough Race
May 2	First Sammamish "Golden Water-Skis" Race
June 26-27	Gig Harbor State Championship Regatta
July 3-4	Whidbey Island Marathon and Regatta
July 31	Green Lake Outboard-Water Ski "Sportscade"
Sept 5	Lake Samish Regatta-Bellingham
Sept 5	Sand Point 100-Mile Marathon
Sept 18-19	Outboard National Championship-Dale Hollow Lake, Tennessee

1948 Sammamish Water-Ski Race competitors (L-R): Lyle Tenny, Tom Brown, Lorraine Stephens, Bill Schumacher, Bob Schmidt with Ibsen Skies before race start on Sand Point Yacht Club dock.

Inaugural Sammamish Slough "Golden Water-Ski" Race

"WATER SKIERS WILL ATTACK SLOUGH TODAY" was the bold headline in the sports section of Sunday's *Seattle Times* on May 5. "The Olympic Water Skiers will challenge the hazards of the Sammamish Slough today with a special race down that 14-mile, twisting course. Starting at 1:30 at Pete's Place on Lake Sammamish, the water skimmers will 'shoot' down the narrow course, towed by high-speed outboards and into Lake Washington to finish at the Sand Point Yacht Club, 90th and Sand Point Way, 30 to 35 minutes later."

This was another dare-devil event put on by Seattle water skiers and raceboat pilots. The event, sponsored by the Washington Athletic Club and supplier of the trophies, was the first "Water-Ski Race" in the Northwest and possibly in the country. Among the skiers entered were Don Ibsen, Bob Schmidt (towed by Al Benson), Bill Schumacher (Ivey), Norma Lions, Wally Panabaker, Harry Swetman, Dud Davidson, Janette Burr, Gene Moore, Tom Brown and Dr. Lou West. Each skier had a separate high-powered tow boat driven by the likes of Jim Harland (skier Don Ibsen), Lin Ivey, John Sheriff, Tom Gould, Otis Clinton, Harold Boulton, Dick Barden, Mike Shain and Al Benson.

1948 Tidbits

The annual Bar Pilots Cruise was run on Sunday, February 22, through a flooded Slough with dredging machinery on each side. Planned flood control work was in progress during the cruise but crews were off that Sunday. The Sammamish River flood control work included clearing flow restrictions in the channel and replacement of the old wooden Bothell Bridge.

Seattle Outboard Club Bar Pilot boats in flooded Slough (foreground)–other boats traveling upstream (background) with dredging machinery idle on both sides of Slough.

An emergency appropriation of $25,000 was allocated for the present dredging and the bridge work cost was estimated at $80,000 for a new concrete structure. United States engineers also announced that they would complete a comprehensive flood control plan for the entire river by early next year. That work was planned to be started when funds were made available. The 1948 SOA sportsmanship trophy was awarded to Commodore, John Michaels.

Bar Pilots assembled on downstream side of Bothell Bridge.

The Lake Sammamish Bar Pilots held their 17th annual cruise under the sponsorship of the SOA and led by Grand Marshall, Jerry Bryant. The group left from their Sand Point headquarters and met in Bothell for the initiation ceremonies. Then continued upstream to one of the Lake Sammamish resorts to warm-up and refresh. A number of boaters came through the Seattle locks from Everett and Tacoma, a 120-mile roundtrip from their launching point, through the locks, upstream to Lake Sammamish, and back to Tacoma or Everett–a courageous journey for the outboarders.

The Henley Connection

The Lake Sammamish resort names changed over the years, which made the race and cruise stopover points on the lake confusing. There were three properties next to each other at the northwest end. I knew about them because of my cousins, the Henley's, who lived just south of the southernmost resort property. The Benson family visited them often. The youngest Henley, Ron, helped me understand the resort's history of ownership and name changes during the running of the Slough Races and Slough Cruises (see photo on next page).

1956 Slough Cruise: (L-R) Al "firewater" Benson (hat), cousin Bill Krietz, cousin's Mrs. Jane (waving) & Mr. Chuck Henley (glasses), son's Phil and Ron (holding boat bow) and a senior Henley (lower right).

1949

What would you think about someone pouring 5 gallons of gasoline into Lake Washington, lighting it on fire and then driving through it in a speeding raceboat with no protection other than the normal race attire; helmet, lifejacket and coveralls… crazy…madness…insanity? By now you've read enough about those dare-devil outboard drivers of the SOA and that they were a special breed. This promotional stunt was the most bizarre and spectacular of them all so far!

"Outboard Racers Brave Flames for Newsreels" was an attention-getting headline in Sunday's *Post-Intelligencer* sports section on April 3, 1949. The article below read: "What with the fire, the smoke and the popping of high speed outboard motors, residents in the vicinity of 123rd and Riviera Pl. N.E. may well have wondered what was going on Friday afternoon. Only this: three daredevil outboard drivers were piloting their bouncy boats through a pool of faming gasoline for the benefit of newsreel cameras that on Sunday will record once again the famous Sammamish Slough Race" (see Published Photo at chapter front).

The flaming gasoline gag was dreamed up by Charley Parryman, "News of the Day" cameraman, and C.L. Edwards, who shoots for Paramount Pictures. The studio editors combined the fire sequence, from the dock of Al Benson's lakefront home, with film shots taken at the Slough Race for a final cut "Short Subject" movie. Short films of this era were used as fillers in-between the main features shown in movie theaters. (Al Benson's raceboat bow, inside flames, is just poking thru in photo below.)

Cameraman Parryman filming on Benson's dock while other photographers shooting on dock to right.

Al Benson, Otis Clinton and Austin Wheeler, after much tinkering and tuning, got their motors revved up and circled out in the lake while some of their friends, under the direction of Parryman, scattered a bucket of gasoline over the water and lighted it with an improvised torch. Wheeler developed engine trouble, but Benson and Clinton came roaring through the sheet of orange flames as black smoke rolled high in the air.

Benson, who returned to shore singed and covered with smoky soot, once again battled flames in a raceboat on water, just like in the 1947 Slough Race. By now he had been known for driving through fire on water. What better moniker to be had than "Firewater," the handle he was given by his neighbors who witnessed the stunt and by his fellow race drivers, all who were amazed after watching the movie in theaters.

Firewater Benson returning from stunt with racing outfit covered in blackish soot.

14th Annual Sammamish Slough Race

The Seattle Outboard race officials were at it again, tinkering with the format of the Slough Race. This year, for the first time in the history of the event, the boats raced downstream, starting from Pete's Place[2] on Lake Sammamish and finishing at the Sand Point Yacht Club. The race, billed as the "Northwest's biggest speed spectacle," was held on April 3, two days after the "Firewater" publicity stunt. Since the current would be with them and the channel had been dredged recently, a new record for the 19-mile course was expected.

Racing downstream for the first time, the competitors found the new direction more hazardous and no faster. With more than 60 entries, only 19 finished as they found it difficult slowing down enough while riding with the current to make the many sharp curves. The overall winner, Johnny Sheriff, was only able to complete the course in 28 minutes, considerably slower than the expected time. Sheriff, veteran driver from Tacoma, was racing in the Unlimited Utility class using a 4-cylinder, 50-horsepower motor. Second overall was Seattle's Otis Clinton in his tiny Class A-Hydro and third place went to another Tacoma pilot, newcomer Clayton Shaw, in the Utility Class. Clinton fared well in his first three Slough races finishing second overall in 1947 and third overall last year. Other class winners were Louie Chichetti in the small utilities, Howard Cole in C-Service Runabout and Howard Price in Class C-Hydro.

---

[2] Pete's Place was a tavern with room and boat rentals on the far northwest end of Lake Sammamish, one-half mile from where the raceboats entered the lake from the Slough.

All the drivers of the faster boats had trouble, including Price, who was thrown completely out of his boat in a turn. However, he managed to get back aboard and under way again, to come through in fine shape. Gene McVicker was another driver thrown out while he was piloting his A-Hydro. A bridge near Redmond, with only a 6-foot wide hole for the boats to squeeze through, proved a bottleneck shortly after the start. Among the other casualties at the start were past winners Lin Ivey and Al Benson whose motors both suffered burned-out pistons.

1949 Sammamish Slough Race Results (in order of overall finish or class)

Place	Driver	Class	Boat #	From	Time
1	Johnny Sheriff	Utility	R-16	Tacoma	28:00
2	Ottis Clinton	A-Hydro	R-141	Bellevue	30:00
3	Clayton Shaw	Utility	R-50	Tacoma	30:01
*	Louie Chichetti	Small Utility	*	Seattle	1st in Class
*	Howard Cole	C-Service Runabout	R-65	Auburn	1st in Class
*	Howard Price	C-Hydro	*	Seattle	1st in Class

1949 Slough Race Program Page 1

1949 Slough Race Program Page 4

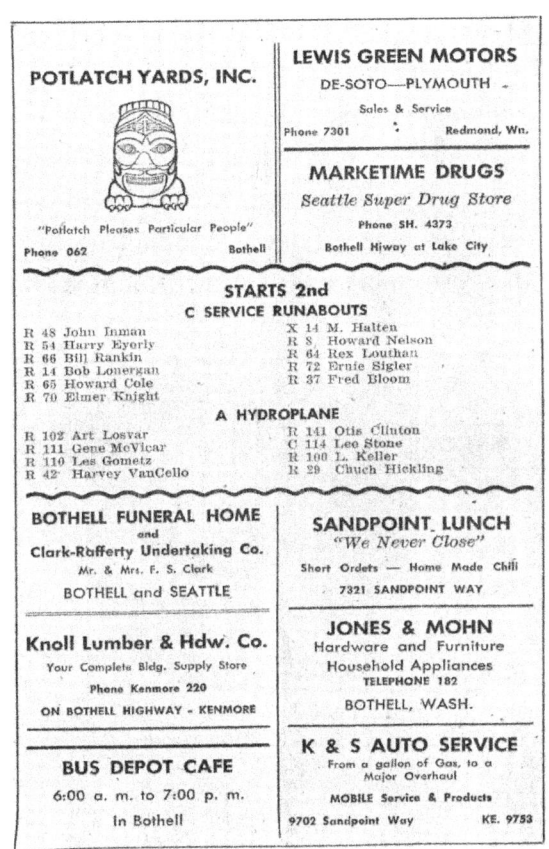
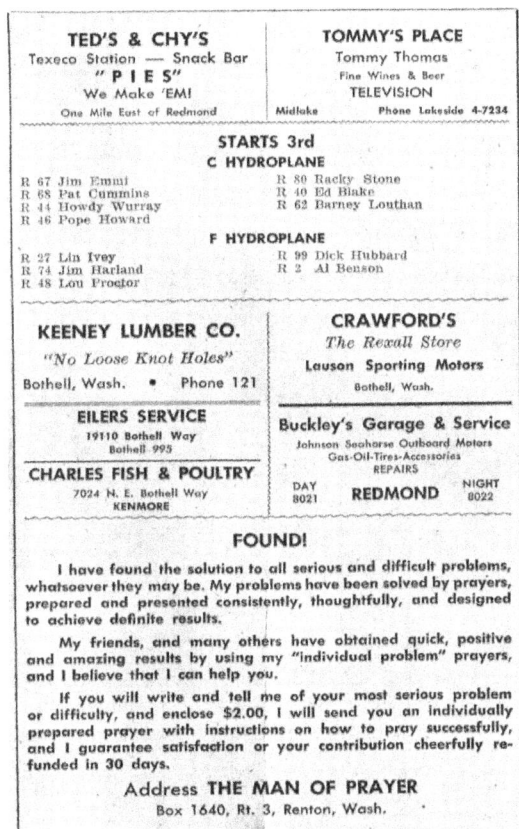

1949 Slough Race Program P-5   1949 Slough Race Program P-6

1949 Race Schedule (Partial)

Jan 2	Annual "Old-Timers" Cruise
Feb 27	Annual Sammamish Slough Bar Pilots Cruise
April 3	14th Sammamish Slough Race
July 10	Seattle Sportscade-Green Lake
July 17	Deep Lake Regatta-Olympia
July 24	Lake Air Park Regatta-Lake Washington East Channel
Sept 25	Mercer Island 100-Mile Marathon

Green Lake Sportscade

Next to the Sammamish Slough Race, the second biggest event of the year was the "Seattle Sportscade", an extravagant affair put on by the Seattle Outboard club. The huge 4-hour water show included outboard and inboard racing, water-skiing and various stunts. "Motorboat Racing, Water Skiing and Fire Test at Green Lake Today," was another one of those catchy headlines that was printed by the *Seattle Times* on July 10. Drivers hail from all along the West Coast, including the best speedboat racers from Canada.

Eighty-six drivers competed in the outboard and inboard races. Outboard classes included A-Hydro, C-Service Runabout, C & F Runabout, C & F Hydro and Utility. The inboards were comprised of 135 and 225 cubic inch classes. In addition, the show included three special water-skiing features by Don Ibsen's Skiquatic Follies and members of the Olympic Water-Ski Club. Another one of those fiery antics like on Lake Washington earlier this year was duplicated on Green Lake. Winding up the spectacular show was the "Trial by Fire," as the performers called it, in which boats and water-skiers went through a wall of flame.

Olympic Water-Ski Club members; Bill Schumacher, Bob Schmidt & Norma Lyons practicing while being filmed by cameraman in Benny Benson's "Sport Craft" cruiser.

1949 Tidbits

Lin Ivey was elected commodore for a third term. Joining him were Jim Harland, vice-commodore; Leonard Keller, secretary; Earl Hanson, treasurer, and Barney Seigel, sergeant-at-arms. Ivey was also voted as the recipient of the SOA Sportsmanship Award for the year.

No animals were hurt or anyone arrested, fined and jailed for setting Lake Washington and Green Lake on fire!

"NEGLECTED BUSINESS, DIDN'T YA?"

Al Benson cartoon by artist-friend Lynn Pitts

1947 Slough Race drivers meeting: (a few of the easier to identify) 1st row, Rockey Stone w/white coveralls & two-tone helmet; 2nd row, Benson center w/strap on helmet, Howard Nelson w/dark helmet & shirt right of Benson; 3rd row, Bill Rankin far right-no hat & white collar, Fred Bloom w/brimmed hat left of Rankin.

1948 Slough Race trophy winners (L-R): John Sheriff (3rd place in class) and first place class winners Al Benson, Otis Clinton, Howard Cole, Jack Hall & Jimmy Benson holding father Al's trophy.

Chapter 9

Al Benson overall winner of 1953 Sammamish Slough Race: (L to R) crewmember Bob Kertis, Al Benson holding "Ben Paris" perpetual trophy, last year's winner Bob Jacobsen.

Snake Dance
1950-1954

"SEATTLE SNAKE DANCE"

"For real thrills, driving or spectating, the Sammamish Slough is a boat racers' snake dance and a spectators' snake pit and big business only for the outboard repair shops"

-By Russ Swanson in BOAT SPORT, October 1952-

A tall and lanky gentleman from Ballard, nicknamed in his younger years as "Tiny," was preparing his Class-E Utility Runabout for the 15th annual Sammamish Slough Race. He was born and raised in the Ballard area as Robert Alvin Jacobsen, a youthful blue-eyed boat racer who owned and operated a boat and motor business in the heart of Seattle's Scandinavian district. "Jake" as he was commonly called, ran the business while his brother, Ed, designed and built boats in the back of the shop, located on Leary Way in Ballard.

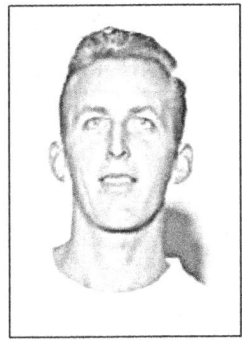

Bob "Tiny" Jacobsen

One of Ed's early builds was a utility boat that he built for brother Bob to race. Bob outfitted it for racing with a hefty four-cylinder, 33 HP Johnson outboard motor, an ideal outfit to run across Lake Washington and up the legendary Sammamish Slough. The final touch for the two-person utility boat was the addition of a raceboat identification number, U-27, that Ed painted in black on each side. "Jake" was now ready for a try in the Sammamish Slough, the "Seattle Snake Dance."

Congestion in the 15th Sammamish Slough Race

The Sunday morning *Times* headline on March, 26, was "Congestion Due Today In Sammamish Slough." This year's version of the Sammamish Slough Race had yet, again, another new twist in the race format. The diabolical race officials set up the race course for a continuous run from Sand Point to Lake Sammamish and back to the starting point. A buoy was placed at the North end of Lake Sammamish around which the racers swung before they headed back down the Slough. A traffic jam was anticipated shortly thereafter for the delight of the spectators but not the drivers.

The faster boats heading downstream were expected to pass the slower boats still coming upstream. This was a very daunting situation as the high-speed boats would meet and pass each other head-on while rounding sharp turns in a space not much wider than two boat-widths. Adding to the already hazardous course was high water and the bridge construction under way in Bothell.

The old wooden bridge in Bothell that had been there for decades was being replaced by a new concrete structure. To help bridge crossers during construction, a temporary footbridge, too low for boats to pass under, was installed for pedestrians to cross the river. Fortunately, the race officials were able to persuade the workers to create a makeshift opening for the raceboats, although it was only wide enough for one boat. This created another traffic jam, causing some boats to bump and bang off the temporary pilings. If those weren't enough hazards, the Slough was swollen and flooded from recent rains and snow melt. The path of the Slough's main channel was hard to determine, which caused some boats to run aground or end up in a pasture among the unsuspecting dairy cows.

Man from Ballard Triumphs in Perilous Slough

The toughest run in the history of the annual Sammamish Slough Race was won by Bob "Jake" Jacobsen. He piloted his Class-E Utility Runabout across Lake Washington, up the flooded and congested Slough, turned around the buoy on Lake Sammamish, met and passed oncoming entries head-on, and returned unscathed to the club's starting dock as the overall winner. He finished in 1-hour and 11 minutes, a slower time than usual, in a contest filled with perils and mishaps.

Only 26 out of the 53 starters finished the grueling 38-mile long course. The other winners included Erv Sigler in B-Utility, Richard Steve in D-Utility, George Hograrth in C-Utility, Max Whitcomb in A-Utility and Ned Brainder in the QD class. The mishaps were a-plenty in the tortuous and flooded river. Billy Bryant had the CU class trophy in his pocket until he turned over in Lake Washington just half-a-mile from the finish line. Bert Michiletti hit a dead head half-a-mile below Bothell that tore off his motor and landed him in an adjoining pasture. Half-a-dozen more hit a protruding snag near the Marymoor Dairy at Redmond in what was deemed the toughest race ever staged by the Seattle Outboard Association.

Slough Race winner Bob Jacobsen with brother Ed navigating the narrow opening under the Bothell Bridge.

Rough going: One obstacle drivers encountered was negotiating through the temporary narrow footbridge break below the Bothell Bridge. Dick Steven above, in his 50-hp craft, is about to make it but a number of raceboats didn't.

1950 Sammamish Slough Race Results (by class)

Place	Driver	Class	From	Boat #	Time
1	Bob Jacobsen w/rider Ed Jacobsen	E-Utility	Seattle	R-27	71:44
*	Dick Steven	D-Utility	Seattle	*	*
*	George Hogarth	C-Utility	Seattle	*	*
*	Art Losvar	C-Utility	Mukilteo	*	*
*	Erv Sigler	B-Utility	Tacoma	*	*
*	Harold Jensen	B-Utility	Seattle	*	*
*	Harold Jensen Jr	B-Utility	Seattle	*	*
*	Jack Headley	B-Utility	Seattle	*	*
*	Max Whitcomb, Jr.	A-Utility	Seattle	*	*
*	Pete Robinson	A-Utility	Seattle	*	*
*	Ned Brainder	QD Class	Seattle	*	*
*	Louis Chicketti	QD Class	Seattle	*	*

Some places, boat numbers and times unavailable

Partial 1950 Race Schedule

Jan 8	Annual Old-Timers Cruise
Feb 19	Annual Bar Pilots Cruise
Mar 26	15th Annual Sammamish Slough Race
May 28	Shadow Lake Regatta-moved from Bitter Lake due to high water
June 25	Tacoma to Seattle Marathon
August 19-20	Green Lake Coast & National Championships
Sept 17	Mercer Island 100-Mile Marathon

Inaugural Seattle Seafair Regatta

Last year's Seattle "Sportscade" on Green Lake turned into this year's *Seattle Seafair* speedboat regatta, part of the new week-long civic celebration sponsored by Greater Seattle Incorporated. Lin Ivey, race chairman of the co-sponsoring Seattle Outboard Association, announced to the press that the regatta, which was run August 18-20, would include prizes totaling $3,850. Jerry Bryant, then president of the "Seattle Salts" and long-time SOA member was a key officer of the Seafair organization. Other race committee members included Max Whitcomb, registration chairman and "Pop" Tuthill, chief race-starter.

1951-Green Lake Aqua Theater

Other events on Green Lake included the national water-skiing championships, Seattle junior crew regatta and the "Aqua Follies" performing in the new Aqua Theater on the southwest end of Green Lake.

Californians Take Home Seafair Prizes

The first annual Seafair boat races were run successfully but unfortunately the boys from California took home nearly all the prizes. Veteran Pat Cummins salvaged the only championship among the Northwest outboard racers. The regatta, which included outboard and inboard events, went off without a hitch except for all the gun jumpers.

Saturday's thrilling F-Runabout race opened the day for the Runabout Coast (Divisional) Championships. The "Fs", the most thrilling and the noisiest, with their 50-65 horsepower motors, required an additional rider who climbed out forward on the deck to keep the bow down. There he hung-on for dear life as the boat sped around the course among all the other competitors. Nineteen of the crowd favorites, sounding like a squadron of growling WWII bombers, hit the starting line but over half jumped the gun in both heats. Harvey Cook of Covina, California, was the winner with Northwest drivers Bob Gilliam sixth, and Al Benson, eighth.

Pat Cummins of Everett salvaged the day for the SOA with a win in the C-Runabout class with Pope Howard, also of Everett, fourth and Rockey Stone of Willamina, Oregon, fifth. Another local, Charles Afdem of Olympia, was first in the C-Service Runabout class with Clayton Shaw and Bill Rankin of Seattle, fourth and seventh respectively. The Californians took all the honors in the B and C Hydro classes. The only accident of the day was the flipping of Seattle's Fred Bloom who escaped injury when he went over in the first turn of the C-Service Runabout class.

Sunday's schedule included the F-Runabout National Championships and the West Coast Championships for the hydro classes. The day's action resulted again with the men from California taking home

1950 Seafair trophy- 1st DU Class not run.

the majority of the prizes. Northwest notables were future Slough Race driver, Bob Gilliam, taking third in the F-Runabout national finals, followed by Seattle's Lou Procter, fourth, and Al Benson, ninth.

In the Coast Divisionals, Lin Ivey was fifth in F-Hydro, followed by Lou Proctor in sixth. In the C-Hydros, Everett's Pope Howard placed second, Rockey Stone fifth,

James Emmi of Seattle, seventh and Pat Cummins ninth. Bill Rankin finished second in the C-Service Runabout's with Charles Afdem sixth and Leigh Stone of Tacoma second in A-Hydro. The 15 finishers in A-Hydro included Bellevue's Chuck Hickling, third; Seattle's Leonard Keller and Austin Wheeler eighth and eleventh and Art Losvar of Mukilteo thirteenth. The regatta prizes were presented during an awards banquet at the New Washington Hotel during the evening after the race.

Governing Body Rule Changes

The National Outboard Association closed its doors at the beginning of World War II leaving the American Powerboat Association as the sole governing body for boat racing in the U.S. No major rule changes were made after the war until December of 1949 when the APBA reorganized and made wholesale revisions to their articles of association and by-laws.

The most sought-after amendment, with the most impact, gave voting rights to individual members, where before only the racing council and clubs could vote. In addition, the body introduced a new category of stock utility outboard classifications which included the JU, AU, BU, CU, DU, EU and FU classes. These new classes were a hybrid of the Utility Runabout classes that the Seattle Outboard Association created back in 1931 and continued to develop up to this point in time.

APBA Stock Utility Class Specifications

Class	Max motor size	Min hull wt.	Min overall wt.	Min wt. (1954)	Min Age limit	Min Age (1954)
JU	7.5 cu. inches	75	190	190	12	9
AU	15 cu. Inches	105	230	265	12	12
BU	20 cu. inches	140	275	305	14	14
CU	30 cu. inches	210	355	350	14	14
DU	40 cu. Inches	280	435	435	14	14
EU	50 cu. Inches	300	465	445	14	14
FU	60 cu. inches	350	525	475	14	14

1950 weights and age limit, which was updated in 1954

Tidbits from 1950

The King County Army Engineers recommended a $1,109.000 improvement project for the Sammamish River. This was the result of a request from the Washington House of Representatives to investigate the project's feasibility and determine a work description for mitigating the yearly flooding of the waterway. This effort was based on decades of requests from Sammamish Valley citizens, culminating in 1946 during a public hearing held in the city of Redmond.

Nothing remarkable was mentioned about either Slough cruise. Lin Ivey was elected SOA commodore for a fourth term. The 19th annual SOA Sportsmanship

Award was presented to restaurant owner, Art Louie, during the final meeting of the year at the Sand Point Yacht Club.

1951

New Blood in Slough Race

Elgin Gates

An unfamiliar name was notable in the sixteenth Sammamish Slough Race. Elgin Gates, a transplant from Southern California and a new member of the SOA, worked for W. C. "Doc" Jones, the Seattle distributor for the young Mercury outboard motor company. Doc enticed Elgin, a veteran outboard racer from Needles, California, to move to Seattle and help him promote his company. Was there a better way to promote the relatively new line of outboard motors? Probably not at the time for an engine ideally suited for boat racing. Competing successfully in the famed Sammamish Slough Race seemed like a great opportunity to attract dealers and sell more motors.

This year as in the past two years, the renowned outboard race started from the end of the SOA's Sand Point Yacht Club's large dock. The dock's first section was a long walkway extending several hundred feet out from shore. A large floating platform was connected to the end, which was lower at about a foot above the water. This structure was originally built and used by the Boeing Airplane Company for docking during the testing of their experimental B-314 Clipper flying boats (see photo on page 540).

Then during the following Clipper Ship era of the late 1930s, the platform accommodated the crew and passengers for loading and unloading. Eventually the outboard club, which had leased the dock and adjacent property, became the dock's beneficiary. The low platform was an ideal starting point for boat racing events because it allowed an easy step into a raceboat and enabled crew members to hang onto the rear-end of the motor until the all-important starting gun fired.

SOA Commodore Art Shorey announced to the press that at least 60 boats were expected to compete, which would be a new record for entries if they all started. This year's race, unlike all the previous, was divided into two heats for all the boats. The first heat started from Sand Point at 1 pm and ended at Pete's Place on Lake Sammamish. The second heat, after refueling, headed back to Sand Point at 2:30 pm.

Monday's headline in the *Times* on April 9 read "Gates Edges Out Benson By Slim Margin in Slough Race." Both Gates and Benson had first and fourth places in their heats but Gates' fourth place run time was one second better, giving him the victory.

Clayton Shaw: C-Utility Winner in Leon Sutter's boat (worked for Sutter in Ballard).

More boats started (57) and finished (31) this year, a new record for the event. The thousands of spectators who turned out saw numerous spills with only one in the serious category. Keith Robinson, 35, of Seattle, was injured when his boat struck a piling under the Wayne Golf Course Bridge. He was taken to Harborview Hospital with head injuries and released, in satisfactory condition, the following day.

1951 Race Results (in order of finish per class)

Place	Driver	Class	From	Boat #	Time
1	Elgin Gates	Unlimited Hydro	Seattle	6-R	28:07
2	Al Benson	Unlimited Hydro	Seattle	R-74	28:08
3	Carl Biber	Unlimited Hydro	Tacoma	39	*
1	Art Losvar	F-Utility	Mukilteo	*	*
2	Robert Sperring	F-Utility	Seattle	*	*
3	Ed Jacobsen	F-Utility	Seattle	*	*
1	Ernie Sigler	D-Utility	Seattle	*	*
2	Jerry Lampkin	D-Utility	Seattle	34-R	*
3	Bob Jacobsen	D-Utility	Seattle	28-R	*
1	Pope Howard	D-2 Utility	Seattle	R-18	*
1	Clayton Shaw	C-Utility	Seattle	10-R	*
2	Ralph Taylor	C-Utility	Seattle	*	*
3	Marv Sperring	C-Utility	Seattle	*	*
1	Richard Schrader	B-Utility	Seattle	*	*
2	Warren Kelly	B-Utility	Seattle	*	*
3	Ken Louie	B-Utility	Seattle	*	*

1	Ned Brainerd	B-2 Utility	Seattle	*	*
2	Johnny Sangster	B-2 Utility	Seattle	*	*
3	Ed Burke	B-2 Utility	Seattle	*	*
1	Art Louie	A-Utility	Seattle	*	*
2	Robert Beatty	A-Utility	Seattle	59-R	*
3	Cliff Plazman	A-Utility	Seattle	*	*

All times and some boat numbers unavailable

Golden Water-Ski Race in Slough

One of the most spectacular aquatic races in the Pacific Northwest, the fourth annual Sammamish Water-Ski Race, was staged on May 6 by the daredevil water skiers of the Olympic Water-Ski club. Twelve contestants, out of the expected twenty-five aptly fit competitors, slipped into their shoes that were permanently attached to wooden planks with rounded turned-up tips in front. No, these weren't converted snow skis; they were designed for skimming over the water while being towed by a speeding water craft tethered by a short rope, the bright idea of recognized inventor, Don Ibsen.

Twelve contestants out of an expected 25, started from the Lake Forrest Park community dock at 2 pm braving the weather and hazardous course in the Sammamish Slough, the same passage the outboarders used in early April. The race, open to all skiers, was divided into two classes according to the speed of the outboard boats that towed them. The slower class included boats with motors up to 33 horsepower and the Unlimited Class was open to more powerful engines, including the new high-revving 4-cylinder Mercurys.

Both men and women came from the Olympic Water-Ski Club, which sponsored the event, until this year when the City of Bothell took it over. A new handicap was introduced this year that required the skiers to pause at the judge's stand in Bothell, take off their skies for an arm and leg count and then hurry-up and restart to Lake Sammamish. The organizers were crazy, just like the diabolical outboard officials a month earlier. They also set up the course with a turnaround buoy in Lake Sammamish, which provided plenty of thrills when skiers were shooting back down the Slough while the slower racers were still going up.

"'Hams' to Air Water-Ski Race On Sammamish Slough Sunday" headlined in the Thursday *Times* on May 3. Shortwave radio transmissions were provided by the West Seattle Amateur Radio Club as they had in the past two races. The volunteer radiomen, which were positioned at various locations along the course, used their portable and mobile units to track the skiers' progress and safety.

Jennings-Benson Win Again

Bob Jennings towed by Al Benson won the Unlimited-Class, the feature race in the annual Water-Ski Race. Benson pulled Jennings to their second win in a row in front of thousands of spectators along the course and in Bothell. Wally Pannabaker towed by Otis Kanson, was second and Bill Schumacher, Sr., towed by Lin Ivey, was third. In the Limited Class, Dr. Lou West of Seattle, finished first followed by Paul Jeffries in second, the only contestants in that class to finish the grueling run. They were towed by Don Ibsen and Henry Kleinberg respectively.

Only seven out of the 12 skiers that started finished. The competitors were watched by several thousand spectators from various vantage points along the Slough and in Bothell where the race finished. There, the race officials were kept informed of the racers' progress by the West Seattle Ham operators. Trophies and prizes were awarded after the last shivering cold contestant crossed the finish line. Most likely they all were happy the ordeal was over, especially after their bodies warmed up with dry clothes and also likely with some type of warmed spirits.

Al Benson's 1st place trophy

The first water-ski event through the Slough was held in 1948 when it was promoted more as an exhibition. For the next two years it ran across Lake Washington from Sand Point but no information covering the race was published. The same goes for the race in 1950, when Al Benson drove the winning raceboat, likely towing Bob Jennings as in this year's race. No records were found about that race either other than Benson's first-place trophy in the photo above.

1951 Race Schedule (Partial)

Jan 7	Annual Old-Timers Cruise
Feb 25	Annual Bar Pilots Cruise
April 8	16th Annual Sammamish Slough Race
May 6	4th Sammamish Water-Ski Race
May 13	Shadow Lake Regatta-moved from Bitter Lake due to high water
June 25	Tacoma to Seattle Marathon
July 15	Devil's Lake Regatta
August 5	Pacific Coast Professional Championships-Lake Washington
August 11	Regional Stock Utility Championships-Lake Washington
August 8	Mercer Island 100-Mile Post Intelligencer Marathon
Sept 15-16	National Outboard Hydro Championship-Nashville, TN

Tidbits from 1951

Three Seattle drivers set world records in the mile trials at Devil's Lake, Oregon, on July 14, 1951. Don Benson set a mark in the JU class, Bob Batie in AU and Elgin Gates in the BU class. Bob Jacobsen won the D-Utility Nationals in Tennessee. The future "fastest outboard driver in the world," Hubert Entrop, was voted in as the 20th winner of the SOA Sportsmanship Award. The old-timer's cruised up the Slough to Pete's Place on Lake Sammamish and the Bar Pilots initiated 14 new members. Both championship races scheduled for Green Lake were moved to Lake Washington due to heavy concentrations of hazardous algae growth.

1952

Slough Race Merry-Go-Round

In a competition full of twists and turn craziness, this years was even wilder. The drivers and boats were caught up in a merry-go-round hunt for a starting point. The race originally was scheduled to start in Portage Bay and go through the Lake Washington Ship Canal. But Seattle officials were denied a request for a temporary lifting of the Mountlake Cut's 6-mile-per-hour speed restriction. Madison Park was the next choice since Greater Seattle, Inc., was sponsoring the event and they wanted the event to start somewhere in Seattle. But alas, the starting site had to be moved yet again, because of the inclement weather.

During the morning of the race, drivers were balking at running in the dangerous waves on Lake Washington that were being whipped up by strong winds. Race chairman Max Whitcomb, Jr., in an effort to save the race, had to scramble to find a more protected site. In what is now a whirlwind saga, the race was delayed and moved to Ward's Resort in Kenmore. One and three-quarter hours later, after every boat was hauled back out of the water and onto trailers at Madison Park, then hastily transported and re-launched in Kenmore, the event finally got under way at 1:00 o'clock in what is now a "merry-go-round"

Bob Jacobsen ready for a start in Kenmore.

land and lake marathon.

The race was divided into two heats, the first from Ward's Resort to Gateway Grove on Lake Sammamish and the second heat, the downstream trip back to Kenmore. Six outboard classes were run including: Unlimited Hydro, A, B, C, and D Stock Runabouts, and a combined class of D-2, E and F Runabouts. No special rules governed the race, only common courtesy was asked for passing in the Slough…yeah sure!

Race Madness Finally Starts

By this time the drivers were already worn out and the race hadn't even started! The 70 or so drivers, some of which needed a swig of spirits to continue, managed to climb into their rigs again in preparation for an actual start. Despite the inclement weather, 57 boats answered the starting gun and hard as it is to believe, they all started at once! The glut of boats roared off the starting line, rounded a buoy and then raced wide-open toward the mouth of the Slough about half-a-mile away in the only stretch of open water wide enough for passing.

1952 Start: Founder Jerry Bryant's cabin cruiser in background.

Al Benson, said to be "one of the all-time racing-greats of the Northwest," gunned ahead into the early lead with Lin Ivey in his wake and Bob "Tiny" Jacobsen close behind. They fought head-to-head in that order up through the narrow and most twisting part of the Slough; past the Wayne Golf Course, Bothell and Woodinville. Most of the golfers stopped their games to watch the outboarders speed by. On that hazardous first section, it was the stretch of water that separated the men from the boys. You get through and you're good in any league.

Approaching and passing under the Bothell Bridge is the most dangerous part the course. We, as drivers, hoped to make it safely around the sharp right-hand turn that is directly under the bridge, while passing between the four huge concrete pillars on each side. Many a driver has met his misfortune here. If you didn't steer to the right soon enough, you'd crash into the pillars, run into the riverbank directly ahead, spin-out or completely flip-over. Then you're in a real predicament because you were at the river's mercy. The current would push you back, tangling you and your boat against the pillars or hopefully just float you back down stream into the grasp of some helpful spectators. Being caught upside down and trapped under your boat was a danger to all of us. It's amazing that a boat racer never drowned here.

Getting back to the duel between Benson, Ivey and Jacobsen; by now Benson and Ivey were way ahead and Jacobsen was lagging about two minutes behind. Ivey took the lead about a mile from where the Slough meets Lake Sammamish when Benson developed engine trouble. From there it was clear sailing for Ivey who gunned by and was first to finish the upriver run at Gateway Grove. Benson managed to finish, limping along with a sick engine.

Art Shorey, commodore of the Seattle Outboard club and official timer, clocked Ivey's Unlimited Hydro *Poison Ivey* at 20:44.3. Less than two minutes later Jacobsen's D-Runabout *Dynah-Mite*, flashed by in 22:36 flat and third was a B-Runabout piloted by Clay Fox in 25:50.06. The other early finishers in order included, Bill Schumacher, Sr., in the *Biffer*, C. W. Coon's A-Runabout and Clayton Shaw's C-Runabout *Fireball*. When the noses were counted the officials found a whopping 25 entries strewn along the Slough. Between runs drivers were given 30 minutes to refuel, make repairs and warm their freezing hands. During that time a Coast Guard patrol craft cleared the stalled boats out in time for the second heat to start.

The return run was again a duel between Benson Ivey and Jacobsen. "Benny" with his engine cured, headed into the Slough first with Lin and "Jake" close behind. Ivey was fighting for the lead about midway down when his boat went out of control and smashed into a river bank. No one's going to be courteous when you're fighting for a lead (its "dog-eat-dog" in racing). Benson continued-on unscathed with Jacobsen hot on his heels. Both were using the new 25 horsepower 4-cylinder Mercury motor, the hottest new engine available compared to Ivey's, which was a prewar 4-60 custom-built by Jimmy Harland. The red-hot duel continued downstream through the treacherous lower section, all the way to the finish line in Kenmore. Benson's R-16 hydro edged-out Jacobsen's 2-R runabout by a scant one second for the win. Their times were 20:55 to 20:56; one of the closest battles ever seen on the Slough.

Smooth and steady Bob Jacobsen was the overall winner based on his two second place finishes in each heat. Benson, the only unlimited hydro to finish the last heat, was second overall because of his sluggish finish in the first heat but with a thrilling first place in the final heat. Out of the 57 starters, 25 finished, a higher than usual percentage. The shortened race with the cold and windy weather failed to keep the spectators away. Race officials estimated the crowd at 50,000, the largest ever to see a Slough race. Their automobiles, near the Slough, were lined bumper-to-bumper on both sides of the highway for more than a mile in some places.

Bob Jacobsen: 1st place overall, heading downstream to Lake Washington.

Chicken Coups to Victory in Slough

From the first boats the brothers built in the family's chicken coup to crafting a Slough Race winner behind the scenes in Brother Bob's Ballard boat shop, Ed Jacobsen was recognized for his boat building skills and expertise. This was very evident when Bob Jacobsen won his second Sammamish Slough Race driving a raceboat designed and built by his brother, Ed Jacobsen. I learned more about Ed's lesser-known boat building history in a phone interview on November 25, 2016. During the conversation with the still sharp 93-year-old, we talked about his boat building, the Slough Race, and association with his late brother, Bob Jacobsen.

Q: Were you the rider in the 1950 Slough Race when your brother won the first time?
A: "It probably was me…I raced with him a number of times."
Q: That race started at Sand Point and rounded a buoy on Lake Sammamish?
A: "Yes, I remember going around the buoy and going back down the Slough."
Q: I see you raced in the 1951 Slough Race and placed 3rd in F-Utility.
A: "I raced one time in a boat that required 2 people back then."
Q: Were they utility boats?
A: "We built a couple of them…they didn't go very fast…we built another one and it was pretty fast, that's the one I drove in the race with my cousin."
Q: Did you build Bob Waite's first hydro?

A: "Yes, he lived next to Bill Farr (on Lake Sammamish) I went over there with Farr (to meet Bob Waite)…I built Waite's boat at his home…he was one of the nicest guys."

Q: Did you build Bill Farr's first boat?

A: "He built the boat from a plan that I gave him and I worked with him" (building the boat at Farr's home).

Q: Farr won in 1954 (Slough Race), was that the boat you designed?

A: "I designed Farr's and helped him with it…he was a finish carpenter and did an awfully good job."

Q: I raced up the Slough in the mid-'50s in the JU Class for 9-14-year old's.

A "Where did you get the boat?"

Q: I raced one of yours.

A: "I designed that little boat and made patterns for it, then I made a jig and he (Brother Bob) had kids putting the boats together."

Q: Was that in the '50s?

A: "Yes, everything I did was in the '50s."

Q: Are you the younger brother?

A: "I am the older brother and I designed and built all those boats."

Q: I have a photo of your newly-built boats stacked up against the shop wall.

A: "That was in the shop on Leary Way (in Ballard), I built all the boats in the evenings…the police would come by and rattle the cages."

Q: Did they think you were a burglar?

A: "They got used to me (working at night)."

Jacobsen's shop stocked with their newly built boats.

Clayton Shaw 1st C-Runabout downstream in Bothell.

Hugh Entrop 3rd B-Runabout in Bothell.

C. W. Coons 1st A-Runabout.

1952 Sammamish Slough Race Results (by class)

Place	Driver	Class	From	Boat #	Time
1	Bob Jacobsen	D-Runabout	Seattle	2-R	43:32
1	Al Benson	Unlimited	Seattle	R-46	*
	(No other finishers in	Unlimited class)			
2	Carl Biber	D-Runabout	Tacoma	39	*
3	Harold Tolford	D-Runabout	Seattle	78-R	*
1	Ray Baker	E,F,D-2 Runabout	Seattle	1-R	*
2	Bill Schumacher, Sr.	E,F,D-2 Runabout	Seattle	X-17	*
3	Ralph White	E,F,D-2 Runabout	Seattle	73-R	*
1	Clayton Shaw	C-Runabout	Tacoma	10-R	*
2	Art Losvar	C-Runabout	Mukilteo	X-11	*
3	Bob Spurring	C-Runabout	Seattle	X-14	*
1	Clay Fox	B-Runabout	Seattle	117-X	*
2	Bob Baite	B-Runabout	Seattle	56-R	*
3	Hubert Entrop	B-Runabout	Seattle	51-R	*
1	C. W. "Jerry" Coons	A-Runabout	Seattle	90-R	*
2	Joe Boyce	A-Runabout	Seattle	14-A	*
3	Richard Osborne	A-Runabout	Seattle	X-12	*

Some places, boat numbers and times unavailable

Golden Water-Ski Race

"Jennings Cops Slough Ski Race" headlined the *Seattle Times* on May 26. Bob Jennings, pulled by this year's Sammamish Slough Race winner, Bob Jacobsen, was declared the winner in the Unlimited Class of the annual Golden Water-Ski Race. It was advertised to have had "one of the year's biggest water-sports crowds in the Pacific Northwest." The daredevil skiers, mostly members of the Olympic Water-Ski Club, were pulled by veteran raceboat drivers of the Seattle Outboard Association.

The fifth annual "wild and woolly" event, sponsored by the Inglewood Country Club, started at 1:00 pm from the country club's dock at the Slough entrance. When the starting gun fired, the dozen or so daredevil skiers sitting on the dock, with their skies tips up in the water and holding their tow line handles tightly, were nervously watching their slack tow line in the water between them and their boat. When the driver started his engine and gunned-it, the line quickly straightened jerking the skier forward off his or her rear ends, hopefully without slivers from the dock. Simultaneously they stood up and were whisked-off upstream to Lake Sammamish.

The speeding competitors braved the cold wind and hazardous turns for 15 agonizing miles each way. They endured the freezing cold water splashing around their legs or even worse, being drenched over your entire body from the numbing spray of a passing boat and skier. While they continued their plight under the most adverse conditions, they were encouraged by the spectators lining the banks and many bridges along the way. When the duo entered Lake Sammamish, they could see their stopping point less than a mile away at Gateway Grove. The skiers cast off their tow line and coasted to a stop in the shallow waters of the resort's beach after they passed race-judges on the dock at the finish line. Then the pilots slowed, coiled up the wet tow lines and headed back to a dock or shore. Here, the skiers rested and warmed up the best they could while the drivers refueled–and made repairs if necessary.

The return run started at 2:30 pm from the resort's floating dock in the same fashion as the upstream run. After the start it's a short distance to the Slough's entrance. This causes the boats to be more bunched together and required them to fall in line as they entered the Slough. The first two-thirds of the return trip is relatively easy. It's that last third that's the killer. A good skier would keep in the center of the boat's wake to minimize the pulling forces on the boat's transom. Moving outside the wake or back and forth would cause the driver to make a steering correction that slowed their progress. The foaming water trail from the motor's propeller was the skier's guide to the center. The teams that made it back finished at the Inglewood dock in the same manner as in the first run.

Bob Jacobsen's smooth-running D-Runabout pulled the other Bob, Bob Jennings of Seattle, across the finish line in first place giving the duo the overall win in the fifth annual golden Water-Ski Race. The winning skier of the D-2 Class was, get this, the future all-time winningest driver of the renowned Sammamish Slough outboard race, Bob Waite! He was pulled by his Lake Sammamish waterfront neighbor who also was a future Slough Race winner, Bill Farr. Among the women skiers, Norma Williams was the leader, even though she spilled at the Bothell Bridge. She was able to climb out of the water safely onto the bank under the bridge and restart with a "deep water start." She was towed by Jim Spinner, future SOA commodore and esteemed local, regional and national racing official. The prizes were awarded after all the contestants dried-out and cleaned up during a dinner at the prestigious Inglewood Country Club.

1952 Ski-Race: Bob Schmidt-Al Benson 3rd place.

Water-Ski Race Results (in order of finish per class)

Place	Class	Skier	Driver
1	Unlimited	Bob Jennings	Bob Jacobsen
2	Unlimited	Bill Schumacher	Lin Ivey
3	Unlimited	Bob Schmidt	Al Benson
1	D-Utility	Bill Farr	Bob Waite
2	D-Utility	Tom Brown	Don Ibsen
3	D-Utility	Dick Langham	Dick Lyman
1	Women	Norma Williams	Jim Spinner
2	Women	Stella Mills	Red Taylor
3	Women	Betty Langham	Bob Oliver

1950s: Jimmy Harland's shop in Seattle at 1114 Aurora Ave N. He and his wife lived upstairs.

1952 Race Schedule (Partial)

Jan 6	Annual Old-Timers Cruise
Feb 24	Annual Bar Pilots Cruise
April 6	17th Annual Sammamish Slough Race
April 27	Lake Sammamish Regatta
May 10-11	Devil's Lake, Oregon Regatta
May 18	Shadow Lake Regatta, Renton
May 25	4th Sammamish Water-Ski Race
June 1	American Lake Regatta
July 20	Deep Lake-Olympia
Aug 8	Seafair Outboard Regatta, Seward Park
Aug 10	Seafair 100-Mile Marathon, Lake Washington
Sept 19-21	Stock National Championships-Lake Merritt, Oakland, CA
Oct 18-20	Outboard National Championships-Lake Alfred, FL

Tidbits from 1952

About 70 boats participated in this year's Bar Pilots cruise, the largest number to date. Prominent young raceboat driver, 12-year-old Don Benson, was the youngest ever to be inducted into the Sammamish Bar Pilots Association. Sammamish Slough pilots J. W. "Jerry" Coons, Bob Jacobsen and Hugh Entrop set 5-mile competition records at Devil's Lake, Oregon, on May 10-11. Coons set the A-Stock Runabout record at 40.476 mph, Jacobsen set the B-Stock Hydro mark at 47.900 mph and Entrop set the D-Stock Hydro record at 55.917 mph.

Art Shorey was elected commodore of the SOA for a second term and held the club meetings at the Lake Forest Park Community Center. He was also honored with the SOA Sportsmanship Award for his outstanding leadership over the past two years.

1953

18th Annual Sammamish Slough Race

A charismatic 39-year old businessman from "Lil Old Lake City" slowly piloted his new *Swift* Unlimited outboard hydro out to the old sunken barge[1] at the end of Ward's Resort's long dock. He was warming-up his engine to hopefully make it easier to start on the first pull. The newer Mercury engines were all equipped with an innovative recoiling starting cord that made them much easier to start. He coasted to a stop and eased up against the 4-foot high barge crowded with spectators, crew members and officials. Using a small paddle, he repositioned his boat with the bow pointing out toward the Slough and the back of the engine near the barge's high side. A designated person had to lie on his stomach to reach down and hold his motor until the official starter finished his countdown and fired the starting gun. This is where all the action and excitement began, when all the boats line up for the start.

Al Benson, who lived just a few miles across the lake, was preparing to compete for the sixteenth time in his favorite race, the 18th annual Sammamish Slough Race. It was the second time since its beginning (1934) that the contest started at the north end of Lake Washington. Benson, who runs a boat and motor shop in Lake City was a past two-time winner hoping to be the first three-time winner of the nationally acclaimed "World's Crookedest Race."

Before this year, the newspaper reporters had made a big deal about the Benson-Jacobsen duel for the coveted Ben Paris Trophy. Which one of the past two-time victors would win for a third time and take permanent possession of the perpetual trophy? The only other two-timer was retired boat racer, Dick Barden, who won in 1945 and 1946. Unfortunately, the duel never occurred because Jake retired from racing in early 1953 to concentrate on his business. Now the main story was only about Benny Benson, would he get another win and take permanent position of the coveted Ben Paris Perpetual trophy?

---

[1] A large rectangular flat-bottomed vessel with blunt ends, once used for hauling sand and gravel.

1953 pre-race preparation at Ward's Resort: (L-R front) John Laird & Doug Calander filling fuel tank of 582-R, Al Benson, unidentified & Bob Kertis connecting steering cables to motor of hydro in middle, Bob Schmidt kneeling next to 51-R, (L-R back) Ken Ferguson (checkered shirt), Dot Benson (Dark scarf) talking to Rockey Stone (dark shirt), Jimmy Benson (white hat), Donnie Benson (skipper hat). Spectators keeping warm inside were watching the action through the resort's ballroom windows.

There was only one word to describe the weather for this year's race–miserable. It was polar bear weather at its coldest. Icy wind whipped up whitecaps on the lakes at both ends of the twisting Slough and in the Slough between the lakes, gusts of wind howled down the necks of the hardy drivers. Officials expected over 100 entries but less half that number registered for the race and a scant 34 finished the first leg. The annual battle of the Sammamish Slough was run in two legs with a breather in between at Gateway Grove on Lake Sammamish. Each leg is scored with points, 400 for first, 300 for second, 225 for third and so on. The winner is based on the highest accumulated point total from both legs.

With the weather playing havoc with Lake Washington, the start had to be pulled closer to shore for safety, most likely because of Johnny Laird's mishap. Laird, a new member of the Seattle Outboard Association, ended his day before the race even started. He flipped in the rough water while warming-up before the start. The original course was set up with a turn buoy 400 yards out in the lake to help space out boats before they entered the Slough. Race officials removed it after Laird's flip to give the drivers a more protected straight shot from the starting line into the Slough.

Benson First Triple Winner

The April 13 *Seattle Post-Intelligencer* sports headline, "Benson Wins Slough Race," closed the book on Benson's goal to be the first three-time winner of the Slough Race, an amazing accomplishment at the time. The article continued: "Al Benson did it again, the old pro with a long and colorful racing career took the 1953 race with a bare 4.2-second edge over Rockey Stone, the Oregonian."

Jack Headley was third in the unlimited class, then Ronald Peterson and Clayton Shaw, the latter because of a very slow downstream run after he finished first in the upstream run. Like Bob Jacobsen last year, "cool-headed Slough veteran" Al Benson won without a first-place in either run. The other class winners behind the unlimiteds were: Carl Biber in D-Runabout; Ed Tolford, C-Runabout; Henry Chevelier, B-Hydro; Bob Jennings, B-Runabout, and Bill Wallace, in A-Runabout.

The upstream leg, 14 miles of twisting river sometimes not more than 20 feet wide, featured a hot battle between the unlimiteds. Lin Ivey, Benson, Stone, Headley, Shaw, Peterson and Bill Rankin fought neck and neck almost all the way up and all finished within two minutes of each other, a remarkable performance despite dodging half-submerged logs, floating debris and sharp corners under bridges along the way.

Lin Ivey in Unlimited F-Hydro *Poison Ivey* passing under Bothell Bridge upstream.

As if the natural obstacles weren't enough for drivers to contend with, a few sadistic fans hurled rocks and other missiles at the passing speedboats. One boat was hit by a bottle narrowly missing the pilot. Despite the juvenile antics of a few spectators, most drivers vowed to come back next year.

On that first heat, Shaw grabbed the lead about half way up and held it to the finish with almost a one-minute margin over Benson who nosed out Rockey Stone of Willamina, Oregon for second-place by a scant two seconds. Headley came in fourth, Rankin fifth and Ivey sixth. Ivey, who was near the lead most of the way despite his motor only hitting on three of his four cylinders, lost most of his time when he made a quick stop to change a sparkplug.

The drivers made repairs and thawed out their hands between heats. Lin Ivey, the hard luck driver of both the '52 and '53 races, ran into more trouble when his temperamental 4-60, a rebuilt pre-war motor, refused to fire up. A dead battery was the culprit, now requiring him to scour the town of Redmond for a replacement but failing to find one, ended his day just like last year when he crashed into a bank.

1953: Al Benson leading Rockey Stone on upstream run in Redmond.

The second leg was the faster of the two with four boats finishing within 17 seconds of each other. Ron Peterson, driving retired Bob Jacobsen's unlimited runabout, won the heat. Nine seconds later Headley flashed by the finish a little more than five seconds ahead of Benson who in turn was about three seconds ahead of Rockey Stone.

Donnie, Jimmy, Al and Dorothy Benson posing for victory photo.   Victory kiss with Ben Paris trophy.

Narrow Escape

The most serious accident of the day occurred at the start of the second heat when Bill Rankin was thrown from his boat. He was speeding across Lake Sammamish toward the Slough when his new "pickle fork" Unlimited Hydro flipped over. The quick action of the crew in a nearby patrol boat saved him from drowning when they pulled him from the cold water.

Bill Rankin piloting Unlimited "pickle fork" Hydro.

An above average number of boats finished with 34 out of 45 starters in the first heat and 33 in the second heat. Nine of them came to some type of grief on the way up; among them were Hal Tolford, the ex-Ballard High fullback, Arleigh Hirsch, Gene Hudson, John Nigri, Mike Cunningham and Jack Lausch of Enumclaw. This year, unlike in the past, all the classes started separately. Sidney Sato, of Carnation, was disqualified from his C-Runabout run when he mistook his starting group and was off a good five minutes ahead of them.

1953 Sammamish Slough Race Results (in order of overall finish)

Place	Driver	Class	From	Boat #	Boat Name	Time
1	Al Benson	Unlimited Hydro	Seattle	104	Mo-Ta-Shun	41:70.6
2	Rockey Stone	Unlimited Runabout	Willamina, OR	R-26	My Girl	41:74.8
3	Jack Headley	Unlimited Hydro	Seattle	X-11	*	42:38.1
4	Ronald Peterson	Unlimited Hydro	Seattle	2-R	*	42:60.1
5	Clayton Shaw	Unlimited Hydro	Tacoma	R-38	*	43:59.2
6	Bill Rankin	Unlimited Hydro	Seattle	X-4	*	*
1	Carl Biber	DU-Runabout	Tacoma	T-56	*	52:51.7
2	Jim Wertz	DU-Runabout	Seattle	53-R	Nightmare	56:92.0
1	Henry Chevalier	B-Hydro	Seattle	X-50	*	61:40.4
2	Duke Polk	B-Hydro	Seattle	586-R	Jerkanamerk	63:85.2
3	Red Taylor	B-Hydro	Seattle	560-R	*	67:47.9
1	Ed Tolford	C-Runabout	Seattle	DU-46	*	*
2	Dick Brunes	C-Runabout	Seattle	*	*	*
3	Pat McCarty	C-Runabout	Seattle	R-120	Iron Pants	*
1	Bob Jennings	B-Runabout	Seattle	56-R	*	*
2	Howard Keltis	B-Runabout	Seattle	*	*	*
3	Bob Schmidt	B-Runabout	Seattle	51-R	Hammerschmidt	*
1	William Wallace	A-Runabout	Seattle	R-23	*	*
2	Richard Osborn	A-Runabout	Hoquiam	154-R	Ding How II	*
3	Cliff Plagman	A-Runabout	Albany, OR	*	*	*

Some boat numbers, boat names and times unavailable

1953 Hard Luck driver Clayton Shaw 5th Unlimited Hydro.

Clayton Shaw "Hard Luck" trophy.

The race winner wasn't usually given the "traditional dunk" (tossed-in by crew members or fellow drivers) at Ward's Resort because the water was only a few feet deep even though the shore is two to three hundred feet away. In this case Benson would get stuck in the mud and be very difficult to retrieve. And if this happened he'd be covered in mud or at least from the waist up. The north end of the lake is very shallow because of the silt build-up that washes down out of the Slough. Dredging is required periodically by the Corps of Engineers to maintain safe passage for the adjacent businesses of Kenmore Air Harbor, neighboring Kenmore Building Materials and Plywood Supply. Unfortunately, the dredging didn't include the waterfront at Ward's Resort.

The waters around the resort were always shallow with thick muddy bottoms. If you dropped something in it like a valuable propeller or spark plug, you could kiss it goodbye as you'd never find it in the mess of thick muddy sludge below. During the winter months when Lake Washington was kept about a foot or so lower, the resort waterfront was shallow with exposed areas of mud flats between the barge and shore. I know this well because I had fallen into it several times during the time I lived and worked there (1959 to 1960) when the property was "Uplake Marina."

Clayton Shaw Receives "Hard Luck" Trophy

Clayton Shaw was awarded a special 1953 Slough Race "Hard Luck" trophy by his fellow drivers. Shaw was leading in the Unlimited class on the downstream run to Bothell and thought he had his first win "in the bag." But he ran over a 4x4 post when he slid too close to a fence that was partially submerged in the Slough, which caused him to slow down and eventually be passed by a number of his competitors. A portion of the post floated down the waterway with his broken-off fin sliced into it. A fellow driver found it and made the trophy which was presented to Shaw during a club meeting later in the month to the delight of the membership.

1953 Race Schedule (Partial)

Jan 4	Annual Old-Timers Cruise
Feb 22	Annual Bar Pilots Cruise
April 12	18th Sammamish Slough Race
April 22	Gateway Grove-Lake Sammamish
May 3	Sectionals Wenatchee
May 10	5th Sammamish Water-Ski Race
June 27	Moses Lake
July 4-5	Regionals-Devil's Lake Oregon
Aug 1-2	Oroville-Lake Osoyoos
August 7-8	Western Divisionals-Green Lake Seafair Regatta
Aug 15-16	Electric City
Aug 10	Mile Trials-Lake Washington East Channel
Aug 29	Mercer Island 100-Mile Marathon
Aug 29-30	Stock Outboard National Championships-Syracuse, NY
Sept 6-7	Devil's Lake Regatta
Sept 18-19	Outboard National Championship-Dale Hollow Lake, TN

1953 Golden Water-Ski Race

For the second time within a month, the outboard motorboat racers ran the Sammamish Slough. But this time they were towing water-skiers. The occasion was the annual race of the Golden Water-Ski Club, which like the recent Slough race, was to be run in two heats. The water skiers were scheduled to leave Ward's Resort in Kenmore at noon for Gateway Grove on Lake Sammamish. At 2:00 pm the skiers, who were still physically and mentally fit, would make the downstream run back to Kenmore.

"Schmidt Shows Way In Water-Ski Race" headlined in the *Times* on Monday, May 11. Bob Schmidt towed by Al Benson won the Unlimited class and Florence West, towed by Red Taylor, took the honors in the Limited class as 21 water-skiers attempted the 28-mile run. The Unlimited class allowed any motor regardless of the power, unlike the limited class that was restricted to 25-horsepower maximum. Schmidt and Benson covered the upstream run in first-place in a time of 25 minutes, 30 seconds, then after a much-needed rest for the skier, returned in a quicker time of 24 minutes and 8 seconds.

Norma Williams, towed by John Laird's underpowered B-Hydro, was thwarted in Bothell when a slow-starting Unlimited passed from behind and narrowly missed running over both of them. It was a scary and dangerous situation because the passing boat ran across their ski-line right in front of Ms. Williams. Luckily, she stopped abruptly after the tow line was ripped from her hands. She crashed into the very cold water unhurt and was picked up by some of her fellow skiers. Laird turned his boat around, restarted, and headed back to Kenmore by himself.

Ms. Williams started with two skis and then dropped one after underway. This is a typical scenario for an underpowered rig as it's much easier to get up on two skies. But once the towboat gets on a plane and the skier is up, one ski is better for the long run. They were never able to restart because Williams only had her one ski. None-the-less, they wound up with national publicity with a cover photo in the July, 1953 edition of *Sea and Pacific Motor Boat* Magazine (see photo on preceding page taken before their troubles started).

Water-Ski Race Results (in order of finish per class)

Place	Class	Skier	Driver
1	Unlimited	Bob Schmidt	Al Benson
2	Unlimited	Bill Schumacher	Lin Ivey
3	Unlimited	Don Ibsen	Doc Jones
4	Unlimited	Burt Ross	Carl Biber
1	Limited	Florence West	Red Taylor
2	Limited	Mike Cunningham	Bud Sullivan
3	Limited	Ray Moore	Dick Brunes
4	Limited	Don Caster	Gary Bartman

1953 Tidbits

Max Witcomb, a Bryant's Marina employee, became the commodore of the Seattle Outboard Association during the 25th anniversary of the club. Jim Spinner was vice-commodore; Harold Tolford, secretary-treasurer and George Orovitz, Sergeant-at-arms. The trustees were C. W. (Doc) Jones, Austin Wheeler, Bill Rankin and Clayton Shaw. This year the APBA celebrated its 50-year anniversary, quite an accomplishment despite the competition from several splinter groups and the now defunct National Outboard Association of the past. A few years earlier in 1948, the national body divided the nation into 16 regions with the Northwest as Region 10. The Northwest region didn't officially organize until 1949 when Lin Ivey, the SOA commodore at that time, was selected as the first chairman. Ivey was also Region 10 chairman this year for a second consecutive year.

1953 Bar Pilots Cruised from Kenmore to Gateway Grove on Lake Sammamish.

Don Benson set another record at Devil's Lake in the A-Runabout class. He set the mile-straightaway mark at 46.039 mph. The first edition of *Northwest Speed News*, a small newspaper dedicated to sports in the Northwest, was published in January of 1953. Russell Swanson, free-lance writer and business partner with photographer Bob Carver, wrote a number of articles about the Slough Race and other outboard events that were published in the newspapers along with articles and photos in most of the popular boating magazines of the time. Jim Spinner was this year's recipient of the SOA Sportsmanship Award and the new Bar Pilots included Slough racers Clayton Shaw, Bill Schumacher, Sr., and 11-year old Bill "Billy" Schumacher, Jr.

1954

19th Annual Sammamish Slough Race

The outboard racing season in the Pacific Northwest has its traditional kickoff with the Sammamish Slough Race. After a full winter of building, repairing, purchasing and experimenting with racing equipment, the annual race brings scores of drivers, veteran and neophyte alike out to Kenmore. Although maps and highway signs refer to it as the Sammamish River, it is really, to some, a meandering fourteen-mile Slough, flowing snake-like through the fertile Sammamish Valley that connects Lake Washington at the lower end to Lake Sammamish at the upper end.

This year the drivers themselves said the race would be the biggest in three decades. Thousands of Sunday motorists converged upon the Sammamish Slough expecting to see the outboard racers smash into the river banks, bridges and sunken logs. As it turned out however, it was safer in the Slough than along the highway from Bothell to Redmond. While the spectators scraped fenders and dented bumpers, the outboarders completed the race without injury to a single boat driver.

Water-Skier Becomes Winning Race Driver

The two-heat race began at 12:00 noon at Ward's Resort in Kenmore. When the starting gun fired, the boats headed out into Lake Washington, rounded a left-turn buoy and swept into the Slough for 14-miles to Lake Sammamish. The return heat started at 1:30 pm and finished for the first time 12 miles downstream in Bothell.

Turns out that a Sammamish water-skier from 1952 became the winning driver in this year's race. Bill Farr, 31-year-old carpenter from Lake Sammamish, beat Fred Bischoff of Everett for the overall victory by a mere 1.1 seconds, the closest in years. It was the first Slough Race for both of the new members of the Seattle Outboard Association. On the upstream run, Farr led most of the way to Lake Sammamish where Bischoff passed him just before the finish line. Rockey Stone was not far behind in third. Farr, driving his new F-Hydro he built from Ed Jacobsen's plans, led all the way downstream and crossed the finish line at Bothell in first-place. Bischoff, who was hot on his heels all the way downstream, was right behind with Stone again in third. Farr and Bischoff were tied in points with a first and a second apiece but Farr had the tie breaker, the best overall time which gave him the win. Farr's time was 33:12 for the shortened course.

1954 winner Bill Farr (1955 photo) near the Bothell finish line.

The race was co-sponsored by The Bothell Chamber of Commerce and the Seattle Outboard Association. Race chairman, Al Benson, modified the race course by moving the finish line from Kenmore to Bothell in hopes of attracting a large crowd for the first Slough Race to finish in Bothell. He also set up loudspeakers up and down the course and enlisted the West Seattle Amateur Radio Club to broadcast the race turn-by-turn from Bothell. It turned out to be better than expected. All the pre-race publicity attracted thousands of fans who lined the Bothell Bridge and on both sides of the river bank up and down the Slough. There was a huge traffic jam with cars parked bumper-to-bumper in both directions on most of the roads nearby.

Race Chairman Al Benson presenting Bill Farr overall winning trophy, Farr's 2 sons in middle.

Bill Schumacher, owner of "Bill's Tasty Home Bakery" in Seattle's Ravenna district, donated all the trophies. When Mr. Schumacher wasn't baking his famous multitiered wedding cakes and pastries, you'd find him water-skiing or keeping in terrific shape at Bob Schmidt's gym. He's known in water sports as an expert water skier, the guy behind the raceboat, but in 1952 he placed second in his class driving a raceboat in the Sammamish Slough Race. Both he and Bob Schmidt, another skier and Slough Race driver, are members of the Olympic Water-Ski Club.

Bill Farr-water skier in 1952 Sammamish Ski-Race.

The day's weather was windy with strong gusts. Jack Shields, who lived across the way on Lake Washington, went bottoms-up on Lake Washington while making his approach to the Slough entrance. Bob Waite, Farr's neighbor, navigated the full length of the Slough, only to suffer a similar fate, on Lake Sammamish. Of the 60 boats that started, 40 finished the first heat and only 33 received the final checkered flag.

Fred Bischoff paddling to start line at Ward's Resort.

Rockey Stone 3rd Unlimited Runabout.

The race is a perennial crowd pleaser and never fails to draw thousands of spectators. Miles of shoreline provide free grandstand seats for all with the more tortuous turns and low bridges drawing the larger crowds. Winding its way through the placid countryside of the Sammamish Valley, the Slough has become one of the most unique race courses in the World.

Don Benson 1st A-Runabout.

Harold Tolford 1st D-Runabout.

This year's course included a new and dangerous hazard in the Slough, a log boom that clogged the existing narrow channel. The log boom held floating logs that were pulled up into Woodinville's Saginaw Sawmill that was built in 1953. The log boom was reminiscent of the past when loggers clogged and blocked the Slough. Now the raceboats had another challenge navigating the Slough, when they battle each other for that skinny lane next to the boom only wide enough for one boat.

1954 Saginaw Sawmill in Woodinville with notorious one-lane channel in Slough.

1954 Sammamish Slough Race Results (in order of overall finish)

Place	Driver	Class	From	Boat #	Boat Name	Time
1	Bill Farr	Unlimited Hydro	Bellevue	224-R	Wee Willy	33:12.0
2	Fred Bischoff	Unlimited Hydro	Everett	R-206	*	33:13.1
3	Rockey Stone	Unlimited Runabout	Willamina, OR	R-26	Over Easy	*
1	Harold Tolford	D-Runabout	Seattle	78-R	Sandbox	*
2	Al Benson	D-Runabout	Seattle	R-78	*	*
3	Carl Biber	DU-Runabout	Tacoma	T-56	*	*
1	John Robinson	B-Hydro	Seattle	*	*	*
2	Ed Jensen	B-Hydro	Seattle	*	*	*
3	Red Taylor	B-Hydro	Seattle	560-R	*	*
1	Ken Ferguson	B-Runabout	Seattle	*	*	*
2	Andy Thompson	B-Runabout	Seattle	250-R	*	*
3	Bob Jennings	B-Runabout	Seattle	56-R	*	*
1	Orin Edson	C-Runabout	Seattle	*	*	*
2	Sid Sato	C-Runabout	Carnation	38-R	*	*
3	Ron Hall	C-Runabout	Seattle	*	*	*
1	Don Benson	A-Runabout	Seattle	29-R	Ill-Eagle	*
2	Del Haack	A-Runabout	Seattle	*	*	*
3	Lance Puckett	A-Runabout	Seattle	*	*	*

Some boat numbers, boat names and times unavailable

1954 Race Schedule (Partial)

Jan 3	Annual "Old-Timers" Cruise
Feb 21	Annual Bar Pilots Cruise
April 25	19th Sammamish Slough Race
May 9	Lake Sammamish Regatta-Gateway Grove
May 23	6th Sammamish Water-Ski Race
May 30	Green Lake Memorial Day Regatta
June 20	Richland Regatta
June 27	Walla Walla Regatta
July 4	Devil's Lake, Oregon
July 18	Regional Championships-Moses Lake
July 31-Aug 1	Lake Osoyoos-Oroville
Aug 6,8	Green Lake Seafair Regatta
Aug 9-10	Mile Trials-East Channel, Lake Washington
Aug 14-15	Electric City
Aug 27-30	Stock Outboard Nationals-Fox River Depere, WI
Sept 12	Lake Sammamish Regatta-Gateway Grove
Sept 25-26	Outboard National Championships, Pasco

Slough Race poster by Lin Pitts.

1954 Golden Water-Ski Race

"Taylor Pulls Taulbee To Ski Victory" was headlined in the *Times* sports section on May 24. George Taylor's outboard runabout pulled Walt Taulbee to victory in the

Unlimited Class of the annual Golden Water-Ski Race on the Sammamish Slough. The team, entering the race for the first time, covered the 28 miles from Kenmore to Lake Sammamish and back in 57:05 some 19 minutes faster than the second-place finishers, Norma Williams towed by Bob Batie with a time of 76:15.

Those were the only two Unlimited teams to finish both heats. Bill Schumacher, Sr., towed by Lin Ivey was awarded third-place overall based on their third in the first heat. Motor troubles and spills forced many teams out of the race–There were no serious accidents or injuries.

Mike Cunningham towed by Art "Bud" Sullivan was the victor in the Limited Class completing the course with a time of 63:65. Eleven-year-old Billy Schumacher skied to second-place behind Red Taylor's boat in 70:31, quite an accomplishment for a youngster. He obviously followed in the footsteps of his father, Bill Sr., who kept in great shape working out at home and in the gym. They lived just north of our home on Lake Washington where they were always practicing their family water-skiing aquatics for the many exhibitions they performed throughout the Northwest.

1954 Tidbits

Harold Tolford, Jr., was elected commodore of the SOA during the American Power Boat Association's 50-year anniversary. Serving with him were George Haack, vice-commodore; Ed Tolford, secretary-treasurer; Ken Ferguson, sergeant-at-arms and Chuck Hickling as trustee. A 50-year history of the APBA was written in the November issue of the 1953 *APBA Propeller* by Mel Crook, then chairman of the inboard racing commission.

Ed (left) & Harold Tolford.

Bill Rankin won the C-Service Runabout Nationals at Pasco, Washington, in September and received the APBA Charles E. Rochester Medal. Jim Benson set the JU Runabout mile record at 26.985 mph at Devil's Lake, Oregon, along with V.J. "Jim" Spinner in the B-Stock Hydro class at 60.482 mph and Bob Batie driving Al Benson's DU Runabout at 59.367 mph.

Doc Jones was awarded the SOA Sportsmanship Award, Don Benson received the club's high-point trophy and Jim Spinner received the "Helldivers Award" (for flipping-over your boat). Jack Colcock, the first Sammamish Slough Race winner in 1934, was selected as the Region 10 chairman.

The first half of the 1950s brought in a new breed of outboard motors for racing along with a completely new class of stock utility runabouts that were introduced by the APBA. This was the first time since before the war that a new outboard motor was introduced (Mercury) that was ideal for racing. The Slough Race crowds and race entries continued to grow along with its coverage by local newspapers, various magazines and the motion picture industry with their short-subject newsreels shown in theaters across the country.

So, goes another year of madness in the Sammamish Slough, a snake dance of sorts, which was called the "Seattle Snake Dance" by local friend of boat racing and free-lance writer, Russ Swanson. His article in the 1952 Boat Sport, titled "Seattle Snake Dance" compared the shape of the Slough to a snake in motion, certainly a fitting description as all of us former drivers will attest.

1954 Howard "Andy" Anderson Unlimited Hydro.

1954-Al Benson D-Runabout 2nd place.

1954 Rockey Stone 3rd Unlimited Runabout.

1954 John "Jack" Swanberg D-Runabout.

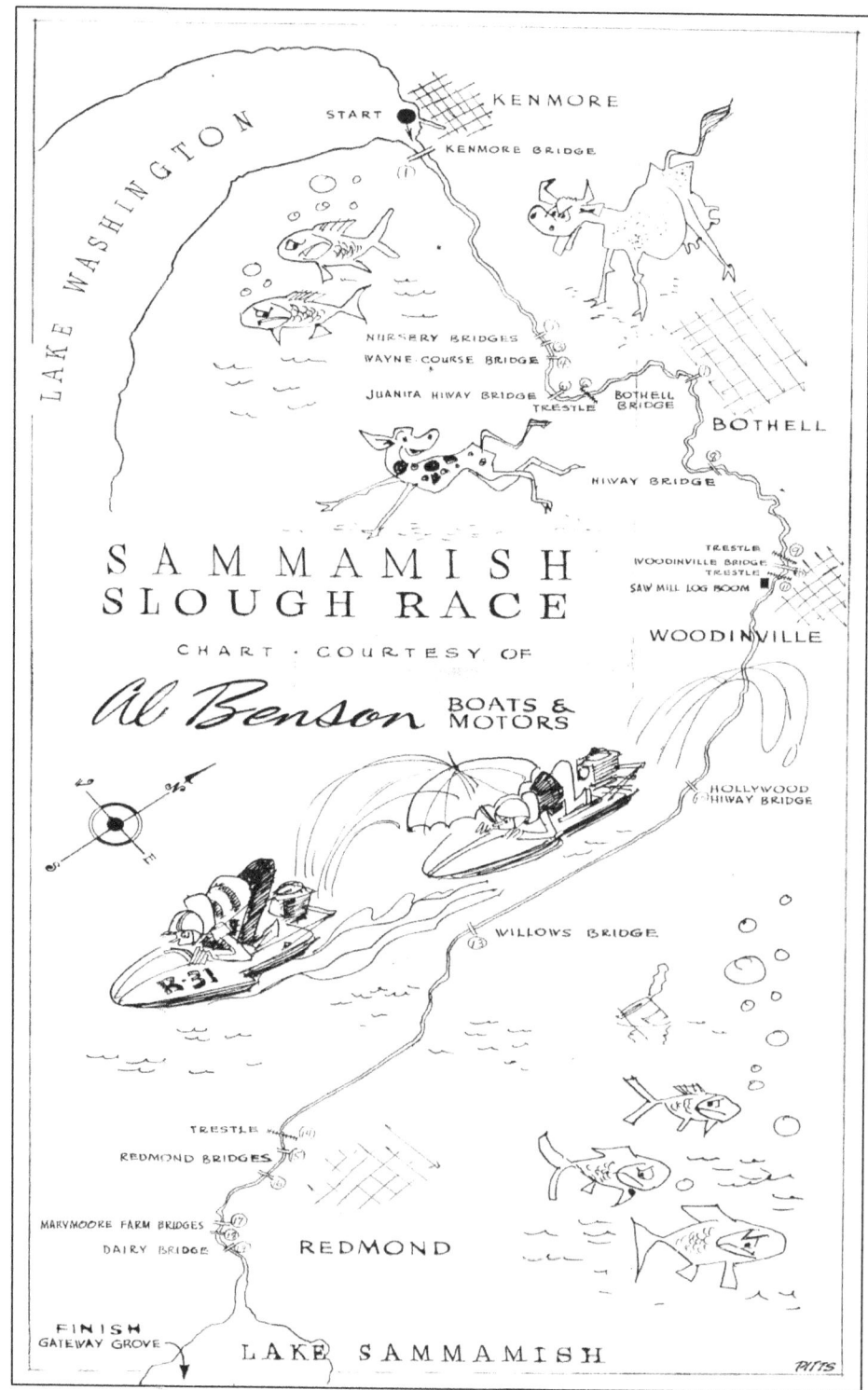

1950s cartoon map of race course by family friend and neighbor, artist Lin Pitts.

1953 Outboard Race at Gateway Grove on Lake Sammamish (not Slough Race)—Great photo by Bob Carver taken from water slide platform.

Chapter 10

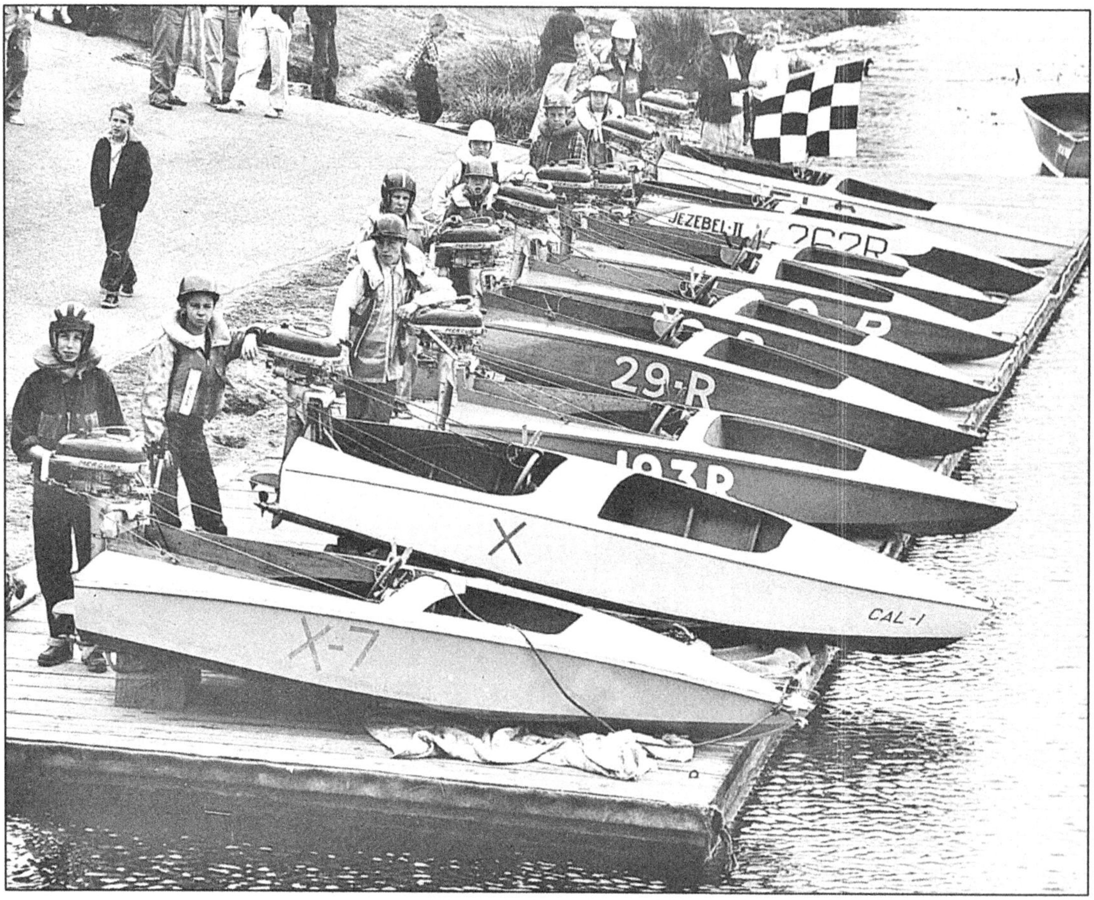

1954 Green Lake JU Class-bottom up: John Freeman, Chuck Lyford, John Ford, Don Benson, Jim Benson, Mike Miller, Bill Schumacher, Herb Chevalier, Keith Balcom & Mr. John Ford Sr. holding checkered flag.

Slaughter in the Slough
1955-1959

"SLAUGHTER ON SLOUGH"
"Bob Rautenberg Skids at Clothes Line-Heads Out of Boat
Joe Trumbly Drydocks at Moorage Available Sign"

-The Seattle Daily Times, April 14, 1958-

Slough Race Draws Top Outboard Pilots

Seattle's outboard racing enthusiasts were busy preparing to invade the 20th annual Sammamish Slough Race. The Slough Race, one of the nation's top outboard events and acclaimed for its wide spectator appeal, already had drawn many entries early in April. Race chairman, Al Benson, announced that notable drivers entered were Bill Farr, last year's winner; Rockey Stone of Willamina, Oregon, second in the unlimited class last year, and perennial competitor, Lin Ivey who says he's going to retire each year but always seems to un-retire for this race–his favorite race.

Ivey, who spends half his time with the powerboat fleet and the rest with the racers, is ready to go with what outboarders term as a "hot" engine. He's taken an antiquated 50-horsepower pre-WWII engine and rebuilt it into a 60-horsepower machine for the Unlimited class. Benson and the other race officials have changed the starting format from a "wild" start, all starting at once, to each class starting at intervals–mainly to facilitate the variety of classes and high number that had pre-registered.

Other entries included Bob Waite and Bud Sullivan in the Unlimited class; Al Benson, Ben Soil and George Taylor in DU-Runabout; Walt Edson and Sid Sato of

Carnation, CU-Runabout; Dan Sizemore, B-Runabout; and Don Benson, Billy Schumacher, Jr., Chuck Lyford and Jim Hale in the A-Runabout division.

Like in years past, the start will be at Ward's Resort in Kenmore, then up the Slough into Lake Sammamish where the boats will finish the first heat at Gateway Grove. There the drivers will knock off for lunch, make repairs if needed, refuel and then head back down the Slough for the finish in Bothell. The Bothell Quarterback Club cosponsored the event along with the Seattle Outboard Association. The race, scheduled for Sunday April 24, was sanctioned by the American Power Boat Association for the first time in its 20-year history.

Something new to the Slough this year will be the introduction of the pint-sized A-Stock hydros into the competition. A large contingent of 20 entries is expected to line up for the start. In the past, the A's weren't considered because of the many hazards that would face the small craft. In the early days Otis Clinton and others raced their small boats successfully through the Slough with Clinton taking second overall several times in the late '40s. Seventy-five drivers were expected to enter the competition that was scheduled to start the first heat at 11 am. The fastest class, the Unlimiteds, was to start first, then down the lineup with the slowest of the seven classes last.

Sullivan Conquers First Slough Race

Art "Bud" Sullivan wore a smile after the race because he knows the secret of winning the Slough Race. Sullivan, 21, kept his D-Stock Hydro at a 50-mph pace throughout the 26-mile course from Lake Washington and back to Bothell. The important thing was…he kept out of trouble.

Sullivan, a carpenter by trade, was a local boy from Kenmore. His employer gave him $500 a year to sponsor his racing, otherwise he couldn't afford it. His Mercury racing engine was originally a 40-horsepower fishing motor he bought used. He told me during an interview that it was well used but after converting it to a racing motor, it ran well on his D-Hydro. He purchased the raceboat after it was wrecked at a regatta in Eastern Washington, then re-built it and the rest is history.

An estimated 15,000 spectators who watched the event, will attest to the race being on the dangerous side. They were lining the banks, on bridges, in cow-pastures and some even perched in trees. Sullivan and seven other unlimited drivers opened the event with a quick turn around a single buoy off Kenmore before entering the Slough. Only six of the boats came out of the turn as Fred Bischoff and Bob Waite collided in the turn and both swamped out of commission, there on the spot. The others who made it around the buoy had to navigate under the Kenmore Bridge and along through a series of S-turns. Farther up they ran between the Wayne Golf Course and around more turns. A mile or so upstream they passed under the notorious Bothell Bridge where the course makes an abrupt right-hand turn under the bridge. At the same time, they had to miss the large concrete pillars on their left while the downriver current pushed their boats toward them. Further up, they encountered a series of S-turns, and a shallow gravely sandbar where Bear Creek emptied into the Slough.

1955 Unlimited start from Ward's Resort (L-R): Al Karelsen 58-R, Bill Farr 224-R, Lin Ivey R-27 *Poison Ivey*, Dick Brunes 760-R *Gotta Go*, Bud Sullivan 626-R, Bob Waite 222-R, Fred Bischoff R-206.

They passed under a total of 19 bridges, while one was under construction in Woodinville with only a 6-foot gap to drive through. Then through a narrow channel alongside the dangerous sawmill log boom in Woodinville, through two straightaway sections leading to Redmond and into Lake Sammamish. They finished their first heat at Gateway Grove on the northwest side of the lake.

Lin Ivey trailed Sullivan by a matter of yards until he reached a point just south of Redmond when his 60-horsepower engine broke a crankshaft and he coasted to a stop, and out of the race for good. Sullivan drove the rest of the way uncontested and won the first heat. On the return run, unlimited drivers Bud Sullivan and last year's winner, Bill Farr, hit the Slough battling neck and neck all the way down to Bothell. Farr finally got his chance and passed Sullivan just before the finish, to thrill the thousands of spectators, to win the second heat. Both drivers finished with a first and second and were tied in points for first-place. Sullivan was declared the victor after race officials added together the heat times and determined his was the quickest.

Close finish with Bill Farr just ahead of Bud Sullivan for first place in the downstream run at Bothell.

The Unlimited drivers weren't the only ones who ran into trouble. Harold Tolford, driving his D-Runabout, took two on the chin. On the trip up the Slough he caught a chine[1] and wound up in the water just below Bothell, a typical hazard if you're not really careful in the turns, especially in right-hand turns in a runabout. The drivers are only used to left-hand turns, which are normal in the regular courses. "I got started up again, but lost the lead and trailed the pack," he said. Then, on the return trip, Tolford led the D's across Lake Sammamish, but climbed a bank on the first downstream turn of the Slough and settled for a tow the rest of the way to the finish in Bothell.

John Robinson, racing in the B-Hydro class, was leading on the downstream run to Bothell, when he was forced into the log boom at the Saginaw Sawmill in Woodinville. A pleasure boat somehow got on the course and blocked the one-lane passage at the boom. Robinson took evasive action and ran up over the logs. He was able to push his rig back

Hal Tolford D-Runabout restarted after incident.

---

[1] A "chine" in boating refers to a sharp change in angle in the cross section of a hull where it meets the water.

into the water and continued on to Bothell managing to take first-place in his class with a badly damaged craft.

Don Benson, on the other hand, had to take a back seat to his dad, Al, who walked off with the first-place trophy in the D-Runabout class. Don's A-Runabout also caught a chine and flipped on the return trip just before the finish line in Bothell. A group of spectators caught it as it barrel-rolled over the bank. When I interviewed my brother later we reminisced. He said, "One or two turns just before the finish at the Bothell Bridge, I caught a chine and rolled over on the bank. I was sailing (though the air) down the Slough and someone grabbed and pulled me out of the water. I staggered back to the boat that they had already up-righted in the water with the engine shut-off. I remember the engine was screaming its heart out; someone must have shut her down. Apparently, my foot caught the throttle wire as I was thrown out and it got kinked, keeping the motor running at full throttle. The crowd coaxed me to get back in, but I wasn't really ready to go! I was dripping wet and dazed a little. I told myself, 'okay, let's go.' I fired her up and still managed to get second place."

Don Benson wet after flip & father Al, glad he's OK.

Billy Schumacher, who was right behind in second at the time, "bounced by" him just before he got back under way for his first victory in the Slough. Ironically, he was driving a special super-lightweight boat that Dad was building for Don earlier in the year. But Mr. Schumacher's money talked him out of it and the rest was history as Billy would have an unbelievable year in setting records, winning championships and receiving a host of awards for his boat racing achievements.

AU winner Billy Schumacher in *Lil Bill* at Bothell finish line in raceboat Al Benson originally built for his son Don.

A field of 51 starters in eight classes answered the gun and managed to twist their way through the serpentine course to Lake Sammamish in the event sponsored by the Seattle Outboard Association. The thousands of spectators, who watched a thrilling race between Bud Sullivan and Bill Farr, witnessed by far the most publicized race to date, all free of charge!

Articles and photos were published in *Boat Sport*, *Speed Age*, *Sea and Pacific Motor Boat*, *Seattle Post-Intelligencer*,

Victor Bud Sullivan posing for photo after race.

Seattle Times, *Mercury Flyer* (for outboard motor dealers), *Bothell Citizen*, Lincoln High School *Totem* Newspaper (Don Benson's High School) and other city papers. A race announcer in Bothell kept spectators informed of the race's progress via loud speakers that were placed along the Slough's banks.

The race was also filmed via helicopter by *Life* magazine (see photo below) and covered by *Sports Illustrated*. Freelance photographers, Bob Carver, Russ Swanson and Bob Miller were taking photos at the start and in various places along the course. *Times* and *PI* staff photographers were stationed near the finish line in Bothell. The Sammamish Slough Race was the public's favorite race to watch in the Pacific Northwest at a time before major-league sports were drawing the crowds in Seattle.

D & B Runabout start with press helicopter above; Jerry Bryant watching on his large yacht's bow-upper right.

Peggy Batie presenting trophy to Bud Sullivan.

D & B Runabouts before start.

13 boat B-Hydro start: John Robinson 509-R won 1st place overall despite slow start (5th from bottom).

260 | Taming of the Slough

Big crowd waiting for finishers in Bothell-judge's stand and finish line across Slough on near side of bridge.

Chuck Lyford in A-Runabout, his first Slough Race.

John Robinson's B-Hydro at Gateway Grove.

1955 Sammamish Slough Race Results (in order of overall finish)

Place	Driver	Class	From	Boat #	Boat Name	Time
1	Art "Bud" Sullivan	Unlimited Hydro	Seattle	626-R	Static I	*
2	Bill Farr	Unlimited Hydro	Bellevue	224-R	Wee Willy	*
3	Al Karelsen	Unlimited Hydro	Seattle	58-R	*	*
1	Al Benson	D-Runabout	Seattle	R-78	*	*

2	George Taylor	D-Runabout	Seattle	108-R	*	*
3	Ken Ferguson	D-Runabout	Seattle	*	Needle Nose	*
1	Sid Sato	C-Runabout	Carnation	38-R	*	*
1	John Robinson	B-Hydro	Seattle	509-R	*	*
2	Harold Davies	B-Hydro	Seattle	*	*	*
3	Hank Chevalier	B-Hydro	Seattle	*	*	*
1	Andy Thompson	B-Runabout	Redmond	250-R	*	*
2	Howard Anderson	B-Runabout	Edmonds	56-R	*	*
3	Gerald Lamplin	B-Runabout	Seattle	*	*	*
1	Ray Holiday	A-Stock Hydro	Carnation	38-R	*	*
2	Bud Stuart	A-Stock Hydro	Seattle	*	*	*
3	Jim Hale	A-Stock Hydro	Edmonds	62-R	*	*
1	V.F. Halsey	DU-2 Runabout	Seattle		*	*
2	Jack Swanberg	DU-2 Runabout	Seattle	109-R	*	*
3	Carl Biber	DU-2 Runabout	Tacoma	T-56	*	*
1	Billy Schumacher	A-Runabout	Seattle	3-R	Lil Bill	*
2	Don Benson	A-Runabout	Seattle	29-R	Ill-Eagle	*
3	Lance Puckett	A-Runabout	Seattle	*	*	*

Some boat numbers, boat names and times unavailable

The historic Cain & Lytle Shingle Mill of the late 1890s was located in Bothell on the Squak Slough just to the East of where the Bothell Bridge is today, on the downtown side of the Sammamish River. The mill could cut an amazing 125,000 shingles and 25,000 board feet of lumber in a day. They used the Slough to float the logs and shingle bolts to a chain conveyor which pulled the material out of the water and up into the sawing area. The mill site below was located where the Sammamish Slough Race judge's stand is in the photo on the preceding page (see arrow pointing toward judge's stand).

1899: Lytle Shingle Mill was located on the site of the race judge's stand shown in photo on preceding page.

Stock Outboard Nationals and Divisionals go to Northwest

The big news for 1955, aside from the Slough Race, was the awarding of the APBA Stock Outboard Nationals and Divisionals to Region 10. The Stock National Championships were slated to run in the Northwest for the first time. The Divisionals were penciled in for Seattle at Green Lake during Seafair week and the grand finale, the Stock National Championships, were slated to run in late August on Devil's Lake at Lincoln City, Oregon.

The credit for obtaining the APBA events was due to the enormous efforts of Region 10 Chairman Jack Colcock (first Sammamish Slough Race winner), Doc Jones (Mercury outboard motor distributor) and SOA commodore and driver, Jim Spinner.

Seafair Western Divisionals on Green Lake

Three Seattle drivers were winners on Saturday August 7, the final day of competition of the Western Divisional outboard races on Green Lake. They were Billy Schumacher in the A-Runabout class, Harold Tolford in D-Runabout and Bill Rankin in the Runabout Free-For-All. On Friday, August 6, Schumacher won the JU-Runabout class, Hugh Entrop in D-Stock Hydro, and Harold Tolford was the victor in the DU-Runabouts after Rockey Stone was disqualified for jumping the gun.

Schumacher, Entrop and Tolford all qualified for the Stock Nationals which were held at Devil's Lake, Oregon on August 27-29. The other winners were all out-of-towners. The results were as follows:

JU Runabout:	Bill Schumacher 1st, Chuck Lyford 2nd, Jimmy Benson 3rd
AU Runabout:	Bill Schumacher 1st, Bill Larson-OR 2nd, Bob Parish-CA 3rd
BU Runabout:	Bill Larson-OR 1st, Gil Ward-OR 2nd, Ward Rogers-CA 3rd
CU-Runabout:	P. Schnurbusch-CA 1st, Sid Sato-Carnation 2nd, Peter Laush-Enumclaw 3rd
DU-Runabout:	Harold Tolford 1st, Paul Woodroffe-OR 2nd, Ned Colett-OR 3rd
A-Stock Hydro;	W. Granberg-CA 1st, Jack Leak-Tacoma 2nd, Bill Schumacher 2nd
B-Stock Hydro:	Robert Brownell-OR 1st, Bob Parish-CA 2nd, Don Atchinson-OR 3rd
D-Stock Hydro:	Hugh Entrop 1st, Dick Brunes 2nd, Paul Woodroffe-OR 3rd
A-Out. Hydro:	Jack Leak-Tacoma 1st, E. Belluomini-CA 2nd, Don Benson 3rd
B-Out. Hydro:	Oliver Dupuis-MT 1st, Don Atchison-OR 2nd, Gil Ward-OR 3rd
C-Out. Hydro:	Bud Wiget-CA 1st, Art Pierre-CA 2nd, Rockey Stone-OR 3rd
F-Out. Hydro:	Bud Wiget-CA 1st, Paul Woodroffe-OR 2nd, Dick Brunes 3rd
C-Ser. Hydro:	Steve Gantner-MO 1st, Art Pierre-CA 2nd, Bill Rankin 3rd
C-Rac Runabout:	Rockey Stone-OR 1st, Bud Wiget-CA 2nd, Roy Hanson-CA 3rd
C-Ser Runabout:	Rockey Stone-OR 1st, Mel Callaway-Spokane 2nd, Oliver Dupuis-MT 3rd
Free-For-All:	Bill Rankin 1st, Fred Bischoff-Edmonds 2nd, Bud Wiget-CA 3rd

1955: Hugh Entrop's amazing world record holding D-Hydro "cabover" designed & built based on Boeing wind-tunnel tests. The revolutionary design, built at his Seattle home, was copied by many but never equaled.

Persistence Rewards Skier Moore

Dick Brunes towed the "old man" of the "Golden Water-Ski" race, Ray Moore, to his first Unlimited-Class victory in the Sammamish Slough on Sunday, May 8. Moore, who had been competing annually in the event for the past decade, never had scored in that class. Racing in the faster Unlimiteds, the two negotiated the hair-pin turns of the Slough without a single hitch. More than half of the field of 23 that started failed to finish. On the trip up the Slough, Brunes and Moore placed second to recent Slough Race winner, Bud Sullivan, who was towing Mike Cunningham. But on the down Slough swing, it was Brunes and Moore all the way.

Two Taylors, George and Red, were the hard luck drivers of the race. Both took bad spills. George hung his Unlimited on a corner at a turn in Woodinville on the up-Slough trip and ended up in the water with his skier, Walt Taulbee. The two had won the title in 1954. Red, ran into a log jam at Woodinville. He was towing young Billy Schumacher, Jr., who was an emerging outboard driver. He and Billy dried-off and watched the rest of the race from the Slough's bank.

Sullivan, after capturing the first heat, got off to a bad start going down Slough when he developed engine trouble. The fact that he crashed into a pier in Lake Sammamish didn't help matters either, but he and Cunningham limped back to Kenmore for third-place in the heat and second overall for the Unlimiteds. Sid Sato of Carnation, pulled Dave Eaden to victory in the limited class.

Race chairman, Bill Schumacher, Sr., and his other officials jammed all the boats into two classes at race time. Earlier, three classes had been slated to go based on pre-entry estimates: Unlimited, B-Hydro and B-Runabout, and the slower DU-2 Runabouts. The change was because the number of entries registered the morning of the race were fewer than expected. The results were as follows:

<u>Unlimited Class:</u> Ray Moore-Dick Brunes 1st, Mike Cunningham-Bud Sullivan 2nd, Mac Millen-Jack Hedley 3rd, Dr. Lew West-Dick Hall 4th.
<u>Limited Class:</u> Dave Eaden-Sid Sato 1st, Bill Semon-Bob Blair 2nd, Gary and Jack Swanberg 3rd, Ron and Don Ibsen 4th.

Devil's Lake Stock Outboard Nationals

"Prize-Laden Outboarders Home" was the small but important headline in the *Seattle Times* on September 4. Most of the weekend coverage was still buzzing about the Seafair Unlimited Hydroplane race run earlier in August. A Detroit boat, *Gale V*, driven by Lee Schoenith, won by a few seconds over Bill Muncey's *Miss Thriftway* and took the Gold Cup back to Michigan, along with the incredible historic coverage of the 360-degree flip of Stan Sayres' *Slow-mo-shun V* during qualifying.

A handful of happy Seattle outboard youngsters, teenage and less, were back in town after the weekend with a load of trophies and some world records from the recent Stock Outboard Championships held on August 28-30 at Devil's Lake, Oregon. Paced by 12-year-old Billy Schumacher, Jr., the Seattle drivers took home four national titles and set three world records. The points totaled by the Seattle contingent were tops for the nation with more than 400 drivers competing in the first Stock Nationals ever run in the Pacific Northwest.

Schumacher was the meet's high-point champion and was awarded the "Muckler Trophy" for his accomplishments. Pretty Ginny Lea Lyford, 12, of Seattle, the only girl driver in the competition, finished third in the Junior Utility Runabout class behind her brother, Chuck, 14, who took second. Schumacher's feats included:

1. National Championship, Junior Utility Runabout
2. National Championship, A-Runabout
3. Bettered world record for JU Runabout in 5-mile competition at 27.217 mph over the former mark of 26.985 mph set by Jimmy Benson in 1954.
4. Set a mile-straightaway record for the A-Runabout class at 46.401 mph.
5. Won fourth place in the A-Hydro competition

Don Benson, 16, won the A-Stock Hydro title and 21-year-old Bud Sullivan, who won the Sammamish Slough Race earlier, was the National Champion in D-Stock Hydro and fellow SOA member, Dick Brunes, was third. Johnny Sangster set a world record for five-mile competition in the B-Stock Runabout class clocking in at 47.493 mph and finished third in the B-Stock Runabout competition. Ken Ferguson (not shown in photo), was third in the D-Stock Runabout class.

1955 National Champions (LtoR): Bud Sullivan 1st DSH, Ginny Lea Lyford 3rd JUR, Chuck Lyford 2nd JUR, Billy Schumacher 1st JUR & ASR, Don Benson 1st ASH. Taller back row: Dick Brunes 3rd DSR and Johnny Sangster 2nd BSR.

Don Benson: A-Stock Hydro National Champion getting a lift to kiss the Devil's Lake Regatta queen to the delight of the guests at the awards banquet after race.

1955 Race Schedule (Partial)

Jan 2	Annual "Old-Timers" Cruise
Feb 20	Annual Bar Pilots Cruise
April 24	20th Sammamish Slough Race
May 8	7th Sammamish Water-Ski Race
May 22	Lake Sammamish Regatta-Lk Sammamish State Park
June 5	Silver Lake
June 18	Fall City-Snoqualmie River
July 2-3	Devil's Lake, OR
July 9-10	Regionals Electric City, WA
July 17	Moses Lake
July 24	Pasco
July 30-31	Oroville, WA
Aug 4-6	Western Divisionals-Green Lake Seafair Regatta
Aug 28-30	Stock Outboard Nationals-Devil's Lake, OR

Sammamish Flood Control Project Gets Budget O.K.

Senator Warren G. Magnuson announced good news for the farmers and residents of the Sammamish Valley on May 5. The Senator said that the Federal Bureau of the Budget had approved a $1,229,000 flood control project for Lake Sammamish. The project plan was to improve the Lake Sammamish outlet, widen the overall river channel, increase the width of Redmond's Bear Creek near its mouth and construct a low levee along the left bank of North Creek.

It was expected to prevent the annual flooding and offset a flood loss of $103,500 annually. Army Engineers said $825,000 was for Federal construction and the remaining funds were to be used for lands and alterations of highways and farm bridges. This was the first major step toward "Taming of the Slough" an event that dramatically changed the Sammamish Slough Race for its duration.

1955 Tidbits

Veteran outboard driver, V.J. "Jim" Spinner, Jr., from Mercer Island was elected commodore of the SOA for 1956 during the club meeting on December 2. The other new officers were Ed Tolford, vice-commodore; Jim Hale, secretary-treasurer and Ken Ferguson, sergeant-at-arms. The club had been holding its monthly meetings at the Capo Club in Lake City since they moved away from the Sand Point Yacht club in 1952.

Commodore Spinner

As it turned out, 1955 was a huge year for the Seattle Outboard Association, with four national championships and a host of world records. At one time the Northwest held all the stock outboard world records. In addition to the highly publicized Sammamish Slough Race and the Western Divisionals and Stock Outboard Nationals at Devil's Lake, Billy Schumacher had one of the most successful years of any outboard race driver in the Northwest to date. A capper for the year was KING-TV's airing of this year's Sammamish Slough Race, and nationwide coverage of the events highlights. The SOA Sportsman Award went to Harold Tolford.

1955: JU Driver Billy Schumacher showing off his winnings for the year.

Son Billy congratulated by father Bill, Sr.

Jim Spinner awarding High Point Trophy.

1956

It was hard to beat last year's successes in outboarding with the Divisionals and Nationals all being run in the Northwest and the triumphs of the Seattle Outboard Association's new crop of young and talented drivers. This year the famous Sammamish Slough Race came of age with its 21st running. This and the Sammamish Bar Pilots Cruise filled the bill along with more major racing events and continued national news reels of the coveted competition.

Commodore Jim Spinner

Maintaining or improving the club's schedule of events was the responsibility of Jim Spinner who was elected commodore of the SOA. Spinner was an extremely likeable person, a successful outboard driver and a good leader. He was equally qualified as a race official for the local, regional and national organizations. Serving behind the scenes with him was Jim Hale as club secretary-treasurer. The other officers were not publicized.

Teenage Drivers and Younger in Slough Race

"Many Teenage Drivers In Slough Race" was headlined in the *Seattle Times* sports section on April 13. Teenage drivers were advertised to be in the majority for this year's Sammamish Slough Race per Al Benson, race chairman. They were expected to represent more than half of the 60-odd entries. "Twenty of 'em never have raced before," said Benson, who allowed the youngsters to race in the classes with a minimum age limit of 14. Faced with the largest entry list it has yet had, the Seattle Outboard Association had to split the regatta into seven staggered sections.

At noon, the "big ones," the Unlimiteds or F-Hydro class, was set to start from Ward's Resort in Kenmore, followed at five-minute intervals by class D-Runabouts, then B-Stock Hydros, A-Runabouts and finally the 35-Runabouts. The upstream heat was arranged to finish this year at Idylwood Resort for the first time. Idylwood was next door to Gateway Grove, the past half-way point for most of the previous races, located about a mile from the Slough entrance on the west shore of Lake Sammamish. They were scheduled to get the starting nod at 1:30 pm for the downstream heat with the usual finish in Bothell.

The excitement was high for the youngsters 8 to 14 who finally got their chance to race in the Slough in the relatively new "Junior Utility Runabout" class, which was run for the first time in the event. The special race, with all the young drivers, including myself, fostered by Al Benson, was slated to start from Kenmore at 12:35 pm and finish to the wave of the checkered flag a few miles upstream in Bothell, among thousands of spectators. The progress of the race was announced over a sound system with loudspeakers set-up along the Slough downstream and upstream from the finishing point.

Another event, an advertised race between Seattle radio disk jockeys, was also planned to make a run to Bothell following the juniors' start. The radio guys were all over this during their live broadcasts. Each participating radio station was constantly chattering about how they were going beat the others in a wild and crazy event and threatening that some surprises were in store for their fellow competitors and to the delight of the spectators in Kenmore and Bothell.

Sullivan to Defend

Bud Sullivan, in *Static II*, an Unlimited class boat, will defend the over-all title. Lin Ivey, always a top contender for the crown, is better known this year as the prospective driver for the *Miss Seattle*, the rebuilt *Slo-mo-shun V,* in the Seafair Trophy unlimited hydroplane race. Ivey will drive the classic "step" hydro (see Chapter 7), the *Thunderbird* (R-74) with his usual custom made, high powered 4-60 engine. Bill Farr, 1954 winner, was looking for his second win and hard-luck driver Bob Waite was after his first win in the annual classic.

The local youngsters entered were Billy Schumacher, 13, Chuck Lyford 14, the first lady of the Slough, Ginney Lea Lyford, 12, Jimmy Benson, 12, Jackie Holden, 10, and local Bothell resident, 8-year-old Charley Walters. And for the first time five Canadian Unlimited drivers from the Vancouver, B.C., outboard club were entered.

Third Try-First Finish-First Victory

He had been trying to win this thing for three years and finally mastered the racecourse. Bob Waite, a young steel products salesman, staged an exciting comeback to capture the overall title in the annual Sammamish Slough Race on Sunday, April 15. Waite, 31, snaked his Class-D hydro over the 26-mile course in 31:53, a new record and did it in a field of nearly 100 boats. He was awarded the Jackens Grill perpetual trophy which Sullivan and Farr had won before him.

The outboard fraternity was pulling for Waite. It was his first race since a serious accident befell him in a race at Silver Lake, the spring of 1955, when he was hospitalized for 10 weeks. This was Waite's first finish in three tries and his first triumph. In his two previous attempts, he had fallen along the wayside on the upstream run between Kenmore and Lake Sammamish. This time Waite made the runs up and down the Sammamish as if he'd owned the river for years, winning both ends of the big race. Closest behind him was newcomer Dick Brunes in second, then veteran Bill Farr, third (1954 titlist) and second time Slough racer Al Karelsen, in fourth place.

1956: Bob Waite crossing Bothell finish line in first place; his first overall win and finish in Unlimited class.

More than half the boats entered failed to finish. Noticeably absent at the finish line (adjacent the Bothell Bridge) were Bud Sullivan, last year's winner, and Lin Ivey. Ivey, slated to drive the *Miss Seattle* unlimited hydro in next summer's Seafair Trophy Race, continued to have bad luck in the Slough Race. On the way up while driving his classy and powerful *Thunderbird* hydro, his boat barrel-rolled onto a bank and threw him into the water. With help from nearby spectators he was able to get the boat back into the water and on his way with minimal time loss. He finished the first heat, but motor trouble like in the past, kept him from making the downstream run.

More spills thrilled an estimated 40,000 spectators up and down the course. It's hard to match Ivey's tribulations. The worst of the many accidents was the experience of Dick Larson right in front of a crowd of thousands in Bothell. Larson plowed into one of the concrete pillars of the Bothell Bridge wrecking his boat and battering his nose. However, except for that skinned-up nose and some sore ribs, he came out well enough to drag the remains of his demolished craft to the bank.

Johnny Robinson and Jerry Pratt of Vancouver, B. C., had similar tales of woe when they both flipped. Robinson, last year's B-Hydro winner, cut a corner too sharp and over he went on the upstream run in his fast B-Hydro. Pratt had double trouble. He went over in a test run before the race and then took an official dunking on the way up the Slough, however, unlike Robinson, Pratt managed to finish both the heats. No one was seriously injured.

Oregon sawmill owner, Rockey Stone, never an overall winner but often in second, captured the D-Runabout class this time. He was in command all the way up and downstream winning both heats. Stone, a championship record-holding veteran driver from Willamina, Oregon, was old enough to be the father of some of the other young winners, particularly Donnie Benson. Donnie, oldest son of race chairman Al Benson, won the A-Hydro division, with a perfect run up and back. Another youngster, Chuck Lyford, upset Billy Schumacher for the A-Runabout title. Schumacher, who placed second, was the reigning national champion and world record-holder in the class.

One of the most exciting races was the Junior Utility class open to 8 to 14-year olds. Harvard Palmer and Jimmy Benson were close all the way, but Palmer nosed-out Benson at the finish, first. Right at the finish line an inboard pleasure craft was cruising along taking jeers from the crowd to "get out of there" as if they were welcome cries. Not seeing the Sunday drivers, Benson and Palmer made the last turn. Then found the small yacht in front of them. They almost drove onto the bank to dodge the intruder. Boos from the crowd and a few choice words from the announcer sent the unwelcome craft and its passengers on the way.

Youngsters Win Arm Load of Trophies

The new crop of young and talented drivers also included the first woman Slough Race driver since its inception, Ginny Lea Lyford, sister of Chuck; Jimmy Benson, brother of Don, and the youngest, Charley Walters. Young Walters is the son of Bud Walters, the local owner-operator of Walters Feed Mill and Boat Shop in Bothell. They were descendants of the pioneering Walters family of Bothell. All the young drivers except for Schumacher and Donnie Benson ran in the Slough Race for the first time. Our fathers, anxious, and our mother's very nervous, were all watching on the starting dock when the starting gun fired. They were relieved when we finished unscathed in Bothell and proud when we were rewarded with an armful of trophies during the presentation ceremonies following the race.

Hooligans Confronted by Bob Carver

Thank goodness for our soon-to-be famous photographer, Bob Carver, who came to our rescue before the race started. On his way up the Slough by boat to his favorite photo shooting site before the race, he discovered a rope that was strung across the river that was tied to trees on both sides by a couple of hooligans. He chased away the two devious young men who were in the process of securing the rope. It was set just high enough to miss the boats but low enough to severely injure the first unsuspecting drivers. Carver removed and confiscated the rope and was able to continue upstream to his spot in time to photograph all the action.

No drivers or race officials knew about the incident until Carver told them after the race. My brother and I learned about it after the race was over. As far as we knew no one caught the men and we were unsure if it was ever reported to the local authorities. The incident was discussed in detail at the next SOA club meeting.

The rope episode was only the beginning of more perils to come in the Slough. Poor control of the Slough with scores of pleasure boats running simultaneously in the narrow and tortuous course almost caused some other serious accidents. They barely missed by inches, head-on collisions with the high-speed boats that were racing toward them.

Prankster Spectators in Slough

This was the first bad year for pranksters in the Slough by a few devious and deranged spectators who threw things at the unsuspecting drivers as they speed up and down the course. A few kids set a very bad example for the mostly appreciative spectators who were entertained for free during a Sunday afternoon. Ed Karelsen, first time Slough Racer, a promising race boat builder and younger brother to fourth place unlimited driver Dave Karelsen, still remembers well his encounters near Bothell, during his one and only run in the Slough Race. During a phone interview in April, 2014, he said:

"They were throwing stuff off the bridges at you when you went under…I had one kid with a rock so big he couldn't lift it up, so an older kid helped him lift it over the side…it almost hit me and missed by only two feet!…then when I got to the straightaway (between Woodinville and Redmond), kids were shooting at me with BB guns…when I got back (finished the race), I said I'm not going to run this anymore!"

Did you also have chicken bones thrown at you? I asked.
"No, that was in Rockey Stone's boat…Yeah; he had a bunch of chicken bones thrown into his boat!"

This also happened to some other drivers during this race. Fortunately, no one was injured because of some spectator shenanigans, but many drivers were shaken by the unexpected experiences. Race officials learned a lesson about racecourse patrol management and safety for future races. Unfortunately, these incidents were only the start of things to come in future races as control of the crowd along 14-miles of river would prove to be difficult in the future.

Pie Fights and Disc Jockeys

The final group of boats left the Kenmore dock about 5 minutes after the JU class started but not without some fanfare. Three boats full of radio personalities (Disc jockeys), were stirring up the audience on the dock behind them. They were putting on a good show with jokes and ribbing. Out of nowhere several pies went a-flying between the comedian competitors. This really got the crowd's attention as more ribbing was going on. At the same time, they got the signal to start and off they went heading into the Slough. Bob Salter and Dick Stokey of radio station KJR led wire-to-wire followed by David Page and Don Einarson, and lastly Don Usher and Jack Hemingway of KAYO. The trailing boat was the official patrol boat that travels all the way up to check for stranded boats and that the course is clear for the second heat.

Disc jockeys ready for the start.

Pies a flying between teams.

KJR team leads the pack of three Disc Jockey boats across finish line in Bothell.

1956 Sammamish Slough Race Results (in order of overall finish)

Place	Driver	Class	From	Boat #	Boat Name	Time
1	Bob Waite	Unlimited Hydro	Bellevue	226-R	*	31:53
2	Dick Brunes	Unlimited Hydro	Kenmore	R-72	Lindy	*

3	Bill Farr	Unlimited Hydro	Bellevue	224-R	Wee Willy	*
1	Rockey Stone	D-Runabout	Willamina, OR	2-R	My Girl	*
2	George Taylor	D-Runabout	Seattle	108-R	*	*
3	Ken Ferguson	D-Runabout	Seattle	R-84	Needle Nose	*
1	Jim Hale	B-Hydro	Seattle	62-R	*	*
2	Kelly Sizemore	B-Hydro	Seattle	262-R	*	*
3	Ed Karelsen	B-Hydro	Seattle	82-R	*	*
1	Dick Leckenby	B-Runabout	Seattle	79-R	*	*
2	Jim Henry	B-Runabout	Edmonds	124-R	*	*
3	Andy Thompson	B-Runabout	Redmond	250-R	*	*
1	Don Benson	A-Stock Hydro	Seattle	V	*	*
2	John Freeman	A-Stock Hydro	Seattle	XX	*	*
3	Bob Kertley	A-Stock Hydro	Seattle	77-R	*	*
1	Chuck Lyford	A-Runabout	Seattle	27-R	CAL II	*
2	Billy Schumacher	A-Runabout	Seattle	3-R	Lil Bill	*
3	Arne Halverson	A-Runabout	Seattle	175-R	*	*
1	Harvard Palmer	JU-Runabout	Seattle	95-R	*	*
2	Jimmy Benson	JU-Runabout	Seattle	59-R	Sparks	*
3	Ginny Lea Lyford	JU-Runabout	Seattle	X	*	*
1	Sid Sato	36 Cu In Runabout	Carnation	38-R	*	*
2	John Swanberg	36 Cu In Runabout	Seattle	109-R	*	*
3	Joe Trumbly	36 Cu In Runabout	Seattle	56-R	*	*
1	Bob Salter & Dick Stokey	Disc Jockey Race	KJR Radio			
2	David Page & Don Einarson	Disc Jockey Race	Unknown station			
3	Don Usher & Jack Hemingway	Disc Jockey Race	KAYO Radio			

1956-Bob Waite overall winner.

Bob Waite's victory kiss from wife, Mary Ellen, holding Jackens Grill perpetual trophy.

Winners L-R front: Dick Leckenby, Bob Waite, Jim Hale, Chuck Lyford and Don Benson. Officials upper L-R: Cricket Callender, Jim Spinner, Jackie Wallace, Betty Kertis, Al Benson. Top: Ed & Hal Tolford.

Chuck Lyford, A-Runabout winner at Bothell finish line.

Don Benson, A-Hydro winner.

Kid Racers Mentored by Al Benson

When I was a youngster at 5 years of age, I bugged my father about having my own boat and motor. My brother had a little 8-foot inboard craft he called *Hot Box*. Eventually dad found me a safe 10-foot double ended duck-hunting boat. He attached a 2x4 board over the deck on one end which stuck out sufficiently for attachment of a small outboard motor. His motor of choice was an air-cooled ¼ horsepower *Elgin*, not speedy but light weight, safe and reliable.

I was instructed to not venture very far out beyond our dock on Lake Washington for safety reasons. So, I complied by running back and forth under the docks. The boat and motor were low enough to clear the docks under-structure in most cases as the lake was lowered in the summer during the boating seasons. It was tricky navigating under the docks because I had to duck my head and still be able to see where I was going. Occasionally, I glanced-off or hit a piling or two.

1956: Al Benson mentoring young drivers: L to R Herb Chevalier sitting, Del Haack, Don Benson, Al Benson, Jim Benson, John Ford.

This and my brother's experience prepared me for the next big venture in my life–outboard racing. As a little 8-year old, I was introduced to the Junior Utility Class, a class my father fostered locally in Seattle that was newly sanctioned by the APBA and part of SOA's new racing program. My brother Don, neighbors Billy Schumacher, John "Butch" Ford and Johnny Freeman, Chuck and Ginny Lea Lyford, Mike Miller, Herb Chevalier, Keith Balcom and Harvard Palmer were the first of the young drivers in the new class designated for 9 to 14-year-olds.

We started using boats designed for the AU Runabout class which were about 10-feet long because they were available at the time and mostly built by the Ballard boat builder and 1950 & 1952 Slough Race winner, Bob Jacobsen. The minimum length for a JU class hull was 9-feet and the motor displacement was 7.5 cubic inches maximum. The engine of choice was the 5-1/2 horsepower *Mark 5* Mercury fishing engine which was introduced in the early 1950s and produced by the Kiekhaefer Corporation in Fond du Lac, Wisconsin. The overall weight restriction was 190 pounds which included the boat, motor and driver. The class was approved by APBA in the early 1950's and Dad, being the entrepreneur, he was, saw an opportunity to bring young blood into the sport of outboard racing and sell more boats and motors. He supplied most of the outfits for the first class of drivers.

Our father set up a starting clock on our dock at our home below Lake City on Lake Washington and proceeded to instruct us how to make a proper start, including his tricks of the trade. My brother and I were hoping he kept a few just for us! The training was complete with starting flags he eagerly waved at us while mother, Dorothy (Dot), was running the clock. The training set a good foundation for the rest of our racing careers, some of whom became very famous like Billy Schumacher, my brother and Chuck Lyford. Most of us were good starters which was half the battle in competition.

1951: JU record holder Don Benson at D-Lake Oregon.

My brother set the first JU mile-trial world record at 22.692 mph on Devil's Lake in Western Oregon on 7/14/1951. He also set a mile-trial record in AU in 1953. Then I attempted to break the record in 1954, also at Devil's lake. It was the record that Butch (John) Ford set when he broke Don's record in 1953 in Seattle.

STOCK OUTBOARD RECORDS
1 MILE AS OF DECEMBER 31, 1951

CLASS	SPEED MPH	DATE	WHERE MADE	BOAT NAME	OWNER or DRIVER	BOAT	ENGINE
Class JU	22.692	7/14/51	Devil's Lake, Ore.	....	Don Benson	Morris	Mercury
Class AU	42.881	11/9/51	Salton Sea, Calif.	Skin Head	Jack Corner	Knapp	Mercury
Class BU	47.462	7/14/51	Devil's Lake, Ore.	Pearly Gates	Elgin T. Gates	Viking	Mercury
Class CU	40.684	11/10/51	Salton Sea, Calif.	Sir Echo	Cag Graham	DeSilva	Elto
Class DU	53.493	9/18/50	Dallas, Tex.	Little Gertie II	Lloyd Huse	Rockholt	Mercury
Class EU	36.022	12/29/51	Miami, Fla.	7-F	Frank Stone	Stone	Evinrude
Class FU	44.280	9/18/50	Dallas, Tex.	....	Roy Buie	Speedliner	Evinrude

One Mile Outboard Records in 1952 APBA Rule Book.

The mile trial set-up requires the entrant to make two passes (one each way) on the course. The average time taken for both directions was used to determine the average speed for the total distance of 2 miles. Buoys with red flags on each end of the 5,280-foot course marked the start and finish points. I remember this attempt well, as I could barely see the marker buoys at the end of the course because the lake was cool and foggy the morning of the run. You could hear people talking from across the lake but not see them because of the limited visibility. Fortunately, it was calm, cold and at sea-level, ideal conditions for record setting. Dad scolded me "you dunderhead" after I returned to the pits because I ran a somewhat zig-zag course over each mile-long run which slowed my speed. A course judge must have ratted-me-out! What could you expect from a 10-year-old who had barely enough muscle to start the engine?

Running straight on the course in a relatively slow-moving boat was a challenge, it seemed like it took forever to make the run! I wished I'd had a radio to listen to some rock-and-roll music instead of the whine of the engine to keep me focused on the task at hand! Actually, it took less than 2-1/2 minutes each way, but that's a very long time for a raceboat. Unfortunately, I was not successful in that attempt.

Later, I was fortunate at Seattle on August 9, 1954, in running the mile-trials on the East Channel course on Lake Washington, east of Mercer Island. I remembered what dad scolded me about, running as straight as possible, which was the shortest and quickest path. The new record was 26.985 mph set in a Jacobsen runabout named *Sparks*, the same boat I won in during the 1957 Slough Race.

Class	Speed	Date	Location	Boat	Driver	Hull	Motor
Class JU Runabout	26.985	8/9/54	Seattle, Wash.	Sparks	Jim Benson	Jacobsen	Mercury
Class AU Runabout	46.039	8/10/53	Seattle, Wash.	J9-R	Don Benson	Jacobsen	Mercury
Class BU Runabout	53.753	8/9/54	Seattle, Wash.	98-R	Bill Larsen	Calkins	Mercury
Class CU Runabout	41.532	2/17/53	Lake Alfred, Fla.	Wang Dang	Bernard Abrams	Abrams	Elto
Class EU Runabout	59.367	8/9/54	Seattle, Wash.	R-78	Robert Batie	Bloom	Mercury
Class FU Runabout	40.655	9/6/53	Devils Lake, Ore.	Nothin' Down	Dick Scandling	Redding	Evinrude
Class PU Runabout	44.280	9/18/50	Dallas, Texas	....	Roy Buie	Speedliner	Evinrude
Class A Stock Hydro.	50.858	8/10/53	Seattle, Wash.	Autta Go III	Jack Leek	Swift	Mercury
Class B Stock Hydro.	60.482	8/9/54	Seattle, Wash.	Thayne	V. J. Spinner, Jr.	Jacobsen	Mercury
Class D Stock Hydro.	69.739	8/11/52	Seattle, Wash.	Auta' Go III	Doug Tenzler	Swift	Mercury

One Mile Outboard Records in 1954 APBA Rule Book.

1955: JU & A drivers with friends at D-Lake, Oregon: Trophy holders and Lyford friends L to R; Chuck Lyford, Eugene Gross, Don Benson, Jimmy Benson (Bill Noble in back) and Ginny Lyford on far right.

As a testament to Al Benson's tutelage, Billy, Chuck, Ginny, Don and I went on to win national honors in outboards, inboards and in Billy's case became a legendary unlimited hydroplane driver. All of Al Benson's mentored JU drivers went on to have successful racing and sporting careers as they matured into their adult lives.

The boat that Don set his first record in, was the same boat that father sold to Bill Schumacher, Sr., who came home Christmas eve with a new boat on top of his car and gave it to son, Billy, on Christmas day (this was the R-6 runabout in the photo on page 277). Later, Dad was building a new lightweight boat that good friend and famous boat-builder, Ed Karelsen, finished. This was after he moved into the "Al Benson Boats & Motors" shop in Lake City (8830 Bothell Way). Dad and Ed were originally building it for Don, but money talks. Mr. Schumacher saw it and had to have it for Billy and the rest is history. Billy ended up setting a number of records in this boat in J-Utility and A-Utility classes along with winning several national championship titles.

1955 Slough Race: Billy Schumacher 1st in A-Utility boat Al Benson and Ed Karelsen originally built for Don Benson.

1956: Al Benson and Don Benson in front of *Al Benson Boats & Motors* in second Lake City shop.

Don't get me wrong we were very appreciative of everything our father did for us and weren't too upset about it as he had to make money to put food on the table and boats on our trailers. We'd set some records and then our competitors who bought outfits from "Pop" as I called him, would go out and break our records! Al Benson, "a renowned racer in his own right," eventually was responsible for fostering some 42 youngsters in the JU class, some of whom had continually held all the JU and most AU and A-Stock Hydro world records

First Lady of the Slough

Ginny Lea Lyford was a war baby born in 1943 to the parents Ginny and Al Lyford of Seattle. Young Ginny Lea was a bundle of energy from her beginnings to this day. Following in the footsteps of her older brother Chuck, she wanted to be, among her other ambitions, a boat racer too. Her father, Alfred "Al," set up brother Chuck with an outboard outfit he purchased from my father. Chuck showed promise with the outfit and his father encouraged and supported him in his racing competition as he grew older.

Ginny Lyford 1955 Nationals

Ginny, sometimes not so discreetly, also had her own ambitions, if not more than Chuck. But Chuck received most of the attention toward boat racing as this was mostly a masculine sport at the time. Not to be outdone, Ginny, a tall and pretty young girl, decided to acquire her own boat even if her parents didn't support it. She purchased, with her own money, an outboard boat and motor from a neighbor to start her new boating adventure. Making a long story short, her father purchased another boat for Chuck from my father. Then Ginny inherited Chuck's first boat and motor, a complete JU outfit that kicked-off her boat racing endeavor. The original boat and motor she purchased herself was just a starter outfit, unsuitable for racing. Ginny's and my parents were good friends during this time, we visited

1956-Ginny Lyford in JU-Runabout 65-R *Miss Take* at Green Lake with mentor Al Benson holding youngest son Jimmy and Don Benson (upper) returning from his A-Stock Hydro heat.

Chuckie (L) & Ginny Lea

Arms instructor

each other's homes occasionally, theirs in the Madrona area and ours below Lake City on Lake Washington.

Her first race was on Green Lake in 1955 along with her other JU (utility) classmates, including me. She quickly moved up a class into the A-Stock Runabout class like the rest of her classmates before her. The faster and more powerful runabouts proved to be a challenge as they could catch a chine and flip over very easily, as all the other runabout drivers, including me, can attest to! As raceboat builder Ed Karelsen said many times, "most anyone can drive a hydro but it takes a real driver to run a runabout." This was true in Miss Ginny's case too, as she had to tame her wild mount at times, which made for some great photo-shoots for the famous Northwest boat-racing photographer Bob Carver. The photo below is one of those where it looks like she is riding a bucking bronco or doing boat wheelies without wheels.

Later, after her boat racing concluded, Ginny Lea became a debutante from Helen Bush School, a Junior Olympic downhill skier, an excellent markperson (an "Annie Oakley" of her time) and one of the few women who became an expert arms instructor for law enforcement, including special weapons and tactics training for *SWAT Teams*. She also was an intervention counselor-teacher and author of "Living On/edge."

1958 Ginny Lea Lyford bouncing completely out of water racing her wild A Runabout during Green Lake regatta.

Debutante

Old-Timers Cruise

The first outing of the year for the Seattle Outboard Association is the annual "Old Timers" cruise up the Sammamish Slough. The event, which usually is run the first Sunday of January, is for fun and work as usually the Slough needs some cleaning to make it passable for the first race of the season, the Sammamish Slough Race.

The photos below show the large turnout of folks who couldn't proceed up the Slough because a fallen tree was completely blocking the waterway. Al Benson, in his boat on the bottom right of the second photo, was leading the club's work crew, which was made up mostly of race drivers. They tied a rope to the trunk of the tree, pulled it over and secured it to the river bank.

Annual Lake Sammamish Bar Pilots Cruise

The Seattle Outboard Association continued its tradition of initiating new Bar Pilot drivers. Their annual affair was run from Kenmore to Lake Sammamish on February 26, with a good turnout of first-time pilots in the Slough. Al Benson, Grand Admiral of the ceremonies, led the group of boats up to Gateway Grove and conducted the proceedings. The men weren't the only new pilots as several ladies were among the large group.

To become a "Bar Pilot" one must first navigate their boat all the way up the winding and hazardous Slough to the designated initiation site. Then the participants were sworn-in by the Grand Admiral by repeating the ceremonial "oath" while all of them were touching the large bent brass propeller (see photo below). The conclusion was taking a swig of the traditional "Slough juice." The drink consists of some distasteful ingredients concocted earlier. I know this because, first I had to drink it for my initiation, and then I made it for this year's occasion. I put a little of every spice I could find in mother's kitchen pantry…not tasty at all!

New Bar Pilots holding the bent propeller while repeating the oath read by Grand Admiral Al Benson.

The ceremony included the changing of shear pins in the early years of the 1930s. A shear pin was a safety device to protect the outboard motors lower unit gears and propeller when a boater ran over something. The device was a small brass pin about one inch long and 3/16 inch in diameter. The pin was inserted through the corresponding holes in the prop and the propeller (prop) shaft. It was made of a soft metal that would shear when the prop hits something in the water, protecting the costlier gears and drive shafts inside the lower unit. The prop nut held it all together.

This exercise was important survival training for novice Slough drivers because hitting something was commonplace. When you sheared a pin the engine's prop would become disconnected from the driveshaft and spin freely with no forward thrust. You were stuck in the water until the pin was replaced.

Notorious Saginaw Sawmill log boom in Woodinville with log blocking channel (looking downstream).

Bar Pilot entering narrow log boom channel (heading upstream).

1956 Race Schedule (Partial)

Jan 1	Annual "Old-Timers" Cruise
Feb 26	Annual Bar Pilots Cruise
April 15	21st Sammamish Slough Race
May 13	8th Sammamish Water-Ski Race
May 20	Lake Sammamish Regatta-State Park
May 27	Green Lake-Inboards & Outboards
June 10	Lake Sammamish-Gateway Grove
July 8	Moses Lake
Aug 10-11	Green Lake Regatta
Aug 11-12	Western Divisionals-Long Beach Marine Stadium
Aug 28-30	Stock Outboard Nationals-Cambridge, MD

Sammamish Water-Ski Race

Water-ski competitors had their day in the Sammamish Slough on Sunday, May 5. The skiers, towed by Seattle Outboard Association drivers, were split into four divisions, the Unlimited and Limited classes, B, C & D. The Unlimited boats started first at noon and the Limited class boats left later in 10-minute intervals. The skiers and their tow boats started from Kenmore on Lake Washington and ran the same two-way 14-mile course that the outboarders ran a month earlier.

Last year's Unlimited winner, Ray Moore-towed by Dick Brunes, won again this year. Bob Blair and Bill Semon, who were second, last year, won in the Limited Class B. They finished the first heat at Gateway Grove on Lake Sammamsih, took a break and then restarted downstream finishing back in Kenmore at 2 pm. The duos that placed among the 84 contestants were as follows:

Unlimited Class: Ray Moore-Dick Brunes 1st, Mike Cunningham-Bud Sullivan 2nd, Bill Schumacher Sr.-Lin Ivey 3rd
Limited Classes: Class B: Bob Blair-Bill Semon 1st, Class C: Mike Knoles-Don Ibsen 1st, Class D: Jim Kleven-Ray Lee 1st

1956 Tidbits

In 1956 a new DU-1 or 36 Class was run in the Slough Race for 30-36 cubic inch motors. Jack Colcock set a 48-limited inboard record of 67.821 mph and was elected APBA secretary for 1957. He joined Jim Spinner, Region 10 chairman and APBA council member, as a member in national organization. Colcock was also a deputy inboard commissioner on the inboard technical committee and on the nominating committee. The Seattle Outboard Association was well represented in the APBA organization. Spinner also was awarded the SOA Sportsman Award for the year.

Billy Schumacher traveled across the United States to Cambridge, MD and won the JU class National Championship for a second time in a row. He also won the Region

10 Hi-Point trophy again and was named to *Yachting Magazine's* All-American racing team for 1956. The Jackens Grill Perpetual Trophy had debuted as the new award for the overall Unlimited class winner in the Slough Race. It was first awarded to Bill Farr in 1954, then Bud Sullivan in 1955 and this year to Bob Waite. It was introduced after Al Benson took permanent possession of the Ben Paris Perpetual Trophy in 1953.

Jacobsen brothers and family in their company-built boats during Old-Timers Cruise.

1957

"Hydro king Bill Muncey tries the putt-putts and winds up in the drink" COMMENT - "Oh take me back to the Gold Cup course, these outboard jobs are too tough for me; they rear and kick like a bucking horse, they rock and roll like Elvis P."

Quoted by Royal Brougham in his 1957 Post Intelligencer "Morning After" column

Jim Spinner was elected for the second year in a row as the commodore of the SOA. During the meeting last year in December, the club decided to return to Kenmore for the start and finish of the Sammamish Slough Race and co-sponsor with the Kenmore Businessmen's Association. (The races finished in Bothell during the preceding three years.)

Gold Cup Winner Enters Slough Race

A headline for the 22nd annual Sammamish Slough Race was that Bill Muncey was entered in the 1957 race. Muncey, who drove the *Miss Thriftway* unlimited inboard hydroplane, won the 1956 Gold Cup in Detroit, Michigan, and brought the prestigious event back to Seattle. He was a dark-horse entry, stepping down to drive a small hydro in the most popular outboard event in the Pacific Northwest. Not to be over-shadowed, Bob Waite, winner of last year's race, was gunning for a second straight victory. Other Unlimited division entries included Bud Sullivan, Bill Farr, and future unlimited inboard hydro jockeys Lin Ivey and Al Benson, who were slated to drive the *Miss Seattle* in future seasons.

"Slough Race Is Tougher Test for Drivers Than Gold Cup-Muncey" was Bud Livesley's headline in the *Times* on Thursday, April 4. Livesley wrote: "The Sammamish Slough is no place for Sunday drivers. Take it from Bill Muncey, a handy man at the wheel of a speedboat; Sunday's Slough run will be a more severe test of a driver's ability than the Gold Cup race.

1957: Bill Muncey and crew celebrating Gold Cup win. Region-10 Chairman, Lin Ivey (skipper's hat) holding Muncey's leg.

"'It's going to be real tough when all that traffic gets out there,' admitted Muncey after a couple of practice runs on the narrow snake-like Slough. 'Of course, the unlimited hydros are "hotter," but for maneuverability, the Slough runs will be tougher than the Gold Cup,' said the man who won the 1956 Gold Cup race with the *Miss Thriftway*.

"The Slough Race will be somewhat of a family affair for the Bensons. Al's sons, Don and Jimmy, also will compete. Don in the A-Runabout division, while Jim will drive a Junior-Utility runabout. There's also the brother team of Richard and Robert Rautenberg in the A-Hydro and B-Hydro events, respectively. Ginny Lea Lyford, driving a JU runabout, is the only woman entrant. Her brother, Chuck, is the defending champion in the A-Runabout division. Also set for action are Bill Schumacher and Bill, Jr. The younger Schumacher is the JU runabout champion and world record holder."

Sometime before the 1957 Slough Race, Ward's Resort was sold to a consortium of owners who were building a brand-new boat marina, Uplake Marina, to be managed by

Al Benson. For the first time, the Slough Race was run next door at the Kenmore Air Harbor because the marina was under construction and the old docks were removed.

Farr Wins Second Slough Race Crown

Take a dash of experience, a splash of nerves, and a measure of help from a pit crew; mix liberally with a ton of luck and you've got the ingredients for a Slough Race champion. That was Bill Farr's recipe on Sunday, April 7. Farr, a finish carpenter of Bellevue, won the overall title for the second time in his Jacobsen-designed D-Hydro with an elapsed time of 38:53. He was followed by Bill Wallace in second and Howard Anderson in third overall.

1957: Bill Farr overall Sammamish Slough Race winner in Unlimited class.

National Berth for Tolford

Sharing laurels with Farr was 33-year-old Boeing model maker, Harold Tolford. Tolford drove his boat named *Sand Box* to victory in the D-Runabout class and qualified for the national marathon in August on Lake Quinsigamond, near Worchester, Mass. He was the first of 16 regional drivers to receive the Mennen Trophy and an all-expenses paid trip to the stock outboard nationals in Massachusetts. The Slough Race, which was sanctioned by the APBA, was one of the qualifying marathon courses.

Seattle Outboard officials lengthened the racecourse this year by moving the finish line back to Kenmore. The race had ended in Bothell the three previous years. Kenmore's businessmen, who wanted more exposure, co-sponsored the event with the Seattle Outboard Association. Their wish was granted, as an estimated 60,000 spectators lined the river banks and bridges to watch the nationally-acclaimed event.

Mennen Co. Ken Wise presents trophy to Tolford.

The Slough course was basically the same as it was when it began in 1934. The width of the Slough varied from 50 feet to as little as 12 feet in several places with the average width roughly 25 feet. The race drivers had to navigate under 19 bridges, which added to their perils; some with very low clearance that required the driver to duck his head as he passed under. It's been said over and over that the snake-like hazardous waterway never fails to give race fans excitement as spectators can watch close enough to get soaked from the spray of the boats' roostertails as they pass by.

One of the crowd's favorite viewing spots was at the Bothell Bridge. Here many of the contestants over the years had failed to maneuver through the tricky right-hand turn directly under the bridge. This year was no exception as veteran driver V.J. "Jim" Spinner, Jr., of Mercer Island, clobbered one of the bridge's concrete piers in his alcohol-burning A-Racing Hydro. He managed to continue on downstream with a damaged hull, only to flip over just shy of the finish line in Kenmore. Despite his misfortunes, Spinner placed third overall on the strength of his upstream run. All the others in his class were either disqualified of failed to finish the upstream run.

Lin Ivey, with first place almost in his grasp after he won the upriver run, had the toughest break of them all. A spectator, thinking his boat was on fire when it backfired as he tried to start for the downriver run, threw water on his motor. Before Ivey could change the spark plugs and get the motor started, his competitors were halfway down the Slough. Bob Waite, last year's victor, flipped during his upstream run, got his boat righted with the help of spectators, and was able to finish at Lake Sammamish. Then he spun-out on the downstream leg managing to finish but not placing.

Bill Muncey, who borrowed a rig from Al Benson, had to paddle across the finish line after he hit a submerged object and was hurled from his D-Hydro during his downstream run through Wayne Golf Course. With the aid of helpful spectators, Muncey and the boat were righted, but the motor's ignition system was flooded and refused to start. The Schumacher's also had their troubles. The elder Schumacher's A-Racing Hydro struck a log and conked out while Billy was thrown from his A-Runabout and was unable to finish. Muncey, who hadn't raced outboards for 17 years, took his dunking in stride. "It was a lot of fun and I'll be back. Maybe with a little more experience at this sort of thing I can keep up with the boys next year."

As was expected, only about half of the 69 starters managed to stay the course from Kenmore to Lake Sammamish and back. The field of entries, which included nine classes, started with the Unlimiteds first and each succeeding slower class leaving in five-minute intervals with the JU-Runabouts last.

Gold Cup champion Bill Muncey driving Al Benson's *Swift* D-Hydro.

The Junior Utility class, like last year, was the only group that finished in Bothell which was for safety reasons and timing. Our times were so slow compared to the other classes that it might have been dark before we finished!

Other class winners included Ted Uerling in B-Hydro; Duke Polk, A-Racing Hydro; John Craven, B-Runabout; John Freeman, A-Stock Hydro; Bob Blair, 36 Cubic Inch, and Jimmy Benson in JU-Runabout. The all-important officials who worked behind the scenes managing the race were Al Benson, chairman; Art Shorey, referee; Keith Nelson, timer; Rod Entrop, starter; Betty Kertis, scorer; Bill Rankin, measurer; Bob Carver, course judge, and Dick Suess, patrol boat captain. For the first time the U.S. Coast Guard helped patrol the course to help minimize spectator misdeeds.

Dick Rautenberg, who placed second in A-stock hydro, got snagged by a kid's fishing line. Yes, it's strange that someone would be fishing while the boat races were under way. Dick told me this story when I interviewed him at his Bothell home in 2015. Dave Culley, three-time Slough Race winner was with us.

"Some kid holding a fishing pole with a hook out caught my collar and I ran all his line off his reel. When I got up to Gateway Grove on Lake Sammamish I unhooked it and threw it away." Both Dave and I then said something like "whoever was following him might have that line fouled up around his propeller because likely a hundred feet or so of line was following Dick all the way up the Slough."

Bob Carver, SOA vice-commodore and renowned photographer, was also working for *Boat Sport Magazine* shooting photos of the race. They were published along with a story about the race in the August of 1957 issue.

1957 Sammamish Slough Race Results (in order of overall finish)

Place	Driver	Class	From	Boat #	Boat Name	Time
1	Bill Farr	Unlimited Hydro	Bellevue	224-R	Wee Willy	38:54
2	Bill Wallace	Unlimited Hydro	Seattle	*	*	39:52
3	Howard Anderson	Unlimited Hydro	Edmonds	222-R	*	40:50
1	Harold Tolford	D-Runabout	Seattle	78-R	Sand Box	51:29
2	Al Benson	D-Runabout	Seattle	64-R	*	*
3	Gil Allen	D-Runabout	Seattle	*	Needle Nose	*
1	Ted Uerling	B-Hydro	Seattle	*	*	55:41
2	Alan McPherren	B-Hydro	Seattle	*	*	*
3	Bob Rautenberg	B-Hydro	Kirkland	*	*	*
1	Johnny Craven	B-Runabout	Seattle	*	*	1:26:41
2	George Huntry	B-Runabout	Seattle	*	*	*
3	Jim Henry	B-Runabout	Seattle	124-R	*	*
1	Duke Polk	A-Rac Hydro	Seattle	*	*	1:21:09
2	Red Taylor	A-Rac Hydro	Seattle	*	*	*
3	Jim Spinner	A-Rac Hydro	Seattle	*	*	*
1	John Freeman	A-Stock Hydro	Seattle	*	*	1:38:41
2	Dick Rautenberg	A-Stock Hydro	Seattle	*	*	*
3	Pat Crane	A-Stock Hydro	Seattle	*	*	*
1	Fred Miller	A-Runabout	Seattle	*	*	1:54:18
2	Larry Knight	A-Runabout	Seattle	*	*	*
3	Kenny Feroe	A-Runabout	Seattle	*	*	*
4	Don Benson	A-Runabout	Seattle	29-R	Ill-Eagle	*
1	Roy Williams	36 Runabout	Seattle	*	*	2:02:37
2	Wally Marten	36 Runabout	Seattle	*	*	*
3	V.F. Halsey	36 Runabout	Seattle	*	*	*
1	Jimmy Benson	JU-Runabout	Seattle	*	Sparks	*
2	Jack Holden	JU-Runabout	Seattle	*	Jolly Jack	*
3	Harvard Palmer	JU-Runabout	Seattle	*	*	*

1957: Jimmy Benson Sammamish Slough Race winner in JU Runabout class.

1957: Rookie Jim Johnson took a bath in Kenmore-old "Bothell Way Pavilion" in background.

"Old-Timers" Cruise

For the first time, the bigger outboard cruisers took part in the annual SOA cruise that traditionally ran on the first Sunday of January. The low clearance bridge at Sanders Farm, which previously blocked their passage, was removed. Participants gathered at Kenmore for a 10 am departure upstream to Lake Sammamish. The entourage, which included 107 boats in freezing cold weather, was a record for the event. They stopped, warmed up to a bonfire and ate lunch at Gateway Grove before heading back downstream to Kenmore.

Seattle Outboard Association "Old Timers" Cruise at Marymoor Farms, Redmond.

More Antics in the Slough

Moviegoers were treated to more crazy antics of Seattle outboard race drivers in the Slough. Hollywood film makers once again spliced together a "short subject" motion picture about the "Crookedest Race in the World," the Sammamish Slough Race.

In the late 1930s to the early 1940s filmmakers concocted stunts with race boats going over the banks of the Slough and through fire on water, as told in earlier chapters. One such stunt by Al Benson was not included in those stories. A Hollywood movie director thought it would be eye-catching and humorous for an outboard motorboat driver to jump the bank of the Sammamish Slough and shoot-through a makeshift chicken coup. At the same time some chickens were released from a cage nearby and it looked like things went afoul when Benson drove through the coup in his C-Runabout named *NO FOOL'N*. It all made for an entertaining showing. Of course, no humans or chickens were injured in the making of the film.

This year, at the age of 12, I was privileged, I think, to be a part of the last newsreel produced about the Slough Race. My father and a film maker set-up some "phony shots," as Dad called them, starring my brother, some other fellow boat race friends and me. The first film clip was of Chuck Lyford who drove his A-Runabout (without the skid fin) up over the river bank and slid toward a golfer who was teeing-off at the Wayne Golf Course. As his boat came to a stop next to the golfer, Chuck rolled out of his boat and scared the daylights out of the so called unsuspecting duffer.

Al Benson in Hollywood "chicken coup" stunt.

The scene ended with the teed-off golfer throwing his clubs in the Slough.

There was another scene where we drove through a clothes line full of clothes. A rope was strung across the Slough with sheets and garments hanging down just high enough to clear our boats. As we drove under the loose hanging clothes, with our heads ducked low, we rose up and grabbed the laundry making it look like we were all caught up in a tangled mess–actually we were. In another scene, a smoke bomb was placed just behind me and set-off. The smoke was billowing while I was stopped alongside the blackberry bushes in the Slough. The other drivers came to my rescue by dousing the smoke, mostly me, using their hands and small paddles to splash the water. A few months later, I was pleasantly surprised when I saw the short subject film at the Lake City Theater.

Schumacher Triumphs in Water-Ski Marathon

Bill Schumacher, Sr., is the new Champion of the Seattle Water-Ski Association's Sammamish Slough Water-Ski Race, held Sunday, April 28. Schumacher won the annual race and foiled Ray Moore's bid for a third straight victory in the unlimited-class feature. Lin Ivey, new unlimited hydroplane pilot, drove the outboard that towed Schumacher. The Schumacher-Ivey combination made the 14-mile run upstream from Kenmore to Lake Sammamish in 22 minutes and the downstream run to Kenmore in 21 minutes. Moore, towed by Dick Brunes, came in second with an overall time of 57 minutes.

Bill Schumacher Sr.

The annual race this year included three divisions, unlimited, limited 32 to 40 miles per hour and limited, less than 32 miles per hour. Mike Reid towed by his brother Fred, won the higher limited class and Bill Semond towed by Bob Blair was first on the lower limited class. The skiers and their drivers braved the usually chilly and wet weather and few finished because of congestion and accidents. Every year someone tangles with the Bothell Bridge. Despite the many spills and beaching, no injuries were reported.

1957 Race Schedule (Partial)

Jan 6	Annual "Old-Timers" Cruise
Feb 24	Annual Bar Pilots Cruise
April 7	22nd Sammamish Slough Race
April 21	Lake Sammamish Regatta
April 28	9th Sammamish Water-Ski Race
July 7	Devil's Lake, OR
July 14	Moses Lake
July 20-21	Columbia River Regionals-Pasco
Aug 2-4	Western Divisionals-Green Lake
Aug 17-18	Lake Osoyoos-Oroville
Aug 25	Silver Lake
Aug 21-25	Stock Outboard Nationals-Worcester, MA
Sept 7-8	Devils Lake, OR

1957 Tidbits

Jack Colcock was elected Secretary of the American Power Boat Association. He was the first Seattle Outboard Association member to be an officer of the national association. Harold Tolford who turned from model airplanes to outboards and won in the Slough Race, finished second in the Stock Nationals marathon on Lake Quinsigamond in Massachusetts and set the C-Service Runabout record at 52.555 mph in D-Lake (was named Devil's Lake), Oregon.

Four Seattle outboard pilots won their respective classes in the Green Lake Western Divisionals on August 2. Jack Holden took the honors in the JU class; John Sangster won in BU-Runabout, Don Benson in AU-Runabout and Red Taylor was first in C-Stock Hydro. Bill Muncey, who also competed in the Slough Race, won the Gold Cup in the Seattle Seafair race. Rod Entrop was awarded the SOA Sportsman Award. Al Benson retired from outboard and limited inboard racing to compete in the Unlimited Hydros. He was selected as the number one driver of *Miss Seattle* with Chuck Hickling as the backup driver.

Lindgren's Bothell Way Pavilion

The popular Bothell Way Pavilion in Kenmore was the place to be if you loved twirling to the rhythms of "old-time" dance music. Accordionist Bert Lundgren and his "old-time dance band" played to the enchantment of dance buffs from the greater Seattle area between 1937 and 1956. Lundgren and his wife Rose bought the facility from Dick Parker (of Parker's Ballroom). They opened their doors every Saturday night for almost 20-years. Dance lovers swung their hips from 9 pm to 2 am to old-time, modern, Scandinavian and square dance music.

The retro-styled dancehall, with two large cupola domes topped with circus-like flags and a large framed sign lettered "BOTHELL WAY PAVILION," was easily recognizable from the Sammamish River (see dunking photo of raceboat R-29, 3 pages earlier). You could catch a bus from Seattle's 9th and Stewart terminal and be there relaxed and ready for dancing without the long drive to the boondocks of Kenmore. Lindgren's orchestra also played every Tuesday evening at Seattle's Trianon Ballroom and Sunday evenings at Seattle's Swedish Club.

1958

Red-headed and freckled Ralph "Red" Taylor was elected as the 30th commodore of the Seattle Outboard Association for 1958. Along with him, famous Northwest freelance photographer Bob Carver was elected vice-commodore; A. E. "Art" Karelsen, secretary, and Mrs. Jackie Wallace, treasurer. Taylor, a longtime Slough Race veteran, ran an outboard sales and service shop in Kenmore. He was one of a few who placed eight times in the event.

Red Taylor

New Marinas in Kenmore

"Uplake Marina" became the new starting location for the 1958 Sammamish Slough Race. It was a brand-new facility in the same location as the old Ward's Resort. The sunken barge and all the old docks were removed and replaced by a modern boat marina complete with 400 moorage slips, gas dock, boat launching, sales, repair, and boat construction. The gas dock at the outer most end of the marina became the new starting point for the Slough Race.

The depth of the water around the docks and beyond was much deeper to facilitate large boats. More than 16,000 cubic yards of silt from the Sammamish River, built up for decades, was removed by dredging cranes. Gone was the thick sludge on the bottom and the mud flats that were exposed when Lake Washington was lowered every winter. You didn't have to worry about getting stuck in the muddy bottom if you fell in. I know this from experience because I lived there as a teenager and ran the gas dock on weekends. On one occasion, the wind blew me and my bike off the long dock as I was riding back to shore after serving a customer. And gone was the old rotten barge and high-dive platform where Bob Carver shot photos of the Slough Race starts in the 1950s.

Another new marina opened this year that instantly became a new hazard for drivers. The Down River Marina, owned and built by Harold Anderson in early 1958, was about a mile up the Slough. It provided moorage for small boats and enticed unsuspecting Slough Racers to come-on-in! If a race driver didn't know better when he passed under the preceding bridge, going upstream, the marina opening looked like the Slough channel straight-ahead.

Knowledgeable pilots knew and prepared for the sharp right-hand turn that began directly under the "Nursery Bridge," right before the new marina. Those that didn't were trapped when they headed into the entrance thinking it was the channel. By then, after realizing their mistake, the driver's reaction was to quickly make a quick but impossible right-hand turn. Unfortunately, they either spun-out or ran up onto the river bank point between the marina and the real channel.

This made for some real excitement for spectators and drivers alike. The crowd on the point had to jump out of the way or be run over. The Nursery Bridge turn became the favorite photo shooting location for Bob Carver and a host of other media and would be photographers. The adjacent photo taken by Bob Carver shows a hydro that spun out and flipped-over after narrowly missing the Nursery Bridge. A bridge load of spectators were watching him below.

Bob Carver photo taken from bridge discussed in proceeding story. Down River Marina opening is in upper left that drivers mistook for Slough channel. This hydro spun-out and flipped-over throwing out its driver.

Record Field Expected for Slough Race

A record number of entries were expected for the annual Sammamish Slough Race on Sunday, April 13. It was a hazardous but scenic drive the outboarders would travel, with hair-pin turns and even golfers offering obstacles because the Slough bisects the Wayne Golf Course.

Bill Farr was prepared to defend his title from last year and hoped to win the event for a third time. Al Benson was the only driver to win three races. This year Benson didn't enter and concentrated on being the chauffer for the new Unlimited Hydroplane, *Miss Pay'n Save*. Farr drove the same F-Hydro as last year but it was re-built into the newer cabover configuration where the driver kneels farther forward.

Race Chairman, Al Benson, announced that prize money amounting to $800, plus another $400 in trophies and merchandise, was expected to draw a field of 100 or more drivers; a record number for the 23-year old event. The Kenmore Civic Clubs co-sponsored the race with the Seattle Outboard Association. Ten classes were scheduled to start at five-minute intervals with a stop on Lake Sammamish at Gateway Grove. The JU-Runabouts would only run upstream and finish in Bothell. The American Power Boat Association sanctioned this event as a qualifying marathon for the winners of the AU, BU, CU and DU classes to be run in the stock outboard nationals. Harold Tolford of Seattle qualified last year and was second at the Nationals in Massachusetts.

Arrowhead Point Resident Conquers Slough In Bargain Hydro

Dick Brunes, a resident of Arrowhead Point on Lake Washington about a mile south from the starting line, mastered the Slough. Brunes finally accomplished what so many others before him, couldn't. In his fifth attempt, he won the overall crown piloting his Unlimited F-Hydro *Lindy* (named after his 5-year old daughter). Brunes, a Kirkland car salesman, bought the bargain hydro a few years ago for $150.

1958 Unlimited Class start (Air Harbor area): Bill Farr 94-R (new cabover-foreground), Bob Waite 226-R (left-not started), Dave Karelsen R-19 (above Waite-not started), 304-R (middle right-unidentified), Andy Anderson R-222 (top right cabover-leading), Dick Brunes 172-R top middle (not started but eventual winner).

Driving skill alone wasn't enough to unsnarl the twisting Sammamish Slough. Brunes was called upon to repair a damaged propeller midway in the race at Lake Sammamish to keep in contention. The clever driver-mechanic used a rock and a hammer to pound out the dents sustained from running over a sand bar near Woodinville. Brunes then zig-zagged back down the Slough never to be pushed and crossed the finish line at Uplake Marina with a record elapsed time of 35 minutes and

58.1 seconds. Bill Farr, last year's champion who came in a distant second, slammed into the same sandbar as Brunes. A burst of speed within sight of the finish line enabled him to pass Dave Karelsen to finished second.

Aside from Bob Waite, the 1956 winner, the faster unlimited hydro jockeys managed to stay astride their craft better than those who followed in the other nine classes. Waite was the "flip" champion but wasn't alone in thrilling the estimated 50,000 spectators who lined every mile of the racecourse. Waite, the steel salesman from Bellevue, flipped twice but managed to eventually finish and place seventh.

Bob Rautenberg's Down River Marina spin and flip in B-Hydro 41-R.

Joe Trumbly's D-Runabout climbing Marina bank scattering spectators at "Moorage Available" sign.

It was an untimely end for two boats that missed their turn and headed toward the new Down River Marina's moorage area. Each driver attempted to turn at the last second but each met misfortune. Bob Rautenberg wheeled his B-Hydro toward the moorage, marked-off by strips of white cloth hanging from a rope (photos on previous page). His hydro skidded, overturned and flipped him into the drink. Joe Trumbly's DU-Runabout went out of control and ran up on the bank at a "Moorage Available" sign scattering spectators. No one was injured but neither boat was able to continue.

Young Benson Beached

Jim Benson, the JU-Runabout winner last year who stepped up into the AU-Runabout ranks also had hard luck. He was running second when he and his boat parted company in the Woodinville "S-turns." He landed half on the bank and half in the water. A couple of his brother's friends helped to right the upside-down boat and empty the water. By the time Benson restarted it was too late to continue because the official patrol boat had just passed him (rules made it illegal to continue if the official passes you when stopped). Two C-Stock hydros threw their rider into the water. Gerald "Red" Halliday was leading the pack when his boat flipped. Les Dunmire had a long walk back to Kenmore when his hydro flipped and sank. His boat was retrieved downstream later by a patrol boat. No one in the race was seriously injured.

Fred Miller in A-Runabout was the only previous winner. Another record was set when Jim Bergman piloted his B-Stock Hydro to the winner's circle with a total time of 46:01.8, wiping out the mark of 55:41 set by last year's winner, Ted Uerling. Dean Mahaffey, Bob Steinbruck and Art Losvar were the only out-of-towners to win. Mahaffey of Roseburg, Oregon, the DU record holder, won in DU-

Dick Brunes overall winner just missing spectator thrown floating beer can in his rebuilt Swift D-Hydro *Lindy*.

Runabout beating current national champion, Oregon's Rockey Stone. Steinbruck of Salem, won in the CU-Runabouts and Losvar of Mukilteo, was the victor in the A-Racing Hydro class. Jack Holden, current JU record holder, won his first Slough Race.

Brunes Got Poor Start

It appeared from the start that hard luck again would strike down Brunes as he was the last boat away from the starting line (see photo two pages back)–the unlimited start overflowed into the Kenmore Air Harbor area because Uplake Marina was still under construction. But the *Lindy* took off like a jet as he caught all the boats except for three as he darted into the Slough. He overhauled two others by the time he reached Bothell and the last, Bill Farr, in Woodinville.

His win was long in coming with back of the pack finishes or DNF's the previous three years. Last year Burnes broke a throttle handle and didn't place. There was more than just the glory of winning; his victory was worth $500 in prize money.

Billy Schumacher 1st BU-Runabout.

1958 Sammamish Slough Race Results (by class)

Place	Driver	Class	From	Boat #	Time
1	Dick Brunes	Unlimited	Kenmore	172-R	36:58.1
2	Bill Farr	Unlimited	Bellevue	224-R	39:33.1
3	Dave Karelsen	Unlimited	Seattle	R-19	39:39.0
1	Dean Mahaffey	DU-Runabout	Roseburg, OR	122-R	42:16.5
2	Sid Sato	DU-Runabout	Carnation	38-R	42:38.2
3	Rockey Stone	DU-Runabout	Willamina, OR	106-R	42:49.6
5	Harold Tolford	DU-Runabout	Seattle	78-R	*
1	Red Taylor	C-Hydro	Seattle	R-89	43:11.0
2	Jody Heise	C-Hydro	Seattle	32-R	43:11.7
3	Victor Phelps	C-Hydro	Seattle	X	45:12.4
1	Bob Steinbruck	CU-Runabout	Salem, OR	106-R	44:23.6
2	Andy Thompson	CU-Runabout	Seattle	18-R	44:25.6
3	Hal Davies	CU-Runabout	Seattle	116-R	46:22.2
1	Jim Bergman	B-Hydro	Seattle	517-R	46:01.8
2	Paul Ambacker	B-Hydro	Seattle	59-R	46:57.2
3	Raymond Cox	B-Hydro	Seattle	149-R	51:32.2
1	Billy Schumacher	BU-Runabout	Seattle	1-R	46:46.2
2	Jim Henry	BU-Runabout	Seattle	250-R	46:54.1
3	John Anderson	BU-Runabout	Seattle	61-R	48:06.9
1	Art Losvar	A-Rac Hydro	Mukilteo	R-112	51:23.2
2	Gerry Wallin	A-Rac Hydro	Edmonds	R-102	54:02.6
3	Duke Polk	A-Rac Hydro	Seattle	R-101	55:58.3
1	Chuck Lyford	A-Hydro	Seattle	21-R	47:54.1
2	Don Benson	A-Hydro	Seattle	R-5	50:37.4
3	Fred Ballinger	A-Hydro	Seattle	229-R	53:06.9
1	Fred Miller	A-Runabout	San Mateo, CA	57-R	62:05.6
2	Larry Leckenby	A-Runabout	Seattle	97-R	63:23.2
3	Alex Cameron	A-Runabout	Portland, OR	32-R	64:31.6
1	Jack Holden	JU-Runabout	Seattle	171-R	*
2	Tiger Bischoff	JU-Runabout	Seattle	83-R	*
3	Jim Zonich Jr.	JU-Runabout	Kelso	J-10	*
4	Charley Walters	JU-Runabout	Kenmore	85-R	*

Some boat numbers and times unavailable

Hugh Entrop-World's Fastest Human in an Outboard

Huge Entrop who raced a B-Runabout in the Sammamish Slough Race in 1952 was the first American to crack the 100 mile an hour mark in an outboard. Entrop set the new record of 107.821 miles-per-hour, June, 1958, on the East Channel of Lake Washington, while piloting his revolutionary 13½ foot Entrop-Jones designed X-Class hydro he built in his basement.

Craig Fjarlie, former Seattle Outboard Association commodore and fellow writer, interviewed Hugh Entrop and wrote a fascinating story about his harrowing experiences during and after his record setting performance. It was published as a three-part series in the Seattle Outboard Association's monthly *Pit Previews*. The following is a true story based on Craig's article and the book, *Iron Fist*, by Jeffrey Rodengen.

Entrop's Intriguing Story

Hubert "Hugh" Entrop's quest for the world straightaway record in an outboard motorboat played out like a mystery novel. He labored relentlessly in his basement for weeks on end creating the most hi-tech and potentially fastest outboard in the world. Entrop, the hero, was unscrupulously chastised by the villain, the CEO of the Mercury Marine outboard motor company.

The CEO was a dominant corporate leader who threatened to have Entrop imprisoned in his Florida compound unless he met the CEO's expectations.

Entrop initially attempted to break the straightaway record on a lake in Florida that proved to be too small. He was unable to reach the speed necessary to establish a new record before he had to slow down or risk running up on the beach. The CEO insisted Entrop continue trying. Entrop knew he was endangering his life running on the private lake. Eventually, the CEO's son-in-law helped Entrop slip out of town.

On June 7, 1958, Entrop ran on Lake Washington in Seattle and set a new outboard world record of 107.821 mph. At first, the CEO refused to acknowledge the new record, but in time was forced to do so when the racing community made the accomplishment nationally known. Entrop's achievement then was used by Mercury Marine for advertising purposes.

Shortly after he set the record, Entrop became affiliated with the competitor, Outboard Marine Corporation, maker of Evinrude and Johnson. Mercury attempted to spy on Entrop and on one occasion they were involved in a car chase. Entrop was able to lose his pursuers and from that point on he could continue his quest for glory on his own terms. He then was able to claim the honor as the "World's Fastest Human in an Outboard Motorboat" once again and lived happily ever after.

June 7, 1958: Hugh Entrop sets outboard world record at 107.821mph on Lake Washington.

First SOA Novice School

"Free Training Course Offered Outboard Drivers" was headlined in the back of the *Seattle Times* sports section. For the first time in its 29-year history, the Seattle Outboard Association officially started training classes for future race drivers. They advertised regularly in the Boat and Motor section of the classified ad pages. Their goal was to recruit and train new members. Most importantly, the club wanted "new blood" or the young members who would promote, run or be a part of the club well into the future.

NEW RACE DRIVERS
A school for outboard racing drivers will start Jan. 24. Register by writing or calling Seattle Outbd. Service—MO. 7070 4100 Rainier Ave. — Open Sun.

The first monthly class was held on January 24 at the Rainier-Genesee Community Clubhouse near Lake Washington. Jim Spinner, Region 10 chairman, and Jim Henry, SOA commodore, organized the novice school along with Harold Tolford and other club members. The course included review of racing rules, driving technique and motor maintenance. Class members took part in an actual race after completing the course. The first novice race, the final exam, was run at Gateway Grove on Lake Sammamish, Sunday, March 30. John "Jody" Heise was named the school's director.

Rookie Russell Rotzler took one of the classes in 1959. His first official race just happened to be the most difficult in the country, the Sammamish Slough Race. Rotzler's schooling proved to be extremely beneficial because he was able to finish in his very first race in the competitive B-Hydro class. He finished

1959: Novice Russell Rotzler's first race was in the Slough Race driving a B-Stock Hydro.

back in fourth place, but as it was said many times before, just finishing the Slough Race was an accomplishment.

Moore, Brunes Win Water-Ski Race 3rd Time

The skier-driver combination of Ray Moore and Dick Brunes returned to their winning ways on Sunday, May 4 in the Slough. The 10th annual Sammamish Water-Ski Race, commonly called the "Golden Water-Ski Race" was expanded to four classes this year, Unlimited, Class-B, Class-C and Class-D.

In racing, all successful drivers take any advantage they can. Rules are the only means of leveling the playing field. But the outboard water-ski races were loosely run. By now the various classifications, other than Unlimited, were subject to stretching the rules by the boat drivers. The classes were based on speed categories rather than engine size as in the outboard races. The speed of the entries was very subjective and not verified, making it fall on the honesty of the driver or boat owner.

Many an entrant fudged a little to gain an advantage in the lower classes. The engine size and boat type were likely factors in the Limited Class determination by the race officials. Because they didn't have any way of certifying a boat's speed, officials had the last word on what class they were actually placed in before the race in, spite of what speed category the boat was registered. In other words, some cheating was involved, but it was mostly a friendly rivalry.

The Unlimited Class team of Moore, riding the slats and Brunes driving the F-Hydro, first won the event in 1955 and repeated in 1956. Their winning time for this year's round-trip between Uplake Marina in Kenmore and Gateway Grove on Lake Sammamish, was 51:23. Bill Schumacher, the defending champion, had a short ride, getting dunked about 100 feet from the start. Schumacher's driver, Ken Ferguson and his boat flipped when their tow-rope was tangled with another boat.

Eye doctor, Lew West and driver Rod Sampson, were the winners in Class-B with a time of 55:05. Class-C honors went to Mike Knoles and driver Don Ibsen (son of water-ski inventor Don, Sr.). and Class-D was won by Jim Kiaven and driver Ray Lee. The only mishap of the 42 teams was skier Harry Wurster, who suffered the loss of several teeth and facial cuts when he slammed into one of the Bothell trestle pilings.

<u>**Unlimited Class:**</u> Ray Moore-Dick Brunes 1st 172-R; 51:23, Rod Preston-Don Reed 2nd A-7; 53:03, Mary Edson-Walt Edson 3rd 7-11, 58:02

<u>**Limited Class-B:**</u> Lew West-Rod Sampson 1st X-2; 55:05, Jack Swanburg-Orin-Edson 2nd 109-R; 57:09, Mike Reed-Fred Reed 3rd B-1; 57:41

<u>**Limited Class-C:**</u> Mike Knoles-Don Ibsen 1st Y-4; 58:50, Chuck Richmond-Bill Anderson 2nd F-1; 63:11, Carol Edson-Adolph Markwitx 3rd C-9; 66:33

Limited Class-D: Jim Klaven-Ray Lee 1st D-6; 73:41, Sandy Proudfoot-Tom Pierce 2nd DXX; 74:22, Bruce Woods-Richard Wright 3rd D-12; 76:55

1958 Race Schedule (Partial)

Jan 5	Annual "Old-Timers" Cruise
Feb 23	Annual Bar Pilots Cruise
April 7	23rd Sammamish Slough Race
May 4	10th Sammamish Water-Ski Race
June 14	Snoqualmie River-Fall City
June 28-30	Devil's Lake, OR Mile Trials
Aug 16-17	Western Divisionals-Long Beach Stadium, CA
Aug 21-24	Stock Outboard Nationals-Miami, FL
Sept 20	Lake Sammamish Regatta
Sept 28	Racing Outboard Nationals-Minden, LA
Oct 9-11	Devil's Lake, OR Mile Trials

1958 Tidbits

Hugh Entrop won the APBA Jack Maypole Memorial Trophy for the largest world record speed increase with his F-Outboard Hydro 1-mile mark set at Devil's Lake, Oregon, in June. His new record of 103.597 mph smashed the old record by more than 30 mph. He also won APBA's One Mile Championship Trophy, the John C. Mulford Trophy and was the first outboard driver inducted into the 100 mph Club. The pinnacle of his year was his induction into the Gulf Marine Racing Hall of Fame sponsored by the Gulf Oil Company.

Other records set at D-Lake in the October trials were Jack Holden in JU-Runabout for the mile at 28.919 mph and the 5-mile mark at 28.072 in his Karelsen built *Jolly Jack*. Billy Schumacher set the BU-Runabout 5-mile record at 48.701 mph. Jim Henry was elected SOA's commodore for 1959 with Austin "Ausie" Wheeler as secretary. Henry also was the recipient of this year's SOA Sportsman Award. Al Benson became the driver of the unlimited hydro, *Miss Pay 'n Save* and placed first in a heat during the Seattle Gold Cup.

1959

Faster Times Expected in Slough Race

The Northwest's most skilled outboard drivers were out again on Sunday, April 7, trying to tame the snake-like Sammamish Slough. If test runs the week earlier were any indication, spectators were in for some real excitement. The challenge of the corkscrew like waterway already had taken casualties. Trial runs up the 14-mile long twisting course between Kenmore and Lake Sammamish resulted in accidents to a number of outfits. All were repaired in time for the noon starting-gun firing for the first of eight classes at the outer dock of Uplake Marina.

One particular incident included Bob Waite's dunking. He was testing his new cabover when it blew-over at 72 mph near his home on Lake Sammamish. Waite, who was thrown clear of his boat and took an unexpected bath, was rescued by some neighbors. They towed him back to his place where he dried out and made repairs in time for the Slough Race, which he had first won in 1956. A host of past winning drivers were expected to enter along with last year's overall champion, Dick Brunes, who had hopes of a second win in a row, a feat only two drivers had achieved–Dick Barden, 1945-46, and Al Benson 1947-48.

Slough Water at Highest Level

Race chairman Al Benson, predicted to the local press, "We're looking for faster times over last year's. The water in the Slough is the highest-ever giving plenty of depth over the usually shallow areas that had caused numerous beaching and bent propellers in the past. The high water will also smooth-out some of the sharper corners allowing for higher speeds and lower overall times."

Rockey Stone and Bob Steinbruck led a contingent of 10 invaders from Oregon. Stone, 1958 national highpoint champion and holder of a handful of world records, was still looking for his first overall win. Steinbruck, current holder of the CU-Runabout competition record, was the winner of his class last year. Stone's last class win in D-Runabout was in 1956. Three of the area's finest young gunners were looking for more wins.

Chuck Lyford, recent record breaker in Jack Colcock's 48 cubic inch inboard, was looking for a second win in the A-Stock Hydro class. Billy Schumacher, another holder of numerous world records and national championships, was a front runner in the BU-Runabout event. Don Benson, another former multiple record holder, national champion and two-time Class-A Slough Race winner, was having another go at it, challenging Lyford in the A-Racing Hydro event. Local Bothell youngster, Charley Walters was looking for his first win in the JU class.

Bob Jacobsen and wife in new Slough Race entry?

The race officials, who usually aren't recognized by the media, included past Slough Race drivers, Jim Spinner, referee, and Chuck Hickling, measurer. Keith Nelson was the timer, Art Kareslen (Ed and Dave Karelsen's father), starter, and Cricket Callender, the scorer. The second heat and return trip, leaving from Gateway Grove on Lake Sammamish, was scheduled to start at 2 o'clock. Mrs. Ruth Karelsen, wife of Ed, was to reign as Queen of the Race. Her husband, Ed, was without a rig for this year and did not compete.

For safety precautions, the West Seattle Amateur Radio Club operated shortwave radios to allow officials to keep tabs on the progress of the drivers. The Coast Guard enforced another safety measure when they closed-off the Slough to pleasure boaters between 10:00 am and the race's conclusion. Dick Suess, past and present patrol boat captain, likely kept the pleasure boaters from entering the Slough on the Lake Sammamish end. Spectators in pleasure boats were still able to travel to their favorite viewing point in the Slough as long as they were on their way before the course was closed.

Huge Crowd Sees Anderson Win Slough Race

A crowd estimated between 30,000 and 75,000 saw Howard "Andy" Anderson jockey his sleek F-Hydro cabover to his first victory in the 24th running of the Slough race. Anderson's elapsed time for the two-way run between Kenmore and Lake Sammamish was 36:06.2, which was 51.9 seconds quicker than Dick Brunes' time last year, but not over the record of 31:53 set by Bob Waite in 1956.

Anderson had his finely-tuned hydro was in front all up and down the course except for when Wade Ashley, who got the best start on the return trip, sprayed his roostertail in Anderson's face for the first mile downstream. But the champ was able to overtake Ashley on the first straightaway north of Redmond.

Andy Anderson's F-Hydro cabover-1st place overall in Unlimited class.

Young Anderson was one of several thousand spectators who witnessed the Sammamish Slough Race in 1953. He was so intrigued, he immediately started building a race boat after returning to his home in Edmonds. Four years later, a near tragedy almost ended the racing career of the courageous driver. He flipped his hydro during a race on Green Lake and suffered a broken back.

An upcoming young driver showed their might be more than one Gold Cup driver in the family. Benson's teenaged son, Don, clipped five minutes off the A-Racing Hydro record with a time of 43:16.3. Only two champs were able to repeat in their respective class. Seattle's Billy Schumacher pushed his BU-Runabout to a faster record time by 2.1 minutes. Ralph "Red" Taylor of Seattle was in a bigger hurry. He trimmed last years' time of 43:11 to 38:47.8 in winning the C-Stock Hydro race.

Slaughter in Slough

Hard-luck driver, Dick Brunes, took another swim in the Slough this year. Only his skill as a driver and mechanic kept the over-all defending champion in the race. While attempting to overhaul Bob Waite on the short straightaway that bisects the Wayne Golf course, Brunes flipped his F-Hydro, *Lindy*. A helpful spectator loaned him tools from his car to repair his damaged motor. Brunes managed to get back underway before Dick Suess in his patrol boat cleared the Slough. Disabled boats were disqualified if Suess passed them before they were restarted in the Slough. Last year's champion was 47th out of the 49 drivers to reach Lake Sammamish. On the return trip his troubles continued. He beached his craft on a bank but was able to re-start and finish fifth in the unlimited class.

Brunes had company on the flip side. The newcomer, Gerald "Red" Halliday and Kelly Sizemore of Maple Valley, both somersaulted into the drink. There were numerous other beaching and conked-out engines. Two Portland drivers in AU-Runabouts were the first casualties this year at the Down River Marina turn. They played tag with the spectators when Alex Cameron, in the lead, passed under the Wayne Golf Course "Nursery Bridge" and missed the sharp right-hand turn, thinking the marina opening was the main channel. He tried to correct like last year's victims but it was too late as he climbed the bank scattering the unsuspecting spectators.

You would have thought they would have learned the lesson from last year's fracas. A few of the panicked crowd standing on a floating dock, shown in photo on the next page, were about to jump out of the way into water on the marina side of the bank. Stan Johnson, close behind, followed Cameron and took the same detour. Johnson's boat punched a hole in the bottom of Cameron's boat. He was able to restart and eventually won this class. Unfortunately for Cameron, the encounter ended his day as he had to sit out the rest of the race with the spectators on the bank.

Stan Johnson's 145-R poking his nose thru Alex Cameron's bottom at Down River Marina.

Only 39 of the 73 entries started, typical for the most hazardous boat racing event on the West Coast. Ironically, mechanical breakdowns almost cost Anderson his long-sought victory, especially after three months of preparation. During the countdown for the start of the return heat, Anderson discovered his throttle return spring had pulled loose. Wendy Ewing, his mechanic, grabbed a pair of plyers and as the starting gun boomed, snapped the spring into place allowing Anderson to start, albeit a little late. Biff Parker beat out Bob Steinbruck, last year's winner in the combined DU-CU Runabout class and Eddie Raymond, mechanic at Uplake Marina, was the victor in BU-Runabout class.

A crowd with various estimates of up to 75,000 saw numerous other casualties. Five boats ran aground, two others went dead in the water and another boat's motor threw a rod, all adding up to a little more than half the field not finishing the most interesting outboard race in the country.

1959 Sammamish Slough Race Results (by class)

Place	Driver	Class	From	Boat #	Time
1	Howard Anderson	Unlimited	Edmonds	222-R	36:06.2
2	Bob Waite	Unlimited	Bellevue	226-R	*
3	Wade Ashley	Unlimited	Seattle	243-R	*
4	Perry Tonsgard	Unlimited	Bothell	R-71	*
5	Dick Brunes	Unlimited	Kenmore	172-R	*
1	Red Taylor	C-Hydro	Seattle	344-R	38:47.8
2	John Robinson	C-Hydro	Seattle	R-24	*
3	Dave Park	C-Hydro	Kent	141-R	*
4	Les Dunmire	C-Hydro	Seattle	90-R	*

1	Biff Parker	DU-CU Run	Tacama	59-R	39:03.4
2	Bob Steinbruck	DU-CU Run	Salem, OR	2-R	*
3	Dean Mahaffey	DU-CU Run	Roseburg, OR	123-R	*
4	Joe Trembly	DU-CU Run	Tacoma	56-R	*
1	Ed Raymond	B-Stock Hydro	Seattle	120-R	40:16.6
2	Keith Spencer	B-Stock Hydro	Bremerton	38-R	*
3	Sam Dupuis	B-Stock Hydro	Seattle	177-R	*
4	Russell Rotzler	B-Stock Hydro	Seattle	121-R	*
5	Clayton Calhoune	B-Stock Hydro	Seattle	27-R	*
6	Maurice Lemke	B-Stock Hydro	Sumner	X	*
7	Chris Sheafe	B-Stock Hydro	Bellevue	147-R	*
8	Joe Croasdill, Jr.	B-Stock Hydro	Bellevue	134-R	*
9	Denton Herlan	B-Stock Hydro	Bellevue	148-R	*
1	Don Benson	A-Outboard Hydro	Seattle	X	43:16.3
2	Clyde Wilson	A-Outboard Hydro	Seattle	169-R	*
3	Mike Jones	A-Outboard Hydro	Seattle	85-R	*
1	Billy Schumacher	BU-Runabout	Seattle	1-R	44:26.2
2	Larry Leckenby	BU-Runabout	Seattle	97-R	*
3	Pat McMullen	BU-Runabout	Bellingham	250-R	*
1	Barry Lewis	A-Hydro	Seattle	99-R	46:49.4
2	Mike Lewis	A-Hydro	Seattle	3-R	*
3	Wendell Ewing	A-Hydro	Edmonds	229-R	*
4	Pete Borg	A-Hydro	Seattle	207-R	*
5	Bob Koening	A-Hydro	Seattle	37-R	*
1	Stan Johnson	A-Runabout	Portland, OR	145-R	57:10.2
2	W.G. Walters	A-Runabout	Kenmore	44-R	*
3	Larry Knight	A-Runabout	Bothell	234-R	*
1	Charley Walters	JU-Runabout	Kenmore	85-R	*
2	John Zonich	JU-Runabout	Longview	J-10	*
3	Jim Reilly	JU-Runabout	Woodinville	87-R	*

Golden Water-Ski Race

The skier-driver team of Lou West and Bud Sullivan conquered rough water, high winds and the defending champions to win the Unlimited class in the Sammamish Water-Ski Race April, 26. Adverse weather conditions and the 28-mile round-trip course between Kenmore and Lake Sammamish took its toll. Forty-three skiers and drivers in three classes started but, only seventeen finished. The win was the first for West, previously a Limited class competitor, and his veteran driver. Their winning overall time up and back was 44:57.

A slip on the dock at Lake Sammamish cost the defending champions a chance for a repeat victory. Ray Moore's foot slipped as they were taking off and he was dunked in the lake. He and his driver, Dick Brunes, made a quick recovery to finish a disappointing second behind Moore and Sullivan. Rod Preston and Don Reed were third. The ski-pilot team of Craig Morrison and Jan Boscvorch won the Class B in

58:36 and finished ahead of the Class A winners of Duane Olsen and Ted Roark who crossed the finish line in Kenmore at 61:48.

Unlimited Class: Lou West-Bud Sullivan 1st, 44:57; Ray Moore-Dick Brunes 2nd, 45:28; Rod Preston-Don Reed 3rd (no time)

Limited Class-B: Craig Morrison-Jan Boscvorch 1st, 58:36; Rod Sampson-Orin-Edson 2nd, 60:09; Mike Reed-Fred Reed 3rd, 62:56

Limited Class-A: Duane Olson-Ted Roark 1st, 61:48; Ron VanHolledeke-Eddie Raymond 2nd, 63:55; Bob Meehan-Stewart Diebert 3rd, 66:0

—Times sketch by Alan Pratt.

1959 Race Schedule (Partial)

Jan 4	Annual "Old-Timers" Cruise
Feb 22	Annual Bar Pilots Cruise
April 19	24th Sammamish Slough Race
April 26	11th Sammamish Water-Ski Race
May 24	Silver Lake
Aug 1	Racing Outboard Western Divisionals-Green Lake
Aug 3	Kilos-Seattle
Aug 9	Stock Outboard Divisionals-Long Beach, CA
Aug 20-23	Stock Outboard Nationals-Green Lake

1959 Tidbits

Hugh Entrop or "Hugo," as he was called by his racing friends, had the most historic two-years of racing in the history of the Seattle Outboard Association. In addition to last year's laurels, he was the F-Hydro National Champion and won the prestigious APBA "Jack Maypole Memorial Trophy" a second year in a row for the largest world-record speed increase in an outboard. He set the F-Hydro 5-mile competition mark on Green Lake during the Outboard Western Divisionals in August. His record of 76.271 mph smashed the old mark by more than 10 mph. His finale for the year was being selected "*Yachting* All-American" for outboard hydros.

Harold Tolford was inducted into the Gulf Marine Racing Hall of Fame. The Stock Outboard Nationals were unexpectedly handed to Seattle because of high water in the originally-selected city, Portland, Oregon. Jack Holden won the JU National Championship on Green Lake and Jim Benson was second in A-Stock Hydro. Billy Schumacher set a new A-Racing Runabout record at 54.282 mph and the B-Racing Runabout record of 67.809 mph in kilometer straightaway runs on Devil's Lake, Oregon, in October.

The SOA Commodore elected for 1960 was Skip Sherwood. Serving with him was John Croasdill as secretary. The other officers were unpublished. Official scorer, Jackie Wallace, received the SOA Sportsman Award, the second woman to win the plaque; Dorothy Dennis, who won in 1935, was the first.

1959 Slough Race (L-R): Chairman Al Benson holding "Jackens Grill Perpetual Unlimited Class" winner trophy, race queen Ruth Karelsen, Andy Anderson holding "Lake City Capo Club Record Overall Trophy".

1955 Devil's Lake National winners Billy Schumacher, Bud Sullivan, Don Benson with mentor Al Benson.

Chapter 11

1960 Sammamish Slough Race: Jim Benson leading in A-Runabout Class heading upstream toward Bothell.

A Driver's View

"Today I was glad I weigh two-forty, it was windy and I had to ride the front of the boat to keep it down. I was steering with my knees. The weight came in handy"

-Bob Waite comment in Seattle Times Sports Section, April 13, 1970-

Ever wonder what goes on before a race starts and what an outboard racer sees and thinks while driving in a Slough Race? The following is a view from the author who raced in his last Sammamish Slough Race in 1960 before moving into the limited hydro ranks.

The Morning of the Race

It was a cool and misty day in Seattle during the morning of April 10, 1960. Our older 1955 Ford station wagon was wet and still dripping from the early morning rain that finally stopped. Dad, brother Don and I had loaded the raceboat trailer the night before in preparation for the next day's Sammamish Slough Race. The day of the race we arrived at the race's starting location, the aging Ward's Resort in Kenmore, fairly early that soggy day in spring.

Jim Benson, age 16

Many of the other drivers already were unloading their boats from the trailers. My brother and I were excited to get going; especially me because I was high-strung and wound-up like a clock. We lifted the boats off the trailer one by one and set them on sawhorses. Dad and mother headed over to the registration area while my brother and I set up our boats. Dad was the race chairman and had to make sure the club's registration people were open for business. Mom was one of the registrars. The race was scheduled to start at noon with the F-Hydros starting first and each succeeding slower class, five minutes later.

Race Registration

Dad returned to make sure we went over to the registration table inside the resort building. We had to enter at the resort's store front and then walk through to the back into the large ballroom on the east side of the building. Our mother, who was helping with registration, was there along with the head scorer, Jackie Wallace, and assistant, Cricket Calendar. They were at a table where we lined up to register. There were drivers standing in line when we arrived. Registration, which is required at every race, is a requirement for the sponsoring outboard club and the national sanctioning organization, the American Power Boat Association (APBA).

We made sure we had our SOA and APBA membership cards. Drivers needed these to show that they were paid-up members and insured by the APBA's underwriter "Lloyd's of London." Mother made us fill-out our registration forms before arriving, to save time during the morning of the race. We were paid-up card-carrying members and only had to pay the standard registration fee of $5. Non-members had to pay more for a one-day registration which included an APBA fee and insurance. If you weren't a member of any club, you had to pay an additional fee. Members of other clubs weren't required to pay a club fee.

1956: Dick Brunes with his D-Hydro at Ward's Resort in Kenmore on the day of the race.

We unloaded Don's A-Hydro *Uplake Jr,* first, because it was on top of the trailer and then my A-Runabout, *Ill-Eagle*. The boats were placed on short sawhorses, one under the bow and one under the transom, for pre-race setup. Then the engine was mounted, steering cables and throttle cables attached, propeller installed and gas tank filled. We started the motor to make sure it was operational before launching, but not for more than a few seconds, otherwise it would over-heat because the engine wasn't in the water where the water pump that cools the motor could pick up water. Then we threw-in the kneeling cushion, life jacket, goggles, safety helmet, a paddle, sponge and some tools in case of an emergency or breakdown along the way.

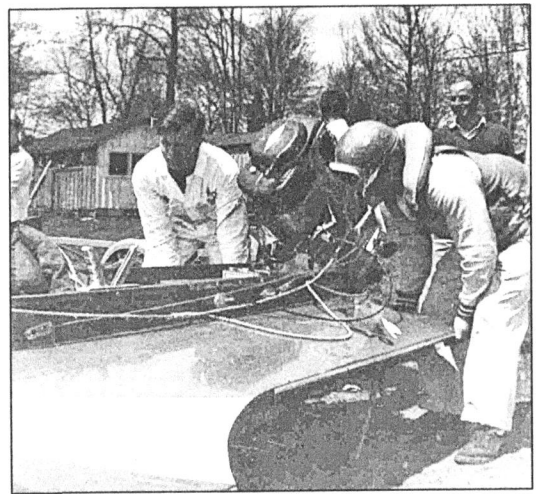
1958: Bill Muncey & crew launching borrowed D-Hydro.

Dad, Don and I, with some help from friends, lifted our rigs over the shore bulkhead and into the water. We held them in place with lines tied to shore. We did this early so dad could leave and go about his business of managing the race. Our boats didn't leak so we could just leave them floating until about 10 minutes before our heat's starting time. At that time, we put on our life jackets and helmets, stepped into our boats, started the engines and idled out to the starting point. We "gunned it" a little on the way to clean out any unburned fuel in the engine. Why? Because fresh fuel in the motor provided more power. By the time we were at the starting area, our engines were warmed up and hopefully still warm enough to start "first-pull" after the starting gun fired.

I paddled my boat out to the end of the starting dock, the large and aging sunken barge, that was rotting and had grass growing in places on the broad deck surface. It was full of spectators, crew members and race officials eagerly watching the start of each heat. The residual smell of burned gasoline and oil was still in the air from the preceding heat, A-Stock-Hydro, my brother's class. I saw him heading into the lead as I was paddling out but I was more concerned about getting a good starting position in front of the barge.

I got the spot I wanted, which gave me the inside position for the run to the turn buoy, straight-out and several hundred yards from the dock in Lake Washington. The same position as number *62-R* (the lower boat in the photo on next page) at the starting barge.

What Everyone Was Waiting for–The Start

Having a good starting position didn't guarantee a good start. Factors are: the motor starting on the first pull of the starting cord, quickly getting the boat on a plane and being fast enough to keep the other boats from cutting you off as you approached the buoy. Five-four-three-two-one, bang! That was the starter's countdown and then the gun fired.

1955: B-Hydros ready for start at Ward's Resort dock.

My engine started on the first pull and I gunned it full-throttle. All the engines of the eight A-Runabouts were roaring in unison. It was loud but not the ear-splitting sound of the F-Hydros, the first class that started. The spray from our propellers was shooting out and soaking the spectators on the barge. I simultaneously stepped over my steering wheel with one leg in the front cockpit to shift my weight as far forward as possible to help the boat get on a plane[1] sooner. I was at a disadvantage at this point because my 100 pounds was a lot lighter than all the other competitors in my class.

1955 Start of the D & B Runabout class.

As the boat was just about on a plane and starting to accelerate, I jumped back into the rear cockpit, still with my hand squeezing the throttle full-on. I crouched down, kneeling with my head down so I could just see what was ahead over the steering wheel. It was the fast-approaching left-turn buoy. Being small gave me an advantage then because I could kneel way down in the cockpit to minimize the wind resistance

---

[1] Once a boat stops pushing water (displacement) and lays down traveling on top of the water (hydroplaning).

(see Schumacher-Benson passing photo later in this chapter). Fortunately, that time I got a great start and everything fell into place.

I was off and speeding toward the buoy, four hundred yards away, with several other boats on my right side all fairly close, about nose to nose. As I reached the buoy with the other boats, I was on the inside at the turn, the most advantageous position for turning. I managed to get around the buoy safely by shifting my weight as far as possible toward the buoy which allowed my boat to turn without catching a chine[2] and flipping-over like many other drivers in the preceding years.

Then it was clear sailing straight ahead into the Slough toward the Kenmore Bridge. I managed to get in front of the pack because I got to the buoy first and the others had to fall in line behind me, "eating my roostertail" (the spray from my engine's propeller). This usually kept the drivers behind, farther back, so they kept out of the spray to see better. Otherwise they had to move to one side or the other to avoid it, slowing them down a little. The channel was wide but only deep enough in the middle section for boats.

Passing under the bridge I could hear the sound of my engine echoing off its underside. Dozens of spectators were watching overhead taking photos and cheering us on. The Kenmore Bridge was the last good long-distance viewing point for the crowd until the bridge before the Down River Marina, which was 1–1/2 miles upstream.

1947 promotion shot taken from Kenmore Bridge with boats heading upstream from Kenmore starting area.

---

[2] The intersection of the bottom and the sides of a flat or V-bottomed raceboat.

We had to negotiate several sweeping right and left turns between Kenmore and the marina, about 1-1/2 miles, but were relatively easy to make, especially if you anticipated the turns by turning just before you reached the bend and hugged the inside to shorten your path. Still in the lead by a boat length or two, I had to make sure I didn't get too close to shore or I would run over a sand bank or worse, rocks in the shallows.

Difficult "Down River Marina" Turn

Now the Down River Marina bridge turn was another story. This was a sharp right-hand turn, very similar to the one I just made in the photo at the beginning of the chapter. A driver needed to be thinking of this turn well before he actually made it because if he didn't hug the right side close to the bridge pilings, the river current would push his boat toward the opposing bridge pilings and river bank, forcing him to slide or run into the marina opening (see photo below). A worse consequence would be a spin-out, like in the photo on the next page. That boat was heading the wrong way, downstream instead of upstream after his spin.

1960: Andy Anderson in Unlimited class taking sharp right-hand turn under Marina Bridge going upstream.

Late 1950s: A-Runabout boat pointing downstream after spinning-out trying to miss overturned boat at Down River Marina during upstream run in Sammamish Slough Race.

Practice, Practice, Practice

How did I learn all this stuff at the young age of 12 when I ran my first Slough Race? Practice, practice, practice and coaching from our father. He would let my brother and me run a boat, up the Slough, during the Slough cruises earlier in the year. In the weeks leading up to the race, we practiced in the river in our raceboats. This was when we made mental notes of the dangerous places; the turns, bridges, sawmill log boom and other notorious places.

Practicing in the Slough wasn't too tricky because we did it when the weather wasn't warm enough for recreational boaters and swimmers. We didn't have to worry much about what could be around the next corner–a kid on an inner tube, another boat or swimmers. Luck played a big part in the Slough Race in its original configuration (before the dredging in 1964). Practicing helped take some of that "luck" out of the race.

There weren't many driving rules in this race. The driver in front had all the advantages and he could block other drivers from passing. Being a good sport at this time was not for drivers whose goal was to win. Leave that for after the race when and if you rationalized cutting-off someone. It was up to the driver behind to find a way to pass, most anything went here short of running over the back of a competitor. This is why I wore goggles, just in case I was behind another boat and in someone's roostertail.

After the marina bridge, there was a short fairly straight section that runs through the Wayne Golf Course (see map

1954 Slough Cruise: Don (driving) and Jim Benson practicing in the Sammamish Slough driving a family pleasure boat.

on page 378). A driver could pass here if he was quick enough but he had to dodge two small golf-course bridges and the Wayne-Juanita highway bridge. The next turn was farther upstream as you approached the Bothell area. It was an easy sweeping left-hand bend with a railroad trestle just ahead. A more difficult sweeping right-hand turn was farther upstream where the driver needed to shift his weight to the right to make the more difficult sweeping right-hand turn, then another easy broad left-hand turn.

Approaching the Treacherous Bothell Bridge

The next hair-raising turn was the sharp switchback turn a few hundred feet before the Bothell Bridge (see photo on next page). Here, it was easy to cut it too sharp and run over the sand bar on the inside of the turn. Approaching and passing under the Bothell Bridge was the most dangerous part of the course. I wanted to make the sharp right-hand turn that was directly under the bridge safely while passing between the large concrete support pillars on each side. If not, all kinds of things could happen, none of them good!

For instance, if a driver didn't anticipate this turn correctly, he'd end up crunching his boat into a pillar, spinning out, or worse getting dunked and a crunched boat. Going upstream, the oncoming current pushes you back toward the pillars on the left. Many a driver met misfortune here by crashing into a pillar, spinning-out because you didn't steer correctly or flipping completely.

During this predicament, you most likely were thrown out into the swirling water and possibly trapped under a half-submerged boat while the strong current either pushed your boat back into the pillars or floated it downstream. Being caught upside down and trapped under your boat was a danger to all of us. Luckily, no one in the race drowned here and we were glad to be wearing the required helmet and life jacket to protect against a header into a pillar or an upside-down experience. The only good thing was when you made a clean run under the bridge.

1964 Bothell: Notorious turn in Sammamish Slough leading to Bothell Bridge.

I found that this turn gave me the first opportunity to pass. An inexperienced driver usually misjudged the current and sharpness of the turn and swung wide to the left. I always hugged the inside of the turn, to the right, by anticipating the current and sharpness by turning my motor before I was under the bridge. If I was close behind another boat, this was where I could make a pass. Continuing from Bothell, we encountered a series of somewhat easy sweeping turns leading you to the next hazard, the S turns approaching Woodinville. These were where the present Interstate 405 bridge crosses the Slough.

Typically, closed-course boat racing always turned left but not in the Slough. The S–turns were a series of snake-like right and left bends. If you don't shift your weight properly and/or hit a swell in the water, you'd end up overturning and possibly ending up on the bank! Runabouts were especially vulnerable because of their sharp chine or edges that intersect between the bottom and the sides that could dig into the water when turning. This combined with the turning force that threw your weight over to the wrong side of your boat, could flip you over in an instant!

I almost ended up on the bank in my first race while traveling upstream in the A-Runabout Class. I caught a chine turning right in the S–turns and instantly flipped over upside down. I was thrown out and almost landed on the bank along with my boat. Luckily for me, there were a few friends of my brother right there watching. But unlucky because the official patrol boat passed me just before the friends righted my boat and I was able to restart soaking wet, head to toe.

If the patrol boat passed you (with a race official looking for drivers in distress), you were disqualified for the rest of the race and were required to return to Kenmore before the downstream heat started. You only received points for a complete run each way. How you finished in the race depended on the points you earned for each run and your time. In case of a tie in points, the best time won.

Reading the Water

"Reading the water" is a term we used in boat racing. A knowledgeable driver should be looking at the water in front of him. He looks for waves from the wind or from another boat in front. Drivers shouldn't steer their boat into a wave sideways because it could catch a chine and flip over, especially in the older style runabouts. To minimize this, we needed to slow down, which was easier said than done in the heat of competition.

Hydros were much more forgiving because they ran higher out of the water and had larger non-trips[3] on their sides. The same goes for rough water from the wind. A driver needed to be careful not to turn into a wave in rough water. Again, catching a chine would result most likely in a driver flipping his boat, or at the least, hooking abruptly, which could force the boat to spin-out and toss its driver in the drink (see photo on next page). Being towed back to Kenmore after flipping was not what you expected to happen in a Slough Race.

---

[3] A series of angled sides located between the bottom and sides of a hydroplane or runabout (at the chines) or on a hydroplane's right and left sponson (the lower outer sides of the boat's front section).

1969: B-Hydro heading upstream, misses turn, spins-out and is flipping over at Bothell Bridge.

Notorious Log Boom in Woodinville

Continuing up the Slough from the S-turns the drivers encountered three bridges. First a railroad bridge, then the highway bridge that connects Bothell to Woodinville and then another railroad bridge. The way under is several easy bends, but beware! The Saginaw Sawmill log-boom in Woodinville is just ahead and a driver needs to be prepared for this next most dangerous part of the Slough.

The log boom took up about two-thirds of the Slough width, leaving six-to-eight feet of channel on the left side (going upstream), only enough room for one boat at a time. If there were two boats side by side approaching the boom, the left-hand boat has the best position because it could enter the narrow channel straight-in. If you were on the right-hand side like my brother a few years earlier, you'd most likely run up on top of the logs and poke a hole in the bottom of your boat before you had a chance to stop. Likely the aluminum skid fin on the bottom middle section would be pushed up leaving a good-sized hole. In this case, his Karelsen-built hydro's bottom was strong enough to prevent a puncture.

In my brother's situation, he shut down his motor while he was stranded half-way up over the logs. He immediately jumped out and pushed his A-Stock-Hydro back into the water. He hoped it would float long enough to re-start and get going fast enough to keep a potential hole on the bottom or sides from preventing him to continue upstream. Luckily, he was able to restart and continue his run, finishing at Lake Sammamish.

The log boom at the Saginaw Sawmill was only in the Slough during the 1950s. It wasn't a hazard for me because I raced only up to Bothell in the JU class and by the time I was too old (over 14) to race in that class, I moved up into the A-Runabout division. By then the mill had shut down and the log boom was gone. Lucky for me I guess?

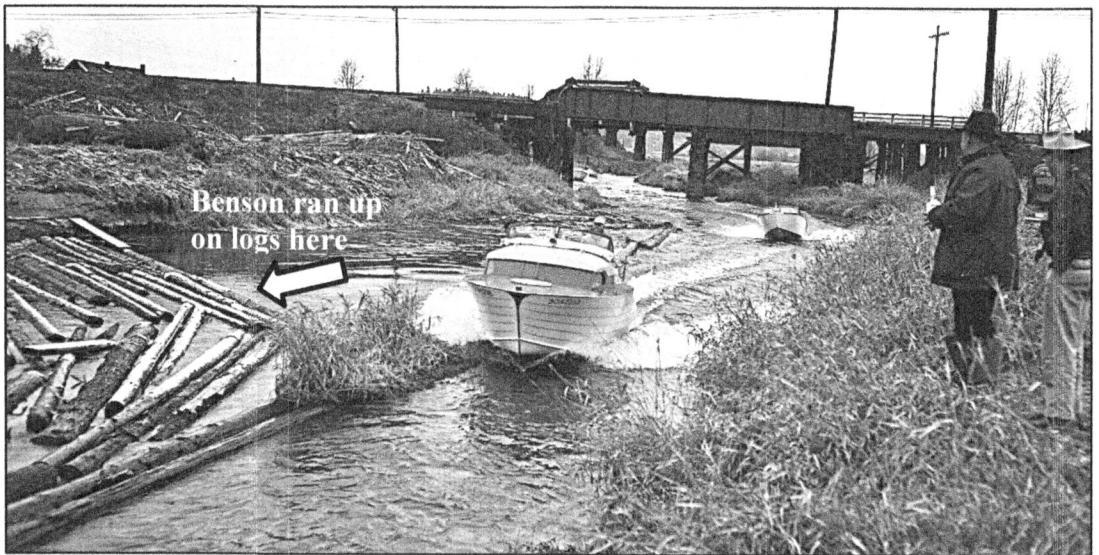

1956 Slough Cruise at log boom in Woodinville: Cruising boat running into log boom next to where Don Benson ran amuck in previous story. The second railroad bridge in foreground and highway bridge is behind.

The Pass

Quite often the straightaways farther up in Redmond were the only places where a driver could pass another boat. This is when I was very glad to have my goggles. If I was behind a boat, had more speed and was catching up, I needed to prepare and think about how I was going to make a pass.

The first straight stretch on the upstream run is the longest, about a half-mile long. Here is where you hoped you were on the tail end of someone's boat at the time so you could use the whole straightaway to pass. A driver needed to get up close to the boat ahead, sometimes right in his roostertail only a few feet behind. Then quickly cut-over to one side and stick your nose ahead of the boat's stern on one side to keep your position and prevent the driver from cutting you off.

Trading Paint

Sometimes it works and sometimes not. If not, you try it again, maybe on the other side or back and forth until you were successful. That's why it's best to pass on the longest straightaway because you had more time to pass. Remember, it was up to the passing boat to find a way to overtake the boat ahead. The driver in front usually tried his best to block you from passing. When runabouts pass closely side-by-side in the narrow Slough, the sides of the boats can touch each other, scraping the paint off one boat and transferring it to the other. This is what we called "trading paint" in racing circles.

After a successful pass, you might have waved as you go by indicating "nice try blocking me, but I'm faster!" At this point you are happy you were successful but now you're thinking: "I'm soaking wet and cold," because the 40-plus mile-per-hour headwind in your face made the wind-chill factor seem like it was freezing. You're thinking, "I wish I was at Lake Sammamish now" because you're looking forward to some dry clothes and hot chocolate. In some cases, maybe in a lot of cases, the more mature drivers were looking forward to some spirits to warm their souls. I don't remember spirits being mentioned in the drivers' meetings as a no-no but at that point I don't think the cold drivers cared. It's not like we had tests for alcohol or other substances back then. It was a traditional or accepted practice.

Just when you think you're in the clear, another boat maybe approached, but the straightaway was coming to an end and there was another shorter one just a few turns ahead. There you could get wet all over again when trying to make another pass.

Mid-1950s: Friendly competition on Lake Sammamish with Jimmy Benson, closest to camera, shaking fist at Billy Schumacher (smiling) while he's passing him on far side-similar to passing in the Slough.

By now you're probably wondering why it took so long to catch up to the slower boats. It's usually because you got a really bad start, ran through some weeds and had to clean them out of your propeller, maybe your carburetor froze up momentarily choking your engine or maybe you ran up on a bank making a poor turn or any number of other unlucky circumstances. There was always something unusual that could happen if you weren't careful, or if you were just unlucky.

At this point I hoped that I was in the lead and didn't have to worry about passing another boat again. There were always stragglers from the classes that started before. That was another hazard, overtaking those slower boats that sometimes moved over if they looked back for some reason. In most instances they were just trying to keep their boat going, in the middle of the course and not thinking about anything else. When you passed them it usually scared the you-know-what out of them. Often, toward the upper end of the Slough, you were just tired of driving and being cold, wanting to get the run over. A driver might take more risks in passing because they were impatient and not thinking about their or other's safety. This is when you could get in real trouble and end your day, on a bank, upside down or in a tree.

Three-Point Hydros

The two straightaways could be a real hazard with a strong headwind and a fast and loose[4] boat, usually in the Unlimited, C- and B-Hydro classes. April was when stiff winds could blow down through the Sammamish Valley, a condition that could upset your hydro's riding ability. Good handling hydros ride an inch or two above the water when they are balanced properly for high speeds. They're called "three-point hydros" because they ride on three points, the bottoms of the two forward sponsons[5] and the tips of the propeller blades. Two or three-bladed propellers are used on raceboats. The boats are designed to catch the air under them because of their built-in lift (the bottom raises upward between the

1973: Bob Waite approaching turn at end of straight stretch floating high with his 240-lb. body forward to prevent blowing-over backwards.

---

[4] An unstable condition created by too much lift or wind pressure under the boat
[5] Projections on racing craft extending outward from the forward hull sides to increase lateral stability in the water, the two-points of a three-point hydroplane with the prop being the third.

sponsons and bow). The boat rides or floats on a cushion of air trapped underneath between the two sponsons and the aft air traps[6].

A gust of wind could upset the boat's balance and send the driver and boat flying over backwards, obviously ending your day. With luck, you landed in the water and not on the river bank or in a tree. This is when you wished you were a 200 plus pounder because you could shift your weight forward far as possible with your head and body leaning over the steering wheel compensating for the extra air flowing under the boat. Bob Waite, a 240-pounder in his 70 mph F-Hydro, is doing just that in the photo on the previous page. Of course, slowing made for a safer ride, but sometimes drivers waited too long to decelerate, the result–blow overs in the straightaways.

At the end of the second straightaway I encountered another series of wider and easier serpentine turns before reaching downtown Redmond and a series of bridges. It was a straight run under the first, which was a railroad bridge and the second, the highway bridge connecting Rose Hill and Redmond. There was another bridge just before the Redmond Golf Course and then two more bridges before you reached the final bridge, a road bridge at Marymoor Farms.

1956 Slough Cruise: Racing-type runabout passes last bridge going upstream at Marymoor Farms.

By this time, I was all by myself and taking it somewhat easier around the bends and under the bridges because no other boats were within sight. The last stretch was a couple of broad bends that led to head of the Slough at Lake Sammamish. As I entered the lake, I could see the finishing area, Idylwood Park ahead, about one-half mile away.

---

[6] The continuation of the inside vertical wall of the sponsons aft to the transom, forming tunnel sides that trap or channel high pressure air underneath, lifting the boat out of the water at high speeds

I was relieved there weren't any boats running in front of me. I was thinking: "I must be in first place." But another boat in my class could have finished ahead of me and already be on the beach. I was relieved again when the checkered flag was waved at me as I passed by the dock at Idylwood. Going ashore, I met my brother who was anxiously waiting for me to finish and was told, "You won the upriver run for your class."

Still soaking from the passes, I changed some clothes, quenched my thirst and ate something. But I couldn't rest much because I had to get ready for the second heat back downstream. My father and mother had traveled to the resort to help us get ready. Dad, the race chairman, was making sure everything was going smoothly and mother was getting the scoring sheets from the first run. Our boats didn't seem to be leaking so we just tied them up to the dock. After a short rest, I refueled and sponged the water out of my boat that was sprayed in during my passes. Don was out at the starting dock, ready for the gun to start his downstream run.

The fastest classes, the Unlimiteds, had already started and were extremely noisy. You can't imagine the sound of a dozen high powered open-exhaust F-Hydros all starting at the same time. The loud screaming sounds were ear-splitting, especially to my ears, echoing between the hills southward down Lake Sammamish. I was tied-up close to the starting line, too close to the loud F-Hydro guys.

Downstream Run Back to Kenmore

After my brother started in the A-Hydro class, I moved my rig over to the starting dock and took position closest to shore, the shortest path from the dock to the Slough entrance. As the starting gun fired, we were off, all the A-Runabout boats that were still able to start. We headed straight for the Slough. I was passed and was eating a roostertail on my way into the Slough in fourth place. Everything was in reverse going downstream. We passed under all the Redmond

1955: Don Benson leading in A-Stock-Hydro class.

bridges all bunched up together in-line. No one could pass anybody until we reached the straight stretches a short distance ahead. I was able to pass a few boats because I was faster in the turns but slower in the open water, the reason I was passed on the way to the Slough.

On the downstream run at the end of the short straightaway is "Halliday Corner." This is where Red Halliday crashed and went head-first into a mud bank on his downstream run in 1960 (see his story in Chapter 12). He was going too fast when he entered the sweeping left and right turns that connect the two straight stretches (see map at end of Chapter 12). His boat hooked and threw him out and the boat behind rescued him. Halliday was a colorful character and well-liked by his fellow club members, so they honored him, I think, by naming the corner after him.

The rest of the way down was about the same as the upstream run, except we now were going with the current. This posed a new problem because we had to slow down a little more at each corner and bridge. If you didn't, the unsuspecting current pushed you deeper into each turn. The downstream drivers learned this in a hurry because it felt really weird compared to the slower run up the Slough. When I reached the long straightaway, I saw a boat ahead of me, but he was too far to catch. I had to be a lot more careful in all the turns and especially at the Bothell Bridge because of the current.

1963: Ralph Payne of Texas learns the hard way about down river currents after hitting a bridge piling next to Down River Marina. Strong currents likely contributed to his accident and bath.

I reached the finish line in Kenmore successfully but another boat beat me to the checkered flag. I wondered if I should have pushed it harder at the upper end of the first run. As it turned out, my thinking was correct because the driver ahead at the finish placed second in the first run. We were tied in points, but his overall time up and down the Slough was a little better because he went faster on the final run. He was declared the A-Runabout class winner.

Our speeds were pretty darn slow compared to the fastest, the F-Hydros. They reached speeds upwards to 70 mph compared to ours, which were in the low-40s. Our total elapsed times were about 50 minutes compared to about 35 minutes for them. The A-Runabouts started in Kenmore 30 minutes after the F boys. The winner had finished by about the time we were in Bothell and were resting comfortably on the beach at Lake Sammamish.

I wasn't discouraged about my second-place finish because this was the first time I made it all the way up and down the Slough in the race. The year before I flipped and didn't finish. It was a learning experience I would think about for a while. But not for long because a few years later I moved from outboards to limited inboards following in the wake of my brother Don, Billy Schumacher and Chuck Lyford, guys I started racing outboards with in the early 1950s.

1967 Jim Benson

All told, there were 63 turns, by my dad's count, and 22 bridges in the original configuration of the Slough between the 1920s and 1963. Most of the hazards were removed by the Slough's dredging in 1964-1965, except for the bigger turns, higher banks, the Bothell Bridge and the remaining straightaways.

For me and most of my friends and competitors, the Slough Race was their favorite boat race, even for the most successful of the unlimited hydroplane drivers such as Chip Hanauer and Billy Schumacher. None of us will ever forget the fun we had learning to drive and compete in the "Crookedest Race in the World."

1953: Seattle Post-Intelligencer newspaper photographer Bob Miller about to photograph Slough Race winner, Al Benson, with 1952 winner Bob Jacobsen at Ward's Resort in Kenmore.

1957 Green Lake: Jim Benson receiving trophy from Seafair Princess for first place in JU-Runabout class.

1967: Jim Benson setting world competition record of 80.142 mph on Green Lake in Seattle driving his Karelsen-built 150 cubic inch limited hydro A-555, *Hilton Hy-Per-Lube* after lapping the field.

Chapter 12

1961: Slough Race winner Wendell "Windy" Ewing (L) holding "Jacken's Grill" perpetual trophy & bride Penny, alongside last year's winner, Howard Anderson, holding "Lake City Capo Club" perpetual Trophy.

Disturbing the Peace
1960-1963

"Heroics, by both drivers and spectators, prevented tragedies...during outboard-speedboat race on Sammamish Slough"

-Bud Livesley of the Seattle Daily Times, April 11, 1960-

SENIOR VICE - PRESIDENT
J. A. COLCOCK, JR.
Seattle, Washington

SECRETARY
V. J. SPINNER, JR.
Seattle, Washington

The big news for the club in 1960 was the election of Jack Colcock and Jim Spinner to officer positions in the American Power Boat Association. Colcock was elected senior vice-president and Jim Spinner, secretary. It was the first time the Seattle Outboard Association had two national officers elected in the same year. Jerry Bryant was the first APBA officer when he was vice president in 1934. The Northwest was fortunate to be well- represented in the national body; other clubs in the nation were surely most envious of the accomplishment.

"Outboards Test Slough Next Sunday"

The sports headline above and all the quotations in the Slough Race story that follows were from Bud Livesley's columns in the *Seattle Times* on April 3, 8 and 11. He wrote: "Navigating the twisty Sammamish Slough is a challenge to even the most cautious skipper. At high speed, taking the kinks out of the meandering Slough has been the undoing of more than one expert speedboat driver. But they never stop trying to unsnarl the 63-turn two-way route between Kenmore and Lake Sammamish. Many are successful but always a few winds up on the beach." Such is the appeal of the Seattle Outboard Association's annual "Taming of the Slough" race.

Howard "Andy" Anderson, last year's winner, will be shooting for his second win in a row, a feat only two have achieved since the race's inception in 1934. Dick Barden was the first in 1945-1946 and Al Benson was the last in 1947-1948. Anderson was expected to be at the Kenmore starting line again on Sunday, April 10 when the first of 11 classes head for Idylwood Resort to complete the first leg of the competition.

Dick Brunes, Billy Schumacher and Red Taylor will also compete. Schumacher and Taylor currently have the fastest times in their respective classes running the Slough. Schumacher, one of the area's experienced youthful drivers, lowered his overall time last year by 2.1 seconds for the BU-Runabouts. Taylor lowered the C-Stock Hydro time from 43.11 to 38.47.8. Other 1959 winners expected were: Biff Parker in the CU-DU runabouts, Ed Raymond in B-Stock Hydro, Don Benson in A-Outboard Hydro, Stan Johnson in AU-Runabout and Charley Walters in the J-Utility class.

Race chairman, Gerald "Red" Halliday, said "the big drivers are capable of speeds over 70 miles per hour. If they get going that fast, there are going to be a few missed turns." He knew because he was one of them. In several pre-race news articles, he warned the spectators to stay back away from the banks when the boats come screaming by.

Course to be Closed

Halliday appealed to spectators to refrain from throwing debris into the Slough during the race as in the past. Trash tossed in by 25,000 to 30,000 spectators who turned out every year had spilled almost as many drivers as the tricky and numerous turns along the course. The Coast Guard will close the Slough to pleasure craft at 10 am, like last year, two hours before the start. And for safety precautions as in the past, the West Seattle Radio Club would be stationed along the course reporting the drivers' status to race officials.

Records In Jeopardy

"More and faster raceboats and a new 'straightaway' start was anticipated to provide more thrills and records," explained race spokesman Al Benson. "In the past, there's been a dogleg from the starting dock at Uplake Marina around a buoy leading into the Slough from Lake Washington. Because the log boom was placed farther out in the lake, the dogleg will be eliminated. More boats will be able to get into the Slough faster. It's going to get somewhat congested, but it will make for a better race."

While the race always attracts the more experienced drivers, many of the entrants will come from the ranks of the recent novice school put on by the Seattle Outboard Association. The rookies got their first chance at competition the week before when they received their competitive baptism in a race on Lake Washington. And for the first time, the 80-cubic inch marathon class pleasure outboards will attempt to unwind the course. The marathon boats are craft of 15-1/2 feet and over, capable of speeds up to 50 miles per hour.

The F-Hydros, fastest of the outboards, will get the racing underway at noon. They will be followed at five-minute intervals by 11 slower classes that include: A, B, C and D-Stock Hydro; JU, AU, BU, CU and DU Runabout; B-Outboard Hydro and the marathon boats. The JU runabouts will finish in Bothell as in the past races. More than 150 boats were expected to enter the Northwest's most popular outboard event.

Andy Repeats

Simply being counted as a finisher in the Sammamish Slough race was an accomplishment in itself. Fifty-one of the 96 starters failed to finish. The most notable exception was Andy Anderson, the 33-year-old Edmonds marina operator. Anderson drove through the twisted Slough in a record time of 35:38 from Kenmore to Gateway Grove on Lake Sammamish and back. He was now one of the select few hydro jockeys successful at back-to-back overall victories, matching the accomplishments of Dick Barden and Al Benson in the 1940s.

Only Kenmore's Don Benson and Charley (Chuck) Walters were repeat class winners. Benson, a future challenger to the mark of three-time overall class victories set by his father, nosed out the defending champion, Seattle's Barry Lewis, to win the A-Stock Hydro division. Benson first won the A-Stock Hydro event in 1956.

Walters, again, showed the way to Bothell for the youngsters in the JU-Runabout class. Ed Raymond, a mechanic at Uplake Marina who took the honors in B-Stock Hydro last year, was second to Bothell's Ray Cox this time.

Brunes Takes Another Dunking

Dick Brunes, Anderson's predecessor as the overall champ in 1958, had his troubles as usual. Brunes flipped his ride in the F-Hydro class for a second consecutive year. But like last year, he was able to re-saddle his mount and finish the race, albeit out of the money. While Brunes and others were unable to tame the Slough, Seattle's Jackie

Holden, 1959 national champion, followed suit with Brunes and the others. He flipped his A-Runabout, a common occurrence for a driver who steps up from the slower JU ranks to the much faster and wilder AU class. I know this because it happened to both my brother Don and me. Tacoma novice driver, Bruce Bille, fresh from a second-place effort in his recent novice race on Lake Washington, won the challenging BU-Runabout event.

1960 Andy Anderson passing under Wayne Golf Course nursery bridge heading to Kenmore finish line.

Thoughtless Spectators

A handful of the estimated 25,000 to 35,000 spectators proved more troublesome to Anderson than the challenges of other drivers and the Slough. "A couple of spectators waded right out into the Slough and splashed water on me as I went past," said Anderson. "Still another threw an object that landed right in front of me and splashed more water in my face. That can be somewhat scary when you're traveling 70 to 80 miles per hour."

Anderson was very concerned when he was the fifth boat off the start. He had spent 18 hours the previous day working over a "sick" engine and was afraid he might have missed something. But by the time Anderson reached the Kenmore Bridge, the first bridge near the Slough entrance, he was in second-place behind Bud Sullivan. He caught Sullivan, 1955 winner, when the Seattle driver spun out at the sharp 90-degree turn just before the Bothell Bridge. From then on, Anderson had the race to himself. Sullivan managed to keep going and finished third behind newcomer Perry Tonsgard.

Heroics Prevent Tragedies

This year's race had injuries and associated carnage. The race chairman, Red Halliday, suffered a dislocated right shoulder when he was tossed 50 feet after his Unlimited class hydro hit the river bank. Harley Batten, a D-Hydro driver, had his left thumb virtually severed when he hit debris in the Slough and lost the skid fin from his craft and crashed into the bank. Lance Puckett, driving his A-Stock Hydro, slammed into one of the pillars of the Wayne Golf Course Bridge, but was uninjured. Dale Hendrickson's hydro was run down by another boat. Hendrickson escaped injury only because he was out of the boat at the time attempting to relaunch and restart the race. Raceboats weren't the only ones in harm's way in the Slough.

Heroics by both drivers and spectators prevented tragedies. Some race officials were forced to abandon an 18-foot patrol boat that was stuck crosswise in the Slough and directly in the path of an oncoming racer in Woodinville.

During the rest period between heats when no race boats were supposed to be running in the Slough, Lynn McMullen, a passenger in a patrol boat returning from Lake Sammamish, had to abandon the craft while stopped in Woodinville. The boat was returning downstream to race headquarters at Uplake Marina with official scoring sheets for the first heat and timing equipment. She was one of the boat's occupants who had to make an emergency exit. The course supposedly was clear, but the unexpected sound of a raceboat was near.

Harrowing Experience

In maneuvering to avoid the river bank and a raceboat stuck on the log boom at the Saginaw Sawmill, the patrol boat ended up wedged between the bank and the log boom. "Then we heard a hydro coming down from the Lake Sammamish end of the Slough," said Miss McMullen. "Apparently it was one that had been beached and the driver managed to get under way again." Miss McMullen, Bonnie Schumacher (one of Billy Schumacher's three sisters), Mike and Debbie Case and children of the patrol boat owner, were among those who jumped before an unsuspecting hydro came around a blind corner and hit their boat. The impact was not severe and the raceboat driver escaped injury.

A rescue attempt was needed as several of the boat's occupants were in the water. Mrs. Case, who was one of them in the cold water, was struggling in the swift current. Sam Dupuis jumped in and rescued her while another person threw a line over to her. It wasn't clear who else was in the water, but it was said that all were taken to a hospital for check-ups and then released. Miss McMullen explained, "No one was hurt, only a few scratches. I was wet, cold and scared."

Race Chairman Halliday Crashes–Rescued

Chairman Red Halliday's prerace prophecy came true, but he didn't think it would be him. Al Karelsen came to his rescue during an incident farther up the Slough in Redmond. "I was running right behind Red," said Karelsen, "when I saw him flip. He was tossed about 50 feet through the air and landed on the bank."

Karelsen, who was running third at the time in the Unlimited class, immediately beached his craft and raced to the aid of the distressed driver. "He was lying unconscious, face down in the mud, when I reached him," said Karelsen. "It's lucky he landed where he did. That mud cushioned his fall; it could have been pretty bad otherwise." Halliday was taken to a hospital nearby and subsequently returned to race headquarters for the presentation of trophies and awards along with a lot of ribbing from his fellow race drivers.

1960 Sammamish Slough Race Results (by class)

Place	Driver	Class	From	Boat #	Time
1	Howard Anderson	F-Outboard Hydro	Edmonds	222-R	35:38
2	Perry Tonsgard	F-Outboard Hydro	Bothell	R-71	*
3	Bud Sullivan	F-Outboard Hydro	Seattle	25-R	*
1	Clyde Wilson	D-Stock Hydro	Seattle	*	*
2	John Owens	D-Stock Hydro	Tacoma	*	*
3	Bill Quam	D-Stock Hydro	Seattle	*	*
1	Roy Williams	DU-Runabout	Bremerton	64-R	*
2	Dean Mahaffey	DU-Runabout	Roseburg, OR	52-R	*
3	Andy Thompson	DU-Runabout	Seattle	250-R	*
1	Bob Vining	C-Stock Hydro	Mercer Island	225-R	*
2	Bob Rautenberg	C-Stock Hydro	Kirkland	*	*
3	Sam Mellison	C-Stock Hydro	Seattle	*	*
1	Harold Davies	CU-Runabout	Bothell	*	*

2	Bob Steinbruck	CU-Runabout	Salem, OR	2-R	*
3	George Stuniga	CU-Runabout	Salem, OR	*	*
1	Glenn Dickerson	B-Outboard Hydro	Seattle	*	*
2	Stewart Lowe	B-Outboard Hydro	Mercer Island	*	*
3	John Croasdill	B-Outboard Hydro	Bellevue	*	*
1	Ray Cox	B-Stock Hydro	Bothell	*	*
2	Ed Raymond	B-Stock Hydro	Seattle	*	*
3	Gerald Riggs	B-Stock Hydro	Renton	*	*
1	Bruce Bills	BU-Runabout	Tacoma	*	*
2	Larry Leckenby	BU-Runabout	Seattle	97-R	*
1	Don Benson	A-Stock Hydro	Seattle	*	*
2	Barry Lewis	A-Stock Hydro	Seattle	99-R	*
3	Pete Borg	A-Stock Hydro	Edmonds	207-R	*
4	Pete Borg	A-Hydro	Seattle	3-R	*
5	Bob Koening	A-Hydro	Seattle	3-R	*
1	Alex Cameron	A-Runabout	Portland, OR	44-R	*
2	Jim Benson	A-Runabout	Kenmore	29-R	*
3	Fred Miller	A-Runabout	San Mateo, CA	57-R	*
1	Charley Walters	JU-Runabout	Bothell	85-R	*
2	Jim Downing	JU-Runabout	Seattle	51-R	*
4	Jim Reilly	JU-Runabout	Woodinville	87-R	*

Some boat numbers and times unavailable

1960 Slough Race winner Andy Anderson being congratulated by his mechanic Wendell Ewing holding Unlimited class perpetual trophies at Uplake Marina race headquarters in Kenmore.

Golden Water-Ski Race

Lou West and Bud Sullivan may be starting a winning dynasty in the Unlimited class of the Golden Water-Ski Race. West the skier and Sullivan the driver, left the competition behind and won the annual Sammamish Water-Ski race for a second time in a row. It was the 12th annual running that started from Uplake Marina in Kenmore, ran up the serpentine course through the Slough to Lake Sammamish, then back downstream to the finish in Kenmore. The duo was never challenged throughout the 28-mile round-trip marathon run on Sunday, April 25.

Don Ibsen, towed by Brother Ron, took the honors in the Class-B competition and Dave DesVoigne skier, and Bud Hughes the pilot, were the victors in the Class-C event. No times were given or the number of entries. The winners all enjoyed receiving their awards during the evening festivities at the Eagle Inn in Kenmore, a restaurant advertised as the "Northwest's most unique dining spot." The race results were as follows:

> **Unlimited Class:** Lou West-Bud Sullivan 1st, Don Schultz-John Freegan 2nd, Mike Plumb-Mike Huff 3rd
> **Limited Class-B:** Ron Ibsen-Don Ibsen 1st, Bob Meehan-Mill Bromfield 2nd, Herm Indrickson-Dave Seefeidt 3rd
> **Limited Class-A:** Dave DesVoigne-Bud Hughes 1st, Dave Jagen-Roger Kireon 2nd, Stew Deibert Jr.-Stew Deibert Sr. 3rd

1960 Don (left) & Ron Ibsen, water-ski champions in B division with awards received at Eagle Inn.

1957: *Miss Seattle* Unlimited hydro launching party at Eagle Inn in Kenmore. Mrs. Freddie Grebbs standing in center under "7" on sign. My mother Dorothy is fifth from right sitting at table. Dad, the unlimited co-driver, is above her crouching behind Freddie.

Eagle Inn Festivities

The legendary Kenmore restaurant was the favorite local establishment for the outboarders and the water-skiers after the races during the 1950s and 1960s. The popular eatery, known for its "special family style chicken dinners" between 1927 and 1962, was owned and operated by George Grebbs and his wife "Freddie." Freddie, as she was called by the "grown-ups," was the vivacious host who always greeted us and insured we were served in the best way. She was the one who made the evening most enjoyable and treated us like family.

I loved to go, not necessarily for the great food, but for the ambience outdoors. They advertised: "Dine under the Trees at Eagle Inn- Outside Dining at Its Best Service to Your Table." You could fish in their pond stocked with small rainbow trout. The east side of the restaurant was where the outdoor dining area was located, complete with waterfall, stream and fishing pond. Families of ducks along with other friendly animals were always around to the delight of us youngsters.

DINE UNDER THE TREES AT EAGLE INN
OUTSIDE DINING AT ITS BEST SERVICE TO YOUR TABLE
For 23 years serving the best in Steak, Chicken, Prime Ribs, Seafood and Salads
Open Sundays and Holidays, 1:00 P. M. — Week Days 5 P. M.
Bothell Hiway at Kenmore

1960 Race Schedule (Partial)

Jan 3	Annual "Old-Timers" Cruise
Feb 21	Annual Bar Pilots Cruise
April 10	25th Sammamish Slough Race
April 24	12th Sammamish Water-Ski Race
April 24	Lake Sammamish-Alexander's Beach
July 11-12	Stock Outboard Regionals-Vancouver, B.C.
July 29-Aug 7	Western Divisionals-Green Lake, Seattle Seafair
Aug 20-23	Stock Outboard Nationals, Rock River-Beloit, WI
Aug 21	Silver Lake
Sept 10	Lake Lawrence-Yelm
Sept 24-25	Outboard Nationals-Lake Ming Bakersfield, CA

1960 Tidbits

Hugh Entrop won the APBA "Jack Maypole Memorial Trophy" a third year in a row for the largest world record speed increase in an outboard. He also was the National Champion in F-Hydro and Harold Tolford was the National Champion in C-Service Runabout. Dave Karelsen set the D-Hydro Kilo record on Devil's Lake, Oregon, at 81.945 mph and the competition record on Lake Lawrence, Yelm, Washington, at 61.181 mph in *R-11*. Lee Sutter set the BU-Runabout mark on Devil's Lake at 52.083 mph in *Sidewinder* and was the B-Stock Hydro National Champion. Gerry Walin set the A-Outboard Hydro Kilo record on Devil's Lake at 71.929 mph and Dick Rautenberg set the B-Stock Hydro competition record on Lake Lawrence in Yelm at 55.317 mph also in *11-R*.

National Champions Harold Tolford (L) C-Service Runabout; Hugh Entrop (far R) F-Hydro.

Jack Colcock was elected APBA inboard vice president and Jim Spinner was elected for another term as secretary. The Northwest Region 10 had the largest number of APBA members and regattas. The traditional Old-Timers and Bar Pilots Slough cruises continued to be popular. Gerald "Red" Halliday won the SOA Sportsman Award and was elected SOA commodore with Jackie Wallace as secretary for 1961.

1961

New Name, Same Place for Race Start

The outboard jockeys were disturbing the peace again when they started from Davidson's Marina (formerly Uplake Marina) in Kenmore at noon on April 10. The Seattle outboard ranks were uneasy because of the pending sale of Uplake Marina, the property where the Sammamish Slough Race started for almost a decade. They were unsure if their 1961 starting location was in jeopardy of being taken from them. Earl Davidson, a rancher from Cody Wyoming, purchased the property in early February and the ownership was in transition. Obviously, my father and Mr. Davidson made an arrangement to allow the races to continue from there, at least for the time being. What was in store for the future races was anybody's guess.

Andy Seeks 3rd Victory in Row

Howard "Andy" Anderson, overall winner the past two years, was shooting for his third win in a row, a feat no one had achieved since the Sammamish Slough race's inception in 1934. Al Benson was the only three-time winner, with victories in 1947, 48 and 53, but they weren't consecutive wins. Anderson, a marina operator from Edmonds, was the first since Benson to score back-to-back victories in the last 13 years. Both of Anderson's performances were records. Last year's record clocking was 35:38, a time that every Unlimited class driver will be aiming to lower.

Former Andy's Boathouse

Andy won last year despite a late start after he was caught off guard with his starter switch turned-off. He managed to start just in time before being disqualified as the next class was about to move to the starting line. Anderson wasn't about to allow that to happen this time. He won't be the only driver seeking a win this year as he'll be contending with a host of other Unlimited class drivers.

Ready and anxious to chase Anderson were two former champions, local driver Dick Brunes and Bellevue's Bob Waite. Brunes, the 1958 winner, has had his troubles staying with his cantankerous hydro the past two years. He's dumped twice but was able to right the ship and finish the race both years. Other contenders, all veterans in trying to tame the Slough, were Red Halliday, Les Miller, Randy and Tommy Thompson of Tacoma, and Seattle's racing brothers, Al and Dave Karelsen.

Red Halliday dislocated his shoulder in last year's contest after missing a turn and being thrown from his mount some 50 feet into a muddy bank. But the big redhead from Edmonds is back for more and will try to be more cautious while passing through what his fellow drivers call, "Halliday Corner," in Redmond.

Ex-Mechanic Thwarts Anderson

When the drivers started their F hydros in Kenmore, it was that signature moment that the crowd was awaiting, the start of the Sammamish Slough Race. Spectators throughout the Sammamish Valley could hear the high-pitched screaming sound of a half-dozen or more 60-plus horsepower engines with their ear-shattering open exhausts as they began their way up into the Slough. For the thousands lining the course, it was a sound that immediately got your heart pumping with excitement and anticipation of seeing the first raceboat round the corner nearest to you. The Sammamish Valley acted like a huge outdoor amphitheater with surround-sound. Residents in the normally peaceful valley that were not interested in the event, most likely felt the outboarders were disturbing the peace.

Bud Walters 3rd Unlimited class, Wendell Ewing won in similar F-Outboard Hydro borrowed from Walters.

Anderson's mechanic for the past two years foiled Andy's bid for an unprecedented third-straight overall victory in the Slough Race. Wendell "Windy" Ewing, 26, was victorious in only his second running of the event driving a borrowed F-Outboard Hydro. Ewing, the ex-mechanic, added insult to injury by setting a new record low time of 35:19 when he broke his ex-boss's record of 35:38 set last year in the 28-mile two-way run between Kenmore and Lake Sammamish. Heavy rains that flooded over the Slough banks and smoothed out the turn's days before the race, likely helped drivers to attain lower times due to higher speeds in the corners (see Ewing's victory photo at beginning of chapter).

Anderson, with a burned-out motor, had to watch the race along with an estimated 40,000 spectators as Ewing won in a "hot rig" owned by Bothell's Bud Walters. Walters was third behind second-place finisher, Bob Waite of Bellevue. Ewing, a surprise late entry, led from start to finish on the upstream run with Les Miller on his heels only a second behind when they finished the upstream run at Idylwood Resort.

It's interesting to note that Ewing was victorious in Walters' rig, an Entrop copy, designed by Sam Bell, that he built himself with help from the revolutionary boat builder, Hugh Entrop. Walters' craft was likely a newer and improved hull, but in this instance, may have been the wrong choice.

Russ Rotzler of Seattle was away first on the downstream run, but later flipped along with Les Miller, leaving a clear path for Ewing to lead the rest across the finish line at Davidson's Marina in Kenmore. Miller was leading two turns from the finish when he and his hydro parted company. He took a swim while his hydro landed high and dry in a willow tree. Miller's spectacular acrobatic flip was one of many incidents in the twisting Slough that took its usual toll with 31 of 82 starters failing to finish.

Bothell's Denton Herland-winner in C-Stock Hydro sliding safely byDown River Marina entrance.

The race was terminated for six other drivers before passing upstream through Woodinville. Perry Tonsgard of Seattle, second to Anderson last year, luckily escaped injury when his craft rammed a piling under the Woodinville railroad bridge. Glenn Dickerson, also of Seattle, spun-out after striking a floating bottle in his path and wound up unconscious on the bank. He was revived by spectators, jumped back into his B-Stock Hydro, restarted and managed to finish in fifth place.

Ducks eye-view of Oregon's Dean Mahaffey winning DU-Runabout class.

The drivers will tell you, it's not the turns and sandbars or the many other natural obstacles that are so hazardous, it's the spectators! They throw beer bottles or cans, rocks, logs, pieces of wood, old tires and even lighted fire crackers. On an occasion, drivers have been shot at with BB guns. Chuck Walters, piloting his AU Runabout, narrowly escaped injury when he ducked under a long leash held by the owner of a dog swimming out into the Slough.

Debris in the water is substantial when spectators numbered almost 40,000, as estimated by King County sheriff patrol Sergeant, E.L. Kirkpatrick. The officer explained to a *Seattle Times* reporter on the scene, "We had more traffic-control problems than in previous years. The crowd lining the Slough was particularly heavy from Woodinville to Lake Sammamish."

Anderson was not the only past winner to be beaten. Bob Vining of Mercer Island, last year's C-Stock Hydro champion, was second to Denton Herland of Kirkland. Roy Williams of Bremerton dropped from first to third among the DU-Runabout finishers. And Bruce Robin Bille of Tacoma was unable to match his victory as a novice last year in a duel with Seattle's Eddie Raymond for the BU-Runabout laurels. Gerald Riggs of Renton, third last year, came out on top as the winner in his B-Stock Hydro.

For the second straight year, Bothell's Harold Davies bettered Bob Steinbruck of Salem, Oregon, the regional high-point champion for the past four years in the CU-Runabout class. Another Oregonian, Dean Mahaffey, settled the score in winning in DU-Runabout. Mahaffey was second to Roy Williams who won last year.

Ewing is a champ without a boat with limited driving experience. He drove an A-Hydro in the Slough Race two years ago and finished third. He told the *Times* reporter, "I owned a B-Hydro, but sold it in 1957. I'm not sure I can afford another now," he said with a smile in the presence of his new bride of two weeks. Ewing went on to say "He didn't decide to compete until he had briefly tested Walters' hydro the morning before the race. I enjoy driving and I figured I had a chance after running the boat." His wife Penny added, "It's all right, my first date with Wendy was at a boat race last year at Green Lake. I suspect he'll be driving a few more races after this."

1961 Sammamish Slough Race Results (by class)

Place	Driver	Class	From	Boat	Time
1	Wendell Ewing	F-Outboard Hydro	Edmonds	R-185	35:19
2	Bob Waite	F-Outboard Hydro	Bellevue	228-R	*
3	Bud Walters	F-Outboard Hydro	Bothell	R-85	*
1	Jim Parks	D-Stock Hydro	Bothell	73-R	38:02
1	Denton Herland	C-Stock Hydro	Kirkland	20-R	35:54
2	Bob Vining	C-Stock Hydro	Mercer Island	225-R	*
3	Al Karelsen	C-Stock Hydro	Alderwood Manor	X	*
4	Red Taylor	C-Stock Hydro	Seattle	R-89	*
1	Gerald Riggs	B-Stock Hydro	Renton	X	40:00
2	Keith Spencer	B-Stock Hydro	Bremerton	38-R	*
3	Louis Green	B-Stock Hydro	Richland	112-R	*
4	Clayton Calhoun	B-Stock Hydro	Seattle	27-R	*
5	Glenn Dickerson	B-Stock Hydro	Seattle	166-R	*
1	Dean Mahaffey	DU-Runabout	Roseburg, OR	52-R	40:13
2	Randy Thompson	DU-Runabout	Tacoma	64-R	*
3	Roy Williams	DU-Runabout	Bremerton	56-R	*
4	Joe Trumbly	DU-Runabout	Tacoma	*	*
1	Harold Davies	CU-Runabout	Bothell	116-R	41:31

2	Bob Steinbruck	CU-Runabout	Salem, OR	2-R	*
1	Eddie Raymond	BU-Runabout	Seattle	120-R	40:48
2	Bruce Robin Bille	BU-Runabout	Tacoma	173-R	*
3	Loren Anderson	BU-Runabout	Seattle	139-R	*
4	Donald Vaught	BU-Runabout	Kirkland	X	*
1	Mike Jones	A-Stock Hydro	Seattle	7-R	44:00
2	Larry Knight	A-Stock Hydro	Seattle	24-R	*
3	Barry Lewis	A-Stock Hydro	Seattle	99-R	*
4	Mike Smith	A-Stock Hydro	Everett	63-R	*
5	Roger Libby	A-Stock Hydro	Seattle	265-R	*
6	Bert Raemer	A-Stock Hydro	Seattle	X-1	*
7	Pete Borg	A-Stock Hydro	Seattle	207-R	*
8	Jamie Van Ellen	A-Stock Hydro	Bellevue	23-R	*
9	Lloyd Peterson	A-Stock Hydro	Everett	215-R	*
10	Paul Tamien	A-Stock Hydro	Seattle	31-R	*
1	Dick Sailors	A-Runabout	Gig Harbor	79-R	48:57
2	Paul Staley	A-Runabout	Bellevue	21-R	*
3	Vern Heikkilo	A-Runabout	Aberdeen	59-R	*
4	Roger Thomas	A-Runabout	Everett	4-R	*
5	John Myers	A-Runabout	Seattle	47-R	*
6	Charley Walters	A-Runabout	Bothell	85-R	*
1	Jim Zonich Jr.	JU-Runabout	Longview	151-R	*
2	Don Armstrong	JU-Runabout	Bundy, B.C.	31-CW	*
3	Ken Abrams	JU-Runabout	Vancouver, B.C.	45-CW	*
4	Jimmy Downing	JU-Runabout	Seattle	277-R	*
5	Steve Knudsen	JU-Runabout	Seattle	45-R	*
6	Don Hughes	JU-Runabout	Edmonds	889-R	*

Some boat numbers and times unavailable

Three in a Row for West-Sullivan Team

The veteran team of skier, Lou West, and driver, Bud Sullivan, made it three in a row by winning the Class-A division (Unlimited) in the 13th annual Sammamish Water-Ski Race on Sunday, April 16. The skier-driver duo toured the 28-mile, round trip distance between Gateway Park on Lake Sammamish and Davidson's Uplake Marina in Kenmore in an elapsed time of 49 minutes and 40 seconds.

In the Class-B division, typically slower than the more powerful Class-A group, Bill Fennel, skier, and Don Due, pilot, were champions with a time of 49 minutes and 33 seconds, 7 seconds faster than the Sullivan-West team. Bill Steffen, towed by Bob Reed, was victorious in the slower Class-C at 56:84.

It's a difficult challenge to make the two-way trip racing alone in an outboard with the many natural pitfalls along the Slough. But the added handicap and hazard of towing a water-skier makes the going extremely difficult.

Bud Sullivan towing water-skier Lou West to victory in Unlimited class.

You may wonder how the water-skiers with single skies make a quick-start after falling in the Slough. From a standing start, the driver must first get his rig on a plane to speed away. This is extremely difficult with a skier attached to your stern with a tow rope. The veteran skiers get up with the aid of another temporary ski to reduce the huge pulling force needed to drag the skier out of the water. Lou West used a disposable three-foot plank with a short piece of rubber inner tube for his foot to slip into. Once he was up, he slipped his foot out of the improvised ski and left it behind as a souvenir. Sullivan kept the short ski tucked inside his cockpit for emergencies.

This was the first year that the event was sponsored by the Lake Sammamish Water-Ski Club, a changing of the guard so to speak. In the previous 12 years, it was sponsored by the Olympic Water-Ski Club of Seattle.

Unlimited Class: Lou West-Bud Sullivan 1st, 49:40; Rod Sampson-Orin Edson 2nd, 50:31; Ray Moore-Dick Brunes, 3rd, 54:04
Limited Class-B: Bill Fennel-Don Due 1st, 49:44; Bob Meehan-Milt Brownfield 2nd, 50:35; Paul and Stu Deibert 3rd, 52:41
Limited Class-A: Bill Steffen-Bob Reed 1st, 56:84; John Pomteo-Ray Lee 2nd, 58:28; Tilly Sprinkle-Dean Sprinkle 3rd, 60:16

Dick Brunes towing Ray Moore-past Unlimited class winners in 1955, '56 & '58.

1961 Race Schedule (Partial)

Jan 1	Annual "Old Timers" Cruise
Feb 26	Annual Bar Pilots Cruise
April 10	26th Sammamish Slough Race
April 16	12th Sammamish Water-Ski Race
April 29-30	Lake Sammamish-Alexanders Beach
Jun 24-25	American Lake Regionals
July 23	Outboard Regionals-Bellingham
July 30	Stock Outboard Divisionals-Port Orchard
Aug 13	Outboard Divisionals-Estacada, OR
Aug 23-27	Stock Outboard Nationals-Guntersville, AL
Sept 13-18	Outboard Nationals-DePue, IL
Aug 18-20	Kilo Trials-Devil's Lake, OR
Sept 10	Lake Sammamish
Sept 23	Lake Lawrence-Yelm

Dick Suess-longtime Patrol Boat Captain.

1961 Tidbits

Past Slough Racer, Bill Muncey, won his fourth Gold Cup driving *Miss Century 21* during Seafair Week in Seattle. Not since the days of legendary Gar Wood "the Gray Ghost," had any driver won four Gold Cups. We mourned the death of Jim Spinner, a good friend of the racing community, past SOA commodore, boat racer and current APBA secretary. Jack Holden was inducted into the Gulf Marine Racing Hall of Fame. "Pop" Tolford was the recipient of the SOA Sportsman Award and Mike Jones was elected SOA commodore for 1962 with Betty Lean as secretary.

1962

Driver in Small B-Hydro Steps Up into Unlimited Class

Lee Sutter was a young University of Washington student from Seattle with plans to go for it all in his first Sammamish Slough Race. He planned to compete in his quick and nimble B-Outboard Hydro, a rig with a high performance two-cylinder engine, but the class was not scheduled for this year's race. The only division he could run in was the fastest class, the Unlimiteds with their much higher- powered 4-cylinder engines.

While Sutter was testing in Kenmore the week before the race, Slough Race spokesman Al Benson told him there would be grumbling from the elite Unlimited drivers because his boat was fast and nimble, a threat to win the whole thing. Although there were no rules against stepping-up into a faster class, it hadn't been done before with a souped-up B-Hydro. Sutter had no choice because the only class his rig would fit into was the fastest class, the Unlimiteds.

While the Seattle Outboard club was running the 27th annual Slough Race on Sunday, April 8, the city of Seattle was finishing last-minute preparations for Opening Day of the Century 21 World's Fair. The world's fair opened two weeks later on Saturday, April 21. The Sammamish Slough Race was but one of hundreds of events to be shown off while Seattle was in the world spotlight. This was by far the biggest event that the Queen City had undertaken. The vision of one young "Husky" freshman wasn't about the World's Fair, but mainly on how he would fare with the veteran Unlimited drivers in his first Slough Race.

Souvenir Medallion

Spectators Affect Race Outcome

Last year only 45 out of 82 starters finished the 28-mile round-trip journey through the meandering waterway between Kenmore and Lake Sammamish. It was a typical toll over the 27-years since the race began. Along the way were numerous natural hazards; strong currents, 63 hairpin turns, 22 bridges, trees, over-hanging branches, stumps, sand-bars, livestock fences, submerged objects, floating deadhead[1] logs and yes, even a golf course that the raceboats wander through.

Unfortunately, in recent years the biggest hazard had been from unthinking spectators among the crowds of tens of thousands who lined both sides of the banks along the 14-mile course. Flying beer cans, dogs on leashes wandering into the Slough and boat-flipping debris have made the already difficult run unnecessarily treacherous. A driver said, "The spectator hazard reached dangerous proportions last year when they threw beer cans, rocks and even lighted firecrackers at the drivers."

The race-sponsoring Seattle Outboard Association, through the newspapers, asked for cooperation from all the spectators not to throw objects at the drivers or in the Slough. The sheriff patrol or race officials should be notified of any violators.

The first of the 70 mile-per-hour plus hydros were scheduled to get under way at noon from Ed Karelsen's Boat Shop (within Davidson's Marina) in Kenmore. The down-stream run from Idylwood Resort on Lake Sammamish was to begin at 2 pm. Jim Henry of Seattle and Fred Mackle of Bellevue were co-chairmen of the race.

Sutter Unsnarls Slough in First Attempt

Bud Livesley's *Seattle Times* sports headline above, told it all the day after the race on April 9. Twenty-year-old Lee Sutter was among a select few to win the

---

[1] A partially or totally submerged log floating in the water.

Sammamish Slough Race in his first try, a feat accomplished by smart driving, good equipment and a lot of luck. Even more surprising was his total elapsed time in competition against the more powerful hydros. His rig had a 20-cubic-inch engine compared to 40-cubic inches for the F-Hydros.

Sutter, second in both runs up and down the river, was clocked at 36 minutes and 43 seconds. Gerald "Red" Halliday, a veteran of five Slough races, was runner-up in 36:51.1. Halliday set the early pace from Kenmore Marina to Idylwood Resort on Lake Sammamish but was third on the return trip. Sutter's margin of victory was a slim 8.1 seconds. On the return trip, 30,000 to 35,000 spectators (estimated by the sheriff's patrol) watched past two-time winner Andy Anderson, lead across the finish line in Kenmore with Sutter close behind in second.

Mishaps Spoil Veteran Driver's Chances

Edmond's Andy Anderson had an encounter with a tree on the upstream run. Swinging wide in a turn and running close to the riverbank, he saw the over-hanging tree in time to duck safely, but a branch slammed against his engine and the leaves clogged up the motor. By the time Anderson unclogged his powerplant and it was purring normally again, he lost almost 25 minutes getting to Lake Sammamish, eliminating any chance he had for a third overall victory.

Bob Waite had a chance for his second overall victory but sheared a pin while leading in the downstream run. He found a nail in his boat and installed it in place of the broken pin while Anderson and Sutter sped by him between Bothell and Kenmore (good reason why most savvy drivers carry tools for emergency repairs). He restarted and managed to finish but not in the running, placing seventh overall.

Wendell Ewing, also of Edmonds, had the opportunity to defend his championship from last year. He never had a chance because his balky engine failed to start and left him stranded at the starting dock in Kenmore. It was a bad day for other defending champs also. Bothell's Harold Davies, shooting for his third straight win in the CU-Runabout class, missed out not far from the starting line. He flipped while rounding the sharp turning buoy that leads into the mouth of the Slough from Lake Washington.

Dean Mahaffey of Roseburg, Oregon, last year's winner in DU-Runabout, was third behind Joe Trumbly of Tacoma and Roy Williams of Bremerton. Dick Sailors of Gig Harbor was fishing himself out of the water after turning-over while Roger Thomas of Everett took the AU-Runabout title. Only young Jimmy Zonich of Longview succeeded where last year's champs failed. Zonich was the JU-Runabout victor for the second straight year in the 14-year-old and under junior class that finished their one-way run upstream to Bothell.

Spectators Scatter for Higher Ground

The most spectacular detour over the bank also occurred at the Down River Marina during an upstream run. Bob Carver captured another of his fabulous action photos when a C-Hydro scared the daylights out of the crowd who was sitting and standing in front row positions on the dangerous marina bank across from the new rebuilt Nursery Bridge. They were in harm's way because this was the dangerous spot where wayward boats ran amuck when they misjudged the sharp right-hand turn after passing under the bridge.

The driver was identified as Don Hansen by the newspapers who most likely obtained their race report from a Seattle Outboard race spokesman. I spoke with Hansen, an automobile businessman, during my early research for this book. He flatly denied it was him. This may be another unresolved Slough Race mystery.

1962-Don Hansen's C-Hydro missed turn, climbs bank, scatters spectators (same photo on book cover).

Other notable drivers in the Unlimited class were future Seattle unlimited hydro drivers, Billy Schumacher and Bob Gilliam, a transplant from Boise, Idaho, who recently moved to the Seattle area. Long-time veteran Slough racer, John Laird, finished in the money driving his alcohol-burning C-Service Hydro. He told me in an interview that the smaller high-performance hydros, like his and Sutter's, weren't as fast as the F's in the straightaways but they could go as fast or faster through the turns making them very competitive. Laird was third overall with a time of 37:55.1

A total of 73 starters raced away from the Kenmore starting line with only 45 seeing the checkered flag at the Kenmore Bridge finish line. Twenty-two never reached Lake Sammamish and another seven, out of commission in the downstream run, were towed back to the finish line with power other than their own–by a race patrol boat. The casualty rate was at its usual high but not because of misbehaved spectators who threw all kinds of debris in the Slough over the past few years.

Race chairman Red Halliday, said, "For once, the Slough didn't look like a brewery; the spectators were the best ever." But still, there was enough natural rubble to cause troubles. Halliday, who finished second, his best to date, had to change a bent propeller at Idylwood and finish with yet another bent prop after running over some "deadheads" on the way back. Roy Williams punched a hole in the side of his DU-Runabout when he had to take evasive action to miss a spectator in the water.

Sutter Was No Rookie

Despite his first-time Slough win, Lee Sutter was hardly a rookie in a speedboat. The ex-Roosevelt High School halfback was one of the nation's top outboard drivers two years ago in 1960. Sutter was national champion in B-Stock Hydro and set a competition record in his BU-Runabout on Oregon's Devil's Lake. Sutter said, "The Slough Race was a ball and I'll be back next year."

Lee Sutter 1st overall Unlimited class driving his Sid-Craft B-Hydro *Sutter's Gold*.

1962 Sammamish Slough Race Results (by class)

Place	Driver	Class	From	Boat	Time
1	Lee Sutter	B-Outboard Hydro	Seattle	R-12	36:43.0
2	Red Halliday	F-Outboard Hydro	Seattle	82-R	36:51.1

3	John Laird	C-Service Hydro	Seattle	R-85	37:55.3
4	Bob Gilliam	F-Outboard Hydro	Seattle	*	38:35.6
5	Jim Parks	F-Outboard Hydro	Bothell	*	39:09.0
6	Andy Anderson	F-Outboard Hydro	Edmonds	R-222	42:30.8
7	Bob Waite	F-Outboard Hydro	Bellevue	228-R	49:37.5
8	Billy Schumacher	F-Outboard Hydro	Seattle	*	60:13.2
1	Red Taylor	C-Stock Hydro	Seattle	R-89	38:48.7
2	Bob Vining	C-Stock Hydro	Mercer Island	225-R	41:09.6
3	Ted Greenlee	C-Stock Hydro	Mercer Island	*	43:12.2
4	Dave Park	C-Stock Hydro	Kent	R-89	44:09.8
5	Gary Bish	C-Stock Hydro	Seattle	*	49:00.1
1	Joe Trumbly	DU-Runabout	Tacoma	*	42:26.4
2	Roy Williams	DU-Runabout	Bremerton	56-R	43:23.1
3	Dean Mahaffey	DU-Runabout	Roseburg, OR	52-R	48:01.6
4	Terry Henderson	DU-Runabout	Bellevue	*	52:16.7
5	Rodney Burton	DU-Runabout	Moscow, ID	*	60:50.6
1	Gerald Riggs	B-Stock Hydro	Renton	*	41:43.4
2	Don Whatmore	B-Stock Hydro	Seattle	*	42:17.5
3	Ray Lee	B-Stock Hydro	Seattle	*	45:58.8
4	Chris Sheale	B-Stock Hydro	Bellevue	*	48:01.0
5	Bob Gromko	B-Stock Hydro	Edmonds	*	48:56.1
6	Don Vaught	B-Stock Hydro	Kirkland	*	50:09.6
7	Ron Anderson	B-Stock Hydro	Port Angeles	*	50:12.0
8	Keith Spencer	B-Stock Hydro	Bremerton	*	50:37.5
9	Jim Clarke	B-Stock Hydro	Seattle	*	55.03.4
1	Gerry Walin	CU-Runabout	Edmonds	*	46:19.8
2	Phil Williams	CU-Runabout	Tacoma	14-R	46:26.3
3	Jan Christ	CU-Runabout	Seattle	*	47:09.6
4	William Kelly	CU-Runabout	Mercer Island	*	48:33.7
1	Al Mar	D-Stock Hydro	Seattle	*	49:09.0
2	Charley Walters	D-Stock Hydro	Kenmore	*	64:36.5
1	Lance Puckett	A-Stock Hydro	Seattle	*	48:26.1
2	Roger Libby	A-Stock Hydro	Seattle	*	51:38.8
3	Jeff Wiggington	A-Stock Hydro	Seattle	*	52:37.0
4	John Leach	A-Stock Hydro	Seattle	*	53:58.4
1	Roger Thomas	A-Runabout	Everett	*	50:43.3
2	Eddie Raymond	A-Runabout	Seattle	*	58:12.2
3	John Myers	A-Runabout	Seattle	*	62:57.8
1	Jim Zonich Jr.	JU-Runabout	Longview	*	*
2	Jim Downing	JU-Runabout	Seattle	277-R	*
3	Steve Knudsen	JU-Runabout	Seattle	45-R	*

Some boat numbers and times unavailable

New Water-Ski Champ Due

New Class A water-ski champions were assured for the 14th annual Golden Water Skis Race when the skiers and drivers wound their way through the twisting Sammamish Slough on April 15. The veterans Lou West, skier, and Bud Sullivan, driver, decided to retire this year after victories the last three consecutive years. Did they want to give the other guys a chance…maybe not?

West admitted during a *Seattle Times* interview, "I'm tired; besides, this is a much too hazardous race for a father of four. It's been fun, but I'm watching from the beach this year." West won't be sitting on the couch, however. He's the race chairman for the annual affair which is sponsored for the second time by the Lake Sammamish Water-Ski Club. And yes, they were giving the others a chance.

Three classes were scheduled to run as in the past few years. The fastest boats, Class A, were set to start first at noon from Gateway Grove on Lake Sammamish. The return run was set to head back upstream at 3 pm from Davidson's Uplake Marina in Kenmore. The classes included: Class A (the Unlimiteds) with speeds 40 miles per hour and faster; Class B, for 30 to 40 mph boats and the slowest, Class C, for 30 and under. It's likely some cheating occurred in the two lower classes because verifying speeds was difficult for the race officials. It was hoped honesty was the best policy but like most sporting events, the competitors usually tried to gain an advantage by stretching the rules.

Last Year's Runner-Up Victorious

Rod Sampson and Orin Edson, last year's runner-up finishers, were victorious for the first time in the wet and wild Sammamish Slough Race. Sampson, skiing behind a boat driven by Edson, won for the first time in the Unlimited or Class A. They covered the 28-mile round trip between Lake Sammamish and Kenmore in 45:55.5. Skier, Lou West, and driver, Bud Sullivan, are the current record holders with a time of 44:57 set in 1959. Bob Meehan of Arrowhead Point, towed by Milton Brownfield, won the Class B division and Bob Sween of Redmond, pulled by Bill Carlson, were first in the Class C group.

Don Schultz Unlimited class boat *#3* with powerful 6-cylinder 60 horsepower Mecury outboard motor.

Unlimited Class: Rod Sampson-Orin Edson, driver 1st, 45:55.5; Bill Fennel-Don Due, driver 2nd; Swan Person-Ken Sanders, driver 3rd

Limited Class-B: Bob Meehan-Milt Brolonfield, driver 1st, 54:27; Willis Jacobus-George Richards, driver 2nd; Dennis Dickerson-Jack Love, driver 3rd

Limited Class-A: Bob Sween-Bill Carlson, driver 1st, 57:03; Bruce Reed-Bob Reed, driver 2nd; Gary Jacobsen-Roger Kheven, driver 3rd

One of many casualties in ski race-notice skier & pilot riding far side keeping crash opening above water.

1962 Race Schedule (Partial)

Jan 7	Annual "Old Timers" Cruise
Feb 25	Annual Bar Pilots Cruise
April 8	27th Sammamish Slough Race
April 15	14th Sammamish Water-Ski Race
May 6	Devils' Lake, OR
May 19-20	Lake Sammamish
June 3	Silver Lake
July 1	Port Orchard Regionals
July 27-28	Green Lake Seattle Seafair
July 30	Stock Outboard Divisionals-Bakersfield, CA
Aug 22-26	Stock Outboard Nationals-Guntersville, AL
Sept 1-2	Lake Lawrence, Yelm
Sept 9	Lake Sammamish
Oct 19-21	Outboard Nationals-Bradenton, FL

1962 Tidbits

Jim Downing was national champion in JU-Runabout and was inducted into the Gulf Marine Racing Hall of Fame. Jack Livie of Edmonds received the SOA Sportsman award. Gerald "Red" Halliday was elected for a second term as commodore for 1963 with Rose Walters (Bud Walters' wife) as secretary.

1963

Race Planned Before Army Tames Slough

One outcome of the looming Sammamish River dredging was known to the Seattle outboarders. When completed, the huge project in the works for almost 50 years, would likely prevent any motor craft from reaching Lake Sammamish. The county Corps of Engineers planned to construct a weir[2] at the Slough's Lake Sammamish entrance. This was a flood control feature to minimize the seasonal water-level fluctuations during the rain storms and snow melts. It was expected that the 1963 race would be the final race to ever reach Lake Sammamish.

The Seattle Outboard Association was planning to sponsor and run its annual Sammamish Slough Race as it had ever since the first race back in 1934. Even though the impending flood-control work on the Sammamish River was only a few months away, it was business as usual. SOA Commodore, Red Halliday, and race officials were focused on running the race, not the future of the Sammamish Slough.

Sutter to Defend

The defending champion, Lee Sutter, was one of many Unlimited drivers expected to compete in the Slough Race for the last time between lakes Washington and Sammamish. Past overall winners, Howard Anderson, Wendell Ewing and Sutter were poised to make their bid for another victory. Halliday, last year's second-place finisher, also had visions of a win; it would vindicate his hard luck in recent years. Anderson won consecutively in 1959 and 1960; Ewing was champion in 1962 and Sutter became the unexpected victor last year.

The Northwest's most popular outboard race was moved from its traditional starting point, Davidson's Uplake Marina, to Kenmore Air Harbor because of logistics. SOA club officials decided to make the move because it was becoming more and more difficult to launch the many raceboats at the crowded marina. The Air Harbor site had better launch facilities, more parking and water-level floating docks, which facilitated easier starts for the contestants.

Bud Livesley of the *Times* quoted longtime Slough driver and race spokesman, Red Taylor, in an article before the race. "We're not certain about the future of the race.

---

[2] A barrier or low overflow dam built across the horizontal width of a river to control water flow.

Certainly, the engineers aren't going to take out all the turns in the Slough. But they probably will eliminate much of the challenge. This probably is the last of the spectacular-type races."

Kenmore Air Harbor's broad shoreline ideal for launching and starting directly in front of their office.

Kenmore Air's marina launching ramp with Al Karelsen's Finecraft-built "bat wing" Unlimited R-11.

Race officials, for the first time, decided to lump all the alcohol burning classes into the Unlimited class. The other seven classes included DU-Runabout, C and B-Stock Hydro, BU-Runabout A-Stock Hydro, AU-Runabout and JU-Runabout. The Unlimited class, perhaps in their last challenging Slough Race, was scheduled to start from Kenmore Air Harbor at noon on Sunday, March 31. This was the second start from the Air Harbor; the first was in 1957. The downstream run was scheduled to start from Gateway Grove on Lake Sammamish at 2 pm. Many of the thrills and spills, which have attracted up to 35,000 spectators during a day of racing, will be eliminated by the widening and deepening, "The Taming of the Slough."

U of W Student Wins in Largest Ever Unlimited Class

No, it wasn't last year's winner, University of Washington student, Lee Sutter. Another UW student, Tom O'Neill, won his first Sammamish Slough Race in record time. Twenty-two-year-old Thomas William O'Neill, piloting his sleek F-Hydro cabover, was the fastest ever–despite losing a turning fin. O'Neill set a course record with an elapsed time for the two-way run between Kenmore and Lake Sammamish of 33:06.6, bettering spectator Windy Ewing's record of 35:19.2 set in 1961.

1963 winner Tom O'Neill with admirer.

"The flying O'Neill" as dubbed by his fellow racers, told *Seattle Times* sports writer Bud Livesley: "I banged into a log or something and lost a turning fin (some Slough Race rigs have two fins, one on each sponson[3], to improve turning in both directions). I had to back off some and Red (Halliday) came at me hard at the finish line." Gerald Milton "Red" Halliday, who finished second overall, was eight-tenths of second behind O'Neill at the Kenmore Bridge finish line. It was the second year in a row that Halliday missed out on a win by mere seconds.

Red Halliday second place unlimited hydro 82-R.

The colorful freckled redhead has a dubious honor in the race. He has a corner in the upper part of the Slough named after him, "Halliday Corner" in Redmond, where he was thrown into the river bank in 1960. He was rescued while unconscious by fellow driver, Al Karelsen, and ended up in the hospital with a dislocated shoulder. He recovered quickly enough to return from the hospital for the post-race award presentations (see map at end of chapter for Halliday's accident location).

Sutter, in relinquishing his title to another Husky, wasn't upset at the result. He was last away from the start and worked his way to third when his engine quit. He spent

---

[3] Projection's on racing craft extending outward from the forward hull sides to increase lateral stability in the water. The two points of a three-point hydroplane with the prop being the third.

the rest of the day watching from the river bank along with some 30,000 other spectators. O'Neill went on to say during Livesley's interview, "Three years ago, (in O'Neill's first Slough Race) I spun-out. A patrol boat ran over and sank my D-Stock Hydro." On this day, he wasn't run over by anyone as he led all the way during his two-way run. His closest competitor was Andy Anderson, Edmonds marina operator, who was the champ in 1959-60.

By lumping together all the alcohol-burning rigs, officials wound up with the largest Unlimited class in history. Seventeen entrants were divided into two "packs for the Slough attack." O'Neill led the first to Lake Sammamish and Anderson led the second pack. Only a dozen of the 17 starters answered the starting gun for the downstream run. O'Neill and Anderson were in a nose-to-nose duel after the start leading into the Slough. Anderson told the *Times*' Bud Livesley. "My engine suddenly went dead, only for a couple of minutes, then I got fired up again, but Tom was long gone."

It was a bad day for other defending champions as well. In all eight classes, not one was successful. Racing only to Bothell, reigning JU national champion, Jimmy Downing, was third behind winner, Steve Knudsen and his nine-year-old kid brother, Mike. There weren't many reports of casualties this year, an indication the toll was somewhat lighter than in past years.

One of the most spectacular crashes was that of Ralph Payne, a newcomer from Corpus Christie, Texas, who was used to the wide-open ranges of the Lone Star State. Payne found the space limited under the new bridge at the Down River Marina. It was a choice of going quickly left or right off one of the support pilings. "Tex" hesitated and slammed into the pillar. The impact, caught by photographer Bob Carver, catapulted him out of his rig and into the water for a souvenir dunking (see chapter 11 for photo). He wasn't injured physically but how does one explain to his boss what happened to the engine of his C-Stock Hydro? It was stolen after the race was over while Payne was helping fellow driver, Bob Gilliam, take his rig out of the water.

1963 Sammamish Slough Race Results (by class)

Place	Driver	Class	From	Boat	Time
1	Tom O'Neill	Unlimited Hydro	Seattle	71-R	33:03.6
2	Red Halliday	Unlimited Hydro	Seattle	82-R	*
3	Bud Walters	Unlimited Hydro	Kenmore	R-85	*
1	Bob Rhoades	C-Stock Hydro	Everett	*	44:42.0
2	Al Hightower	C-Stock Hydro	Alderwood Manor	*	*
3	Murray Pietz	C-Stock Hydro	Bellevue	*	*
1	Rodney Burton	DU-Runabout	Moscow, ID	*	43:07.0
2	Dick Williams	DU-Runabout	Beaverton, OR	*	*

3	Phil Williams	DU-Runabout	Seattle	R-61	*
1	Don Whatmore	B-Stock Hydro	Seattle	*	41:17.0
2	Ron Anderson	B-Stock Hydro	Port Angeles	*	*
3	Don Vaught	B-Stock Hydro	Kirkland	*	*
1	Bob Montoya	BU-Runabout	Sumner	*	46:12.0
2	Bruce Robin Bille	BU-Runabout	Seattle	14-R	*
3	George Christ	BU-Runabout	Edmonds	*	*
1	Barry Lewis	A-Stock Hydro	Seattle	*	44:00.0
2	Dennis Lee	A-Stock Hydro	Seattle	*	*
3	Bob Wartinger	A-Stock Hydro	Seattle	*	*
1	Dave Swanson	A-Runabout	Everett	*	49:50.0
2	Ralph Olson	A-Runabout	Seattle	*	*
3	Bob Taylor	A-Runabout	Seattle	*	*
1	Steve Knudsen	JU-Runabout	Seattle	45-R	*
2	Mike Downing	JU-Runabout	Seattle	*	*
3	Jim Downing	JU-Runabout	Seattle	1-R	*

Some boat numbers and times unavailable

Last Sammamish Slough Racing Event

Sammamish water-ski competitors likely thought their event would be the last racing event ever to be held in the Sammamish Slough, at least as far as running all the way to Lake Sammamish was concerned. The 15th annual Golden Water Skis Race was held on April 7, earlier than in the past. The big storyline was the veteran team of Lou West, 42, and Bud Sullivan, 28, decided to come out of retirement and give it one last try. Last year West said he was getting too old to water-ski the twisting 2-way (28 miles total) event between Kenmore and Lake Sammamish. They still hold the record low time which they set in 1959.

During an interview before the race, *Seattle Times* columnist Bud Livesley asked the 42-year-old West about competing again. West said, "Bud's just a kid at 28, he's capable of it. I'm not that positive about me." Dr. Lou West, a Seattle dentist, has been at it since the beginning of the event back in 1948. He's the veteran among the Northwest's top water-ski competitors.

Could "Old Man" of Slough Win Again?

In what was expected to be the final West and Sullivan show in the Sammamish Slough, the old favorites took their final curtain call as winners for a record fourth time. The Seattle dentist won going away in a record elapsed time of 42:32, almost two and-a-half minutes quicker than their old record. They were followed by Swan Person, skier, and Don Saunders, driver, with newcomer Bobbie Waite rounding out the unlimiteds in third place. She was towed by her well-known father, 1956 Sammamish Slough Race victor, Robert "Bob" Waite.

The three classes, A (Unlimited), B for speeds 40 mph and under, and C for speeds less than 30 mph were run on Sunday, April 7. The speedier Unlimiteds left the starting line at Idylwood Resort on Lake Sammamish at 11 am. The upstream return run from Davidson's Uplake Marina on Lake Washington in Kenmore started at 2 pm. The other classes left in 10-minute intervals with the slowest departing last.

Unlimited Class-A: Dr Lou West-Bud Sullivan, driver 1st, 42:23; Swan Person-Don Saunders, driver 2nd 49:58; Roberta "Bobbie" Waite-Robert "Bob" Waite, driver 3rd 51:22
Limited Class-B: Bob Meehan-Milt Brolonfield, driver 1st, 47:17; Ron Ibsen-Don Ibsen, driver 2nd 49:34; Stew Deibert Jr.-Stew Deibert Sr., driver 3rd
Limited Class-A: Bob Reed-Bill Stephan, driver 1st, 59:09; Mike Nedley-Bruce Reed, driver 2nd 60:17; Tillie Sprinkel-Dean Sprinkel, driver 3rd 62:46

1963 Golden Water-Skis Race: Limited class boats congested in Sammamish Slough below Bothell.

Gateway Grove-Idylwood Resorts Becomes Beach Park

Gateway Grove, developed in 1927 by the Charles Enos family, was the stopping point for the Slough Races from its beginning in 1934 to 1963. The small vacation resort, consisting of about a dozen cottages, was located on the Northwest end of Lake Sammamish. It was a popular getaway for families escaping Seattle's urban sprawl.

The resort was sold to Chandler and Myrtle Pickering, who spruced up the resort with a 40-foot slide and high-dive platform in the early 1950s. Photographer, Bob Carver, took photos from the top of the slide giving a panoramic view of the site during an outboard race in 1953 (see photo at end of Chapter 9). King County purchased Gateway Grove and its neighboring property, Idylwood Resort (Park), in 1969, combined them into Idylwood Beach Park and gave the property to the City of Redmond in 1994.

Air Harbor Puts Kenmore on Map

When I lived next door to Kenmore Air Harbor in the late 1950s to early 1960s, I was always fascinated with the operation and its seaplanes. I'll never forget those familiar sounds of the engines as they took off and flew by along the shores of Lake

Washington. The powerful growling sound of the "Kenmore Beavers" reverberated up and down the lake for miles. You might have thought if you didn't know better that a vintage World War II bomber was flying nearby from Boeing Field in Seattle.

Even before, when I lived and grew up on the lake several miles northwest below Lake City, I remembered those oh-so familiar rumblings. But at that time when I was in my teens, I didn't know much about the famous local seaport, Kenmore Air Harbor, on the very north end of Lake Washington.

My first direct encounter with the "world's largest seaplane-based airline" was when I started my sophomore year at Bothell High School. That's when I met Leslie Munro, the attractive brown-eyed daughter of the airline's owner, Ed Munro. We were competitors then (friendly) and I didn't even know it as they also had a fledgling boat marina business, Kenmore Marina, right next door. My father's racing friend of the 1950s, George Sylvester, was the marina manager and mechanic. The Munro's only son, Gregg, told me he liked the Slough races as a youngster when they were run from their marina. He told me, "I loved eating the hotdogs."

1952 Ed Munro family: (L-R) Ed and wife Ruth, Margie, Leslie and Gregg posing on their 1940s *Noorduyn Norseman* seaplane. Their home on left in late 1950s was next door to our marina, Uplake Marina in Kenmore. The Noorduyn Norseman was a single-engine Canadian bush plane designed to operate from unimproved surfaces. Distinctive stubby landing gear protrusions from lower fuselage made it easily recognizable.

I loved their company perspective: "Our airline is different. For starters, we build our own planes… Our fleet is the envy of pilots worldwide. Tickets aren't necessary. Just tell your name. Don't look for departure gates. There aren't any. We'll direct you to a picnic table where you'll meet your pilot and fellow passengers. Feed the ducks 'til it's time to go." I experienced their family-like culture when I took a business flight to the San Juan Islands in the early 1990s. I even was able to reconnect with my father's friend and business competitor, the owner and founder, very likeable Mr. Ed Munro.

San Juan Island Bucket List Flight

If you've never taken one of their touring flights, or any flight, I highly recommend one. It's one of those items that should be on your "bucket list," a lifetime adventure and experience that you'll never forget. I was lucky to be working on an engineering project that took me to a former co-worker's model shop at Friday Harbor in the San Juan Islands. I was doubly fortunate that I worked with an engineer co-worker who was a part-time pilot for Kenmore Air.

I scheduled my flight with my former high school classmate and neighbor, Leslie (Munro) Banks, who was the reservations manager at the time. I made a request for my pilot to be the engineering co-worker friend who flew part-time for them. Leslie made it happen. My co-worker, Lytle the pilot, took an afternoon off from work to fly me and another passenger to the San Juan Islands.

"Kenmore Beavers" waiting at Kenmore dock.

Before the flight, I checked-in at the small two-story office just a few feet from Lake Washington. I met Leslie and got re-acquainted with her father, Mr. Ed Munro, and then preceded just like their company statement implied, outdoors to the plane without a ticket. But instead of meeting at one of their picnic tables and feeding the local water fowl, I met Lytle outside in front of the office on the floating departure dock. He'd just finished checking-out and warming up the sleek and sparkling clean seaplane, with the distinctive Kenmore Air white and yellow markings. We were ready for takeoff. He helped me step from the dock onto one of the two large pontoons where I stepped up into the co-pilot's seat. Lucky me, I didn't have to arm-wrestle anyone for the seat because I was the only passenger leaving from Kenmore.

Flying into Lake Union terminal in Seattle.

Lytle climbed in on the other side, restarted the engine and taxied away from the dock heading south on Lake Washington. Before you knew it we were up and away flying down the lake, past Sand Point, banked a right turn by Madison Park, over the Mountlake Cut and down into Lake Union to pick up the other passenger. How could I have known then that I would be writing about our path to Lake Union? We flew low, over the original Slough Race course path between Kenmore and Madison Park. Our flight from Kenmore to Lake Union gave me another chance to experience a take-off and landing in the water, a wonderful smooth glide-in and a slight bounce as we kissed the water below landing among the boats on Lake Union in the heart of Seattle. After landing and loading at Lake Union, we took off for a memorable scenic flight to Friday Harbor in one of their reliable Cessna commercial float-planes

Before you knew it, the passenger was helped off the floating dock up into our seaplane and we were off again heading directly to Orcas Island, well almost. Orcas Island was our first stop, which was the Lake Union passenger's destination, a company meeting at the historic Moran Mansion at Rosario on the East Sound. But on the way we took a shortcut. Pilot Lytle knew I had a cabin on the east side of Lummi Island, the eastern-most island of the San Juans that overlooks Bellingham to the east. The passenger knew we were off-course because she had been to the Orcas meeting place earlier. I told Lytle about my place before we left and he remembered, giving us a bonus tour around the island. The Orcas stop was just a few miles west of Lummi Island, a very short but rewarding detour for me... Thank you Leslie (Banks), Gregg Munro and pilot, Lytle!

Flying over Friday Harbor on San Juan Island.

World's Largest Seaplane-Based Airline

Kenmore Air started its humble beginnings in 1946, a year after WWII ended. It was a time when outboard speedboats from Madison Park were racing by the fledgling facility at the extreme northern end of Lake Washington. The outboarders were on their way into the mouth of the Sammamish Slough and heading upstream to the race finish line at Gateway Grove on Lake Sammamish. My father, Al Benson, was one of the hardy speed boaters who traveled by the seaplane facility. Twelve years later he was part of a group of business owners who purchased the swampy property bordering the air harbor on its west side.

In 1947, when my father won his first Slough Race, the race started for the first time in Kenmore at the Kenmore Boathouse, next door to Kenmore Air, which was on the east side of the boathouse property. Ed Munro founded the company with two partners. They started fixing small airplanes and providing flying lessons. Soon after that, they purchased their first used seaplane, which they restored and started air service to remote locations, including charter flights. The company, still owned and operated by the Munro family, eventually became the largest commercial seaplane base in the world with flights to remote locations throughout the Pacific Northwest, Western Canada, and Alaska.

The year 1963 was a defining milestone for the air harbor, when they acquired their first *Beaver*, the classic and reliable de Havilland seaplane fitted with pontoons for water landings. It was defined as "a utility transport aircraft (bush plane) with a powerful single engine for short takeoffs and landings" that was originally manufactured in Toronto, Canada.

Kenmore Air is known for its remanufacturing and modification program they established for surplus and used Canadian de Havilland *Beavers*. Their Kenmore *Beavers* are renowned throughout the world and the company has the enamored position as the world's premier seaplane operator to this day.

1948: Kenmore Air Harbor property, Kenmore Boathouse on right with long dock (future 1950s Ward's Resort)

1963 Race Schedule (Partial)

Jan 6	Final "Old-Timers" Cruise
Mar 3	Annual Bar Pilots Cruise
March 31	28th Sammamish Slough Race
April 7	15th Sammamish Water-Ski Race
April 28	Lake Sammamish-Redmond
July 13-14	Outboard Divisionals-Olympia
July 28	Stock Outboard Divisionals-Sumner
Aug 2-3	Seafair-Green Lake
Aug 21-25	Stock Outboard Nationals-Boston, MA
Aug 23-25	Outboard Nationals-Moses Lake, WA
Sept 8	Lake Sammamish, Issaquah

1963 Tidbits

Popular Gerald "Red" Halliday was reelected club commodore with Linda Walters as secretary. Linda was Rose and Bud Walters' daughter. Kirkland's Dick Rautenberg and Seattle's Hal Tolford won National Championships that took place in Moses Lake. Rautenberg took the honors in A-Outboard Hydro and Tolford in C-Service Hydro. The SOA Sportsman Award was presented to "Seattle Sam" Dupuis.

Final Slough Race?

The Sammamish Slough Race was traditionally the first SOA event of the year, the kick-off race for the next season, ever since 1934. It was a tradition now in jeopardy of being lost for good due to mankind's tinkering of the land and nature–the impending Sammamish River flood control project.

The massive project called for dredging to widen and deepen the channel and include a wide weir at the Lake Sammamish entrance to minimize the lakes' seasonal level changes. It would prevent any watercraft from accessing Lake Sammamish through the Slough, a change that would eliminate all navigational travel between the lakes as it was done for over the past half century.

The King County Corps of Engineers had scheduled the work to begin in June, not long after the outboard and water-ski events concluded. One change that was known for sure was, this year's races would be the last traditional runs that traveled all the way between Lake Washington and Lake Sammamish.

Let the Dredging Begin……

Chapter 13

1964: Bothell Landing in Sammamish Slough <u>before</u> dredging & widening by Army Engineers.

1965: Bothell Landing in Sammamish Slough <u>after</u> dredging & widening by Army Engineers.

The Taming
1964-1965

"Boatmen Penalized"
"Because some boat-operators closed their eyes and ears to official warnings, one of the area's popular waterways has been closed to pleasure boating for the remainder of the season."

"Boatmen who follow the rules must be denied entry, along with those who do not. It's an old story."

-Seattle Times, June 26, 1964-

Dredging of the Sammamish River began in earnest during June of 1963. The long wait was over for the residents, farmers and businessmen of the upper Sammamish Valley. They hoped that the annual flooding of their fertile land would be mitigated by the widening and deepening of the river. The planning process, that was first investigated by engineer's Cowie, Tibbetts & Crawford in 1888, had been in the works for some 75 years. The political hassling of words was over and finally turned into action. Over the years a lot of baby steps had been taken with token dredging undertaken in the decades before.

"Sammamish Flood Project Given Boost"

The above headline was over a story by Dick Trowbridge of the *Seattle Times* on June 14, 1956. He wrote about the "long pending Sammamish River flood-control project" that was considered by the congressional subcommittee in Washington, D. C. on May 8, 1956. The project originally was recommended by the Seattle Army Engineers District Office in 1949. The project also would include widening the outlet of the Sammamish River at the Lake Sammamish end and Redmond's Bear Creek.

State legislators Alfred Westland and Thor Tollefson said, "the effort would protect 2,500 acres of farmland and create some 1,900 acres of potential residential sites." Tollefson was instrumental in arranging surveys by the Army Engineers, which were completed before the dredging started.

Presidents Eisenhower & Kennedy Approve Flood-Control Project

President Eisenhower eventually signed a special bill in 1958 that eliminated the many projects that had been thrown into the original bill at the last minute. This paved the way for construction to begin by the Army Engineers after an appropriations bill was approved for financing the project. A lot of numbers were given in newspaper reports that were confusing. In the final analysis, approximately $3 million was appropriated which consisted of federal money and state matching funds. President Kennedy gave final approval in 1963.

Final Slough Race?

The Sammamish Slough Race had started in 1934 and was traditionally the first SOA event of the year, the season's kickoff race. It was a tradition now in jeopardy of being lost for good due to mankind's tinkering of the land and nature in the impending "Sammamish River Flood-Control Project."

1963 Tom O'Neill wins what some thought would be the final Sammamish Slough Race.

Project Plan for Taming the Slough

The massive project called for dredging to widen and deepen the channel including the construction of a weir[1] near the Lake Sammamish entrance along with an adjacent shallow and wide transition zone to minimize the lakes' seasonal level changes. The new configuration at the Slough's entrance would prevent any watercraft from

---

[1] Low overflow dam built across a stream or river to raise or control the level of the water upstream.

accessing Lake Sammamish through the Slough, a change that would eliminate all navigational travel between the lakes, including raceboats. The project was scheduled to take at least two years.

The flood-control work was planned to help reduce the annual flooding, which backed up into Lake Sammamish. Under low water conditions the Slough dropped about 12 feet in its 14-mile-long channel (the level between Lake Sammamish and Lake Washington). During high water, the drop exceeded 20 feet. In times of exceptional flooding, such as in 1933, the Slough crested two feet over its banks.

Flood-Control Project Details

The work between 1964 and 1965 included the following:

- Existing bridge modifications and new bridge construction.
- Weir construction with transition zone near Lake Sammamish entrance.
- Straightening and deepening dredging between Wayne Golf Course and Marymoor Park (Dredging between Wayne and Lake Washington not feasible due to established private homes and docks on or near waterway).
- Removal of earth to eliminate some sharp river bends.
- Removal of all vegetation in county right-of-way on both river sides.
- Riverbank reconstruction with higher rock-reinforced features.
- Erosion prevention with grass plantings along riverbank water lines.
- Facilitation of county river-bank access with graveled surface.
- Riverbank erosion prevention by watercraft speed-limit and enforcement of watercraft speed.

There was a proposal for a river trial but it was not completed as part of this project.

The King County Corps of Engineers scheduled the work to begin in June of 1963, not long after the 28th annual Sammamish Slough Race was completed. One monumental effect of the impending project was known; the 1963 race would be the final Slough Race to travel between lake Washington and Lake Sammamish.

No one knew what the waterway would be like or even if racing could resume after the work was completed. The big question for the Seattle Outboard Association and Slough Race fans all over the Northwest was: Will there ever be another race after this year?

Army to 'Tame' Sammamish Slough

The headline above Bud Livesley's story was in the *Seattle Times* on March 3, 1963. Livesley wrote, "One of the area's top sporting attractions soon may give way to progress. Dare-devil outboard-speedboat drivers, as for so many years in the past, will engage in their favorite pastime, 'taming of the Slough' next month. But thereafter, the Sammamish Slough Race just won't be the challenge it has been in the past.

"What many speedboat drivers have failed to accomplish, the Corps of Army Engineers starting in May, will; straighten the river that meanders through fields and farms and a golf course for 14 miles from Lake Sammamish to Lake Washington. The Army's 'attack' on the Slough is for flood-control. Only a few of the 30-odd hairpin turns will be eliminated. 'Mostly' said an army spokesman, 'we are going to widen and deepen the river.' But he admitted the river will be so much wider that the turns will be considerably gentler and sweeping. The river will be widened about twice its present width of 25 feet."

Seattle Outboard officials scheduled their final Slough Race for March 31. They would decide the race's future after an inspection of the "damage" done by the engineers. In the past, finishing the race was the challenge. Last year (1962) only 45 of the 73 starters saw the checkered flag at the finish. It was the "wreckage" of boats on the sand bars, literally up in the trees and skipping across meadowlands that lured as many as 35,000 spectators in past events.

Livesley's comment at the end of his article was: "Will the engineers take the 'tiger' out of the Slough and leave a lazy; unchallenging stream fit only for cruisers?"

The project actually began in early 1963 with bridgework by the Army Corps of Engineers and the Northern Pacific Railroad. County engineers started on the Marymoor bridges by converting four of its wooden one-lane bridges into one two-lane concrete bridge. The railroad modified four of their bridges beginning in Redmond, all a "prelude" to the actual dredging, which began in mid-June.

None of the outboard drivers who competed in the Slough knew what the waterway would be like or even if racing could resume after the work was completed. The project was scheduled to be ongoing for at least the next two years. The big question for the Seattle Outboard Association and Slough Race fans all over the Northwest was: Will there ever be another race after this year?

The Dredging Begins...

The Seattle J.A. Jones and Osberg Construction companies were awarded the contract as low bidders for channel improvements to the Sammamish River on June 29. And soon began their dredging work. In the meantime, the Redmond and Wayne golf Courses were having their issues with the proposed project in August, 1963.

1963 dredging, widening & deepening by Seattle's J.A. Jones and Osberg Construction companies.

Golf Courses Challenge Dredging Alongside Their Property

John Graham, owner of the Redmond Golf Course, had his problems with the Army Corps of Engineers because they planned to slice away into Redmond's 12th hole including their work on Bear Creek, which ran the length of the fairway. Graham objected obstinately to the work plan. The Corps tentatively altered their blueprints to accommodate his objections. He told a *Times* newspaper reporter, "I've been here 14 years and the flooding never has been a problem on the golf course. They tell me it runs in cycles; about every 15 years." Graham said he was optimistic that the revisions would be acceptable and most likely never raised any further concerns as nothing more was published in the *Times* newspaper.

Gordon Richards, whose family owned Wayne Golf Course, went to court and successfully received a court order to halt work through the course. He obtained a temporary restraining order from Superior Court Judge, Theodore S. Turner, to stop the engineer's work. Richards contended that the Corps had agreed to begin the work between November and January, the off-season for the course. But he said that "The County and the engineers appeared to be getting ready to begin work in early August." The King County Deputy Prosecutor, William Paul, Jr., said the county would resist the golf courses court order.

2016 "Google Earth" aerial view of Wayne Golf Course in Bothell, Washington bisected by Sammamish Slough showing "Down River Marina" and old "Nursery Bridge" location.

In the interim the new nine holes at the Wayne Golf Course opened on August 16, 1963 despite the engineers' dredging that continued through the middle of the golf course. Wayne golfers were permitted to play the new holes despite the construction work that was on-going. The golf course lost its bid for an injunction to keep the Corps of Engineers from beginning their work on the project. Richards said in *Times* newspaper article on August 13, 1963, "The flood-control work will cut only slightly into the ninth fairway and will add about 30 feet to a narrow section of the eighth fairway." No further concerns were made public from the golf course.

Speed Limit Placed in Slough

King County Army Corps of Engineers placed a 5-mile-per-hour speed limit on the Sammamish River for the duration of their flood-control work. The restriction was expected to be enforced for at least two years while the construction work was in progress. Their issue was that the wakes of the speeding boats would erode the soft riverbanks and plantings along the sides of the waterway. Signs were posted at both ends of the river and in various places along the waterway.

Dredging was suspended for a few weeks during late October, 1963 to allow salmon to travel upstream for spawning. The work was resumed following the spawning period and the Army Corps of Engineers continued their huge project where some work had begun in May. The $3 million job was being supervised by the County engineers. King County is responsible for about a third of the cost. The following "Troubleshooter article" was published in the *Times* on December 17, 1963.

LAKE SAMMAMISH LEVEL: "The water level in Lake Sammamish varies greatly during the year. Sometimes we can't use our docks, bulkheads and boats. Can anything be done about it?"—B. J.

TROUBLESHOOTER: Complete control of the lake level would require a dam at the Sammamish River outlet, and flood problems would be created in the river, Army Engineers say. They add that the river flood control project, which is scheduled for completion next year, will cut three feet from the maximum flood peak in the winter months, thereby helping to reduce fluctuation in the lake level. The extreme low-water periods will continue, however.

Taming of Slough Meaning

To the newspaper readers and writers, the "Taming of the Slough" meant the boat racers had successfully navigated the twisting Slough by winning the annual event. To the Seattle Outboard club members and raceboat drivers it meant something quite different. It meant the meandering waterway was now much easier to traverse in their speedboats. To them it was the end of an era where luck meant just as much to their success as their driving skills. But now the annual tradition of running over logs and encountering other hazardous obstacles was about to be minimized. The race would never have its mystique of the past; it will now be tamer and easier to navigate.

Famed Slough Race Called Off–Flood-Control Work Has Priority

The headline above was for the *Times*' Bud Livesley's column on April 1, 1964. He wrote: "One of the season's most fascinating speedboat races has been eliminated this year, at least. The Sammamish Slough Race, most testing of the campaign for outboard-speedboat drivers, has given way to the Corps of Army Engineers and a round-the-clock task of completing a flood-control project.

"The 14-mile river, from Lake Washington to Lake Sammamish, never again will offer the man-made and natural hazards to outboarders as in the past, but there probably will be a race again next year. 'We tentatively had scheduled the race Sunday (April 5),' said race spokesman and American Power Boat Association regional chairman Hal Tolford, 'but after conferring with Army officials, it was agreed the race should be called off for this year, at least. But we're hoping to resume the event next year.'

"In the past, the race had provided a spectacular test of endurance and speed, with spills and thrills at virtually every turn along the snake-like river. Spectators numbering 30,000 to 40,000 lined the river bank from Kenmore to Redmond to speculate which would be the ultimate victor–man or nature. It was touch and go even for the most capable driver. Two years ago, 73 rigs set out to conquer the Slough; 45 were successful.

"Tom O'Neill, 22, a dare-devil sophomore at the University of Washington, set a record of 33 minutes 3.6 seconds last spring for the round trip run in winning the overall championship for the fastest of the outboard rigs, F Hydros. The engineers probably have taken much of the 'fun' out of the race by widening, deepening and eliminating most of the kinks in the Slough. But the 'buzz boys' will have another go at 'Taming the Slough' in years to come."

Kenmore River Residents Ask for Permanent Speed limit

Residents along the Sammamish River in Kenmore asked the county to affix a permanent 10-mile-per-hour speed limit on the river after the flood-control work was finished. They said the restriction is necessary to protect their property along the riverbanks. They added that a provision should be put in place to lift the speed limit for authorized boating events only. The county previously had placed a 5-mph speed limit for the duration of the construction period.

Sammamish River Boaters Get Warnings & Closure

An article in the *Seattle Times* on June 19, 1964, warned boaters using the Slough. It stated: "Boat operators were warned that unless they cooperate in obeying the 5-mile-an-hour county speed limit on the Sammamish River, the waterway may have to be closed to boating. Sheriff Jack Porter said he may join with the Corps of Army Engineers in seeking closure of the river during flood-control work.

"Officials had complained that wakes from speedboats were damaging banks faster than they can be constructed. Chief William Walsh, head of the sheriff's criminal division said, 'The sheriff had added an airplane patrol to its boat patrol of the river.' He also said, 'The engineers complain particularly about water-skiers in the river. No water skiing is allowed in the waterway.'

"Boat operators who refused to obey the speed limit on the Sammamish River were blamed for an order to close most of the river to all pleasure boating. The Army Engineers announced that the river was to be closed to boating from Thursday, June 25, 1964 to midnight, November 15. The closure extended from the Wayne Golf Course to Marymoor Farm, about two-thirds of a mile below Lake Sammamish."

This was a protective measure to prevent further damage from boat wakes during the construction period. Rock facing, sodding and seeding of the banks were expected to be completed and stable by late November. The Corps and Sheriff Porter tried to persuade pleasure boat operators to hold their speed within the 5-mph limit, but to no avail.

Another *Times* article published on June 23, 1964, quoted an announcement from the Sheriff's office: "Numerous disregards of this necessary curtailment of activity resulted in the closure order to stop further costly damage to the soft banks and delay in the construction progress." Barricades and blinker lights were installed at the downstream bridge in the Wayne Golf Course and at the bridge in Marymoor Farm upstream from Redmond. Access will be allowed between Lake Washington and the Downriver Marina on the lower end of the river. No access was possible from Lake Sammamish because of the wide and shallow weir that was constructed just downstream from the lake. "Boatmen who followed the rules were denied entry, along with the violators who did not." It's was a familiar old story….

Project Status

The projects progress was the topic of the *Times* "Troubleshooter" April, 28, 1964.

"How is construction work on the Sammamish Slough coming along? Is the channel open to boat traffic all the way yet?"—Ken Ayres.

Troubleshooter: The total project is about half-way completed now, with work a little ahead of schedule, Army Corps of Engineers spokesmen say. Dredging is in progress between Woodinville and Redmond. Some small boats could get around the drag lines and pipe-line dredge, engineers say, but the travel is hazardous, and excessive traffic could prove damaging to the soft banks which have been cleared. The contractor hopes to complete the project by the end of this year.

The five-mile-an-hour speed limit all along the channel still is in effect to protect property and construction work, and sheriff's officers investigate speed violations.

Bridge Modifications

Reshaping the riverbed required modifications to a few manmade structures in addition to the efforts to reduce the drainage problems. The Sammamish was crossed by 22 bridges, nine of them private and four others were railroad spans, which all had to be strengthened along with their foundations overhauled as a safeguard against erosion. Some of their piers were replaced to provide more channel clearance.

The old wooden highway trestle near Woodinville was removed in anticipation of the new freeway construction and interchange over the Slough. Previous efforts to mitigate the flooding, particularly the county's dredging in 1948, straightened some of the worst spots. Now more corners were smoothed-out and the dredged earth was used to fill former swampy areas.

The Sammamish River of 1965 bears little resemblance to the same stretch at the beginning of the last century when logs were rafted or towed down the river from one lake to another. Bothell was then regarded as a port served by steamboats making round trips daily to Seattle. Its citizens felt cheated when the water level was lowered in 1916 as a result of Lake Washington being lowered. Now there were boats on the Sammamish, but they are the smaller outboards with increasing numbers and speed. Several marinas had been built in Kenmore and one in the river; probably the harbinger of other businesses in the future.

1932: King County dredging in Woodinville (looking downstream at Railroad Bridge.)

Sammamish to Stay Closed-More Dredging Sought

The Corps of Engineers said the Sammamish River will continue to be closed until June of 1965, a move to allow sufficient root growth in the recently seeded and sodded areas to withstand the wave-wash from speedboats. The river had been previously closed to boats during the summer of 1964 because of the damage caused by the boat drivers who ignored the speed limit. It had been scheduled for re-opening in the fall. The closure wasn't expected to affect the lower river basin between Lake Washington and the marina just downstream from the Wayne Golf course.

Additional dredging to open the Sammamish River to heavier boat traffic between the Kenmore Bridge and Lake Washington was requested and granted to the Corps of Army Engineers by the King County Commissioners in December of 1964. The current depth of the Slough's outlet at Lake Washington was inadequate for their maintenance equipment and needed dredging because the Corps was responsible for maintaining the waterway. Additional funds were needed before this project could begin. But as in the past, lack of funds and bureaucratic red tape thwarted the effort for many years after the project was approved. Again, it's the same old story… except environmental concerns have complicated the matter to such an extent that further dredging may never occur.

Race and Cruises Never to Reach Lake Sammamish Again

To many outboard drivers and club members, the severe challenge of running the Slough was tamed and would never be the same. Many chose to never participate again in the event that was run under the same conditions since it began in 1934, for some that even included the annual cruises that began in 1929. The nostalgic navigations up and down the twisting Sammamish Slough to Lake Sammamish were now blocked by a dam–the tradition was gone, lost forever.

No more drinking of the "Slough Juice" and sayings of the Bar Pilots oath ending in "So help me Sammamish Slough." Their voices won't be heard on a cold and moist

1956 Bar Pilots repeating oath.

winter day at a resort on the north end of Lake Sammamish. No more running over logs in a borrowed boat, no more handing out "Bar Pilots certificates," or induction ceremonies somewhere along the Slough. The last Slough Cruise and boat race to reach Lake Sammamish was in March of 1963. That was when young Tom O' Neill won the overall outboard race in record time; a record that will stand forever because it was now impossible for powerboats to make the two-way run between Lakes Sammamish and Washington again.

Sammamish River Dredging Timeline

1888: Cowie, Tibbetts & Crawford investigate scheme[2] to drain upper Squak Slough.

1911: King County Drainage District #3 (upper Sammamish River) approved.

1911: King County appropriates $30,000 to dredge upper Sammamish River but project never started due to impending Lake Washington Ship Canal project.

1912: Sammamish River farmers pay $60,000 to dredge upper river stretch between Redmond and Woodinville.

1916: Lake Washington Ship Canal Completed with Lake Washington lowered 9 feet, Squak Slough transformed into narrow meandering waterway.

1920: Seattle Port Commission's defunct $1,750,000 "Bothell Waterway Plan" never materializes due to taxpayer objections.

1929: Seattle Outboard members clear Slough for unobstructed cruising up waterway.

1934: King County Corps of Army Engineers completes partial dredging between Woodinville and Bothell.

1949: Seattle Army Engineers recommend Sammamish flood-control project

1956: Long pending Sammamish River flood-control project (estimated at $1,045,000) recommended by U.S. Congressional sub-committee with support from Washington State Congressmen Alfred Westland and Thor Tollefson.

1956: President Eisenhower vetoes flood-control bill because of numerous projects thrown into bill at last minute.

1956: Revised Rivers & Harbors Bill approved by President Eisenhower-$83,000 goes to Sammamish Basin project.

---

[2] From *Seattle Post-Intelligencer* newspaper article printed, Thursday, August 18, 1892. Cowie, Tibbetts & Crawford were likely engineers studying the upper Squak Slough (ditch) drain scheme for the King County drainage district commissioners. Article found in Library of Congress' "Chronicling America" 1888-1914.

1959: Washington State congressmen Thomas Pelly and Jack Westland push public works appropriations for Sammamish River flood-control project.

1961: Seattle District of the Army Engineers given $50,000 in federal funds for pre-construction planning of straightening, deepening and clearing the Sammamish River.

1961: U.S. House appropriations committee approves $58,000 for start of Sammamish River project with a total cost of $1,060,000. King County will provide $712,000.

1962: King County Park Board recommends replacing narrow bridges crossing Sammamish River at Marymoor with one two-lane structure.

1962: State Game Department recommend footpaths along both sides of river.

1963: Northern Pacific Railway bridgework begins.

1963: Army Engineers begin road bridge work.

1963: Seattle J. A. Jones Construction and Osberg Construction awarded $2,469,850 contract for Sammamish River channel improvements.

1963: King County Engineers impose 5-mile-per-hour speed limit to Sammamish River during construction period.

1963: Sammamish River dredging suspended to allow spawning salmon to go upstream.

1963: Wayne Golf Course owners, John Graham and Dave Richards, get court order to halt work on river adjacent their golf course.

1963: Old Sammamish Valley Drainage District #3 dissolved (deemed unnecessary due to government funding for Sammamish River dredging project).

1963: Wayne Golf Course loses court case seeking halt to Sammamish flood-control work near course–remains open during dredging project.

1963: Stoen Construction of Monroe supplies 60,000 tons of rock for Sammamish River flood-control project.

1964: Army Engineers close Sammamish River to all boating traffic for the duration.

1964: Dredging of the Sammamish River outlet in Kenmore was proposed and approved but financing was an ongoing saga thru late 1970s.

1965: Engineers continue Sammamish closure through summer of 1965.

1965: Sammamish River reopens to watercraft in summer of 1965.

1964 Tidbits

Popular Ray Lee was elected commodore of the Seattle Outboard Association for 1965. He succeeded Red Halliday who held the office the last two years. He was joined by Fred Mackle, vice commodore; Ken Ferguson, treasurer; Linda Walters, secretary and Dave Jenkins, sergeant-at-arms. The four SOA directors elected to the board included longtime Slough Racer John Laird and Earl Garrison, Bill Downing and Bill Meyers.

Commodore Ray Lee

Hal Tolford

Harold "Hal" Tolford was C-Service Hydro national champion in 1964 and was elected to the "Gulf Marine Racing Hall of Fame" for a second time; a stellar achievement for one of the club's most active members. He also was the acting APBA Region 10 chairman, a position he held for a number of years.

If you ever needed racing fuel, Tolford was the "go-to guy." He concocted his toxic but wonderful smelling fuel in his garage. His high-potency racing fuel consisted of about four quarts alcohol, two quarts Castrol (racing oil) and a quart of some other volatile solvent like acetone to mix it all together. It's a good thing the local fire department never inspected his garage because it was full of flammable chemicals, including 55-gallon drums full of alcohol.

Hugh Entrop won the APBA Jack Maypole Memorial Trophy for an unprecedented fifth time when he obliterated his old F-Hydro kilo[3] record. He set his new mark at 110.485 miles per hour on Devil's Lake in Oregon. His outboard record was faster than most of the limited hydros except for the high powered 7 liters, 266 and 225 cubic inch classes. Entrop most likely retired the trophy this year. Lee Sutter was the only other Slough Race driver to set a record. He set the BU-Runabout UIM[4] five-mile competition record at 55.249 mph. Bev Downing was the SOA Sportsman of the Year.

H. J. "Pop" Tolford Leads Novice School

Hal Tolford's father, Harold "Pop" Tolford, Sr., was one of the volunteer-mentors and teachers in the SOA "Novice School." The acclaimed school that the outboard club founded in the mid-1950s was the only program of its kind in the United States. The classes, led by Tolford, Sr., were open to anyone interested in boat racing.

---

[3] Kilo: Straight-a-way record 3,281-foot-long course (approx. 5/8th of a mile). A safer and shorter record distance verses the mile, usually producing higher speeds.

[4] UIM: *Union Internationale Motonautique*, the world powerboat racing governing organization.

It was one of the Seattle Outboard's most giving and popular programs, one that most of the new raceboat drivers graduated from and were thankful as participants. It produced national champions, world-record holders and a number of "hall of famers." The program continues to this day and is admired by the national body (APBA), and boat racing clubs throughout the nation.

1965 Tidbits-World Records Galore

Ray Lee was elected commodore of the Seattle Outboard Association for a second term in a row. He had his work cut out for him because the club members had just completed setting a host of records in Devil's Lake, Oregon and on Lake Lawrence in Yelm, Washington. SOA drivers set 12 world records and won many awards in the 29 races sponsored by the club during the year, all of which Lee and his officers had to document and submit to APBA headquarters for approval. The SOA annual awards banquet was held at the American Legion Post No. 1 facility at Seventh Avenue and University Street in Seattle on November 27, 1965.

The officers that were re-elected with Commodore Lee of Seattle were: Vice Commodore, Fred Mackle, Bellevue; Treasurer, Ken Ferguson, Seattle; Secretary, Linda Walters, Bothell and sergeant-at-arms, Dave Jenkins of Seattle. The board of directors elected included: John Laird, Bellevue; Earl Garrison, Edmonds; Hal Tolford, Seattle; Howard Anderson, Edmonds and Lee Sutter of Seattle. John Laird was the SOA Sportsman for the Year.

Dennis Lee 2nd Pennsylvania Nationals

World records set by SOA Sammamish Slough Race drivers at Devil's Lake, Oregon included: Lee Sutter, Tom O'Neill and Gerry Walin. Sutter set the B-Hydro UIM competition record at 73.170 mph and an A-Racing Runabout APBA kilo mark of 69.800. O'Neill set the D-Stock Hydro APBA competition record at 68.285 mph. Walin set the A-Outboard Hydro UIM competition record at 68.965 mph, an A-Outboard Hydro UIM kilo mark at 81.506 and an A-Racing Runabout APBA kilo record of 74.008. Dick Rautenberg set a B-Stock Hydro competition record of 58.823 mph at Lake Lawrence. Dennis Lee was second in A-Stock-Hydro in the Pennsylvania Nationals.

1963 overall Slough Race winner Tom O'Neill with wife Helene in his record breaking D-Stock Hydro.

Sammamish River Quietly Reopens

Finally, after 53 years since the Sammamish Valley farmers paid for their own dredging of the "Squak Slough," the long-awaited Sammamish Valley flood-control project was completed by the King County Army Corps of Engineers with the funds approved back in 1948. There were no bands or fanfare to celebrate the occasion, just the removal of the Barricades and blinker lights that blocked the river.

The enthusiasm for the river opening was tempered with reality that the Slough entrance at Lake Washington was still too shallow for navigating in the summer months. On the positive side, the SOA, led by Commodore Ray Lee, was creative enough to find a way to continue the long tradition of staging the Sammamish Slough Race.

Drivers…Get Ready to Start Your Engines!

Chapter 14

1965 JU champion Janis Lee, 12, with proud parents, mother Juanita & father, SOA commodore Ray Lee.

High Speed Chase
1966-1970

"Walters, a 'Watcher' No Longer,
Wins Slough Race"

-Bud Livesley of the Seattle Daily Times, April 16, 1966-

"Old Time" Snake Dance Returns to New Digs

It's over baby, all the widening, deepening and digging is over. The questioning about if there will be another dance is passé. It's about to happen again as it's been three years since the old dance. Finally, after decades of political hassling and cries from concerned residents and property owners of the Sammamish Valley, the work was completed to mitigate the flooding. The King County flood control project, in the planning for decades and with funds approved in 1948, was completed in the summer of 1965 by the Seattle District of the Army Corps of Engineers.

The bad news was, navigating all the way to Lake Sammamish was impossible. The good news? The SOA was resourceful in finding a way to continue the Slough Races, albeit with a shorter, straighter route without reaching Lake Sammamish. Although dredgers straightened the channel and the waterway achieved the ranking of a "river," the Slough Races resumed after a three-year hiatus.

The renowned race with classes for outboard hydros and runabouts was scheduled to get under way at noon on Sunday, April 17, from the marina at Kenmore Air Harbor. But this year the speedboats took a breather at Marymoor Park instead of at one of the northern resorts on Lake Sammamish. The Army Engineers created a shallow dam between Marymoor and the Lake Sammamish entrance to help control the lake level fluctuations. The shallow dam, built up with rocks for several hundred feet in length, made it impossible for any motorized craft to pass over the long and shallow spillway to reach the lake.

Ray Lee, commodore of the sponsoring Seattle Outboard Association, told the *Sammamish Valley News* on March 24, 1966, "Close to 60 entries are expected, we expect it will be a much faster race because of the straightening of the Slough." The main reason the times would be lower was because the round-trip course was almost two miles shorter. All the classes would race up the river to Marymoor Park where they would either be pulled out or parked on the riverbank. Then the rigs were refueled and readied to start their return run downstream and finish at the boat-ramp on the southwest side of the Kenmore Bridge.

"As well as being faster," Lee said, "The races will be more dangerous this year because of the rocky banks on the many turns; before you just landed in the mud when you missed a turn." Lee also said, "He thought the races would be more popular spectator-wise since more riverside area had been opened during the dredging and straightening operations."

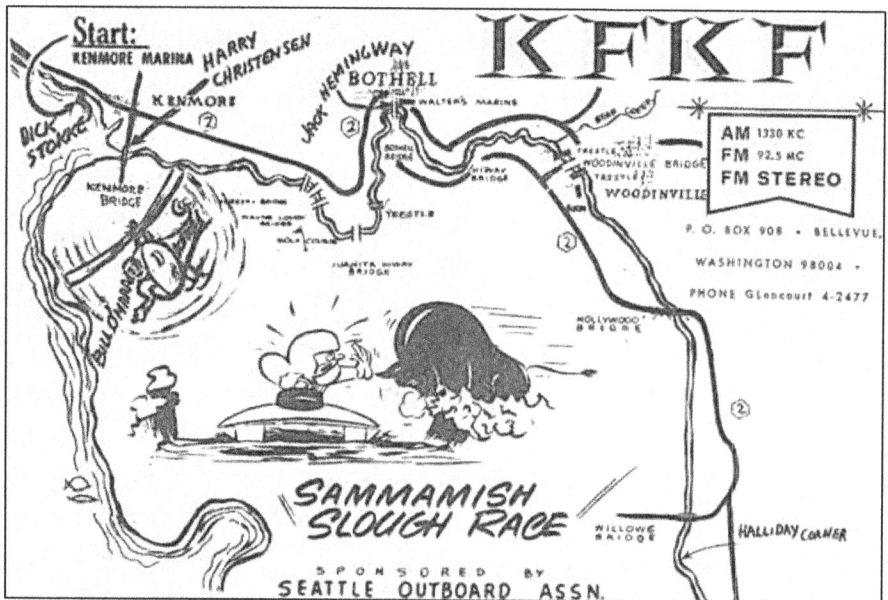

Bellevue radio station KFKF broadcast the race live by helicopter with longtime sports announcer "Bill O'Mara" calling the action from high above the race course.

Bellevue radio station KFKF covered the race by helicopter with Bill O'Mara broadcasting in the air; announcer Dick Stokke at the Kenmore starting line; Jack

Hemingway, Bothell; Johnny Forrest, Marymoor Park, and Harry Christensen at the Kenmore Bridge finish line. This was the first time a Slough Race was covered in the air and on land via a live broadcast from start to finish.

Fred Mackle of Bellevue and Red Halliday of Bothell were race co-chairmen. They needed to receive permission to run the event since the boats raced partly in the city limits of Redmond and would violate the city's new seven mile-per-hour maximum speed ordinance. Ray Lee was quoted in a *Sammamish Valley News* article. "I realize the Sammamish is a river, but the Slough Race had too much history on its side." (They continued to call it the Sammamish "Slough" Race.)

'Taming of the Slough' Resumes

The above headline and following article by Bud Livesley was published in the *Seattle Times* on Sunday, April 17, 1966. "Being a wife, mother and pal in a sports-oriented family is not always easy. Take for example the cases of Mrs. Ray Lee and Mrs. Lee Sutter. They await today's Sammamish Slough Race for outboard speedboats with contrasting emotions. 'I'll probably be on the beach chewing my fingernails,' Mrs. Lee said. 'Lee and I will be spectators but I wish he were driving,' 'I think it would be exciting,' Mrs. Sutter said. Why the difference?

"Mrs. Sutter, married only a month and a half, never has seen her husband race; Mrs. Lee, over the years has seen hundreds of races. But it will be different today. Three among the 60 to 70 racers who will attempt to tame the Slough will be Ray, husband; Dennis, 19, son, and Janis, 13, daughter. 'This is the first time all three have been in the race. I'm not sure I like the idea,' Mrs. Lee admitted. However, the racing Lees are an experienced trio. Father is commodore of the sponsoring Seattle Outboard Association; Dennis was second nationally last year in A-Stock hydros and Janis has been racing JU runabouts for a couple of years.

"They will not race against each other today. Ray will pilot a B-Stock Hydro; his son an A-stocker and Janis a JU. 'The JU's will race only to the Bothell Bridge,' Mrs. Lee pointed out. 'I'll probably meet Janis there and we'll have each other's company while the men try to keep their rigs in the water.'"

The article continued: "The Slough Race is hazardous, but not foolhardy. Besides, the Army Engineers, busy as beavers the past couple of years, had taken much of the snarl out of the previously snarly Slough. The once-meandering river that connects Lake Washington and Lake Sammamish is not so meandering any more. The engineers, for flood-control reasons, have deepened and straightened the river that winds 14 miles through Sammamish Park, a couple of golf courses, acres of fertile dairy land and through the cities of Bothell, Woodinville and Redmond. Still, in the past, a toll has been extracted in the for-fun test between man and machines and the twisty Slough. Mostly, however, it was machines that suffered. Injuries to drivers tossed out on sand bars or in nearby trees have been minor.

"Gerald 'Red' Halliday, a veteran Slough-tamer, suffered a broken arm a few years ago. But Halliday, a former SOA commodore, didn't want to miss the excitement for anything. He was in the lineup when the race resumed at noon for the first time since 1963" (he has his own corner with his namesake "Halliday Corner," see the "KFKF program map in a preceding page). "'Lee (Sutter) isn't racing because he doesn't want to risk his new boat in the Slough.' Mrs. Sutter said. 'It's not true that his bride won't permit it. I wanted him to race.' Lee Sutter was a carefree student at the University of Washington in 1962 when he entered his first Slough Race. He surprised everyone– including himself, by winning the whole thing." The Livesley article continued…

"Wendell Ewing, hanging tight around the 63-turns along the 28-mile roundtrip tour, set a record of 35 minutes 19.2 seconds for elapsed time in winning in 1961. Ewing since has retired from racing. But the last-time victor, Tom O'Neill, was on hand to test the engineer's renovated river course. O'Neill, in winning the 1963 race, set a record of 33:03.6 that will stand forever (because the course is now shorter).

"This year's race will be four miles shorter than in previous years. The racers will go only as for as Marymoor Park, less than a mile shy of Lake Sammamish. The upstream journey for the first of eight classes of outboards (was) planned to get under way at noon from the Kenmore Marina. The downstream return trip (was) scheduled to leave Marymoor at 2 o'clock."

The "Jolly" Man of the Slough

Wallace "Bud" Walters was victorious in the 1966 renewal of Sammamish Slough Race on Sunday, April 17. He was the first winner to test out the new $3-million course, courtesy of the King County Army Engineers. An unlikely looking candidate for honors as a raceboat jockey; he was then 48 years young and full figured at well over 200 pounds. He was one of the Northwest's most successful and popular drivers, grinning from ear-to-ear behind his gold framed glasses. He conceded in an interview with the *Seattle Post-Intelligencer's* Bill Knight shortly after his victory:

"'I've been in the Slough Race a half a dozen or so times, but this is the first time I've ever won.' The windy conditions didn't make it easy as he almost hit a patrol boat coming downstream just north of Woodinville. 'Coming into the wind on the way down you'd be bouncing over the waves and catching the wind under the hull so you had to go at about half throttle,' he said."

Walters, a good natured and "jolly" man from Kenmore, tamed an angry Sammamish Slough with unusual whitecaps whipped-up by 25 mile-per-hour winds. The trees that once protected the waters in the straightaways were removed allowing the wind to whip-up waves in the long straight sections. He still managed to pass by defending champion, Tom O'Neill (last winner in 1963) near Woodinville and led the rest of the way to Kenmore for the overall victory, 43 seconds ahead of second-place finisher, Wendell Ward. He won in a total time of 29 minutes and 3 seconds running the course that the Army Corps of Engineers had spent the past two years dredging and straightening.

Walters set the new course record in the natural amphitheater some 12-miles long each way in the Sammamish Valley, which included miles of unobstructed views. Families of spectators could lay out their picnic blankets and bask in the sun (when it was out) while watching a day of entertaining boat racing along the newly seeded banks of the Sammamish River, all for free.

Champion-Bud Walters replacing his wet shoes.

Bud Walters, 1966 unlimited overall winner, successfully passing by concrete pillars at Bothell Bridge.

O'Neill was just one of the 20 drivers from the field of 49 starters who failed to finish. He had engine troubles on the second leg after winning the upstream run handily. Several others ended up in the cold water. Two-time winner, Howard Anderson, winner in 1959 and 1960, hit a log after the start when he was heading into the Slough from Lake Washington. The boat went out of control and he bailed out just before hitting a large rock. Two scared occupants of a patrol boat that Walters almost hit in the middle of the course also bailed out (unhurt) during the upstream run.

Of the 11 who entered the Unlimited class, swiftest of the afternoon, only Walters, Ward and Charles Dockhorn made it back without a tow. Tom O'Neill won the first leg but spun-out on the downstream run. He and Bob Waite ended up with dead engines and Dave Jenkins flipped in the windy straightaway below Halliday Corner. There were a lot of drivers with sore knees from bouncing over the choppy waves.

Walters was the senior member of one of the area's prominent boating families. His son, Charley, 19, had been a top outboard contender for several years and a daughter, Linda, was secretary of the outboard club and a past competitor herself. Knight of the *Post-Intelligencer* also quoted Bud Walters' wife, Rose, shortly after she gave her soaking wet husband a hug (following his victory dunking): "In fact after getting his son interested in racing about 10 years ago, Bud decided to take up the sport as a contender himself. He thought that as long as he was going to be around he might as well do it himself."

Rose Walters likely was not with Bud back in 1939 during his first Slough Race at the age of twenty-one. The following story was printed in the *Bothell Citizen* on Wednesday, April 5, 1939. "If it hadn't been for an unexpected bend or two in the river Sunday (April 3), Bud Walters would have won a prize in the putt-putt boat race. The curve at the bridge was too much for him and the boat tried a shortcut across the bend, which resulted in the engine sheering off a pin and spoiled the race for Bud." History tells us that Bud was a competitor some 27 years ago.

1966 Slough Race: Ray Lee 3rd place B-Stock Hydro Class.

It was a historic day for the Lee family of boat racers. Papa Ray, a bread delivery driver, took third place in the B-Stock Hydro class, Dennis led the pack in A-Stock Hydro and Janis took third place in JU-Runabout. They were the first family trio to all place in the same race. My family in the 1950s raced together several times in the same event but we never all placed in the same race, only two of us.

Dennis Lee & dad Ray holding A-Hydro. **Janis Lee in JU-Runabout 45-R built by her father.**

The renewal of the Slough Race was a maiden voyage for some and "old hat" for the veterans, except the old hat was now a new hat (the revised Slough) that fit more efficiently. The race was postponed in 1966 to give the fisherman time for their opening season. But the fish likely were in no mood for biting in their new surroundings as they also were checking out their new digs. This time it was son Charley Walters who was proud of his father when dad brought home the overall winner's hardware, the coveted Jackens Grill and Capo Club perpetual trophies.

1966 Sammamish Slough Race Results (by class)

Place	Driver	Class	From	Boat #	Time
1	Bud Walters	Unlimited Hydro	Kenmore	R-50	29:03
2	Wendell Ward	Unlimited Hydro	Bothell	*	29:46
3	Charles Dockhorn	Unlimited Hydro	Seattle	*	32:26
1	Phil Williams	Unlimited Runabout	Seattle	R-61	33:12
2	Ken Ferguson	Unlimited Runabout	Seattle	*	33:72
1	Don Haack	C-Stock Hydro	Redmond	*	32:31
2	Mike Moreland	C-Stock Hydro	Playa Del Ray, CA	*	32:74
3	Tom Berryhill	C-Stock Hydro	Seattle	*	37:49
1	Bob Thorn	B-Stock Hydro	*	*	32:72
2	Dan Mackle	B-Stock Hydro	*	*	33:27
3	Ray Lee	B-Stock Hydro	Seattle	35-R	33:48
1	Earl Garrison	BU-Runabout	Seattle	*	33:32
2	Steve Greaves	BU-Runabout	Seattle	3-R	46:01
3	Tim Fagan	BU-Runabout	Seattle	*	*

1	Dennis Lee	A-Stock Hydro	Seattle	R-45	38:72
2	Lance Puckett	A-Stock Hydro	Seattle	*	39:32
3	Keith Knowilton	A-Stock Hydro	*	*	40:60
1	John Myers	A-Runabout	Seattle	R-1-77	43:88
2	Neil Bass	A-Runabout	*	*	44:24
3	John Hammond	A-Runabout	*	*	51:85
1	Mike Downing	JU-Runabout	Seattle	*	16:52
2	Drew Thompson	JU-Runabout	Seattle	*	18:49
3	Janis Lee	JU-Runabout	Seattle	45-R	*

Some towns, boat numbers & times unavailable

The article below was from Don Duncan's column in the *Seattle Times* on April 6, 1966

> They are billing the Sammamish River outboard race as the "Sammamish Slough Race" once more after three years without a neck-breaker due to dredging by the Army Engineers. Purists favored "river," but promoters felt there was too much tradition connected with "slough."

1966 Race Schedule (Partial)

Annual Old-Timers and Bar Pilots Cruises discontinued

April 10	29th Sammamish Slough Race
May 1	Lake Sammamish-Alexander's Beach
May 22	Cottage Lake
June 26	Green Lake Regatta
July 24	Stock Outboard Divisionals-Port Orchard
Aug 5-7	Outboard Nationals, DePue, IL
Aug 18-21	Stock Outboard Nationals, Prineville OR
Sept 4-5	Silver Lake, Everett
Sept 17-18	Lake Lawrence-Yelm
Sept 25	Lake Sammamish-Redmond
Oct 1-2	Devil's Lake Kilos

1966 Tidbits

Seattle's Mike Downing had a stellar year, one of the best of any past SOA club member. He set a new JU-Runabout 5-mile competition record at 27.795 mph, the J-Stock Hydro record at 29.470 mph, the JU-Runabout kilo record at 32.003 and the J-Stock Hydro kilo at 31.949. He was also JU-Runabout and J-Stock Hydro National Champion and named to the Gulf Marine Racing Hall of Fame. This was the first year the new J-Stock Hydro class was run at a national event. Harold Tolford won his fourth National Championship (three in a row in C-Service Hydro). Gerry Wallin, another Slough Race driver, set the world speed record for an outboard at 131.051 mph, the A-Outboard Hydro kilo record at 84.107 mph and was inducted into the Gulf Marine Racing Hall of Fame. Lee Sutter set a BU-Runabout 5-mile competition record at 55.762 mph and Don Benson won the 280 Inboard National Championships on Lake Washington driving Bruce McDonald's *Hilton Hy-Per-Lube*.

The traditional Old-Timers and Bar Pilots cruises were discontinued after the dredging of the Slough. And it is most likely that the notorious log-boom in Woodinville was removed before or during the dredging. No information was found that indicated when it actually was removed. Fred Mackle received the SOA Sportsmanship Award. Stuart Lowe was elected the SOA commodore for 1967 with Bob Waite, vice-commodore; Charley Gilbert, treasurer and Joan Haack secretary.

1967

Lynnwood Junkman First-Time Winner

In the early 1960s, my father retired from driving the big unlimited hydros and began managing the *Miss Exide* unlimited racing team for the Stoen Brothers, Glenn and Milo. My brother moved into limited inboard racing and I quit racing outboards to concentrate on graduating from high school and starting college at the University of Washington. The only outboard racing equipment we had at the time was a boat trailer full of equipment, an A motor and two Class-A boats, my older Jacobsen A-Runabout *Ill-Eagle* and the A-Hydro *Uplake Jr.*, Ed Karelsen's first of its kind kit-boat.

1959: Al Benson driving *Miss Pay'n Save*

Ed Karelsen and Chuck Hickling produced a popular A-B class kit hydro that anyone handy at woodworking could build. The *Uplake Jr.* was the prototype, a semi-cabover that was fast and quick in the turns. I had a lot of success with it, winning the Canadian nationals and second in the U.S. nationals on Green Lake in 1959.

My father decided it was time to sell the last of our outboard racing equipment because it wasn't being used much. He sold it to an eager buyer, Mr. Frank Jenkins, a second-hand dealer in Lynnwood with a son who yearned to race outboards. Young Dave Jenkins began his career racing the equipment my father sold them. Long story short and a few years in the learning curve, young Jenkins became a successful boat racer. Not necessarily because of our racing equipment but because, with the help of his father and others, he learned how to be successful driving his secondhand racing equipment. Dave told me a few years later: "I ruined all your good racing equipment learning how to race."

Twenty-year-old Jenkins captured his first victory in the 30th annual Sammamish Slough Race. He won with a record time of 27:17.2 in the "tamer" Slough driving a used Karelsen hydro he purchased from previous Slough Racers, Dr. Charles Dockhorn and Andy Anderson. Jenkins powered his new boat that had a reputation for being a bit wild at times with a powerful Class-F motor. Bud Livesley of the *Times* quoted him in an article the following Monday: "You might say it was my first real try in this race. I had the motor and the boat this time and it worked out much better than last year." Livesley added, "That was an understatement; he tamed both his boat and the Slough!"

1967: Dave Jenkins R-29, 1st place overall Unlimited lass.

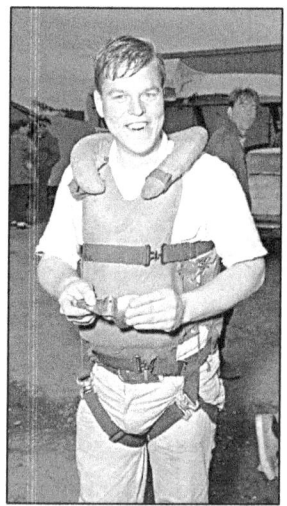
Dave Jenkins

A year ago, competing in the Unlimited Hydro division with an underpowered engine, he wasn't so fortunate. He blew over backwards in a long straightaway near Redmond. Livesley stated in his article: "Yesterday he just blew over his rivals, including the defending champion and the old man of the river, Bud Walters. Walters, last year's winner at 48, nursed a sick engine to third place." The article went on with a quote from Halliday: "Me, I'm always the bridesmaid. I've been second in three of the last four races. It was an easier run (this year)."

Bud Walters agreed it was easier. "The wind wasn't such a factor. It was darn cold, but the wind wasn't as stiff, especially coming downstream. But I never could catch Dave and Red, not with only three of my four cylinders putting out."

The boat entries were the lowest in decades this year. Out of the 42 that started from Kenmore Marina, only 33 reached Marymoor and fewer made it back to the finish at the Kenmore Bridge. Casualties were limited; mostly it was engine troubles sidelining the competition. Ray Lee experienced a whack on the nose even though he wasn't in the race. The ex-commodore was helping a driver when he was hit in the face by the driver's helmet. Race Chairman Fred Macke's son Don was thrown from his boat but managed to climb back in to finish second in the B-Stock Hydro class. Lee found some solace to his bruised nose. His son Dennis won the A-Stock Hydro class and daughter Janis won the JU's that finished a short and safe run only to Bothell.

Jenkins didn't win any money but he was elated to receive the two perpetual trophies for his victory, the Jackens Grill trophy for the Unlimited class winner and the Lake City Capo Club trophy for being the overall winner. Later in the year he probably made some nice pocket change selling his well-publicized winning raceboat.

Dick Rautenberg 1st place Unlimited Runabout.

John Myers 1st place A-Racing Runabout.

Last Lady of the Slough

Janis Lee, in a boat built by her father, Ray, won the JU-Runabout class. It was a bittersweet win for the petite 5-foot-2 14-year-old. Seattle Outboard race officials were concerned about the low turnout for this race and began to ponder about how to increase participation and provide more excitement for the spectators. As it turned out Miss Lee won the last Junior Runabout class to run in the event. She was also the "last lady" to ever race in the Slough.

1967 Janis Lee 1st place JU-Runabout.

1967 Sammamish Slough Race Results (by class)

Place	Driver	Class	From	Boat #	Time
1	Dave Jenkins	Unlimited Hydro	Seattle	R-29	27:17.2
2	Gerald (Red) Halliday	Unlimited Hydro	Seattle	82-R	29:00.6
3	Bud Walters	Unlimited Hydro	Kenmore	R-50	35:12.8
1	Dick Rautenberg	Unlimited Runabout	Mountlake Terrace	R-69	29:30.5
2	Gordon Matias	Unlimited Runabout	*	*	31:59.6
3	Ken Ferguson	Unlimited Runabout	*	*	32:17.6
1	Don Haack	C-Stock Hydro	Redmond	*	30:34.2
2	Bob Haack	C-Stock Hydro	Redmond	*	31:07.5
3	Ron Johanson	C-Stock Hydro	*	*	31:30.2
1	Wes Hausman	B-Stock Hydro	*	*	31:52.8
2	Dan Mackle	B-Stock Hydro	*	*	33:30.0
3	Bob Wartinger	B-Stock Hydro	Seattle	*	33:30.2
1	Earl Garrison	BU-Runabout	Seattle	*	32:17.4
2	Tim Fagan	BU-Runabout	Seattle	*	33:06.4
3	Mike Cruver	BU-Runabout	Seattle	*	36:22.0
1	Dennis Lee	A-Stock Hydro	Seattle	R-45	36:03.4
2	Lance Puckett	A-Stock Hydro	Seattle	*	36:37.6
3	Barry Lewis	A-Stock Hydro	*	*	37:05.4
1	John Myers	A-Racing Runabout	Seattle	R-1-77	40:53.8
2	Bill Kelly	A-Racing Runabout	*	*	40:05.0
3	Steve Greaves	A-Racing Runabout	*	3-R	48:46.4
1	Janis Lee	JU-Runabout	Seattle	45-R	*
2	Mike Ragan	JU-Runabout	Seattle	*	*

Some towns, boat numbers & times unavailable

Family and Sibling Rivalries

During the Sammamish Slough Races of the 1950s, families and siblings began competing together in the Slough. The first who competed in the same race were Al Benson and oldest son Don in the 1954 race. Don outdid his father by winning for the first time in the A-Runabout class while Al, was second in D-Runabout. They both competed in the 1955 race with the tables turned. This time father Al was the winner in D-Runabout and Don came in second in the A-Runabout division despite flipping completely over and ending up in the drink. He was in first place at the time, but managed to climb back in, restart and finish.

In 1956 father Benson took a breather from the event to help his two sons who both competed in the first sibling rivalry of the renowned race. Don won again but this time it was in the A-Stock Hydro class. Younger brother, Jimmy (your author), was second in the first-ever JU-Runabout class event. All three ran in the 1957 race when Jimmy was the headliner of the Benson bunch. He was first in the JUs; father Al was second in D-Runabout and veteran Don was out of the money this time in the A-Hydro class.

The next sibling rivalry occurred in the 1955 event between Chuck and Ginny Lee Lyford, who both competed in the Slough Race for the first time. Chuck was first in the A-Runabout class and Ginny Lee was third behind Jimmy Benson in the JUs. This was the first and only time that two families with multiple racing members competed in the same race. The next challenge was between brothers Bob and Dick Rautenberg in 1957. Older brother Bob was third in the B-Hydro class and Dick was second in his first Slough Race in the A-Hydro division. The next rivalry was between Jim and Mike Downing in 1963. Younger brother Jim got the best of his older brother Mike in the JU class, with a second and Mike was third.

The Ray Lee family came onto the scene in 1966. They were the first family trio to all place in the same race. Dennis was the champion of the family with his first win in the A-Runabout class. Father Ray was third in B-Stock Hydro and daughter Janis was third in the JUs. In 1967, both Dennis and Janis were victors in their respective classes. Janis was first in the JUs and Dennis was first in the A-Hydros. The Haack brothers, Don and Bob, battled it out in the C-Stock Hydro event. Don was first in 1967 and 1968 and Bob was second and fourth. The last siblings were the Christ brothers in 1968. As it turned out, the Lee family was the second and last family trio to ever run in a Slough Race.

1967 Race Schedule (Partial)

April 9	30th Sammamish Slough Race
April 23	Lake Sammamish-Redmond
May 21	Silver Lake-Everett
June 4	Lake Goodwin-Everett
July 23	Stock Outboard Divisionals-Port Orchard
July 28-29	Green Lake Seattle Seafair
Aug 23-27	Stock Outboard Nationals-Essex, Md
Sept 10	Silver Lake-Everett
Sept 13-18	Outboard Nationals-DePue, Ill
Sept 16-17	Lake Lawrence-Yelm
Oct 1	Lake Sammamish-Redmond
Oct 7-8	Devil's Lake, Ore. Kilos

1967 Tidbits

Charley Walters of Bothell, named after his pioneering Bothell grandfather, won the F-Racing Runabout Outboard Nationals. Harold Tolford, Jr., made it four in a row after winning the C-Service Hydro Nationals again. Mike Downing won two in a row by taking the J-Stock Nationals and Gerry Walin set the B-Outboard Hydro kilo record at 90.940 mph. Janis Lee also ran in the Stock Nationals placing second in JU-

Runabout. Fred Mackle was the recipient of the SOA sportsman award. Rick Sandstrom was elected SOA commodore for 1968 with Joan Haack as secretary.

Two Slough Race pre-teenagers from the 1950s, Billy Schumacher and Jim Benson, were national champions in inboards, both in boats built by past Slough Racer Ed Karelsen. Schumacher won the 1967 Gold Cup and was national high point champion in the *Miss Bardahl* unlimited hydro. Benson was the 1967 national high point champion in his *Hilton Hy-Per-Lube* 150 cubic inch limited inboard hydro and was awarded the APBA Interstate Championship Trophy. Both drivers were inducted into the Gulf Marine Racing Hall of Fame.

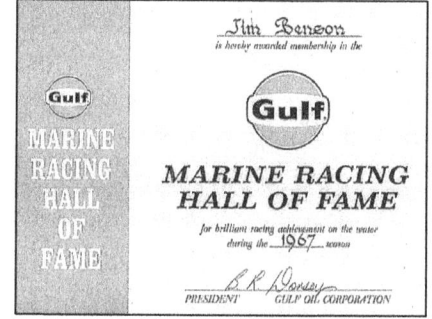

1967: Jim Benson and his 150-limited inboard hydro at Seattle Hot Rod & Boat Show- APBA *Interstate Championship Trophy* (center)-simulated driver in raceboat cockpit.

Water-Skiing Banned in Slough

You may have noticed that there's been no mention of the water-ski races since 1963. Water-skiing in the Sammamish River was banned during and after the dredging because of the speed limit restriction. Only special permission allowed any high-speed activity in the river. As of 1967, the Seattle Outboard club was the only organization with an approved event.

The 15-year tradition of the water-ski races ended after the Army Engineers straightened much of the river. It was mainly because of the new speed restrictions and complaints from riverside residents. Also, organizers and participants of the Golden

Water Skies Race that began in 1948 were getting older and their arthritic bodies were speaking to them and saying, "No more water-skiing!" Interest was dwindling among the old guard of water-skiers and new blood wasn't being sought at the time. No ski-races were in the wind for the foreseeable future.

1968

Is the Slough Race Going to the Dogs?

Gerald "Red" Halliday's dog "Snookie" eagerly awaiting a ride in her master's F-Outboard Hydro.

The Sammamish Slough Race has seen its share of unusual drivers but this tops them all. Could a Labrador retriever be the next zany boat racer in the Slough? If you asked Red Halliday's dog "Snookie," you would have likely received a confident "Woof." Snookie was a large 100-pound very friendly pooch who thought she could do a lot of things we humans can do. One of them was riding with her master in his fast F-Hydro cabover.

Her owner was preparing to compete in this year's Slough race. There was nothing in the race rules about this but as of then she only was a recreational rider during testing. Of course, she had the standard safety attire, a life jacket, helmet and goggles; what did you think she'd wear? This wasn't the only human-like stunt she performed. She loved to ride on Red's motorbike.

Bud Livesley, *Seattle Times* sports columnist, wrote in his article on March 20, 1968: "Motorists, at first are startled. Then, as the motorbike scoots past, there is bewildered amusement. But seeing is believing and yes, that was a man and a dog on the motorbike."

Livesley quoted Halliday: "I was bragging about Snookie to a friend Ray Lee (former Seattle Outboard commodore and boat racer). Finally, Ray said, 'If that dog is so great, why doesn't she ride the bike with you?' There was no argument from Snookie. She rode behind me all the way home and has enjoyed our outings ever-since. But like I was telling Ray, Snookie is the best hunting dog around. Now I suppose, she's also the best bike rider around."

A few months later Halliday fitted Snookie with a safety helmet to comply with Washington State law. Red cut out the front of the helmet to clear her nose and fitted her with the goggles, the same equipment used in her ride in her master's outboard hydro.

Snookie riding behind master Halliday

The *Times* article ended with an answer from Halliday about whether he could win the race for the first time with his dog as a co-pilot: "'I don't know,' Halliday said after a trial spin with Snookie on Lake Washington off the Kenmore Marina. 'I've never won the race. I've always been a bridesmaid–four seconds (second place finishes). Snookie's weight might hold me back. But I must admit she'd be a swell companion.' Regardless, Snookie is a doggone cooperative dog, and riding in a speedboat would be easier than a motorbike–even for a dog as talented as Snookie."

Celebrities, War Canoes, Pleasure Craft Compete in Slough Race

The Seattle Outboard Slough Race officials decided to shake-up the race format for this year by adding a variety of different racing classes to increase the dwindling number of entries to add more excitement for the spectators. One of the new classes race organizers added was a Celebrity's class for local and renowned members of the unlimited hydro ranks (notable former drivers in the Sammamish Slough Race). Race organizers were hoping that Jerry Bryant, the originator of the famous race, would also compete.

Among the list of entries were Billy Schumacher, last year's unlimited hydro national champion in *Miss Bardahl*, Bill Muncey, multiple national champion driver of *Miss Thriftway*, and past unlimited hydro drivers, Chuck Hickling and Al Benson. Local radio station disc jockeys rode with each celebrity as a so-called mechanic. It was thought the radio personalities would help with the race promotion by bantering about in their broadcasts as to who was going to whip who to the finish line. Then after the race the winners would be able to boast about their success on the air during their radio programs, adding some prestige for the winning station.

The most unusual class ever run since the race's beginning in 1934, were 25-foot "dugout" canoes driven by native Indians, all powered by outboard motors–no paddling allowed. Race organizers were expecting entries from the Quinault and Quileute tribes. For the first time in history logs would move up the waterway (against the current) instead of floating downstream as in the logging days of yore.

"War Canoe" driven by local Indian tribal member powered by modified 2-cylinder outboard motor.

The third group of new entries was for the first time open to anybody in an outboard pleasure boat, sometimes called "Sunday drivers," powered by a minimum of 50-horsepower engines. This group was divided into four classifications with 50 to 150 horse-power engines, with their classes starting fastest to slowest: Combined U-2/OPC, Family-J, Needle Nose and Family-E. Many of the drivers were members of the Seattle Marathon Association, co-sponsors of the race along with the Kenmore Chamber of Commerce. Race organizers hoped the addition of these classes plus the others would far exceed last year's low total.

The JU class (Junior Utility Runabout) for the youngsters that only ran upstream to Bothell was dropped from the schedule, partly because of dwindling entries and partly because of the complication with a separate finish line in Bothell. They competed over a span of 11 years, between 1956 and 1967.

As of four days before the race, the previous record of 120 entries had been surpassed with more pouring in daily. In fact, there was a second day of pre-registration at the Kenmore public launching area (at the Kenmore Bridge) from noon to 4 pm on Saturday before the race

The upriver run was scheduled to start from Kenmore Marina and round the usual left-turn buoy at the mouth of the Slough. Ten classes would leave at five-minute intervals starting at noon. The competitors who finished the first leg would regroup at Marymoor Park and restart downstream, heading to the finish line at the Kenmore Bridge boat launch in the same starting class position as their upstream order.

Local Boy Scout troops stationed more than 100 youngsters along both banks of the Slough. Their duties included handing out free race programs to the thousands of spectators and providing assistance to wayward race drivers who were out of commission, ended up in the drink or landed on the bank.

Many unlimited hydroplanes were on display at various locations along the Slough to promote the event. It was planned that preceding the Celebrity Class, the miniature *Miss Bardahl* hydroplane would make an exhibition run. Incidentally, Schumacher's full-size *Bardahl* canoe that was on display cost about $50,000.

Jenkins Heads List of Unlimited Class Drivers

Last year's victor, Dave Jenkins, was among this year's favorites to be the overall winner in the Unlimited Hydro class. Jenkins, a second-hand dealer from Lynwood, had a different rig for this year, a newer cabover he had built for last year's Nationals in Essex, Maryland. It was a replacement for last year's winning boat, which he sold for a profit. What you would expect from a typical "picker," a skillful negotiator of buying and selling used merchandise.

Dave was looking forward to a second-straight win to put him in a select group of two-time Slough Race winners. It was a feat only a few had accomplished before him. They included Dick Barden (1945-1946), Al Benson (1947-1948) and Howard Anderson (1959-1960).

1968-Dave Jenkins

Jenkins, 21, who learned the family business from his father, had quickly learned the sport of boat racing over the past five years since the purchase of the families first racing outfit from Al Benson. At first, he was a naïve young rookie with a stocky body, too heavy to be competitive in the underpowered Class-A boats. But now his body size just fit the larger hydro classes, giving him an advantage sometimes as he could move his burly body forward as needed to keep his F-Hydro from blowing-over in the high-speed straightaways of the Slough.

Jenkins Victorious Despite Early Dunking

It took about three weeks of continuous work for Thomas Penn, a Quinault Indian, to dig-out a 25-foot log in the making of his Indian fishing canoe. It took about $5,000 to purchase a 16-foot high-powered pleasure craft such as Chuck Hickling drove in the Celebrity class of the Sammamish Slough Race on Sunday April 7.

In the words of Dave Jenkins (describing the racing), "It takes a well-tuned stocker" (D-Stock Hydro engine). Whatever, Jenkins had what it took to win his second straight overall victory in the 31st annual spectacle. Tom Penn in his new canoe didn't as he took second to a 30-year-old hand-me-down canoe driven by John Bryson. Hickling, driving the first inboard raceboat in a Slough Race along with his radio disc jockey, also wasn't successful as he ran aground and beached due to faulty steering in the Celebrity class.

Jenkins, in a sometimes-cantankerous F-Hydro, became the fourth driver to win back-to-back, joining the ranks of previous winners Anderson, Benson and Barden. It wasn't easy, though, because of his dunking in the upstream run. He flipped when he was leading after passing under the Willows Bridge near Redmond.

He was quoted by Bud Livesley of the *Seattle Times* on April 8: "Was I surprised. I hit something and-pow! There I was in the water." The soaking wet 190-pounder swam over to his upright boat, pushed it over to the bank, jumped back in and restarted with a damaged propeller. He still managed to finish second in the upstream run, behind Don Hansen of Edmonds, because of his big lead.

At Marymoor Park, he replaced the cracked propeller, changed his clothes, and then got a great start for the downstream run. He left all the other competitors behind and had a commanding lead as he crossed the finish line at the Kenmore Bridge. Later in the pits at Kenmore Marina, Jenkins got a second dunking from his crew members. Only this time he was happy to be tossed in the drink, unlike his upriver experience earlier in the day.

Dave Jenkins gets a second dunking after his victory by fellow crew members

Another winner was Ken Ferguson in the Unlimited-Runabout division. "Fergie," as he was called by his fellow boat racers, was among only two finishers as the Slough was brutal for this class of nine starters. Don Haack beat his brother Bob in C-Stock Hydro, Bob Thorn won in B-Hydro and George Christ beat his brother Jan in B-Utility.

Lee Wins Three In A Row

Dennis Lee won the A-Hydro class, the first driver to win their class three years in a row. It was the first time in several years that only one member of the Lee family competed. Kid-sister, Janis, had to cheer him on from the bank because unfortunately for her, the JU class was eliminated. Some of Lee's success, aside from good driving and equipment, was because of his use of an improvised "engine dynamometer."[50]

Dennis Lee paddling to the starting line in A-Hydro

Dennis and fellow race driver, Craig

---

[50] Instrument attached to outboard propeller shaft used to measure foot-pounds of torque produced by the engine.

Selvidge, built a makeshift dynamometer to compare the performance of various engines they rebuilt. They used it to determine the best motor for racing and setting records. It was a very innovative method at the time and became a tool used by most motorsports competitors who wanted an edge over their competition.

Billy Schumacher with disc-jockey Jim Kelly about to pass boat ahead in Bob Jacobsen's donated boat.

Al Benson with disc-jockey Bob Hardwick hanging-on in boat donated by Advance Outboard.

The Slough took its usual heavy toll. Only 59 of the 115 starters finished even though the Slough was supposed to be tamer since the dredging in 1964-65. Joining Hickling as a spectator on the bank was unlimited hydro driver, Bob Gilliam of Bothell who got a bath and was out of contention early after misjudging the Downriver Marina turn a few minutes after the start. Bud Walters, 1966 winner, also received an unexpected bath. He flipped just after he passed under the Bothell Bridge on his way upstream.

The celebrities had their fun scaring the daylights out of their disc-jockey mechanics. Billy Schumacher, with KOMO's Jim Kelly onboard, piloted Bob

Jacobsen's donated entry to victory even though he started last in both heats. KVI's popular radio host, Bob Hardwick, was hanging-on for dear life in a boat driven by his friend and business partner, Al Benson, to second place. Hardwick was an investor in "Lake Union Boat Charters" where Benson was the sales manager. Benson, who started the JU class in the 1950s, tutored Schumacher when he began racing.

Chuck Hickling with disc jockey mechanic in first & only inboard entered in Sammamish Slough Race.

Logs Race Up Slough

The estimated 50,000 spectators witnessed the most unusual event ever to run in the Slough. Logs raced up the Slough against the river current for the first time in history. In years past loggers only floated them the easy way–downstream. Native Indians driving their racing canoes, made from tree trunks (solid logs), were the latest entries in the race. They powered their "dugouts" with outboard motors that were clamped on the rear. The back ends of the canoes were squared-off so outboard motors could be mounted.

Indian canoes heading upstream passing under Bothell Bridge.

Jim Jackson, operator of the Moclips, Washington, shake mill where eight of the entries worked, shut-down the Saturday night shift so his employees could compete in the Slough Race. "Can't let work interfere with our racing" was Jackson's quote in Bud Livesley's sports article written April 8 in the *Seattle Times*.

The crowd of thousands that lined the banks of the Slough was delighted by the unusual sight of a half-dozen or more long sleek canoes whizzing by at high speeds, something unusual in the long standing outboard racing event. Slow-moving logs aren't what they used to be.

1968 Sammamish Slough Race Results (by class)

Place	Driver	Class	From	Boat #	Time
1	Dave Jenkins	Unlimited Hydro	Seattle	R-29	*
2	Don Hansen	Unlimited Hydro	Edmonds	*	*
3	Frank Boyle	Unlimited Hydro	*	*	*
4	Bob Waite	Unlimited Hydro	Bellevue	228-R	
5	Gerald (Red) Halliday	Unlimited Hydro	Seattle	82-R	*
6	Bob Gilliam	Unlimited Hydro	Bothell	*	*
1	Ken Ferguson	Unlimited Runabout	Seattle	*	*
2	John Laird	Unlimited Runabout	Bellevue	R-62	*
1	Don Haack	C-Stock Hydro	Redmond	*	*
2	Bob Rhoades	C-Stock Hydro	*	*	*
3	Mike Moreland	C-Stock Hydro	Playa Del Ray, CA	*	*
4	Bob Haack	C-Stock Hydro	Redmond	*	*
5	Thomas Berryhill	C-Stock Hydro	*	*	*
1	Bob Thorn	B-Stock Hydro	*	*	*
2	Gene Laes	B-Stock Hydro	*	*	*
3	Doug Mahurin	B-Stock Hydro	Seattle	*	*
4	Jim Allen	B-Stock Hydro	*	*	*
1	George Christ	BU-Runabout	Edmonds	*	*
2	Jan Christ	BU-Runabout	Edmonds	*	*
3	Darrell Sorenson	BU-Runabout	*	*	*
4	Mike Cruver	BU-Runabout	Seattle	*	*
5	Steve Greaves	BU-Runabout	Seattle	*	*
1	Dennis Lee	A-Stock Hydro	Seattle	R-45	*
2	Mike Jones	A-Stock Hydro	Seattle	*	*
3	Terry Wolcott	A-Stock Hydro	*	*	*
4	Keith Knowition	A-Stock Hydro	*	*	*
1	Tom Walker	Family E	*	*	*
2	Stan Murray	Family E	*	*	*
3	Randy Zavaies	Family E	*	*	*
4	Gordon Mauhl	Family E	*	*	*
5	Bill Stephen	Family E	*	*	*
1	Bob Ballinger	Needle Nose	*	*	*
2	Ed Geddes	Needle Nose	*	*	*
3	Stu Deibert	Needle Nose	*	*	*
4	Jay Pederson	Needle Nose	*	*	*

	Driver	Class	Town		
5	Larry Lewis	Needle Nose	Seattle	*	*
1	Rick Adams	FamilyJ	*	*	*
2	Norm Boddy	FamilyJ	Seattle	*	*
3	Bill Hauta	FamilyJ	*	*	*
4	Lanny Lindros	FamilyJ	Kirkland	*	*
5	Dick Hoffman	FamilyJ	*	*	*
1	Bob Best	U-2/OPC Combined	*	*	*
2	Jerry Chichetti	U-2/OPC Combined	Seattle	*	*
3	Gerry Walin	U-2/OPC Combined	*	*	*
4	Dick Heintzelman	U-2/OPC Combined	*	*	*
5	E.E. Fowell	U-2/OPC Combined	*	*	*
1	John Bryson	Indian Canoes	*	*	*
2	Thomas Penn	Indian Canoes	*	*	*
3	Michael Jackson	Indian Canoes	Moclips	*	*
4	Ralph Capoeman	Indian Canoes	Taholah	*	*
5	Norman Capoeman	Indian Canoes	Taholah	*	*
	Driver	*Class*	*Disc Jockey-Station*		
1	Bill Schumacher	Celebrity Class	Jim Kelly-KOMO		
2	Al Benson	Celebrity Class	Bob Hardwick-KVI		
3	Earl Wham	Celebrity Class	Dick Curtis-KOL		
4	Red Loomis	Celebrity Class	Jack Morton-KVI		
5	Chuck Hickling	Celebrity Class	*		
*	Bill Muncey	Celebrity Class	*	*(No report they raced)*	
*	Bob Miller	Celebrity Class	*	*(No report they raced)*	

Some towns, boat numbers & times unavailable

Red Loomis with KOL's Jack Morton being crazy at Bothell in Puget Sound Marina boat.

Steve Greaves learning the Slough in B-Utility.

Outboard Championships Return to Seattle

One of the biggest outboard races in the country, the U.S. Stock National Championships, returned to Seattle's Green Lake. The last time they were held here was in 1959. The first ever national event conducted in Seattle occurred on September 24, 1933, at Green Lake. At that time in history it was the Runabout National Championships that were run in conjunction with the Pacific Coast Championships. Six runabout classes competed this year the amateur and professional divisions: C-Service, F-Service and E-Service Runabouts for both classes.

The most recent national regatta held in the Northwest was the Outboard National Championships at Moses Lake on August 23-25, 1963. The last Stock National Championships were held at Green Lake on August 20-23, 1959.

Last Lady of Slough Is National Champion

"Joining the ranks of first time National Champions was a wee, 110-pound junior elect at Shorecrest High School," was part of an article written by Bud Livesley in the *Seattle Times* on July 29, 1968. Janis Lee was the only driver from the Northwest to win a National Championship on Green Lake that day. She piloted her JU-Runabout, *Janny's J*, to victory on Sunday, the final day of the three-day regatta in a light-weight raceboat built by her father. Janis won both heats by a large margin beating the likes of one of the most famous unlimited hydro drivers of all time, Chip Hanauer, who placed a few positions behind her. Other competitors from the Seattle area didn't fare so well. Charley Walters placed fourth in the DU-Runabout class, Dave Jenkins fifth in C-Stock Hydro and John Myers was fifth in D-Stock Runabout.

1968: National Champion Janis Lee leading in J-Stock Hydro competition.

1968 Race Schedule (Partial)

April 7	31st Sammamish Slough Race
May 5	Lake Sammamish-Vasa Park, Bellevue
May 19	Cottage Lake, Woodinville
April 23	Lake Sammamish-Redmond

June 2	Lake Goodwin-Everett
July 13-14	Stock Outboard Divisionals-American Lake, Tacoma
July 7	Moses Lake
July 25-28	Stock Outboard Nationals-Green Lake, Seattle
Aug 2-4	Outboard Nationals-DePue, IL
Sept 14-15	Lake Lawrence-Yelm
Sept 22	Lake Sammamish-Vasa Park, Bellevue
Sept 28-29	Devil's Lake Kilos-Lincoln City, OR

Slough Race Celebrity Class Notables

Billy Schumacher, driver of Bob Jacobsen's Celebrity class entry, drove the *Miss Bardahl* unlimited hydroplane to his second straight national championship (1967 & 1968). Al Benson, driver of Advance Marine's Celebrity class boat, was a former driver of the *Miss Pay'n Save* and *Miss Seattle* unlimited hydros. He was known as the first three-time Sammamish Slough Race winner. He would have been the first four-time winner if the 1960-70s rules were in place in the 1950s.

The 1966 and on winners of the race always came out of the unlimited hydro ranks no matter if another class winner had the fastest overall time. Al Benson won the unlimited class in 1947, 1948, 1952 and 1953. Bob Jacobsen was deemed the overall winner in the D-Runabout class in 1952 because he had a slightly faster overall time; the year Benson won in the Unlimited Hydro class.

1968 Tidbits

Janis Lee had a year that would be considered exceptional for a male driver. She won the J-Stock-Hydro Nationals on Green Lake in Seattle, set the J-Stock-Hydro kilo record at 36.168 mph on Devil's Lake in Lincoln City, Oregon, and capped her year as an inductee into the 1968 Gulf Marine Racing Hall of Fame.

Gerry Walin set a kilo record on Devil's Lake in B-Outboard-Hydro at 98.329 mph. He was another Slough Race driver inducted into the Gulf Marine Racing Hall of Fame for the year. Jim Downing was awarded the Sportsmanship Trophy. Rick Sandstrom was reelected commodore with Tom O'Neill, vice commodore; Charley Gilbert treasurer and Sue Cummins secretary.

Janis Lee receiving Gulf Marine Hall of Fame award

1969

Jenkins Goes for Three In-A-Row

Winning the Slough Race three times in a row has proven to be elusive. Dave Jenkins the "Lynnwood junkman," would try to be the first ever to win the classic race for three-consecutive years. The "tamed" Slough had become more of a speed run verses the original route that required more skill (and luck) plus speed because of the continuous turns and encroaching banks.

The Indian canoes were on the slate for the second year in a row but last year's Celebrity class was not scheduled. Apparently, their careers and arthritic bodies prevented them from another run. The loss of the celebs and other outboard class participants were substituted by more pleasure boat class entries and the OPCs, (Outboard Performance Craft) like last year.

"Barefoot Bob" Foils Jenkins' Bid

Robert Ned Waite, in his early working days, delivered parts for Totem Pontiac on a motorcycle. This time he delivered the goods in his fast F-Outboard Hydro. "Barefoot Bob" as nicknamed by his fellow race drivers, won his second Slough Race, 13-years since he first won in 1956. The tamer Slough proved to be more to his liking because he led wire to wire in a record time of 20 minutes, 24 seconds for the two heats of the 12-mile course even though it was a windy day

It was another bid spoiled for past two-time winners as last year's winner Dave Jenkins, who was hoping for three in a row, came in behind Waite for second-place. Winning two times remained a rarity. Waite joined four others who had won at least two times: Dick Barden (1945 & 1946), Al Benson (1947 & 1948), Bob Jacobsen (1950 & 1952) and Bill Farr (1954 & 1957).

Waite, 44, an 18-year veteran of outboard racing, overcame several minor problems to win both of his heats in the 32nd annual event. The wind this year, as sometimes in the past, was a real problem for the fast hydros because it was blowing hard against them on the way upstream. Barefoot Bob had to ride with his body forward, overhanging the steering wheel, to keep the boat from flipping-over backwards most of the way to Lake Sammamish. This year the drivers drew for starting positions and Waite was lucky as he got to pick the No. 1 position. His *228-R* was first out of the pits at the Kenmore Bridge boat launching area, partly because of his more efficient "quick start lift."[51]

Waite's other problem was a surprising encounter with water-skiers at the upper end of the course in the upstream leg. He caught up with them before reaching Marymoor Park but was able to get by after he slowed down and they pulled over. He still was going too fast for crossing the wake and flew nearly 40 feet. Luck was on his side again because he landed safely and kept going. Surely that got Bob's heart pumping a little faster.

When he was asked by *Times* sportswriter Del Danielson after the race why he raced barefoot, he replied: "Well, you're going to get wet anyway and your feet warm up quicker if you don't have (wet) shoes on." Danielson also wrote in his article "a helicopter hovering over the race course clocked Waite at 80 miles an hour on the straightaways."

1969 Overall Winner Bob Waite kissed by his wife Mary Ellen (right) and "Miss Seattle Boat Show" at Kenmore Bridge pits.

---

[51] Lifting a race boat's stern and engine out of water to lessen propeller water forces–helps engine starting (see next pages for more details and photo)

This was the first year the boats started at the Kenmore Bridge boat launch, a likely move by race officials to avoid starting in the rough water on Lake Washington from Kenmore Marina during the last few years. The race had started at one of the Kenmore sites for 22 years (at the north end of Lake Washington) since 1947. It was an effort to make the race safer.

But danger was still lurking throughout the Slough for the 100 entries in 11 classes. Out of the 69 finishers, the most in Slough Race history, Gary Whitehead, for the second year in a row, ran amuck under the Bothell Bridge. Gary Cummins, son of 1941 Slough Race winner Pat Cummins, Mike Scott and Steve Cotter provided entertainment for the spectators. Cummins' boat ran aground hitting a sandbar with enough stopping force to throw out the engine's batteries clear out of the boat. He was uninjured but the incident ended his day. The three others hit the drink when their boats flipped-over in the turns and others were towed back to the boat-ramp pits.

By the early 1970s Bob Carver had switched to using newer fast-action, multiple frame-per-second, 35-millimeter cameras. No more question about whether he got that precise shot or not. With a through-the-lens camera you could easily see exactly what you were shooting and shoot several shots per second, getting all the action in-between. Bob took the three sequence-photos below of Mike Scott in about one-second (taken from a four-shot array).

Bob Carver's sequence photos of Mike Scott taking a bath in his B-Hydro at Bothell Bridge.

"Quick Start Lift"

The high-powered four-cylinder Class-F outboard motors were hard to start in the water. This was due to their high-compressions and the combined restrictive force of the propeller pushing against the water. To overcome this, crewmembers would lift the back end of the boats out of the water during the starting process. It took two or more strong persons to lift and another to manually start the engine (with a starter rope). The person starting the engine had to pull the rope with a lot of oomph to insure the engine crankshaft turned quickly to suck-in enough fuel for a quick start; he usually got wet in the process (see Bob Waite photo below–the starter is the person moving away on the right just after powerfully pulling the starting rope).

Anyone standing behind the boat within 50 feet or so would get thoroughly doused from the propeller spray along with the deafening high-pitched sound screaming from the open (not muffled) exhaust pipes. After the engine started and reached high revs (revolutions per minute), the crew would launch the rig after utilizing the "quick start lift" by throwing it forward into the water. They hoped the engine wouldn't quit because of the sudden restrictive forces from the weight of the craft and the water acting on the propeller. (The highly modified Class-F engines were temperamental to start.) Waite was shown squeezing the hand throttle (with left hand) fully to open the motor's carburetor valves "wide open" for maximum power during the start.

Bob Waite in his F-Hydro getting a "quick start lift" for downriver run at Marymoor Park.

The objective of this start method is to get the motor started on the first pull along with a quick launch to get the driver and craft first out into the Slough. Unfortunately, sometimes the engine would die (stop) during the launching, usually because the motor wasn't tuned properly or driver error. This left the competitor at a disadvantage, behind some or all of the other boats at the start. Anytime this type of start was attempted the crew had to be extremely careful to stay away from the razor-sharp propeller that was spinning at over 10,000 rpms.

Indian Canoes Almost Run Over

The Indian canoes that were invited back after last year's colorful performance added some unexpected drama to the day. They got out on the course a little too early preparing for their start. They started too early, at the same time the marathon boats were making their running start a few blocks from the Slough entrance on Lake Washington. The marathoners, who were speeding 50-miles-per-hour, had to dodge their way through the bunch of canoes that had started from the boat-ramp, likely raising the canoe drivers' heart-rates a bit. Fortunately, no collisions occurred and no one was run over.

After spending the winter getting his racing outfit in shape, Charley (Chuck) Walters, now of Fall City, had to exert a little extra effort just to place second in the F-Runabout class. Chuck ran out of fuel about 30-yards from the Kenmore Bridge finish line and paddled the rest of the way feverishly with his hands to edge-out John Myers who was fast approaching in third place. Dick Rautenberg of Mountlake Terrace, who won the Runabout class, had trouble but a big early lead on the downstream run gave him the margin for victory. He burned a piston and that slowed his speed about 25 miles an hour. He narrowly edged Walters at the finish.

Howard Anderson takes 1st in his Anderson Marine *Invader* runabout in the combined U-2/OPC Class.

Howard Anderson, former two-time overall winner (1959-1960), took it easier in his smooth-riding OPC runabout, showing off his new line of boats to the crowd. He won driving in the combined U-2/OPC class piloting his hot 15-foot *G-W Invader* rig powered by a 125 HP Mercury motor. The crowd was down from previous years, partly because of the uncertain whether and because Seattle's first major pro team, the Pilots was playing the Chicago White Sox. Apparently, the crowd was well behaved as there were no reports of incidents, a better sign of the times. Unruly or drunk fans inclined to throw things at the boats stood a higher chance of being spotted.

1969 Sammamish Slough Race Results (by class)

Place	Driver	Class	From	Boat #	Time
1	Bob Waite	Unlimited Hydro	Bellevue	228-R	20:24.0
2	Dave Jenkins	Unlimited Hydro	Seattle	R-29	*
3	Ralph (Red) Taylor	Unlimited Hydro	Seattle	*	*
4	Jerrat Neupart	Unlimited Hydro	*	*	*
5	John Heisc	Unlimited Hydro	*	*	*
1	Dick Rautenberg	Unlimited Runabout	Mountlake Terrace	*	32:27.2
2	Chuck Walters	Unlimited Runabout	Fall City	R-62	*
3	John Myers	Unlimited Runabout	Seattle	R-77	*
4	Scott Poindexter	Unlimited Runabout	*	*	*
5	John Laird	Unlimited Runabout	Bellevue	R-62	*
1	Mike Moreland	C-Stock Hydro	Playa Del Ray, CA	*	46:07.2
2	Doug Moreland	C-Stock Hydro	Playa Del Ray, CA	*	*
3	Dave Cordell	C-Stock Hydro	Playa Del Ray, CA	*	*
4	Dave Park	C-Stock Hydro	Redmond	*	*
5	Steve Calter	C-Stock Hydro	*	*	*
6	Bob Weiss	C-Stock Hydro	*	*	*
7	Bob Gierke	C-Stock Hydro	Edmonds	*	*
8	James Clark	C-Stock Hydro	*	*	*
1	Wes Hausman	B-Stock Hydro	*	*	56:30.2
2	Bob Wartinger	B-Stock Hydro	Seattle	*	*
3	Don Mackle	B-Stock Hydro	*	*	*
4	John Hawkins	B-Stock Hydro	*	*	*
5	Doug Mahurin	B-Stock Hydro	*	*	*
1	Jan Christ	BU-Runabout	Edmonds	*	66:59.6
2	George Christ	BU-Runabout	Edmonds	*	*
3	Mike Currie	BU-Runabout	*	*	*
4	Allen Greathouse	BU-Runabout	Seattle	*	*
1	Terry Wolcott	A-Stock Hydro	*	*	81:63.4
2	Chip Hanauer	A-Stock Hydro	Bellevue	*	*
3	Craig Selvidge	A-Stock Hydro	*	*	*
4	Lance Puckett	A-Stock Hydro	*	*	*
5	Dennis Lee	A-Stock Hydro	Seattle	R-45	*
1	Andy Anderson	U-2/OPC Combined	Edmonds	S-7	101:05.4
2	Jerry Chichetti	U-2/OPC Combined	Seattle	*	*
3	Dick Heintzelman	U-2/OPC Combined	Olympia	*	*
4	Bob Reed	U-2/OPC Combined	*	*	*
1	Tom Losvar	FamilyJ	Mukilteo	*	114:19.4
2	Len Gariach	FamilyJ	Lynnwood	*	*
3	Bill Hauta	FamilyJ	Redmond	*	*
4	Jerome Norton	FamilyJ	Kirkland	*	*
1	Tom O'Riley	Family E	Seattle	*	132:54.8
2	Harold Jandszak	Family E	Seattle	*	*
1	Ted Woodward	Needle Nose	Seattle	*	137:36.2

2	Ed Geddes	Needle Nose	Marysville	*	*
3	Larry Lewis	Needle Nose	Seattle	*	*
4	Ralph Stocker	Needle Nose	*	*	*
5	David George	Needle Nose	*	*	*
6	Larry Edwards	Needle Nose	*	*	*
7	Norm Boddy	Needle Nose	*	*	*
8	Sunny West	Needle Nose	*	*	*
9	Fred Burr	Needle Nose	*	*	*
1	Leland Schmidt	Family F	Mukilteo	*	151:90.8
2	Stan Murray	Family F	Seattle	*	*
3	Norm Boddy	Family F	Seattle	*	*
4	Richard Newark	Family F	*	*	*
5	Gordy Mauhl	Family F	*	*	*
6	Mike Kent	Family F	*	*	*
7	George Brehm	Family F	*	*	*
8	Ken Ryan	Family F	*	*	*
9	Scott Harris	Family F	*	*	*
10	John Abbott	Family F	*	*	*
11	Murph Baldwin	Family F	*	*	*
1	Ralph Capoeman	Indian Canoes	Taholah	*	170:74.0
2	Michael Jackson	Indian Canoes	Moclips	*	*
3	Peter Kalama	Indian Canoes	Queets	*	*
4	Cliff Jackson	Indian Canoes	*	*	*
5	Robin Moiler	Indian Canoes	*	*	*
6	John Bryson	Indian Canoes	*	*	*
7	Howard Hudson	Indian Canoes	*	*	*

Some towns, boat numbers & times unavailable

Veteran driver John Laird with mechanic Mike Alm in F-Runabout Class.

1969 Tidbits

Dick Rautenberg was elected, SOA commodore, and Janis Lee, secretary, for 1970. John Laird, Harold Tolford and Bob Waite of the SOA were presented lifetime club memberships for 20 years of continued membership. David Nelson won the SOA Sportsmanship award. Janis Lee set the 5-mile competition record at 32.503 mph in J-Stock Hydro and the UIM Kilo record at 38.239 mph on Devil's Lake in Oregon. Her older brother, Dennis, set the A-Stock-Hydro UIM Kilo record at 59.183 mph. Charles "Chuck" Walters set the UIM Kilo record in B-Racing-Runabout at 79.329 mph.

1969 Race Schedule (Partial)

April 13	32nd Sammamish Slough Race
July 25-28	Stock Outboard Nationals-Hinton, W. Va
July 25-26	Green Lake
July 27	Estacada, Oregon
Aug	Devils Lake, Oregon
Sept 7	Silver Lake-Everett
Sept 13-14	Lake Lawrence-Yelm
Sept 21	Lake Sammamish-Vasa Park, Bellevue
Sept 27-28	Devil's Lake-Lincoln City, Oregon

G. W. INVADER
THE HOT ONE

Driven to first place in Sammamish Slough race by Howard Anderson.
NOW OFFERED FOR SALE
15' G. W. INVADER competitive model, Merc. 1250 Super Bp. Tach, stainless prop., battery, 12 gal. tank, bucket seats, foot throttle and trailer. Complete ready to win more races.
$3495

Anderson Marine
At Ferry Dock, Edmonds 778-3191

1970

Waite Bids for Second Straight in Slough

Could Bob Waite get his second straight and third win overall? That was the question before the 33rd running of the Sammamish Slough Race. That and yes, race officials were tinkering with the format of the competition once again, like in so many years in the past. Race chairman Red Halliday said in a *Times* article on April 12: "We are going to have the marathoners start out in the lake (Lake Washington) and race around a barge (a large sand-barge a few hundred-feet from shore) before heading into the river. It should add a little excitement to the race." All the other classes started from the boat launch area next to the Kenmore Bridge.

The action was scheduled to start at noon as usual with the F-Outboard Hydros heading out first. Then all the succeeding slower outboard classes were to follow in five-minute intervals. The OPC classes were set to start after the A-Stock Hydros, the last outboard class of the day with the Indian canoes rounding out the 11 classes, last off the starting line. Halliday told the *Times*: "We want to keep things moving." It was anticipated to be a quicker race than a few years ago because along with the course being shorter (22-miles round trip), the average speed of all the classes was faster. More than 80 boats were expected to compete in what was still one of the most popular events in the Pacific Northwest.

Barefoot Bob Leads the Pack

Bob Waite, in his old reliable homebuilt *228-R* cabover, drew a number from the race referee's hat for his starting position during the drivers meeting, likely the lucky first or second starting position. After a few instructions and cautions from the referee in the meeting, everyone scurried around getting their rigs ready for the start. The first boats, the F-Hydros, were carried from the pits into the water and lined-up in order of their starting positions with the lowest number upstream closest to the Kenmore Bridge.

The drivers waded out into the water and climbed aboard into their cockpits and sat or kneeled anticipating the five-minute to start signal, an air-horn blast. During the 15-second countdown, the crews lifted the boats out of the water preparing for the quick start. It was a daunting job because Bob weighed 240 along with the weight of the boat, his wet clothes, and a full tank of fuel. The total was about 600 pounds or 150 each per the four crewmembers.

At the same time another crew member wrapped the starting cord three-quarters of a turn around the engine's open flywheel and prepared to pull as forcefully as he could at the sound of the starting signal. The OPC boys were a lot more advanced with their electric starters and powered lower units that tilted in or out with the push of a button. They were real softies compared with the "old-school" outboards. Rules didn't allow those modern conveniences for the outboarders and the added weight of a battery and starter motor could slow them down a little.

At the blast of the starting horn, all hell brook loose! Most all the engines quickly started in unison with their ear-splitting open exhausts instantly causing the spectators, crew and family members to wince and cover their ears. The crowd upstream knew they were coming because they could hear the high-pitched screaming sounds echoing up the Sammamish Valley, several miles upstream. In years past, a shotgun or starting cannon (firing blanks) was used as the starting signal. Outboard race officials changed over to using hand-held air horns during the later years of the Slough Race.

Bob Waite's guy yanked hard with the starting rope and his engine roared after the first pull, shooting water out almost 50 feet behind dousing anyone in its path while the stern was out of the water during the quick start lift. He got on a plane and was off and running after his crew threw him forward into the water, boat and all. He led the way under the Kenmore Bridge and quickly zoomed out-of-sight after passing around a corner about 1,000 feet upstream with all the others in hot pursuit.

That wonderful smell of burnt racing fuel mixed with Castrol motor oil had saturated the air all over the pits, a reminder of that familiar smell from the old prewar "4-60" engines of the past. The folks watching from the bridge got a whiff or two also after the noisy high-pitched rigs passed underneath.

Gaining the lead at the start was a huge advantage because it was still hard to pass in the Slough even though it was tamer. Waite led all the way to Marymoor Park and back for his third win and second straight, partly because of his good starts, but mostly because he was faster and luckier than the rest. Dave Jenkins came in third in the Unlimited class still trying to get his third win but his luck charms likely had lost their luster as he had been trying for a number of years to get back to his winning ways of the late 1960s. Luck still played a part in the race but not nearly as much as racing in the old untamed configuration. Gary Cummins, son of well-known and successful 1941 winner Pat Cummins, finished second.

Laird Wins in Unlimited Runabout

Waite wasn't the only repeat winner. Mike Moreland of California won again in the C-Stock Hydro class and John Laird got his first win in the Unlimited Runabout class. Laird a longtime veteran Slough pilot with mechanic-rider, Mike Alm, traversed the 22-mile round-trip journey out in front all the way to the finish line in Kenmore. John started racing the Slough back in 1953 and has competed for 18-years in the historic event, second longest behind Red Taylor's twenty-year run.

1970 Slough Race: John Laird in *R-62* with rider-mechanic Mike Alm leaning forward going upstream

He finally got his win and somehow managed to keep from being tossed into the drink as is customary for the winners. Laird's mechanic-rider, Mike Alm, who was a shirt-sleeve relative to Bob Waite's wife Mary Ellen, was kneeling alongside Laird. His racing experience was as a long-time member on Bob Waite's crew.

The mechanic gets out of the cockpit and up over the bow to help the runabout get on a plane during the starts. Then he moves back and parks himself behind the driver during the runs, usually getting a black and blue rear-end from being pushed against the protruding engine mounting clamps and sitting on the gas tank. However, in this case, John's boat had a wide cockpit enabling Alm to ride side-by-side with him. He also moved forward and leaned toward the corner when turning, which helped a lot with the cornering ability of the boat (see photo on opposite page).

Laird's First Boat In Dump-Truck

John Laird began his boat racing career in 1951 in a little home-made C-Hydro he built from boat plans he acquired from "Champion Boats," a California company that made kit-boat plans. His brother Jim hauled the rig back and forth to the race sites where John competed, all nestled nicely in the bed of his old dump-truck

Laird's first boat in brother's truck

Laird, who at the time knew nothing about boats or motors, bought his first engine, a pre-war C-Service motor from my father's gas station-boat shop in Lake City.

Hanauer Wins A-Hydro Class

When you've been dominant in your class and winning for a while as was the case for Dennis Lee, and someone passes you by and seems to know more about being faster than you do, then it's probably time to retire. So was the case last year for Dennis Lee, he retired. This year Chip Hanauer took over the reins as the front runner in the A-Stock Hydro class, winning it for the first time as one of the young up-and-coming Seattle Outboard drivers. Gold Cup unlimited hydro driver, Bill Muncey, was his idol.

Late 1970s Hanauer & Muncey

1970 Sammamish Slough Race Results (by class)

Place	Driver	Class	From	Boat #	Time
1	Bob Waite	Unlimited Hydro	Bellevue	228-R	23:00.0
2	Gary Cummins	Unlimited Hydro	Kenmore	*	*
3	Dave Jenkins	Unlimited Hydro	Seattle	R-29	*
1	John Laird	Unlimited Runabout	Bellevue	R-62	*
2	John Myers	Unlimited Runabout	Seattle	R-77	*
3	Dave Tonge	Unlimited Runabout	*	*	*
1	Mike Moreland	C-Stock Hydro	Playa Del Ray, CA	*	*
2	Bob Weiss	C-Stock Hydro	*	*	*

3	Bob Gierke	C-Stock Hydro	Edmonds	*	*
1	Roger Wendt	B-Stock Hydro	*	*	*
2	John Hawkins	B-Stock Hydro	*	*	*
3	Bob Wartinger	B-Stock Hydro	Seattle	7-R	*
1	Jan Christ	BU-Runabout	Edmonds	1-US	*
2	Al Greathouse	BU-Runabout	Seattle	*	*
3	Greg Simmons	BU-Runabout	*		*
1	Chip Hanauer	A-Stock Hydro	Bellevue	*	*
2	Walt Taylor	A-Stock Hydro	*	*	*
3	Stephen Straight	A-Stock Hydro	*	*	*
1	Tom Williams	OPC-T	*	*	*
2	Henry Zacharios	OPC-T	*	*	*
3	Greg Horn	OPC-T	Seattle	*	*
1	Ed Geddes	OPC-UI	*	*	*
2	Tom Losvar	OPC-UI	Mukilteo	656	*
3	Fred Adams	OPC-UI	*	*	*
1	Kerry Ballantine	OPC-SJ	*	*	*
2	Bill Hauta	OPC-SJ	*	*	*
3	Red Johnson	OPC-SJ	*	*	*
1	Larry Lewis	OPC-SE	Seattle	442	*
2	Steve Murry	OPC-SE	*	*	*
3	Ted Woodward	OPC-SE	*	*	*
1	Mike Jackson	Indian Canoes	Moclips	*	*
2	Cliff Jackson	Indian Canoes	Moclips	*	*
3	William Johnson	Indian Canoes	*	*	*

Some towns, boat numbers & times unavailable

In Memory of Jerry Bryant

The Sammamish Slough Race and unlimited hydro drivers lost a good friend in November, 1970. Jerry Bryant, founding father of the Slough Race and first Seattle Gold Cup chairman, died the day before Thanksgiving at Doctor's Hospital with most of his family by his side. Slough Race drivers and organizers fondly remember Jerry watching over them from his 42' Chris-Craft cruiser *Alexa* out in Lake Washington. He usually anchored a few hundred feet out from the Kenmore starting line where he oversaw almost every race for some 36 years (between 1934 and 1970).

1970 Race Schedule (Partial)

April 12	33rd Sammamish Slough Race
April 19	Sammamish Water-Ski Race Revival
May 17	Cottage Lake, Woodinville
May 24	Columbia River, Quincy
May 31	Silver Lake, Everett
July 24-26	Green Lake "Best of Boat Racing"
Aug 22-23	Stock Nationals-Beloit, Wisconsin
Sept 20	Lake Lawrence, Yelm
Sept 25-26	Devil's Lake-Lincoln City, Oregon

Laird's Humorous Inside Story

John Laird, 18-year Slough racer, told me a funny story about a high strung and nervous Unlimited class driver, Buz Dupea (pronounced "Do pay") about to start in the Slough Race. "During the start in shallow water, we were holding the back of his boat out of the water, trying to fire-up his motor using a quick start lift. Buz was kneeling forward with his hand holding the throttle wide-open and impatiently waiting for us to drop him into the water for his take-off along with the other boats but couldn't figure out why he wasn't moving and all the other boats were throttling away.

"He turned around and frantically yelled as loud has he could, 'Let me go! Let me go!' The screaming noise from the other four-cylinder open-exhaust F-Hydros was so loud he didn't realize that his engine hadn't started. His crew on the dock, frustrated with aching backs from holding the heavy hydro out over the water, considered dropping the boat in and letting Dupea try to start it by himself."

Eventually, after the crewmember pulled a few more times on the starting cord, the engine fired and he was off and running, albeit behind all the other boats. By then Dupea was last into the Slough and didn't finished the race in the money.

1970 Tidbits

The Sammamish water-ski race returned this year but no results were published. Dick Rautenberg was elected SOA commodore, Janis Lee secretary, Dave Jenkins sportsman of the year and Rick Sandstrom APBA Region 10 chairman. Bob Waite was national high-point champion in F-Runabout, Red Taylor in C-Hydro and Harold Tolford was chairman of the Stock Outboard division. Craig Selvidge set the A-Stock-Runabout UIM competition record at 48.780 mph and UIM Kilo record at 55.511 mph.

Your author retired from driving limited inboards with a win at Green Lake in the 5-Liter class during the Seafair race in July. It was a bittersweet win as he was never able to attend the trophy presentation after the race. A crash in the second heat sent him to the hospital (with a severe concussion and back injuries) after a spill just before the start. It was too late to re-run the second heat because of the Seattle Park Board's 6:00 pm curfew. Race officials called the race based on the first heat results which Benson won.

Doctors and family urged his retirement after almost 20-years of racing. Following a year of recovery, Benson turned to race officiating as an official APBA timer for outboard and unlimited regattas, a duty he assumed for the next 25 years until he retired for good after 34 years of service in boat racing.

Chapter 15

1972: Strange Slough Race where Dave Culley finishes Unlimited class in canoe.

End of an Era
1971-1976

"Everybody has problems in this race-mechanical troubles, spinouts, engines won't start, debris in the water. Usually the winner is the guy with the fewest problems"

-Bob Waite, April 12, 1970-

Bob Waite, who didn't wait for anybody, went for three in a row like so many others in the past. He hoped good luck was on his side and this year he would be the first to accomplish the feat that eluded so many before him. Only one driver, Al Benson, had won three races, but not three in a row.

The annual kickoff for the outboard racing season, the Slough Race, was set to start at noon Sunday April 18. More than 80 entries had signed up for 11 classes that were to start at the Kenmore Bridge boat-ramp and run to Marymoor Park in Redmond and back. The usual outboard hydros and runabouts plus the OPC boys and Indian canoes were scheduled to compete for prizes in the 34th staging of the event.

F-Hydro driver Bud Walters, overall winner of the 1966 affair who was coming out of retirement, and Dave Jenkins still trying for his third win, would try to thwart Waite's efforts by providing plenty of competition. Race officials were hoping the spectators would behave by not throwing objects into the Slough. In recent years, drivers had been forced to deal with bottles, cans, rocks, wood and even old tires thrown-in from the banks. This was particularly a problem during the return run because some unruly spectators had been drinking longer.

Luck Inspires Elusive Three in a Row?

Bob Waite got a good draw and start from the Kenmore boat launch utilizing the "quick start lift" method. He drew the No. 1 starting position from the referee's hat. His engine started on the first pull enabling him to be first out into the Slough, a huge advantage because it was still hard to pass in the Slough even though it had been tamed by massive dredging. He was in the lead just before the first turn about one-half mile into the Slough, a tricky right-hander, when two boats came roaring by him, one on

Unlimited Hydro start at Kenmore Bridge boat launch; Bob Waite (far right) starting in No. 1 spot

Luck was on his side as both the faster drivers, Jody Hiese and Jim Allen, ran straight instead of taking the sharp right turn up the main channel. Allen's chewed life jacket was the scary evidence of him being tossed from his cockpit and Hiese driving right over the top of him. They mistook Swamp Creek's opening straight ahead and both ended up in the muddy muck of the creek's outlet into the Slough. Waite kept going vigilantly around the turns up through Bothell and sped his way to Marymoor Park in first-place.

The Ballou Show

A number of other drivers weren't so lucky. Tom Ballou caught the immediate attention of photographer Bob Carver when he got too cozy with the Bothell Bridge in the Unlimited-Runabout Class. Carver was shooting from the bank across the Slough.

You would think after some 34 rousing years of competition that you had seen it all, but this year like in the past gave the spectators something different at the usual place. Tom Ballou misjudged his turn at the Bothell Bridge and entertained the crowd. His boat caught a chine, spun-out, then…clunk…and crunch! The sickening sound (to a driver) of his D-Runabout hitting the bridge pillars.

The many spectators lining the banks were spellbound after seeing Ballou's "dipsy doodle" under the bridge. He ricocheted off a pillar, crashed-in the right side of his boat, and was hurled into the water. The finale was Ballou swimming after his boat that flipped upside-down and was drifting downstream. One would think the crowd would have given him a perfect 10 score or at least something encouraging for his efforts; most likely lots of clapping.

Bill Carver's editing of father Bob's 6-sequence array of Tom Ballou getting dunked after hitting the Bothell Bridge, spinning out and flipping upside down.

Eileen Crimmin, accompanied by photos from renowned photographer and business partner, Bob Carver, wrote a very entertaining three-page article about this year's race which was published in the July, 1971, issue of *Powerboat* magazine. The following are excerpts of what she wrote: "Its survival (the Slough Race) defies all logic; therefore, its survival must depend on that most unquenchable of human qualities–fun!

And fun was had during the April 18th running…which was won by Bob Waite for a third consecutive time…Waite watchers were delighted that this veteran of (nearly) 20 years of Slough competition was the one to achieve this unique triumph.

"Waite-watchers had no connection to Weight Watchers, you understand, except in a sort of reversal during which Waite had gained weight to around 240 pounds, every one of which helped him win the race on the windy straightaways when he literally spread his bulk across the boat's bow to keep the sled from blowing over."

From Crimmin's article, you understood that the race conditions were again windy and bore some of the blame for the many mishaps in addition to Ballou's show. Of the 13 Unlimited Hydros which started, only five finished. A similar fate resulted with mishaps in the Unlimited Runabout Class where only two out of the eight crossed the finish line at Kenmore. And the estimate for the OPCs was a 45 percent casualty loss.

Waite passing under Kenmore Bridge for 3rd consecutive win.

Buzz Dupea's misfortunes started farther upstream. He encountered what most thought would never happen again when he ran over a floating tire. Well, so much for spectators behaving. Dupea's propeller attempted to cut through the rubber but as a result, the boat suddenly stopped and launched Dupea who skidded across the water. He ended up in the hospital with rib and arm injuries. Joining him there for observation purposes was Norm Boddy, whose OPC hit the bank during his return run. Randy Zavales along with Ballou took the top honors for the most spectacular accidents. Zavales, who was trying to beat the fellow who was supposed to buy his brand of boat but instead purchased another type, caught the right sponson of his OPC pickle-fork[52] and tore it off completely after hitting the Down River Marina bridge (old Nursery Bridge). What was coincidental, Zavales' boat builder was watching the incident right in front of his shop near the bridge.

Cattails Curtail Culley

Dave Culley, 27, still trying to master the Slough, learned how tough it was to finish a heat. He only made it about a half-mile up the Slough. Dave told me the following story. It was during a book interview in September of 2015 at Lake Pleasant RV Park in Bothell. My wife Carolyn, our two small dogs and I were staying for the month interviewing former Slough Race drivers. Culley recounts his 1971 Slough run, one he vividly remembered driving his hi-powered F-Hydro, the fastest class in the race:

"It was 1971 and I was going up the Slough. First, I never ran the engine before the Slough Race or tested because it was too cold. I was going up there (had started the race) and I locked the throttle about half-throttle and reached back to adjust the carburetor. And then looked up and, geez, the bank was coming and so I turned the (steering) wheel to the right real fast and I fell out! The boat ended up across the river in some bushes, still running. And geez, I had hip boots on and I tried to swim across the river and all these boats were going by and the boots were holding me down."

I said: "You're lucky you didn't drown." Culley said: "Yeah, I never wore hip boots again." I asked: "So you were going upstream?" Culley continued: "I was just a quarter-mile up from the Kenmore Bridge…in the R-59 boat…and it's over up in the weeds, half on the water and half on top of the cattails. I couldn't see it but it was still running, screaming away at half throttle. So, I finally got over there and I took one hip-boot off. I couldn't move any more with hip-boots full of water and I'm wading through the cattails and whatever, I hit the throttle and stopped the engine. That's before we had tethers[53] on them to electrically stop them.

"So, I drug the boat back down to the water and finished adjusting the carburetor with half the boat's transom on the bank and the other half over the water (to clear the propeller). So, the prop was about half way out of the water and I got in the boat, locked the throttle again and started it up. I scooted the boat forward off the bank (with body weight lunging forward) and I took off again. So anyway, I got going again and

---

[52] Bow cut-away feature between sponson's to reduce air-lift and dangerous blow-over accidents. First hydro of this type used in Slough Race was driven by Bill Rankin in1953 (see Chapter 12).
[53] Cord attached between the driver and engine's kill-switch to quickly stop the engine for safety.

try to compose myself, and now I was soaking wet. I got up to Woodinville with the boat running pretty good but I was way behind, and right by the lower train bridge, I burned a piston and came to a stop with one hip-boot on and one still back there (in Kenmore) somewhere in the mud. Then I threw the other boot away. So, now I'm in my socks wading around in the bushes on shore.

I asked "What happened next?" "Well they came (the official rescue boat) after all the other boats came by and towed me back down to the pits along with two or three other boats in a train. We tied ropes onto one and another and they towed us down slowly (back to Kenmore). Just another cold wet day!" Obviously, this was one of the driver's worst nightmares or most embarrassing moments, being towed back to the pits in front of all your competitors, family and friends.

Walters Knew Waite's Secret

Fourth-place finisher, Bud Walters, revealed one of Waite's secrets to success in the Slough in a quote in Eileen Crimmins' *Powerboat* article: "He's got the right rig. He only uses that outfit for the Slough Race. It will turn left and right. Most boats are built for a circle course only and will not turn left easily, and (to the) right badly or not at all." Waite confirmed in the article that his hydro was indeed a talented and flexible hull. Nonetheless, Waite justified his victory by saying his win was still due to "luck."

He told Crimmin: "Sure it's luck. There are so many possibilities in a race like this with a dead-engine start, the 22-mile length, wind, debris, driving error and equipment failure. It has to be luck. For instance, I drew the No. 1 starting position, Luck. Then my motor fired up on the very first pull, Luck. When Heise and Allen passed me on that corner I didn't get drawn into their problems with the bank, Luck. The boat stayed on the water and the motor didn't quit, again Luck." Crimmin finished the conversation stating: "When he was reminded that that his outfit was the same rig he'd used for all three wins–same hull, engine and prop–and that likely his winning combination resulted from a degree of experience and skill, he just grinned and puffed on his victory cigar."

Interest in the Slough Race was still high but all the major-league sports in the area had taken away many of the spectators. Many of which were April baseball fans. Newspaper reports of outboard racing had been relegated to the back pages with some results but minimal race summaries. The exception was the *Seattle Times'* Del Danielson who covered all boat racing; powerboat and sailing events. But the crowds were still lining the banks in the thousands on both sides along the course.

It still depended on the weather which was often cold, windy and wet during April, unpredictable at the least. The 1970 race was no exception as it was another cold and windy afternoon of racing. Everyone was bundled up with warm clothes. The crews still had to dawn their waist-high waders and turn for cover when the engine finally started to avoid being drenched while helping the F-Hydro boys get started.

"Wart" Gets First Win

Bob Wartinger in B-Hydro at Bothell.

Bob Wartinger, like Entrop and Tolford who came before him, were all Boeing employees and world record setters in outboards. "Wart" as he was affectionately called by his close boat racing friends, finally got the win that had eluded him since he started racing in the Slough. Maybe some of Bob Waite's luck rubbed off on him. Driving his well-tuned B-Hydro, he won his class for the first time since he started running the Slough in around 1967. He's placed third, second and another third before this year's win.

Young Hanauer's Second Win

Chip Hanauer, born Lee Edward Hanauer, who was a youngster who started racing in the JU-Runabout class in the mid-1960s, got his second consecutive win. He drove to victory in the A-Stock Hydro class, leading the way in both heats. Unlike some, he used his best equipment because he was in it to win. Many drivers didn't run their best stuff because of concerns about the hazardous conditions that could ruin their equipment. Hanauer's winning ways were a preview of his future where he became one of the most famous boat race drivers of all time.

I interviewed Chip while researching Slough Race drivers in April of 2015. He told me: "The Slough Race was one of my favorite racing events. But I cheated in the Slough, I used my best equipment." Well that wasn't cheating at all, it was smart racing. Aggressive competitors use their best abilities whenever they compete.

Almost all the Slough Race winners used their best equipment without regard to the many hazards. Motivated race drivers don't enter a race to get second-place or just to finish. I told him my brother and I along with our other racing friends (Schumacher and Lyford) all used our best equipment–just like him. Teenager Hanauer (17) and middle-aged Bob Waite (47) had something in common. They both had won their classes two and three times in a row respectively. Very likely both were thinking ahead about next year's race. Could they continue their win streaks?

John Meyers second-place Unlimited Runabout.

1971 Sammamish Slough Race Results (by class)

Place	Driver	Class	From	Boat #	Time
1	Bob Waite	Unlimited Hydro	Bellevue	228-R	22:29.2
2	Frank Boyle	Unlimited Hydro	*	*	*
3	Mike Smith	Unlimited Hydro	*	*	*
4	Bud Walters	Unlimited Hydro	*	R-50	
1	Dick Rautenberg	Unlimited Runabout	Mountlake Terrace	R-69	*
2	John Myers	Unlimited Runabout	Seattle	R-77	*
3	Norm Gilmore	Unlimited Runabout	Bothell	*	*
1	Mike Moreland	C-Stock Hydro	Playa Del Ray, CA	*	*
2	Bob Gierke	C-Stock Hydro	Edmonds	*	*
3	Ron Johnson	C-Stock Hydro	*	*	*
4	Robert Weiss	C-Stock Hydro	*	*	*
1	Bob Wartinger	B-Stock Hydro	Seattle	*	*
2	Darrell Rupnow	B-Stock Hydro	*	*	*
3	Don Mackle	B-Stock Hydro	*	*	*
4	Terry Noll	B-Stock Hydro	*	*	*
1	Bryan Demoray	B-Stock Runabout	*	*	*
2	Jan Christ	B-Stock Runabout	Edmonds	1-US	*
1	Chip Hanauer	A-Stock Hydro	Bellevue	*	*
2	Steve Straith	A-Stock Hydro	*	*	*
3	Brad Roberson	A-Stock Hydro	*	*	*
4	Steve DeSouza	A-Stock Hydro	*	*	*
1	Jim Fox	OPC-S Runabout	*	*	*
2	Henry Zacharios	OPC-S Runabout	*	*	*
3	Fred Adams	OPC-S Runabout	*	*	*
4	Stu Diebert	OPC-S Runabout	*	*	*
1	Greg Horn	OPC-SJ	*	*	*
2	Bill Hauta	OPC-SJ	*	*	*
3	Larry Alexander	OPC-SJ	*	*	*
4	Joe Paris	OPC-SJ	*	*	*
1	Don Burns	OPC-UNL	*	*	*

2	Kery Ballantine	OPC-UNL	*	*	*
1	Larry Lewis	OPC-SE	Seattle	442	*
2	George Abbott	OPC-SE	Kent	*	*
3	Craig Nelson	OPC-SE	*	*	*
4	Norm Boddy	OPC-SE	Seattle	*	*
1	Robin Moiler	Indian Canoes	*	*	*
2	John Ballen	Indian Canoes	*	*	*
3	Cliff Jackson	Indian Canoes	Moclips	*	*
4	Glen Jacksom	Indian Canoes	Moclips	*	*

Some boat numbers, place, times & names unavailable

1971 Race Schedule (Partial)

April 18	34th Sammamish Slough Race
April 2	Sammamish Water-Ski Race Revival
Jun 6	Upper Columbia River-Bridgeport, WA
July 30-31	Green Lake-"Best of Boat Racing"

Army Engineers Dredging Report

Seattle Army Engineers were proposing to dredge about one-half mile of the Sammamish Slough channel between Lake Washington and the Kenmore Bridge next summer (1972). The effort would allow boaters who had to paddle because of shallow water between the Kenmore Bridge public boat launch and the marinas in Kenmore, before they could use their outboard motors.

There were environmental impact concerns because the dredging would destroy two acres of marsh and temporarily interfere with fish life by muddying the water. The project's proposed $50,000 cost was to be split between the federal government and the county. Comments on the project were asked to be mailed to the district office in Seattle.

1971 Tidbits

Bob Wartinger set the B-Stock Hydro 5-mile competition record at 63.604 mph. Gerry Walin was the first to break the 100-mph

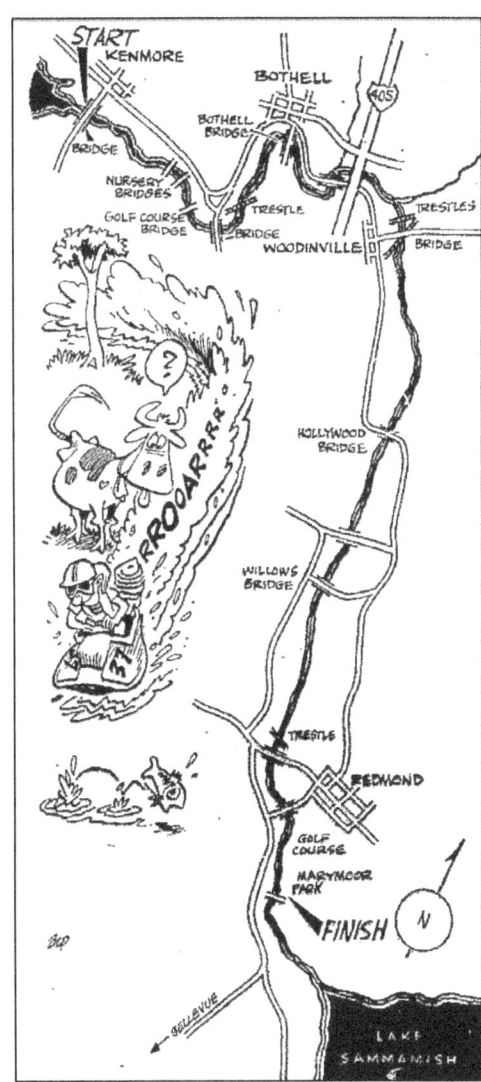

1971 *Seattle Times* Slough Race map: 11 miles from Kenmore boat launch to Marymoor Park.

barrier for the UIM Kilo straightaway run in B-Outboard Hydro at 100.089 mph. Future Slough racers Craig Selvidge and Earl Garrison set records. Selvidge set the A-Stock-Runabout UIM Kilo record at 55.511 mph and Garrison set the B-Stock Runabout UIM Kilo record at 71.033 mph. Jimmy Harland, one of the SOA's most interesting and active characters, died August of 1971. One of many interesting things about him was that he was one of the first in the U.S. to receive an international sharpshooting certificate.

Del Danielson of the *Times* reported in his "Make Mine Water" column on July 2: "Line of the week comes from the profile on Bill Muncey in the press kit for the *Atlas Van Lines* unlimited team: 'Bill has been a popular figure in Seattle for more than 15 years (he raced in the Slough Race in 1957). 'In fact, a recent State of Washington poll found he was second only to the President of the United States (Richard Nixon) in popularity in his adopted State.' (That's what it said. Honest.)"

Intermittent reports of the Slough Race were heard on radio station KFKF-AM. Bob Waite was the SOA sportsman of the year and Jim Daniels was elected SOA commodore for 1972.

1972

"Waite Watchers" for Fourth Consecutive

Not so little Robert Ned Waite, all 240 pounds of him, was the favorite for four in a row. If he were to be successful you could say he really did own the Slough. No one else could have said that, nobody since the race began in 1934. No one could have thought this was possible because luck played such a big part for all the drivers who won this historic event, even in its later tamer configuration. The other Unlimited drivers likely wished they were in Bob's bare feet and probably thinking of passing the hat to collect enough cash to bribe him to quit racing the Slough. But anyone who knew him well knew better because he loved to compete and win, the more the better.

The annual April outboard dash had a new name and sponsor for this year. The sponsor was the Rainier Brewery and the name, "The Sammamish River Race and Rainier Beer Cup." Waite, who would be among the Unlimited class drivers owned the past trophy that was presented to the winner. He took permanent possession last year after winning for the third straight time.

The 35th annual race was scheduled to commence at noon on Sunday, April 15 at the Kenmore Bridge boat-ramp. More than 80 entries had signed up for 11 classes before the day of the race. In the past, upwards to 50,000 spectators watched from vantage points all along the banks of the Slough. The 22-mile round trip zig-zag run to Marymoor Park and back would give Waite a chance to extend his three-year win streak, which also gave his competitors an opportunity to dethrone the barefoot grandfather from Bellevue. Bud Walters, 1966 winner, was expected for this race and Dave Jenkins, 1967 and 1968 winner, planned to try again for his third win. Dave Culley wanted to just finish the event. He had tried since 1968 but luck had not been on his side, mostly because of an uncooperative motor. So far, Dave had not even finished the upstream run to Marymoor Park.

Granddaddy Waite Rules

As Del Danielson of the *Times* said in his column April 17, "Like old Man River, Bob Waite just keeps rollin right along. Braving drenching showers of rain, snow and hail, Waite yesterday rolled to his fourth consecutive Sammamish Slough Race victory." He must have been inspired by his cheering granddaughter of 2-1/2 years because the 48-year-old veteran was first out of the Kenmore Bridge pits and led all the way to Marymoor Park and back with a respectable time of 23:27.8.

Little Miss Charlene Cross, Waite's granddaughter and his daughter Bobby, were the family cheering section this year. Bob's wife, Mary Ellen, who was usually by his side during the starts both in Kenmore and Marymoor, was recovering from serious injuries from an auto accident. The granddaughter, who had been waiting for almost four hours for the 60 or so drivers to finish the four-hour program, provided the victory kiss.

Bob Waite crossing finish line in Kenmore for fourth straight Slough Race victory.

After an unprecedented four in a row most everyone in the know would agree that Waite indeed owned the Slough but not if you listened to him. He still said after the race that luck had much to do with it and he hadn't paid his dues yet, maybe in the next year if he can make it five in a row? Chuck (Charley) Walters, now of Fall City, came in second. You may find this hard to believe but Dave Culley was an unofficial third after he crossed the finish line in a canoe…I'm serious, he was paddling a canoe!

Infamous Culley Canoe Caper

Would you have ever imagined that someone who drove an 80-mph hydro in the Slough Race completed his run by paddling a canoe across the finish line? No, it wasn't one of the Indian canoes that Dave Culley borrowed when he used his conked-out F-Hydro as collateral. Here is Dave's account of the most unusual Slough Race finish in history based on my September 2015 interview at Phil Williams' "Performax Marine shop/museum in Puyallup, Washington. This was a gathering of a bunch of old Slough Race cronies including Don Benson, Culley, John Laird, Wayne LaChapelle Clayton Shaw, Phil Williams, Williams' son Charley and me.

Dave began: "Well, I was up the river (Sammamish) about a mile and again, the engine failed on me" (like in 1971 only this time on the downstream run). "I had too many carburetors on the engine and it was kind of temperamental, but it would go pretty fast. Anyway, the engine quit and I pulled into these people's yard and they had a party going on…I might-a-had a couple of beers, it was another cold and wet day.

"So, they had this yellow canoe there and I thought (and said), 'Geez, could I just borrow your canoe? I'll bring it back…I'll leave my boat here (as collateral).' So, I thought, well you know, if I put my life-jacket and helmet back on, they (the race officials at the finish line) really can't say anything" (about it being against the rules) because I had entered the race.

"So, I paddled down about a mile and I could hear Waite (Bob Waite) coming down on his return trip and I was

1972 Slough Race: Dave Culley's Unlimited class finish in Kenmore.

paddling like crazy. He finally passed me and then somebody else passed me. But I managed to come under the Kenmore Bridge in third place."

I said, "You did, in the canoe?" Dave continued: "Yeah but they didn't fully score me (the officials at the finish line) they just didn't have any sense of humor. So, I had to tow the canoe back up (with a patrol boat) to trade it back for my boat. I'm only about 50-feet from the finish line in the photo" (taken by Bob Carver next to the Kenmore Bridge).

I told Dave in a later interview: "Your paddling form looked really good in Carver's photograph…I heard it snowed that year?" "It started snowing about half-way down after I started paddling" (in the canoe), he said. "And I worked up quite a sweat paddling (with all his racing gear on, helmet, visor, lifejacket and warm clothes) and by the time he (Bob Carver) shot the picture, I had a lot of practice!"

Meanwhile, back upriver at Marymoor Park the rest of the classes were starting their return trip downstream. Longtime Slough veteran, Red Taylor, finished first overall in the Unlimited Runabout class with Dick Rautenberg second and two-time overall winner Dave Jenkins third. The next starters were the C-Stock Hydros–and Bob Gierke of Edmonds finally got his win. (Three-straight class winner, Mike Moreland of California, wasn't mentioned in the results. He possibly had troubles or didn't make the trip north this year.)

Seattle's Bob Wartinger led the pack at the start of the B-Stock Hydro class and was the first to receive the checkered flag after crossing under the Kenmore Bridge at the finish line and, Jan Christ of Edmonds, was not far behind. Christ's victory in the first heat and his combined points and quickest time gave him the overall victory. Wartinger was second and Ed Klopfer was third.

Bob Wartinger leading, with Jan Christ & Ed Klopfer next, B-Hydro class downriver start at Marymoor.

Hanauer's Humble Beginnings to Fame

Chip Hanauer, now a veteran of the Slough, won the A-Stock-Hydro class for the third year in a row, a feat only three others had accomplished. Dennis Lee, also competing in the A-Stock Hydro class was the first (1966-1968), Bob Waite in the Unlimited class (1969-1971) second and Mike Mooreland of California, in the C-Stock Hydro class (1969-1971) third.

The Bellevue 18-year old, was sharing his driving time between outboards and limited inboards, driving in the 145-cubic inch class. His dream job was competing in the big boats, following in footsteps of his idol, Bill Muncey, driving in the Unlimited-hydroplane circuit. Chip told his affable father, Stan, at the age of 10 that he wanted to race boats. He was quoted by *Times* reporter Craig Smith in an article published on July 12, 1980. Smith's article began: "When Chip Hanauer (then 26) was 10 years old and told his father he wanted to race boats, he was told: 'If you make the decision and you get hurt, I don't want any complaints about the sport.'

Chip Hanauer's 1968 SOA membership card.

"Now 16 years and several injuries later, Chip still is as excited about boat racing as ever, and he doesn't complain. Last Sunday (July 6, 1980), he suffered his second injury in four years of unlimited driving when *The Squire Shop* exploded when he was trying to start for a practice lap before the *Gold Cup* in Madison, Indiana. His left eye was hurt but doctors have said it was only temporary–not permanent. 'There is a price to racing boats and that is dealing with pain sometimes,' said Chip, who has broken ribs, sliced tendons and injured a leg racing in everything from outboards to unlimiteds."

As it turned out, Hanauer, one of the most famous boat race drivers of all time, competed in the Sammamish Slough Race for the last time and moved on to racing limited inboards and then to his famous era, driving the "big boats," the Unlimited Hydroplanes.

1972 Sammamish Slough Race Results (by class)

Place	Driver	Class	From	Boat #	Time
1	Bob Waite	Unlimited Hydro	Bellevue	228-R	23:27.8
2	Chuck Walters	Unlimited Hydro	*	*	*
1	Red Taylor	Unlimited Runabout	Seattle	*	32:44.0
2	Dick Rautenberg	Unlimited Runabout	Mountlake Terrace	R-69	34:52.6
3	Dave Jenkins	Unlimited Runabout	Lynnwood	*	*

1	Bob Gierke	C-Stock Hydro	Edmonds	*	*
2	Maurice Shuman	C-Stock Hydro	Edmonds	*	*
1	Jan Christ	B-Stock Hydro	Edmonds	*	*
2	Bob Wartinger	B-Stock Hydro	Seattle	*	*
3	Ed Klopfer	B-Stock Hydro	Seattle	*	*
1	Chip Hanauer	A-Stock Hydro	Bellevue	*	*
2	Rick Christensen	A-Stock Hydro	Eatonville	*	*
3	Mark Kirchner	A-Stock Hydro	*	*	*
1	Greg Horn	OPC-B	Seattle	*	*
2	Ed Brinson	OPC-B	Bellingham	*	*
3	Tom Losvar	OPC-B	Mukilteo	656	*
1	Larry Lewis	OPC-C	Seattle	442	*
2	Norm Boddy	OPC-C	Seattle	*	*
3	George Abbott	OPC-C	Kent	*	*
1	Bill Allen	Combined S. Run	*	*	*
2	Lany Ingalls	Combined S. Run	Seattle	*	*
3	Greg Selvidge	Combined S. Run	Edmonds	*	*
1	Cliff Jackson	Indian Canoes	Moclips	*	*
2	Glen Jackson	Indian Canoes	Moclips	*	*
3	Robin Moiler	Indian Canoes	*	*	*

Some boat numbers, place, times & names unavailable

<u>1972 Race Schedule (Partial)</u>

April 16	35th Sammamish Slough Race
April 23	Sammamish Water-Ski Race
July 30-31	Green Lake-"Best of Boat Racing"
May 14	Cottage Lake Stock Outboard Divisionals

557 Moorage, Storage
DRY Storage up to 30'. Complete work facilities. $20 minimum, $1.50 ft. Craig Craft Boats, Edmonds Waterfront, 778-2275.

Outboard Racing News Scarce

Outboard racing news and race reports in the newspapers were hard to come by during this time-period, likely due to lack of interest by the news media and fewer reports given by the SOA. To be fair to the boat club, major-league and college sports got most of the attention from the columnists. And famous photographer, Bob Carver, was shooting less often. But the Slough Race was still getting a write-up or two, keeping the public aware of outboard racing and that it was still active and thriving in the Northwest.

1972 Tidbits

John Laird set the Kilo straightaway record in C-Service Runabout at 54.699 driving *Rain Karen* at Devil's Lake, Oregon. Lee Sutter set the A & B-Racing Runabout Kilo straightaway records at 75.780 mph and 82.396 mph respectively and the C-Stock Hydro Kilo record at 73.857 mph the same day, also at Devil's Lake. He was inducted into the Gulf Marine Racing Hall of Fame for his accomplishments in the outboard category. Don Haack was voted sportsman of the year and Red Taylor was elected SOA commodore for 1973, a position he also held 15 years ago in 1958.

1973

Waite in Unchartered Territory

Was five in a row in the cards for Grandpa Waite? Bob Waite was in uncharted territory; no one could even have dreamed of winning five Slough Races, not even the *Tarot* fortune telling cards. What about that guy from California? Could Mike Moreland be as dominant as Waite in his C-Stock Hydro class?

The 36th edition of the Sammamish Slough Race was slated to start at noon on Sunday April 8, as in the past four years from the boat launch area next to the Kenmore Bridge. The return run was planned to start at 2 pm from Marymoor Park, the same location since the grand Slough dredging of the mid-1960s.

Rapid Robert, another of his nicknames because it's the name painted on the side of his F-Runabout, has had a stranglehold on the annual April regatta for outboard racers. Last year he won his fourth straight, his fifth overall victory. He still said it was mostly because of luck because his old engine continues to start on the "first pull," but many around him are saying "he owns the Slough" regardless of luck.

Race officials scheduled 16 classes combined into 10 heats of racing over the 22-mile round trip course. Everything from the traditional outboards to various Outboard Performance Craft entries started in five-minute intervals, including the fast and nimble OPC Unlimiteds. The quickest outboard and OPCs were vying for a new trophy that was presented for the first time to the driver of the fastest entry, regardless of the class. To make the event fair, the OPC class made a standing start from the beach like the traditional outboards, unlike the last few years when they milled around out in Lake Washington and then made a "flying start" into the Slough.

Referee's Pre-race Instructions

Rick Sandstrom, referee for the 1970s Slough races and veteran outboard pilot, instructed the competitors during the drivers' meeting before the race. "For safety reasons, in case of an accident or breakdown, they should move their boat to the nearest bridge." A race official would be on every bridge with a two-way radio to report incidents and status. Sandstrom also initiated the draw (from his hat) to determine the starting positions from the pits in Kenmore. No draw was needed for the downriver start at Marymoor. The drivers' upstream finish order determined their starting position for the return trip. First place got the best location–in front of all the other boats. The second-place boat got the next best spot and so on.

Waite Wins–Not Fastest

Bob Waite was first out of the gate and quickest up the Slough to the Marymoor stopover location but the return start was a different story. Barefoot Bob didn't get a good start because of a cantankerous starting engine. It took a number of pulls to get him started. By then some of his competitors were hightailing it around the first corners at full speed. Old reliable had seen better days. He was fifth out of the pits but managed to pass several rigs on his way through Redmond. Somewhere along the way farther downriver he passed the leader, Dave Culley, who was first out of the Marymoor pits.

Waite's start at Marymoor: His old reliable engine didn't start first pull this time.

Even with the poor downriver start, Bob Waite sped to victory as the Unlimited Hydro class winner; the first five-consecutive winner in Slough Race history. Longtime veteran Dick Rautenberg finished second and Dave Culley was third. Barefoot Bob's two-way time of 22:54.2 was slower than in the past because of his starting troubles and his string of finishes as the quickest class up the Slough came to an end.

Potter's Modern Putt-Putt Fastest

Waite's string of finishes as the quickest class up the Slough finally ended. Dave Potter driving his sleek tunnel-hull, powered by a 200 plus horsepower Merc "Twister,"[54] won the OPC Unlimited class with the fastest time of the day. This year's race, which offered a new trophy for the fastest overall time, brought out some of the Unlimited OPC rigs powered by state-of-the-art factory racing engines.

Potter, 19, a Pacific Lutheran University economics major and one of Seattle's up and coming OPC drivers, sped up and down the course in the quickest time ever at 20:03.0. Stu Diebert of Mountlake Terrace, had the second fastest time of 22:00.4 and Tom Losvar of Mukilteo was third. Losvar is the son of Art Losvar who raced and won the Utility Runabout class 31 years ago in 1942. Bob Waite, driving his aging home-built hydro, was third overall with a time of 22:54.2.

Potter's Mercury "Twister" engine was a high performance 6-cylinder factory racing engine that was approved by the APBA for the OPC Unlimited class based on a limited production run of at least 100 motors; a requirement in the early 1970s APBA Rule Books.

Waite Undisputed "King of the Slough"

Bob Waite-"King of the Slough."

As far as this book is concerned, Bob Waite was the overall winner because of his traditional Unlimited outboard class victory. Now it can be said indisputably that Waite owned the Slough. His six Unlimited class victories, with five-straight, most likely will never be matched. The King was quoted by the *Times*' Del Danielson the day after the race: "It took me a couple of minutes to get started. The old engine didn't start on the first pull. I guess my luck ran out after four years of having everything go right."

Mike Moreland, from Playa Del Ray California, loved to come to the Northwest and compete in the Slough Race. He ought to; he's been coming for seven years and has dominated

---

[54] Mercury 6-cylinder factory racing engine produced in limited quantity expressly for racing; included in-out power trim, remotely adjustable by driver using rocker switch on steering wheel.

the C-Stock-Hydro class. This year was no exception as the Californian took the first-place hardware back to the Golden State for the fourth time, a feat no other C-Stock driver had accomplished in the Slough Race and no one else except Bob Waite. The rest of the class probably wished he had stayed home.

Jan Christ of Edmonds won for the second straight year in the B-Stock Hydros, Earl Garrison was best in the combined B-Stock and C-Runabout class and Bryan Anderson was the leader in A-Stock Hydro. Dave Culley, who rounded-out the field of six Unlimited finishers in third, was happy. It was the first time he finished the problematical race. He was behind in the first heat because of engine troubles but his luck improved with a second in the downriver heat.

Jan Christ 1st B-Hydro

Tunnel Boats Come of Age

"Tunnel boats" were a newer class of outboard raceboats regulated by the APBA. Their hulls are tunneled underneath all the way from bow to stern–a cross between a runabout and hydro. These rigs float on a cushion of air at high speeds similar to hydros and corner extremely well because of their large non-trip sides that extend the entire length of the boat. One of their most unique features is attached to their outboard motors; a "power trim and tilt system."

A small electric motor drives hydraulic fluid through one or two cylinders that are mounted between the engine's lower unit and transom mount. It pumps hydraulic fluid back and forth to the cylinder(s) that tilts the outboard motor in and out; all activated by a rocker-switch mounted to the boat's steering wheel. The driver can control the riding attitude with a push of a switch while in the heat of competition.

Tunnel boat riding on cushion of air.

The ideal trim position, when the boat is fastest, is right on the ragged edge of being dangerous. In this trim attitude, the boat has the most freedom from the water's drag forces. But a slight change, such as a wave or gust of wind, could cause the boat to blow-over backwards–the driver's worst nightmare. It's a dilemma between going as fast as possible and still being safe, like NASCAR drivers feathering their speed to keep their tires from slipping or spinning out of control. In the tunnel boat's case, it could turn into a very wet experience for the driver and possibly severe injuries.

One veteran old-timer said: "It looks like the OPC boys will take over the Slough. Those rigs cost lots of money, but they sure go fast. With electric starting they always start when they're supposed to. If we put up prize money for the Slough Race, I'll bet we'd have a whole creek full of those OPC things."

The Loaner Engine That Kept-On Winning

Dave Culley told me an interesting inside story about his Class-F "Scott-Atwater" loaner engine. It goes like this: "In 1972 I burned a piston in my engine (his Slough Race engine) and I didn't have an engine to go to the next race. So, this friend of mine, Larry Swinford (OPC-SI class winner in 1973-75 races), loaned me a Scott-Atwater powerhead to put on my Mercury lower unit, which I fit on with an adapter plate. So, I ran this Scott and it ran pretty well; I ran it the rest of the summer. I won more races with it those days than I did with my Mercury. It didn't go as fast but it was way more dependable.

Culley-"Team Atwater"

"So, I went back to my Mercury the following year and Dick Rautenberg came along and said 'Geez, I burned a piston in my outboard (race engine).' I said, 'No problem, I got a Scott.' So, I put it on his boat at Silver Lake (Everett) and he went out and won. So then Buzz Dupea came along a year or so later and said 'Geez my engine doesn't run well, what'll I do?' No problem, we got a Scott. So, I passed that same engine to Buzz and he went out and won. That was the loaner engine that wouldn't give up. It didn't go very fast, but everybody had fun so I came up with these hats with *Team Atwater* printed on the front." Could Culley need another hat in the future, possibly *Team Mercury*?

The total of 49 entries was the lowest in recent years. In the past years, more than 120 competitors raced on a Sunday in the Slough. There was talk about the longevity of the 39-year-old event. Because of dwindling entries and complaints from residents along the Slough, there was considerable discussion about discontinuing one of the most famous long-running boat races in the country.

1973 Sammamish Slough Race Results (by class)

Place	Driver	Class	From	Boat #	Time
1	Bob Waite	Unlimited Hydro	Bellevue	228-R	22:54.2
2	Dick Rautenberg	Unlimited Hydro	Mountlake Terrace	*	27:48.2
3	Dave Culley	Unlimited Hydro	Kent	R-59	28:04.6
4	Roger Compton	Unlimited Hydro	Vashon	R-69	28:17.4
5	Jim Clark	Unlimited Hydro	Seattle	*	31:52.8
6	Paul Tilzer	Unlimited Hydro	Bothell	*	46:38.2

1	Richard Kack	Unlimited Runabout	Bremerton	*	38:47.0
2	Norm Gilmore	Unlimited Runabout	Bothell	*	51:32.8
1	Mike Moreland	C-Stock Hydro	Playa Del Ray, CA	*	48:10.4
2	Bob Gierke	C-Stock Hydro	Edmonds	*	50:57.8
1	Jan Christ	B-Stock Hydro	Lynnwood	*	58:32.2
2	Steve Uhrich	B-Stock Hydro	Kirkland	*	58:47.6
3	Mark Gordon	B-Stock Hydro	Seattle	*	61:03.3
4	Jim McDonald	B-Stock Hydro	Corvallis, OR	*	74:32.8
1	Earl Garrison	B & 25SS Runabout	Edmonds	*	70:59.2
2	John Myers	B & 25SS Runabout		R-77	73:32.2
1	Bryan Anderson	A-Stock Hydro	Seattle	*	83:51.0
2	Greg Selvidge	A-Stock Hydro	Edmonds	*	84:37.0
3	Larry Ingalls	A-Stock Hydro	Seattle	*	86:27.6
4	Rick Christenson	A-Stock Hydro	Eatonville	*	86:45.2
1	Dave Potter	OPC S & U Comb	Seattle	226	20:03.0
2	Stu Diebert	OPC S & U Comb	Mountlake Terrace	*	22:00.4
3	Tom Losvar	OPC S & U Comb	Mukilteo	656	24:19.8
1	Robert Schey	OPC-SE	Everett	*	56:26.6
2	George Abbott	OPC-SE	Kent	*	57:04.6
3	Larry Lewis	OPC-SE	Seattle	442	59:10.8
4	Fred Burr	OPC-SE	Seattle	*	60:38.6
5	Clyde Jacobs	OPC-SE	Seattle	*	65:49.2
1	Greg Horn	OPC-SJ	Seattle	*	32:48.0
2	John Abbott	OPC-SJ	Renton	*	33:24.4
1	Larry Swinford	OPC-SI	Seattle	930	48:13.8
2	Tom Cain	OPC-SI	Bremerton	*	59:01.4

Some boat numbers, place, times & names unavailable

Wartinger-de Souza in Hospital

Bob Wartinger, a Boeing Airplane Company manager, had his troubles when he hit the bank, not the Kenmore or Bothell bank but the Sammamish Slough bank. Wartinger, one of 16 racers who didn't finish, hit a submerged log that ripped off his turning fin and hurled him face first into the muddy shoreline. Bob recounted his harrowing experience:

"I was out in front in B-Stock Hydro on the downriver run back to Kenmore–had been first on the upriver run and got a good start out of Marymoor (the downstream run). The boat ended up partly in the water and out (on the bank). I was face-planted into the shoreline muck (out of the boat). I knew something was wrong with my neck so I just stayed still, knowing that someone would be along to help." Mishaps like this are the reason boat racers are required by the APBA to wear helmets and life jackets.

Wart continued: "I could hear the other guys behind me roar past. Ed Klopfer was at the rear of the pack and he stopped to see if he could help. He's one of the great guys I met and knew through racing. I asked him to take off the prop and stick it in my lifejacket (which he was still wearing) because I knew that when the boat was towed to Kenmore and the guys put it away, the competition might look at the numbers on the prop and order a duplicate–the things you worry about when you are young and competitive.

Bob Wartinger upstream at Bothell in B-Stock Hydro.

"The EMTs showed up, stabilized my neck, got me into the ambulance and took me to Northwest Hospital. In the emergency room, the nurses were pulling off my boots and lifejacket, which were full of mud. One of the nurses exclaimed, 'what is this?' holding the prop up in front of my eyes. I had forgotten about asking Ed to tuck the prop away inside the jacket…I explained to the nurse what happened–she may still be shaking her head years later. The X-rays showed a compression of the C2 (upper neck) vertebra and I was popped into bed for the night.

"Steve de Souza, who was running C-Stock Hydro was in the class ahead, slid into a rocky bank (created for erosion control) near the Bothell Bridge turn and absolutely destroyed a new C-Hydro. I glimpsed the wreckage as I went by on my way down and saw that the boat was part way up the bank.

"After I was in bed at Northwest Hospital for about an hour, in hobbles Steve. He sat down on the floor, leaned against the wall and we told each other our stories of the day. He was released and going home, not spending the night, and stopped by to see what was up with me. I remember that he said he was really sore.

"The next morning, I was visited by my regular doctor and was able to get out of the hospital with a one-night stay. He told me to stay pretty still at home for at least a week, no driving, going to work, etc. At one week, I went back to work at Boeing…It definitely was a painful injury for a while. I went to rehabilitation for a few weeks to heal up…my doctor said it might take three months to get the muscles in shape.

"My wife Jan, at the time, was very supportive during the recovery…After about two months (of intense rehabilitation) I was itching to race; so, I asked some friends to pick up the boat and they took it to Lake Ming in Bakersfield, California. I flew down and raced the boat feeling pretty sore after a couple of heats and took it easy. As I remember, I didn't tell Jan that I was going to race, probably implied that I was going to watch."

Yeah right, that's a man for you. We don't listen to what we're told a lot of the time, well maybe most of the time!

KJR radio station's Emperor Smith presenting Bob Waite wining Slough Race trophies.

1973 Race Schedule (Partial)

April 8	36th Sammamish Slough Race
April 22	Sammamish Water-Ski Race
May 13	Cottage Lake-Woodinville
June 3	Silver Lake-Everett
June 16-17	Moses Lake Regatta
July 20-22	Green Lake-Heidelberg "Best of Boat Racing"

1973 Tidbits

Ski-raceboat driver, Jay Maxwell, who used to work for Bob Jacobsen (1950, 1952 Slough Race winner) was victorious driving his OPC in the Sammamish Water-Ski Race towing John Garrett in the C class. Maxwell would make a significant impact in the Sammamish Slough races during the upcoming years.

Jay Maxwell towing Mike Garrett to first-place in Class-C of 1973 Water-Ski Race.

Two Slough Race drivers set Kilo straightaway records in Modesto, California. Bob Wartinger set the 25SS Hydro mark at 65.996 mph and future Slough Race driver, Barry Woods of Vancouver, Washington, broke the century mark for OPCs at 116.538 mph. My good friend, Dave Culley, won the well-deserved SOA Sportsmanship Award for the year, which was presented during the December SOA meeting at the Kirkland Eagles hall. The club commodore for 1974 was not identified.

1974

New Start Location for Slough Race

The outboard flotilla of the Pacific Northwest was set to converge on Lake Washington, except this year they would start from a new location. Sammamish Slough Race officials continued their long tradition of tweaking the marathon-like event by changing the starting point location again. The new site was at Lake Forest Park, about 1-mile across Lake Washington from the Kenmore public boat launch area, the seventh different site since the race began in 1934.

During the preceding weeks, race co-chairmen Dick Rautenberg and Chuck (Charley) Walters of the Seattle Outboard Association published articles through the news media about the venue change. This year the Slough Race would start at noon on Sunday, April 7, from the beach at the Lake Forest Park Civic Club.

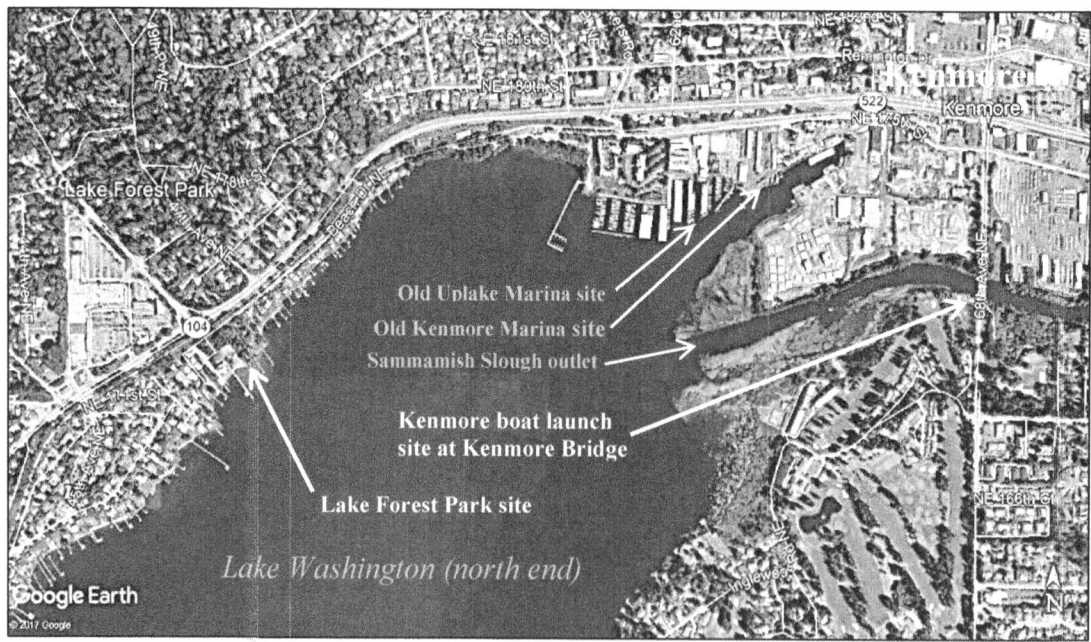

New Slough Race start location at Lake Forest Park across from Kenmore.

There had been complaints from the locals about traffic congestion and from recreational boaters who were unable to use the public boat launch because it was full of race personnel vehicles, raceboats and trailers, which blocked access for the recreational boaters during race day. And local officials wouldn't give the club exclusive use rights for the 1974 race. This coupled with the site's limited space and the added congestion from the OPC boat entries, forced the venue change.

In years past, the OPC boats launched from other areas, milled around in the lake and then made running starts into the Slough. This gave them an advantage for winning the fastest time trophy. This year race officials required the marathon drivers to make standing starts form the beach just like the outboarders, making the race starting procedure equal for all entries. There wasn't a need to draw for starting positions. Every class started from the shore, in line with each other and after starting, they headed straight across the lake into the Slough.

No Clear Favorites This Year

Fans and officials wondered if Bob Waite could continue his win streak or would there be a new winner. It was obvious to some that Bob's older equipment was becoming unreliable and his luck fading. Aside from the newer high-tech marathon boats, there were newer and faster Unlimited outboard hydros that Waite's competitors were still fine-tuning and making them more reliable and possibly the next winner.

Both of the race co-chairmen (Rautenberg & Walters) and Dave Culley were among the list of contenders. Culley had a new Jones cabover and an unproven, highly modified racing engine. They and others were thinking about dethroning Waite, the crafty old veteran. It was anyone's grab in the Unlimited OPC class. Seattle's Dick Sharp and Henry Zacharies of Surrey, B.C., were gunning for last year's winner, Seattle's up-and-comer, Dave Potter. Bob Wartinger was aiming for another win in the B-Stock Hydro class. Would California's Mike Moreland make the long trip north again?

"Cattail Culley" Prevails

Dave Culley of Kent, head guru of the *Valu-Mart* Unlimited Hydroplane, finally got his win although it wasn't easy. Culley took a day-off from his frantic duties of preparing for the coming "thunderboat" season and scooted to his first overall victory in the Slough Race. This time, his fortunes were better than in 1971 when he ended up in the cattails shortly after his start.

Dave had a handicap right from the start. All the other drivers left him in their wakes because it took three "cranks" (pulls of the starting rope) to start his engine. He had a couple of crewmembers holding the backend of his boat out of the water, but it didn't help because of the cranky engine. In a recent interview, Dave gave me the following inside story about his two-way run through the Slough.

"By the time I started, everyone was gone. I passed a few boats by the time I got to the river and a few more in the Slough" (the beginning stretch between the entrance and first turns) "I caught up to Waite" (had his usual quick start and was in the lead) "before the marina and golf course (Wayne) and was following him–I had speed on him.

"As I was following him I was thinking where am I going to pass him? It wouldn't be until Woodinville before I could make a pass" (mostly winding turns between this point, Bothell and on). "So anyway, I was close behind and right after he went under the marina bridge, his engine stopped and I almost ran over him! Because he stopped so fast, I went off (maneuvered) to the left of him and hit the golf course walking bridge (a piling) and it collapsed."

I said: "The bridge collapsed?"

Dave Culley driving his Unlimited class hydro across the finish line in first place at Kenmore.

He said: "No my boat collapsed. Part of the sponson deck and non-trip, but I kept going and thought I've got to be careful here. So, I'm going slower–pretty slow around and through Bothell and, darn if I didn't foul a spark plug! I'm now running on 3-cylinders (4-cylinder Mercury engine) and limping up towards Woodinville. And here comes Charley Walters up behind me. I thought he would pass me but it was pretty tight through the Woodinville train bridges so I just moved over and he went by. I was on his wake and my engine started running better but I couldn't pass him. So, he beat me on the leg up (to Marymoor) and I came in second."

I asked if he patched-up his boat with 100 mile-an-hour duct tape (while the other classes were finishing and during the breather period between runs). Dave replied: "I used a piece of aluminum, duct tape and anything else I could find and then changed spark plugs and leaned out the engine" (adjusted carburetors before final leg start).

"One-hundred mile-an-hour duct tape" was an old saying by boaters who used the very sticky and strong tape to patch and hold together pretty much everything. It has been used in the past to patch the Unlimited "thunderboat" hydros that sped well over 100 miles-per-hour in the Seattle Seafair races. Dave continued about his return run:

"I came off second behind Walters at the start and immediately passed him. I was thinking I had to get way ahead of him because I didn't know how far he was ahead of me on the uphill leg (timewise). So, I had to go as fast as I could the whole way (to the finish). I had no mishaps coming down. It just ran good and I never saw anyone again…finishing at the Kenmore Bridge boat ramp" (his first overall victory).

Charley Walters, nicknamed "Honkers" by his racing friends (it was the name of his boat), had a chance for victory because he beat Cully by 1-1/2 minutes going up. But mechanical issues delayed him. He told the *Times*' Del Danielson after the race: "A wire came loose on the engine. I hooked it back up and got going again, but the vibration knocked it off again. I finally had to stop and beat it on with a rock (he wasn't carrying any tools). 'But it seemed pretty good' he said with a grin, it's the best I've done."

Dave Jenkins, with a third on the upriver run and a second on the downriver run, finished second overall. Walters, with his second-place finish on the upriver run and a fourth on the downriver run, finished third overall. Bob Waite managed to get his engine restarted on the upstream leg but finished back in the pack.

Bob Wartinger heading upstream floating on cushion of air won B-Stock Hydro class for second time.

Norm Gilmore of Kirkland, was the winner in the Unlimited Runabout class and Don Haack, who hadn't made a showing since 1968, was victorious in C-Stock Hydro. And Bob Wartinger was successful in gaining his second victory in the B-Stock Hydro event.

Marathon Boats Still Quickest

The OPC boys had the fastest time again. Dick Sharp of Mountlake Terrace, a veteran OPC driver who entered the Slough Race for the first time, took the honors in the combined OPC J & U class with the fastest overall time to date. The longtime Bryant employee was clocked at 20:03.0 in the featured marathon class. His time in his Evinrude factory powered craft bested Dave Potter's time from last year.

Greg Horn, from Seattle, won for the third time driving this time in the OPC-SJ division. Seattle's Don Sullivan, son of 1955 Slough Race winner, Bud Sullivan, was victorious in OPC-SE, Clyde Jacobus of Seattle won the OPC-SD class and Seattle's Larry Swinford, the engine loaner to Dave Culley the year before, made it two in a row in the OPC-SI category.

Dick Sharp Team Evinrude factory *Scotti Hull* powered by V-6 *Evinrude Super Strangler* engine.

Unsung Heroes Behind the Scenes

What you haven't heard about were the unsung heroes of the Slough Race. These were the hardy souls, the crew, who braved the cold water and weather to help their driver get going. They were the ones who moved the boats and equipment from the trailer to the beach and back, held the boats in the water at the pits, lifted the heavy rigs at the start and cheered them on, with their fingers crossed, to the finish.

Notice Bob Waite's crew in the foreground of the photo on next page waiting to give him a quick start lift. His wife, Mary Ellen (arms folded), was all dolled-up wearing makeup, earrings and a lovely fur hat to keep warm, all while wearing chest-high waders preparing for her hubby's lift. Mr. Waite obviously was not about to observe the "River Speed Limit" sign with a posted speed of 7 miles-per-hour.

Yes, they were the dedicated souls who wiped the oil off the engine, out of the bilge and packed all the stuff back onto the trailer after the race. Then gave you a hug or a high-five for a job well done regardless of how you finished. These were the spouses, children, relatives and friends who tirelessly gave their all for the good of the sport.

Bob Waite is obviously about to ignore River Speed Limit sign while crew nervously awaits Marymoor Park start-Bob's wife Mary Ellen is wearing fur hat, ear rings and chest-high waders.

1974 Sammamish Slough Race Results (by class)

Place	Driver	Class	From	Boat #	Time
1	Dave Culley	Unlimited Hydro	Kent	R-59	24:06
2	Dave Jenkins	Unlimited Hydro	Seattle	*	No time
3	Chuck Walters	Unlimited Hydro	Brier	*	*
1	Norm Gilmore	Unlimited Runabout	Bothell	*	*
2	Dave Brown	Unlimited Runabout	Seattle	*	*
3	Scott Ingram	Unlimited Runabout	Seattle	*	*
1	Don Haack	C-Stock Hydro	Redmond	*	*
2	Bob Gierke	C-Stock Hydro	Edmonds	*	*
3	Bob Weiss	C-Stock Hydro	Issaquah	*	*
1	Bob Wartinger	B-Stk-25SSHydro	Seattle	*	*
2	Red Taylor	B-Stk-25SSHydro	Seattle	*	*
3	Ed Klopfer	B-Stk-25SSHydro	Seattle	*	*
1	Bryan Anderson	A-Stock Hydro	Seattle	*	*
2	Rick Christiansen	A-Stock Hydro	Eatonville	*	
3	Greg Selvidge	A-Stock Hydro	Edmonds	*	*

1	Dick Sharp	OPC-J & U Comb	Mountlake Terrace	175	*
2	Dave Potter	OPC-J & U Comb	Seattle	226	*
3	Henry Zacharies	OPC-J & U Comb	Surrey, BC	*	*
1	Greg Horn	OPC-SJ & UI Comb	Seattle	31	*
2	Tom Losvar	OPC-SJ & UI Comb	Everett	656	*
3	John Abbott	OPC-SJ & UI Comb	Renton	*	*
1	Don Sullivan	OPC-SE	Seattle	325	*
2	Tom Stanley	OPC-SE	N. Vancouver, BC	*	*
3	Bob Bollinger	OPC-SE	Kirkland	*	*
1	Clyde Jacobs	OPC-SD	Seattle	*	*
2	Spencer Weaver	OPC-SD	Seattle	*	*
3	Ray Kramer	OPC-SD	Seattle	*	*
1	Larry Swinford	OPC-SI	Seattle	930	*
2	Ed Vollan	OPC-SI	Edmonds	*	*

Some boat numbers & times & unavailable

OPC Boats Unique To "Old-School" Outboards

The must-have "engine trim feature" in the tunnel boats was almost too easy to use. The driver, with the trim button usually located on the steering wheel, could easily, with the touch of a finger, change the boat's riding level at high speeds. Sometimes you could get into real trouble because it was so easy to use.

Occasionally the trim setting was set too close to the ragged edge, where a slight change of conditions would cause the boat to blow-over backwards. In this instance, as the boat's bow began to rise, it was too late for the driver to make a correction with the control switch. You'd be sailing through the air, and about to get dunked. This resulted in some bad accidents and some casualties (see Bob Carver sequence photos at end of this Chapter).

Bruce Klopfer OPC blow-over at Black Lake Race.

1974 Race Schedule (Partial)

April 7	37th Sammamish Slough Race
April 21	Sammamish Water-Ski Race
June 16	Crescent Bar on Columbia River
July 8	Desert Aire Regatta-Columbia River, Vantage
July 26-27	Green Lake Seafair Regatta
Sept 21-22	Devil's Lake Time Trials

Seattle Times Articles

This book owes a lot to the *Seattle Times* newspaper. A good share of the stories and statistics were based on articles written by the *Times* journalists. A complete history of the Sammamish Slough Race and related parallels of history wouldn't have been complete without them. Thanks to all the many reporters who wrote those wonderful and colorful articles about the "Crookedest Race in World."

1970s *Seattle Times* Building-Fairview and John.

1974 Tidbits

Earl Garrison, who won the Slough Race BU Runabout class two in a row, set a straightaway record of 65.000 mph in 25 SS Runabout class. Penny Rautenberg won the sportsmanship award and was elected club commodore for 1975. She was the fourth woman to be voted as sportsman of the year. Dorothy Dennis was first in 1935, Jackie Wallace 1959 and Bev Downing in 1964.

1975

Penny Rautenberg-First Woman Commodore

Commodore Penny

Penny Rautenberg was the first woman to be elected commodore of the Seattle Outboard Association, the 47th club leader. All 46 previous commodores, since the club's beginning in 1929, were men. George Brown, owner of Brown's Boathouse in Madison Park, was the first. His boathouse on Lake Washington was the original starting point for the Sammamish Slough Race. Penny was extremely well qualified for the job as she had been deeply involved with the club and race management since 1959.

Penny was heavily involved with the Slough races, especially in 1975 because it was her first year officially running the club as the commodore. She was extremely busy, still juggling family life and work along with her passion, helping in all aspects of boat racing–especially the Sammamish Slough Race. She knew that since the Slough Race was the first race of the year, its success would lead the way for the rest of the season.

1976 Commodore Penny Rautenberg

Penny was supporting race Co-Chairmen, husband Dick Rautenberg, and Charley Walters. Her responsibility was race control where she directed and communicated from the pits to race officials stationed along the Slough and at the Marymoor Park finish line. You could easily recognize her with her wavy blonde hair and a two-way radio pinned to her ear that was constantly blaring in between her communications. She was the force behind the race, "Race Control Central," controlling most of the activity in concert with Rick Sandstrom, the race referee.

Field Boosted for 38th Running

Two classes of first-time "amateur" boat competitors were added to the lineup for the 38th running of the classic Sammamish Slough Race. That was the headline news reported to the papers by veteran Slough Race driver Chuck Walters, only this year he wouldn't be racing because he was the race co-chairman. The 1975 race format was the same as last year except for the new classes that were added. The starting time was set for noon on Sunday, April 13, with the boats leaving from the Lake Forest Park Civic Center beach.

Owners of stock outboards, "Sunday drivers" or pleasure craft, who wanted to take a try at taming the Slough, were invited to register early on the day of the race. The two new classes were only for amateurs; designated Local I for 64 and under horsepower engines and Local II for 65 and over. Both divisions were only for non-racing type hulls with two passengers. The driver and passenger were required to wear an -approved life jacket and helmet.

The outboards and the OPC tunnel boats would again compete for bragging rights and the fast time trophy. The traditional Unlimited Hydro that accumulated the most points would be declared the overall winner as had been customary regardless of the fastest time. Dave Culley, last year's winner, was the favorite for the outboarders and Dick Sharp and Dave Potter were the picks for the OPC boys.

The race program included five classes of the outboard hydros and runabouts and five of the tunnel boats, including two categories combined in the Unlimited division (U-Unlimited and UJ). The Unlimited outboards would start first with all the other class; Unlimited Runabout, C-Hydro, B & 25SS Runabout, A-Hydro, OPC-Unlimited, UJ, SI, SE, SD, Local 1 and Local II starting five minutes later respectively. The return run from Marymoor Park was scheduled to start at 2:30 pm in the same order.

Celebrating a successful day of racing at Lake Lawrence: (L-R) Andy Anderson, Penny, "Little Andy."

Some of the OPC factory sponsored drivers were planning on entering the Slough Race for the first time, potentially finishing with faster times than ever with their latest high-performance factory racing engines. The "King of the Slough," Bob Waite, was not in the lineup because he was recovering from back surgery that was planned to correct years of wear and tear on his aging body. Dick Rautenberg, who was registered in the Unlimited Hydro class, was up for the challenge again and so was someone out of the past, 1963 winner Tom O'Neill. And there were rumors that a radio personality might enter if he could be persuaded.

Penny's Beginnings in Racing

Penny Kingdon, while attending Edmonds High School at the age of 18, witnessed her first boat race, the 1959 Slough Race with husband-to-be, Wendell Ewing. Penny, an attractive and vivacious teenage waitress, was the eye of many a boat racer who frequented "Al's Diner." The popular Edmonds eatery was across the street from "Andy's Boat House" where Ewing was a mechanic. Eventually they married and after attending more boat races, Penny caught "boat racing fever," a desire to become a part of the exciting sport–a passion that has lasted for 58 years and counting.

A racing season or two later and during her early volunteer work for the club, Penny met a seasoned race driver, Dick Rautenberg. They became friends and after one thing led to another, they married. Soon after, she joined the SOA and began contributing by assisting with registering and scoring duties at the club's regattas.

This time period was the true beginning of Penny's successful calling as boat race official extraordinaire, even though she was uneasy about being near the water. Penny almost drowned swimming with some friends at age 12. She says: "I like being around the water but not in it." Over the years she had been involved with every facet of racing. Raising a family while having a full-time job was extremely difficult but adding another nearly full-time activity of boat racing management was something only a super-woman could achieve. This year, 1975, the club membership persuaded her to become the first woman commodore "the head honcho."

Culley Repeats as Traditional Winner

Dave Culley made it two in a row by winning the traditional overall title in the outboard Unlimited class. He told me that he got a great start from Lake Forest Park, headed across the lake on relatively smooth water, and into the Slough never to be headed. He never saw anybody during his run all the way upstream, it was a fast smooth and uneventful run to Marymoor Park. His crew was on the dock at the start encouraging him by holding up a sign, "Go Culley."

1975: Dave Culley about to cross finish line at Kenmore boat launch in first-place.

For the return run he got the No.1 starting position because of his first-place finish during the upstream run. His runs were lonely but he was happy about never encountering any problems either way, the first time that happened. His time was not published in any of the newspapers, only those of the first three OPC finishers. Maybe a sign of the times since the OPC boys were fastest for the last two years. Tom O'Neill was second and Dick Rautenberg came in third.

Three-consecutive winner, Don Haack of Redmond (1966-1968), took the honors in C-Stock Hydro; newcomer Drew Thompson won the combined B-Service and 25SS Runabout class and veteran, Steve Straith, won the A-Stock Hydro class. Drew Thompson's father is Andy Thompson, the former B-Runabout winner of 1955.

1975: Dave Culley leading the pack in Unlimited Hydro class at downstream start from Marymoor Park. Waiting OPC boats, which started after outboards, were on left Slough bank.

OMC Goes Against Their Word

The popularity of OMC (Evinrude-Johnson conglomerate) racing engines in the 1960s and 1970s flew in the face of a comment made in 1943 by the Vice-President for the company. He vowed to "Never make another Evinrude or Johnson racing motor again and furthermore he guaranteed they wouldn't make any spare parts either." So much for OMC never making racing engines again.

Kiekhaefer Corporation, maker of a complete line of factory Mercury racing engines since 1949 and rival, OMC, maker of factory Evinrude and Johnson racing engines were fierce competitors. Both were vying for top sales of their lines of factory racing outboard motors. APBA had approved racing classes for use of their limited quantity production high-performance motors for the outboard performance classes (OPCs). They both sponsored factory race drivers who were setting world records and vying for bragging rights in their respective divisions.

First timer Barry Woods, a factory pilot for OMC, entered the 1975 Sammamish Slough Race expressly for the purpose of setting the fastest time and the bragging rights that goes to the winner of the Unlimited OPC class. Barry planned to use his best tunnel boat and motor at the time, which included a 17' Glastron tunnel hull and a highly modified Evinrude V-6 cylinder engine. But he was leery about using his best propeller for fear of damage from running over rocks, sandbars and the other notorious Slough debris he had heard rumors about.

His "pickle-fork" tunnel hull boat incorporated all the latest high-tech equipment, including in-and-out tilt motor control right from his steering wheel. These controls allowed him to adjust or trim his ride attitude to maximize his speed and acceleration. He also was equipped with a two-way radio for communication with his crew on shore.

1976: Barry Woods leading over 100 boats driving Unlimited OPC factory *Team Evinrude Molinari/Saffa* with V-6 Evinrude engine in two-day marathon on Lake Havasu in Arizona.

Mad Scramble OPC Start

Race officials sent a patrol boat up the Slough after the last traditional outboard class started; the A-Stock hydros. They wanted to insure the Slough was clear of all racing craft and spectator boats before the start of the Unlimited OPC class. It was imperative that there was a safe path for the high-speed OPCs who were about to attain speeds upwards to 100 mph in the straightaways.

It was a mad scramble at the start from the beach at Lake Forest Park. All the boats lined up abreast of each other only a few feet apart. At the sound of the starter's horn they pushed their electric starting buttons to fire-up the 150-plus horsepower racing engines. It was a muffled whine of a dozen or so motors all starting in unison with Dave Potter, Barry Woods, Dick Sharp and Henry Zacharias leading the way across the white caped waters of Lake Washington.

The real horsepower rating of these motors was a secret, but those in the know knew the factory engines might put-out more than 200 horsepower. The Unlimited class motors were not well regulated by rules during this time. The APBA rules limited them to 99 cubic inches of displacement but aside from that almost anything could be done to squeeze more power out of them. They were real beasts of power.

Potter, who got a great start, led the way into the Slough with Woods in hot pursuit. They continued this way through Bothell and Woodinville and into the straightaways near Redmond. Woods was in Potter's roostertail and trying to overtake him but he didn't quite have enough acceleration to make the pass.

At this point his competitive spirit got the best of him and radioed back to his crew who were about to drive up to Marymoor. Barry told me in an interview: "I radioed to my crew, while running behind Potter, to bring up our best 3-bladed propeller for the downriver run." Potter continued to lead the rest of the way and crossed the finish line at a Marymoor Park in first-place. Woods finished close behind in second-place and Sharp was third.

Slough Slays Some, But Not Woods

A hot battle for the OPC class win was instore for the downstream run. Potter had the No. 1 starting position (based on his first in the upstream run) and Woods, now with his best prop, had the No. 2 spot. Potter got the jump at the start but Woods pulled into the lead with better acceleration as they got up to speed. Barry needed to push it hard all the way to beat Potter's upstream run time to claim a class victory.

Woods, a 34-year-old demolition and concrete cutting contractor from Vancouver, Washington, led with a commanding lead all the way downstream. He crossed the finish line at the Kenmore Bridge with Potter a distant second. Both drivers were tied in points with a first and second. The earlier radio call to his crew gave Woods the margin of victory and a new course record of 17:43.00, eclipsing Dick Sharp's record time of last year.

The rest of the day's action, headlined in the above sub-heading, was based on an article written by *Seattle Post-Intelligencer* columnist Bill Knight on April 11. Knight began: "Tom Cain started yesterday's Sammamish Slough boat racing madness by leaping into the water to rescue an unconscious driver. He finished it on a Wayne Golf

Course fairway, perched in his boat still clutching the throttle. Barry Woods set a record fast time in the Unlimited OPC class and Jack Morton, a KVI radio personality, started out going for a joyride and ended up as slightly damaged goods after his boat ran aground and he was pitched into the grass."

Rounding out the OPC class winners were John Abbot in UJ; Larry Swinford, SI; Bill Kelly, SE and Jan Norvold in the SD category. Jay Maxwell of Seattle, a veteran Slough driver who had previously competed the past five years in the water-ski races, won his first Slough Race class driving a tunnel ski-boat in the new Local I division. Ken Planque was the victor in the Local II class. Barry Woods was awarded the fast time trophy and Dave Culley the traditional overall prize to the winning Unlimited Hydro. Maxwell will play a major role in the next Slough Race.

While Potter and Woods were battling it out in the first section of the Slough, another battle was taking place on Lake Washington about half way across the lake. Tom Cain's date with destiny began shortly after the start of the Unlimited OPCs. He got a bad start and was well behind the others when Henry Zacharias of Surrey, B.C., blew-over backwards. He was the first driver to reach him and saw that Zacharias was lying face down in the water apparently in deep shock and "really spaced out."

Newspaper copy of Tom Cain skidding up riverbank (L)–high and dry on Wayne Golf Course fairway (R).

Zacharias was treated for cuts and shock and later released from a local hospital. The boat flipped high in the air, pitched the driver out, and fell back on him in the water. A typical blow-over accident that wasn't surprising because of the strong head wind and rough water (see similar blow-over photo by Bob Carver at the end of chapter). Larry Swinford, who also had a bad start, joined Cain in the rescue. Now, soaking wet and undaunted, Cain climbed back into his rig, re-started and he and Swinford resumed racing. Near the Wayne Golf Course, just after the Down River Marana turn, Cain hit a wake, went out of control, slammed into a bank and was hurled, boat and all, about 50 feet up and over onto a fairway, an astonishing feat only to be seen in a Slough Race (see photo on preceding page).

Jack Morton ended up with a few cuts and bruises when riding with Tom Losvar in a V-bottom marathon boat. The boat hooked on the return run, hit a rock, bounced a few times and slammed into a grassy bank. He asked Knight of the *Post-Intelligencer*, "Who ever got grass stains from a boat race?"

Staging Race Not Easy

The tireless work of planning and running a regatta was seldom discussed in the newspapers or boating magazines, first there's the scheduling-way in advance, and finding race sites, local sponsors and getting commitments. Then filling out all the paperwork to obtain a race sanction from APBA, the national governing body, permissions from local city authorities, police, and safety by insuring an ambulance was on site at all times.

Then there was driver registration, race site set-up, patrol boat operator recruiting, race official duty assignments and volunteer recruiting. One set-up that's wasn't required for a Slough Race was a race-course survey for official records along with placing and anchoring buoys. What's different from a normal race is the length and access of the 12-mile long course. The course is usually inspected the day before to insure no unsafe obstacles are present in the Slough.

During the early years of the race, members of the outboard club would spend a Saturday or Sunday the week before to clean-out the Slough. Many times, they had to cut-away fallen trees or remove wayward logs that were blocking the Slough (see "Old-Timers Cruise" in year 1956 of Chapter 10).

Timing and Scoring

Race timers and scorers were stationed at the upper end of the race course (Marymoor) where they start the timing at the designated start time (always at noon). The timers would one-by-one stop their watches individually as each boat crosses the finish line per class. Keeping track of which boats were in each heat was difficult. The scorers observed and documented each entry by boat number with a time. Later they organize their summary sheets by class (they knew from registration what boat numbers were in each class). This takes a lot of skill and knowledge of the boats and different classes because by the time the boats finish, the slower boats get passed and all the classes get mixed up–it was very confusing.

Then the process is reversed for the return run. The scorers, timers and stop watches are returned to the Kenmore finish line, usually by boat down through the Slough to the finish line. They start their stopwatches at the pre-determined time when the downstream run is scheduled to start. Then after the race has completed the scorers all meet together and determine what the actual times were by subtracting the time intervals, five minutes for every class starting after the first class, the Unlimited hydros. Confusing, yes, that's why it's so important to have experienced and competent personnel. A mistake could cost a driver a win or placing.

In some races only, the overall winner's time was given, in others the winning time of each class and still others with a time for every finisher. The later was the case for the 1973 race where most likely the stopwatches had split second hands. One or two timers could record the times because they had "a split" or a second "stop button." A race official with a two-way radio was needed at all bridges to help stranded drivers and report race status and for safety reasons.

Stopwatch with split second hand

Newspaper Views Varied by Club

During the mid-1970s Slough races, the two Seattle newspapers covered the race differently. The *Times* favored the outboarders and the *Post-Intelligencer*, the marathoners. Their articles and results were written based on the respective boat club's race reports with each giving the results of their classes first. The results in this book are based on the *Times'* articles because the *P-I* articles were not readily available, only a few that were saved by my mother and some from the race drivers or their families.

1975 Sammamish Slough Race Results (by class)

Place	Driver	Class	From	Boat #	Time
1	Dave Culley	Unlimited Hydro	Kent	R-59	No time
2	Tom O'Neill	Unlimited Hydro	Seattle	177-R	*
3	Dick Rautenberg	Unlimited Hydro	Mountlake Terrace	*	*
1	Dave Jenkins	Unlimited Runabout	Seattle	*	*
2	Dave Tonge	Unlimited Runabout	*	*	*
3	Earl Garrison	Unlimited Runabout	Edmonds	*	*
1	Don Haack	C-Stock Hydro	Redmond	*	*
2	Steve DeSousa	C-Stock Hydro	Edmonds	*	*
3	Bob Gerke	C-Stock Hydro	Edmonds	*	*

1	Drew Thompson	B-Ser-25SSHydro	Seattle	*	*
2	Bob Maschmedt	B-Ser-25SSHydro	Seattle	*	*
3	Greg Selvidge	B-Ser-25SSHydro	Edmonds	*	*
1	Steve Straith	A-Stock Hydro	*	*	*
2	Dan Kirchner	A-Stock Hydro	*	*	*
3	Bryan Anderson	A-Stock Hydro	*	*	*
1	Barry Woods	OPC-Unlimited	Vancouver, WA	35	17:43.0
2	Dave Potter	OPC-Unlimited	Seattle	226	18:11.4
3	Dick Sharp	OPC-Unlimited	Mountlake Terrace	175	19:32.1
1	John Abbott	OPC-UJ	Renton	*	*
2	Lee Davies	OPC-UJ	*	482	*
3	Stu Diebert	OPC-UJ	Mountlake Terrace	*	*
1	Bill Kelly	OPC-SE	*	*	*
2	Tom Stanley	OPC-SE	N, Vancouver BC	*	*
3	Larry Lewis	OPC-SE	Seattle	442	*
1	Jan Norvold	OPC-SD	*	*	*
2	Spencer Weaver	OPC-SD	Seattle	*	*
3	Ray Kramer	OPC-SD	Seattle	*	*
1	Larry Swinford	OPC-SI	Seattle	930	*
2	Doug Kamm	OPC-SI	*	*	*
1	Ken Planque	Local I	*	*	*
2	Mike Price	Local I	*	*	*
3	Bruce Klaper	Local I	*	*	*
1	Jay Maxwell	Local II	Seattle	XX	*
2	Tom Losvar	Local II	Everett	*	*
3	Wayne Peeters	Local II	*	*	*

Some boat numbers, place, times & names unavailable

1975 Race Schedule (Partial)

April 13   38th Sammamish Slough Race
April 20   Sammamish Water-Ski Race

1975 Tidbits

Bob Wartinger was awarded the 44th SOA Sportsmanship award. Slough Race fastest time holder, Barry Woods of Vancouver, Washington, set a world competition record in the modified unlimited OPC class at 88.620 mph in Eufaula, Alabama, on September 1.

The OPC marathon boats have their own club (Northwest Outboard Association) and a separate race schedule. The Slough Race was the only event in the Northwest where they competed with the Seattle Outboard Association drivers.

Race officials (L-R): Rick Sandstrom-referee and Dick Rautenberg-chairman.

1976

Rough Water on Lake Greets Drivers

The 39th annual Sammamish Slough Race was scheduled to start from the beach at the Lake Forest Park Civic Center for a third year. Race co-chairmen Dick Rautenberg, Chuck Walters and Burt Fraley, with second-term SOA commodore Penny Rautenberg as race control, planned to run this year's event. Fraley was in charge of the OPC boat activity and the others the traditional outboard activities.

The weather report for Sunday morning on April 11 was for stiff southerly wind conditions that were expected to whip up whitecaps at the north end of Lake Washington, not what race officials or race drivers wanted to hear.

The race was set to start from the beach at noon with a smaller field than in past years, about 59 entries. The entries consisted of five traditional outboard classes, four OPCs and two for Local I and II drivers. As in the past four events, the racers made a standing start from the beach, headed across the north end of Lake Washington into the mouth of the Sammamish Slough and wound their way upstream to Marymoor Park.

As predicted, the water was getting rough before the start. Dave Culley told me that he tried to persuade the traditional Unlimited outboard drivers to all take it easy across the wind-blown whitecaps and then hit the throttles wide open as they entered the calm water in the mouth of the Slough. Yeah, right! No one wanted to do that so it was a battle to see who could go the fastest skimming across the windblown whitecaps.

All but Rautenberg Braved Whitecaps

At the sound of the starting horn, half a dozen F-Hydros roared away from the beach. Their engines with open exhaust were screaming away, echoing their deafening high-pitched sounds to the excitement of the spectators on the beach and dock. It was disturbing the peace for most of the local lake residents to the north and south, including up the hillside along Sheridan Beach.

Culley, whose crew gave him a quick-start-lift, got a great start and jump on all the other Unlimited Hydros. He hightailed it across the lake at full-throttle without any concern about the wind-swept whitecaps. His 12-foot Jones cabover handled Lake Washington's rough water well. He didn't worry about a blow-over; the only thing on his mind was being first into the Slough. Dick Rautenberg decided to pull out because he knew his hydro wasn't suited for the rough water they would encounter at the start.

Bob Waite, who couldn't compete last year because of doctor and wife's orders following back surgery, got a bad start. His cranky engine and sore back kept him behind all the others at the start. His aging engine finally started after a few more cranks by a crewmember, but by then he was all by himself, way behind his competitors. You would bet he wished he had those fancy trim features the tunnel boats had so he could tilt-in his engine to keep from blowing-over in the wind.

1976: Bob Waite's late start against the wind in whitecaps at Lake Forest Park.

Culley was way out in the lead and all by himself when he finished his upstream run at Marymoor. He knew he had an advantage because of his first-place finish. He got the No. 1 position for the start of the downriver run, an advantage he would need because of the Slough gremlins lurking in the bushes downstream. Soon after his crew showed up they rested, hydrated and maybe had a few beers along with the bucket of fried chicken that Dave provided. Then, refreshed, they prepared for the return run.

On the downstream run near Bothell, Dave's boat went out of control and slammed to a stop partly up a steep bank into a bunch of weeds and bushes, the boat's transom and engine was still in the water with the motor running slowly. "It pitched me out over the right side with my feet on the ground still holding the throttle and steering wheel" (he was leaning half in and half out of the boat). "I kept the engine running and pushed the boat back into the water, jumped back in and kept going. There were leaves, branches and sticker bushes all over the boat."

Dave's chances for victory apparently had gone by the wayside but he continued on running, but slower and still in the lead. Bob Wartinger, in his borrowed D-Stock Hydro, had passed all the other boats ahead of him, except for Culley, after they conked out or became stranded. Culley was still ahead of Wartinger but his outfit was running poorly–much slower. Wartinger, who almost caught up to Culley, was in his wake at the finish line for second-place. He was the only other finisher in the traditional Unlimited Hydro class.

Culley Wins 3 in a Row

When Culley, from Kent, Washington, finished, there was no fanfare at the Kenmore Bridge finish line, just a wave of the checkered flag and Dave's friendly return wave to the officials as he and Wartinger sped by. Penny Rautenberg, SOA commodore and race referee, was among the officials on the shore at the Kenmore boat launch finish line who witnessed Culley's third win, very satisfying for him, but a lonely end to his successful day of racing.

1976 Dave Culley: Slough Race first place in Unlimited Hydro class just before finish at Kenmore Bridge.

Culley and Wartinger continued slower out of the Slough and across the lake to the pits at Lake Forest Park. It was even lonelier there for the first drivers. All the race officials were in Kenmore timing and scoring, the boat crews were driving back from Marymoor and all the spectators were gone because the start was the only part of the race that kept them there. Most everyone knew that by the time the boats finished they would be strung out and it would just be just a formality at the finish. Dave told me about his victory greeting at Lake Forest Park: "There was nobody there!"

When Culley and Wartinger arrived at the pits, they jumped out of their rigs into the water, waded to shore and parked their boats bow-first onto the beach. Then they walked wearily across Lake City Way to fetch their vehicles and trailers that were parked in the shopping center. Space was limited at the civic center, so most of the drivers were instructed to park elsewhere. Only a few select rigs, like out-of-towner Barry Woods, had permission to park near the beach.

There were no reports about the starts and order of finish for the other classes except for the Unlimited tunnel boat start. Their high-speed run into the strong headwind across Lake Washington provided most of the day's excitement. The drivers with finger-tip control of their engine trim had a huge advantage for staying upright and preventing blow-overs because their potential 100 mph speeds coupled with the strong headwind made for precarious driving conditions.

Two groups of race officials timed and scored the race. The first group, including Penny Rautenberg and one of the race chairmen, started the race at Lake Forest Park. The other group was stationed at Marymoor Park awaiting the boats to finish the upstream run. The Lake Forest Park group drove over to the Kenmore boat launch after all the classes started to perform the timing and scoring for the finish.

A patrol boat ran up the Slough after the last traditional outboard class started–the A-Stock hydros. This was to insure the meandering waterway was clear of all racing craft and spectator boats and there was a clear path for the high-speed Unlimited OPCs. They were about to start and attain speeds upwards to 100 mph in the straight stretches.

Burt Fraley's OPC raceboat.

Woods Cuts Slough-Second Time OPC Victor

Barry Woods cut his way up and down through the Slough to his second straight victory. Woods, who during the week cuts through concrete for a living with powerful diamond bladed saws, cut through the Sammamish Slough in an even more powerful raceboat over the weekend. His factory "Team Evinrude" Unlimited class OPC won handily, powered by a near 200 horsepower, Super Strangler V-6 Evinrude, clamped onto the transom of a 17-foot Scotti tunnel hull craft. Although his time was slower this year, a two-way clocking of 19:04.9, it was still impressive with his flying speeds approaching 100 mph in the upper straightaways of the Slough.

Woods told *Seattle Post-Intelligencer* reporter Bill Knight after the race: "It was a more tiring race this year than last. The setup we ran wasn't as fast (as last year) and we had a kind of lousy run coming down. We didn't get the acceleration out of the turns. But we didn't have any problems. It was a great day–a great race and these are great people (the race committee)."

1976: Barry Woods in 1st place cutting under Bothell Bridge in Unlimited OPC class.

Maxwell Takes Shortcut-Spectators Scramble

The real story of the Slough Race was what unfolded about a mile and a half upstream during the second-to-the-last heat in the Local II class for rigs with 65 and over horsepower engines.

The story begins early Sunday morning on April 11, 1976. In the immortal words of Skip Fornier as told to the *Post-Intelligencer's* Bill Knight the day after the race, "It was a helluva way to spend a Sunday." Fornier was a neighbor of Jay "Pepe" Maxwell who lived in a Lake City apartment complex just above Maxwell. Slough Race driver, Maxwell, told me the following in an interview during September of 2015:

"I was in a great part responsible for the final demise of the Slough Race. I followed the Slough Race for a long time when I lived close to Bob Jacobsen (1950 & 1952 Slough Race winner) and worked for him performing odd jobs." The 6-foot something "gentle giant," born in Ballard of Scandinavian ancestry, told me: "You were supposed to have an observer on board (basically ballast). I had my skier lined up who I pulled in the Sammamish Ski-Race for several years but he pulled out early the morning of the race. So, I conned my neighbor upstairs, Skip Fornier, into coming with me. He had no idea what was instore for him," and neither did Maxwell!

His boat, a 16' Barracuda tunnel boat, powered by a powerful 6-cylinder Mercury engine, was the same craft he drove winning his class during the Sammamish Water-Ski race of 1973. Pepe told me during the interview:

"When we were about to start, I told Skip to just get back there and hang-on." He rode with his back pinned against the transom and hung on for dear life to the ski-rope support bars on each side (see photo on page 478).

Maxwell told me he was driving his Barracuda craft downstream, when it took a shortcut over the bank on a turn just before the Wayne Golf Course. His boat was handling poorly, especially in the turns, because he was using a back-up propeller this year–he ruined his best prop in a race the year before.

As he made a right-hand turn approaching the Bothell-Juanita highway bridge, his boat hooked violently to the right. The resulting force propelled him and his rider up and over the bank cutting-off a bend in the river. They slid at a fast pace over rocks and grass, somewhere between 100 and 200 feet in an arc. A small crowd of spectators who were partying and watching the action scattered in several directions, all fleeing for safety up the bank to higher ground. Unfortunately, one fan who was down lower in or near the water, was hit broadside by the oncoming boat as he was running up the bank for safety. He ran right into the path of boat as it was skidding across the bank.

Maxwell's accident location in 1965 Slough photo.

The spectator, Ron Clausen, was a freshman pole vaulter for the University of Washington. This day he vaulted himself right into the hospital. Clausen was transported first to Northwest Hospital and eventually to Harborview Hospital for his trauma-care treatment. The student sustained cuts, bruises, a broken leg and a pelvis injury.

After things settled down, Maxwell and his rider, Fornier, recovered somewhat from their shocking experience. They pushed the boat back into the Slough, straightened the bent prop, restarted and limped back to Lake Forest Park. There they reported the incident to race officials, loaded the boat on the trailer and headed home still shaken by the accident, not knowing the consequences of their actions.

Jay Maxwell and rider Skip Fornier in Local II OPC class during downriver run from Marymoor Park.

In the following weeks a lawsuit ensued where the insurer, APBA, the SOA and the local city officials were named. Maxwell was involved in the lawsuit only to the extent of a deposition where he explained what had happened. Eventually, after several years of go-arounds between the plaintiffs and defendants, the litigation was settled out-of-court by APBA's insurer. Clausen, who originally filed for $150,000 in damages, settled for the cost of his medical expenses in 1979, after three years of litigation.

On April 15, 1994, some 18 years later, Craig Smith of the *Times* quoted Clausen who was at the time was a quality assurance manager for Boeing. The title of Smith's article was "UNPREDICTABLE 'SLOUGH RACE' A BYGONE RITE OF SPRING:" "Clausen...who lives in Kirkland, said his vaulting was 'never the same' after the accident and he never competed again. The former two-time state prep champion from Shorecrest High School lost his Husky scholarship and said he had to drop out of school. He declined to say how much he received in the settlement but said the sum basically covered his medical expenses.

"Clausen said: He had regularly attended the race and always had enjoyed it until the accident. 'It wasn't my intent to shut the race off, but I had to get the bills paid and it did kind of ruin my pole-vaulting career.'"

1976 Sammamish Slough Race Results (by class)

Place	Driver	Class	From	Boat #	Time
1	Dave Culley	Unlimited Hydro	Kent	R-60	24:10.6
2	Bob Wartinger	Unlimited Hydro	Seattle	*	26:19.6
3	Dan Kirchner	Unlimited Hydro		*	31:12.2
1	Dave Jenkins	Unlimited Runabout	Seattle	*	29:43.6

2	Craig Selvidge	Unlimited Runabout	Edmonds	*	33:18.0
3	Steve Greaves	Unlimited Runabout	Seattle	*	40:00.8
1	Don Haack	C-Stock Hydro	Redmond	*	30:43.5
2	Steve DeSousa	C-Stock Hydro	*	*	30:55.1
3	Gerry Borden	C-Stock Hydro	*	*	32:42.0
1	Jan Christ	A-Stock Hydro	Lynnwood	*	43:17.2
2	Mark Kirchner	A-Stock Hydro	*	*	*
3	Jerry Hopp	A-Stock Hydro	*	*	*
1	Darrel Sorenson	24 SS Runabout	*	*	43:23.9
2	Jeff Reins	24 SS Runabout	*	*	*
3	Drew Thompson	24 SS Runabout	*	*	*
1	Barry Woods	OPC-SST	Vancouver	35	19:04.9
2	Dick Sharp	OPC-SST	Mountlake Terrace	175	25:31.6
1	Stu Diebert	OPC-UJ	Mountlake Terrace	*	22:12.1
2	Rick Adams	OPC-UJ	*	213	24:58.5
3	Randy Zavalas	OPC-UJ	*	280	26:00.8
1	Greg Horn	OPC-SE	Seattle	31	25:09.6
2	Fred Stevens	OPC-SE	*	*	25:18.2
3	Dick Lee	OPC-SE	*	316	25:42.4
1	Ray Kramer	OPC-SD	Bellevue	*	*
2	Jan Norvold	OPC-SD	*	*	*
3	Gary Hansen	OPC-SD	*	*	*
1	Larry Christensen	Local I	*	*	*
2	Steve Whiteman	Local I	*	*	*
3	Bob Jacobsen	Local I	Ballard	*	*
1	Mike Price	Local II	*	*	*
2	George Batterfield	Local II	*	*	*
3	Greg Hamper	Local II	*	*	*

Some boat numbers, place, times & names unavailable

1976 Race Schedule (Partial)

April 11	39th Sammamish Slough Race
April 17	Sammamish Water-Ski Race
July 31	Green Lake Seafair Regatta
Sept 12	Silver Lake-Everett
Sept 18-19	Lawrence Lake-Yelm
Sept 25-26	Devil's Lake Kilo Regatta-Lincoln City, Ore.

1976 Tidbits

A number of world 5-mile competition records were set on Lake Lawrence in Yelm, September 18-19. Harold Tolford set marks in C-Service Hydro and Runabout at 57.692 and 53.019 mph. Bob Wartinger bettered the B-Mod Hydro record at 62.630. Kilo straightaway records were broken at Devil's Lake on September 25-26. Earl Garrison of Edmonds sped to 58.443 mph in 15SS-Runabout, Harold Tolford at 62.156 mph in C-Service Hydro and Bob Wartinger in B-Mod Hydro at 71.598 mph and in his

C-Mod Hydro at 71.835 mph. Penny Rautenberg was elected to a second term as SOA Commodore and Howard Shaw was given the SOA Sportsmanship Award.

Race Control Central

A few years later, still acting as "Race Control Central," Penny married Andy Anderson, the 1959 and 1960 Slough Race champion. They were a strong team at managing and running boat races on the local and national circuit. Andy was the APBA professional racing chairman and Penny the secretary for 13 years. They both were honored with the highest honor given by the APBA, induction into the "Honor Squadron." Penny was elected SOA Commodore for three more times including 1978, the clubs 50-year anniversary. Her five terms (1975, 1976, 1978, 1979, 1982) were the most for an officer since the club was formed back in 1929.

1977

Sad News-Historic Race Ends

"Traditional Slough Race dropped from schedule" was the headline printed in the *Times* sports section on March 10, 1977. Seattle Outboard Association spokesman, Dick Rautenberg, reported the sad news, for outboard race drivers and fans in the article following the headline:

"The Sammamish Slough Race is about to become extinct. The annual kickoff event to the outboard-racing season in the Pacific Northwest has been dropped from this year's race schedule because of insurance problems according to a spokesman for the Seattle Outboard Association.

"'It looks like the end of a long tradition,' said Dick Rautenberg, a longtime organizer and participant in outboard racing. A spectator, Ron Clausen, was injured during last year's race. Clausen, a University of Washington pole vaulter from Seattle, suffered a broken leg when a boat went out of control and hit him. He since has dropped out of school."

The accident was only a contributor to the race's ending. There were issues that compounded the club's difficult decision. When the APBA's insurer found out about the risky race, they discontinued coverage of the event. In order for the club to continue to run the race, they would have to find another insurer, likely much costlier.

The city of Redmond imposed a 7-mph maximum speed limit following the litigation that ensued after the accident, which required the club to obtain permission to continue the event. In addition to getting permissions from the four cities along the river, the club would have to place barricades on both side of the Slough for its entire length both ways; a total of 24 miles of fencing, which would be impossible to afford.

The main draw for spectators was that they could watch the race within a few feet of the dangerously close speeding raceboats, almost literally inside the action. Nice for the crowd as long as no one got injured, but very dangerous as was the case in Mr. Clausen's experience. In addition, there would have to be security personnel stationed all along the fence to keep the crowd from crossing into the protected area. All this of course, would be prohibitively expensive and impossible to control.

And so, the "Crookedest Race in the World"; "the bygone rite of spring," that ran over a span of 42-years (1934 to 1976), witnessed by some 400,000 spectators during its lifetime, was cancelled and never to be run again.

Sammamish River Outlet Dredging Cancelled

Dredging of the Lake Washington outlet of the Sammamish River was cancelled because of "bureaucratic red tape." Efforts to start the project were continuously delayed because of environmental concerns and lack of finding a disposal site for the thousands of yards of material that would be dredged. The delay was a similar story of political fighting that had lasted since the early 1900s about the river's dredging woes.

The channel that had been neglected for years was unnavigable since the 1960s. Unfortunately for boaters it will stay that way for the foreseeable future. As far as this book is concerned, the long history of the Sammamish River's dredging and maintenance history that was in the planning and construction stages since 1911 and occurred sporadically until the final dredging in the 1964-1965 period, is closed.

Snow Leopard mother & cub.

"Sasha Loses It"–Green Lake Racing Goes Bye-Bye

Green Lake suffered the same fate as the Slough Race in 1985. After the demise of the Sammamish Slough Race the Seattle Outboard Association focused their attention on their biggest event of the year, the traditional Green Lake race. But in the not-to-distant future they would find out their days of racing on the most ideal racecourse in the country were numbered. Residents had been complaining for years about the noise, parking issues, pollution and the cost of city services associated with the event.

The Seattle Park Board finally put an end to powerboat racing on Green Lake. The final blow was the death of a leopard cub born to "Sasha," a five-year-old snow leopard. "Sasha Loses It" was headlined in a history article written for historylink.org. The article stated:

"On November 15, 1984 the Seattle Park Board voted 5-2 to permanently ban hydroplane racing on Green Lake," because the cub's mother apparently abandoned her cubs due to noise from the boat race; even though it was found later that the cub died from a genetic defect. The leopard's death was the final blow to boat racing on the lake. A 59-year tradition that started in 1925 and ran continuously from 1925 to 1984 was lost to the whims of a cute little snow leopard.

1977 Tidbits

Slough Race drivers Ed Klopfer and Dick Sharp joined the APBA 100 MPH Club in the SST Tunnel Boat Class at Devil's Lake, Oregon. Klopfer of Seattle averaged 106.275 mph and Sharp of Woodinville averaged 103.330 mph.

Making good use of the old Kirkland ferry, *Leschi*.

1978: Seward Park marathon race (L-R) 213-Rick Adams, 157-Dick Sharp, 413-Burt Fraley, 482-Lee Davies.

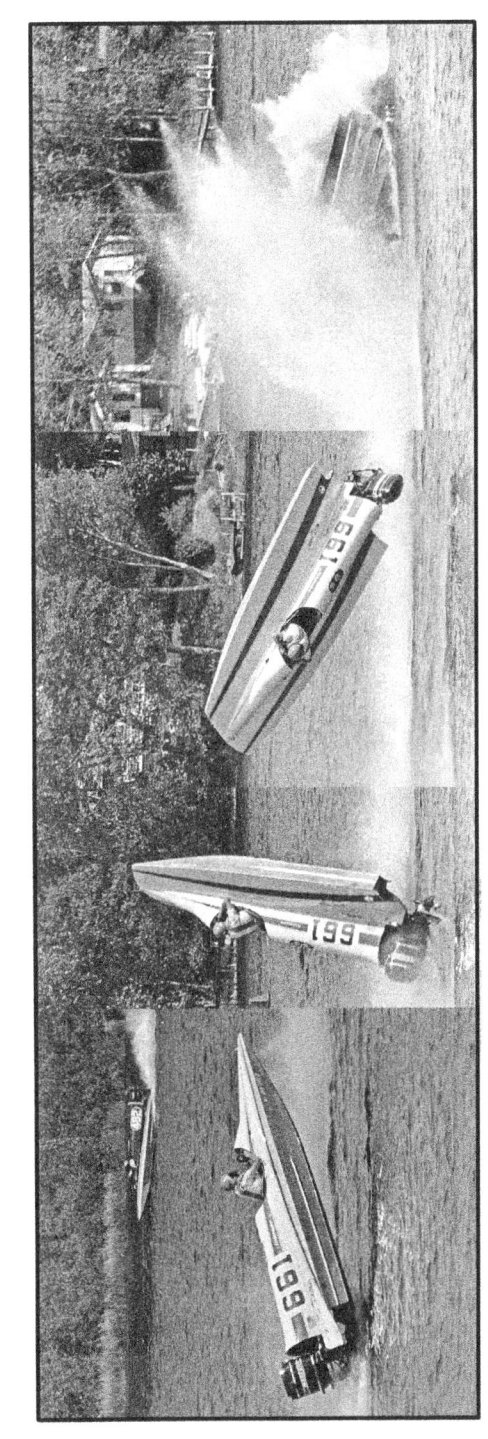

1976 Bob Carver photographs (4 shots out in 8 sequence arrays): Taken at Black Lake, Wash. OPC regatta of Bruce Klopfer blowing-over in Unlimited-J class, driving 16' Miles Master GB hull. Klopfer escaped with only minor injuries.

Chapter 16

Bob Carver returning from Green Lake still wet after Bob Batie ran over him (see photo on opposite page) carrying all his gear along with his Speed Graphic camera.

The Bob Carver Story
1917-1981

"The Man Behind The Photos"

"One of racing's most famous unknowns is a stocky balding red-head of ready grin and lightning reflexes, Bob Carver"

-Eileen Crimmin, APBA Propeller, April 1963-

Picture yourself out in the middle of a lake in a small boat only a few feet away from high-speed raceboats whizzing by at over 100 miles per hour. You're sitting on a small chair with your professional grade 4x5 Speed Graphics camera focused out to about twenty-feet while all your thoughts are keenly fixed on the fast approaching raceboat hurtling directly toward you. Then in an instant you know you have to bail-out into the water or risk being run over… And so, it was in the life of Bob Carver as a free-lance photographer who put his life in danger every time he was in his little boat, shooting photos of high-speed raceboats, hoping to get that "Pulitzer Prize" shot.

1954: Photo taken just before Carver was run over on Green Lake by Bob Batie in Benson's wild D-Runabout.

The above is a real-life story about one of the heart-pumping and dangerous consequences of a profession that is directly in the "line of fire." The photo on the left was taken by Carver during an outboard regatta on Seattle's Green Lake in the mid-1950s. What wasn't recorded was Bob being knocked out of his boat with his camera in hand into the algae-prone waters to avoid being run over. Batie, a good friend of my father, was the driver of my father's Switzer Craft, an odd looking but wild riding D-Runabout. The boat was just his style as he was a sometimes wild and crazy driver just like my dad. My brother and I ran the boat at home for recreation.

A number of us raceboat drivers liked to get action shots. We knew the closer the better for Carver to get that ideal shot. So, some of us purposely sped by him as close as possible. In this instance close was too close as Batie's boat caught a chine, hooked left and leaped directly into Carver's boat, knocking him into the water, camera and all. The boats weren't any worse for wear but both driver and photographer hit the water. When Batie came up for air, he said something like "Cuddles, did you get the shot?" When Carver came up for air he luckily had his camera in hand and hoped he got it. Although there were several accounts of this accident, mine is based on my memory of how it happened according to my conversations with Carver and Batie.

When I was working in Ballard during my inboard racing years, I would visit Carver at his Northlake office just above Gas Works Park. We would reminisce about the "olden days" when he was closest to my father. The most fun times were when he was first shooting the Sammamish Slough Races and was a working member of the Seattle Outboard Association as its vice-commodore. We discussed the latest boat racing gossip and which boats were most likely to be his subjects at the next boat race.

One of his gifts was his knowledge of a good or bad riding raceboat. He studied our boats while we were competing, learning which boats weren't riding properly or if its driver was driving out-of-control. These were the likely subjects that he would pan with his high-speed camera for a possible "spill shot." That may sound cruel but that was his business and he was just a bystander. You didn't want to be on his list of candidates because that meant he thought you were going to be in trouble at some point in a race. Fortunately, I wasn't on his radar, even though I had an accident that ended my boat racing career in a 266-limited inboard in the early 1970s. Yes, he got a shot of the tail end of the accident, but it wasn't spectacular, only some spray and a driverless broken-up boat floating aimlessly without power.

Bellingham Roots

Robert Wesley Carver was born in Bellingham, Washington, on March 23, 1917, as an only child to Foster and Myrtle Carver. Bob's family was well known in the area. His dad, Foster, served two terms as the Whatcom County Assessor. There, Bob grew up as a young boy, attended grade school, junior high school and was valedictorian at

Bob-grade school

Bob-High School

Newlyweds-Norma & Bob

Bellingham High School. After graduating from high school, he attended the University of Washington. A few years later he met his soulmate, Norma Coughlin and they got married in Ballard, a northwest Seattle neighborhood.

Four years later in July of 1945, he was drafted into the Army and then was honorably discharged in August of 1946 as a technical sergeant. Bob and Norma lived in Ballard raising four children; daughter Lynn, first son William, second son Casey and fourth child, son Keith.

Bob's first jobs were at Ballard Marine Railway as a shipyard pipe fitter, a bookkeeper for the Pittsburgh Paint Company and then was drafted into the Army where his love affair with photography started.

Carver family with children Lynn and Casey-photo taken by oldest son, Bill.

Bob-Army Sergeant

As a noncommissioned ordnance officer serving on St. Lucia Island in the British Indies, he didn't see any action. Things were pretty dull so to fill his time, he began shooting pictures at the suggestion of an Army buddy who worked in the base's darkroom. Bob learned the art of developing and printing working alongside his friend.

After being discharged from the army in 1946, he bought a camera for $18 and began taking outdoor shots. One day his friend, Russ Swanson, asked him to shoot some photos of outboards during a local race. The two snapped their shutters from a diving platform as the raceboats roared by. To Bob's surprise, the pictures turned out good.

He had returned to selling paint in the late 1940s for the Pittsburg Paint and Boone Paint

Army time on St. Lucia Island.

Morris Rosenfeld

Companies but his love, other than for his wife Norma and family, was shooting photos. He was influenced by his idol, legendary Morris Rosenfeld, who produced spectacular photos of boat-racing for *Yachting* and *Motorboating* magazines in the early 1900s. Bob's admiration for Rosenfeld inspired him to start taking photographs seriously. My late friend and APBA historian, Fred Farley, said in his "Tribute to Bob Carver" for the Hydroplane and Raceboat Museum in Seattle: "A friend once commented that Bob's work was the equal of Rosenfeld's." Farley said that Carver replied: "That is the finest compliment anybody ever paid me in my life."

1940s Carver home in Ballard Heights.

While working in the paint business, Bob was taking pictures as a hobby, which led him into his side business, free-lance photography in the early 1950s. He built a dark room and photo processing lab in the basement of his Ballard home where his magic with photos began and flourished. His developing chemicals probably permeated not only his lab, but upstairs in their home, likely a sore subject at the dinner table.

He teamed up with friend Russell "Russ" Swanson in the late 1940s. Swanson's greatest contribution to the duo, in addition to his photography, was his freelance writing. He began his career while working for Jerry Bryant at Bryant's Marina producing promotion material. Together they supplied racing photographs and stories for local and national media outlets, including *Boat Sport* magazine. One of their published works was a story about my family's boat racing, "Outboard Racing Family Style" in 1953.

The Bob Carver Story

My father at some point became acquainted with Bob Carver either through Swanson or at one of the Seattle Outboard Association's regattas in the late 1940s. Their association soon turned into a lifelong friendship. They were close during the 1950s when dad was race chairman of the Slough Race's when they started at Ward's Resort and the former Ward's Resort, Uplake Marina in Kenmore.

In the early to mid-1950s Slough Races, Carver would perch on top of the elevated swimming platform on the old barge at the outer end of the dock at Ward's Resort. There he shot photos of the starts, usually with some of the spectators watching behind to visually tell his story. It was crowded on the platform as there was barely enough room for him, my dad and the race starter. Then he would venture by small boat up the Slough to his favorite location after all the classes had started and we (the boat racers) were on our way. He would take his action shots from a bridge or along the river bank upstream.

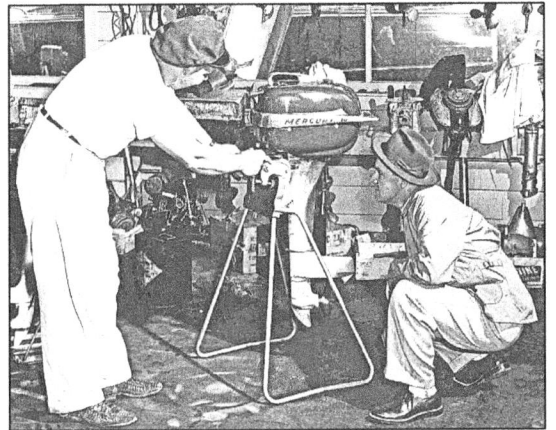
1953 *Boat Sport* photoshoot at Al Benson's Lake City shop-Bob Carver kneeling-Benson demonstrating.

Public photographs of Carver were rare. The earliest found was during a photo shoot for *Boat Sport* in 1953 at my dad's first outboard shop in Lake City. Bob was partners with Russ Swanson at that time. Bob usually took the photos and Russ would write the articles–they were a great team. During the boat races, they would both take photos. Later-on during the Slough Races, Russ would be at the starting barge and Bob would be positioned somewhere on the Slough. After the friendly end of their partnership, Bob usually positioned himself in Bothell taking photos, often with friends or family members with their own cameras.

He was known throughout the world for his ability to capture incredible action photos, recording the split-second action as a moment of history. You could easily recognize one of his photos because of the clarity and crispness of his prints along with

1953 Boat Sport magazine photo of Benson family, Don (left) mother Dorothy & Jimmy.

his captivating compositions. Throughout this book you are treated to his masterful artistry with over 75 of his outboard racing photos beginning in the early 1950s through the late 1960s.

1958: Carver's famous "Flying Mercs" water ski jump shot on Puget Sound near Des Moines, Washington.

One of his most unusual and controversial shots was taken from under a water-ski ramp when he was shooting a promotional shot for an outboard boat and motor manufacturer at Betts Marina on Puget Sound in 1958. He caught one of those once-in-a-lifetime action shots from underneath a floating water-ski jump where he photographed the boat a split second after its transom[55] with two engines running was ripped-off the boat's stern (the back part of the boat). Waves at the time raised the

---

[55] The surface that forms the rear of the craft where an outboard motor is held in place by screw-on clamps or metal bolts.

jump to a point where the lower units of the two Mercury motors, ("Mercs,") impacted the bottom edge of the ramp. The speeding boat combined with the impact of the engines caused the mishap.

A split second later Carver captured the two separated halves of the boat with the driver still looking forward. The pilot was Jack Leek, a well-known Tacoma outboard driver and expert mechanic. The back of his helmet and life-jacket collar are barely visible in the space between the two outboard motors. The right-hand side of the

Normal shot of boat flying over water ski jump (photo taken from shore side of jump).

windshield is adjacent Leek's head. One of the engine's gas tank is visible through the sheared-off rear section's lower-right where the transom was intact before the impact. Leek turned around to see his craft split-in-two a moment later.

The shots prior to the mishap were side shots like the one above. About the time driver Leek and the promotion crew had decided to end the shoot and pack it up, Carver asked if he would make one last jump. This time Carver positioned himself in his small boat at the very end of the jump almost under the top of the ramp. He wanted a shot from underneath as the boat was passing overhead. Leek thought that since he had made this jump without incident about 20 times before, it would be safe to make another. And the rest was history.

The man behind the camera.

The "Flying Mercs" shot, was not to be made public as it was deemed bad advertising for the manufacturer. It's been said that after Carver took the shot he immediately went back to his shop and developed the photo. He left Leek stranded on the bow of the boat trying to hold the rear end out of the water to keep it from sinking. Carver told him he would send help and hurried his way to shore and immediately drove back to his shop in Seattle to find out if he captured the moment on film.

He brought several prints to the Seattle Outboard Association's next meeting where he excitedly showed them to the club members. Unbeknownst to him, this was a historic showing of one of his most famous boating-stunt photographs never to be published. After seeing the accident photo, the company instructed Carver to never publish the photo, the now famous "Flying Mercs" photo. The story goes-on that he eventually published it some 10 years later after the outboard motor company's president retired. It was one of those incredible shots capturing a split second of history that was unintended for the public eye.

Carver in newer larger boat donated from Art Louie's Sporting Goods store in Lake City.

In the mid-1950s my dad provided Carver a pram[56] type boat to enable him to maneuver around on the lakes and other race courses to get close-up shots somewhere in the middle of the racecourse. This opened up a whole new class of shots that were intimate and action packed. Somewhere along the way, the boat's name became *Cuddles*, likely from his boat racing friends who thought he looked nice and cuddley in his small boat. The name stuck because the rest of the bigger boats he obtained, per gratis for advertising purposes from local boat dealers, all bear the same name.

---

[56] A small utility boat with a transom bow rather than a pointed bow

1962: Don Hanson, boat number *XX* in the Sammamish Slough Race D-Hydro class.

Carver became so popular that other boat and motor shops in the area did one-upmanships to get their advertizing on the side of his boat, which they donated. Notice the stool he's sitting on in the previous page's photo. It's an innovative swivel seat that turns freely from side to side enabling him to smoothly follow his subjects for better shots.

One of his most noteworthy photos was the one on the cover of this book. He was shooting this at one of his most favorite positions; across from the Down River Marina on the South Slough bank next to the Wayne Golf Course nursery bridge (I sometimes call this bridge the Marina Bridge). Many times, his sons Bill and Casey, were by his side shooting their own photos hoping to make the newspapers. They still were striving to be published as father Bob was the one who got the shot (above) of the crowd avoiding the raceboat sliding by under them.

Carver-Crimmin Dynamic Duo

Bob Carver

In the late 1950s Bob quit the paint business to go full-time into commercial photography. By then his brilliance behind the camera was legendary. He had a broad spectrum of clients in the marine, sports, industrial and publication arenas. He soon outgrew his small lab and office at his Ballard home and moved his operation to the Christy-Lambert building on Westlake Avenue.

Eileen Crimmin

There, he set up a larger darkroom and had enough room for an office.

In 1960, he hooked up with free-lance writer, Eileen Crimmin. She shared space in Bob's section of the building but soon their businesses grew to the point where Eileen needed more space and moved into another section of the building. They soon became partners in all kinds of photo-journalism projects and combined their business resources, although both had separate commercial businesses. They became recognized as a dynamic-duo in their business. Bob took most of the photographs and Eileen wrote the articles.

Carver's Genius

In 1963 Eileen Crimmin wrote an article, "The Man Behind The Photos," for the American Power Boat Association after they honored him with an award plaque for his outstanding contributions in photography. It was published in APBA's *Propeller* magazine in April, 1963. The following are excerpts from her article: "One of racing's most famous unknowns is a stocky balding red-head of a ready grin and lightning reflexes, Bob Carver.

APBA Award plaque

"Racers who know the photos well know the photographer not at all because the congenial 'Cuddles' follows the rule of all top artists and gives the publicity spotlight to the flipping, speeding boats and drivers he photographs. Carver's ability to capture spills in the split 1/1000ths second of occurrence, as well as his uncanny depth perception enabling him to secure the proper focus, soon had racers clamoring for prints.

"How does he do it? Is the question asked most frequently by racers and non-racers alike? His talent begins with racing knowledge-he predicted for years that the now disintegrated unlimited, *Miss Seattle Too*, (see photo at end of chapter) would be on its head one day and ends with the superior timing that clicks the shutter at exactly the right moment.

"As admitted master of his field, Carver serves boat racing at major races by being 'on assignment' for as many as seven magazines, various newspapers and both wire services, in addition, that is, to his capacity as official APBA photographer. Specialist though he is, Carver is far from limited to action photos. The

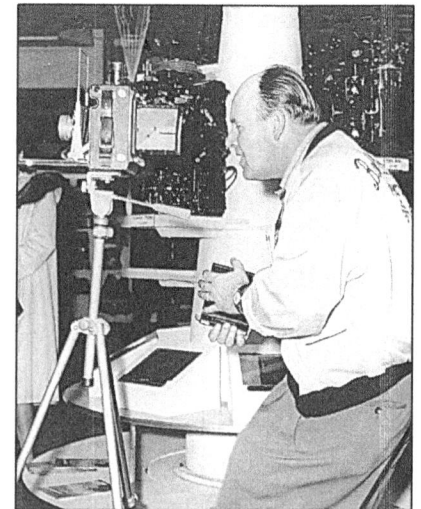

Carver shooting at Seattle Boat Show.

business world taps his occupational skill as a free-lance commercial photographer. All these photos, from festival queens to logging trucks, bear the same distinctive stamp of realism caught with depth and clarity that characterizes his spill shots.

"Anyone wishing to convince himself of the impact 'Cuddles' has made upon racing need only examine press media prior to 1948. Boat racing photos? There were only a few. Contrast this with the month of July 1959 when more than 110 Carver photos appeared in magazines, newspapers and regatta programs! Or the hydroplaning book in which 64 Carver photos outnumbered those of all other contributors!

"At the APBA's annual meeting (1963) in Miami Beach, Fla., past President Red Peatross presented a plaque to Bob (see photo on previous page) "in appreciation for contributions to APBA," thus officially recognizing his outstanding work and the attention his photos have focused on the sport and on the Association. In an era when pictorial coverage was often the only coverage of an event, boat racing owes much to the little man who had splashed it across the press of the world and continued to keep it there, Bob Carver."

He Shoots by Ear

Carver has said "he shoots his photographs by sound." Yes, he does his homework on his subjects and pans them at races. But his true genius is his uncanny ability to capture on film the precise moment of the extreme action. And to top it all, he did it with a camera that shoots only one photo at a time, not like today's cameras that shoot continuously at multiple frames per second. The true essence of his fame was his instincts.

Carver was quoted in an Associated Press article written by Jack Hewins, December 11, 1960: "I shoot my pictures by sound. Once I bet a friend I had gotten a picture of an accident that happened behind my back. When the film was developed, I collected. I've

1973 Bob shooting with newer equipment, Multi-frame Nikon camera with telephoto lens.

learned that an accident can happen any instant and to never relax while on the water. I learned that lesson when I was sighting with an unloaded camera. Through the glass, I saw one of the most beautiful accidents I've ever missed.

"I don't think it's any more dangerous out there with the hydros than it is crossing a busy street. I'm always too busy to be frightened, but afterwards I'm a nervous wreck.

That's when I get scared–afterwards. People ask why I keep it up and I can't give them an answer. I guess I'm either stupid or mercenary."

Racing Photos Didn't Pay Bills

Although boat racing photography made him famous, his commercial business paid the bills. Shooting the sport he loved didn't bring enough food home for a family of six. What sustained his income was his superb primary business in the fish boat, marine, pleasure boat, general business, commercial and industrial photography fields. His racing photography legend garnered his plentiful commercial business.

Cuddles in the Calaboose

Like so many urban legends, this one had a mind of its own and continues to the present day by good friends of Bob "Cuddles" Carver. The story had many versions because of its telling over and over by many of whom are in the hereafter. It was the subject of several Seattle Outboard Association club meetings in the early 1950s after a weekend race on Lake Osoyoos in Oroville, a border town in Eastern Washington.

Cuddles, somehow ended-up behind bars on the wrong side of the border in British Columbia. He was locked-up in a Canadian jail just north of the race course. Who would ever think a mild mannered, lovable and cuddly man like Carver would end up in the brig?

I was there with my family and a group of other boat racers staying at the Edgewater Motel in Oroville. Our family was racing there at the time. We had a nice water-side room on the shore of the lake. The Chuck Hicklings, Jim Spinners, Ed Karelsen and Carver were all staying there. Carver most likely was saving his pennies and sleeping in his car at the parking lot just outside our rooms.

The story starts shortly after the first day of racing when Carver was nowhere to be found. I'm sure my parents and other friends thought he was still out in the lake napping in his little boat, *Cuddles*, after a long day of photographing. He might have been sipping some spirit-like beverage to ease his sore body after sitting all day in the middle of the lake.

The race site in Oroville was one of our favorites because it wasn't too far from Seattle, just far enough away to be in different surroundings. The motel was comfortable for a few night's stay in the summer. The regatta was usually a two-day race where we would stay until Monday, the day after the race, for a traffic-free drive back to Seattle over Stevens Pass. My brother and I loved the place because the lake was always warm, fun to swim in, and just a few steps away from our hotel room. The weather was always very warm and dry. I loved the familiar smell of sagebrush that was so common in Eastern Washington. Every time we traveled there for a boat race, we'd start smelling the scent not long after driving over the mountain pass.

As it turned out Bob probably was sleeping in his little boat and somehow floated north across the border ending up onshore in Canada. Apparently, the Canadian authorities apprehended him and took him directly to the local law establishment just across the border, including his boat. He was able to make the traditional phone call to someone at our motel.

Carver's 9' pram donated by Al Benson.

As the story continues, the local authority that confiscated his pram and all its belongings, including the beverages, was concerned about someone whose namesake was painted on the bow of his boat–*Cuddles*. Carver, called on the phone and said, "Come and get me. They don't want someone here named Cuddles in their establishment!" A short time later, dad and likely others drove the short distance across the border, chuckling all the way, to rescue their friend, Cuddles and *Cuddles* the boat. Carver was the talk of the motel group long into the evening while they were sipping the spirits and joking about Bob's hilarious experience. The "Legend of Cuddles in the Calaboose" goes on and will never be forgotten because of this book.

Carver & Crimmin-Awards and More

Bob Carver won many awards during his career, in addition to the APBA honor. The Seattle Outboard Association made him a lifetime member in recognition of his longtime publicity efforts. As a team, Carver and Crimmin won two national media awards. Later, Crimmin won several individual awards with Bob's photos, which were inseparable from her body-of-work. She wrote numerous articles for *Motor Boating* magazine and other boating articles ranging from recipes to racing. In the later years of her professional career, she wrote articles and manuals about how to write, including one's family history, historical papers and business-related articles. She helped me with my early writing for my family history and resumes for future employment. She was a fun person to talk to, always outgoing and very personable. I usually learned something when I talked to her.

1971 Eileen Crimmin & Bob Carver at Seattle Center covering a sporting event.

She and Bob were the people in boat racing circles who knew all the gossip. Many boat racers and friends would drop by for the latest news, sometimes when we were acquiring photos and sometimes for a lunchtime chat. Bob always treated me like family. He gave me a lot of photos for my personal collection as well as for promotion of the Seattle Inboard Racing Association's regattas. I was publicity chairman for a few years in the late 1960s. Bob was always enthusiastic about showing me his latest masterpieces, usually in his darkroom still wet and hanging to dry.

1964: Bob precariously atop stepladder in 16' boat.

In their joint business, their boating was done in a 16-foot Pacific Mariner pleasure boat with a 60-hp Mercury outboard motor for power; the same motor Slough Race drivers ran at over 70 mph. They both couldn't fit into the little 9-foot pram *Cuddles*. This boat was rigged with a stepladder securely attached by guy-wires for shooting large yachts, tugboats and most any other vessel high in the water. Eileen did the driving as she had experience driving her family's classic Chris-Craft as a youth. It probably was a little touch-and-go with the throttle while Bob was standing high on-top of the ladder, keenly focused on his shot.

Carver's Large Format Camera

Once you understand the time-consuming and complicated use of Bob Carver's camera, you begin to appreciate how talented and skillful he actually was; his genius. We're talking about a one-shot wonder here! The camera he used was a large format (4-inch by 5-inch film size) "Speed Graphic" model made by the Graflex Company, similar to the famous "press camera" of the day. It was American made, in Rochester, New York. No surprise at the time.

Variations of this model were in production between 1912 and 1973, with the most significant improvements occurring in 1947. Bob purchased his first Speed Graphics model in the early 1950s, most likely the latest "Pacemaker" model with top and side mounted rangefinder. It included a "focal plane shutter" capable of speeds of 1/1000ths of a second. This was Carver's favorite camera that he used in the early part of his era and was used by most photographers of his day and by professionals all over the world including most of the press. You weren't in the game without one.

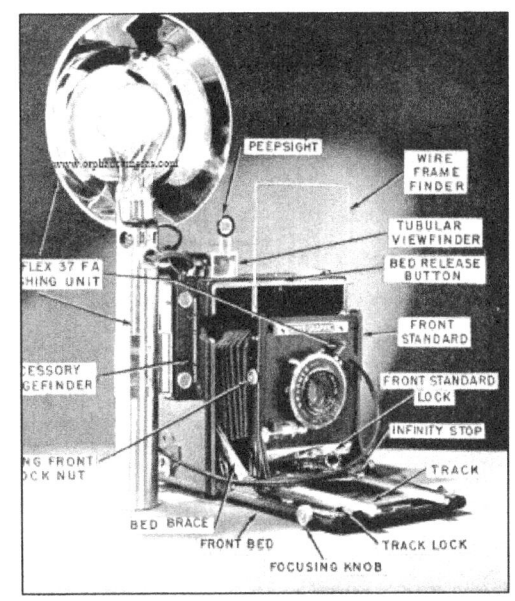

Carver's 1950s Speed Graphic Camera w/flash.

Today, it is considered a "slow camera." Setting the focal plane shutter speed required selecting both a shutter slit width and a spring tension. Each exposure required the photographer to change the "sheet film holder" (separate two-shot film container), open the lens shutter, cock the focal plane shutter, remove the dark side slide from the inserted film holder, focus the camera, aim and release the shutter (snap the picture). Although the film holder contained two film sheets, only one shot could be made in a fast action scene. This was why Carver was so remarkable–he got his shots one at a time, not like today's automatic power-driven, multi-shot cameras.

The camera included interchangeable lenses and accordion-like bellows that expanded and contracted when the focusing knob was adjusted. The unique focal plane

Rear mounting accessory for sheet film holder on Graphlex.

shutter was a type of photographic shutter that was positioned directly in front of the film. The sheet film holder was a removable cartridge-like container that held two sheets of film (one on either side). Each film sheet was protected from light by sliding covers.

Before Carver shot a photo, he would pull out the film cover on one side of the attached film holder and then shoot the first picture followed by reinserting the film cover to protect the exposed film. Next, he removed the film pack, turned it around and re-inserted it. Then he removed the second film cover to shoot the second shot. The final step is to reinsert the second film cover and remove the used film holder. He then inserted an unused holder and started the process over again and again, a very time-consuming process.

Film holders with removable covers.

Carver would pre-load dozens of his film holders at his office the day before a shooting. If he ran out of film holders, he had unloaded spares that had to be loaded on site or in his boat using a special black bag accessory with arm sleeves. He'd place unused film sheets into the bag, slip his arms in, remove the film sheet covers and load the film holder by feel. It was a time-consuming process. Carver was an extremely busy man during his boat-racing photo shoots. He had to be in almost athlete-like shape to perform his work as a professional high-speed action photographer.

1960: Carver holding flash camera on left with telephoto cameras, accessory bag and tripod on right.

Carver Gets High for Photos

One of Carver's more unusual opportunities was his commercial photoshoot on top of the 600-foot tall Seattle Space Needle during its initial painting. In the photos below you see the painter rigged-up in safety gear but where's Carver's gear? A life jacket and helmet wouldn't help him here. One of his talents was good balance and knowing how to steady himself under extreme conditions. All that experience came in handy high atop the Seattle Space Needle in dizzying nose-bleed territory.

1970s: Worker rigged-up and painting on top of Seattle Space Needle.

Bob Carver: Sometimes you just had to enjoy the view before going to work.

Eileen Crimmin wrote a very nice life story of Bob Carver for Seattle's *Fisherman's News* publication when he died in 1981. She summed-up his wonderful work career with the following: "Carver enjoyed career tenure with firms like Bayliner Marine, Marco, Mercury Outboard, Pacific Marine Supply (Shwabacher), Peterbilt, Ray Marine and many others including the *Seattle Times* newspaper. The *Times* staff photographers refused to accept boat-racing assignments, saying, 'Get Carver!' So, the *Times* did.

"Bob was survived by his wife Norma, three sons, Bill, Casey and Keith and grandson Robbie, all of Seattle; a daughter, Lynn (Carver) John and granddaughters Amy and Lori, all of Spokane; friends everywhere and the aforementioned millions of persons who for 32 years thrilled to the excitement and clarity of every Bob Carver photo they happened to see."

Hugh Entrop (left) famous outboard world speed record holder, Casey (Bob Carver's second son) & Bob on right after long day baking in sun shooting action photos of local outboard race.

Bill Carver-Family Historian

Bob Carver's oldest son, Bill, a retired Boeing mechanical engineer, has been a huge contributor and collaborator for this book. Bill supplied hundreds of his dad's magnificent photos while I provided our family photos that were missing from his archives. Bill has collected, preserved and restored most of his dad's photos that remained after his passing. Father Bob condensed his collection and sold most of his non-boat racing collection to downsize during his later years. However, he kept his favorites, mostly of his close boat racing friends and other favorites. He died in 1981.

Bill Carver, Bob's oldest son.

Bill has been a great resource to writers and collectors who have kept his father's images in the public eye. He has provided most of the historic photographs without compensation to honor his father's legacy. We've also exchanged many articles about the Slough Race and of his father's history. Bill helped me immensely with my preliminary and ongoing research for the book.

Thank You Bill! I couldn't have visually told the story without your father's wonderful photographs! A few of my favorites are shown on the following pages…

1956: Incredible photo of Hugh Entrop getting dunked in his skipping F-Hydro at Moses Lake.

1957: Mira Slovak piloting unlimited hydro *Miss Wahoo* completely out of the water at Lake Chelan.

504 | Taming of the Slough

1950s Johnny Sangster in B-Runabout.

1950s Harold Tolford's D-Runabout *Sandbox*.

1962: Dallas Sartz driving *Miss Seattle Too* in accident on Lake Washington. He survived!

The Bob Carver Story | 505

Early 1950s: Bill Rankin in his classic F-Hydro *Thunderbird*.

1958: Dick Brunes steering his D-Hydro with feet & holding throttle open with left hand at Green Lake.

1963: Mira Slovak test-driving new *Miss Exide* Unlimited hydroplane on Lake Washington.

Epilogue

2014 "Kenmore Hydroplane Cup" poster by artist Amberly (Gaul) Culley.

Return to the Slough
2014-2017

*"Unpredictable Slough Race-
A Bygone Right of Spring"*

-Craig Smith of the Seattle Times, April 15 1994-

The only racing up and down the Slough these days are raft races and foot races along the Sammamish River Trail. The actual Sammamish Slough Races of old are only a distant memory, except for the recent exhibition "Return to the Slough" event co-sponsored by the Seattle Outboard Association, a "season opener" each year.

The inaugural Slough revival event was planned for closed course races to be run at Log-Boom Park in Kenmore and token exhibition runs up and down the lower part of the Slough. Current and past drivers competed in the Slough runs which started from the mouth of the Slough on Lake Washington.

Amberly (Gaul) Culley
event founder.

None of this would have happened if it weren't for Amberly (Gaul) Culley, daughter-in-law to former three-time Slough Race winner, Dave Culley. The exuberant, fun-packed artist (her poster on left) was the brains and enthusiasm behind the event, the 2014 Kenmore Hydroplane Cup. She almost single-handedly revived the legendary races of the past, which were run between 1934 and 1976. They were run from Madison Park in Seattle to Lake Sammamish and back; a 25- to 50-mile marathon event in its early days.

Her tenacious drive and infectious personality brought the Seattle Outboard Association, the City of Kenmore and the surrounding communities all together to pull off what most thought was impossible, a revival of the bygone days of the Sammamish Slough Race. The highly anticipated Kenmore Hydroplane Cup was held on April 5, and staged in conjunction with the City of Kenmore, Seattle Outboard Association, American Powerboat Association and the Hydroplane and Raceboat Museum.

The Brainstorm

Amberly's brainstorm for this ambitious event began early in 2013. The lightbulb turned on when she was in the planning stages of a grant-sponsored art project that would memorialize the Slough Race in a public artwork. She recently was awarded an artist's grant from King County's 4Culture public development authority. The budding artist, because of her father-in-law's rich history in boat racing, thought: "Why not rekindle the historic race with an event advertised as a 'Return to the Slough' event?" Amberly's theme, which fit perfectly with her existing artwork project, was to reconnect the local communities with the history of the Slough Race.

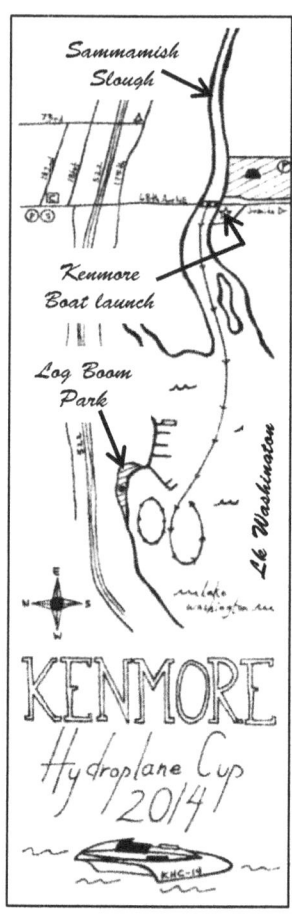

Megan Tanner's event map.

2014: Kenmore Cup exhibition runs downstream (photo taken from Kenmore Bridge).

They Humored Her at First

Amberly began her quest by trying to convince her father-in-law, Dave Culley, that she could pull off the event. He probably thought she was crazy. After all, resurrecting the Slough Race was deemed impossible. So, when she asked him to go around with her to gather support for the endeavor, he politely went along and humored her–he didn't really believe it was possible. When Dave's old Slough Race cronies heard the news, they thought "Yeah sure, this was never going to happen," just like Dave. They knew why and how the race ended and thought like everyone else, it would be impossible in the present day's environment.

Well, long story short, Amberly got the necessary authorizations to proceed. Though, this was just the beginning of an arduous year-long effort with extensive planning, approvals, promotion and volunteer recruiting needed to be successful. She couldn't do all by herself, as she had up to this point. She enlisted a well-rounded team of Jan Shaw (race chairman), Megan Tanner (logistics and volunteer manager) and Brent Hall (marketing and sponsorship director) for the 2014 spectacle.

A Slough of Boats

Former and current outboard drivers participated in the exhibition runs. The field included Bob Waite's restored F-Hydro and a few Indian canoes. They launched at the newly renovated Kenmore Public Boat Launch shortly after the dedication ceremonies. The drivers fired up their rigs and warmed-up heading toward the mouth of the Slough (toward Lake Washington) about 800 yards downstream. They circled back slowly and then squeezed their throttles roaring up to speed past the boat launch and under the Kenmore Bridge while a crowd of spectators waved from above. They headed upstream about 700 yards, turned around slowly at a buoy and then raced back downstream finishing to the wave of the checkered flag by an official at the boat launch.

2015 Event: (L-R) Jan Shaw-chairman, Rick Sandstrom-referee.

The schedule was set up for a group run of all the participants to be followed by individual timed runs and closed-course races. This was the Seattle Outboard Association's kickoff for their season of racing. It was an opportunity for the participants to test their outfits and entertain the spectators–not a true competitive event like the old Slough Races of the past.

Closed course races were scheduled to run around a set of buoys located off Log Boom Park, which is at the north end of Lake Washington. The plan was to have the exhibition runs start from the boat launch and travel out of the Slough across Lake Washington to the Park. Then the boats were to circle around a buoy and return back into the Slough and finish upstream just before the Kenmore Bridge.

But the weather gods played out a different story. They whipped-up whitecaps with strong southerly winds that blew up Lake Washington, right into the faces of the spectators who were watching from the dock and shore all bundled up braving the cool and windy weather. The biggest waves were at the north end of the lake, right where the closed course was set up. Only a few runs were made early in the program because of the winds that revved-up shortly after the first round of boats started. The closed-course races had to be cancelled because of water too rough for driver safety.

Past and present race officials were on hand to conduct the racing events. Jan Shaw, longtime race official and APBA Region 10 Chairman, was in charge of the racing activities with veteran official, Rick Sandstrom, serving as the race referee. Jan is another woman heavily involved in boat racing just like Penny Anderson had done before her. She is a lifetime member of the SOA and has been a key official in most every aspect of outboard racing. All the day's activities were held under the watchful eye of the proud race originator, Amberly (Gaul) Culley. The old cronies, including her father-in-law who didn't believe she could pull this off, all had to eat some crow!

2015 Event: Dave Culley and son Darryl before start.

Bob Waite's restored winner-previously 228-*R*.

2014 Kenmore Cup Participants

Driver	Class	From	Boat # or Name
Dave Culley	Unlimited Hydro	Woodinville	R-60
Kyle Lewis	Unlimited Hydro	Seattle	R-96
Dwight Malhiot	Unlimited Runabout	Seattle	R-147
J. Michael Kelly	Unlimited Runabout	Seattle	16-R
JW Myers	Unlimited Runabout	Seattle	R-77
Pat Gleason	B Utility Runabout	Seattle	19-R
Nate Brown	Inboard Runabout	Seattle	17
Freddie Kalama	Indian War Canoe	*	*Redwing*
Doug Reed	Indian War Canoe	*	*Loyal-C*

City of Kenmore Lecture

Amberly Culley organized a lecture that was held at Kenmore City Hall on April 7, 2013, to promote the upcoming 2014 "Kenmore Cup." A panel of former drivers and a race official spoke to an overflowing crowd that included many former drivers, including famous unlimited hydro driver Chip Hanauer.

Steve Greaves was the moderator with Andy Anderson, Penny Anderson (Andy's wife), Dave Culley, John Laird, and Lee Sutter as the panelists who spoke about their Slough Race experiences. They answered numerous questions asked from the standing room only crowd of 500 or so in the packed Kenmore City Hall.

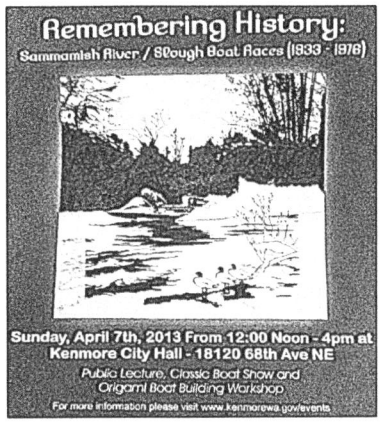

Amberly Culley's 2013 lecture poster.

Slough Race trophies on display.

Organizer Ms. Culley greeted the attendees who were able to gaze at some of the old Slough Race trophies on display in the lobby. The upbeat affair included a number of dusty Slough Race boats from the past that were taken out of storage. Dozens of former Slough Race drivers, most of whom were grayed, balding or bearded, including my brother Don Benson, were part of the audience.

Permissions Difficult to Attain

Staging the last Slough Races of the 1970s was difficult but nothing compared to all the hurdles and red-tape needed to be overcome for the 2014-2017 revival events.

Amberly told me recently that people in the know asked her, "How the heck were you able to do this," (obtaining all the permissions and approvals to stage the event).

Amberley's plan was to schedule this event for the first or second week of April; the same time period that the races were run since 1948. It was a seemingly impossible task for the present day. You can see below the many approvals and actions that were required for staging an event that is and was affected by so many requirements.

Approvals-Actions:
- Land and water use permission from the Puyallup Indian Tribe.
- Sound study on industrial noise compared to outboard racing engine noise.
- Water sample tests before and after the event.
- City of Kenmore use permit.
- King County Sheriff's approval (for traffic control).
- Coast Guard approval.
- Department of Fish and Wildlife approval.
- SnoKing Watershed Council (Snohomish & King County overseers of Sammamish River & tributaries).
- Sponsorship by the Seattle Outboard Association (SOA) and American Power Boat Association (APBA).

The studies and testing were the responsibility of Jan Shaw, who was the acting APBA Region 10 chairman and the Kenmore Cup chairperson. The rest of the activities were all accomplished by Amberly Culley, event originator and organizer. Tribal approvals were required because the Puyallup Indian Tribe owns treaty rights to the area around the Kenmore boat launch property.

Boat Launch Renovation Ceremony

Since about 1997, King County and Kenmore had been planning to extensively renovate the Kenmore boat launch facility. It had been an unimproved public boat launch with limited vehicle and trailer parking for years. It had served as the starting and finishing site for the Sammamish Slough Races from 1969 through the last race in 1976. The site at that time was graveled, not paved. The project was drawn out for some 17-years because of the long planning process that was plagued with political hassling and formalities.

The day's opening ceremonies, led by master of ceremonies Chip Hanauer, began with a specially-composed song, *Ripple*, the sounds of the Sammamish Slough, by local composer Rulon Jones. Then a Native American ritual was performed by

Puyallup tribal elder, Donna Star, with Amberly (Gaul) Culley alongside and other dignitaries including Kenmore mayor, David Baker.

Unlimited hydro legend Chip Hanauer-event Master of Ceremonies.

The tribe, "Sts'ahp-absh" (people of the Sammamish Slough) who originally lived on this site, was eventually integrated into the Puyallup Indian Nation. The Puyallup tribe still has the water and fishing rights to Lake Washington and the Sammamish River outlet.

Amberly, with grant funds from the 4Culture organization, told me, "My work ('The return to the Slough' painting) was not just because of my Native American heritage. It was about deepening a person's relationship to the place where they live–all because I was responding to a grant proposal on that specific topic." The topic was reconnecting Kenmore and surrounding residents back to the past when they raced or were among the thousands of spectators who enjoyed the "Crookedest Race in the World."

2015 Kenmore Cup and On

The second annual April Kenmore Cup was sponsored and run again by the Seattle Outboard Association in conjunction with the City of Kenmore. Amberly (Gaul) Culley, the originator, was the consultant for the event. Jan Shaw, the regatta chairman and APBA region chairman, ran it pretty much as originally set up by Amberly.

Jan was able to extend the Slough run to Squires Landing, about a quarter-mile farther upstream at the Swamp Creek outlet area. The closed-course races that were unable to be run in the inaugural program were moved eastward to a more protected area of Lake Washington (still in Kenmore) closer to the Slough entrance. The parking and shuttle services provided by the City of Kenmore were discontinued for cost reasons.

Dave Culley Dipsy-Doodles

The action in the 2014 to 2017 events was tame compared to the fiery drive-throughs, spectacular flips, spinouts and crashes of the past. All except for Dave Culley's unexpected run into the trees just upriver from the Kenmore boat launch. Culley, driving his beautiful mahogany and yellow-blue trimmed Karelsen F-Hydro aptly named *The Never Again* 7, did his version of a "dipsy-doodle" in front of the crowd lining the Kenmore Bridge.

Dave, who was making a run downstream, swerved abruptly to miss a string of ducks, which resulted in a high-speed spin-out into some low-hanging tree branches on the bank. The spectators on the bridge watched as Culley disappeared into the trees.

Dave told me about his dramatic accident in a phone conversation after he returned home from several weeks of rehabilitation.

"I was just up from the Kenmore Bridge…I was coming down the river and I had to move a little bit (toward the bank on his left) because there were some ducks swimming from my right to the left…and that put me toward the bank a little more. I had to make a right turn (to correct his path back to the center of the Slough). Well, a smart guy would let off the throttle but I didn't do that…I was rolling right along (going fast).

"I had power-tilt on the boat (like the OPC marathon boats). I can tilt it from one degree under to five degrees under. Anytime over 80 mph I kick it under, otherwise it will get loose (bow rises and could blow-over). So, I had it kicked under and if I would have had it kicked out, it wouldn't have ridden so hard on the sponson. All that added up…and I just got seconds to think about all this stuff, but I should have known better. It snapped to the right so fast that it pitched me out the left side, I didn't even know what happened…all I know, I was in the water real fast."

The action seemed to go in slow motion for a number of seconds until he was thrown out from the boat's front left side, tossing him half in the water and half into tree branches overhanging the Slough. A photographer took several seconds of high speed sequence shots of the accident, which were displayed on the Seattle Outboard Association's internet website. The sequence photos showed the complete action from start to finish, including multiple shots of the rescue by the safety patrol boat responders.

The safety crew was quickly on the scene and carefully placed Dave onto a stretcher board and into the rescue boat. He was in shock and soaking-wet in his racing gear. Culley suffered a sev-

2015: Dave Culley's damaged F-Hydro.

erely broken leg and was taken directly to a hospital. After several weeks in a rehab facility, he was discharged to his home, but it took physical therapy for a number of months to enable his 70-year-old body to go about normal activity again.

To date, this was the only mishap of the annual springtime affair. We can joke about it now but it was a serious accident and no laughing matter at the time. Especially, when Dave was able to get out of the house and see his beautiful Karelsen cabover damaged with half its left side missing, deck damage and numerous minor scrapes.

Culley holding his F-Hydro's cowling after the accident—none the worse for wear.

Culley's Fire Breathen' Engine

Culley's Fire Breathen' 850 engraved on engine head of race motor used in the 2014- 2115 Slough Race Kenmore Cups.

Dave Culley had a special motor he built up from a factory Mercury racing engine for his F-Hydro. The base engine originated from an 85hp, four-cylinder 1100cc recreational motor specially modified by the factory for racing in the mid-1970s. Dave modified it by further enlarging the intake and exhaust ports, adding custom pistons and his creation, a custom polished and finned aluminum cylinder head. Dave always liked to add humor to his adventures. He engraved "Culley's Fire Breathen 850" onto the back of the cylinder head. The arrow in the photo points to the special engraving.

The Never Again 7 Hydro

Dave's damaged custom-designed Ed Karelsen hydro is shown on the previous page. It included state-of-the art features specially designed for right turns on race courses. In addition to the powerful custom motor, it incorporated: left-of-center hull balance (for turning), engine electric-screw power-tilt, a rear rudder (turned with the engine) and rear sponsons. The rear sponsons created a tunnel on the bottom rear section for added hull lift. The hydro, built in 1985, was capable of speeds over 110 miles per hour.

Slough Race Memorials

John Laird, longtime Slough racer and the historian-caretaker of the Race, has done a number of things to remember the Slough races of old. His vision of memorializing the race was to build and place mementos in parks alongside the Slough. He eventually was able to achieve his goal but it wasn't easy.

Entrance sign to Brackett's Landing Park.

Donated park benches at Brackett's Landing Park on Sammamish River by the Jacobsen-Laird-Waite families.

2015: Slough Race park bench plaque.

Park Benches-Storyboard

Laird worked for months with city and county leaders to gain approval to place Slough Race memory benches somewhere along the Slough. Eventually he received permission to place them at Brackett's Landing in Bothell on the north side of the Sammamish River. Family members of former race drivers donated plaques, attached to the two park benches, with names of the drivers inscribed. He also

John laird holding Bothell Museum storyboard.

created a framed Slough Race storyboard for the Bothell Historical Museum to further memorialize the famous local event with photographs and accompanying history stories.

The four photos on the storyboard are shown in earlier chapters of this book. See these photos in Chapters 9, 10 and 14. The pictures, from left to right on the storyboard are: Bob Waite's 1956 overall win, John Laird's 1970 Unlimited Runabout class win, 1956 winners and overall winner Bob Jacobsen in 1952. The storyboard was donated to the Bothell Historical Museum by the Seattle Outboard Association.

2015: Rear view of Culley's rig with Mercury racing lower unit without powerhead.

Williams' Outboard Racing Museum

Past Slough Race class winner, Phil Williams, has a wonderful museum in his boat and motor shop in Puyallup, Washington. Inside "Phil's Performax Marine" facility is a collection of restored antique outboard racing motors, boats, photos, trophies, posters and other memorabilia. Although it is a private museum, the public is welcome to the shop at 5113-66th Ave E.

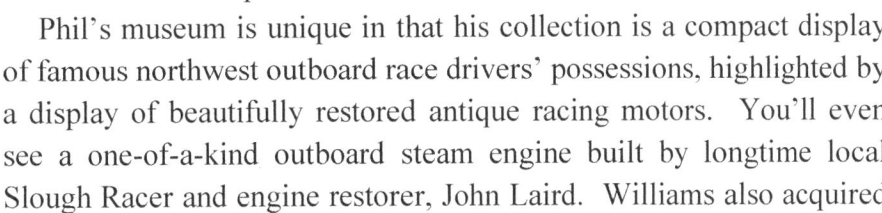
Phil Williams

Phil's museum is unique in that his collection is a compact display of famous northwest outboard race drivers' possessions, highlighted by a display of beautifully restored antique racing motors. You'll even see a one-of-a-kind outboard steam engine built by longtime local Slough Racer and engine restorer, John Laird. Williams also acquired Hugh Entrop's "the fastest human in an outboard" world-record plaque and the historical APBA "Jack Maypole Memorial Trophy." The Maypole trophy was awarded for the yearly highest increase of a speed record. It was retired to Entrop after he won the award three years in a row.

Outboard history is usually a forgotten sport because as old raceboat drivers pass on to outboard heaven, their memories fade away and their keep-sakes get lost.

2015: Phil's Performax Marine and museum in Puyallup, Washington.

The "Hydroplane & Race Boat Museum" in Kent, Washington, is huge, likely the largest of its kind in the U.S., nonetheless, there isn't enough room for outboard history because it is full of unlimited and limited hydro memorabilia. Phil's shop-museum in Puyallup is one of a few local and accessible outboard showplaces because it is displayed at his business unlike some private collections that reside in collectors' homes or other facilities.

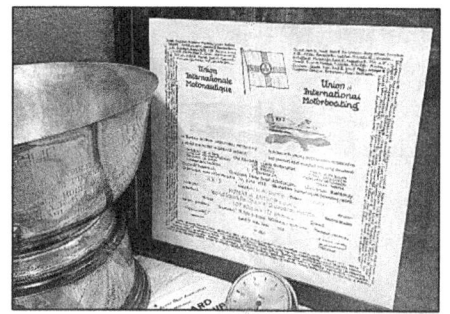

Hugh Entrop's world speed record awards in museum-APBA *Jack Maypole Trophy* left.

Phil, his wife Karen, and son Charlie maintain and run the shop where a few old-time outboarders congregate most every week to rekindle their friendships, reminisce with their racing stories and brag about their past racing accomplishments. A visitor also might run into a current successful outboard driver, way back in the shop, tuning up his racing engine in the well-equipped engine service department. I took the photographs in this section during a fun and entertaining reunion with past Slough Race drivers and friends who were interviewed for this book.

2015: Restored antique outboard motors in front office.

Phil Williams' Shop-Museum Photos

2015: Bob Waite's retired F-Hydro and F-Runabout

2015: Howard Anderson's retired F-Hydro.

Old-cronies meeting area amongst antiques.

2015: Some old-cronies gathering weekly at Williams' shop: (L-R) Don Benson, John Laird, Clayton Shaw, Phil Williams, Dave Culley, Wayne LaChapelle and Jim Benson (kneeling), your author.

The Kenmore Hydroplane Cup continues to be an annual affair for the Seattle Outboard Association. It's their first-of-the-season kickoff event that is still held in Kenmore. Jan Shaw, the ever-present racing official, remains the acting chairman for the event. Past and present outboarders, fans and your author hope this tradition continues into the foreseeable future.

We former outboarders, present racers and fans alike, look forward to the ongoing story of remembering the most famous outboard race in the Northwest and most likely in the country--"The Crookedest Race in the World," the Sammamish Slough Race.

Charlie Williams with the last memento of the famous Sammamish Slough Race.

2016: Amberly (Gaul) Culley posing in front of Slough Race mural she painted on St. Vincent de Paul building in Kenmore, Washington.

Hydroplane & Raceboat Museum Photos

2015: Hydroplane & Raceboat Museum in Kent, Washington-Miss Wahoo unlimited hydro replica on left.

2015: (L-R) Jim Benson (your author), Dave Williams (museum director), Don Benson holding pieces from Miss Seattle Too accident (see Carver photo of the accident in "Bob Carver Story" chapter).

Author's Hall of Fame Selections

Chuck Lyford   Chip Hanauer   Jerry Bryant   Penny Rautenberg
Bob Carver   Al Benson   Bob Waite   Don Benson
John Laird   Dave Culley   Ed Karelsen   Hugh Entrop
Andy Anderson Janis Lee   Bob Wartinger Billy Schumacher
Harold Tolford Jack Colcock   Bill Muncey

Slough Race Hall of Fame
(Your Author's pick of local SOA drivers)

"There are those that look at things the way they are, and ask why? I dream of things that never were, and ask why not?"

-Robert Fitzgerald Kennedy-

Andy & Penny (Rautenberg) Anderson: The Andersons were a dynamic duel. Penny is a unique woman in Seattle Outboard Association history. She was the first woman commodore and served for five years, a Slough Race chairman and "control central" during its last years and a longtime boat racing official. Penny served in nearly every office within the APBA and the SOA. She won several awards for her 58-years of dedication to boat racing, including the highest honor–induction into the prestigious APBA Honor Squadron. Andy was a longtime boat racer and official, a national champion and world record holder. He owned Anderson Marine, formerly Andy's Boat House, in Edmonds. He like Penny was inducted to the APBA Honor Squadron for 55-years of contributions to professional outboard racing.

Penny the official

Andy and Penny Anderson

Al Benson: "Benny" raced in the Sammamish Slough for over 30-years, became the first three-time overall winner, first four-time unlimited class winner and was the Northwest JU Runabout class originator. He was a lifetime Seattle Outboard Association member, two-time club commodore, publicity chairman and performer-stuntman in numerous Hollywood movie film clips. Al was Slough Race chairman, and outboard boat and motor dealer during the 1950s and father to boat racers Don and Jim Benson. He also drove the unlimited hydros *Miss Seattle* and *Miss Pay'n Save*, was boat manager for the *Miss Exide* unlimited team, co-owner and operator of Uplake Marina in Kenmore, limited-inboard driver and a world-record holder. Later in life, he was a tugboat operator in Ketchikan, Alaska.

Al "Benny" Benson

Don Benson: Don won his class in every Sammamish Slough Race from 1954 to 1960 except once when he finished second after flipping while in the lead just before the finish. He won national championships in outboards and inboards, set multiple world records in both and was one of the most experienced and successful drivers in the Northwest winning in all types of outboards and limited inboards. He was highly sought after to drive other owner's raceboats and before retirement he drove vintage inboard raceboats until 2013. Don was a master automobile and boat mechanic by trade. In your author's opinion, he was the best boat race driver of his time. And yes, he is my brother.

Don Benson

Jerry Bryant: Jerry was the creator of the Sammamish Slough Race and Sammamish Slough Cruises. He was a local and national outboard race driver during 1920s and 1930s, but never drove in the Slough Race and was the "Grand Admiral" of Sammamsih Slough Cruises. Bryant was co-founder and lifetime member of the Seattle Outboard Association and Puget Sound Outboard Cruising Club. He served as Seattle Outboard Association commodore and longtime race official along with wife, Ann, who also was an outboard race driver. Bryant was 1930s APBA officer, president of Seattle Boat Builders Association, Northwest Marine Dealers Association and Seattle Salts, Maritime Man of the Year and a charter member of the Stanley S. Sayers Hydroplane Hall of Fame. He was the first Seattle Seafair race chairman, president of Greater Seattle and Seattle Chamber of Commerce. Jerry was director of the Washington Athletic Club and owner-president of his nationally known, Bryant's Marina.

Ann Bryant   Jerry Bryant

Bob Carver: Bob was a gifted photographer and good family friend, a lifetime member of the Seattle Outboard Association and club VP. Without Carver's wonderful pictures, we wouldn't have his visual history of boat racing, including his masterful split-second action shots. His legacy is thousands of impeccably focused photographs, hundreds in this book and countless more published all over the world. His gift was capturing the precise moments of action using a large format camera that took one picture at a time. This book and numerous other publications couldn't have told their stories without them.

Rare photo of Carver at 1950s Slough Race.

Jack Colcock: Jack was the first winner of the Sammamish Slough Race in 1934. He drove outboard and inboard raceboats and attained multiple world records in inboards. He was a master carpenter, high-end home builder, and an inboard-outboard boat builder. His inboard raceboats, driven by Chuck Lyford, won three national championships. Colcock served terms as APBA vice-president and secretary, chairman of inboard technical committees and APBA Region 10 chairman.

Jack Colcock

Dave Culley: Dave won the last three Sammamish Slough Races (1974, 1975 and 1976)–only the second to win it three times in a row. He is one of the few original Slough Racers (driving his unlimited cabover) to participate in the "Kenmore Cup," the Slough Race revival event in 2014 and 2015. He was the *Miss Budweiser* unlimited hydro crew chief, crewmember for other unlimited hydro teams, Seattle Outboard race driver and a master mechanic by trade. He has the distinction of being the only boat racer to complete a Slough Race paddling a canoe across the finish line (see his story in Chapter 15).

Dave Culley

Chip Hanauer: Chip was one of the most famous unlimited drivers of all time and a three-time class winner in the Slough Race. He began boat racing in the JU class for 9 to 14-year-olds in the mid-1960s. He played football at Newport High School, but his favorite sport was boat racing. He taught special education after graduating "cum laude" from Washington State and then was a full-time raceboat driver and heart-throb for teenage girls. Hanauer's unlimited career included 61 victories and an unprecedented seven straight Gold Cups. Chip was a champion driver of *The Squire Shop*, *Atlas Van Lines*, *Miller American*, *Miss Budweiser* and won six limited-inboard championships. At the time he was the second winningest unlimited driver next to Bill Muncey, his idol. He copiloted with Muncey in outboard marathon races and with Chuck Lyford at the "24-Hours of Daytona" sports car race. Chip was inducted into the Motorsports Hall of Fame in 1995, a longtime Seafair Race commentator and "The Boat Guy" on TV.

Chip Hanauer

1980 Chip with Saurra Benson

Hugh Entrop: The Seattle native was the greatest smasher of world records in outboard history and first American driver to break the 100 mile-per-hour speed barrier. He retired APBA's "Jack Maypole Trophy" for the largest record-speed increase three years in a row driving his revolutionary cabover hydro design. Hugh, the fastest man

Hugh Entrop

in an outboard for a number of years, was a Boeing Company model maker who utilized the Boeing wind tunnel to perfect his designs. His awards included: multiple outboard national championships, numerous world records, induction into the "Gulf Marine Racing Hall of Fame" and being honored as a "Yachting All-American" for outboard hydros. Entrop took up photography as a hobby during his retirement and spent time out in the middle of Northwest lakes with his good friend, Bob Carver, photographing raceboats in action (see group photo in "Bob Carver Story" chapter).

1950s: Hugh Entrop before start in D-Hydro class at Eastern Washington race.

John Laird: John is a veteran raceboat driver who competed in 23 Slough Races. He is a lifetime member of Seattle Outboard Association, multiple world record holder and boat racing historian. He is well respected by all ages of boat racers, helpful to all in the sport, a caretaker-promoter of Sammamish Slough Race history and my good friend. John is a master engine builder and restorer of vintage outboard motors. He is responsible for the park benches on the Sammamish River at Bothell's Brackett's Landing with plaques honoring past Slough Race drivers.

John Laird

Janis Lee: Janis is one of two women who drove in the Slough Race and was the "Last Lady of the Slough." Janis, driving boats built by her father, Ray, won national honors and set a number of world records. Young Miss Lee was a national champion at age 13 and was rewarded for her stellar racing career as an inductee into boat racing's "Marine Racing Hall of Fame". With help from her father's boat building expertise and older brother Dennis' engine building skills, she became the most famous woman race driver of her time in the Northwest (1964-1969).

Miss Janis Lee

Chuck Lyford: Chuck was a good family friend and boat racing competitor I reconnected with after 30 years of going in different directions. We made dozens of phone calls and emails during the writing of this book until his untimely death in a car race accident, June 2017, in Spokane, Wash. He was one of those "Most interesting people in the world."

Chuck Lyford

His life was filled with adventure and risks, including his passion for boat racing, airplane racing, car racing and as a P-51 mercenary fighter pilot in Central America where the Nicaraguan Air Force honored him with the rank of colonel. Among his many racing honors, he was a three-time national champion in limited hydroplane racing, two-time class winner in the Sammamish Slough Race, national champion Reno air racer, Northwest champion car racer, driver in the 24 Hours of Daytona race with Chip Hanauer, and with his copilot wife Pam, was a two-time road race champion at the "Rally of the Incas" in the mountains of Argentina at elevations up to 16,000 feet.

1965 Reno air race: Lyford flying his *P-51 Mustang-Bardahl Special*

1969 Mercenary war fighter pilot in El Salvador, Central America

He was boat manager and crew chief for the revolutionary unlimited hydroplane *U-95*, his dream financed by Jim Clapp. It was powered by twin side by side helicopter turbines via a single gearbox and propeller shaft. With World War II engines becoming scarce, Chuck was a key figure in the sport's advancement to turbines. His love of flying was an adventure in itself. He flew a host of unusual airplanes including:

1960 & 1961 7-Liter inboard National Champion *Challenger*

Chuck and Pam "Rally of the Incas"

his personal high-speed twin *Piper Aerostar 700*, a *P-51 Mustang* Reno air racer, twin engine *P-38 Lightning* fighter, twin engine *F7F Tigercat* fighter, huge 4-engine *Martin PBM* amphibian and the infamous "*Lear Jet*" he barrel-rolled performing a "fly-over" in Seattle. My father was responsible for his start in racing when he provided Chuck's dad, "Al," with their first raceboat in 1952. Chuck was a fierce competitor, but always respectful of his fellow racers, charismatic, fun loving and a great storyteller.

He wrote his philosophy of life in an email to me: "Jim: As you can see my life is something like a dream come true. I was able to accomplish most of everything I ever dreamed of. Luck had a huge amount to do with it, as I survived so many accidents and close calls. Living on the edge puts a nice zest in one's spirit. If life gets boring, risk it." He will be profoundly missed by all who knew him.

Chuck leading at Pacific Raceways

Chuck after flying a *Tigercat F7F* fighter

Gliding in *P-38* with engines-off for photo

The Lyford's 58' Twin turbine yacht *Nothing More*

The Lyford's *Aerostar 700* personal airplane

U-95 turbine powered unlimited hydro

Chuck flying huge 4-engine *Martin Mars PBM* flying boat

Bill Muncey: Bill is the most famous unlimited hydroplane driver of all time. He brought the "Gold Cup" back to Seattle in 1956 driving the *Miss Thriftway*, which he drove to multiple national championships. He also piloted *Miss Century 21* and *Atlas Van Lines* to national championships. He drove other unlimiteds including, *Notre Dame,* and *Miss U.S.* He raced in the 1957 Slough Race and drove limited inboards locally. His career included eight Gold Cups, seven U.S. National Championships, four World Championships, 62

Bill Muncey

victories, induction into the APBA Honor Squadron and the International Motorsports Hall of Fame. Bill owned and managed his own Thriftway grocery store and an auto parts store on Mercer Island where he lived on Lake Washington across from the Stan Sayers hydroplane pits. Muncey's off-duty love was music. He played saxophone in various Seattle venues, including the Seattle Symphony hall and in his basement with band friends. He composed music, which was played by various

Bill Muncey driving *Miss Thriftway* unlimited hydro.

bands in the Northwest. He died the defending World Champion in a blow-over accident while leading the final heat of a race at Acapulco, Mexico in 1981, the only unlimited race ever run south of the U.S. border.

Billy Schumacher: Billy was the most successful boat racer of the first JU class, the Benson-Lyford-Schumacher clan from the shores of Lake Washington, all started by my father. After driving limited hydros for a few years, he stepped-up into the unlimited ranks as the youngest driver in the early 1960s with various rides in outclassed boats. His talent was revealed when he drove the *Miss Bardahl* for Ole Bardahl, winning two consecutive national championships with the "Teeny Bopper" crew. The media and friends began calling him

Billy as teenager

"Billy the Kid" after his first championship. Later, he piloted the *Pride of Pay'N Pak*, OPC international "Tunnel Boats" and the *Weisfield's-Olympia Beer* winning his third national championship. Billy then drove the *Parco's O-Ring Miss* before retiring to run his family's bakery businesses. Later he and his wife Jane, were successful running their own unlimited hydro team, winning four races.

1968 National Champion Billy Schumacher piloting *Miss Bardahl.*

Harold Tolford: Hal was a lifetime member of the Seattle Outboard Association, served two terms as commodore and competed in the Slough Race during the 1950s. He was a Gulf Marine Racing Hall of Famer, five-time National Champion, world-record holder, and maker-supplier of outboard racing fuel for outboard racers. He built his own raceboats and was employed by the Boeing Company as a model maker. He held various APBA official and technical committee positions. His fuel concoctions gave way to delicious food cookery–his family regarded him as the "best cook in the Northwest."

Harold Tolford

Bob Waite: "Rapid Robert" or "Barefoot Bob" as he was called was the "King of the Slough"; a six-time overall Slough Race champion. Waite was the first driver to win three in a row and the only driver to win five times in a row with wins in 1956, 1969, 1970, 1971, 1972 and 1973. He was well respected, easy to talk to, helpful to others but extremely competitive. Bob hated to have anybody in front of him, even when driving to regattas in his car. He was a good auto driver but while hurrying to race locations, he scared the daylights out of crew members who rode with him. If you lived near Lake Sammamish, you would hear him testing his loud open-exhaust raceboats from his home on the northwest side of the lake. Waite was a West Coast salesman in the steel banding and wire business for U.S. Steel. He didn't care much about winning championships or breaking records; his obsession was winning. Bob retired many Slough Race perpetual trophies and was the winningest driver in Slough Race history. He owned the Slough Race, and yes, he competed and won achieving his own destiny!

1969-Bob Waite receiving kisses for 2nd Slough win from wife Mary Ellen (right) & Miss Boat Show; "to the victor goes the spoils"

Ed Karelsen: Eddie, as he was called by his friends, is a lifetime Seattle Outboard Association member best known as one of the premier raceboat builders in the Northwest. He raced the Sammamish Slough Race and built outboard raceboats at Benson's boat and motor shop in Lake City and at Kenmore's Uplake Marina in the early days of his career. Ed built the first fast-turning limited hydros in the 1960s and unlimiteds including three-

Honor Squadron Award

Ed Karelsen

time national champion *Miss Bardahl* in the years following. I was fortunate to drive his first limited inboard hydros, a 150 and two 266's. After retiring from boat building, he donated his time to help young hydro drivers design and build J-Stock hydros for the novice drivers with their parents and fellow club members. He received a number of national awards including the American Power Boat Association's highest honor as an "Honor Squadron" inductee for his contributions to the sport.

Bob Wartinger: Wartinger, another Boeing worker, set 133 records in outboards–likely the most during his time of racing in the U.S. "Wart," as called by friends, raced the Slough in the 1960s and 1970s. He's one of those "thinkers" who knew how to get the most out of his equipment–one of many reasons for his success. His career included three World Championships, 24 US National Championships, the world's speed record for fastest man in an outboard, two-time UIM Gold medalist and an inductee into the APBA Honor Squadron and Hall of Champions. His 1989 record was an incredible speed of 176.550 mph. Later Bob competed in international outboard marathon events throughout the world including wins at Rouen, France and St. Petersburg, Russia. He's still an active powerboat race driver and official, President of the Safety and Medical Commission of the Union of International Motorboating (UIM), for 28 years, a world educator on lessons learned from safety improvement programs and author of "Driver's Guide to Boat Racing Safety" and "Safe Champions."

Bob Wartinger

1989: Bob Wartinger driving world's fastest outboard hydro.

☆ In Memory Of ☆

The following are Slough Race *Hall of Famers who passed-on since the original race ended in 1976.*

Andy Anderson (1927-2013) Al Benson (1914-1988) Jerry Bryant (1907-1970) Bob Carver (1917-1981) Jack Colcock (1911-1993) Hugh Entrop (1923-2003) Chuck Lyford (1941-2017) Bill Muncey (1928-1981) Harold Tolford (1924-2010) Bob Waite (1924-2012)

Appendix

P. O. BOX 94   KENMORE, WASH.

A-B 3 POINT HYDROPLANE KITS

LENGTH	9 Feet
BEAM	57½ Inches
WEIGHT	100 Pounds
POWER	7½ to 25 H.P.

EASY TO ASSEMBLE!
No Special Tools Required!

The NEW HICKLING-KARELSEN Three Point Hydro Kit is designed for the Home Builder who does not have power equipment and special tools. All one needs is a hand saw, small plane and a hammer to complete the kit. Although this Hydro is a proven Trophy winner in both A & B Classes in competition racing, it was designed with the non-racer in mind. The boat is safe in reasonable conditions with stock motors up to 25 H.P.

The Kit comes complete with all parts except the outer skins and fasteners. All parts are cut to size with little or no trimming to do.

PACKAGED HYDRO FRAME KITS

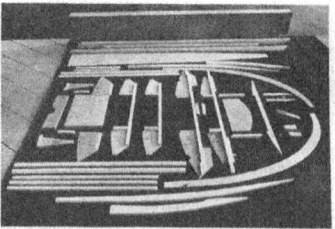

KIT PRICE - $79.50
F.O.B.

SOLD BY

UPLAKE MARINA
P. O. BOX 57
KENMORE, WASH.

Slough Race Overall Winner by Year

	Year	Date	Overall Winner	Start Location	Finish Location	Time	Miles
1	1934	Mar 3	Jack Colcock	Brown's-Madison Park	Gateway Grove-Lk Sam	46:00	25
2	1934	April 4	Buster Sill	Brown's-Madison Park	Gateway Grove-Lk Sam	44:43	25
	1935		No races run				
	1936		No races run				
	1937		No races run				
3	1938	May 15	Jack Corcoran	Brown's BH-Madison Park	Gateway Grove-Lk Sam	None	25
4	1939	April 2	George Thompson	Brown's BH-Madison Park	Brown's BH-Madison Park	None	50
5	1940	Feb 25	Pope Howard	Fisher's BH-Madison Park	Shamrock Grove-Lk Sam	39:00	25
6	1941	Feb 23	Pat Cummins	Fisher's BH-Madison Park	Shamrock Grove-Lk Sam	36:03	25
7	1942	Mar 1	Lin Ivey	Fisher's BH-Madison Park	Shamrock Grove-Lk Sam	34:31	25
8	1943	Feb 21	George Lansing	Fisher's BH-Madison Park	Shamrock Grove-Lk Sam	None	25
9	1944	Feb 20	Don Critser	Fisher's BH-Madison Park	Shamrock Grove-Lk Sam	None	25
10	1945	Feb 25	Dick Barden	Fisher's BH-Madison Park	Shamrock Grove-Lk Sam	39:00	25
11	1946	Feb 24	Dick Barden	Fisher's BH-Madison Park	Shamrock Grove-Lk Sam	58:44	25
12	1947	Mar 30	Al Benson	Kenmore Boathouse	Shamrock Cottage-Lk Sam	22:32	14
13	1948	April 18	Al Benson	Sand Point Yacht Club	Pete's Place-Lk Sam	24:57	19
14	1949	April 3	John Sherriff	Pete's Place Lk Sam	Sand Point Yacht Club	28:00	19
15	1950	Mar 26	Bob Jacobsen	Sand Point Yacht Club	Sand Point Yacht Club	71:00	38
16	1951	April 8	Elgin Gates	Sand Point Yacht Club	Sand Point Yacht Club	28:07	19
17	1952	April 6	Bob Jacobsen	Fisher's BH-Madison Park	Fisher's BH-Madison Park	42:00	50
18	1953	April 12	Al Benson	Ward's Resort-Kenmore	Ward's Resort-Kenmore	None	28
19	1954	April 25	Bill Farr	Ward's Resort-Kenmore	Bothell Bridge-Bothell	33:12	26
20	1955	April 24	Bud Sullivan	Ward's Resort-Kenmore	Bothell Bridge-Bothell	None	26
21	1956	April 15	Bob Waite	Ward's Resort-Kenmore	Bothell Bridge-Bothell	31:53	26
22	1957	April 7	Bill Farr	Kenmore Air Harbor	Kenmore Air Harbor	38:53	28
23	1958	April 13	Dick Brunes	Uplake Marina-Kenmore	Uplake Marina-Kenmore	36:58	28
24	1959	April 19	Howard Anderson	Uplake Marina-Kenmore	Uplake Marina-Kenmore	36.06	28
25	1960	April 10	Howard Anderson	Uplake Marina-Kenmore	Uplake Marina-Kenmore	35:38	28
26	1961	April 9	Wendell Ewing	Uplake Marina-Kenmore	Uplake Marina-Kenmore	35:19	28
27	1962	April 8	Lee Sutter	Uplake Marina-Kenmore	Uplake Marina-Kenmore	36:43	28
28	1963	Mar 31	Tom O'Neill	Kenmore Air Harbor	Kenmore Air Harbor	33:03.6	28
	1964		No race-dredging				
	1965		No race-dredging				
29	1966	April 17	Bud Walters	Davidson's Marina-Kenmore	Davidson's Marina-Kenmore	29:03.0	24
30	1967	April 9	Dave Jenkins	Davidson's Marina-Kenmore	Davidson's Marina-Kenmore	27:17.2	24
31	1968	April 7	Dave Jenkins	Kenmore Marina-Air Harbor	Kenmore Marina-Air Harbor	None	24
32	1969	April 13	Bob Waite	Kenmore Boat launch	Kenmore Boat launch	20:24.0	24
33	1970	April 12	Bob Waite	Kenmore Boat launch	Kenmore Boat launch	23:00.0	24
34	1971	April 18	Bob Waite	Kenmore Boat launch	Kenmore Boat launch	22:29.2	24
35	1972	April 16	Bob Waite	Kenmore Boat launch	Kenmore Boat launch	23:27.8	24
36	1973	April 8	Bob Waite	Kenmore Boat launch	Kenmore Boat launch	24:52*	24
37	1974	April 7	Dave Culley	Kenmore Boat launch	Lake Forrest Park	24:06*	25
38	1975	April 13	Dave Culley	Kenmore Boat launch	Lake Forrest Park	None*	25
39	1976	April 11	Dave Culley	Kenmore Boat launch	Lake Forrest Park	24:10*	25

*1973-1976 OPC unlimiteds ran fastest overall times: 1974-Dave Potter 20:03.0; 1974-Dick Sharp 19:38.6; 1975-**Barry Woods 17:43.0 (fastest ever)**, 1976-Woods 19:04.9

Statistics-Oddities-Timeline

Number of races: 39
Starting and finish locations:
- Madison Park to Lake Sammamish; 25 miles (1934-1946)
- Kenmore Boat House-Ward's Resort-Uplake-Marina-Davidson's Marina (all same start location) in Kenmore to Lake Sammamish; 14 miles (1947, 1953, 1958-1962, 1966, 1967)
- Ward's Resort to Lake Sammamish finishing in Bothell; 26 miles (1954-1956)
- Sand Point to Lake Sammamish; 19 miles or 38 miles two way (1948-1951)
- Madison Park to Lake Sammamish finishing at Madison Park; 50 miles (1952)
- Kenmore Air Harbor to Lake Sammamish finishing at Bothell; 26 miles (1954)
- Ward's Resort to Lake Sammamish
- Kenmore Air Harbor to Lake Sammamish finishing at Kenmore Air Harbor; 28 miles (1957, 1963)
- Kenmore Bridge Boat Launch to Marymoor Park and Back; 24 miles (1969-1973)
- Lake Forrest Park Civic Center to Marymoor Park to Kenmore Boat Launch; 25 miles (1974-1976)

Longest Race: 50 miles (from Madison Park to Lake Sammamish and back (1939)
Shortest Race: 14 miles (from Kenmore to Lake Sammamsih (1947)
Most Starters & Finishers: 115 starters-58 finishers (1958)
Estimated total number of entries in all races: 2,000
Estimated total number of spectators in all races: 400,000
Most 1st, 2nd & 3rd Place Finishes: Al Benson (8), Red Taylor (8), Bob Waite (8), Bob Wartinger (8)

Oddities

Old-Time Slough Race Vocabulary:

Over the years newspaper columnists and reporters have had a special vocabulary (pet names) pertaining to the race drivers and their boats. Some of their gems are listed below:

Names	*Definition*
Wave-Hoppers:	Outboard drivers
Wave-Wallopers:	Outboard drivers
Putt-Putt Screwballs:	Outboard drivers
Water Bugs	Outboard drivers (Bud Livesley-*Seattle Times*)
Pop-Poppers:	Early outboard motors
Shooting-Shingles:	Outboard raceboats
Flying Shingles:	Outboard raceboats
Snarling Sea Steeds	Outboard raceboats by *Seattle Star* columnist H.E. Jamison
Slaughter on the Slough:	The annual Sammamish Slough Race
Dipsy Doodle:	Raceboat turns over or upsets during a race (when boat & driver did something it wasn't supposed to)
Upsy-Daisy	Raceboat turns over or upsets during a race by *Times'* Chick Garrett

The Bygone Rite of Spring: The annual Sammamish Slough Race by Craig Smith of the *Seattle times*
Aquatic Bucking Broncos: Outboard drivers by *Seattle Star* columnist H.E. Jamison
Egg Beater Racing: The annual Sammamish Slough Race by *Seattle Star* columnist H.E. Jamison

Historical Timeline

1864 - L. B. Andrews family canoe journey through Squak Slough.
1876 - First steamboat in Squak Slough was side-wheeler "Mud Hen".
1887 - Seattle-Lake Shore & Eastern Railway extended to Woodinville.
1906 - First scheduled passenger-freight runs by steamer "City of Bothell" & scow "Squak".
1911 - U.S. Court contempt proceedings against Loggers blocking Slough.
1911 - King County Drainage District Number 3 formed for Sammamish River Region.
1911 - Defunct Sammamish Drainage Project never started.
1911 - Loggers blocking Slough served US Court Injunction.
1912 - Valley Farmers dredged and straightened Squak Slough for $60,000.
1916 - Lake Washington lowered 9'- All commercial traffic on Slough eliminated
1920 - Bothell Waterway $1,750,000 Plan by Port Commission never materializes.
1929 - Seattle Outboard Club organized and first Slough Cruise.
1930 - Seattle Outboard Club changes name to Seattle Outboard Association (SOA).
1932 - SOA builds clubhouse on Lake Washington.
1934 - Jack Colcock: first Sammamish Slough Race winner.
1941 - Olympic Water-Ski Club established.
1946 - Dick Barden: first two-time Slough Race winner.
1947 - First race start in Kenmore.
1948 - Race starts at SOA's new Sand Point Yacht Club.
1948 - First Sammamish Slough Water-Ski race.
1949 - First and only race starting at Lake Sammamish.
1953 - Log boom placed in Slough by Saginaw (Sawmill) Timber Products
1953 - Al Benson: first three-time Slough Race winner.
1955 - National television broadcast of Slough Race (KING TV)
1956 - Ginny Lea Lyford-first woman Slough Race driver.
1957 - First Slough Race start at Kenmore Air Harbor
1958 - Down River Marina on Slough opens
1960 - Marymoor Park opens after King County acquires Marymoor Farms
1963 - Last Slough Race to Lake Sammamish.
1963 - Last Slough Cruise's
1965 - Final Slough dredging/straightening project completion.
1966 - First race to Marymoor Park and finish at Kenmore Bridge boat launch.
1968 - First & only Celebrity Race entries
1969 - First race start at Kenmore Bridge.
1971 - Bob Waite: First 3-time consecutive Slough Race winner.
1972 - Bob Waite: First and only 5-time Slough Race winner.
1974 - First race start at Lake Forrest Park.
1975 - Barry Woods' OPC quickest ever in Slough Race
1976 - Dave Culley wins last three Slough Races.
1976 - Final Sammamish Slough Race.

Commodores of the Seattle Outboard Association

#	Year	Name	#	Year	Name	#	Year	Name
1	1929	George Brown	38	1966	Ray Lee	76	2005	Craig Fjarlie
2	1930	L.S. Davis	39	1967	Stuart Lowe	77	2006	Dwight Malhiot
3	1931	S.V.B. Miller	40	1968	Rick Sandstrom	78	2007	Dwight Malhiot
4	1932	S.V.B. Miller	41	1969	Rick Sandstrom	79	2008	Dwight Malhiot
5	1933	L.S. Davis	42	1970	Dick Rautenberg	80	2009	Sheryl Rucker
6	1934	Jerry Bryant	43	1971	Dick Rautenberg	81	2010	Jim Nilsen
7	1935	Latham Goble	44	1972	Jim Daniels	82	2011	Jim Nilsen
8	1936	S.V.B. Miller	45	1973	Red Taylor	83	2012	Jim Nilsen
9	1937	George Brown	46	1974	*Not Identified*	84	2013	Dwight Malhiot
10	1938	George Brown	47	1975	Penny Rautenberg	85	2014	Daren Goehring
11	1939	*Not Identified*	48	1976	Penny Rautenberg	86	2015	Daren Goehring
12	1940	Lin Ivey	49	1977	Steve Straith	87	2016	Daren Goehring
13	1941	M.A. "Pop" Tuthill	50	1978	Penny Rautenberg	88	2017	Daren Goehring
14	1942	M.A. "Pop" Tuthill	51	1979	Penny Rautenberg	89	2018	Ron Magnuson
15	1943	M.A. "Pop" Tuthill	52	1980	Howard Shaw			
16	1944	Leonard Keller	53	1981	Howard Shaw			
17	1945	Al Benson	54	1982	Penny Rautenberg			
18	1946	Al Benson	55	1983	Dave Cossette			
19	1947	Lin Ivey	56	1984	Dave Cossette			
20	1948	John Michaels	57	1985	Tom O'Neill			
21	1949	Lin Ivey	58	1986	John Myers			
22	1950	Lin Ivey	60	1987	George Smith			
23	1951	Art Shorey	61	1988	George Smith			
24	1952	Art Shorey	62	1989	Bob Montoya			
25	1953	Max Whitcom	63	1990	Bob Montoya			
26	1954	Harold Tolford Jr.	64	1991	George Smith			
27	1955	Harold Tolford Jr.	65	1992	Patrick Gleason			
28	1956	Jim Spinner	66	1993	Patrick Gleason			
29	1957	Jim Spinner	67	1994	Sam Houghtaling			
30	1958	Ralph "Red" Taylor	68	1995	Missi Diamond			
31	1959	Jim Henry	69	1996	Susan Rautenberg			
32	1960	Skip Sherwood	70	1999	George Thornhill			
33	1961	Gerald "Red" Halliday	71	2000	Jeff Kelly			
34	1962	Mike Jones	72	2001	Carl Lewis			
35	1963	Gerald "Red" Halliday	73	2002	Jim Nilsen			
36	1964	Gerald "Red" Halliday	74	2003	Tony Perman			
37	1965	Ray Lee	75	2004	Craig Fjarlie			

SOA Sportsmanship Award

Year	Name	Year	Name	Year	Name
1932	Gene Hatton, Jr.	1969	Davin Nelson	2005	Dick Rautenberg
1933	Bill Harrison	1970	Dave Jenkins	2006	Troy Holmbug
1934	Latham Goble	1971	Robert Waite	2007	Drew Thompson
1935	Dorothy Dennis	1972	Don Haack	2008	Drew Thompson
1936	Don Dunton	1973	Dave Culley	2009	Drew Thompson
1937	Jimmy Harland	1974	Penny Rautenberg	2010	Drew Thompson
1938	Wes Loback	1975	Bob Wartinger	2011	Kay Brewer
1939	Pope Howard	1976	Howard Shaw		Dave Salnon
1940	Fred Carlson	1977	Howard Shaw	2012	Ron Magnuson
1941	Fred Bloom	1978	Steve Uhrich	2013	Ron Magnuson
1942	Leonard Keller	1979	Earl Garrison	2014	Ron Magnuson
1943	M.A. "Pop" Tuthill	1980	Robert Waite	2015	Ron Magnuson
1944	Al Benson	1981	Earl Garrison		
1945	Al Benson	1982	Al Clarke		
1946	Bill Rankin	1983	John Karelsen		
1947	Bill Rankin	1984	John Myers		
1948	John Michaels	1985	Allan Rautenberg		
1949	Lin Ivey	1986	Art Losvar		
1950	Art Louie	1987	Art Losvar		
1951	Hugh Entrop	1988	Bobby Sandvig		
1952	Art Shorey	1989	Les Morgan		
1953	Jim Spinner	1990	Jeff Kelly		
1954	C.W. "Doc" Jones.	1991	Patrick Gleason		
1955	Harold Tolford Jr.	1992	Earl Garrison		
1956	Jim Spinner	1993	Art Losvar		
1957	Rod Entrop	1994	Art Losvar		
1958	Jim Henry	1995	Nelse Lunstrum		
1959	Jackie Wallace	1996	Nelse Lunstrum		
1960	Gerald "Red" Halliday	1997	Nelse Lunstrum		
1961	Pop Tolford		Col. Ray Yager		
1962	Jack Livie	1998	Diamond Racing		
1963	"Seattle Sam" Dupuis	1999	Nelse Lunstrum		
1964	Bev Downing	2000	Roy Blackwell		
1965	John Laird	2001	Bill Blackwell		
1966	Fred Mackle	2002	Jamie Nilsen		
1967	Fred Mackle	2003	Bill Blackwell		
1968	Jim Downing	2004	Zach Malhiot		

Photo Credits

Abbreviations: APBA (American Power Boat Association), BFC (Benson Family Collection), BHM (Bothell Historical Museum), BLP (Bothell Landmark Preservation Board), BS (*Boat Sport Magazine*), CT (Cinema Treasurers), GE-JB (Google Earth-Jim Benson), HO (Historylink.org), HRM (Hydroplane & Race Boat Museum), JBF-ECB (Jerry Bryant Family & Eileen Crimmin's book *Bryant's*), JFC (Jacobsen Family Collection), JL-BS (John Laird-Blackstock Scrapbook), KHS (Kenmore Heritage Society), MOHAI (Seattle Museum Of History & Industry), MOHAI-1 (PEMCO Webster & Stevens Collection-Seattle Museum Of History & Industry), MOHAI-2 (*Post-Intelligencer* Collection-Seattle Museum Of History & Industry), NWM-JB (New Wave Media-Jim Benson), PI (Seattle *Post-Intelligencer*), PMB (*Pacific Motor Boat Magazine*), PSMHS (Puget Sound Maritime Historical Society), SGC (Steve Greaves Collection), SMA (Seattle Municipal Archives), SPM (*Sea And Pacific Motor Boat Magazine*), SPR (Seattle Parks and Recreation), SS (*Speed and Spray Magazine*), ST (*Seattle Times*), VC (Peter Hunn's book *The Vintage Culture of Outboard Racing*), WO (Wikipedia.org) WHS (Woodinville Heritage Society).

Front
Dedication	BFC
Table of Contents	BFC
Page 3	Jim Benson
Page 4	BFC

Chapter 1
Page 0,2,3,5^2,6	BHM
Page 5^1,10	MOHAI
Page 7	ST
Page 8	KHS

Chapter 2
Page 0,1,3,4	ST
Page 2	Peter Hunn-VC
Page 5	APBA
Page 6,7	JBF-ECB

Chapter 3
Page 0	JBF-ECB
Page 2,5,6, 8,13,14, 16-18,20,22,29	ST
Page 3	BFC
Page 7	WO

Chapter 4
Page 0	Jim Benson
Page 2,16	ST
Page 6,10,11,15 18-19,22	JL-BS
Page 8,20	JBF-ECB
Page 12	BFC

Chapter 5
Page 0,14	ST
Page 1,7	JBF-ECB
Page 2,12	MOHAI-1
Page 5	BFC
Page 6	APBA
Page 7,10,16-21	JL-BS
Page 11	Jim Benson

Chapter 6
Page 0	Peter Hunn-VC
Page 1-4,6,10	JBF-ECB
Page 14,16	JL-BS
Page 18,19	ST
Page 19,21	BFC

Chapter 7
Page 0,35	MOHAI-3
Page 4,6,9^3,11-31,39-46, 48-51	BFC
Page 5	Cinema Treasurers
Page $9^{1,2}$,33	WO
Page 10	HO
Page 47	SPR

Chapter 8
Page 0-6, 10-11, 15-19, 23-24, 26-31	BFC
Page 8, 21-22, 26	MOHAI-2
Page $9^{1,2}$, 20	WO
Page 12	Priscilla Droge-KHS
Page 13	KHS

Chapter 9
Page 0,31^{1-2},36^1	Bob Miller
Page 1,12^1,15	JFC
Page 3^1	PMB
Page 3^2	PI
Page 4,18,21-23,28, 29,30^1,31^{3-4}, 36^{2-5}	Carver-Swanson

Page 5	HO	Page 14	George Carkonen-SGC
Page 6,7,10, 12²,24¹⁻², 34,35	BFC	Page 19	Jim Benson
Page 8,14,16	Clayton Shaw	Page 22	Lee Sutter
Page 19	Peter Hunn-VC	Page 28	Erin O'Neil
Page 24³	SS	Page 32-35	Kenmore Air
Page 26	SPM	Page 37	Dick Rautenberg
Page 30²	Carver-Swanson-SGC	*Chapter 13*	
Page 32	WHS	Page 0	Annette Eaton
Page 37	Bob Carver	Page 2,17²	Erin O'Neil
Chapter 10		Page 5,12¹⁻²	BHM
Page 0, 11,13-16,18,23, 26, 27¹28¹, 30-32,34, 38-40,42, 45,47,48,51¹, 55,57, 61¹	Bob Carver	Page 6	Jim Benson
		Page 9,16	Bob Carver
		Page 15,17¹	Janis (Lee) Ely
		Chapter 14	
Page 3-4¹,5,6¹,7¹,8², 21-22,24,27²,61	Bob Miller	Page 0,6¹,7,11³,20²,25,26,	Janis (Lee) Ely
		Page 2,33,36,37¹	John Laird
Page 4², 8³	BS	Page 5	PI
Page 6²,7², 7³, 8¹	Carver-Swanson	Page 9	Bob Miller
Page 9	BLP	Page 10¹	Penny Anderson
Page 25, 28²,36,46	BFC	Page 10²,15,17,18,20¹, 21,22,24¹,28,29,31	Bob Carver
Page 29	Ginny (Lyford) Asp		
Page 35,37,53	APBA	Page 11¹	Dick Rautenberg
Page 41	Jim Benson	Page 11²	Kathy Myers
Page 43, 44¹,51²,59	ST	Page 14,37²	HRM
Page 49	Billy Schumacher	Page 6²,16,34	ST
Page 51³	Russell Rotzler	Page 24²,30	Steve Greaves
Page 54	Bev Schadt	*Chapter 15*	
Page 60,62	SGC	Page 0,12,20,26,34,35,44	Dave Culley
Chapter 11		Page 2,4,11,17,18, 23¹,29,43	SGC
Page 0,1,4²,7,8	Carver-Swanson		
Page 2,3	Jim Benson	Page 3	Bill & Bob Carver
Page 4¹,18	Bob Miller	Page 7,13,19¹,22,27	Bob Wartinger
Page 5,19¹	BFC	Page 8	Kathy Myers
Page 6, 14	SGC	Page 28,30,53	Bob Carver
Page 9	BHM	Page 9,15	ST
Page 11-13,15-17,19²,³	Bob Carver	Page 14	HRM
Chapter 12		Page 19²	APBA
Page 0,13,17,21,24,25, 27,31	Bob Carver	Page 23²,48	Pepe Maxwell
		Page 24	GE-JB
Page 1,10,18	APBA	Page 31¹	SMA
Page 4,7	SGC	Page 31²,32,33, 50	Penny Anderson
Page 8	Don Ibsen	Page 36	Barry Woods
Page 9¹	Bob Miller	Page 38	PI
Page 9²,11	ST	Page 40	Jim Benson
Page 12	John Laird	Page 41	Dick Rautenberg
		Page 46	Burt Fraley
		Page 47	BHM

Page 51	Emmanuel Keller	*Hall of Fame* (other than previously credited)	
Page 52	NWM-JB	Page 1[1,2]	Penny Anderson
Chapter 16		Page 1[3],2[1,3]	BFC
Page 0,3[4],	Bill Carver	Page 2[2]	JBF-ECB
Page 1,3[1-3,5],4,6-11, 13-18[1],19-21	Bob Carver	Page 3[4]	Saurra Benson
		Page 4[1],7[4]	Bob Carver
Page 5	Carver-Swanson	Page 5	Chuck Lyford
Page 18[2]	Jim Benson	Page 6	Ginny (Lyford) Asp, Chuck Lyford
Epilogue			
Page 0,4[3],5,14[2]	Amberly Culley	Page 7[1,2]	BFC
Page 1,3,4	Bill Carver	Page 7[3,4]	Bill Schumacher
Page 2[1]	Magen Tanner	Page 8[2],	SGC
Page 2[2]	John Paramore	Page 8[3]	Jim Benson
Page 7	WO	Page 8[4]	Bill Carver
Page 8-14[1],15	Jim Benson	Page 9	Bob Wartinger

1938: Boeing B-314 *Clipper* experimental flying boat was docked at Mathews Beach-same dock used by the Sand Point Yacht Club-Courtesy of Wikipedia.org.

Index

American Power Boat Association (APBA), 6, 24, 29, 39, 53, 58, 68, 85, 100, 248, 254, 295, 298, 316, 335, 380, 494, 512, 531

Anderson, Howard (Andy), 189, 261, 288, 291, 298, 307, 309, 312, 320, 334, 337, 338, 340, 341, 354, 357, 360, 363, 388, 396, 400, 408, 421, 422, 442, 463, 480, 511, 522, 531, 533

Anderson, Penny (Rautenberg), 5, 381, 464, 465, 467, 476, 478, 479, 484, 510, 511, 523

Army Engineers, 220, 266, 337, 372, 374, 376, 380, 381, 384, 385, 386, 391, 393, 394, 404, 439,

Barden, Dick, 159, 160, 161, 170, 175, 176, 184, 185, 186, 187, 189, 196, 201, 205, 234, 306, 336, 337, 408, 417, 533, 535,

Benson, Al (Benny) 9, 128, 130, 134, 135, 137-142, 148, 149, 151, 152, 155, 156, 159-161, 166-171, 174-176, 178-185, 189, 192-194, 196-203, 205, 207-210, 212-214, 219, 222, 224, 226, 230, 232, 234-239, 241, 242, 244, 247-249, 253, 257, 260, 268, 269, 271, 275, 276, 279, 280, 282, 283, 286-292, 293, 295, 297, 305, 306, 312, 313, 333, 336, 337, 345, 352, 368, 399, 402, 407-409, 411, 412, 414, 416, 417, 431, 489, 497, 522, 523, 531, 533-537

Benson, Don, 225, 233, 242, 246, 247, 248, 252, 254, 257, 258, 261, 262, 264, 265, 274, 275, 276, 277, 278, 279, 280, 291, 295, 301, 306, 310, 313, 326, 330, 336, 337, 341, 399, 442, 511, 519, 521, 522, 524

Benson, Dorothy (Dot), 139, 143, 150, 152, 159, 166, 170, 171, 173, 174, 235, 238, 277

Benson, Jim (Jimmy), 213, 235, 248, 252, 262, 264, 269, 271, 274, 276, 278, 290, 291, 300, 312, 314, 315, 322, 327, 332, 333, 341, 403, 404, 519, 521, 523

Blackstock, Carl, 51, 69, 71, 75, 77, 78, 79, 80, 81, 93, 99, 100, 113, 114, 115, 116, 119, 128, 129

Bothell Bridge, 11, 14, 106, 124, 125, 133, 147, 148, 184, 196, 205, 206, 217, 226, 232, 236, 244, 255, 257, 261, 270, 289, 294, 322, 323, 325, 331, 332, 339, 393, 395, 411, 412, 419, 432, 433, 452, 476, 533,

Brown, George, 23, 32, 35, 120, 123, 125, 142, 461, 536

Brunes, Dick, 239, 242, 255, 262, 2 63, 264, 265, 270, 273, 285, 294, 298, 299, 300, 301, 304, 306, 307, 308, 309, 310, 311, 316, 336, 337, 338, 345, 351, 505, 533

Bryant, Ann, 33, 51, 52, 55, 58, 59, 63, 71, 73, 76, 81, 85, 109, 114, 120, 150, 524

Bryant, Jerry, 23, 26, 27, 30, 32, 33, 34, 36, 37, 38, 39, 40, 41, 43, 46, 47, 48, 49, 52, 56, 57, 61, 68, 69, 73, 75, 76, 77, 78, 79, 80, 81, 85, 87, 88, 93, 102, 106, 107, 109, 112, 113, 114, 115, 117, 118, 118, 120, 121, 124, 125, 131, 133, 136, 137, 144, 145, 149, 150, 158, 171, 199, 206, 218, 226, 335, 407, 428, 488, 522, 524, 531, 536

Burr, Mrs. Francis, 41, 42, 46, 49, 51, 52, 55, 58, 63, 109, 120

Carver, Bill, 502, 545

Carver, Bob (Cuddles), 252, 258, 271, 272, 281, 290, 291, 296, 297, 355, 363, 365, 419, 432, 443, 445, 484-502, 522, 524, 526, 531

Clinton, Otis, 181, 182, 196, 197, 198, 199, 200, 202, 205, 208, 209, 210, 213, 254

Colcock, Jack, 40, 44, 45, 87, 90, 92, 93, 94, 99, 101, 102, 144, 115, 124, 133, 248, 262, 285, 295, 306, 335, 344, 522, 525, 531, 533, 535

Crimmin, Eileen, 34, 433, 434, 436, 485, 493, 494, 497, 498, 502

Culley, Amberly (Gaul) , 2, 506, 507, 508, 509, 510, 511, 512, 513, 545, 520

Culley, Dave, 9, 290, 430, 435, 441, 442, 447, 449, 450, 453, 455, 456, 458, 459, 462, 464, 465, 468, 470, 472, 473, 474, 475, 478, 507, 509, 510, 511, 513, 514, 515, 517, 519, 522, 525, 533, 535, 537,

Cummins, Pat, 65, 66, 75, 78, 80, 87, 89, 99, 100, 101, 112, 113, 114, 115, 118, 119, 122, 128, 137, 141, 143, 146, 147, 148, 149, 151, 152, 153, 154, 155, 156, 160, 161, 185, 189, 219, 220, 416, 419, 426, 427, 533

Dennis, Dorothy, 91, 99, 107, 109, 110, 111, 112, 113, 114, 115, 117, 118, 120, 312, 461, 537,

Down River Marina, 296, 297, 299, 308, 309, 319, 320, 321, 331, 347, 355, 363, 378, 435, 469, 493, 535,

Entrop, Hugh (Hugo), 230, 233, 262, 263, 302, 303, 305, 311, 344, 347, 387, 502, 503, 517, 518, 522, 525, 526, 531, 537,

Evinrude, Ole, 21, 27, 28, 39, 40

Evinrude, Ralph, 27, 28, 40, 44

Farr, Bill, 229, 232, 243, 244, 245, 247, 253, 255, 256, 258, 260, 269, 270, 274, 286, 287, 288, 291, 297, 298, 299, 301, 417, 533,

Flying Boat (Clipper Ship), 164, 177, 190, 191, 202, 203, 221, 528, 540

Gateway Grove, 84, 87, 88, 92, 94, 95, 97, 132, 133, 137, 199, 226, 227, 231, 235, 240, 241, 242, 247, 251, 254, 255, 260, 268, 283, 285, 290, 292, 298, 303, 304, 307, 337, 350, 358, 361, 365, 368, 533

Goble, Latham, 87, 91, 93, 98, 99, 101, 107, 108, 109, 110, 111, 113, 115, 118, 122, 122, 128, 131, 536, 537

Greaves, Steve, 397, 402, 413, 414, 479, 511,

Green Lake Races, 23, 28, 35, 42, 44, 52, 56, 74, 76, 97, 98, 100, 111, 117, 118, 128, 150, 204, 211, 218, 240, 247, 262, 266, 285, 294, 295, 311, 344, 370 398, 403, 414, 424, 428, 439, 453, 460, 479, 481, 484, 485

Halliday, Gerald (Red), 300, 308, 331, 336, 339, 340, 344, 345, 346, 354, 356, 359, 360, 362, 363, 370, 371, 387, 393, 394, 396, 400, 402, 405, 406, 413, 424, 536, 537

Hanauer, Chip, 332, 415, 422, 427, 428, 437, 438, 444, 445, 511, 512, 513, 522, 525, 527

Harland, Jimmy, 32, 56, 57, 58, 63, 66, 69, 70, 75, 78, 86, 87, 113, 114, 115, 118, 119, 120, 122, 123, 124, 125, 131, 133, 134, 135, 148, 149, 150, 159, 205, 212, 227, 233, 412, 440, 537

Hickling, Chuck, 44, 118, 119, 175, 176, 196, 220, 248, 295, 307, 399, 407, 409, 411, 414, 496,

Ibsen, Don, 124, 181, 204, 205, 212, 223, 224, 232, 242, 264, 285, 304, 342, 365,

Ivey, Lin, 124, 126, 127, 128, 130, 131, 136, 137, 138, 141, 142, 143, 146, 147, 148, 160, 161, 168, 175, 184, 185, 186, 189, 193, 203, 205, 210, 212, 218, 219, 220, 224, 226, 227, 232, 236, 237, 242, 248, 253, 255, 269, 270, 285, 287, 289, 294, 533, 536, 537,

Jacobsen, Bob (Jake), 214, 215, 216, 217, 218, 222, 225, 226, 227, 228, 229, 230, 231, 323, 233, 234, 236, 237, 276, 278, 286, 306, 333, 411, 412, 416, 417, 479, 516, 517, 533

Jenkins, Dave, 387, 388, 396, 399, 400, 401, 402, 408, 409, 410, 413, 415, 417, 422, 426, 427, 429, 431, 441, 443, 444, 457, 459, 470, 478, 533, 537

Karelsen, Ed, 272, 274, 279, 281, 333, 305, 307, 325, 353, 399, 404, 496, 513, 515, 522, 530

Keller, Leonard, 112, 116, 123, 141, 142, 148, 154, 155, 156, 157, 166, 170, 171, 172, 175, 212, 220, 536, 537

Kenmore Air Harbor, 240, 288, 300, 360, 361, 365, 366, 367, 368, 369, 391, 533, 534, 535,

Kenmore Boat House, 194, 195, 369, 533

Kenmore Boat Launch, 3, 432, 439, 474, 475, 512, 513, 533, 534. 454, 464

Kenmore Marina, 354, 366, 394, 401, 406, 408, 409, 419, 454, 533,

Laird, John, 235, 236, 241, 355, 356, 357, 387, 388, 413, 422, 423, 426, 427, 429, 442, 445, 511, 516, 517, 519, 522, 526, 537

Lake Washington Ship Canal, 3, 5, 16, 17, 225, 386

Lee, Dennis, 364, 388, 397, 398, 402, 410, 413, 422, 427, 444,

Lee, Janis, 390, 397, 398, 401, 402, 403, 415, 416, 423, 429, 522, 526,

Lee, Ray, 285, 304, 305, 351, 357, 387, 388, 389, 392, 393, 396, 397, 401, 403, 406, 536

Losvar, Art, 143, 154, 155, 156, 158, 159, 160, 161, 170, 180, 187, 188, 218, 222, 230, 300, 301, 448, 537

Lyford, Chuck, 252, 254, 260, 262, 265, 269, 271, 274, 275, 277, 278, 293, 301, 306, 322, 522, 525, 527, 531,

Lyford, Ginny Lea, 109, 264, 265, 271, 274, 276, 278, 280, 281, 287, 535

Marathon, 100-Mile, 65, 74, 97, 135, 138, 144, 170, 177, 178, 180, 181, 198, 199, 204, 211, 218, 224, 233, 240

Marymoor, 13, 217, 292, 329, 375, 376, 381, 386, 391, 392, 393, 394, 401, 408, 409, 418, 420, 426, 431, 432, 439, 441, 443, 446, 447, 451, 456, 459, 462, 463, 464, 465, 467, 469, 472, 473, 474, 475, 478, 534, 535

Maxwell, Jay (Pepe), 453, 468, 471, 476, 477, 478

Miller, Bob, 258, 333

Miller, S.V.B., 21, 23, 24, 27, 28, 32, 35, 43, 44, 45, 46, 53, 61, 62, 64, 68, 73, 77, 81, 85, 86, 97, 99, 107, 117, 120, 536

Movies, Race Promotion, 4, 6, 33, 182, 207, 208, 268, 293, 294

Muncey, Bill, 264, 286, 287, 289, 290, 295, 317, 352, 407, 414, 427, 440, 444, 522, 525, 529, 531

National Outboard Association (NOA), 26, 28, 32, 47, 53, 54, 55, 62, 64, 67, 75, 78, 87, 100, 109, 114, 116, 142, 170, 220, 242

Northwest Outboard Association, 28, 29, 32, 34, 36, 41, 46, 53, 56, 57

Myers, John, 350, 357, 398, 401, 402, 415, 421, 422, 427, 438, 451, 536, 537,

O'Neill, Tom, 362, 363, 380, 388, 389, 394, 395, 396, 416

Pan American, 177, 191, 202, 203

Potter, Dave, 448, 451, 455, 458, 460, 462, 467, 468, 471

Rankin, Bill, 130, 148, 159, 170, 175, 187, 193, 199, 213, 219, 220, 236, 237, 238, 239, 242, 248, 262, 290, 431, 505, 537

Rautenberg, Dick, 41, 111, 287, 290, 291, 344, 370, 388, 401, 402, 403, 421, 422, 423, 429, 438, 443, 444, 447, 450, 454, 455, 463, 464, 465, 470, 472, 480, 536, 537, 471

Reinell, Bertha, 42, 43, 44, 109, 120

Saginaw Sawmill, 246, 256, 284, 325, 326, 339, 535,

Sand Point Naval Air Station, 3, 90, 95, 163, 164, 165, 176, 189, 190, 191, 202,

Sand Point Yacht Club, 163, 165, 176, 177, 192, 199, 200, 202, 204, 205, 209, 221, 533, 540

Sandstrom, Rick, 404, 416, 429, 446, 462, 471, 509, 510, 536

Schumacher, Billy, 243, 248, 254, 257, 261, 262, 263, 264, 267, 269, 271, 274, 276, 277, 279, 285, 287, 289, 301, 305, 306, 308, 310, 312, 319, 327, 332, 336, 355, 357, 404, 407, 408, 411, 529

Seattle Outboard Association, 5, 6, 23, 41, 44, 45, 52, 53, 58-65, 72, 75, 77, 79, 81, 82, 85, 86, 88, 90, 91, 97, 98, 100-102, 107-109, 111, 113, 117, 123, 126, 131, 133, 136, 139, 140, 142, 146, 151, 151, 158-160, 162, 166, 167, 169-172, 174, 177, 179-181, 183, 185, 193, 196, 199, 202, 203, 217, 218, 220, 231, 235, 242,-244, 254, 258, 266, 268, 282, 283, 285, 288, 292, 295, 296, 298, 302, 303, 311, 335-337, 353, 360, 375, 376, 387, 388, 392, 393, 454, 461, 471, 480, 481, 486, 489, 492, 496, 497, 507, 508, 510, 512-514, 517, 520, 523, 524, 526, 530, 535-537

Seattle Outboard Club, 24, 32, 33, 35, 36, 38, 40, 535

Shamrock Grove, 137, 144, 147, 158, 159, 533

Sharp, Dick, 455, 458, 460, 462, 467, 471, 479, 482, 483, 533

Shaw, Clayton, 175, 209, 210, 219, 222, 227, 230, 236, 239, 240, 242, 243, 442, 519

Shaw, Jan, 509, 510, 512, 513, 520

Sheriff, Johnny, 32, 143, 148, 175, 196, 205, 209, 210, 197, 198, 213

Slough Dredging, 54, 111, 112, 143, 205, 206, 296, 312, 332, 360, 370, 372, 373, 374, 375, 376, 377, 378, 379, 382, 383, 384, 385, 386, 389, 392, 395, 399, 404, 439, 481, 535

Spinner, Jim, 232, 242, 243, 248, 262, 266, 267, 268, 275, 285, 286, 289, 291, 303, 307, 335, 344, 352, 496, 536, 537

Spreckels, Adolph, 58, 66, 67, 69, 70, 78, 90, 91, 117, 170,

Steinbruck, Bob, 300, 301, 306, 309, 310, 341, 349, 550

Stone, Rockey, 157, 175, 200, 201, 202, 213, 219, 235, 236, 237, 239, 243, 245, 247, 249, 253, 262, 271, 272, 274, 300, 301, 306,

Suess, Dick, 290, 307, 308, 352

Sullivan, Art (Bud), 242, 248, 253, 254, 255, 256, 258, 259, 260, 263, 264, 265, 269, 270, 285, 286, 287, 310, 311, 313, 339, 340, 342, 350, 351, 357, 358, 364, 365, 458, 533

Sutter, Lee, 344, 352, 353, 354, 356, 360, 362, 387, 388, 393, 394, 399, 445, 511, 533

Russ Swanson, 7, 215, 243, 249, 258, 488, 489

Taylor, Ralph (Red), 222, 232, 239, 241, 242, 248, 263, 291, 295, 296, 301, 308, 309, 336, 349, 357, 360, 422, 426, 429, 443, 444, 446, 459, 534, 536

Tolford, Harold (Hal), 230, 238, 242, 246, 247, 248, 256, 262, 266, 267, 288, 289, 291, 295, 298, 301, 303, 312, 344, 352, 370, 275, 380, 387, 388, 398, 403, 423, 429, 437, 479, 504, 522, 530, 531, 536, 537,

Tuthill, MA (Pop), 51, 73, 75, 120, 123, 134, 135, 141, 142, 150, 158, 166, 170, 171, 177, 178, 179, 185, 218, 536, 537

Uplake Marina, 194, 240, 287, 296, 298, 300, 304, 306, 309, 336, 337, 339, 342, 345, 350, 358, 360, 365, 366, 454, 489, 523, 530, 533

Waite, Bob, 9, 228, 229, 232, 245, 253, 255, 269, 270, 273, 274, 275, 286, 287, 289, 298, 299, 306, 307-309, 315, 329, 347, 354, 357, 364, 365, 396, 399, 413, 417, 418, 420, 422-427, 429, 431, 432, 434, 436-438, 440-442, 444, 446-450, 453, 455-459, 463, 473, 509, 516, 517, 522, 530, 531, 533-535, 537

Walters, Bud, 271, 247, 310, 346, 349, 359, 363, 370, 391, 394, 395, 396, 397, 400, 402, 411, 431, 436, 438, 441, 533

Walters , Charley (Chuck), 269, 271, 301, 306, 310, 337, 341, 348, 350, 357, 396, 397, 403, 415, 421, 422, 424, 442, 444, 454, 455, 456, 457, 459, 462, 472

Ward's Resort, 194, 195, 224, 225, 226, 235, 239, 240, 241, 243, 245, 254, 255, 268, 287, 296, 315, 316, 318, 333, 396, 489, 533, 534

Wartinger, Bob, 364, 402, 422, 428, 437, 438, 439, 443, 445, 451, 452, 453, 455, 457, 458, 459, 471, 474, 475, 478, 479, 522, 531, 534, 537

Williams, Phil, 357, 364, 397, 442, 517, 519

Woods, Barry, 453, 466, 467, 468, 471, 475, 476, 479, 433, 535

World War II, 142, 162, 166, 171, 179, 180, 181, 190, 200, 527

Made in the USA
Las Vegas, NV
31 January 2023